THE
PHYSICIANS' MANUAL FOR PATIENTS

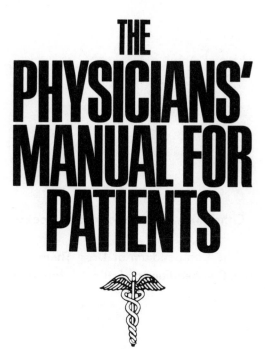

Other Biomedical Information Books:

The Compendium of Drug Therapy
The Compendium of Patient Information

THE PHYSICIANS' MANUAL FOR PATIENTS

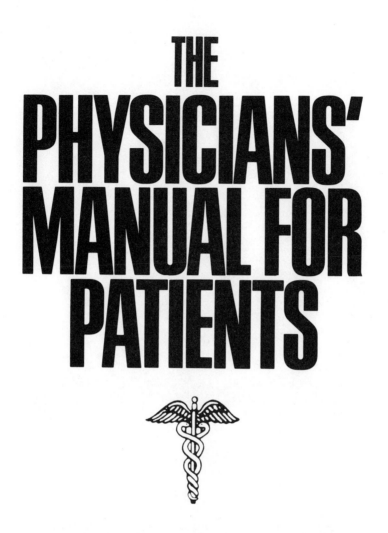

A Biomedical Information Corporation™ Book

Genell J. Subak-Sharpe, Editor

Morton Bogdonoff, M.D., and Rubin Bressler, M.D.,
Medical Editors

Times
BOOKS

Library of Congress Cataloging in Publication Data

Main entry under title:

The Physicians' manual for patients.

Includes index.
1. Medicine, Popular. I. Subak-Sharpe, Genell J.
II. Bogdonoff, Morton D., 1925-   . III. Bressler,
Rubin. IV. Biomedical Information Corporation. [DNLM:
1. Medicine—Popular works. WB 120 P578]
RC81.P58 1984   616   83-40098
ISBN 0-8129-1102-4

Designed by Doris Borowsky

Manufactured in the United States of America

  85 86 87 88 5 4 3 2

ACKNOWLEDGMENTS

EDITORS

Rubin Bressler, M.D.
Professor and Head
Departments of Medicine and
  Clinical Pharmacology
University of Arizona Health Sciences Center
Tucson, Ariz.

Morton D. Bogdonoff, M.D.
Professor of Medicine
Cornell University College of Medicine
New York, N.Y.

Genell J. Subak-Sharpe, M.S.
Vice President/Editor
Biomedical Information Corporation
New York, N.Y.

MEDICAL ADVISORY BOARD

ALLERGY
Louis Tuft, M.D.
Clinical Professor of Medicine
  (Emeritus)
Formerly Chief of the Allergy Clinic
Temple University Medical Center
Philadelphia, Pennsylvania

CARDIOLOGY
Mark A. Goodman, M.D.
Director, Coronary Care Unit
Nassau Hospital
Mineola, New York

James V. Warren, M.D.
Professor of Medicine
The Ohio State University
College of Medicine
Columbus, Ohio

DERMATOLOGY
George W. Hambrick, M.D.
Chief of Dermatology
New York Hospital
Cornell University Medical College
New York, New York

FAMILY MEDICINE
John H. Renner, M.D.
Director, Family Practice Residency
  Program
St. Mary's Hospital
Kansas City, Missouri

GENERAL SURGERY
Robert E. Hermann, M.D.
Head, Department of General Surgery
Cleveland Clinic Foundation
Cleveland, Ohio

INTERNAL MEDICINE
Marvin Moser, M.D.
Clinical Professor of Medicine
New York Medical College
Valhalla, New York

NUTRITION
Jules Hirsch, M.D.
Professor and Senior Physician
The Rockefeller University Hospital
New York, New York

OBSTETRICS AND GYNECOLOGY
William J. Ledger, M.D.
Chairman, Department of Obstetrics
  and Gynecology
New York Hospital
Cornell University Medical College
New York, New York

OSTEOPATHIC MEDICINE
Robert E. Mancini, Ph.D., D.O.
Associate Professor and Chairman
Department of Pharmacology
  and Toxicology
New York College of Osteopathic
  Medicine
Old Westbury, New York

PEDIATRICS
Rudolph L. Leibel, M.D.
Assistant Professor
  and Associate Physician
The Rockefeller University Hospital
New York, New York

PSYCHIATRY
William A. Frosch, M.D.
Professor and Vice Chairman
Department of Psychiatry
Cornell University Medical College
Medical Director, Payne Whitney Clinic
New York Hospital
New York, New York

RHEUMATOLOGY
Joseph A. Markenson, M.D.
Assistant Professor of Medicine
Hospital for Special Surgery
Cornell University Medical College
New York, New York

Special Tributes

Over the last two years, scores of people have been involved in the creation of this book and the parent *Compendium of Patient Information.* While it is impossible to cite all of the many dedicated writers, medical artists, researchers and others who have worked so diligently on this book, there are some whose contributions cannot be overlooked. These include Susan Carleton, associate editor; Judith Adams, Penny Andrew, Amy Aronson, Diana Benzaia, Judy Ann Cohen, Barbara Fogel, Jane Hershey, John Kelly, Suzanne Loebl, Helene MacLean, Adele S. Paroni, Emily Paulsen, Tia Powell, Daniel Simon, Jay Soltz, Jamie Talan, Caroline Tapley and Lois Wingerson, all medical writers. Joan Simpson, as Executive Art Director, supervised a superb group of medical artists and illustrators, including Douglas Cramer, Robert Demerest, Marsha Dohrmann, Carol Donner, Nancy Lou Gahan, Cas Henselman, Masako Herman, Barbara Knight, Cynthia Mason, George Schwenk, Ray Surges, Hugh Thomas, and Beth Willert. Special tribute also is due John A. Gentile, Jr., Publisher of the *Compendium of Patient Information,* and Howard H. Rich, President of Biomedical Information Corporation.

Introduction: The Meaning of Health

We are in the midst of a health revolution that is changing both the practice of medicine and the way all of us live. Only a few decades ago, health was looked upon as a matter of fate: If you were blessed with good health, it was chalked up to luck; if not, physicians were called upon to do what they could—which wasn't much—and the outcome was considered beyond earthly control.

Today, of course, the situation is vastly different. Tremendous medical advances of the last forty years now make it possible to treat, and often cure, diseases that were once considered a certain death sentence. One-time killers, such as polio, tuberculosis, diphtheria, or small pox, are now all but extinct. A vast array of drugs—unheard of a few decades ago—now make it possible to overcome life-threatening infections, while others enable people with chronic, often disabling diseases, such as arthritis, high blood pressure, diabetes, and many forms of mental illness, to enjoy full, productive lives.

Although most experts agree that Americans have the world's best medical system, health care in this country is coming under increasing public criticism. People are often frightened or confused by the new medical technology. Many are sometimes left feeling that their doctors fail to give them the individual attention and concern they have come to expect. Cost is also a major factor. The nation's total health bill is now about $320 billion a year, and rising at an alarming rate. In 1982, health care cost an average of $1365 for every man, woman, and child in the United States. Medical costs for the impoverished and elderly are threatening our Social Security and social welfare systems. Even though we live in the world's wealthiest nation, the sad fact is there are millions of Americans who simply cannot afford to pay their medical bills, and often go without needed care until the crisis stage.

Against this backdrop, it's little wonder that the need for change is perceived on every front. One of the most important changes, in our opinion, is the growing realization that maintaining good health is an individual responsibility. People now know that good health is not luck or something the doctor brings about. Instead, it's rooted in how we live from day to day— what we eat, drink, or smoke; how we play, cope with stress, control our environment. And when illness does strike, each patient must act as an informed partner to the physician if optimal results are to be achieved.

This book is designed specifically to help you become that informed partner. It is an outgrowth of *The Compendium of Patient Information,* collections of patient guides published by Biomedical Information Cor-

poration and distributed to more than 125,000 physicians nationwide. These guides provide basic background information on more than two hundred common disorders—everything from acne to vertigo and warts. They are not intended to replace or supersede the advice and therapeutic directions of your own physician; instead, they should be used to supplement your doctor's educational efforts, and to provide a concise resource for future reference.

A word of caution: Although the information in this book is based on current medical knowledge, and has been extensively reviewed by medical specialists, it should not be used to alter a prescribed regimen or course of treatment. We are confident, however, that this book will become your major source of reliable, practical health information.

—the editors

Contents

Section One:
General Background Health Information

---

1. How to Find a Doctor

All too often, the choice of a doctor is made when you are sick, or in pain, or worried, or in a hurry. But this is an important decision and deserves careful attention. You should choose a doctor while you are healthy and have time to gather information, weigh alternatives, and evaluate impressions. (The same considerations apply to a reappraisal of your current doctor.)

While you may need the services of a specialist on occasion, it is important, first of all, that you have a doctor who oversees your general health: a primary-care physician. This is the doctor who should be aware of your complete medical history; your family situation; your living environment; your occupation and its possible stresses and hazards; and your overall state of health, both mental and physical, over a period of time. This is also the doctor who should refer you to a specialist, when appropriate.

Your primary-care physician should be both competent and caring in his or her treatment of you. He or she should be knowledgeable, experienced, and up to date in the scientific aspects of medicine. He or she should also practice the "art" of medicine and be aware of you as an individual, rather than simply as a collection of signs and symptoms. He or she should emphasize preventive medicine, teaching patients about good health and how to obtain and maintain it.

It is not possible, of course, to come to a conclusion about a doctor's ability and attitudes until you have met him or her. However, when choosing a doctor, it is advisable to make inquiries and use these as the basis for an informed guess that a particular individual might be the right

1

doctor for you. After these preliminaries are completed, a visit can be scheduled.

FORMAL QUALIFICATIONS

The doctor chosen as the primary-care physician may be either an internist (a specialist in internal medicine) or a family practitioner. (Family practitioners treat people of all ages, not necessarily families as such.) Both internists and family practitioners are qualified to provide basic, comprehensive health care and maintenance. Patients with problems beyond the knowledge or ability of these "generalists" are referred by them to specialists for a second opinion or for treatment. Ideally, the same doctor should treat all the adult members of a household; a family practitioner may also care for the children.

Doctors train for family practice by doing postgraduate work in such fields as preventive and internal medicine, gynecology, pediatrics, orthopedics, and minor surgery. The postgraduate training of an internist places more emphasis on the gastrointestinal and genitourinary systems, the endocrine glands and their function, disorders of the heart and lungs, and such diseases as diabetes and arthritis. The doctor chosen should have obtained certification in an appropriate American specialty board or should be board-qualified (having completed the postgraduate training but not yet having taken the examination). This information is available either from the doctor's office or from reference books in larger libraries.

FINDING NAMES

The most common sources of doctors' names—friends and family—are not necessarily the most reliable, although they may provide useful information about doctors' personalities. You should follow up such suggestions with your own evaluations.

Local medical societies will provide you with a list of licensed medical practitioners in the area, and the same list may be available at the local library. Such a list provides information on the physicians' specialties and location—but tells nothing about the doctors' respective competence. Further sources of lists are hospitals, which can provide the names of internists and family practitioners on the staff, and medical schools, whose faculty members often have private practices. In addition, public interest groups in some communities may be able to provide not only a list of names but also information on many of the practical considerations that should enter into the choice of a doctor.

PRACTICAL CONSIDERATIONS

A conveniently located office and office hours that are compatible with your own schedule are obviously factors in the choice of a doctor, as are doctor's fees. While it is impossible to predict the cost of an illness, the basic cost of health maintenance—the regular office visit—should be something that you can comfortably pay.

If you or a member of your household is housebound or unable to travel without great difficulty, the doctor chosen should be willing to make house calls. Further considerations are the efficiency of the doctor's answering service, the attitudes toward patients of the office personnel, how readily you can get an appointment, and how long you have to sit in the waiting room.

HOSPITAL AFFILIATION

An important factor is the hospital with which the doctor is affiliated, since, if you become seriously ill, it is to this hospital that you will be admitted. The hospital should not be too far distant. Preferably, it should be affiliated with a medical school or with a specialty training program. Such hospitals are likely to have well-qualified specialists on the staff and to be familiar with the latest techniques and equipment.

However, community hospitals—especially those that have programs of continuing postgraduate education—may also provide excellent care.

The hospital at which the doctor of your choice has admitting privileges should be fully accredited by the Joint Commission on the Accreditation of Hospitals.

AGE AND SEX

The doctor's age and sex should be taken into consideration. Some people strongly prefer to be seen by a doctor of their own sex; for others, this factor is unimportant. As to age, young doctors are. more likely than older doctors to be up to date in their knowledge. Older doctors, on the other hand, have more clinical experience; if they participate in the continuing education programs available through many of the medical schools, they may also be in touch with the latest advances. In any event, it is advisable to choose a doctor who is not likely to die or to retire while you are a patient.

MEETING THE DOCTOR

It is usually possible, in an initial interview, to decide whether or not a particular doctor is someone with whom you can be comfortable. Your reaction to the doctor as an individual should be the decisive factor in your choice. A superbly qualified physician will be of no help to you unless you can relate to him or her. (In this connection, it should be remembered that more than 60 percent of all the complaints brought to primary-care physicians have an emotional or psychological dimension.) This is not to say that you should see the doctor as a friend but rather as someone to whom you can talk comfortably about intimate concerns. Your doctor should give you his or her undivided attention, should be willing to answer questions in language that you can understand, and should treat you warmly and unhurriedly.

If the visit includes a history-taking and a physical examination, you will be able to arrive at further conclusions. Questions about your smoking and drinking habits and your patterns of sleep and exercise—together with appropriate recommendations for promoting good health—show that a doctor places emphasis on preventing illness, the most important aspect of health care. The thoroughness and consideration with which a doctor performs a physical examination provide valuable clues about his or her competence and attitudes toward patients.

GETTING A SECOND OPINION

Getting a second opinion is one of your rights as a patient. There are many circumstances in which it is entirely appropriate for you to exercise this right and ask your doctor for a referral to another physician. In so doing, you are not challenging your doctor's judgment; rather, you are taking a responsible attitude toward your health and well-being.

Doctors also get second opinions, with their patients' permission. Primary-care physicians consult with colleagues who are specialists in appropriate areas—or refer patients to these colleagues—if they are unsure of their diagnoses, or uncertain about a proposed course of treatment, or confronted with a difficult decision. Similarly, specialists seek the advice of other specialists in their own or related fields.

Surgery

One of the times when it is most important to get a second opinion is when surgery is proposed as the treatment for an ailment or as an aid in diagnosis. All surgery, however minor, carries some risk of disability or even death.

About 80 percent of the surgery done in this country is elective, that is to say, non-emergency. Thus there is time to get a second opinion on the procedure that has been recommended and to consider poss-

HOW TO FIND A DOCTOR—CHECKLIST

	YES	NO
Does the doctor have certification from a recognized medical society?	____	____
Is the doctor affiliated with a hospital?	____	____
Is it a teaching hospital?	____	____
Is it a community hospital with a postgraduate education program?	____	____
Is it a fully accredited hospital?	____	____
Is the hospital conveniently located?	____	____
Is the doctor's office within a convenient distance?	____	____
Is the office near public transportation routes?	____	____
Is parking easily available near the office?	____	____
Are the doctor's office hours compatible with your schedule?	____	____
Does an associate or partner cover for the doctor when he or she is unavailable?	____	____
Is the answering service reliable?	____	____
Will the doctor make house calls?	____	____
Can you get an appointment within a reasonable time?	____	____
Do you spend excessive time in the waiting room before an appointment?	____	____
Are the office personnel attentive and courteous?	____	____
Is the office clean and attractive?	____	____
Can you afford to pay the doctor's fee?	____	____
Does the doctor answer your questions courteously and clearly?	____	____
Would you feel comfortable discussing intimate concerns with the doctor?	____	____
Is the physical examination thorough and respectful?	____	____
Does the doctor emphasize the preventive aspects of health care?	____	____
Could you work well with the doctor to maintain your health?	____	____

ible alternative medical treatments. In the final analysis, an individual should decide whether or not to undergo elective surgery by weighing the risks and benefits: Do the potential benefits of the operation outweigh its risks?

It is especially important to get a second opinion from another qualified surgeon when the suggested operation is one of several that are often done unnecessarily. Operations that are often done for insufficient reason, exposing patients to unnecessary risk, include hysterectomies, gallbladder surgery (cholecystectomies), hernia repair, tonsillectomies, and operations on the back, on varicose veins, and on hemorrhoids.

If the consultant who is asked for a second opinion disagrees with the original surgeon, it may be helpful to obtain a third opinion. Most insurance policies that cover a consultant's fees allow for this possibility.

Serious and Potentially Fatal Illness

A second opinion should be sought if a doctor diagnoses a serious chronic illness, or a disease that may be fatal, or a disease that is extremely rare. If the diagnosis is of a malignancy, it may be advisable to have the advice of two cancer specialists, especially if the first is pessimistic about recovery.

No Diagnosis

It is also advisable to ask your doctor for a referral to a specialist if your doctor is not able to make a diagnosis within a reasonable length of time. Two or three visits should be sufficient for a doctor to make a diagnosis or to decide that your problem is outside his or her area of expertise.

Risks and Benefits

Patients have the right to know the risks and benefits of any procedure that it is proposed that they undergo. It is therefore appropriate to ask for a second opinion if a doctor does not give you satisfactory answers to your questions about the risks (including the costs) and the potential benefits of a procedure—for example, an expensive or potentially dangerous test.

Where to Get the Name of a Specialist

Your regular doctor should provide you with the name of a specialist to whom you can go for a second opinion. Other sources of names are hospitals (preferably teaching hospitals), medical centers, and medical schools. It is perfectly in order to telephone the office of the head of the appropriate service or department and ask for names of specialists in the field.

SUMMING UP

The choice of a primary-care doctor is an all-important decision since this man or woman will be the one to oversee your medical care, to decide when you should see a specialist and which specialist you should see, and to admit you to the hospital and be your advocate while you are there. He or she will also help you maintain good health and prevent illness, the most important part of medical care.

Obviously, the doctor you choose should be well qualified, competent, and caring. It is also essential that he or she be someone with whom you are comfortable. The importance of a good working relationship with one's doctor cannot be overstated.

2. Warning Signs of Cancer

COMMON CHARACTERISTICS

Cancer is not a single disease, but instead a family of different diseases that have one characteristic in common: uncontrolled cell growth. This rapid proliferation of cells occurs at the expense of the body's normal cells and the normal body systems.

If cancer is detected early, the chances that treatment will be effective are greatly enhanced. Some cancers—lung cancer, for example, and cancer of the pancreas—are very difficult to diagnose early since they produce no noticeable symptoms until they are quite well advanced. However, many other common cancers—such as those of the breast, bowel, cervix, and skin —can be detected early enough for a complete cure to be possible. It is therefore very important to be aware of the signs that may—or may not—be warning signals of cancer, and to report them promptly to the doctor if they appear.

Some of the more common warning signs of cancer include:

• *Unusual bleeding or discharge.* This is a particularly common warning sign of uterine or cervical cancer. Any unusual vaginal bleeding that is not specifically related to menstruation should be promptly investigated by a doctor. Bleeding associated with gynecologic cancer does not follow any pattern—it can occur at any time, can be light or heavy, and may or may not be accompanied by a discharge. Pain is usually not one of the early symptoms of gynecologic cancer. Blood in the stool or urine also may be a sign of cancer and also should be investigated by a doctor.

• *A lump or thickening of the flesh in the breast or elsewhere.* Most breast cancer is initially discovered by the woman herself as a lump or thickening in the breast. (It should be noted, however, that most breast lumps turn out to be cysts or other benign growths; even so, they should be seen by a doctor to rule out the possibility of cancer.) Many childhood cancers begin as unexplained lumps or swellings. Hodgkin's disease and lymphomas may be detected when lymph glands become tender and swollen.

• *A sore that fails to heal.* Skin cancer commonly begins as a small sore that does not heal. More advanced cancers also may appear as a chronic sore.

• *A change in bowel habits.* Any change—diarrhea, constipation, change in stool size, shape, or color—that persists for more than a few days should be investigated.

• *Hoarseness or chronic coughing.* This is an early sign of cancers of the larynx, throat, and lung. Smokers should be particularly wary of such symptoms, which are often hard to distinguish from the so-called smoker's cough. Any cough that lasts for a few days and that produces blood should be promptly investigated.

• *Abdominal distress or difficulty in swallowing.* Intestinal and esophageal cancers often start with chronic indigestion or problems in swallowing.

• *Any significant new growth on the skin, or a change in a growth, mole, or skin marking.*

MOST COMMON CANCER SITES

IN MEN
1. Lung
2. Prostate
3. Colon and rectum
4. Urinary tract
5. Blood and lymph system

IN WOMEN
1. Breast
2. Colon and rectum
3. Lung
4. Uterus
5. Blood and lymph system

Skin cancers and melanoma—cancer of the pigment cells—often begin with a change in a mole or the appearance of dark, mole-like growths.

• *Any loss of weight that cannot be explained.* A number of cancers are diagnosed following a sudden drop in weight. Loss of appetite is also a warning sign of some cancers.

• *Unusual bruising.* Leukemia is often heralded by an increased tendency to bruise. Unusual paleness is another warning sign, especially in children.

• *Unexplained chronic pain, especially in the bones.* Multiple myeloma, bone cancer, and leukemia are often accompanied by a deep, aching sensation, especially in the back. In addition, a number of cancers, particularly breast and ovarian cancers, spread to the bones.

• *Chronic fever.* A fever is usually a sign of infection, and since many cancers affect the immune system and make a person more vulnerable to infections, a chronic, low-grade fever is often a warning symptom. Any lingering fever that lasts for more than a few days should be investigated.

The occurrence of any of these signs should not automatically be interpreted as a diagnosis of cancer. Such a determination can be made only by biopsy or other appropriate tests. In most cases, the warning is of some condition other than cancer. Even so, the symptoms should be investigated promptly. Many people who fear they may have cancer procrastinate; in fact, studies indicate that a majority of people tend to put off seeing their doctors about conditions that are clearly abnormal—often for months. Where cancer is concerned, such a delay may be critical.

REGULAR CHECKUPS

A regular medical checkup may detect an early cancer before an individual notices any warning signal. The Pap smear, which should be part of every woman's annual checkup, is a reliable means for early detection of cancer of the cervix. (If this cancer is caught sufficiently early, the cure rate is nearly 100 percent.) A routine rectal examination may detect cancer of the prostate before a man experiences any problems. And an annual check for occult (hidden) blood in the stool is a vital screening tool for cancers of the colon and rectum in both sexes after age forty.

A routine checkup, however, should not be thought of as a substitute for an immediate investigation of alarming symptoms. If one of the warning signs of cancer makes its appearance, an individual should act promptly—don't wait until the next checkup to have the symptom checked.

SUMMING UP

Early detection and prompt treatment are all-important in cases of cancer. It is the responsibility of the individual to recognize the warning signs of cancer—changes in bodily function or appearance that persist for more than two weeks. It is the individual's responsibility to see his or her doctor at once if any of these signals appear.

3. Preparing for a Physical Exam

The routine medical examination of a healthy individual has two primary objectives: to maintain health and to detect disease before symptoms appear. During the course of routine checkups, serious but unsuspected diseases have been found in millions of Americans. When disease is diagnosed at an early stage, it can often be cured or controlled before severe damage is done. Moreover, treatment is likely to be less expensive.

In the past, an annual checkup was the rule for all adults. Today, most doctors schedule routine reexaminations according to the individual's age and health status. It is generally recommended that a complete "base-line" examination be performed early in adult life, providing a measure against which future changes can be assessed. Thereafter—as a general rule for low-risk, asymptomatic patients—a checkup should be scheduled every five years in early adulthood, every two or three years in middle age, and annually after age sixty or sixty-five.

A checkup is also advisable if you acquire a new physician. While you should, if possible, have your health records transferred, it is also helpful to have a complete examination so that the new physician has base-line information about your condition.

A complete medical examination usually takes from three-quarters of an hour to an hour, exclusive of any follow-up tests or X-ray examinations that may be ordered. The examination is usually done by a private physician or by a nurse practitioner working under the supervision of a physician. It includes a detailed medical history, a thorough physical examination, and a number of tests.

THE MEDICAL HISTORY

The history, which may take fifteen to thirty minutes, is considered by many doctors to be the most important part of the examination. More than half of all illnesses can be detected on the basis of the history alone. A complete history is taken at the time of the initial checkup and is updated at subsequent ones.

You will be asked—and should answer without reserve—a variety of questions about your family's history of health and disease, your personal history and habits, (smoking, sex, diet, sleep, for example,) your past health, and the functioning of your body parts and organ systems (eyes, heart, lungs, bowels, and so forth). The history may take the form of a lengthy questionnaire; your doctor will review this with you, asking more detailed questions on any topics where your answers differ significantly from the norm. The medical history provides the doctor with important background information about your body; it also helps supply a focus for the physical examination, the next stage of the checkup.

THE PHYSICAL EXAMINATION

You will be asked to undress. The doctor will carefully look at, listen to, touch, and probe the body, both to assess your general health and to detect early signs of disease. This part of the examination takes ten to fifteen minutes.

Measurement of blood pressure is a routine part of the physical examination. Hypertension (above normal blood pressure) is a significant risk factor in heart disease, stroke, and kidney failure. A manual examination of the rectum is also routine; this may be supplemented with visual inspection through a sigmoidoscope, which enables the doctor to extend examination of the lower bowel to a depth of twelve inches. The rectal examination can detect hemorrhoids, polyps, and cancer. (Rectal and colon cancer, if found early, are often completely curable.) It provides information about a woman's uterus and ovaries; in men, it reveals the state of the prostate gland.

For women, the checkup always includes a careful visual and manual inspection of the breasts, to detect any cysts or tumors, and a pelvic examination. The walls of the vagina and the opening of the cervix are examined visually through a speculum, and a manual examination is done to check the uterus and ovaries for any unusual growths.

TESTS

Specimens of blood and urine, a stool sample, and, for women, a cervical smear are obtained at the time of the physical examination and are sent to a laboratory for analysis. The blood analysis provides information about silent infections and disorders in numerous organ systems and can reveal the presence of conditions such as diabetes and anemia. The cholesterol level in the blood provides a valuable indicator not only of specific malfunctions (for example, kidney disease, underactivity of the thyroid gland) but also of the presence of one of the major risk factors in heart disease. Analysis of the components of the urine provides a measure of the function of the heart, kidneys, and

COMMON MEDICAL TESTS

Below are common medical tests that are performed on a routine basis and are often included in a physical examination. Individual circumstances may dictate other tests that are not listed here.

TEST	PURPOSE
Breast exam	Detect any lumps or other abnormalities
Blood pressure measurement	Detect high blood pressure (hypertension)
Electrocardiogram	Study heart function, particularly electrical activity
Biopsy	Microscopic examination of body tissue
Blood lipid tests	Measure levels of cholesterol and triglycerides in blood
Sigmoidoscopy	Visual examination of rectum and lower portion of colon
Pap smear	Microscopic examination of cells shed from cervix or other organ (may be done on bronchial cells in heavy smokers).
Fecal blood	Examination of small stool samples to detect microscopic blood
Urinalysis	Examination of urine for sugar, protein, or other substances
Complete blood count	Analysis of numbers of red and white blood cells, platelets, and other blood components.
Exercise stress test	Measure of heart's work capacity
Mammography	Special X-rays of the breast
Pelvic examination	Visual and manual examination of vagina, cervix, and other female reproductive organs

pancreas and may indicate infection or malfunction in any part of the urinary tract. Even in the absence of any bowel symptoms, the stool sample may reveal inflammation in the colon or bleeding in the gastrointestinal tract due to ulcers, hemorrhoids, or cancer. The Pap test, in which cells from a woman's vagina and cervix are examined microscopically, is a valuable tool in the detection of cervical cancer; its regular use has greatly reduced the death rate from this common malignancy.

Other tests may be done on the basis of symptoms, the findings of the physical examination, or the patterns of disease suggested by the medical history. The mammogram, for example, is one of the most common tests recommended for women over forty. This simple X-ray of the breasts can pick up early cancers that are not noted in the physical examination; of these, 95 percent are curable.

At one time, a chest X-ray was considered an essential part of the medical checkup. However, increasing concern about the effects of radiation on the body has resulted in diminished use of this test. In the absence of respiratory symptoms or exposure to substances that damage the lungs (asbestos, for example), most physicians do not include a chest X-ray in the checkup.

An electrocardiogram (ECG) may be ordered if the physical examination and routine tests suggest an abnormality in heart function. This recording of the heart's electrical activity may be made

A Guide to Common Medical Tests

This guide is based on the findings of four major studies comparing the effectiveness of periodic exams with their risks and costs.

o recommended by one or two of the four studies

● recommended by three or all of the four studies

AGE	BREAST EXAM	MAMMOG-RAPHY	PELVIC EXAM	PAP SMEAR	RECTAL EXAM	SIGMOID-OSCOPY	FECAL BLOOD	BLOOD PRESSURE	CHOLESTEROL LEVEL
20	o		o	o				o	
21	o		o	o				o	o
22	o		o	o				o	
23	o		o	o				o	
24	o		o	o				o	o
25									
26	o		o	●				o	
27									
28	o		o	o				o	o
29	o		o	o				o	
30	o		o	o	o			o	o
31									
32	o		o	●				o	o
33									
34	o		o	o				o	
35	o		o	●	o			o	o
36	o		o	o				o	o
37		o							
38	o		o	o				o	
39									
40	●		●	●	o		o	●	o
41	o		o	o	o				
42	●		o		o		o	o	
43	o		o		o				
44	●		o	o	o		o	o	o
45	o		o	o	o		o	o	o
46	●		o	o	o		o	o	
47	o		o	o	o		o	o	
48	●		o	o	o		o	o	o
49	o		o		o		o	o	
50	●	●	●	●	o	o	●	●	o
51	●	●	o		o	o	●	o	
52	●	●	o	o	o		●	●	o
53	●	●	o	o	o		●		
54	●	●	o	o	o		●	●	
55	●	●	o	o	o	o	●	o	o
56	●	●	o	o	o		●	●	o
57	●	●	o	o	o		●	o	
58	●	●	o	o	o		●	o	
59	●	●	o	o	o	o	●	o	
60	●	●	●	●	o		●	●	o
61	●	o	o		o		●	o	
62	●	o	●	●	o		●	●	
63	●	o	o		o	o	●	o	
64	●	o	●		o		●	●	
65	●	o	o	●	o	o	●	●	o
66	●	o	●	o	o		●	●	
67	●	o	o	o	o	o	●	o	
68	●	o	●	o	o	o	●	●	
69	●	o	o		o		●	o	
70	●	o	●	●	o		●	●	o
71	●	o	o	o	o	o	●	o	
72	o	o	o		o		●	o	
73	o	o	o		o		●	o	
74	o	o	o	o	o		●	o	
75	o	o	o	o	o	o	●		o

These recommendations apply to the low-risk patient without symptoms. Your physican may wish to alter the frequency or perform other tests.

while resting or while exercising on a treadmill or stationary bicycle. The latter —the so-called stress test—is considered by most cardiologists to be the more valuable. (See the accompanying chart for common tests and how often they should be performed.)

PREPARING FOR A CHECKUP

When you call to make an appointment for a checkup, the nurse may give you special instructions, asking you to fast for a certain time before arriving, for example, or to empty your bowel. It is important to follow these instructions in order to assure the accuracy of test results. It is also important that you do not go on a crash diet or suddenly undertake a strenuous exercise program to try to "get in shape" for the examination. Such efforts could distort the test results and endanger your health.

You should check your health insurance policy to see whether it covers a routine examination. Most policies do not. However, if any abnormality is found in the course of the examination and the doctor records it on the claim form, you may be compensated for part of the cost.

Before the appointment, make a list of any questions you may have about your body and its functioning, and do not hesitate to let your doctor know what concerns you. Two-way communication is essential to good medical care.

SUMMING UP

A complete medical checkup includes a history, a physical examination, and a variety of tests. Its primary purpose is to prevent and detect disease. It also, however, provides you with an opportunity to establish and then to maintain a good working relationship with your doctor.

It is no longer generally considered necessary for all adults in good health to have a complete medical examination every year. Rather, the frequency of checkups and the performance of tests are tailored to the individual's age and well-being and the presence of any risks to health.

4. Stocking Your Medicine Chest

A well-stocked medicine chest should be an important part of any household. All too often, however, drugs are kept in a bathroom medicine cabinet that is jammed with unused medicines left over from previous illnesses, a few bandages and other first-aid supplies, a collection of cosmetics, razors, dental products, and assorted other items that are handy to keep in the bathroom. If this describes your medicine cabinet, it's time to do some housecleaning and to organize a medicine chest that is exclusively for drugs and emergency supplies.

SORTING OUT

The first step in organizing and stocking your medicine cabinet should be to take stock of what you already have. Look first at the prescription drugs. Set aside those that are currently being taken or are used periodically for recurring problems, such as asthma or arthritis. *Discard the rest.* While throwing out leftover medicines may appear wasteful, the fact is that many can become hazards when they are saved for future use.

Generally, doctors prescribe only as much medicine as is needed for a particular illness. This is particularly true of antibiotics, where the general rule is "use it or throw it out," unless specifically instructed otherwise. Many antibiotics quickly lose potency; for example, the liquid antibiotics that are often prescribed for children may be good for only two weeks.

The composition of others, such as tetracycline, change with age. In addition, most prescriptions are written for a specific episode of illness. You may think you have the same thing, but the diagnosis may be different or require a different treatment than before. Therefore, you should not take a prescription drug for any illness other than the one for which it was originally intended unless specifically instructed to do so by your doctor.

Nonprescription drugs also should be sorted out. Look for date codes and discard those whose effective date has passed. When buying nonprescription drugs, write the purchase date on the label. Go through your medicine chest at least once a year and throw out those that are more than a year old.

Look for any changes in smell, color, or consistency or any other alterations. Aspirin that has a vinegary smell is beginning to go bad and should be thrown out. Liquid medicines that contain alcohol may become more condensed as the alcohol evaporates—if the mixture seems thickened or has a thick skin on top, throw it away. Any tablets or capsules that are crumbling, partially melted, or otherwise changed should be discarded. The same is true of ointments or creams that have caked or changed in composition. Effervescent medicines that have lost their fizz also should be thrown out.

WHAT TO BUY

Individual needs often dictate what drugs should be kept on hand. For exam-

WHAT TO HAVE ON HAND

Obviously, selecting health care items for the family medicine chest is a matter of common sense. Here are some suggested items that will meet the needs of most families:

Nondrug products

Adhesive bandages of assorted sizes
Sterile gauze in pads and a roll
Absorbent cotton
Adhesive tape
Elastic bandage
Small blunt-end scissors
Tweezers
Fever thermometer, including rectal type for a
    young child
Hot water bottle
Heating pad
Eye cup for flushing objects out of the eye
Ice bag
Dosage spoon (common household teaspoons
    are rarely the correct dosage size)
Vaporizer or humidifier
First-aid manual

Drug Items

Analgesic—aspirin and/or acetaminophen. Both
    reduce fever and relieve pain; only aspirin can
    reduce inflammation.
Emetic (to induce vomiting)—syrup of ipecac to
    induce vomiting and activated charcoal. Read
    the instructions on how to use these products.
Antacid
Antiseptic solution
Hydrocortisone creams for skin problems
Calamine for poison ivy and other skin irritations
Petroleum jelly as a lubricant
Antidiarrhetic
Cough syrup—nonsuppressant type
Decongestant
Burn ointment
Antibacterial topical ointment

The medicine chest might also include antinausea medication if any family member is prone to motion sickness, a laxative, and some liniment. Seasonal items, such as insect repellents and sunscreens, round out the list.

ple, a family with young children will have different needs from those of an older couple. Make a list of drugs—both prescription and nonprescription—that are used on a regular basis and make sure that these are in adequate supply. In addition, every well-stocked medicine chest should have items that are used in an emergency: antiseptic, assortment of bandages, ipecac syrup and activated charcoal (for poisoning emergencies), sterile cotton swabs, sunburn or other burn medications (remember, however, that you should not apply ointments or other sticky substances to anything other than very minor burns), and other supplies that may be indicated by individual needs (such as a snake-bite or bee-sting kit). Replace antiseptics often. Some, such as hydrogen peroxide, lose their potency after being opened. Others, such as tincture of iodine, contain alcohol, which quickly evaporates. The condensed antiseptic may cause burns.

Make a list of those nonprescription medications that you use occasionally or would find convenient to have on hand

should the need arise: painkillers, antacids, laxatives, antidiarrheal or antinauseant agents, and allergy medications all are examples of drugs that many people may need from time to time and that can be purchased in small quantities for possible future use.

WHERE TO KEEP YOUR DRUGS

All medicines should be stored according to directions on the label. Do not refrigerate unless instructed to do so. Most drugs should be kept in a dry place with an even temperature. *The bathroom is usually the worst place in the house in which to keep medicines.* Its extremes in heat and humidity hasten the deterioration of drugs, especially those that have been opened. In addition, the bathroom medicine cabinet is readily accessible to young children—save it for toothpaste, shaving supplies, and other such items, and look for some other place to serve as a medicine chest. A high shelf in a hall closet usually is a good place in which to keep medicines. Many people have found that keeping drugs locked in an overnight case or similar container that can be placed on a closet shelf is both convenient and safe.

Always recap tubes and bottles tightly and keep drugs in their original containers. Discard the cotton padding that is placed under the lid in many pill bottles; it will absorb moisture and hasten deterioration. But do not remove the little white disc containing silica gel that is placed in many bottles—it is designed to keep the pills dry. (Be careful not to consume the disc; its contents are not harmful, but it can cause choking or an internal obstruction.)

SUMMING UP

The items in your medicine chest depend largely upon individual needs and common sense. It's not necessary to have an at-home pharmacy; on the other hand, a supply of often-used nonprescription drugs in addition to those prescription medicines that are currently being taken under a doctor's supervision and emergency supplies should be stored in a safe, convenient place at home. You should go through your medicine chest periodically, discarding all the old or doubtful nonprescription medications as well as all leftover prescription drugs unless your doctor has specifically instructed you to save them. Even so, don't take any prescription drug without specific instructions from your doctor. Although the symptoms may seem the same as in the past, the problem may be different or require a different approach.

5. Drug Information for Senior Citizens

GENERAL CONSIDERATIONS

As a group, people over sixty-five years of age take three times more medication than younger persons, primarily because they are affected by chronic disease to a greater extent. It is not uncommon for an older person to take several different prescription medications daily, in addition to one or more nonprescription or over-the-counter preparations. Multiple drug use of this kind has the potential of producing adverse reactions, particularly if there is no single doctor supervising the use of all the drugs. However, by being knowledgeable about the drugs you are taking and by playing an active part in the treatment process, you can help your doctor help you derive the greatest benefit from your medications, while avoiding undesirable side effects.

WHAT YOUR DOCTOR SHOULD KNOW

When your doctor prescribes a specific drug for a particular condition, the selection is based on various factors, including your age, weight, and state of health. You can assist your doctor in selecting the most appropriate drug by making sure that he or she is aware of any problems—particularly any allergic reactions—that you may have had in the past with specific medications, and also by making sure that he or she knows what prescription medications and over-the-counter preparations you are currently taking.

Of course, if the doctor is your regular physician, he or she will have a record of your medical history and drug use and will be aware of any potentially dangerous combinations of medication. However, it is important that you inform your regular doctor about any medication prescribed by another doctor or by a dentist. It is equally important to give complete information about current drug use to any doctor whom you are seeing for the first time, a specialist, for example.

WHAT YOU SHOULD KNOW

Most doctors are more than willing to discuss your condition with you and to provide basic information about the drugs they prescribe. However, many people find after they have left the doctor's office that they cannot remember all the information and instructions they were given. Therefore, it is advisable to take notes during your doctor's explanation of your condition and to ask your doctor to write down instructions for taking medications. You should never hesitate to ask questions. If you have not heard or have not understood something, ask that it be repeated or explained.

Specifically, you should know the following about each of the medications you are taking: the name of the drug and its strength; the condition for which it has been prescribed; the benefits you can expect; what the possible side effects are and which should be reported promptly to your doctor; how much medication you should take and when you should take it; any special instructions about taking the drug; its cost. You should also know if

there are any foods or beverages (such as alcohol) that should be avoided while taking the medication; if any of your usual activities (such as driving or operating machinery) should be discontinued; and if interactions with other medications—including over-the-counter drugs, vitamins, and dietary supplements—are to be expected.

YOUR PHARMACIST

If possible, use the same pharmacist for all your drug needs, thus ensuring that there is a record of all your past and present medications. You should also ask your pharmacist if there are any special storage instructions for your medication—if it should be refrigerated, for example, or kept in dark-colored glass bottles. (In general, it is wise not to remove medications from their original containers.)

Most prescriptions are filled in child-resistant containers. However, if there are no small children who are at home or who visit, you can ask your pharmacist to fill your prescriptions in regular containers.

TAKING YOUR MEDICATION

In order to derive the full benefit from your medication, it is essential that you follow your doctor's instructions precisely. You should not stop taking a medication after a few days if you feel better, or reduce the dosage if you feel worse, or take a double dose if you forget a previous one. As an active participant in your treatment, it is your responsibility to take your medication when and as prescribed.

If you have problems with vision, ask a

MONTHLY MEDICATION CALENDAR

Fill in names of drugs.

Check off each dose when you take it.

Breakfast	1	2	3	4	5	6	7	8	9	10	11	12	13	14	15	16	17	18	19	20	21	22	23	24	25	26	27	28	29	30	31

Lunch																															

Dinner																															

Bedtime																															

friend or relative to copy the prescription labels in large print and, perhaps, in different colored inks. These new labels can be taped over the original ones to make it easier to distinguish one drug from another.

It may help you to remember which of your medications to take when if you place the instructions you received from your doctor in a prominent position for easy reference. If the medication schedule is complicated, a drug calendar is useful. Marked with the names of the drugs and the times of day they are to be taken, the calendar should provide a space for checking off each dose as it is taken. Another memory aid is a set of prescription bottles or an empty milk carton labeled with the times of day (or days of the week) that medications are to be taken and filled with the appropriate dose. You may find it helpful to set an alarm clock for the time that the medication is to be taken.

It is generally not advisable to put a day's medications together in one box. One pill may easily be mistaken for another with a similar appearance. Moreover, some drugs may lose their potency if kept in such a manner.

It is important not to share your prescription medication with anyone and not to take someone else's medicine. It is also important not to use medication remaining from a previous illness. Even though your present symptoms may seem identical to those of a former illness, only your doctor can evaluate whether your current problem is in fact the same and whether the same drug should be used to treat it. Further, some drugs decline in strength over time and may even become totally ineffective.

SIDE EFFECTS

In addition to their beneficial actions, many, if not all, drugs have some undesirable side effects. Not everyone taking a specific drug will develop a particular side effect, and many bad reactions are temporary or only mildly uncomfortable. However, other side effects are more serious and may indicate that there are problems associated with a particular drug. Therefore, if you experience any untoward symptom that you think may be drug-related, you should inform your doctor. If the problem proves to be caused by your medication, your doctor may change the drug or alter the dosage. You should never stop taking a drug, or change the dosage, without consulting your doctor.

NONPRESCRIPTION DRUGS

Over-the-counter products for the relief of problems ranging from arthritis to influenza to constipation are widely used in the erroneous belief that they are not drugs and can do no harm. However, these drugs—as well as vitamins, dietary supplements, and even home remedies—can have undesirable side effects and may interact adversely with prescription medications. Thus, it is very important to ask your doctor's advice about such products and to inform him or her about any nonprescription drugs and preparations you may be using.

SUMMING UP

Modern drugs can combat many diseases and can be used to manage many long-term illnesses. However, they can also produce undesirable and even dangerous side effects.

There is much that an elderly person can do to derive the greatest benefit from necessary medications and to minimize the possibility of misuse and unwanted reactions. A person who is well informed is more likely to use drugs properly and to become an active participant in his or her own drug therapy.

6. Designing a Fitness Program

Medically, there are any number of good reasons to exercise on a regular basis. Regular exercise adds to cardiovascular and pulmonary fitness, strengthens weak or damaged muscles, often reduces feelings of emotional tension and depression, and makes weight control easier, thereby helping to eliminate the attendant health hazards of obesity. But if you ask the millions of joggers, swimmers, tennis players, golfers, or other amateur athletes why they exercise, most would probably reply: "Because it makes you look and feel good!" And, indeed, the best way to flatten a stomach, firm up thighs, slim down flabby hips and arms, improve skin tone, and generally look fit, trim, and healthy is regular exercise.

WHO SHOULD EXERCISE?

Seventy years ago, half the American population worked in jobs that met their daily exercise needs. Today, only 2 percent have jobs meeting this need, and it is believed that this figure will fall still lower in the future as more and more labor-saving devices enter our homes and offices. Most authorities feel that nearly all Americans could benefit from more exercise—including those who already do exercise. According to a recent study by the President's Council on Physical Fitness, 55 percent of Americans engage in some form of physical activity. But only 28 percent pursue that activity frequently enough to derive any health benefit from it.

Of course, there are people who should not engage in exercise unless prescribed and planned by a physician. This group includes people with certain forms of musculoskeletal injuries and disorders and certain chronic diseases such as heart disorders, asthma, or obstructive pulmonary disease.

If you are in good health but over the age of thirty-five or forty and have heretofore led a sedentary existence, a medical plan for the exercise schedule is probably desirable. If you are over forty, that consultation may include an exercise stress test, especially if you smoke or have high blood pressure, elevated blood cholesterol, or a personal or family history of heart disease—all factors that increase the risk of a heart attack. The test involves taking an ECG (electrocardiogram) while walking on a treadmill or pedaling on an exercise bicycle and climbing. The results give a good indication of how the heart will respond to the increased stress of exercise. (See Chapter 191, "The Exercise Tolerance Test.")

CHOOSING THE RIGHT EXERCISE

Exercise generally improves cardiovascular fitness, uses excess calories, enhances joint flexibility, and increases muscular strength and endurance. Before selecting an exercise, you must first decide what you want it to do for you. According to the experts, the key criterion should be boosting cardiovascular fitness. The best exercises for strengthening the heart are continuous and aerobic in nature: walking, biking, jogging, swimming, jumping rope, aerobic dancing, racquet sports, soccer, and basketball.

Sit-ups, knee bends, leg raises, and other types of calisthenics are best suited to building joint flexibility. However, many joggers also find that calisthenics are an

Benefits of Exercise

Aerobic Exercises

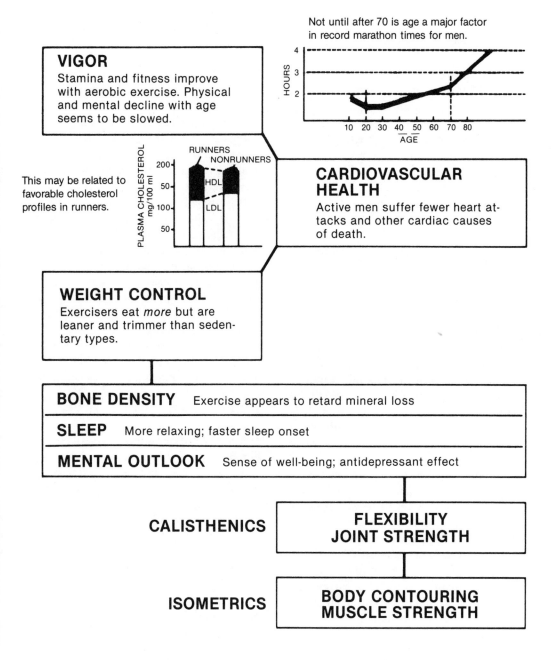

Not until after 70 is age a major factor in record marathon times for men.

VIGOR
Stamina and fitness improve with aerobic exercise. Physical and mental decline with age seems to be slowed.

This may be related to favorable cholesterol profiles in runners.

CARDIOVASCULAR HEALTH
Active men suffer fewer heart attacks and other cardiac causes of death.

WEIGHT CONTROL
Exercisers eat *more* but are leaner and trimmer than sedentary types.

BONE DENSITY   Exercise appears to retard mineral loss

SLEEP   More relaxing; faster sleep onset

MENTAL OUTLOOK   Sense of well-being; antidepressant effect

CALISTHENICS

FLEXIBILITY JOINT STRENGTH

ISOMETRICS

BODY CONTOURING MUSCLE STRENGTH

Over 35? Check with your doctor before starting an exercise program.

ideal warm-up exercise. By combining them with running, it is possible to design an exercise program that provides both cardiovascular and musculoskeletal benefits. Weight training is a good way to build muscle strength and endurance and to reshape the body's contours. But it is also a stop-and-go activity, which means that it is not an efficient calorie-burner and that it provides little cardiovascular support.

Most recreational sports—such as bowling, softball, and weekend tennis—have the same stop-and-go disadvantages. They may be useful for relieving emotional tension or desirable as outdoor activities, but they may not increase cardiopulmonary capacity if not played vigorously enough. Golf may provide limited aerobic benefits if one does not use golf carts and walks at a brisk pace.

CREATING AN EXERCISE PROGRAM

Don't pick an exercise just because it is fashionable or even because you have read that it is good for you. You must enjoy what you do; otherwise you will not keep it up. There are enough options within each exercise group to suit most tastes. If running bores you, swimming, walking, bicycling, or handball may be more interesting. If you don't find calisthenics challenging enough, weight training, combined with an aerobic exercise, may be a good substitute.

A good way of making a program work is to set aside a certain time each day or every other day for your exercise. Specific scheduling will help create a sense of discipline. It also helps to exercise with friends or in an organized program. The added company alleviates the boredom of solitary exertion. Finally, it is useful to set specific goals for yourself, providing a target to work toward and a standard against which to measure your progress.

Each exercise session should include warm-up and cooling-down routines, so that starting and stopping strenuous activity do not come as a shock to the system. The best warm-up is a good ten minutes (or more) of stretching, followed by a few minutes of calisthenics or jogging. As the workout comes to an end, walk or jog lightly until you feel that respiration and heartbeat have leveled off before coming to a complete rest.

HOW MUCH EXERCISE?

Most exercise physiologists believe that cardiovascular-respiratory fitness is best improved and maintained by vigorous exercise four or five times a week. But there is also evidence that comparable benefits may accrue from intensive, briefer workouts (thirty minutes), three times a week—provided that the exercise is continuous and sufficiently rigorous. Of course, the definition of rigorous will vary according to an individual's age and sex. But as a general rule, the exercise should make you work at 60 to 80 percent of your maximum aerobic capacity. This can be measured by taking your pulse immediately after exercising; for persons between the ages of thirty and sixty, a pulse rate of 115 to 160 indicates the optimal performance range.

SUMMING UP

A final word of caution: don't overdo it. For beginners, this means starting slowly and progressing gradually. If your ultimate goal is to run four or five miles three times a week, give yourself six to eight weeks to reach that target. Even experienced amateur athletes must be careful not to overexert themselves. Fatigue and injuries should never be ignored. Although there is much talk about "working through" the pain among competitive (and amateur) exercisers, the most important thing is to remain attuned to your body and to heed the strain or pain messages it sends you.

7. Dealing with Alcoholism

COMMON CHARACTERISTICS

Alcoholism is said to exist when the patient becomes physically dependent upon drinking alcohol; in the simplest terms, an individual who *must* have a drink in order to "get going" or to "make it through the day" is an alcoholic.

Alcoholism is the nation's major addiction problem and one of our leading causes of death. It has a major effect on the lives of people close to the alcoholic, particularly family members and co-workers. Drunken driving—frequently an outgrowth of alcoholism—claims thousands of innocent lives each year.

Drinking during pregnancy—even a moderate three ounces of liquor per day—can damage the unborn. Furthermore, excessive consumption of alcohol increases the chance of a number of different cancers, particularly those of the liver, stomach, and bladder. The risk is even greater for people who both drink and smoke.

One of the major difficulties in treating this disease is that the line dividing social drinking from alcoholism may be exceedingly narrow.

HEALTH IMPACT OF ALCOHOL

Alcohol also impairs function of the brain and the central nervous system. Although its initial emotional effect may be euphoric, alcohol actually is a central nervous system depressant. When taken in sufficient quantity, alcohol causes a numbing of the senses (anesthesia); indeed, before the discovery of anesthetics, alcohol was the only means a surgeon had of dulling pain.

Almost all the alcohol a person ingests is absorbed into the bloodstream. It is then transported to the liver, where it is metabolized. The liver at first becomes more effective at handling increased alcohol intake, but eventually the amount of alcohol can overwhelm the liver's capacity. At this point, the liver becomes infiltrated with fat, which may be followed by an active inflammation. If the alcohol overloading persists for a long enough time—perhaps two or three years; the exact duration is not known—cirrhosis sets in. Cirrhosis is characterized by irreversible scarring of the liver, and a cirrhotic liver also may eventually become cancerous.

Advanced alcoholism may cause a type of dementia known as Korsakoff's psychosis, as well as a number of other serious illnesses. These include a type of heart disease known as cardiomyopathy; foot drop (peripheral neuritis); seizures; bleeding ulcers of the stomach, esophagus, and small intestine; and bone marrow depression resulting in lowered production of white blood cells.

Alcoholics sometimes have nutritional problems. Since alcohol contains calories but no other nutrients, many heavy drinkers are overweight. In some cases the alcoholic drinks instead of eating. Although alcohol stimulates the appetite when taken in small, dilute amounts, it becomes an appetite suppressant when consumed in greater quantity. Alcohol damages the liver and interferes with its ability to absorb and store such vitamins as B_{12} and folic acid, as well as its ability to convert some vitamins into their active chemical form. Even when the alcoholic eats, he or she does not get the full nutritional value of the food and may develop certain vita-

21

min and mineral deficiencies, particularly of folic acid.

DIAGNOSIS OF ALCOHOLISM

Many studies have indicated that an alcoholic is often the last person to admit that drinking has become a problem. Nevertheless, these patients will come to the doctor's office for an unrelated medical problem—hypertension, seizures, gastritis, ulcers, or other complaints. Admitting that excessive drinking has become a problem is, however, the first and major step in successful treatment.

Several self-administered tests have been developed by the U.S. government, Alcoholics Anonymous, and others to help the patient decide whether he or she has a drinking problem. Questions that may be asked include: Do you ever drink because you have problems? Do you drink when you get angry at others who are close to you? Do you often prefer to drink alone? Are you doing poorly at your job or in school? Do you ever try to stop drinking or to drink less and fail? Have you begun to drink in the morning before work or school? Do you gulp your drinks? Do you often get drunk, even when you do not mean to?

TREATMENT

Alcohol withdrawal results in delirium tremens (D.T.'s), characterized by trembling, agitation, acute mental distress, anxiety, and hallucinations. Not all alcoholics experience D.T.'s, but as a precaution, withdrawal should not be attempted without medical help. Delirum tremens may develop at this time and requires urgent attention. Fortunately, there are detoxification clinics in most hospitals. Once an alcoholic has gotten through the detoxification or initial withdrawal stage, there are a number of self-help groups, especially Alcoholics Anonymous, to aid in abstaining from further drinking.

Alcoholics Anonymous, the oldest and most successful self-help group, has helped millions of people since it was founded in 1935. Today, the organization has forty thousand local groups in 110 countries, and total membership is estimated at one million. The organization keeps no records of its members, and any personal information is kept confidential. (For phone numbers, see your local phone book.)

Alcoholism can also be treated by drugs, primarily disulfiram (Antabuse). This drug, when taken regularly, will make the patient extremely ill when he or she consumes alcohol. If your doctor prescribes this drug, be aware that alcohol is contained in many foods (in sauces, for example) and in some medications, including cough medicine and mouthwashes, which should be avoided.

ALCOHOLISM AND "IMPORTANT OTHERS"

Alcoholism, according to some psychiatrists, is often a family affair in which a nondrinking partner, without realizing it, helps the alcoholic to continue his or her addiction. This situation is referred to as collusion, and it must be brought to the attention of the nondrinking partner before an alcoholic can be cured. It is therefore crucial for family members to seek help for an alcoholic even if he or she does not admit to a drinking problem.

SUMMING UP

Alcoholism is a major addiction problem and cause of death in the United States. It can lead to many health problems such as malnutrition, cirrhosis, heart disease, dementia, and even cancer of the liver. In order to cure alcoholism, the individual must first admit that drinking has become a problem. Then, with the help of family, friends, and support groups, such as Alcoholics Anonymous, the individual must begin to change his or her behavior and attitudes toward drinking.

Mechanisms of Antabuse Therapy

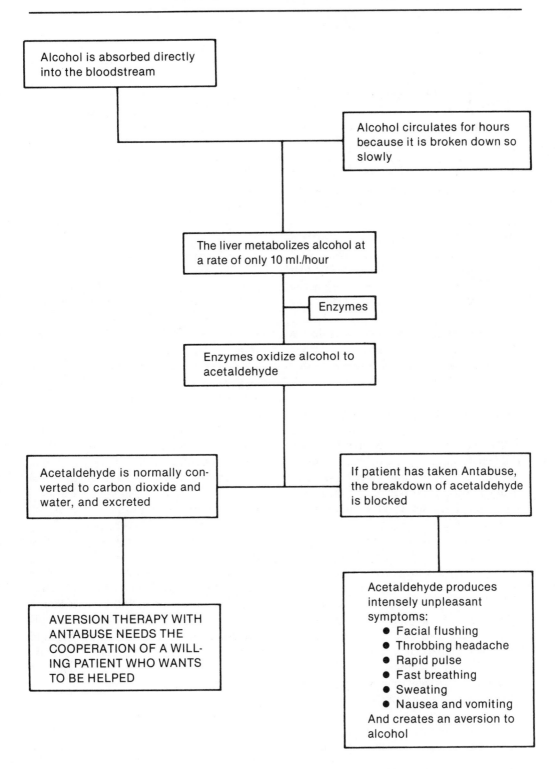

Alcohol is absorbed directly into the bloodstream

Alcohol circulates for hours because it is broken down so slowly

The liver metabolizes alcohol at a rate of only 10 ml./hour

Enzymes

Enzymes oxidize alcohol to acetaldehyde

Acetaldehyde is normally converted to carbon dioxide and water, and excreted

If patient has taken Antabuse, the breakdown of acetaldehyde is blocked

AVERSION THERAPY WITH ANTABUSE NEEDS THE COOPERATION OF A WILLING PATIENT WHO WANTS TO BE HELPED

Acetaldehyde produces intensely unpleasant symptoms:
- Facial flushing
- Throbbing headache
- Rapid pulse
- Fast breathing
- Sweating
- Nausea and vomiting

And creates an aversion to alcohol

8. Smoking and Health

COMMON CHARACTERISTICS

The U.S. Surgeon General recently called cigarette smoking "the most important health issue of our time" and "the chief preventable cause of death in our society," contributing to 325,000 premature deaths every year. Indeed, there is no doubt that quitting smoking is the single most important step that smokers can take toward improving health and prolonging life. Your doctor can help you quit, but first you must truly want to. Understanding the impact of cigarettes on your body may help.

Cigarette smoke contains more than a thousand different chemicals. The latest scientific research clearly documents that the effects of many are detrimental.

EFFECTS OF CIGARETTE SMOKE

Cigarette smoking is both psychologically and physically addictive. Nicotine reaches the brain within seven seconds of being inhaled. The body's production of adrenaline increases, resulting in the heart beating faster and blood pressure rising. At the same time, other biochemical responses yield increased activity of cells in the spinal cord, which leads to a decrease in muscle tone and a feeling of relaxation.

However, the feeling of relaxation only appears to be felt by people who are already addicted to nicotine. The pleasure apparently stems primarily from the relief of withdrawal symptoms. When you stop smoking cigarettes, symptoms of withdrawal may occur within hours or days of the last cigarette. These include restlessness, sleep disturbance, gastrointestinal upset, drowsiness, headache, amnesia, and impairment of concentration and judgment—all similar to the symptoms seen on withdrawal from other addictive drugs.

The variety of symptoms indicates the many body organs that are affected by nicotine and the other chemicals in cigarette smoke, and there is increasing evidence of long-term detrimental effects on these organs.

THE HISTORY OF EVIDENCE

In 1964, the first U.S. Surgeon General's report indicating that cigarettes posed a serious health risk was issued, resulting in the first health warnings on cigarette packages. Specific health effects that have been documented include:

• Smoking is implicated in about 30 percent of all cancers in human beings, including 75 percent of all lung cancer. It is also a major risk factor in cancers of the larynx, mouth, esophagus, bladder, pancreas, kidney, stomach, and uterine cervix. The smoker's risk of developing lung cancer is ten times greater than the nonsmoker's. After quitting, the cancer risks gradually decrease and return to normal within seven to fifteen years.

• Smoking is considered the primary cause of most cases of chronic obstructive pulmonary disease in the United States, which includes emphysema and chronic bronchitis. A smoker's cough will begin to disappear within a few weeks of quitting and, for those who already have lung disease, the rate of deterioration may decrease.

• Smoking is one of the major risk factors in the development of coronary artery disease and heart attacks in this country. The

Health Effects of Smoking

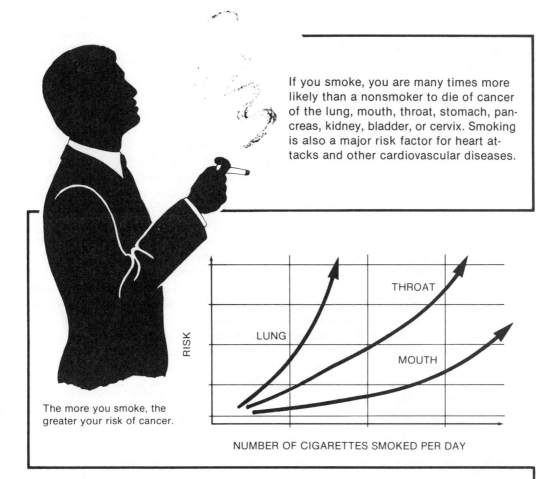

If you smoke, you are many times more likely than a nonsmoker to die of cancer of the lung, mouth, throat, stomach, pancreas, kidney, bladder, or cervix. Smoking is also a major risk factor for heart attacks and other cardiovascular diseases.

THROAT

LUNG

MOUTH

RISK

The more you smoke, the greater your risk of cancer.

NUMBER OF CIGARETTES SMOKED PER DAY

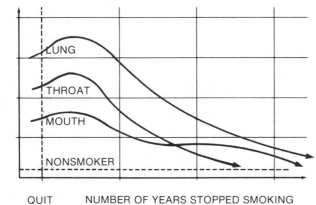

If you give up smoking, your chances of avoiding cancer become nearly as good as a nonsmoker's.

RISK

LUNG

THROAT

MOUTH

NONSMOKER

QUIT   NUMBER OF YEARS STOPPED SMOKING

latest Surgeon General's report estimates that smoking may account for 120,000 of the 600,000 deaths from heart disease in the United States each year. Additionally, women who smoke and take contraceptive pills greatly increase their risk of heart attacks and blood clots. Smoking affects many of the disease mechanisms related to heart disease, including heart rate, blood pressure, and the heart's susceptibility to abnormal rhythms. The risk of heart disease drops sharply within the first year of quitting smoking.

• Smokers are nearly twice as likely as nonsmokers to have stomach and duodenal ulcers. Curing ulcers is far more difficult among smokers, and deaths due to ulcers are twice as common among them as among nonsmokers. After quitting smoking, ulcers are more likely to heal rapidly and completely.

• Cigarette smoking is harmful to the unborn fetus. Smoking mothers have more stillbirths and babies of low birthweight. Smoking interferes with the blood and oxygen supply to the fetus and also has been associated with an increased risk of miscarriage, prematurity, crib death, cleft lip and palate, and other birth defects.

• Smoking contributes significantly to gum disease and impairs the ability to taste and smell. These effects are reversed soon after quitting.

DECIDING TO QUIT

Although the percentage of Americans who smoke has declined over the last two decades, an estimated 54 million Americans continue to smoke. About half have tried to quit at least once. In addition, the number of women and teenagers who smoke has increased. Clearly, quitting is not easy. Yet millions of Americans have achieved that goal and reaped the reward of a healthier life.

A variety of techniques and programs to help you quit are now available. Some are sponsored by nonprofit organizations such as the American Cancer Society, the American Heart Association, the American Lung Association, the Seventh Day Adventists, and local hospitals. These programs are free or inexpensive. Commercial programs run by profit-making organizations such as SmokEnders seem to work better for some people, possibly because some individuals may place greater value on something for which they are paying. Your physician can tell you about any special programs in your area and may provide special help to enable you to cope with withdrawal symptoms, if needed.

A number of studies have found that quitting all at once, or "going cold turkey," is the most likely to succeed. But overall more than 90 percent of those who quit will take up smoking again, although some methods have a higher success rate than others. Those who backslide should not be overly discouraged, however, because each successive attempt to stop seems to have an increasingly improved success rate.

WEIGHT GAIN

Many people, especially women, fear they will gain weight after stopping smoking. While there may be a modest weight gain in the first few weeks, this can be avoided or reversed by increasing physical activity and resorting to filling but low-calorie foods such as fresh fruits and vegetables.

SUMMING UP

Cigarette smoking presents clear and documented dangers to your health and well-being. If you decide to quit, you will feel better in the long run and probably live longer, too. While quitting is not easy, it pays to keep trying until you succeed.

Section Two:
Cardiovascular Problems

9. Risk Factors for Heart Disease

GENERAL CONSIDERATIONS

In the last decade, there has been a dramatic decline in the number of deaths from heart attacks. In 1970, nearly a million Americans died of cardiovascular disease; now the annual toll is about 600,000. The causes for this improved mortality rate are unknown, but most experts believe that the increased awareness of cardiovascular risk factors and their correction have played an important role in cutting the death toll.

WHAT ARE THE RISKS?

Eventually, about half of all Americans develop some form of heart disease. The most common is a hardening of the arteries caused by a buildup of fatty deposits along the vessel lining. This is a slow process that usually takes many years to develop into serious disease. If the coronary arteries, which supply blood to the heart muscle, become severely blocked by the fatty

deposits, warning symptoms of heart disease may appear. These include shortness of breath, chest pains (angina pectoris) that are relieved by rest, or a combination of the two. In many people, however, there are no warning signs—the first symptom of heart disease may be a heart attack. This is why it is important to identify and correct possible risk factors before they reach this stage.

In recent years, a number of these risk factors have been identified. Some of them, such as age, sex, and family history of heart disease, are things over which we have no control (see chart). But there also are a number of factors that can be modified or eliminated, and such action appears to reduce the probability of a heart attack. The three most important controllable risk factors are high blood pressure, high levels of blood cholesterol, and cigarette smoking. In fact, many experts attribute the recent decline in cardiovascular deaths to the fact that more people than ever before are now being treated for high

Risk Factors for a Heart Attack

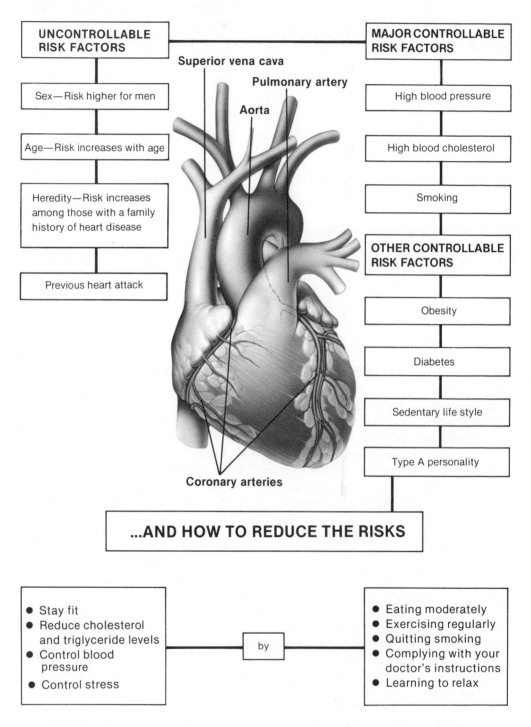

UNCONTROLLABLE RISK FACTORS		MAJOR CONTROLLABLE RISK FACTORS

Superior vena cava

Pulmonary artery

Aorta

Sex—Risk higher for men		High blood pressure
Age—Risk increases with age		High blood cholesterol
Heredity—Risk increases among those with a family history of heart disease		Smoking
		OTHER CONTROLLABLE RISK FACTORS
Previous heart attack		Obesity
		Diabetes
		Sedentary life style
		Type A personality

Coronary arteries

...AND HOW TO REDUCE THE RISKS

- Stay fit
- Reduce cholesterol and triglyceride levels
- Control blood pressure
- Control stress

by

- Eating moderately
- Exercising regularly
- Quitting smoking
- Complying with your doctor's instructions
- Learning to relax

blood pressure. Changes in the American diet that have reduced the consumption of butter, eggs, and animal fats—and consequently lowered the average blood cholesterol—and a reduction in smoking by middle-aged men also are credited with lowering the toll. Since the likelihood of developing heart disease increases when two or more risk factors are present, modifying the controllable ones helps reduce the hazard of those over which we have no control.

ROLE OF DIET

Studies have shown that population groups whose diets are rich in cholesterol and other animal and dairy fats have more heart attacks than those whose diets are low in these saturated fats. Americans, whose diets are high in meat and eggs, have a higher incidence of heart disease than the Japanese, who tend to eat very little meat and other animal and dairy fats.

Studies have also shown that high blood cholesterol—more than two hundred milligrams per milliliter of blood—can be lowered by modifying the diet. This means eating more fish and poultry while cutting consumption of red meat, eggs, butter, and other dairy fats and increasing consumption of fruits, vegetables, and cereal grains. Substituting polyunsaturated cooking oils (corn, safflower, or sunflower oil, for example) for lard or hardened shortening and using margarines whose labels indicate a high ratio of polyunsaturated to saturated fats (for example, four to two) instead of butter or margarines with less favorable ratios (e.g., equal or two to three) also help to lower blood cholesterol.

ROLE OF HIGH BLOOD PRESSURE

People with high blood pressure have a marked increase in heart attacks and strokes. The cause of most high blood pressure is unknown, but it usually can be lowered by the use of antihypertensive drugs, reduced salt intake, and weight loss in people who are overweight. Controlling high blood pressure is an important preventive measure because it increases the work load on the heart and also directly contributes to hardening of the arteries (arteriosclerosis).

ROLE OF CIGARETTE SMOKING

Since 1964, when the Surgeon General reported that cigarette smokers on the average had a 70 percent greater chance of having a heart attack than nonsmokers, many other studies have confirmed that cigarette smoking is a major risk factor. This risk increases with the number of cigarettes smoked, and recent studies have found that low-tar, low-nicotine cigarettes do not lower the risk of heart disease. Stopping smoking is now considered one of the best things you can do to help prevent a heart attack.

OTHER RISK FACTORS

Sedentary Life Style

Although evidence linking a sedentary life style to increased likelihood of heart disease is indirect, physically active people are known to have wider coronary arteries, which presumably would not be as prone to blockage as those of sedentary people. Also, conditioning the heart by aerobic exercise (jogging, swimming, cycling) leads to more efficient pumping and an increased capacity of the heart to withstand stress or increased work loads.

Type A Personality

In recent years, much discussion has focused on the relationship between the type A personality, characterized by anxiety, impatience, and perfectionism, and the risk of a heart attack. Although many assessments have confirmed this relationship, scientific proof definitively linking personality type and the development of heart disease is yet to come.

Diabetes

People with diabetes, a serious disease in which the body cannot regulate its blood sugar (glucose), have a higher incidence of coronary disease and heart attacks. The incidence is increased further if the diabetic has other risk factors.

Obesity

The Framingham Study recently concluded that obesity alone increases the risk of heart disease—a hypothesis that has been debated for years. Since obesity often coexists with hypertension, diabetes, and a sedentary life style, weight control is an important factor in reducing a number of coronary risk factors.

Sex and Age

Some risk factors, such as age and aging and a person's sex, are unavoidable. Statistics show that men under age forty-five are ten times as likely to develop coronary artery disease as women in the same age group. Between ages forty-five and sixty,

however, the sex difference diminishes. After age sixty, the incidence of coronary artery disease is about equally distributed between men and women.

Family History

An inherited susceptibility is also an important risk factor that cannot be avoided. Some manifestations, such as high blood pressure or an inherited tendency to have very high blood cholesterol levels (familial hypercholesterolemia), can be controlled by drugs and diet.

SUMMING UP

The relationship between heart disease and certain risk factors, such as high blood cholesterol, hypertension, and cigarette smoking, has been established by many studies. Because coronary artery disease is the leading cause of death (via heart attacks) in the United States, prevention takes on a special importance. Reduction of dietary fat, cessation of cigarette smoking, control of hypertension, weight loss, and exercise are all steps that help check the development of atherosclerotic coronary disease and reduce the risk of heart attack.

10. Angina

COMMON CHARACTERISTICS

Angina pectoris, commonly referred to as angina, is a temporary pain or tightness that starts in the chest and sometimes radi-

ates to other parts of the body, particularly the arms, neck, jaw, and back. It comes on suddenly—often in response to exertion, emotional stress or exposure to cold—and is usually of short duration. It is caused by

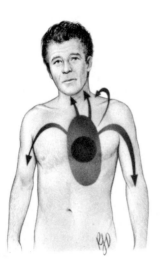

Anginal pain typically begins in the area of the heart, spreading through the midsection of the chest. Pain also may radiate to the arms, neck, jaw, and back, as shown here.

a reduction in blood flow through the coronary arteries, the blood vessels that nourish the heart muscle. This reduced blood flow results in a reduction in oxygen reaching a portion of heart muscle, which, in turn, causes the pain.

Although episodes of chest pain may be very frightening, it should be emphasized that angina is only one of many possible causes. Indigestion, anxiety, muscle disorders, infection, and structural abnormalities are just a few of the many causes of chest pain. This is why a number of tests may be required before it is determined that the chest pains are, indeed, angina. Even then, there are different types of angina, and distinguishing the specific type involved may be a factor in prescribing the most effective treatment.

CLASSIC ANGINA

The most common form of angina is associated with coronary artery disease. As we grow older, our blood vessels tend to "harden" or lose some of their elasticity, a process known as arteriosclerosis. They also may become narrowed or clogged

with deposits of fatty material. These are gradual processes that may go on for years, even decades, without causing any problems or symptoms. But if the narrowing progresses to the stage where 75 percent or more of the artery is blocked, the result may be angina or a feeling of breathlessness. Typically, classic angina is brought on by exertion or other activities that cause the heart to work harder; for example, the increased blood flow required to digest a large meal. Cold weather, emotional upsets, and anxiety are other common factors that may provoke angina.

VARIANT ANGINA

Variant angina is not necessarily related to exercise or other stresses. It may come on while asleep or sitting quietly or performing exercise that is usually well tolerated. This type of chest pain, which is sometimes referred to as Prinzmetal's angina, has puzzled doctors for many years. Recent studies, however, indicate that it is often caused by a spasm or constriction in the coronary artery, which cuts off the blood flow and results in pain like that of classic angina.

UNSTABLE ANGINA

Some patients experience both classic effort-induced angina and variant angina, with attacks coming on during periods of exertion as well as during restful times. Others experience an acceleration of symptoms, with attacks occurring more and more frequently after less and less exertion. These syndromes are generally referred to as unstable angina, which usually requires more intensive treatment because it is associated with a higher risk of heart attacks than classic, stable angina. It should be noted, however, that heart attacks often occur in people who have never experienced any chest pain, and, conversely, there are many people who live with angina for many years without having a heart attack.

TREATMENTS OF ANGINA

In most instances, the angina will subside with rest. If an attack occurs, stop whatever you are doing and rest until it passes. Angina caused by coronary spasm may not respond as well to rest as classic angina. Aside from rest, there are three major approaches to treating angina: lifestyle changes, drugs, and surgery.

LIFE-STYLE CHANGES

If you smoke, you should make every effort to stop. Smoking stimulates the heart to work harder; it also causes other changes that many researchers think may be instrumental in triggering chest pain and heart attacks. People who are overweight are usually advised to lose weight gradually by eating less and exercising more. However, a person with heart disease should not embark on a weight reduction or exercise program without close medical guidance. Avoiding stressful situations or learning relaxation techniques are still other life-style modifications that may be recommended.

DRUGS TO TREAT ANGINA

The two major classes of drugs used to treat angina are nitrates and beta blockers. Nitrates come in several forms: as nitroglycerin or other tablets that may be slipped under the tongue to bring relief during an attack, as an ointment to be absorbed through the skin to prevent or relieve an attack, or as long-acting tablets or capsules to be taken orally to prevent an attack. Recently, still another form—a disc applied to the skin to provide a steady release of the drug over a period of several hours—has become available.

Beta-blocking drugs help prevent angina attacks by slowing the rate at which the heart beats, thereby reducing the heart's work load and lowering the amount of oxygen it needs. These drugs should be taken exactly as instructed and should not be stopped abruptly.

Another class of antianginal drugs known as calcium-blocking agents appears to be particularly effective in controlling the type of angina associated with coronary spasm. All muscles require varying amounts of calcium in order to constrict; by reducing the amount of calcium that enters the muscle cells in the coronary vessel walls, the spasms that choke off the heart's blood supply may be prevented.

SURGICAL TREATMENT

In some patients, coronary bypass surgery may be recommended. This operation entails taking a portion of a vein, usually from the leg, and grafting it to the coronary artery to bypass the clogged area. Many factors are considered in deciding whether or not to operate, including the extent of coronary disease, degree of disability from the angina, and age and general physical condition of the patient. (See Chapter 15, "Coronary Artery Bypass Surgery.")

SUMMING UP

Angina is a common manifestation of a progressive narrowing of the coronary blood vessels. It also may be caused by a temporary spasm of these vessels. Most angina patients can be effectively treated through a combination of life-style changes and drugs. No one treatment works for all patients; each person must be evaluated by his or her doctor, who can then prescribe the treatment.

11. High Blood Pressure

COMMON CHARACTERISTICS

High blood pressure, or hypertension, is often referred to as the silent disease because it has no symptoms until it reaches an advanced state. Very often, it is detected during a routine doctor's visit or high blood pressure screening program. Even then, several measurements may be needed to make a definite diagnosis of hypertension, which is defined as blood pressure that is persistently elevated over what is considered normal.

Blood pressure is the force that is exerted by the blood against the vessel walls. It is measured by using a simple instrument called a sphygmomanometer, which consists of an inflatable cuff that goes around

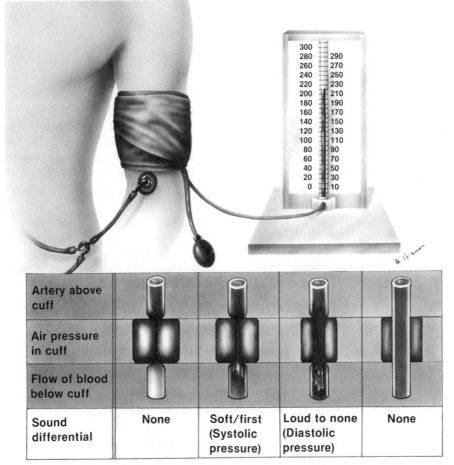

Artery above cuff				
Air pressure in cuff				
Flow of blood below cuff				
Sound differential	None	Soft/first (Systolic pressure)	Loud to none (Diastolic pressure)	None

An instrument called a sphygmomanometer is used to measure blood pressure. It consists of the cuff, which is applied to the arm and tightened, a column of mercury, and a stethoscope, which is used to listen for the various sounds of blood moving through the arteries.

the upper arm and a column of mercury or a pressure dial. When the cuff is inflated, it tightens around the arm and momentarily blocks the flow of blood through the main artery of the arm. As the cuff is slowly released, the person taking the blood pressure uses a stethoscope to listen to the returning blood flow. One sound signals the maximum force that occurs with the heartbeat. This is the systolic pressure, the higher of the two numbers in a blood pressure reading. The second or lower number, referred to as the diastolic pressure, reflects the lowest amount of pressure, which occurs between heartbeats.

Everyone's blood pressure varies during the course of a day. As would be expected, it is usually lower when resting or engaged in quiet activities, and it may spurt up during a sudden burst of activity, such as running to catch a bus or exercising. Age also affects blood pressure; it is generally lower in children and gradually rises as we grow older. Although there is some disagreement over how high is too high, the average normal blood pressure for healthy children is about 90/60, while the normal adult average ranges from 100/85 to 135/90. A diastolic pressure over 95 in an otherwise healthy adult is regarded as suspiciously high, and a reading of 140/100 usually would be diagnosed as hypertension that should be treated. Many experts feel that any diastolic pressure that is consistently over 95 should be treated.

CAUSES OF HYPERTENSION

It is estimated that more than 35 million Americans have hypertension. In the large majority of cases, the cause of the high pressure is unknown. Doctors refer to this most common form of the disease as primary or essential hypertension. There are some unusual instances, however, in which the high blood pressure may be caused by kidney disease, tumor, or some other identifiable cause. This is known as secondary hypertension, and treating the underlying

cause usually will cure the high blood pressure.

While the cause of primary hypertension is unknown, a number of factors appear to increase the risk of developing it. These include a family history of high blood pressure or strokes at an early age, cigarette smoking, obesity, and excessive salt intake. Altering or avoiding these risk factors will not necessarily prevent hypertension, but all are thought to play some role. Cutting salt intake, stopping smoking, or losing weight may be sufficient to prevent borderline high blood pressure from developing into frank hypertension. This is particularly true for adolescents or young adults whose blood pressures may be in the higher end of the normal range.

TREATMENT OF HYPERTENSION

Over the last few years, dozens of highly effective antihypertensive drugs have been developed that have truly revolutionized the treatment of this disease. At one time, the only treatments available for high blood pressure were surgery, which was not very effective, or an extreme restriction of salt intake, which in some cases meant living on a diet of mostly fruit and rice. Now most cases of high blood pressure can be brought under control with drugs, which may be prescribed singly or in combination.

There are three major categories of antihypertensive drugs:

• Diuretics, "water pills," which rid the body of excessive salt and reduce the volume of blood that must be pumped through narrow blood vessels, relieving some of the pressure on them.
• Beta blockers and other agents, which act on the nervous system to stem the outflow of impulses from the brain that cause blood vessels to constrict or work elsewhere to block their effect.
• Vasodilators, which act directly on the

muscles in the blood vessel walls, allowing them to relax and expand, or "dilate."

In addition, a new class of drugs, known as renin-axis blockers, has recently become available that interferes with the formation of a powerful vessel-constricting substance in the body and also with the action of the hormone aldosterone, which causes the body to retain salt and water.

Since there are many antihypertensive drugs and combinations, an effective treatment that lowers blood pressure with a minimum of unpleasant side effects almost always can be found. Therefore, if you experience a side effect such as unusual tiredness, dizziness or faintness upon standing, depression, or any other untoward symptom that you think may be related to your antihypertensive drugs, report it to your doctor. It may be only temporary, or it may be something that can be remedied by altering the regimen. In any case, remember that the treatment is usually for life.

The drugs will keep the high blood pressure under control, but they do not cure the disease. If you stop taking the drugs, the blood pressure will return to its previous level or go even higher. Therefore, it is particularly important that you follow your doctor's instructions and that you return for periodic checks.

SUMMING UP

High blood pressure is the most common serious disease in the United States. Once diagnosed, however, most cases can be brought under control through the use of antihypertensive drugs and, where appropriate, through life-style changes such as stopping smoking or losing excess weight. Treatment is usually for life, but if high blood pressure is brought down to normal and kept there, the patient can expect to live a normal life with no major interference with day-to-day activities.

12. Cardiac Arrhythmias

COMMON CHARACTERISTICS

Under normal, healthy conditions the human heart beats sixty to one hundred times a minute. In the course of a day, the heart pumps an equivalent of two thousand gallons of blood, carrying essential oxygen and other nutrients to all of the body's cells. Ultimately, the brain coordinates this complex process, but the heart also has its own semi-independent power station. Most of this electrical activity is

carried out by pacemaker cells located in the upper righthand portion of the heart muscle known as the sinus node. From the sinus node, beat impulses are relayed to other areas of the heart via special groups of interlocking relay cells.

To have a properly functioning heart, all four of the heart's chambers must receive the beat signal in the proper sequence. The chambers are divided into the right atrium and ventricle and the left atrium and ventricle. The pair on the right side of the heart pumps oxygen-depleted blood coming back from the rest of the body into the lungs for fresh oxygen. The pair on the left side moves freshly oxygenated blood returning from the lungs to the many organs of the body.

Many factors affect the heart rate, or the number of heartbeats per minute. The rate goes up when we exercise or are emotionally aroused and goes down when we rest or sleep. Irregularities, however, also can originate within the heart itself. This type of disturbance is known as an arrhythmia, and it can affect not only the rate at which the heart beats but also its pattern of beating.

Most people experience skipped beats or minor palpitations from time to time; these generally are of no medical significance. Other types of arrhythmias, however, are potentially quite serious.

SINUS RHYTHM DISTURBANCES

Some rhythm disturbances are due to a malfunction of the heart's pacemaker cells. These commonly occur in one of two forms: bradycardia, in which the heart beats at an abnormally slow rate; and tachycardia, in which it pulsates at one hundred or more beats per minute. In itself, neither condition is particularly worrisome. In fact, a slow heart rate is often found in highly trained athletes whose hearts have been conditioned to beat more slowly, pumping a greater volume of blood per beat. In some older people, however, an abnormally slow beat may be a sign of an underlying disease. In such cases, there is usually a telltale rhythm of fast beats followed by slow ones. And while this pattern in not necessarily a cause for concern, in some individuals it can lead to loss of consciousness or dizziness due to poor output of blood from the heart. In these cases, an artificial pacemaker may stabilize the heartbeat.

Tachycardia arising in the pacemaker cells also may be harmless. The exceptions include an accelerated rapid heartbeat, which may indicate congestive heart failure, or conditions in which there is both a rapid beat and some other problem involving the heart and blood vessels.

ATRIAL RHYTHM DISTURBANCES

Though the relay cells in the atrium chamber are designed to pass on beat impulses sent out by the pacemaker cells, sometimes they acquire the ability to produce a beat on their own. Since such beats occur just before the "true" heartbeat, they are known as atrial premature beats. Commonly associated with the heavy use of tobacco, alcohol, or coffee, these beats disappear once the stimulants are removed. However, when they are accompanied by palpitation, fluttering in the chest, rapid heartbeat, dizziness, or shortness of breath, they may indicate underlying heart disease. In such cases, treatment with drugs may be indicated.

Potentially far more serious is atrial fibrillation, a condition in which the muscles of the atrium contract in an erratic, uncoordinated fashion. In most instances, it can be corrected by drugs; at times, it may be necessary to employ a technique called cardioversion, a type of electrical shock designed to restore normal rhythm. One major complication of atrial fibrillation is blood clotting. Usually, these clots form in the left atrium and then move out into the general circulatory system, where they can produce a potentially serious blockage. Anticlotting drugs are therefore often prescribed for people with this condition.

In persons with narrowed coronary arteries, the onset of atrial fibrillation may produce chest pain, particularly if the heart rate speeds up dramatically. This combination of symptoms is frequently a warning sign of pending heart failure or a heart attack. The rapid beat must therefore be slowed immediately with either drugs or a medical procedure.

Cardiac Arrhythmias

Most people occasionally experience skipped beats or minor heart palpitations, and these generally have no medical significance. Other rhythm irregularities that originate in the heart itself may require treatment. The irregularities usually can be diagnosed by taking an electrocardiogram (ECG), a test that records the electrical activity of the heart.

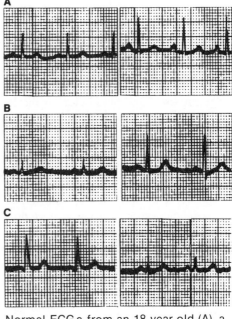

Normal ECGs from an 18 year old (A), a 40 year old (B), and a 51 year old (C).

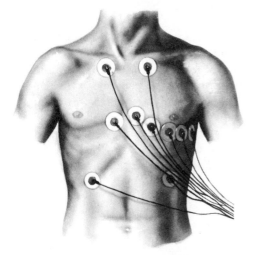

Placement of chest electrodes to take an ECG. Electrodes also may be placed on the legs and lower arms.

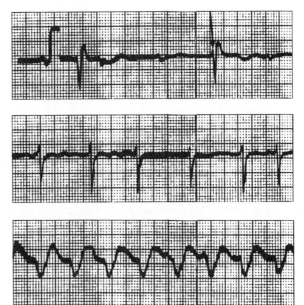

ECG showing complete heart block resulting in a slower than normal heart rate of 32 beats per minute

ECG taken during atrial fibrillation, showing a very irregular rhythm

ECG showing ventricular tachycardia (rapid heart rate) of 136 beats per minute and complete heart block

Another significant rhythm disturbance is atrial tachycardia, in which the muscles of the atrium beat much faster that those of the ventricle, producing an erratic heart rate. Symptoms such as a sense of fullness in the chest, light-headedness, and chest flutters are also common. Problems often associated with this disturbance include rheumatic heart defects, hyperthyroidism, pneumonia, and blood clots in the lungs. Drug therapy is often the most effective treatment.

VENTRICULAR RHYTHM DISTURBANCES

The relay cells in the ventricles, like those in the atria, also may acquire the ability to produce a heartbeat on their own. Called a ventricular premature beat, this condition may be traceable to excessive use of caffeine, cigarettes, or alcohol. But since it can also be the sign of a serious cardiac disorder, it should be investigated. Prompt medical attention is crucial in cases of ventricular tachycardia. As its name implies, this problem involves rapid beating of the ventricles (usually over 100 to 120 beats per minute), and the danger is that the rate may increase even further, leading to ventricular fibrillation and possibly death.

SUMMING UP

Disturbances in heartbeat and heart rhythm are among the most common forms of cardiac disorders. While not all such disturbances have medical significance, some can be extremely serious unless they receive proper medical attention. Drug therapy is often used to treat various forms of arrhythmias, and strict adherence to the dosage instructions given by your doctor is most important.

13. What Happens During a Heart Attack

COMMON CHARACTERISTICS

Each year, more than a million Americans suffer heart attacks. Although heart disease remains the leading cause of death in the United States, great strides have been made in the last decade, both in treating heart attacks and in helping people who have suffered one resume a full, active life.

The most common type of heart attack is caused by a coronary thrombosis, which occurs when a clot (thrombus) blocks one or more of the blood vessels that nourish the heart muscle. As a result of the lack of blood, part of the muscle may be damaged, and its ability to contract may be lost. This is known as a myocardial infarction. If the infarct is small and the electrical impulses that control the heart's contractions (beats) are not disturbed, chances for recovery are excellent.

CORONARY ARTERY DISEASE

Coronary thrombosis is one of the manifestations of coronary artery disease. As we grow older, our blood vessels tend to lose their elasticity, a process known as arteriosclerosis. The arteries may also become narrowed or clogged with deposits of fatty material called atheromas, a condition called atherosclerosis. Atherosclerosis is progressive and usually does not produce symptoms until there is significant blockage in the blood flow. Sometimes, in fact, the first symptom of this heart disease is a heart attack.

Although the specific cause of atherosclerosis is not known, it has been found that certain risk factors help in identifying population groups that are more likely to develop it. Three major risk factors are high levels of cholesterol and other blood fats, high blood pressure (hypertension), and cigarette smoking. Others include diabetes, obesity, a sedentary life style, aging, being male, and heredity.

Atherosclerosis begins forming as a fatty streak on the inner wall of an artery, usually at its branching-out point, and disturbs the smooth flow of blood. As patches of fatty tissue build up, the inner wall becomes narrower, which inhibits blood flow in a more significant way. An artery continues to narrow as the tissue buildup progresses, and in time, the fatty deposit becomes a hard mass of fatty tissue with a

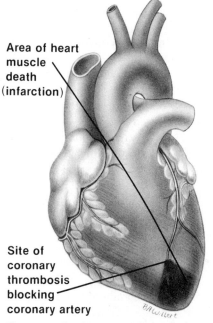

Area of heart muscle death (infarction)

Site of coronary thrombosis blocking coronary artery

The pain of a heart attack usually begins as a feeling of tightness or pressure in the center of the chest, spreading to the back, jaw, and arms. Other symptoms, such as sweating and nausea, also may be present.

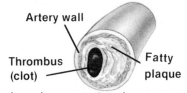

Artery wall

Thrombus (clot)

Fatty plaque

An enlarged cross section shows a coronary thrombosis, or clot formation, blocking a portion of an artery that nourishes the heart muscle. This is most likely to occur in an artery that is severely narrowed by deposits of fatty material (plaque).

tough outer lining of cells—a plaque. As plaques spread and thicken, they erode the wall of the artery, which interferes with blood flow and makes it increasingly turbulent. This turbulence may trigger the blood to form a clot (thrombus), partially or completely blocking the artery. Further, a fragment of the clot (embolus) may be carried by the bloodstream and block an artery at some distant, narrower point.

Heart attacks sometimes occur in people with little or no coronary artery disease. Some experts believe that a spasm or sudden constriction of the coronary artery may be the cause of these heart attacks. It appears that a spasm may occur in a coronary artery that is totally free of atherosclerosis (as well as in one that is heavily affected by that condition), and this would explain why many people suffer angina and other cardiac problems without any evidence of underlying blockage in the arteries.

SYMPTOMS OF A HEART ATTACK

A heart attack can come on gradually, preceded by several attacks of angina over days, weeks, months, or even years. (Angina is the name given to the chest pain that arises when the muscular wall of the heart is temporarily deprived of sufficient oxygen.) But a heart attack may also occur without any apparent warning, and in people who have never previously experienced any chest pain.

Typically, the pain of a heart attack is a sensation of constriction in the central chest area; it may vary in intensity from a feeling of tightness to one of agonizing crushing or bursting. The pain may be continuous, or it may last a few minutes, fade, and then recur. It commonly spreads to the back, jaw, and left arm. Although a heart attack may be precipitated by physical or emotional stress, the pain, unlike that of angina, does not subside when the stress ceases.

Pain is commonly accompanied by shortness of breath, sweating, nausea, dizziness, and pallor. (Some people experience a heart attack without any of these symptoms. This is known as a silent infarct, which may be confirmed by changes in an electrocardiogram or certain other hospital tests.)

A MEDICAL EMERGENCY

Most deaths from heart attack occur within minutes to hours after the onset of symptoms. Therefore, when sudden and severe chest pain occurs, an ambulance should be called immediately and the individual taken to a hospital. Denying that these symptoms represent a life-threatening illness may cause a delay that could be fatal.

One of the major causes of death from coronary thrombosis is the development of abnormal heart rhythms in the hours immediately following the attack. Emergency treatment, therefore, concentrates on stabilizing the heart rhythm, as well as on relieving pain and preventing shock.

In the hospital's intensive care or cardiac care unit, the rate and rhythm of the heart will be continuously monitored by an electrocardiograph machine. Blood tests to detect enzymes released from the heart aid in assessing the infarct further, and various medications may be given. Mood changes and feelings of apprehension are very common following a heart attack, and a mild tranquilizer is often given to the patient.

Depending on the severity of the attack, the patient may be allowed out of bed within three or four days and be discharged after two weeks. Bed rest for more than a short time should be avoided, where possible, because it results in a rapid loss of the body's muscle tone and in increased heart rate on exertion. Physical activity is gradually increased, and most patients are able to return to their full range of normal activity within a few months.

LONG-TERM TREATMENT

Depending on such factors as the patient's age and general physical condition and the extent of the heart damage, a variety of different approaches may be taken to deal with the underlying coronary artery disease and to reduce the possibility of another heart attack.

Changes in Life Style

A number of steps can be taken to prevent or slow down the progression of heart disease. These include stopping smoking, exercising regularly, and adopting a low-cholesterol diet.

Drug Treatment

The use of drugs depends upon the nature of the heart attack and underlying coronary disease. Antihypertensive drugs may be prescribed to lower the blood pressure. Other drugs may be given to improve heart function, prevent chest pain, or lower the level of blood cholesterol.

Other Treatments

A number of other treatments, including coronary bypass surgery, are available. Obviously, their use depends upon individual needs.

SUMMING UP

Heart attacks are a common occurrence, particularly among middle-aged and older men. An understanding of the risk factors involved in coronary artery disease, and the adoption of appropriate preventive measures, may reduce the likelihood of an attack. If the typical pain of a heart attack does strike, prompt treatment greatly improves the chances of survival. Modern treatments enable most heart attack patients to resume a full, active life, although some changes in life style probably will be required.

14. Life After a Heart Attack

GENERAL CONSIDERATIONS

In many of the more than 27 million Americans who suffer from heart disease, the first sign that anything is amiss is a heart attack. Improved techniques for treating heart attack victims ensure that more and more coronary patients return to productive, enjoyable lives. However, modern medical care is not the only factor in successful recovery from a heart attack; much also depends on the emotional and psychological response of the patient himself or herself. It is important to understand the psychological problems that may be encountered and their role in coping with heart disease.

THE ROLE OF DENIAL

The classic symptoms of a heart attack—severe, crushing chest pains, pain radiating down the left arm, nausea, and sweating—are commonly taken to be those of a case of indigestion. The first reaction of many victims is to reach for an antacid. When this fails, all too many try some other home remedy—a heating pad, pacing the floor, doing pushups, drinking strong coffee or alcohol—in short, almost anything but getting the emergency coronary care needed to save their lives or minimize the damage of the heart attack. The typical heart attack patient delays for an average of nearly four hours between the initial chest pain and getting to a hospital. Since half of all deaths from heart attack are thought to occur within the first four hours, it is easy to understand that such delay may prove fatal.

Many victims delay because they simply refuse to believe that a heart attack could happen to them—in other words, they deny the obvious. Overcoming the tendency to denial may well be the most significant step that a coronary patient can take in ensuring his or her successful recovery. It is important to learn the symptoms of a heart attack and, if they occur, to get immediate medical attention. If your chest pains are a case of indigestion mimicking a heart attack, it is far better to have this confirmed in a hospital than to err in the opposite direction and be pronounced dead on arrival.

THE ROLE OF ANXIETY

Virtually every person who has suffered a heart attack suffers also from anxiety, a mental condition that resembles fear. Anxiety usually occurs during the first few days of hospitalization and is manifested by intensified feelings of apprehension, alertness, and worry. This state of mind is completely understandable; anyone who has had a heart attack is likely to be worried by a number of questions: Will I keep my job? Will I still be able to be an effective spouse or parent? Am I going to die?

The best way to overcome such anxiety is to ask your doctor to explain exactly what is happening and what you may expect. It is a frightening experience to be in a coronary care unit, surrounded by monitors, tubes, and other apparatus. However, once you know the function of these devices, they become less anxiety-provoking. The same is true when you understand what has happened to your heart.

Studies have found that many heart attack victims harbor myths that add greatly to their anxiety. For example, they believe that their hearts are irreparably damaged, or even that a hole in the heart now permits a permanent leak in the pumping system. With an explanation of what happens during a heart attack, and of how the heart can form scar tissue to repair the damage, such anxiety can be greatly relieved.

Other myths hold that activities such as vigorous exercise or sexual intercourse are forbidden to anyone who has suffered a heart attack. Again, the facts belie the myths. Most heart attack victims can resume normal sexual relations. As for exercise, each year a dozen or more runners completing the Boston marathon are people who have had heart attacks in the past. While this does not mean that everyone

who suffers a heart attack will be able to return to such vigorous exercise, it does indicate that having a heart attack does not mean that you must resign yourself to being a cardiac cripple.

Knowing what has happened and what you may expect in the future is perhaps the most effective means of easing the anxiety that is a natural part of the psychological response to a heart attack. In some instances, tranquilizers may also be prescribed to help alleviate anxiety. Although many patients, especially men, think that taking tranquilizers is a sign of weakness, it should be stressed that the state of mind is a very important factor in regaining physical health. Therefore, if a tranquilizer is considered necessary, it should be regarded in the same light as any of the other drugs that are commonly given to cardiac patients.

Denial also plays a part in overcoming the anxiety that follows a heart attack. In contrast to the denial that prevents a heart attack victim from seeking immediate medical help, here denial may have a positive effect since it enables patients to overcome fear and anxiety. Denial is one of the mind's normal ways of handling stress; coronary patients who are able to deny anxiety have a better chance of surviving hospitalization after a heart attack than those who cannot do so. Denial is also an important factor in the ability to see the positive aspects of leading as normal a life as possible.

THE ROLE OF DEPRESSION

Depression and anxiety often go hand in hand. The type of depression that follows a heart attack can usually be attributed to a keen sense of loss—loss of strength, energy, independence. Again, knowing what to expect is helpful. For example, many heart attack patients are dismayed at how weak they feel after they leave the hospital, not realizing that anyone—even an athlete in peak physical condition—will feel weak and will tire easily after two or three weeks in bed.

POSTCORONARY EXERCISE

Exercise is an important part of cardiac rehabilitation. A specific exercise program should be tailored to the individual patient and should not be undertaken without a doctor's approval. The following principles apply to most postcoronary exercise programs.

1. *Early mobilization.* Most heart attack patients are encouraged to get out of bed, if only for a few minutes, within a day or two of the coronary event.

2. *Start gradually.* A moderate walking program usually begins while still in the hospital. Within two or three weeks of discharge, most patients who are recovering from an uncomplicated heart attack are able to walk for several blocks.

3. *Don't overdo.* Stop when you feel tired or have any symptoms, such as shortness of breath or chest pain.

4. *Gradually increase your exercise capacity.* Ask your doctor to tell you your safe maximum pulse rate. Learn to take your pulse, and gradually work up to the target rate. Assume, for example, that your target rate is 120 beats per minute. Exercise for more than fifteen or twenty minutes at this heart rate has a conditioning effect on both the heart and lungs.

5. *Exercise regularly.* Set aside a half-hour to an hour at least four times a week for a workout.

6. *Find physical activities that are enjoyable.* Many heart attack patients feel more comfortable exercising in a controlled setting, such as a cardiovascular rehabilitation program at the Y or a clinic. Others enjoy solitary walks, bicycling or swimming with friends or family members, playing tennis, jogging, or some other activity.

7. *Return gradually after a layoff.* Even a week or two of inactivity reduces your body's ability to extract oxygen from the blood (oxygen uptake). If you stop exercising for more than a few days, resume your program gradually, rather than picking up where you left off.

8. *Avoid hot showers, steam baths, and saunas immediately after exercise.* The heat can put too much of a burden on the cardiovascular system; wait until your heart rate and circulation have returned to normal before showering.

9. *Always include a warm-up and cool-down period in each exercise session.* This gives your body a chance to adjust to the different levels of physical activity and also helps to avoid muscle cramps and strain.

Many doctors feel that a program of physical conditioning is one of the best ways to overcome the depression that follows a heart attack. A few decades ago, patients were told that they would have to "take it easy" for the rest of their lives. Today—depending, of course, on the extent of the heart damage—the more likely course is to get the patient up and moving around as soon as possible. Even while still in the hospital, a patient may be started on a conditioning program. Finding that it is safe to do such things as walk up a few stairs, exercise on a bicycle or a treadmill, or engage in certain sports, the cardiac patient realizes that he is not as vulnerable as he had feared.

It is important that all post–heart attack exercise programs be designed by a physician or exercise physiologist to meet the needs of individual patients. Some people are able to start jogging within a relatively short time of their heart attacks; others must be content with more leisurely forms of exercise. The important point is that the vast majority of persons who have suffered a heart attack are indeed able to resume an active life. It may not be as fast-paced or as competitive as before, but it is definitely not the life of a cripple.

SUMMING UP

A number of psychological difficulties are commonly encountered by those who suffer a heart attack. Denial is a frequent response to the initial chest pain of the attack itself, and almost all patients suffer from anxiety and depression at different periods during the recovery stage. Very often, an understanding of what has happened during the heart attack, what is happening in the hospital, and what may be expected to happen in the future will greatly ease psychological distress. In addition, a carefully designed physical conditioning program frequently has benefits not only for the body but for the mental state also.

15. Coronary Artery Bypass Surgery

COMMON CHARACTERISTICS

Coronary artery bypass surgery is a procedure in which one or more healthy blood vessels are removed from a part of the body—usually the veins of the leg—and grafted on the heart's surface to bypass one or more clogged or partially blocked coronary arteries. After this procedure, the heart muscle can receive a normal amount of blood, thus reducing or eliminating angina and perhaps preventing further deterioration of the cardiovascular system. Once considered an extreme measure, coronary bypass surgery is now performed on about 170,000 people each year, usually with good results. However, it is not a cure for heart disease in general, and it is not indicated for all heart patients. Your doctor will help you to decide if and when such surgery is indicated for your specific problem.

WHEN SURGERY IS INDICATED

Most doctors agree that a coronary bypass is a difficult but practical measure for heart patients with severe disabling angina or for patients whose left main coronary artery is severely diseased. Angina occurs when the heart muscle does not receive adequate oxygen-rich blood. It is a temporary pain or tightness in the chest that comes on suddenly and sometimes radiates to the arms, neck, or back. Often, angina is brought on by exertion or emotional stress; sometimes, it comes on during restful times. Usually, angina can be treated with drugs such as nitrates or beta-blockers, which either increase the blood flow to the heart muscle or reduce the heart's oxygen needs. However, in cases of disabling or uncontrolled pain, a doctor may recommend a bypass operation.

Before deciding whether a coronary bypass operation is indicated, the doctor will want to make a careful study of the patient's medical history and current physical condition.

As part of the preoperative exam, there will be the standard tests given to all surgical candidates. For the coronary bypass patient, special emphasis will be placed upon the angiogram and other tests to pinpoint

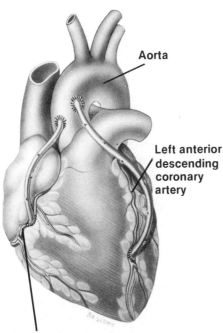

Aorta

Left anterior descending coronary artery

Right coronary artery

In coronary bypass surgery, a portion of healthy blood vessel is grafted to the heart's coronary arteries to bypass severely occluded sections. The drawing above shows a typical double bypass, in which grafts have been attached to the aorta to bypass diseased portions of the right coronary artery and the left anterior descending artery. In most cases, the grafts are made from healthy sections of the external saphenous vein in the leg. The vein may be taken from the upper or lower leg or both. Other veins in the leg take over the function of the portions that have been removed.

the diseased arteries and provide other information about the heart. If the test results indicate that the candidate could probably benefit from coronary artery bypass surgery, the next step for doctor and patient is to prepare for the operation itself.

THE CORONARY BYPASS OPERATION

You will enter the hospital a few days before the actual operation takes place.

This will allow adequate time for tests and for you to learn about your postoperative therapy, which will include special breathing and coughing regimens. Psychologically, too, it is good to have a chance to become familiar with your hospital staff and surroundings. It is always normal to feel nervous before an operation. You should never be afraid to ask your doctor questions about the procedure itself and the possible aftereffects.

Before the operation, your doctors will outline the steps of the bypass. You will have much of your body hair shaved and will be instructed to shower with special antibacterial cleansers. You will be given a sedative shortly before the surgery. The operation is conducted while you are under general anesthesia. You will feel nothing while the bypass surgery is going on.

A coronary bypass usually takes between four and six hours to complete. The operation is performed in several steps and, at one point, involves the use of a heart–lung machine. After the operation, the patient will spend at least a few days in the hospital's intensive care unit. This is standard procedure. Various wires will be attached to the chest to allow constant monitoring of the heart rate to make sure that the grafted vessels are working properly and the heart rhythm is regular. A breathing tube, which is awkward but not painful, is usually used for the first twenty-four-hour period.

STEPS TO FULL RECOVERY

Coughing and deep breathing are an essential part of recovery therapy. Coughing helps to loosen lung secretions. Hospital therapists and nurses will help you learn the proper techniques. The first few days will be fairly uncomfortable; this is true for anyone who has undergone surgery. Soreness at the incision sites is common, as is a certain amount of fatigue. However, most patients are soon taking mild exercise and eating normally.

After a week, the stitches are removed from the chest and leg areas. The skin will probably look red and swollen for several weeks; in about two months, most of the discoloration should disappear. The hospital stay itself is normally about two weeks. During most of that time, visits are permitted. Each hospital sets its own policy. Your doctors will be making frequent checks on your progress, too.

LIFE AFTER BYPASS SURGERY

Surgery is not the final answer for the cardiac patient. Maintaining good habits is important to help prevent the newly grafted vessels from becoming diseased. Stopping smoking is of great importance; in fact, many surgeons will not perform a coronary bypass unless a patient stops smoking. Diet and exercise also are important. Your doctor may help you to work out ways of cutting down on cholesterol and salt in your daily diet. This will also help to reduce blood pressure and keep your weight within a healthy range. Regular exercise that increases the flow of oxygen to the heart can be highly beneficial as well as psychologically rewarding; plan a moderate program of exercise that can be increased as you go along. It is important not to overdo any strenuous activity, and your doctor can help you to set correct limits.

In the period immediately following the operation, most patients feel let down and weak. Some of this is due to your large muscles not being exercised. Mild to severe depression can arise from facing the problems of the daily routine or worrying about the future. Talking to your doctor should help allay fears about such things as sexual relations (which can usually be resumed shortly after surgery), returning to work, and resumption of a regular routine.

Patients are encouraged to resume as normal a life style as possible, with perhaps some minor modifications. This should reassure both you and the people with whom you live and work. In fact, a bypass operation often means the start of a more active and complete life.

SUMMING UP

Coronary artery bypass surgery can be of great benefit to cardiac patients whose discomforts cannot be controlled with drugs or other kinds of therapy. It is a surgical procedure with a low mortality rate and a high frequency of good results for patients with angina. After bypass surgery, you may require little or no medication and may well be able to sustain a greater level of physical activity than before.

However, coronary bypass surgery is not for everyone who suffers from cardiovascular disease, nor can the operation alone rid a person of the risk of future problems. Diet, exercise, giving up cigarettes, and, above all, having a positive attitude about leading a healthier life play crucial roles in maintaining a vigorous heart and circulatory system.

16. Disorders of the Heart Valves

GENERAL CONSIDERATIONS

The human heart has four sets of valves. These structures control the flow of blood passing in and out of the various sections of the heart. When, at rest or after exercise, you hear the thumping of your heart, it is the sound of the valves closing. Various illnesses may damage the heart valves, or abnormalities may be present at birth. At one time, these heart disorders were largely untreatable. However, in the past twenty years, cardiovascular medicine and surgery have evolved, and now many valvular problems can be treated with medication or, frequently, with valve-replacement surgery.

HOW HEART VALVES WORK

The heart is actually a muscle that contracts with every beat. These contractions force movement of blood, aided by the valves. As the heart contracts, blood passes into the lungs through the pulmonary valve, and into the general circulation through the aortic valve. In between beats, these valves close, and the mitral and tricuspid valves open to permit blood to enter the heart from the veins. At the next beat, the mitral and tricuspid valves close and the aortic and pulmonary valves open again.

Most valvular problems are due either to stenosis or to incompetence. A valve is stenosed when it thickens, narrowing the valve opening, which inhibits the flow of blood. A valve is incompetent, or insufficient, when it does not close properly, causing some of the blood that has passed through it to leak back. Stenosis or incompetence may force the heart to work much harder in pumping blood throughout the body.

CAUSES

Historically, the most significant cause of valvular damage was rheumatic fever. This is a disease caused by streptococcal bacteria, which often follows an upper respiratory infection. The antibodies produced to combat the streptococci attack not only the invading bacteria but also the healthy tissue of the heart and the joints. Today, such damage is largely preventable by the prompt treatment of "strep throat" infections with antibiotics.

Another cause of valvular defects in the past was damage due to advanced syphilis; but now, syphilis is commonly controlled by antibiotics in the early stage of the disease. A variety of congenital birth defects may produce valvular problems as well.

Today, the most common causes of valvular disease are degenerative changes produced by aging and heart attacks and certain infections leading to bacterial endocarditis.

SYMPTOMS AND TREATMENT

An individual whose heart valves are not functioning properly may tire easily. As the problem intensifies, the primary symptom may become breathlessness—occurring at first during exertion but, as the disorder progresses, even during rest. Without treatment, the condition may cause abnormal heart rhythms and congestive heart failure. Tiny blood clots may develop in the valvular areas, which may

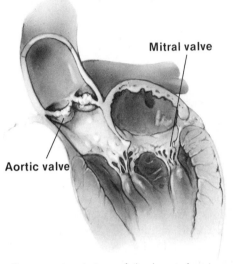

Cross-sectional view of the heart showing disease of the mitral and aortic valves.

block minute arteries and contribute to heart attack or stroke.

The mitral valve is the most vulnerable to damage. Mild stenosis (narrowing) or incompetence may not require treatment. Your physician may, however, recommend prophylactic antibiotics before any dental or medical surgery to prevent further infection and damage. If symptoms of congestive heart failure occur, such as breathlessness or swelling caused by fluid retention (edema), a low-salt diet and/or diuretics may be prescribed to help prevent fluid buildup in the body. If abnormal heart rhythms occur there are antiarrhythmic drugs that can help regulate the heartbeat and anticoagulants to help prevent the formation of blood clots. Severe damage may warrant surgery, either to widen a stenosed valve or to replace the diseased valve with a prosthetic one.

The second most likely candidate for damage is the aortic valve. In addition to experiencing symptoms similar to those of mitral valve damage, the individual may also suffer angina, a mild to severe pain in the chest. Again, mild aortic valve damage may not warrant treatment, although it may be necessary to curtail strenuous activity and antibiotics may be prescribed before any surgery to prevent infection. Severe aortic disease can be treated only with valve-replacement surgery.

Narrowing and incompetence of the tricuspid valve are less common and tend to occur only in conjunction with other valvular diseases. Symptoms and treatment usually parallel those of mitral valve damage. The pulmonary valves are but rarely affected and ordinarily require replacement only if there is a congenital defect.

VALVE-REPLACEMENT SURGERY

Valve replacement entails major surgery. The damaged valve is replaced either by a tissue substitute, constituted from an animal part, or by a completely artificial valve made of metal and plastic. Convalescence may take several months.

While the artificial valves are not quite as efficient as the natural ones, they have given thousands of people renewed energy and an extended life. In fact, many who were severely disabled by valvular disease have been able to resume active lives.

SUMMING UP

Valvular disease is a serious ailment that needs no longer be considered hopeless. Through modern medicine and surgery, most patients may carry on productive lives while taking careful preventive measures.

17. Congestive Heart Failure

COMMON CHARACTERISTICS

The heart is among the most durable of our organs. In the course of an average lifetime, the heart beats an estimated three billion times. Over the years, this labor produces some wear-and-tear changes in the heart's structure. But such changes—which come with normal aging—are quite different from congestive heart failure. Heart failure—a breakdown in the heart's ability to pump blood—is usually produced by disease. While it occasionally occurs suddenly, it more typically emerges slowly and insidiously over time. As the heart fails, circulation becomes impaired, producing a succession of increasingly painful and often disabling symptoms, which are highly treatable but can result in death if uncorrected.

CAUSES

The normal heart is usually able to meet any temporary extra demand simply by beating faster and more vigorously. Jogging, swimming, and other physical exercise, for example, create extra burdens that any healthy heart can respond to immediately and with ease. The danger arises when a burden becomes continuous or excessive, as in cases of sustained high blood pressure (hypertension), where the effort to keep pushing blood through inelastic blood vessels so overtaxes the heart that it begins to fail. Any local insult to the muscle of the heart, such as would result from a blockage in a coronary artery (a heart attack), can weaken the strength of the heart's contraction and thus produce heart failure. Heart failure can also result from damage or a structural change in one of the heart valves, which may have been caused

by rheumatic fever or a bacterial infection and may lead to internal obstruction or to valvular leakage.

Even disorders that are not directly related to cardiac function can result in heart failure. A case in point is severe anemia, a problem that decreases the blood's oxygen supply and may dangerously overwork the heart by forcing it to circulate underoxygenated blood around the body at an increasingly exhausting pace. Severe vitamin B deficiency has also been implicated in heart failure, as has a hyperactive thyroid. In an already weakened heart, chronic infection with

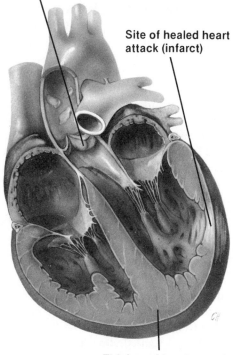

Diseased aortic valve

Site of healed heart attack (infarct)

Thickened heart muscle

Heart showing some of the hallmarks of congestive failure.

recurrent fever may also produce heart failure.

SYMPTOMS

As the heart's pumping action grows weaker, blood no longer circulates in an adequate flow to the body's major systems. The result is a series of increasingly debilitating symptoms, many of which seem to have little to do with heart disease. Some problems originate in the brain, where the body's respiratory centers, lacking adequate oxygen, begin malfunctioning. The kidneys, too, may no longer effectively filter excess fluid out of the blood. Or the fault may be with the damaged heart itself, which is unable to move the now increasingly waterlogged blood at its usual brisk pace through the circulatory system. Consequently, the water begins backing up into the lungs, liver, and tissues of other organs, producing one of the most telltale signs of heart failure—congestion. This is why physicians often refer to the disorder as *congestive* heart failure. Its most common symptoms include:

- *Shortness of breath.* Medically, this symptom is known as dyspnea, and it is often the earliest warning signal of heart failure. Usually, it appears gradually. In fact, the patient rarely notices it, until the first time he is left breathless by climbing a flight of stairs or must stop at the end of a short walk to catch his breath.
- *Rapid heartbeat.* At about the same time, he may also notice that his heart occasionally beats very rapidly. This is called tachycardia; it is another early symptom of heart failure, and it occurs because the overtaxed cardiac muscle attempts to compensate for its inability to pump the normal amounts of blood per beat by beating more frequently.
- *Swelling.* Caused by the buildup of fluids, this symptom announces itself by an unexpected and seemingly unaccountable weight gain of five, ten, or fifteen pounds.

Usually, the ankles are the first place the swelling shows up; typically, they become puffy and bloated during the day, then return to normal with sleep. As the swelling increases, excess weight may also become noticeable on the arms and legs.
- *Nocturnal breathlessness.* This occurs in two forms, both of which are associated with the later stages of heart failure. The less serious and less dramatic type is related to sleep position: If a person lies flat on a bed with only a single pillow, he may awake coughing and choking. Far more terrifying, however, is to be awakened by a feeling of imminent suffocation. Known as paroxysmal nocturnal dyspnea, this sensation is usually accompanied by a racing pulse, and it may last anywhere from a few minutes to an hour or more.

TREATMENT

As with most disorders, the earlier that congestive heart failure is diagnosed, the more likely treatment will succeed. This is why it is important to be able to spot the first signs of the disorder and to seek prompt medical attention when they appear. More than likely, your doctor will recommend one or more of the following steps.

- *A complete physical.* Often, the most effective way to treat congestive heart failure is to treat its underlying cause, and the chief purpose of a thorough examination is to identify that cause. If the cause is high blood pressure, for example, lowering it will almost automatically make the heart failure more amenable to treatment. On the other hand, if the underlying problem is a heart attack, bed rest and a program of coronary care may be instituted.
- *Medication.* An effective treatment of progressive heart failure is a drug called digitalis. When given in small doses, digitalis not only slows the heart's rate but also increases the force of each beat, so that each of these beats can move more blood.

In certain cases, nitroglycerin may also be prescribed to ease the discomfort. New vasodilator drugs, which widen the blood vessels, are also increasingly used for easing the load on a failing heart. Diuretics are used to reduce fluid retention.

• *Life-style adjustment.* When appropriate, a physician may also recommend weight loss, suggest that salt intake be restricted since it promotes water retention, and urge that the individual rest frequently during the day.

SUMMING UP

Congestive heart failure—related to a relative breakdown in the heart's ability to pump blood—is a highly treatable condition when its symptoms are recognized promptly and brought to a physician's attention. In most cases of early detection, it is a reversible syndrome that can be improved with proper treatment and life-style adjustments.

18. Congenital Heart Defects

COMMON CHARACTERISTICS

A congenital abnormality is a defect that is present at birth. It is estimated that eight out of every one thousand babies are born with some type of congenital heart defect. The abnormality may be minor, requiring no treatment or restriction of activity. On the other hand, it may be so severe that no effective treatment is available and the infant will die. Between these extremes, there is a range of congenital heart defects of various degrees of severity. Some have become increasingly amenable to surgical treatment, offering new hope to families.

CAUSES

The fetal heart begins to develop early in pregnancy. By about the fourth week, it starts to twitch and then to beat; by the sixth week, the four heart chambers are recognizable; by the end of the third month, its development is complete. Any abnormality of development during these weeks may cause a congenital heart defect.

When a baby is born with a heart defect, parents are often distressed about their own possible role in causing the disorder. However, it is seldom that anything parents do—or fail to do—has any causal relationship to the baby's problem. In fact, in 90 percent of cases, the causes of congenital heart defects remain unknown.

Some congenital heart defects are known to be associated with disturbances in oxygen supply to the mother, or with infections such as German measles (rubella), or with specific injuries or nutritional deficiencies. Sometimes a defective chromosome is associated with the problem, as in Down's syndrome. Several drugs, when taken early in pregnancy, have been shown to lead to heart abnormalities in babies. Therefore, no woman who is pregnant or thinks she may be pregnant should take any medication unless it has been approved by a physician.

Finally, there is a tendency for congenital heart defects to run in families. If either parent has or has had a congenital heart defect, the risk that a child will be affected is about one in twenty. Thus, if you or any of your immediate family members has such a problem, you might wish to consult a genetic counselor before starting a pregnancy.

SYMPTOMS

Frequently, a baby with a congenital heart defect has no symptoms, and the abnormality is discovered during a routine examination. In other cases, the symptoms are marked at birth—or may become severe in early infancy. The presence of symptoms is not necessarily related to the need for treatment; many children with no symptoms at all require surgery to prevent later problems, while others who have symptoms may outgrow the problem without treatment.

A classic indication of a congenital heart defect is cyanosis, a blueness of the skin and mucous membranes caused by an excess of underoxygenated blood in the circulatory system. The birth of such a "blue baby" may be a medical emergency. More often, the symptoms are less obvious. For example, an infant with mild heart failure —a less than normal output of blood from the heart—may have problems feeding, because sucking is difficult, and may therefore be underweight. Infants with severe heart failure may have rapid and distressed breathing. Many children with congenital heart defects become breathless on exertion, or even at rest. Their physical development is often below average.

DIAGNOSIS

The physician may detect the presence of a congenital abnormality through the simple use of a stethoscope, which picks up normal heart sounds and abnormal ones such as murmurs. (Murmurs do not necessarily signal heart abnormalities: "innocent murmurs" are heard in about 60 percent of normal infants.) Different congenital abnormalities generally produce recognizably different and characteristic murmurs, and in most cases the doctor can detect which abnormality is present.

A clearer picture may be derived from diagnostic tests. These include chest X-rays, which show the shape and size of the heart; electrocardiograms, which show electrical impulses produced by the heart and can reveal thickening of its chambers; and ultrasound examinations, which show the thickness of the heart chamber walls,

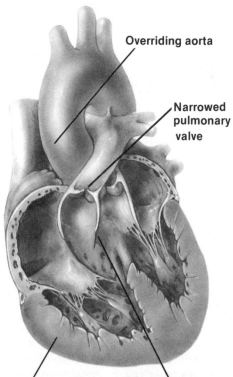

Overriding aorta

Narrowed pulmonary valve

Thickening in the wall of the right ventricle

Opening in the wall between the left and right ventricles

In Fallot's tetralogy, four abnormalities occur together. The aorta is displaced so that it overrides the ventricles and receives both arterial and venous blood. The valve between the pulmonary artery and the right ventricle is abnormally narrow, and there is an opening in the wall between the ventricles, which allows blood to flow from the left chamber to the right, permitting excess blood to flow into the lungs. The wall of the right ventricle is also thickened.

the size of the chambers, and the condition of the valves. Sometimes cardiac catheterization, an examination in which a catheter is passed along a blood vessel until it reaches the heart, is required.

TYPES OF DEFECTS

Eight types of defects are most common in infants. *Congenital aortic stenosis* is a narrowing of the aortic valve and sometimes of the aorta itself. This restricts the flow of blood to the body generally. *Congenital pulmonary stenosis* is a narrowing of the pulmonary valve—or, less frequently, of the pulmonary artery or the upper right ventricle —that restricts the flow of blood to the lungs. In *ventricular septal defects* and *atrial septal defects,* there are holes in the wall within the heart that separates the left and right chambers. These holes disturb normal flow within the chambers, leading to an excess of blood circulating in the lungs, which, in turn, leads to fibrosis of the pulmonary vessels. While about a quarter of all ventricular holes close spontaneously, such closure is less common for atrial defects.

Coarctation of the aorta is a constriction that limits the blood supply to the lower parts of the body. *Patent ductus arteriosus* involves a failure of the ductus to close after birth. In the womb, the ductus prevents circulation of blood through the fetus's lungs, which are not needed since oxygen is supplied through the placenta. After birth, the ductus normally closes. If it does not, blood from the aorta flows through the open ductus into the pulmonary artery and results in excess blood passing through the lungs. In *Fallot's tetralogy,* four abnormalities occur together: a

hole between the ventricles, aortic displacement, a narrowed pulmonary valve, and a thickening of the wall of the right ventricle. In the defect known as *transposition of the great arteries,* the locations of the aorta and pulmonary arteries are switched. Here, oxygenated blood coming from the lungs returns to the pulmonary arteries instead of passing through the aorta to the peripheral tissues. There is usually a hole in the septum, allowing some oxygenated blood to reach the aorta.

TREATMENT

Except in the case of very small holes in the heart, or when patent ductus arteriosus is detected early and occasionally closed with drug treatment, most congenital heart defects require surgery to correct the abnormality. If the disorder is not so severe as to demand immediate surgery, the operation may be delayed until the child is five years old or older, when he or she is larger and better able to withstand the stress of open heart surgery.

SUMMING UP

In most cases of congenital heart defects, the cause of the abnormality is not known. Drugs, infections such as rubella, and hereditary factors are implicated in about 10 percent of the cases.

With modern surgical techniques, the success rate for heart operations in children is very high. Most children who have effective surgical treatment for a congenital heart defect can expect to live normal lives.

19. Cardiac Pacemakers

COMMON CHARACTERISTICS

Since their introduction in the 1960s, cardiac pacemakers have saved many thousands of lives. In the United States alone, they are worn by half a million people whose hearts beat too slowly to supply adequate circulation to vital organs. Once a pacemaker is installed, it provides the essential electrical impulse that keeps the heart pumping at an efficient rate. Recent pacemakers are about one inch thick, weigh about five ounces, and are powered by lithium batteries that last up to ten years. Implantation is accomplished without opening the chest in a majority of cases, and proper functioning is checked from the outside by electronic instruments. In the latest models, which contain a radio transmitter and receiver, the doctor can even find out whether the pacemaker needs adjusting, and if so, the necessary changes can be made by sending the proper signals into the device without removing it.

WHO NEEDS A PACEMAKER

The healthy human heart beats about seventy to eighty times a minute. The electrical impulses that energize this activity originate in the part of the right atrium (sometimes called *auricle*) known as the sinoatrial node. It is here that the specialized cells are located that act as the heart's natural pacemaker. In a fraction of a second, the electrical impulse is transmitted throughout the left and right atria, causing them to contract, and then passes through the specialized fibers in the atrioventricular node. From here the electrical wave is conducted into the walls of the ventricles, resulting in their contraction. These are

the electrical impulses that are pictured in an electrocardiogram (ECG). (The discovery in the nineteenth century that the electrical discharge from the two cardiac nodes made it possible to measure the action of the heart by means of electrocardiography provided the basis for the great advances in cardiology.)

When the ECG indicates interference with the conduction system anyplace along its natural path, the aberration may not yet have produced any symptoms noticed by the patient. But where the interference is more than mild, the result is a slower than normal heartbeat.

SLOW HEARTBEAT

The technical name for this condition is bradycardia, and while in the strictest sense it is said to exist when the rate goes below sixty beats a minute, many people function without any noticeable symptoms with a heartbeat of fifty to fifty-five per minute. However, when the rate goes below that, the result is a general feeling of fatigue and lack of energy.

Slow heartbeat may be caused by certain drugs prescribed for a prior condition, by slow impulse transmission by the cells in the sineatrial area of the natural pacemaker, or by some degree of heart block.

HEART BLOCK

Heart block, also called atrioventricular block, is the condition in which there is a disruption—mild or major—in the transmission of the electrical signals between the upper and lower chambers of the heart, resulting in a slowdown of pumping ability. Heart block is usually caused by scarred heart tissue resulting from rheumatic fever, from the irreversible damage done by a heart attack (myocardial infarction), or from surgical repair of the heart.

When the condition is mild, medications acting as stimulants on the nervous system can compensate for the deficiency. However, when the heart block has reached the point where the flow of blood to the brain is so insufficient that dizziness and blackouts occur (Stokes-Adams syndrome), medical therapy is inadequate, and an artificial pacemaker is needed.

TYPES OF PACEMAKERS

There are now two main types of pacemakers, but they are constantly being improved for longevity, versatility, and convenience. Demand pacemakers (also called synchronous) are currently the most popular. They are designed to send impulses only when the heart goes below a previously determined rate (usually sixty-eight to seventy-two beats a minute). No impulses are sent when the heart maintains that rate naturally. The asynchronous pacemaker sends electrical impulses at a fixed rate no matter whether the heart's own beat is too fast or too slow. A major refinement in pacemaker design is expected to enable the instrument not only to correct a slow heartbeat but to adjust itself automatically so that it can correct any sudden functional disturbance in the heart's electrical system.

INSERTING THE PACEMAKER

The majority of pacemakers now in use are of the transvenous type, which are implanted without opening the chest. The procedure is simple and one of the safest in all surgical practice, requiring a total of about four days in the hospital if there are no other problems.

The batteries—or power pack—are placed under the skin below the collarbone. The wires from the batteries are

The wires attached to the power pack are passed through a vein in the arm into the right ventricle of the heart.

The power pack for the pacemaker is inserted under the skin below the collarbone.

B.A. Willett

passed through a vein in the arm into the heart's right ventricle. In a small fraction of cases, an incision must be made in the chest so that the electrodes can be placed directly on the heart muscle near the top of the left ventricle.

PACEMAKER CHECKUPS

The power packs in the earliest pacemakers had to be replaced every two years, but the present-day lithium packs may last as long as ten. Once the pacemaker has been put in place, the patient visits the cardiologist twice a year for an electrocardiogram and for a checkup with a minicomputer that can tell whether everything is working properly. Beginning with the third year, the doctor may suggest visits three times a year, and in the fourth year, four times a year. When the batteries show signs of wearing out, they can be replaced through a small incision in the skin made under local anesthetic. If any sign of dizziness or fainting occurs, the doctor should be notified at once. If the doctor cannot be reached, the patient should go to the nearest hospital emergency room.

PRECAUTIONS

The wearer of an artificial pacemaker leads a completely normal life unless circumscribed by restrictions because of other heart conditions, such as heart disease or angina. Older models were more sensitive to magnetic fields than the newer ones are. However, pacemaker wearers should discuss necessary precautions and carry a doctor's note exempting them from security checks at airports and other checkpoints. Museums and other public places

with electric eye installations usually post signs that alert pacemaker wearers to keep their distance.

SUMMING UP

The perfecting of the cardiac pacemaker is considered one of the greatest medical advances of the last few decades. It has increased the longevity and enhanced the life style of thousands of people whose hearts were no longer able to perform efficiently. The pacemaker is simple to implant and, once in place, easy to ignore, especially if one concentrates on the freedom from unpleasant symptoms and the ability to enjoy normal activities.

20. Rheumatic Fever

COMMON CHARACTERISTICS

Rheumatic fever is an inflammatory disease that affects the connective tissue in various parts of the body, especially in the joints and the heart. Although the disease may affect adults, its primary victims are children between the ages of six and ten years.

Once a widespread, crippling, and even life-threatening disease, rheumatic fever is now comparatively rare. This is due in part to antibiotic treatment of the initial streptococcal infection and also to general improvements in living conditions and diet that have increased resistance to the bacteria responsible for the disease.

ROLE OF STREP THROAT

An attack of rheumatic fever can usually be traced to an upper respiratory infection with fever and a sore throat that occurred and apparently cleared up two to three weeks earlier. It is not the cold and runny nose that are the danger signals but rather the sore throat. However, in some cases the streptococcal throat infection is without symptoms.

A sore throat can be caused by many types of infection, but that which causes rheumatic fever—a strep throat—is due to a particular strain of streptococcal bacteria: beta-hemolytic streptococcus (group A). In some children, for reasons that are not clear, the antibodies produced to combat the streptococci attack not only the bacteria but the connective tissue of the joints and, less commonly, the heart.

Certain signs distinguish strep throats from other sore throats: the onset is usually sudden, swallowing is painful, and the glands in the neck are swollen. There is usually a high fever, between 101 and 104°F. Headache, nausea, and vomiting may accompany the throat discomfort. When a child has these symptoms, a throat culture should be taken. If the culture shows the presence of beta-hemolytic streptococci, treatment with antibiotics should be begun immediately and be continued for at least ten days. If such treatment is not given, rheumatic fever may follow.

It should be emphasized that only a few children who are infected by the group A streptococcus actually do go on to develop rheumatic fever. Those who do, have a susceptibility that appears to be in part inherited. For most children, then, prompt

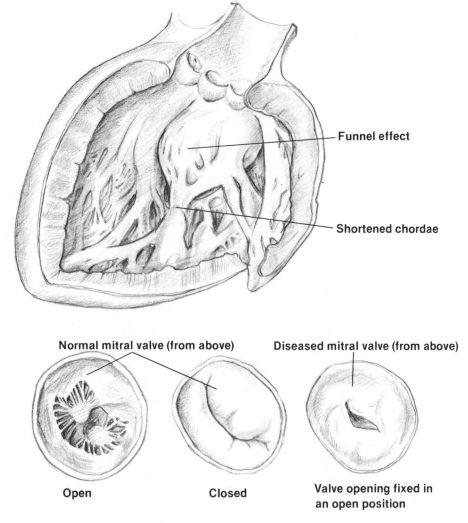

The most common serious result of recurrent rheumatic fever is mitral valve disease. The valvular leaflets and chordae become fused and thickened. The chordae are shortened and the leaflets held downward, creating a funnel effect. The valve opening is reduced and remains fixed in an open position.

antibiotic treatment is a precautionary measure—but an important one.

SYMPTOMS

To diagnose rheumatic fever, a doctor looks for any of the following four symptoms, known as the Jones criteria:

• Arthritis, usually of sudden onset, and most often located in the knees, ankles, elbows, wrists, or hips;
• Inflammation of the heart (carditis);
• A nonitching rash, which may be flat or may be slightly raised, appearing in circular or spiral shapes most often on the trunk or thighs (erythema marginatum);
• Spasmodic movements of the voluntary muscles (chorea).
Each of these symptoms is discussed below.

The joints, or the heart, or both may be affected. When the joints alone are involved, several become swollen and tender. (The child will also have a fever and a poor appetite and, in general, feel ill.) After about twenty-four hours, the inflammation usually disappears from the joints originally affected but migrates to others. The wrists, elbows, knees, and ankles are most commonly involved, but occasionally the hips and shoulders are affected also. This characteristic pattern of fever and joint pain gave the disease its name, at a time when *rheumatism* was the term used to describe any chronic pain or swelling of the joints.

If the heart alone is involved and the case is a mild one, there may be no symptoms at all. Sometimes only fatigue, pallor, and malaise are noted. There is a danger, in such circumstances, that the condition may go undiagnosed. In more severe cases involving the heart, the child will be breathless on exertion or when lying down, and the legs and ankles will swell, indicating that fluid is accumulating in the tissues (edema). This edema is a sign of early congestive heart failure.

In some cases of rheumatic fever, there is a transient, recurring red rash, usually on the chest, abdomen, back, or thigh. A late sign (six months to one year) is chorea—a disorder causing involuntary twisting and arching movements of the hands, arms, and face. In severe cases, particularly when the heart is involved, nodules may appear under the skin over bony prominences such as the elbows, knees and knuckles.

Rheumatic fever may run an acute course and then subside completely. However, repeated exposure to beta-hemolytic streptococci may lead to a recurrence or to frequent flare-ups.

CONSEQUENCES FOR THE HEART

Of the areas of inflammation that may be involved in acute rheumatic fever, the only one where the tissue changes may lead to a chronic problem is the heart. After repeated episodes of inflammation, the affected valves become severely scarred and narrowed and may cease to function properly, occasionally ultimately requiring valve-replacement surgery.

TREATMENT

Today, rheumatic fever is largely a preventable disease. Sore throats that are suspected of being caused by a streptococcal infection should be checked and a culture taken; if they prove to be caused by group A beta-hemolytic streptococci, the patient should be treated promptly with antibiotics to prevent rheumatic fever.

If rheumatic fever does occur and the attack is mild, bed rest at home will usually be sufficient. If the attack is more severe, hospitalization may be indicated. Aspirin may be given to ease joint pain and, when the heart has been affected, may be continued after the joint inflammation has subsided. If the heart is seriously affected, a course of powerful anti-inflammatory drugs, such as steroids, may be prescribed. In all cases, an antibiotic is given to kill any bacteria that may remain from the original throat infection and to guard against further attack.

During an attack of rheumatic fever that affects the heart, it is essential to rest and remain quiet, so as to put as little demand as possible on the heart. Depending on the extent of the damage, it may be weeks or months before the child can return to a normal routine. If there has been no heart damage, all normal activities can be resumed. If heart damage has occurred, the physician may advise the patient about which activities should be permitted. Many recovered rheumatic fever patients have persisting heart murmurs as evidence of heart valve involvement. While these patients' activity may be somewhat restricted, other recovered patients face no restrictions whatsoever. Long-term medication is usually required; if so, the doctor's instructions should be carefully followed.

SUMMING UP

With effective diagnosis and prompt antibiotic treatment of the initial streptococcal infection, rheumatic fever can now largely be prevented. Antibiotic treatment —on a long-term basis—has also enormously reduced the rate of recurrence of this disease. Although in some cases valvular heart disease develops, with modern treatment most affected children can live normal or nearly normal lives.

21. Mitral Valve Prolapse

COMMON CHARACTERISTICS

Mitral valve prolapse (MVP) is a common and usually benign heart condition. It is also known as Barlow's syndrome (named for the physician who, in 1968, described the association between MVP and a number of its possible complications) and as the "click-murmur syndrome," describing its characteristic sounds as heard through a stethoscope.

An estimated 4 to 7 percent of the population has MVP, the great majority without any symptoms at all. More women than men are affected, for reasons that are unknown, and a hereditary predisposition seems to be involved. Because MVP is so prevalent, some authorities have speculated that the condition is simply a normal variant in heart structure rather than a syndrome as such.

THE MITRAL VALVE

The mitral valve—so called because its two leaflet flaps look like a bishop's miter —is located on the left side of the heart. In the resting phase between heartbeats, blood moves through this valve, which then closes. The ventricle then contracts strongly, sending fresh oxygenated blood out through the heart's main artery (the aorta) for distribution through the body. If the mitral valve fails to close com-

Mitral Valve Prolapse

A tightly closed mitral valve normally ensures that, with each beat (contraction) of the heart, blood moves from the left ventricle to the aorta. If the valve is prolapsed, however, and fails to close completely before the ventricle contracts, there is a backflow into the atrium. This flow can be heard through the stethoscope as a murmur, sometimes preceded by a clicking sound.

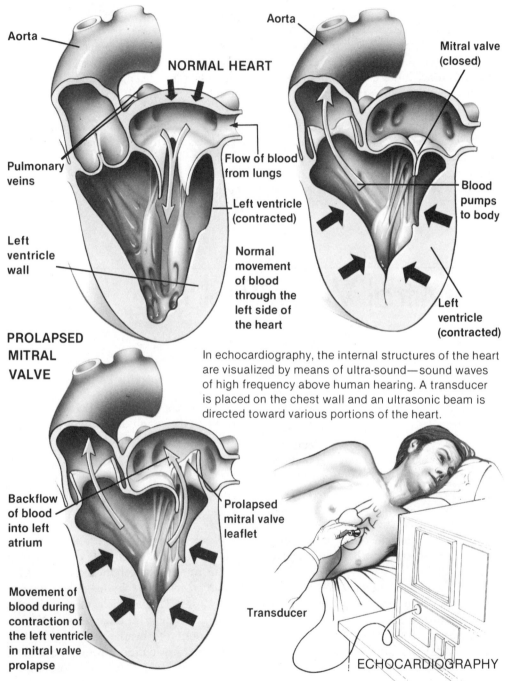

NORMAL HEART

Aorta

Pulmonary veins

Left ventricle wall

Flow of blood from lungs

Left ventricle (contracted)

Normal movement of blood through the left side of the heart

Aorta

Mitral valve (closed)

Blood pumps to body

Left ventricle (contracted)

PROLAPSED MITRAL VALVE

In echocardiography, the internal structures of the heart are visualized by means of ultra-sound—sound waves of high frequency above human hearing. A transducer is placed on the chest wall and an ultrasonic beam is directed toward various portions of the heart.

Backflow of blood into left atrium

Prolapsed mitral valve leaflet

Movement of blood during contraction of the left ventricle in mitral valve prolapse

Transducer

ECHOCARDIOGRAPHY

pletely before the contraction occurs, as in MVP, there is a backflow of blood from the ventricle into the atrium. This flow can be heard through a stethoscope as a murmur, sometimes preceded by a clicking sound.

CAUSES

Until recently, most cases of MVP were thought to be due to structural defects in the valve caused by rheumatic fever or a congenital condition. But physicians are now recognizing that brief murmurs, and occasionally clicking sounds, are present in many otherwise completely healthy individuals. In these cases, the mitral valve is not damaged; rather, some part of a normal valve is pushed too far back (that is, prolapsed) as the heart contracts.

The great majority of people affected with MVP remain completely asymptomatic throughout their lives; in some cases, even the "classic" murmur and click are not present. A small number, however, develop troublesome symptoms; in very rare cases, severe complications may occur.

SYMPTOMS

Chest pain is one of the two most common symptoms of MVP. Typically, the pain is described as being "sharp" or "stabbing." It may last for a few hours or a few days and is not brought on by exertion. The cause of the pain associated with MVP is not known. Some authorities have suggested that it may be due to an abnormality in the bony structure of the chest or to changes in the tone of the muscles of the chest wall. Despite the pain, the prognosis for those with MVP is extremely good. Knowing this, many people have learned to live with chest pain. In other cases, medication, usually a beta-blocking agent, may be prescribed.

Palpitations—disturbances of the normal heart rhythm—may also be associated with MVP. Frequently, these are completely benign and treatment is not needed. More serious arrhythmias may be treated with standard antiarrhythmic drugs.

COMPLICATIONS

Though extremely rare, several serious complications have been associated with MVP. One is progressive mitral insufficiency (regurgitation), which, like MVP, involves a backflow of blood into the atrium. In mitral insufficiency, however, the heart wall enlarges in an attempt to deal with the extra work load, and there may be fatigue, shortness of breath, or, in extreme cases, the symptoms of congestive heart failure. Mitral insufficiency can usually be treated medically with the prescription of diuretics to help the body carry off accumulating fluids; occasionally, surgery is necessary to replace the valve with an artificial one.

A well-recognized complication of MVP is infective endocarditis (inflammation of the lining of the heart, which affects the valves in particular). It is for this reason that those who have MVP with both a constant murmur and a click should be sure to have antibiotic treatment before undergoing any procedure—dental or surgical—that might release harmful bacteria into the bloodstream.

SUMMING UP

In the vast majority of cases, mitral valve prolapse remains a benign condition without any symptoms or problems. Even individuals who suffer occasional symptoms such as chest pain or palpitations rarely require treatment or develop serious complications. In the rare cases in which complications do develop, a wide range of effective therapies is available.

22. Pericarditis

COMMON CHARACTERISTICS

Pericarditis is an inflammation of the pericardium, the sac that surrounds and contains the heart. The pericardium is composed of two layers of membrane separated by a film of lubricating fluid. It enables the heart to move freely in relation to adjacent organs as it performs its normal functions. When inflammation occurs, the action of the heart is impeded, and while symptoms vary with the cause, the typical manifestations of pericarditis are chest pain and shortness of breath (dyspnea).

CAUSES OF PERICARDITIS

Acute pericarditis is usually traceable to a prior condition: bacterial infection elsewhere in the body (often staphylococcus of the bone marrow, a condition called osteomyelitis), pneumonia, or a lung abscess. It also may be the result of a heart attack or the aftermath of a trauma to the chest, such as a penetrating wound. Pericardial inflammation sometimes develops because of the spread through the bloodstream of tubercle bacilli even when tuberculosis of the lung is not present. (This diagnosis can be confirmed when a tuberculin test gives a positive result.) Pericarditis may also be a secondary effect of radiation or drug therapy, or of tumors in the lungs or breast. It may be associated with kidney failure (uremia), and it may be a consequence of heart surgery. Acute primary pericarditis is usually caused by virus infection.

Acute pericarditis may be characterized by a marked increase in the fluid contents of the pericardial sac (effusion) or, conversely, by a drying out and roughening of the membranes.

SYMPTOMS AND DIAGNOSIS

While symptoms vary with the cause of the inflammation, the patient usually feels a chest pain that may travel to the back and shoulders. The pain is intensified by movement and deep breathing and more or less subsides when the body is at rest. Breathlessness and coughing may be accompanied by fever, a faster pulse, and a change in blood pressure. When the inflammation produces "dry" pericarditis, the membranes develop deposits of fibrin, the protein material that causes the blood to clot. It is this fibrinous matter that creates the "rubbing" sound the doctor hears when listening to the heart with a stethoscope.

The doctor can often diagnose acute pericarditis on the basis of the patient's description of symptoms, aided by the stethoscope and confirmed by an electrocardiogram. X-rays will indicate changes in the outline of the heart distended by fluid accumulation, and the presence of pericardial fluid is also indicated by the results of echocardiography, a quick, safe, and noninvasive technique based on the use of ultrasonic waves.

TREATMENT OF ACUTE PERICARDITIS

When the cause is determined, treatment proceeds accordingly. For example, antibiotics are prescribed for bacterial pericarditis. Early in the course of tubercular pericarditis, isoniazid combined with streptomycin or rifampicin will control the spread and worsening of the condition. When laboratory diagnosis of antibodies has determined the cause to be viral (coxsackie virus or echovirus), the best treatment is strict bed rest. When pericarditis is associated with a heart attack or heart surgery, bed rest may be the only requirement. In all cases, aspirin or an equivalent may be given to ease pain and reduce temperature when high fever is present.

CHRONIC PERICARDITIS

When symptoms of acute pericarditis have been neglected and treatment delayed, or when inflammation has continued over a long period for whatever reason, pericardial tissue becomes scarred

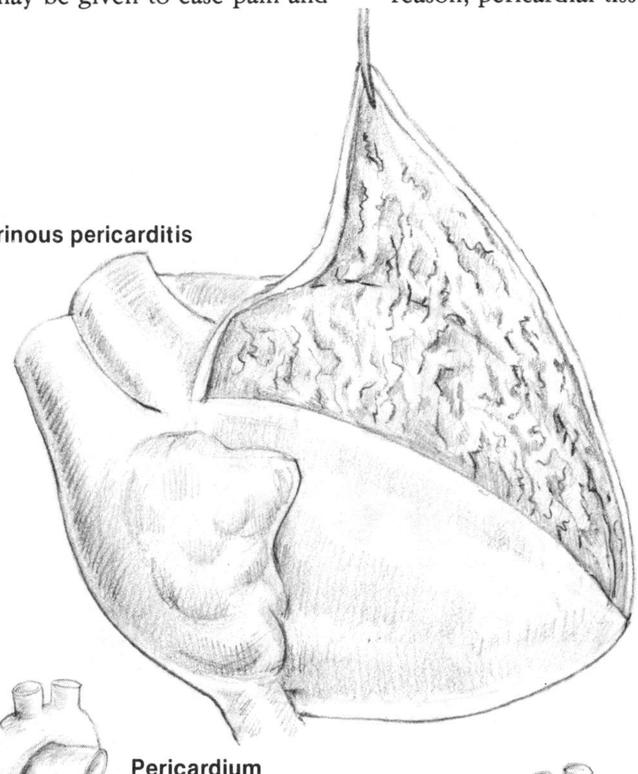

Fibrinous pericarditis

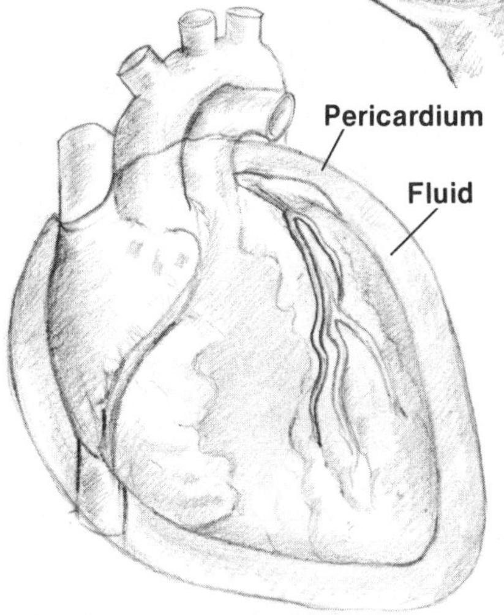

Pericardium

Fluid

Cardiac compression resulting from fluid

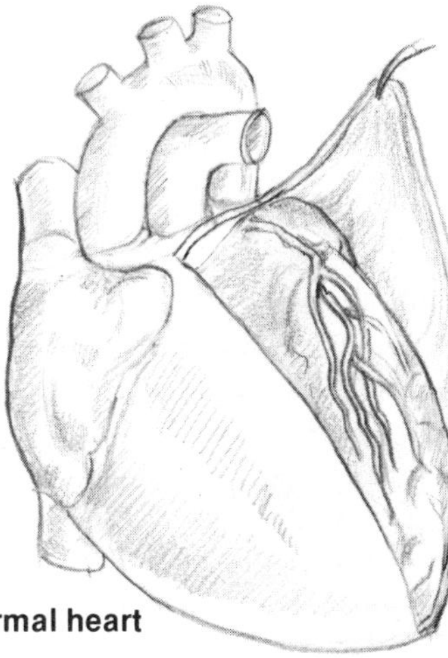

Normal heart

and eventually constricted. In chronic constrictive pericarditis, interference of heart function leads to liver enlargement and a generalized condition of edema.

Constrictive pericarditis, which may be tubercular in origin, causes calcium and fibrous deposits to form around the heart, limiting its movements. Another form of chronic pericarditis causes the heart to become anchored to surrounding tissues by the formation of adhesions.

Sometimes chronic pericarditis can be relieved and eventually improved by medication, bed rest, a salt-free diet, diuretics, and drainage of accumulated fluids. However, when it has reached the constrictive stage, surgery is called for. The procedure, technically a pericardiectomy, strips off the diseased portion of the membrane, thus enabling normal heart function to resume and thereby eliminating the secondary effects on other organs of the constriction. (The surgical procedure for draining the accumulation of excess fluid or effusions is called a pericardiostomy. In this operation, the pericardium is opened for drainage but otherwise remains intact.)

SUMMING UP

Most instances of acute pericarditis are a manifestation of infection elsewhere in the body. Once its nature is determined, the secondary inflammation can be controlled and cured by proper medication and bed rest. The danger lies in neglecting the body's signals until the inflammation becomes serious. Any sudden onset of chest pain and shortness of breath with or without fever should always be called to a doctor's attention without delay. Prompt diagnosis is especially important when the cause is the tubercle bacillus, since early treatment with anti-TB drug therapy successfully prevents complications.

23. Potassium and the Heart

GENERAL CONSIDERATIONS

Potassium is a naturally occurring mineral found in every human body and in a wide variety of foods. It is one of the essential substances needed to maintain the body's internal balance of fluids and chemicals. A constant internal environment, in which the various chemicals and fluids are in a state of balance, is necessary if the cells are to carry on their vital functions. Any marked change in the concentration and content of water and chemicals within the body leads to drastic changes that modify our ability to function normally.

THE ROLE OF POTASSIUM

Potassium, like sodium, is necessary to human life. The human body requires about equal amounts of both sodium and potassium. The typical American diet, however, provides much more sodium than needed and about the right amount of potassium, which is found in fruits, vegetables, some meats, dairy products, and a

Potassium and the Heart

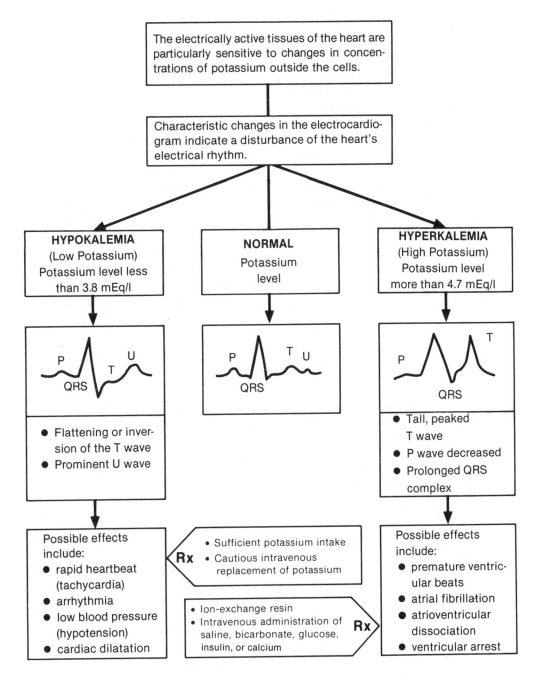

The electrically active tissues of the heart are particularly sensitive to changes in concentrations of potassium outside the cells.

Characteristic changes in the electrocardiogram indicate a disturbance of the heart's electrical rhythm.

HYPOKALEMIA
(Low Potassium)
Potassium level less
than 3.8 mEq/l

NORMAL
Potassium
level

HYPERKALEMIA
(High Potassium)
Potassium level
more than 4.7 mEq/l

- Flattening or inversion of the T wave
- Prominent U wave

- Tall, peaked T wave
- P wave decreased
- Prolonged QRS complex

Possible effects include:
- rapid heartbeat (tachycardia)
- arrhythmia
- low blood pressure (hypotension)
- cardiac dilatation

Rx
- Sufficient potassium intake
- Cautious intravenous replacement of potassium

- Ion-exchange resin
- Intravenous administration of saline, bicarbonate, glucose, insulin, or calcium
Rx

Possible effects include:
- premature ventricular beats
- atrial fibrillation
- atrioventricular dissociation
- ventricular arrest

variety of other foods. In addition, the increasingly popular salt substitutes usually contain potassium as a sodium substitute.

Because potassium is found in sufficient amounts in the average diet, a true dietary deficiency of potassium is very rare. However, hypokalemia, a deficiency of potassium in the blood, may occur under a number of specific circumstances that are unrelated to diet. Certain drugs, especially some of the diuretics used to treat high blood pressure, frequently lead to potassium reduction.

Signs of potassium deficiency include lethargy, muscular weakness, increased nervous irritability, a feeling of mental disorientation and irregular heartbeats. To

FOODS HIGH IN POTASSIUM

Food	Portion	Potassium (mg.)
Apricots, dried	20 halves	850
Apricots, raw	3 medium	440
Avocado	1/2 avocado	340
Banana	1 medium	560
Beef, lean round	3-4 oz.	400
Bran, cereal flakes	1 cup	1,200
Cantaloupe	1/2 of 5 in. melon	230
Cocoa, dried	2 tsp.	1,400
Dates, dried	1/2 cup	790
Figs, dried	1 large	780
Ham, cured, cooked	3-4 oz.	340
Lentils, dried	1/4 cup	780
Lima beans, green, frozen	3/4 cup	489
Orange	1 medium	350
Peaches, dried	1/2 cup	1,100
Prunes, dried uncooked	10 large	600
Radishes, raw	10 small	260
Salmon, canned	3-4 oz.	300
Sardines, canned	3 ounces	560
Spinach, raw	3-4 oz.	780
Tomato, raw	1 small	230
Tomato juice	1 cup	240
Tuna canned	3-4 oz.	240
Turkey	3-4 oz.	310-320

prevent serious problems, potassium supplements may be recommended, especially if the deficiency is likely to continue, as might be the case in patients taking certain types of diuretics for high blood pressure.

IMPORTANCE OF BALANCE

Just as too little potassium can have serious consequences, excessive blood levels of potassium also can lead to complications. If the kidneys and circulatory system are functioning properly, it is virtually impossible to produce a dangerously high level of potassium in the blood through diet alone. High potassium levels may occur, however, in patients taking prescribed potassium supplements. But if potassium levels are too high, they must be treated to avoid a possible progression to more serious problems. Therefore, it is imperative that the patient follow the physician's dosage recommendations.

SOURCES OF POTASSIUM

The recommended dietary allowance (RDA) of potassium for adults is in the range of two to six grams per day, depending on body weight. The average American adult consumes 4.5 grams of potassium per day, which is well within these suggested guidelines. The best dietary sources of potassium are bananas, orange juice, raisins and other dried fruits, meats, peanut butter, bran, dried peas and beans, and potatoes. Cocoa, coffee, and tea also contain significant amounts of potassium (see accompanying table for more specific amounts).

TREATMENT OF POTASSIUM DEPLETION

An estimated two million Americans regularly take potassium supplements. Most are patients with high blood pressure, where potassium levels are lowered by their antihypertensive medications. In many instances, increased consumption of potassium-rich foods is all that is required. For others, however, additional potassium in the form of prescription supplements is needed. This is a determination that must be made by a physician.

SUMMING UP

Potassium is an essential mineral that is found in a variety of foods. The average healthy person consumes adequate potassium. However, a number of diseases and other circumstances, including the use of certain drugs, may upset the body's natural balance of fluids and chemicals and lead to a potassium imbalance. Unless corrected, this imbalance can have serious consequences.

24. Strokes and Mini-Strokes

COMMON CHARACTERISTICS

Stroke is the general term used to describe an interruption in the flow of blood to the brain. A mini-stroke, known medically as a transient ischemic attack, is a temporary interruption that passes in a few minutes but is often a prelude to a stroke. A stroke is always a medical emergency, which may result in permanent damage to a number of body functions depending upon what part of the brain is affected.

TYPES OF STROKE

A number of causes may decrease or totally shut off blood flow to the brain. The most common, however, is blockage of the blood supply by a clot or by a cerebral hemorrhage.

Blockage from a clot (cerebral thrombosis or cerebral embolism) is one of the more common types of stroke. Very often, the clot forms in a blood vessel that is already narrowed by arteriosclerosis (hardening of the arteries). The portion of the brain normally fed by the affected artery begins to die, producing corresponding disruptions in the emotional, intellectual, or physical functions. Typically, cerebral thrombosis occurs during sleep, and the damage becomes apparent when the victim awakens. The condition is often associated with high blood pressure—a prime factor in the development of arteriosclerosis.

An embolism is another kind of clot, which differs from a thrombosis in that it forms at one site—usually the heart or large arteries of the neck—breaks off, and is carried by the bloodstream until it lodges in the smaller vessels of the brain. Composed of fatty plaque fragments or other bits of loose material (detritus) from the cardiovascular system, an embolism usually strikes when a person is awake and active. It is particularly common in individuals recovering from a heart attack. Rheumatic heart disease and infections and inflammations of the heart valves also increase the risk of embolism.

As its name implies, a cerebral hemorrhage involves a form of bleeding within the brain. It is the most serious form of stroke, killing an estimated 75 percent to 90 percent of its victims. Cerebral hemorrhage is often associated with high blood pressure, which, through the years, weakens the walls of the arteries in the brain until one or more of them develops small, balloon-like outcroppings (aneurysms). When an aneurysm ruptures, the flow of blood to the rest of the brain is interrupted. Moreover, the blood spills out onto the surrounding brain cells, causing further damage. A cerebral hemorrhage commonly occurs during waking hours and is usually accompanied by severe headache, a sense of forboding or doom, vomiting, and paralysis. As the bleeding progresses, the victim may lose consciousness.

TRANSIENT ISCHEMIC ATTACKS

Though cerebral hemorrhage usually strikes without warning, other forms of stroke are preceded by brief and passing spells of impaired brain function. These are known as transient ischemic attacks, or TIAs. A TIA causes no permanent damage, but it is a warning that something is seriously amiss and should never be neglected or shrugged off. Usually, TIAs result from a narrowing in the arteries of the neck through which blood flows to the brain. This narrowing can be corrected surgically if discovered in time—before a major stroke occurs. Some drugs, particularly those that have a blood-thinning and anticlotting action, also may be given to prevent a stroke.

TIAs produce a wide range of temporary symptoms, including blurring or dimness of vision, difficulties in reading or pronouncing certain words, dizzy spells, and motor impairment. A loss of limb control or coordination on the same side of the body—such as the sudden inability to move both the left arm and left leg—is strongly suggestive of a TIA.

WHO IS AT RISK?

The majority of strokes occur in persons over sixty-five, who are most likely to have incurred degenerative changes in the cardiovascular system. However, strokes may occur at any age, even in newborn babies. Among children, they are often the result of congenital heart disorders; they may also be caused by sickle-cell anemia, which is most prevalent among blacks.

Among young adults, hypertension—often as a result of or in association with atherosclerosis—is the most frequent cause of strokes. Obesity may be another contributing factor. Women who take oral contraceptive pills are at higher risk of stroke than those who do not, especially if this is coupled with heavy smoking. Doctors usually recommend that women with a family history of high blood pressure avoid oral contraceptives. In addition, a range of other diseases, including diabetes mellitus and meningitis, may increase the possibility of stroke.

TREATMENT

Because the effects of stroke are so severe and may be permanent, prevention is a primary objective. If high blood pressure or arteriosclerosis is present, such prevention may consist of dietary changes, exercise programs, and drug therapy if necessary. Certain drugs may also be prescribed to serve as blood thinners or anticoagulants, which lessen the danger of clotting. Some studies indicate that aspirin may be an effective anticlotting agent in men who have suffered TIAs. Aspirin may have negative side effects, however, and you should consult your physician rather than start your own program of self-medication.

Congenital cerebral aneurysms, which sometimes occur in clusters, frequently cause strokes in younger patients. These clusters of weakened vessels are often removed surgically after the acute stroke is stabilized.

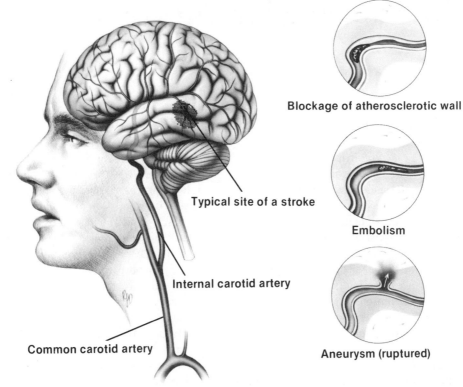

Blockage of atherosclerotic wall

Embolism

Typical site of a stroke

Internal carotid artery

Aneurysm (ruptured)

Common carotid artery

Bypass surgery may be recommended as a preventive measure when narrowing of the neck arteries has been detected. It is designed to provide alternate routes for the blood that normally flows through these clogged vessels. Newer operations include translocating small blood vessels to increase the blood supply to certain areas of the brain.

IF A STROKE OCCURS

Once a stroke patient is stabilized and the immediate danger is over, attention is focused upon rehabilitation. The sooner one begins relearning functions that have been impaired by the stroke, the better. This is particularly true of speech and the use of limbs. While the process may seem slow and frustrating, it is important not to give up. There are many excellent stroke rehabilitation clinics located throughout the country, and most hospitals have trained therapists who can help in the rehabilitation process.

SUMMING UP

Stroke is always considered a serious condition, even though many stroke patients make a full recovery. Recognizing the warning signs and taking early, preventive steps remains the best treatment. This is particularly true of people with a family history of stroke or those who have high blood pressure.

25. Infective Endocarditis

COMMON CHARACTERISTICS

The word *endocarditis* means inflammation (-itis) of the endocardium, the internal lining of the heart, which includes the valves. Infective endocarditis, then, is an endocardial inflammation caused by an infection. In almost all cases, the infection centers on a heart valve, leaving the rest of the endocardial surface unaffected. (In rare instances, the infection develops on a defect in certain blood vessels serving the heart, or on the endocardium at the site of an injury or defect.) Depending on the virulence of the bacteria causing the infection, the course of the disease may be either acute or moderately acute (subacute).

Infective endocarditis occurs most often in people who have certain types of preexisting heart damage or defect. The disease can be cured if it is treated promptly, but the outlook is poor if it goes unrecognized or untreated.

SUSCEPTIBILITY

Those most susceptible to infective endocarditis include people with damaged heart valves (usually as the result of rheumatic fever), some types of congenital heart disease, mitral valve prolapse, and degenerative heart disease. Individuals who have artificial heart valves or pacemakers are also at risk, as are some hemodialysis patients and addicts who "main-line" drugs.

BACTERIA IN THE BLOODSTREAM

Infective endocarditis is caused by bacteria entering the bloodstream. The type of bacteria that most often causes endocarditis *(streptococcus)* normally inhabits the mouth and the upper respiratory tract. Other bacteria that are commonly involved are the *enterococci* (which normally inhabit the genitourinary and gastrointestinal tracts) and the *staphlococci* (which are found on the skin). These ubiquitous bacteria may enter the bloodstream when surgery is performed on the mouth, the throat, the heart, the genitourinary tract, or the gastrointestinal tract. Other portals of entry are provided by tooth extraction, cystoscopy (passing an instrument up the urinary tract to view the inside of the bladder), abscesses of the teeth and skin, upper respiratory or pelvic infections, and injections of narcotics.

The average healthy person runs little risk of developing infective endocarditis from any of these problems or procedures. Under normal conditions, the heart is not easily infected. For example, bacteria commonly enter the bloodstream during dental treatment, but in the vast majority of instances no harm is done and no complications arise.

However, when the endocardium is damaged, bacteria circulating in the bloodstream may adhere to the abnormal surface, where conditions are suitable for their growth. The area may be a tiny clot on the roughened surface of a defective valve, for example, or a clot on the suture line holding an artificial valve in place. It is thought that, as the initial bacterial colony becomes covered with more and more clotted blood, the clots form a barrier protecting the bacteria from the body's immune system. An established infection may, therefore, take a long time to eradicate.

SUBACUTE ENDOCARDITIS

The subacute form of the disease is a slowly progressing or "smoldering" infection, usually affecting heart valves that are congenitally defective or have preexisting damage. This form most often follows dental procedures—tooth extraction in particular.

The onset is slow and deceptive. At first, an individual may feel that he or she merely has a viral illness because the only signs are a low-grade, intermittent fever and a feeling of fatigue. These signs may persist for weeks. As the disease progresses, however, chills and pains in the joints may occur, mimicking a flare up of rheumatic fever. Thin red lines (splinter hemorrhages) under fingernails and toenails, and small red or purplish spots (petechiae) on the skin are common. The ends of the fingers may become thicker and broader and there may be blood in the urine.

If an unexplained fever lasts for more than a week in a person with a known heart murmur, infective endocarditis should be suspected and the doctor should be notified. Delaying until advanced symptoms have appeared can be dangerous.

ACUTE ENDOCARDITIS

The acute form spreads rapidly through the heart valves. It usually develops in the course of blood poisoning (septicemia) from serious infections such as pneumococcal pneumonia, abscesses, or meningitis. It may also occur as a complication of open-heart surgery or other surgery involving infected tissues.

The symptoms of acute endocarditis are similar to those of the subacute form, but they appear rapidly and almost simultaneously.

TREATMENT

If endocarditis persists, it can develop into congestive heart failure, severe anemia, kidney failure, or blood clots (emboli) in the brain or the lungs—all of which may be fatal. However, if the disease is properly treated with antibiotics, almost all patients with the subacute form are cured. The mortality is greater in the acute form.

It is vital to detect the infection at the earliest possible time and to start treatment. The choice of antibiotics depends on identification of the causative agent and laboratory "sensitivity" tests that show which drug is effective against it. Sometimes the safest course is to start antibiotics before the causative bacterium and its sensitivity are known—perhaps even before the diagnosis of endocarditis has been confirmed. Occasionally, surgery may be necessary, as, for example, when an infected artificial heart valve must be replaced.

Heart viewed from above

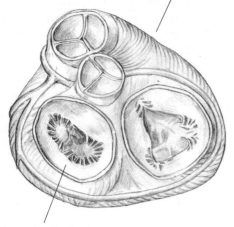

Normal mitral valve

Mitral valve with vegetation caused by bacterial endocarditis. Vegetation may prevent proper functioning of valves and, if untreated, may eventually result in death.

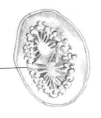

In all cases, a basic requirement is prolonged antibiotic therapy, often administered intravenously. The cure of endocarditis, unlike that of other infections, depends on the ability of the drug to work unaided by the body's immune system. Some people may be cured in a few weeks, while others may have to be treated for far longer periods.

PREVENTION

There is no certain way to prevent endocarditis. However, it is possible to minimize the likelihood of infection.

The risk of the disease occurring is greatest when bacteria enter the bloodstream during tooth extraction and certain surgical procedures involving the mouth, nose, throat, and the genitourinary and gastrointestinal tracts. Therefore, if you know that you are susceptible to endocarditis, you should inform your dentist or doctor before undergoing any such procedure. He or she will then prescribe appropriate antibiotics, to be administered both before and after the operation or extraction. The goal is to eliminate bacteria in the bloodstream before they can infect an abnormal endocardium—and, if need be, to cure a very early infection.

Some doctors believe that patients with valvular disease should have all their teeth removed, as a preventive measure. The majority, while they do not recommend that sound teeth be extracted, stress the importance of good routine dental care to keep teeth and gums healthy. "Jet spray" toothbrushes should be avoided and dentures should fit well.

A further important preventive measure is to treat any infection of the skin, mouth, nose, or throat promptly. This minimizes the possibility that the infection will spread into the bloodstream.

SUMMING UP

Although anyone can develop infective endocarditis, this serious infection occurs most often in people who have certain kinds of preexisting heart damage or defect. The onset of the disease may be insidious; often the first symptoms are a persistent low fever and a feeling of fatigue. In its acute form, however, the disease develops rapidly, with fever and other symptoms (painin muscles and joints, splinter hemorrhages, petechiae) appearing almost simultaneously. In either case, it is vital that endocarditis be recognized and treated promptly. Antibiotic therapy is effective in the majority of cases.

Prevention of endocarditis in susceptible individuals consists of three basic measures: antibiotics given before and after dental work and surgery; regular dental care; and prompt treatment of infections of the mouth, skin, and upper respiratory tract.

Arthritis and Other Musculoskeletal Disorders

26. Back Pain

COMMON CHARACTERISTICS

Back pain, which afflicts four out of five Americans at one time or another, is second only to headache as a common disorder characterized by pain. Pain in the upper spine may accompany an injury; however, for the overwhelming majority, the pain originates in the lower back, or lumbar region.

Recent studies indicate that fewer than 15 percent of cases of lower back pain are traceable to structural defects, such as ruptured disks, arthritis, or tumors. In most cases, the disability arises from weakness of the musculature surrounding the spine. Therefore, the most important aspect of treatment for muscle-based back pain involves strengthening and protecting these supporting muscles. With a doctor's guidance, well-informed and motivated patients can carry out most of the treatment themselves.

HOW THE PAIN ORIGINATES

The spinal column is made up of twenty-four separate and nine fused vertebrae, held together with tough bands of tissue called ligaments. Nerve roots pass through openings at the side of each vertebra. Thus, a wrench of the back or a failure of muscular support may result in the painful "pinching" of a nerve. The sciatic nerve—which extends from the lumbar area into the buttock, leg, and toes—is particularly vulnerable to pressure. (The condition known as sciatica is a frequent companion to lower back pain, usually associated with a ruptured disk.)

Pain also is generated where muscles go into spasm. While such spasms may occur as a protective reflex, they intensify discomfort by choking off circulation and setting up an inflammatory response. Stress of any kind—physical or psychological—may cause spasms in underexercised muscles.

BASIC CAUSES

Recurrent back pain—leading to the deterioration of the muscles supporting the spine—usually can be traced to a specific condition. These include—singly or in combination—a sedentary life style, obesity, poor posture, and a general lack of muscular tone. The type of exercise taken by usually sedentary people often fails to strengthen muscles supporting the lower back. Indeed, such popular weekend sports as tennis, golf, and skiing may actually promote back problems.

TREATING THE PAIN

Typically, acute low-back pain comes on suddenly and without apparent reason. Symptoms of sciatic nerve involvement— twinges, numbness, burning—may also be present. For such cases, a regimen of bed rest, hot baths, and aspirin or a prescribed painkiller usually provides relief. A short course of muscle relaxants may be recommended. If sagging abdominal muscles need support, a girdle is helpful.

In about 90 percent of all cases, low-back pain subsides within two months. However, if the circumstances that caused it are not altered, it is likely to recur.

PREVENTING A RECURRENCE

As soon as possible after the acute pain subsides, exercises should be undertaken to strengthen muscles in the back and abdomen. A long-term weight-reducing plan may also be advised (see Chapter 27, "Exercises for a Bad Back"). Yoga, meditation, and breathing exercises may help reduce tension and stress.

If your daily routine involves many hours of standing, check your posture in profile. Your chest should be raised, buttocks tucked in, and stomach flat. Sedentary workers should have a chair with armrests, support for the lower back, a movable upper section, and an adjustment for height, so that feet can rest on the floor. When picking things up, bend at the knees only. If the object is heavy, hold it close to flexed abdominal muscles. Sports involving sudden body movements should be avoided in favor of walking, jogging, cycling, or swimming.

CHRONIC DISABLING PAIN

When diagnostic tests determine that the cause of severe and unremitting back pain is nerve damage, tumor, arthritis, or bone inflammation, therapy involves more extensive treatment, which may include surgery, drugs, and physical therapy.

Very often, longtime sufferers from back pain of unidentifiable origin become "lower back cripples," limiting their activities and life style for fear of provoking pain. If the back becomes an excuse for avoiding responsibilities or confronting

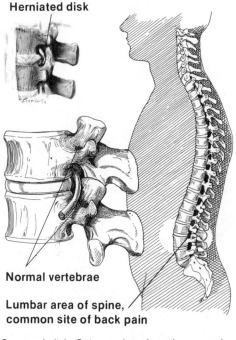

Herniated disk

Normal vertebrae

Lumbar area of spine, common site of back pain

Ruptured disk. Pain results when the central cushion of gelatinous material in the disk ruptures (herniates) and presses on the adjacent nerve root.

underlying problems, professional counseling should be considered.

SUMMING UP

Back pain is one of our most common health problems, but it can usually be resolved by proper exercise, heat, diet, and other conservative measures. While 90 percent of all back pains dissipate within a few weeks, precautions should be taken to prevent their recurrence. Less frequent causes of lower back pain include arthritis, tumors, and structural or neurological defects, which require clinical treatment.

27. Exercises for a Bad Back

GENERAL CONSIDERATIONS

Back pain is one of the most common causes of disability in the United States. At any one time, about seven million Americans are under treatment for back pain, and it is estimated that seventy million Americans have experienced at least one severe episode of backache.

Various factors contribute to back problems, and a number of treatments are available (see Chapter 26, "Back Pain"). Fortunately, most people can overcome back problems through a common-sense program of exercise, weight control, and, when appropriate, drugs for pain relief. Perhaps the most important of these approaches, however, is a program of exercises—performed on a regular basis—that is designed to strengthen back and abdominal muscles.

PRECAUTIONS

Before undertaking a back exercise program, several cautions should be noted:

First, exercises should not be initiated without having your doctor's instruction to do so. There are many types of back problems, and the exercise regimen should be designed specifically for you. Exercises that have helped a neighbor or friend may not be right for you; indeed, certain problems may even be exacerbated by the wrong exercises.

Second, exercise programs should start gradually and then be performed regularly. At the beginning, you may be instructed to do an exercise only two or three times. Once the routine is established and your back and muscles become accustomed to the exercises, you probably will be instructed to do each exercise five to ten times each day.

Third, care should be taken to make sure the exercises are properly performed. Small details, such as the placement of your arms or legs, angle of your neck and chin, and direction and sequence of movement are important. A physical therapist, doctor, or other health professional skilled in exercise therapy should give the initial instructions and periodically check to make sure the exercise technique is correct.

Fourth, stop if an exercise or movement

produces pain. Pain is usually a warning that something is amiss. Many people have the mistaken notion that the pain will go away if they continue or even step up the exercises. Exercises that strengthen and tone muscles do not need to be strenuous or painful to produce results; in fact, most back exercises use easy, nonstrenuous motions.

Fifth, exercises should be continued even after the acute back problem is under control. For most people, this means a lifelong endeavor. Many people make the mistake of stopping the exercises once they overcome the back pain. Within a few weeks or months, the muscles are again out of condition, and the problem recurs. Most exercise regimens take only ten to fifteen minutes to perform.

BASICS INVOLVED

Most exercises are performed while lying on a hard surface, preferably the floor. A very firm mattress also may be used, and some people do their exercises before getting out of bed in the morning.

The exercises are designed either to strengthen specific groups of muscles or to increase flexibility by stretching muscles and ligaments. The exercises should be performed slowly and in a relaxed manner.

Pelvic tilt. Pull in the stomach so that the small of your back is flat on the floor. Then, tightening the buttocks, raise your hips. Hold for a count of 10. Relax. Repeat up to 20 times.

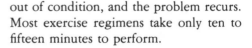

Knee-to-forehead. Grasping one knee with both hands, bring it to the chest. At the same time, raise the shoulders off the floor and touch your forehead to the knee. Return slowly to the starting position. Repeat, alternating legs, up to 10 times.

Bent-leg sit-ups. With the arms extended, raise the trunk about 30 degrees off the floor. Relax and repeat up to 20 times.

Lower back stretch. Bring one knee as close to the chest as possible. Return it slowly to the starting position. Relax. Repeat up to 10 times for each leg.

Leg raises. Bring one knee to the chest. Extend the leg, then bend the knee and return to the starting position. Relax. Alternating legs, repeat up to 10 times.

A motion to relax muscle tension is usually included in each exercise, and sometimes the sequence in which the exercises are performed is important in achieving the best results.

The exercises illustrated here are typical of those included in most bad back programs. Remember, however, that an exercise program should not be initiated without a doctor's recommendation.

SUMMING UP

Back pain is one of our most common causes of disability, but most back disorders can be successfully treated. Regular exercise is generally considered the most effective means of preventing future episodes of back pain. However, exercises should not be started without a doctor's recommendation. Once a regimen has been designed, it should be started slowly, with a gradual increase in the number of times each exercise is performed. If an exercise causes or increases pain, it should be discontinued at least temporarily until you have had a chance to check with your doctor.

28. Scoliosis

COMMON CHARACTERISTICS

Scoliosis means abnormal curvature of the spine. Some people have an abnormal spinal curvature that is so minor that it is barely noticeable and does not interfere with normal posture and gait. In a small percentage of patients, however, scoliosis is progressive, and can become severe enough to cause deformity and even interfere with the function of the lungs because of chest wall compression. Fortunately, there are now a variety of techniques to treat the earliest stages of scoliosis and prevent the pronounced deformities often seen in the past.

FINDING THE CAUSE

Normally, when viewed from behind, the spine is aligned perfectly straight up and down. When a slight lateral curve develops, it is called scoliosis.

The most common form of scoliosis develops for unknown reasons, usually between the ages of ten and fourteen years, when pubertal growth is very rapid. This type of scoliosis tends to run in families and is far more common in girls than in boys. In the United States, scoliosis is estimated to affect more than 2 percent of teenagers, and most suffer little deformity. However, in its severe form, scoliosis tends to be progressive, and it can cause back pain and cosmetic deformity and even interfere with breathing.

Scoliosis also may be caused by some specific disorders affecting the muscles along the spine. Imbalance of muscle tone tends to pull the spinal column out of normal alignment. Historically, polio and tuberculosis were frequent culprits; however, as the incidence of these diseases has been reduced in our country, so has their contribution to abnormal spinal alignment. The muscular response accompanying vertebral arthritis and bone or nerve tumors also can cause scoliosis.

A small percentage of cases are present at birth, caused by congenital malformation. These include the absence of half a vertebra, unequal leg length, and faulty function of a hip joint.

DIAGNOSIS

Scoliosis is often first detected during a routine physical examination. But parents should be aware of how their children's backs are developing, especially during the adolescent growth spurt. The child's back should be carefully observed, both while standing and bending forward. The spinal column should appear straight when the youngster "stands tall." Note particularly whether one shoulder is higher than the other, or whether there is any protrusion of a shoulder blade, a waist crease that appears deeper on one side, any hump on the back, the appearance of one arm being longer than the other or one hip being more prominent.

If parent or physician spots any curvature, it should be monitored regularly. X-ray films may be taken to chart any progression. Most cases are minor and require little, if any treatment. For example, if the cause is unequal leg length, treatment may simply involve using a shoe lift for the shorter leg. However, if the scoliosis is of the progressive type, prompt intervention is important. The more the spine is deformed, the longer corrective measures will be needed.

TREATMENT

If the curvature is caused by a spinal abnormality, the underlying problem must be identified and treated. Treatment may arrest or reverse the scoliosis.

The scoliosis that develops in adolescence, however, can sometimes be difficult to treat and may warrant several approaches. One, physical therapy, improves posture and tones up spinal muscles but will not improve structural scoliosis. The youngster also may have to wear a spinal brace, which is fitted by an orthopedist. The brace gently nudges the spine into a normal position over the course of months of wear. As progress is made, the brace is periodically readjusted. Most youngsters adapt easily to its use, which can help prevent the need for surgery. Those who require neck support usually are fitted with the Milwaukee brace, which encases the wearer from the top of the neck to the pelvis and is made of leather or plastic with metal rods. If neck support is not needed, a plastic brace—which is less conspicuous because it begins below shoulder level—may be worn. However, both should be used twenty-three hours a day and removed only for bathing.

A newer approach involves using electrical stimulation to correct the spinal curvature. A specially fitted device that administers low amounts of electrical current to the back muscles, strengthening them to realign the spine, is worn at night. This treatment is still new and in the research stages.

The new molded plastic brace that is now used to treat scoliosis affecting the middle and lower back.

Early diagnosis, followed by appropriate bracing and exercise, has reduced the need for scoliosis surgery. With age, however, the spinal column becomes less responsive to bracing. Then, surgery may be required to correct the deformity. This usually involves inserting rods on either side of the spinal column. The patient must spend ten days to two weeks in bed after surgery. In some cases, a plaster cast may have to be worn following the operation. However, once the cast is removed, the good results are permanent. While surgery is best performed when the patient is still a teenager, it can be successful even later in life.

SUMMING UP

Scoliosis usually is a minor problem for most people but should be monitored by a physician. Recent advances have made treatment more effective and less inconvenient than in the past. With prompt care, debilitating deformity almost always can be avoided.

29. Rheumatoid Arthritis

COMMON CHARACTERISTICS

Rheumatoid arthritis is a systemic disease characterized by painful, swollen, inflamed joints. It can occur at any time from infancy on, affecting not only particular joints and muscles but, in extreme cases, vital organs as well. It most commonly occurs between ages twenty and thirty-five, with women three times as vulnerable as men until the age of fifty, when the difference narrows. Of the 6.5 million Americans affected, about one-third are free of symptoms for long periods of time; of the children with juvenile rheumatoid arthritis, two-thirds recover completely by adulthood.

No one knows exactly why rheumatoid arthritis occurs or how to prevent it. However, the disease is most likely to occur in genetically susceptible people when some factor disturbs their immune system. An increasing number of researchers believe that this factor may be a virus, with particular emphasis focused on the Epstein-Barr virus, a herpes-like organism that is commonly associated with infectious mononucleosis. Thus, while osteoarthritis is a wear-and-tear disease essentially restricted to the weight-bearing joints, rheumatoid arthritis is best described as an autoimmune disease, which means the body attacks its own tissues. The result is not only stiffness and pain in specific areas but general malaise and fatigue as well as fever and weight loss.

CLASSIC RHEUMATOID ARTHRITIS

While there may be differences of opinion about what triggers the onset of rheumatoid arthritis (some specialists think it begins as part of another severe illness; some associate it with unusual emotional stress; still others point to infectious agents), there is general agreement about what happens once the autoimmune system goes awry.

30. Osteoarthritis

COMMON CHARACTERISTICS

Osteoarthritis, also known as degenerative joint disease, is one of the most common ailments associated with getting older, and it is therefore most common in those parts of the world where people live the longest. More than fifteen million Americans see their doctors because of osteoarthritis each year, and more than twice that many are affected by it to some degree. However, it rarely results in serious disability.

Osteoarthritis is essentially a "wear-and-tear" disorder. In typical cases, symptoms appear after age fifty, and usually in the large joints that bear the most weight—hips, knees, shoulders, and spine.

Pain and stiffness are at their most uncomfortable upon arising in the morning and are likely to be intensified during damp, cold weather. (This does not mean, however, that symptoms are likely to disappear in a warm, dry climate.) Redness and swelling of the affected joints may also occur. Joints, particularly in the fingers, may become permanently gnarled by osteoarthritis, but this almost never interferes with their function. Painless bony bumps, known as Heberden's nodes, may appear symmetrically on the fingers of both hands or on toe joints as well.

CAUSES OF OSTEOARTHRITIS

When a person is young and spry, the joints between the bones swing freely like efficient, well-oiled hinges. Stresses and strains are absorbed by the cartilage pads that provide cushioning and lubrication at the ends of the bones where they constantly come together as the parts of the body make their coordinated movements.

Over the years, these protective layers become eroded, lubricating fluids diminish, and the result is a sensation often described as "creaking" at the joints. In addition to a decrease in smoothness of function, small growths, or spurs, may develop on the bones in the area of the joints. These are ten times more prevalent among women than men and are likely to aggravate an already uncomfortable condition.

SIGNS AND SYMPTOMS

Since the weight-bearing joints are the ones most commonly affected, stiffness and discomfort in the knees and hips are likeli-

Heberden's node, showing spurry growth in the finger joint

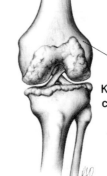

Knee joints in which the cartilage is wearing away

est to occur first, especially in the overweight person or in someone whose life style involves long stretches of standing or walking. A visit to the doctor for diagnosis normally includes close inspection of painful areas as well as X-ray examination of the joints in question. (When X-ray pictures are taken for diagnosis of some other condition in younger patients, they usually reveal the beginnings of cartilage erosion in the weight-bearing joints at a stage that does not yet produce associated symptoms.) Other than X-rays and visual examination, there are no other diagnostic tests for osteoarthritis.

TREATMENT OF OSTEOARTHRITIS

Where overweight exists as a contributing factor, efforts should be made to lose the extra pounds and keep them off. Application of warm, moist heat, slow and gentle massage to the affected joints, and a reduction (not a total cessation) of normal activities are ways in which patients can help themselves when there is an intensification of discomfort. Where pressure on the weight-bearing joints can be diminished through postural adjustments, special exercises may be recommended.

DRUG THERAPY

Although inflammation is not one of the initial symptoms of osteoarthritis, as the joint degeneration progresses, swelling, redness, and other signs of inflammation may occur. When this happens, anti-inflammatory drug therapy may be recommended.

Aspirin.

Patients who can tolerate high doses of aspirin may be treated with this drug alone. However, patients on anti-inflammatory aspirin therapy, which may involve taking sixteen or more tablets a day, should be aware of possible side effects, among which the most common are ring-

ing in the ears, heartburn, and other gastrointestinal upsets. To minimize gastrointestinal complications, the aspirin should be scheduled after meals. Acetaminophen, in smaller dosages, may be recommended as an alternative to aspirin.

Nonsteroidal Anti-inflammatory Agents.

These are relatively new drugs that relieve the pain and joint inflammation of osteoarthritis. It is the physician's role to match the patient with the particular drug that will be most suitable and effective without adverse effects. Sometimes drugs are used in combination, but whatever the procedure, supervision by the doctor

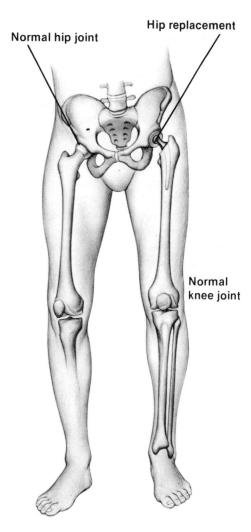

Normal hip joint

Hip replacement

Normal knee joint

is usually indicated if maximum benefit is to be achieved.

Steroids.

In those few cases where other measures fail, steroid drugs (cortisone) may be injected into the damaged joint for temporary relief. However, long-term treatment with steroids is not recommended for osteoarthritis.

SURGERY

When an older person suffers such severe osteoarthritis that most normal activity becomes impossible, surgical replacement of the affected joints may be considered. Hip replacement, in which the entire hip joint or head of the femur is replaced, is the most common operation of this type. The replacement joint is made of plastic and metal parts and is held in place by special plastic cements. The artificial joints allow the previously immobilized patient to be relieved of crippling pain, and most activities can be resumed following physical therapy and regaining of muscle function.

More recent joint replacements include the knee—a joint that is more complicated than the hip and, consequently, poses more engineering problems in replacing. However, the newer artificial knee joints are providing good results, both in terms of pain relief and restoration of function.

TRAUMATIC ARTHRITIS

Closely related to osteoarthritis, traumatic arthritis is usually the result of excessive joint use combined with injury. It is commonly seen in athletes—Joe Namath's knees and Mickey Mantle's throwing arm are two famous examples. Rest will usually resolve the problem, although in some instances drugs or surgery may be required, particularly in the case of athletes who need to regain quickly the use of the injured joints.

SUMMING UP

For millions of people, osteoarthritis is an inevitable condition of aging. Most cases can be handled by rest and common sense. Anti-inflammatory drugs—both nonprescription painkillers such as aspirin or acetaminophen and prescription nonsteroidal anti-inflammatory agents—may be used during flare-ups.

Osteoarthritis rarely turns into a crippling disease, but as newer and more effective drugs are available for reducing aches and pains to a minimum, there is little reason for allowing this particular cause of physical discomfort to be a dominating factor in determining one's life style in advancing years.

31. Exercise and Arthritis

COMMON CHARACTERISTICS

There are many different types of arthritis, ranging from the relatively common osteoarthritis and rheumatoid arthritis to the rare ankylosing spondylitis, a condition affecting the spine. The common feature of these diseases is inflammation of the joints. Indeed, the word *arthritis* is derived from the Latin and means inflammation of the joints.

Today, most forms of arthritis can be controlled, often by a combination of therapies that include drugs, rest, exercise, and, in severe cases, surgery. Since arthritis has a tendency to stiffen and deform the affected joints, exercises have been specifically designed to prevent these effects.

The exercises described here were developed by the Arthritis Foundation and illustrate the types of exercises that might be recommended. However, you should follow your doctor's instructions in exercising because the level and type of activity depend upon the specific joint involvement.

TYPES OF EXERCISE

Exercises for arthritis fall into four general categories: (1) range-of-motion exercises that preserve or restore joint mobility; (2) strengthening exercises for the muscles surrounding a joint; (3) stretching exercises to rehabilitate a stiffened or deformed joint; and (4) functional exercises that help in performing routine tasks, such as buttoning clothes or opening faucets.

RANGE-OF-MOTION EXERCISES

An exercise often recommended to maintain mobility of the hands, elbows, and shoulders involves standing with the hands at the hips and slowly raising them, with palms facing outward to shoulder height and then over the head. This is followed by clasping the hands behind the neck and moving the elbows as far front and back as possible.

Common household items can double as useful exercise aids. For example, a broom can be used in a common range-of-motion exercise that involves standing with your back against the wall, with heels, buttocks, shoulders, and head touching the wall. Grasp the broom with both hands facing in the same direction and raise it over your head. Then move the broom along the wall as far down on each side as possible.

Since hands are frequently afflicted, it is important to keep the finger and wrist joints mobile. An exercise designed to retain wrist motion involves placing the hands on a hard, flat table, then spreading the fingers wide (palm down) on the table. With the palms on the table, lift the index finger. Then bring the fingers together and, with the wrist and arm on the table, lift all of the fingers, including the thumb.

Still another exercise that is used to retain finger mobility and strength involves opening and closing the hand, then making a fist. Extend the fingers and touch each one to the thumb, making an "O."

HIPS AND KNEES

Exercises to retain mobility of the hips, knees, and legs are often complicated by the fact that these are weight-bearing joints and one must be careful not to place extra stress on them. Therefore, many are done from sitting or lying positions.

One basic exercise aimed at limbering

the spine, knees, and hips involves lying flat on your back with knees flexed. Slowly pull up one knee at a time, aiming to touch the nose with the knee. Keep your back as straight as possible, but don't strain it. This exercise also strengthens the legs. A variation calls for lying on your back, again with knees flexed. Raise the knee toward the chest, using your hands to pull it toward you, if necessary. Bend both the knee and hip as far as possible.

Another exercise designed to straighten and tighten knees can be done while sitting on either a bed or the floor. Sit up, bracing yourself with your arms and hands placed behind the buttocks. Raise both legs about one inch from the floor, keeping them as straight as possible. Put a rolled towel under your legs if you find you are unable to straighten them otherwise.

Still another sitting exercise involves sitting in a chair with the feet flat on the floor. First, raise your toes as high as you can while keeping the heels down. Then keep

---

Here is a series of basic exercises for arthritis sufferers designed to stretch and strengthen painful joints. Some of them may prove to be too difficult to perform fully; if so, do only as much and stretch only as far as you feel is comfortable. Stop immediately if any exercise causes pain.

Breathe easily with the exercises—holding your breath tends to make the muscles tighten up and constricts your range of movement. And go slowly: These exercises are more effective when they aren't rushed. Before starting any program of arthritis exercises, check with your doctor or physical therapist to make sure that the movements are right for you.

For Arthritis of the Neck

1. Stand or sit with back straight. Slowly bend head forward and tuck chin in toward chest. Repeat 10 times.
2. Stand or sit with back straight. Tuck chin in, then slowly turn head to one side and then to the other. Repeat 10 times.
3. Stand or sit with back straight. Tuck chin in. Slowly bend head to one side, so that the ear is moving toward the shoulder. Keep shoulder relaxed; do not shrug it toward the ear. Bend head to other side. Repeat 10 times.

For Arthritis of the Feet

4. Lie on back on a firm surface with toes pointed upward. Pull entire foot toward body as far as is comfortable. Then point toes away from body as far as is comfortable. Repeat 10 times for each foot.
5. Lie on back with toes pointed upward. Turn foot in as far as is comfortable so that the sole faces toward the other foot. Then turn foot out as far as is comfortable so that the sole faces away from the other foot. Repeat 10 times for each foot.

For Arthritis of the Shoulder, Elbow, and Wrist

6. Stand (or sit, if necessary) with arms at side. Slowly raise arms sideward in a wide arc, keeping palms up. Bring arms as high overhead as is comfortable, but do not lift or shrug shoulders. Lower arms to side and repeat 10 times.

7. Stand (or sit) with arms at side. Slowly swing arms forward as high as is comfortable without shrugging shoulders. Clasp hand if necessary to make lifting easier. Repeat 10 times.

8. Bring arms out to side and bend elbows to make a 90 degree angle, with palms up and facing forward. Without moving torso, swing forearms and hands downward, then back up again. Repeat 10 times.

9. Start with arms out in front, keeping the elbows straight and the palms up. Bend elbows and try to touch palms to shoulders. Repeat 10 times.

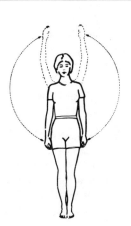

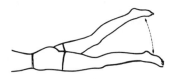

For Arthritis of the Knee and Quadriceps Muscle Atrophy

10. On a firm surface, lie on back with legs relaxed and a few inches apart. Straighten one leg and push the back of the knee down to the mat. Hold for a count of 10 and then relax. Repeat 10 times for each leg.

11. Lie on back with legs relaxed and a few inches apart. Straighten one leg and lift up to 45 degrees. Hold for a count of 10 and then relax. Repeat 10 times for each leg.

12. Lie on side with legs relaxed. Straighten top leg and lift it as high as it will comfortably go. Hold for a count of 10, then lower slowly and relax. Repeat 10 times for each leg.

13. Lie on stomach with hips flat on the floor. Keep involved leg as straight as possible and raise it as high as it will comfortably go. Hold for a count of 10, then lower slowly and relax. Repeat 10 times.

your toes down and lift your heels as high as possible. Next, starting with your feet flat on the floor, lift the inside of each foot and roll the weight over on the outside of the foot. While doing this exercise, try to keep your toes curled down if possible.

OTHER RECOMMENDATIONS

Even though exercises are very important, the way you move and hold yourself throughout the day and night also are important. So is rest, which is as important for arthritis patients as exercise. Rest frequently to alleviate stress placed on the joints and learn to listen to the pain—it tells you when you are overdoing. Above all, when specific exercises tend to cause more pain and increase the inflammation surrounding a specific joint, the exercise should be terminated and the joint should be rested until the inflammation subsides. Other pointers include:

• *Avoid overstraining the joints.* Do not carry heavy packages or walk more than is comfortable. If you are overweight, try to slim down. An extra ten pounds, for example, puts a great strain on inflamed joints.
• *Pay attention to your posture.* Stand erect, head high. Avoid slumping forward with stooped neck and pelvis.
• *Sit straight,* make sure the chair gives proper support and is a comfortable height.
• *Sleep on a firm mattress.* If need be, use a bed board under the mattress.
• *Wear comfortable well-fitted shoes with low or flat heels.*

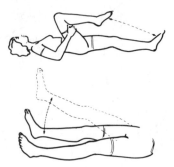

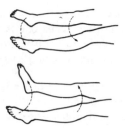

For Arthritis of the Hip

14. Lie on back on a firm surface. Slowly draw knee up toward chest, using hands under the back of the knee to help pull. Hold for a count of three, then lower leg and straighten knee. Repeat 10 times for each leg.
15. Lie on back with legs together, toes pointed upward. Bring one leg out to the side as far as is comfortable, keeping knee straight and toes pointed. Return to starting position. Repeat 10 times for each leg.
16. Lie on back with knees straight, toes pointed upward. Roll the entire leg in as far as is comfortable, then roll entire leg out. Repeat 10 times for each leg.

32. Gout

COMMON CHARACTERISTICS

Gouty arthritis usually starts as acute pain and inflammation in a single joint, often the big toe. Gout is related to the body's inability to dispose of excess uric acid, a waste product of body metabolism.

Normally, uric acid is extracted from the blood by the kidneys and then excreted in the urine. In gout, however, there is an abnormally high level of uric acid in the blood, a condition called hyperuricemia. This may be because the patient is not excreting it as fast as normal, or it may be due to an overproduction of uric acid. In either instance, needlelike uric acid crystals form in the joints and are ingested by white blood cells, causing inflammation and excruciating pain.

Generally, an attack of gout begins suddenly, without warning, as exquisite pain in a single joint. Most frequently, it occurs in the joint at the base of the big toe (podagra). Within a few hours, the patient may be unable to bear even the slight touch of bed sheets on the affected area. Swelling occurs, and the overlying skin may grow markedly red, dry, and shiny. A fever of up to 101° F may accompany the episode.

Untreated, an attack of gout may last as long as four or five days before gradually subsiding. Intervals of four to six months or longer between attacks are common, especially during the early stages of the disease. Initially, only one joint is usually affected, but without treatment, both the frequency of the attacks and the number of affected joints tend to increase. Sites, in addition to the toes, that are commonly afflicted include fingers, ankles, and knees. Uric acid crystals in the urine and the formation of kidney stones, composed predominantly or entirely of uric acid (urate stones), are other manifestations.

WHO IS SUSCEPTIBLE?

More than a million Americans suffer from gout. It is seen most often in middle-aged men, many of whom are overweight and have a family history of the disease. Some population groups, most notably the Polynesians, seem to suffer from a particularly widespread incidence of gout, while others, such as the Scots, are virtually unaffected. Women very rarely have gout, and when it does occur, it is generally after menopause. The use of certain drugs, such as some of the diuretics used to treat high blood pressure and some cancer drugs, may increase the risk of gout; the same is true of certain diseases where there is a rapid turnover of cells, such as leukemia, psoriasis, and lead poisoning.

DIAGNOSIS

Gout often can be diagnosed on the basis of symptoms alone—a swollen, ex-

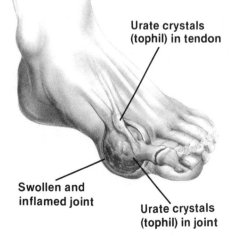

Urate crystals (tophil) in tendon

Swollen and inflamed joint

Urate crystals (tophil) in joint

traordinarily painful big toe is the classic case. Blood tests may confirm a high level of uric acid, although an acute attack of gout may appear with normal blood levels of uric acid. These cases may be more difficult to diagnose, especially if joints other than those in the feet are affected. Diagnosing gout in these cases may involve drawing out some joint fluid with a needle and identifying the uric acid crystal using polarized light microscopy.

TREATMENT

The treatment of gout has four distinct phases. The first is directed at controlling the inflammation and swelling that occur during an acute attack. Oral or intravenous colchicine—a drug that stops white blood cells from ingesting uric acid crystals—may be used during this phase. Nonsteroidal anti-inflammatory drugs also may be prescribed during the acute phase. Aspirin, however, should not be used since it may increase uric acid levels in the blood. Ice or hot compresses may be applied to the affected joint where the severity of the attack permits; otherwise the area should be shielded from any direct contact.

The second stage in the treatment, which can only be undertaken once inflammation has been controlled, is the analysis of the particular nature of the gout that involves determining whether the gout is due to the overproduction or the underexcretion of uric acid and whether there are any other determining factors, such as a related illness that is triggering the gout.

The third stage involves normalization of uric acid levels in the blood. Drugs are used either to reduce the production or increase the excretion of uric acid. Once levels have been returned to normal, the drug dosage may be lowered, but generally the medication must be taken for life to insure against further attacks of gout or formation of kidney stones from uric acid deposits in the kidneys. Finally, the patient should understand that, although gout can be controlled, there is no permanent cure. Prevention of recurrent attacks requires a lifetime commitment to medication therapy. Diet also is somewhat important. Certain foods that are high in purines should be avoided. These include organ meats, such as liver, brains, heart, and kidneys, certain seafoods, and legumes, such as dried peas, beans, and lentils. Alcohol intake should be limited.

Stress also can play a role in triggering an attack of gout. Many people find that an emotional upset is invariably followed by an attack of gout. The same may be true of overindulgence in wine or beer. Most gout patients quickly learn what seems to trigger an attack and how much medication is needed to prevent attacks.

SUMMING UP

Gout is a particularly painful form of arthritis that tends to run in families. It usually afflicts middle-aged men and is caused by excessive uric acid in the blood. The feet, particularly the joints in the big toes, are most frequently affected, although other joints also may be involved. Drugs are used both to treat an acute attack and to prevent recurrences. Diet also is important in the overall control of the disease.

33. Infectious Arthritis

COMMON CHARACTERISTICS

Unlike rheumatoid arthritis and osteoarthritis, whose cause continues to remain a medical mystery, infectious arthritis can be traced to a specific invasive agent that attacks the synovial membrane lining of the joints. The agent that causes the inflammation and the ensuing discomfort may be bacterial, viral, or fungal. Or it may be an infectious agent spread by a tick, as in the case of Lyme arthritis.

Acute infectious arthritis may be a direct result of a staphylococcus infection, more common in children than adults, or it may be secondary to pneumonia, gonorrhea, hepatitis B, or "strep" throat. In the young, it may follow or accompany rubella (German measles) or mumps.

Chronic infectious arthritis may accompany tuberculosis. The on-again off-again symptoms may also occur when certain microbes or mold spores (fungi) find their way into the bloodstream, for example, as a result of an injection with a contaminated needle, or during surgery. It is characteristic of practically all types of infectious arthritis that the disease can be controlled and cured when the cause is identified.

SYMPTOMS

Whatever the source, the symptoms are more or less the same: pain and stiffness in the joints with swelling and/or fever. The affected areas may feel warm and tender to the touch. Chills and fever together with a general malaise may be produced by the primary infection, or they may be an additional manifestation of an underlying cause of the arthritis.

DIAGNOSIS

Where signs and symptoms point to infectious arthritis, an unequivocal diagnosis and identification of the cause can be made by withdrawing (aspiration) a sample of the synovial fluid from the affected joint. In addition, the disease-bearing organism may also be identified by laboratory analysis of sputum and blood. Since people suffering from rheumatoid arthritis are especially vulnerable to bacterial arthritis, it is important to find out the source of the infection and treat it at once.

A diagnosis of gonorrhea-related (gonococcal) arthritis may be deduced if the patient has had a recent episode of gonorrhea or symptoms, such as a urinary infection, that may have been caused by gonorrhea. This source of the disease should not be excluded even in very young children who may have been infected by a parent or other adult. (Since some women can be gonorrhea carriers without themselves having symptoms, they can transmit the disease unknowingly to others.) A diagnosis of gonococcal arthritis is usually confirmed by a smear test. When this is the cause, only one joint may become inflamed, and when the synovial fluid is withdrawn, it is thick with pus. The pus will also contain gonococcal bacteria.

TREATMENT

Since joint tissue can be irreversibly destroyed if infectious arthritis is not brought under control promptly, it is considered advisable to begin antibiotic treatment at once, before the identification of the cause. Where gonorrhea is involved, it is of prime importance to determine whether

MOST COMMON TYPES OF INFECTIOUS ARTHRITIS

CAUSATIVE ORGANISM	COMMON SYMPTOMS	JOINTS AFFECTED MOST OFTEN
Gonococcus	Fever, joint pain, rash on extremities; may follow attack of gonorrhea	Knees, wrists, ankles, hands, elbows, hips, and shoulders
Meningococcus	Spiking fever, chills, joint and muscle pain	Widespread joint involvement
Mumps virus	Joint pain one or two weeks following mumps	Knees, hips, ankles, other large joints
Pneumonococcus	Swollen, red, and painful joints; seen more often in children than adults	Usually knees, ankles, other large joints
Staphylococcus	Swollen, painful joints	Joints that have received steroid injections to treat other forms of arthritis
Streptococcus	Swollen, red, and painful joint; may follow "strep" throat	Knee or other large joint
Tubercle bacilli	Joint pain, usually within 3 years of tuberculosis infection during childhood	Hip, knee, elbow, and wrist

the strain is penicillin-resistant before beginning treatment. In such cases, tetracycline or ampicillin may be the antibiotic of choice.

When sputum and blood samples reveal that the arthritis is related to tuberculosis, therapy to arrest the TB should begin at once.

When laboratory findings indicate the presence of staphylococcus or streptococcus bacteria as the cause of joint inflammation, appropriate antibiotics are prescribed. In severe cases, continued withdrawal of synovial fluid for analysis is recommended until the sample becomes sterile, that is, totally free of the infectious agent. Where the inflammation is so acute that surgical drainage is necessary, the affected joint—often the knee or hip—may require rehabilitation through physical therapy.

SUMMING UP

Infectious arthritis, unlike most other forms of the disease, has an identifiable cause, namely, an invading microorganism that attacks the joint linings. Once the organism—usually a bacterium, but other possibilities include viruses and fungi—has been identified, treatment consists of giving antibiotics to eradicate it. Prompt diagnosis and treatment are important to prevent joint damage.

34. Lyme Arthritis

COMMON CHARACTERISTICS

Lyme arthritis is a relatively newly discovered disease and one that is now known to be spread by a particular type of tick. While Lyme disease has much in common with other types of arthritis, it is now categorized as a distinct disorder, with a known cause and specific symptoms that may vary from mild to severe and from acute to chronic.

The disease was first identified in 1975 following an epidemic in Lyme, a Connecticut town on Long Island Sound. The Yale University scientists who identified the disorder before determining its cause named it for the town. Since that time, most reported cases have occurred on the East Coast, although there have been outbreaks in the Midwest and West. Most cases occur in wooded or marshy areas from May to early August.

About half the patients with Lyme disease have arthritis-like symptoms. Others may develop heart or neurological problems. Early recognition of the disease and treatment usually assure full recovery without complications. So far, no deaths have been attributed to the disorder.

CAUSE OF LYME ARTHRITIS

Lyme arthritis was recently discovered to be caused by a tiny tick called *Ixodes dammini.* The tick is about the size of a dot and looks like a moving speck of dust. It is much smaller than the ordinary dog tick, and its usual host is likely to be a rabbit or deer. Although Lyme arthritis is often called a new disease, it is more likely an old one that remained unidentified because only a few people who are bitten by the tick actually develop symptoms. Also, many people have very mild symptoms that may be mistaken for flu or other transitory ailment unassociated with the bite.

SYMPTOMS OF LYME DISEASE

Lyme disease begins with the appearance of a small red lump at the site of the tick bite. The red spot may grow to a diameter of as much as five inches, and as it increases in size, the circumference becomes a brighter red than the rest. Similar spots may appear elsewhere. The affected area is hot, but it does not itch. At the same time, most patients develop a general malaise, with fever and chills, stiff neck, and headache. Some suffer from nausea and vomiting, sore throat, and backache early in the course of infection.

Within a few weeks (sometimes a few months and, in rare instances, as long as two years) after the appearance of the red spot, half the victims begin to suffer from inflammatory arthritis, with attacks of pain and swelling, especially in the knees, but other joints may also be involved. If the disease is not cured at the outset, the attacks may continue over a period of years.

About one-fifth of all people with Lyme disease develop neurologic complications before the arthritis sets in, with self-limiting paralysis of nerves of the face (Bell's palsy), arms, or legs or inflammation of the lining of the brain (encephalomeningitis). In approximately one case in ten, the disease leads to cardiac abnormalities by attacking the heart's electrical conduction system and thereby producing palpitations.

DIAGNOSIS

Even when the patient's history contains circumstantial details that link the symptoms to Lyme disease, it still becomes necessary for the doctor to differentiate it from the onset of rheumatoid arthritis or multiple sclerosis, many of whose symptoms it shares. This differentiation is accomplished through a study of the patient's previous history and the findings of various blood tests.

TREATMENT FOR LYME DISEASE

Early recognition and prompt treatment with penicillin or tetracycline can prevent the development of more disagreeable and long-lasting effects. Aspirin can be helpful in reducing discomfort, and where joint inflammation has proceeded to the point where movement is impeded, fluid withdrawal and corticosteroid injections can hasten healing. Long-term medical supervision is recommended so that complications can be dealt with as soon as they occur.

PREVENTION OF LYME DISEASE

Like other tick-borne diseases, Lyme disease is best prevented by avoiding wooded or marshy areas during warm weather. When walking in such locales, or in tall grasses, wear protective clothing—long pants tucked into high socks and long-sleeved shirts tucked into pants. When dogs are permitted to run loose in the woods or other tick-infested areas, they should be checked regularly for ticks.

Where local health authorities have posted instructions during the summer, about avoiding the dangers of tick-borne diseases, the instruction should be followed by everyone in the family of whatever age.

SUMMING UP

Lyme disease can be extremely uncomfortable, but if recognized promptly, anti-

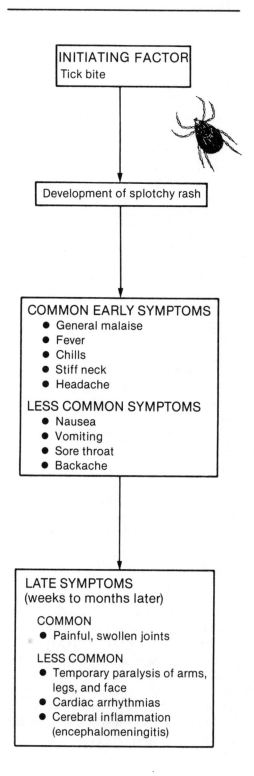

Natural Course of Lyme Arthritis

INITIATING FACTOR
Tick bite

Development of splotchy rash

COMMON EARLY SYMPTOMS
- General malaise
- Fever
- Chills
- Stiff neck
- Headache

LESS COMMON SYMPTOMS
- Nausea
- Vomiting
- Sore throat
- Backache

LATE SYMPTOMS
(weeks to months later)

COMMON
- Painful, swollen joints

LESS COMMON
- Temporary paralysis of arms, legs, and face
- Cardiac arrhythmias
- Cerebral inflammation (encephalomeningitis)

biotic treatment can limit the intensity of the symptoms and prevent long-lasting effects. Lyme arthritis rarely causes irreversible damage to the joints and usually clears up when the cause is identified for correct medical or other therapy. Since early treatment is important, a doctor should be consulted when symptoms first appear.

35. Arthritis of the Spine

COMMON CHARACTERISTICS

Spondylitis (from the Greek *spondylos* meaning vertebra) is a chronic and progressive arthritis that typically attacks the small joints of the spine. It is often referred to as ankylosing (from the Greek *ankylos* meaning crooked or bent, as in *angle*) because the inflammation may eventually cause a fusing of the affected joints, with resultant curvature of the spine. (Ankylosing spondylitis is sometimes called Marie Strümpell's disease.)

In typical cases, spinal joints stiffen to the point where movement becomes difficult and painful. When stiffness affects the ribs, the full expansion of the lungs becomes difficult and breathing is impaired.

Onset usually occurs in the early teens or young adulthood, although cases among children under ten have been reported. About two people per thousand are affected, with males predominating. Recent studies, however, indicate that more women suffer from spondylitis than had previously been estimated. The earlier disparity in figures may be attributable to the fact that in women the disorder was thought to be rheumatoid arthritis.

CAUSE OF SPONDYLITIS

Like rehumatoid arthritis, which occurs far more frequently, the cause of spondylitis is unknown. However, it is known to run in families, especially in the male line, and recent genetic research shows that people with a particular gene (technically identified as histocompatability antigen HLA-B27) are three hundred times likelier to be stricken by the disorder than people with a different heredity. Since this "genetic marker" is present in about 90 percent of all spondylitis patients, screening for B27 enables the doctor to make a correct diagnosis early in the disease when the other findings and symptoms might be ambiguous. It should be understood that only a significantly increased *susceptibility* to the disease is inherited and not the disease itself.

SYMPTOMS OF SPONDYLITIS

In rheumatoid arthritis, pain and immobility result from inflammation and ensuing thickening of the synovial membrane that normally lubricates the joints. In spondylitis, symptoms are produced by inflammation of the ligaments that bind the spinal vertebrae or the larger joints—especially the hips, knees, and shoulders—which are affected in about one-fifth of all cases.

Pain and stiffness in the lower back and other affected joints are the first indications, typically increasing rather than decreasing after periods of rest, so that getting out of bed in the morning becomes more and more uncomfortable. In some cases, when inflammation of the lower spine triggers muscle spasm, the normal curvature of this area may be forced into a rigidly straight position that imposes additional restrictions on movement.

As the disease progresses, further soreness and immobility may occur with the fusing and distortion (ankylosing) of the affected joints. When the spine is the locus of this ongoing process, it becomes more and more rigid, causing a curvature that forces the patient to stoop in such a way that the rib cage becomes incapable of proper expansion.

DIAGNOSIS OF SPONDYLITIS

In addition to the patient's history of painful stiffness and immobility, the doctor finds the affected area sore and tender to the touch. In the early stages of the disease, X-rays do not provide clear evidence, but as it progresses, the pictures will reveal a narrowing and distortion of the joints in question. Early diagnosis is made easier by genetic screening for the HLA-B27 antigen, which is present in more than 90 percent of all spondylitis patients.

TREATMENT FOR SPONDYLITIS

Because spondylitis is chronic and progressive and usually occurs before age thirty, correct diagnosis and prompt treatment are critical in helping the patient achieve a normally productive life. While treatment does not "cure" this arthritis, it can reduce some of the inflammation and alleviate much of the pain, thereby enabling the patient to embark on an essential exercise program. When performed every day, these exercises can maintain

normal posture and circumvent the potentially crippling effects of progressive tissue rigidity.

Medical Treatment

Aspirin is usually tried before other drugs are prescribed. When it can be tolerated in large doses, it acts both as an analgesic and an anti-inflammatory agent. The pain must be reduced if the patient is to get the rest and sleep essential for the maintenance of physical stamina. Where aspirin does not work, stronger prescription anti-inflammatory drugs, usually phenylbutazone (Butazolidin) and indomethacin (Indocin), may be given. These drugs must be used with care since they are very powerful and can produce adverse reactions. Before either one is prescribed, the patient should undergo a complete physical and laboratory checkup. If considered a suitable candidate for either of these drugs, the patient should follow the doctor's instructions carefully, reporting any negative side effects immediately. The usual procedure is a one-week trial. If during that period symptoms do not signifi-

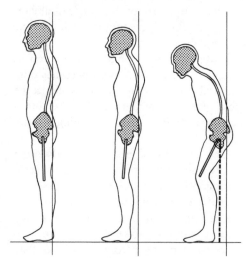

The normal spine (left) is highly flexible and allows a person to bend or stand upright. The drawing in the middle shows a mild curvature caused by spondylitis; the more severe curvature is shown at the right.

cantly diminish, or if the severity of the side effects is greater than the severity of the symptoms, the medication is discontinued in favor of alternative treatment.

Exercises

The range of exercises covers as many aspects of spinal mobility as possible. Correct upright posture is stressed, deep knee bends are included, and back movements from the neck downward are part of the daily routine. Where spinal curvature has begun to affect rib expansion, exercises are introduced that encourage deep abdominal breathing. For best results during sleep, specialists recommend a firm mattress and no pillow.

Unconventional Adjuncts

Some people have found that they can do the exercises with less discomfort if they supplement the aspirin with self-help techniques, such as meditation, biofeedback, or self-hypnosis.

PROGNOSIS AND COMPLICATIONS

Spondylitis usually continues for years, with episodes of inflammation alternating with periods when the disease is totally quiescent. When the inflammation flares up, it may affect general health, causing weight loss and fatigue. In some cases, eye inflammation (iritis) occurs. This complication requires prompt attention to prevent impairment of vision. In fewer than one patient in twenty-five, the inflammatory episodes involve the aortic heart valve, a complication that must be surgically treated without delay.

The most disabling aspect of untreated spondylitis is the fusing of the affected areas to the point where rigidity makes normal movement and posture impossible.

SUMMING UP

While spondylitis, like other forms of arthritis, is chronic and progressive, it need not be disabling. With early diagnosis and treatment, the prognosis for most patients is excellent. There are many ways of controlling pain and inflammation, and where good health and morale are maintained, exercises can keep deformity to a minimum. Most patients lead normal lives and participate in vigorous activities of their choice.

Additional information is available from the national office of the Arthritis Foundation, 3400 Peachtree Road, NE, Atlanta, GA 30326. Chapter offices are maintained in many cities, and their offices can be located in local telephone directories.

36. Osteoporosis

COMMON CHARACTERISTICS

Osteoporosis is a disease of aging, involving a decrease in bone tissue mass which, in turn, results in bones that fracture easily —even spontaneously. The disease affects some fifteen million people in the United States. Osteoporosis is much more common in women than in men, more common in older people than in the middle-aged, and more common among whites and Orientals than blacks. Among whites, people of northwestern European extraction, particularly fair-haired and fair-skinned individuals, seem to be most vulnerable.

BONE

Bone is not an inert tissue, as was once thought, but one that is constantly rebuilt and resorbed in very complex ways. Bone formation requires calcium, vitamin D, phosphorus, hormones, and a proper environment. The contribution made by calcium—in association with vitamin D—seems to be the most important. A hormone, estrogen, promotes and participates in the uptake of calcium into bone, while other hormones and chemicals (parathyroids and corticosteroids) promote calcium loss. Calcitonin secreted by the thyroid controls bone resorption.

Bone loss in some degree is an almost inevitable consequence of aging. In osteoporosis, however, bone loss considerably exceeds bone formation.

CAUSES

Exactly what causes the accentuated bone loss of osteoporosis is unknown.

There appear to be many contributing factors. Hormonal imbalances, which affect the uptake of calcium and phosphorus, seem to be primarily involved. Another major cause is probably an inadequate supply of protein, minerals, and vitamins over a number of years. To remain in calcium balance, postmenopausal women need to ingest six servings of milk, cheese, or other calcium-rich dairy products a day. In women, menopause, with its accompanying decreases in production of the hormone estrogen, is clearly a factor. (Almost one in six postmenopausal women has osteoporosis, and the disease develops early in women who have a premature menopause due to surgical removal of the ovaries.) Prolonged bed rest, immobilization, and inactivity also promote bone loss, even in young people. The effect of these factors is very marked in the elderly.

SYMPTOMS

Osteoporosis is a "silent" disease, often remaining undiscovered until a fracture occurs. The first symptom is usually lower back pain, often severe and aggravated by carrying anything heavy. This pain is due to the spontaneous collapse (crush fracture) of one or more of the spinal vertebrae. After a few days, the pain generally subsides.

Over time, the continued collapse of the vertebrae results in loss of height and the curvature of the spine that is commonly referred to as widow's hump. In the later stages of the disease, there is often a chronic, aching pain in the lower back due to the stress that the vertical compression places on the muscles and ligaments attached to the spine.

A hip fracture that results from a minor fall is another sign that osteoporosis is present. The incidence of hip fractures is especially high among elderly white women: five of every thousand white women aged sixty-five to seventy-five suffer such fractures annually.

TREATMENT

Treatment aims at arresting or at least slowing the progress of the disease. It involves increased calcium intake, drug therapy, physical therapy, and exercise.

Physicians usually advise that at least six glasses of milk or servings of other high-calcium foods such as cheese or yogurt and a small supplement of vitamin D be taken daily. Oral calcium supplements are usu-

ally given; estrogenic hormones, which decrease bone resorption, also may be prescribed. For postmenopausal women, estrogen-replacement therapy can help to retard the disease. This therapy should be carefully monitored by a physician because it may increase the risk of strokes, blood clots, uterine bleeding, and endometrial cancer. Sodium fluoride taken in conjunction with calcium supplements appears to stimulate bone formation, but the long-term safety and effectiveness of this form of treatment are not yet known.

Exercise is very important. For bedridden patients, those confined to wheelchairs, and many others whose ability to move is restricted, physical therapy should be given on a regular basis. Walking is good exercise for those who do not want

Height (inches)

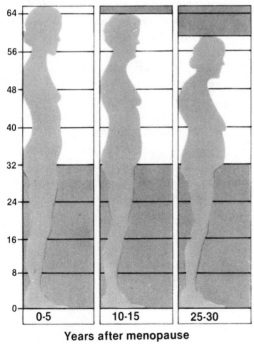

Years after menopause

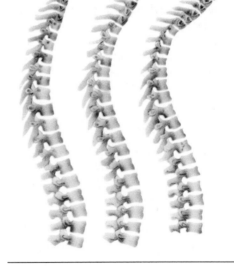

As the spinal column becomes more compressed, people with osteoporosis become progressively shorter. This chart shows the typical height loss in a postmenopausal woman with osteoporosis.

Progressive spinal changes in osteoporosis. As the spine becomes more compressed, hairline fractures of the vertebrae are likely to occur, sometimes resulting in severe back pain.

to take part in active sports or cannot do so.

PRECAUTIONS

For elderly patients with osteoporosis, every precaution should be taken to avoid accidental falls. If glasses are necessary for general vision, they should always be worn. A walking stick or frame should be used if the patient's gait is at all unsteady. Shoes and slippers should have skid-resistant soles. It is wise to install handrails in bathrooms and sturdy banister rails along all stairs, inside and outside.

PREVENTION

In order to reduce the risk of post-menopausal osteoporosis, many physicians advise women in their forties to increase their calcium intake from the usual 800 milligrams a day to 1,200 milligrams a day. This corresponds to approximately one and one-third quarts of milk. Since many women do not care to take such a large amount of milk (or its equivalent in yogurt and cheese), and some are allergic to all dairy products, the use of calcium supplements is often indicated.

Exercise is also helpful as a preventive measure, since it keeps both bone and muscle healthy. To be effective, exercise need not necessarily be strenuous, but it should be regular.

SUMMING UP

Bone loss to some degree is an almost inevitable part of aging. In osteoporosis, however, the process is accentuated, and the diminished bones—especially those of the spine and hip—fracture easily.

New treatments are being developed that may increase bone formation and so reverse osteoporosis. Meanwhile, however, the object of treatment is to arrest or retard the progress of the disease. Current treatment involves an increased intake of calcium, various hormones, and physical therapy and exercise. Preventive therapy, for premenopausal women, consists of a diet high in dairy products (often supplemented with calcium tablets) and regular exercise.

The number of elderly people in the United States is growing rapidly and will continue to do so in the future. Osteoporosis—an age-related disease—is fast becoming a major health problem.

37. Juvenile Rheumatoid Arthritis

COMMON CHARACTERISTICS

Juvenile rheumatoid arthritis, also called Still's disease, is an inflammation of the joints affecting about 250,000 children under the age of sixteen in the United States. While its cause is unknown, it is presumed to result from a disturbance in the body's immune system. The immediate circumstance that produces the pain, swelling, and stiffness of the joints and the accompanying redness of the skin surface is a condition called synovitis, in which the synovial membranes that line the spaces between the joints become inflamed. When this occurs, the membranes swell and the synovial fluid thickens, eventually damaging the soft tissues, especially the cartilage, ligaments, and tendons that surround and protect the bones.

While the disease itself is not hereditary, a genetic predisposition is thought to exist. In children as in adults, rheumatoid arthritis may be triggered by an infectious illness, invasion by a virus not yet identified, an injury, or a profound emotional shock. There are, however, several differences in symptoms and results depending on the age of onset. Juvenile rheumatoid arthritis may interfere with growth, especially when the larger joints are affected or when treatment is delayed. Another difference is that the disease in children is often accompanied by high fever and a rash that comes and goes as temperature rises and falls. Younger victims are more likely to suffer complications such as swelling of the lymph nodes, enlargement of the spleen, and eye inflammation. Yet with prompt and proper treatment, most children are completely recovered before adulthood. Only in about 15 percent of all cases is there some degree of permanent stiffness, and in those, continuing physiotherapy usually can maintain mobility of the joints.

RECOGNIZING ONSET

Because children often complain of unaccountable aches and pains, develop a mysterious fever that comes and goes without explanation, or become irritable and easily fatigued, parents may ignore the early evidence of rheumatoid arthritis. It's a very tricky ailment, and sometimes even a doctor has to perform several tests before an unequivocal diagnosis can be made that differentiates it from other disorders with similar symptoms.

While parents needn't hover over every deviation from good health, they should be alert to the following symptoms:

• Consistent or occasional complaints about feeling stiff and achy in the joints of the fingers, toes, wrists, and knees, especially in the morning. (The larger joints of the shoulders and hips are less likely sites of inflammation in the young.)
• Swelling and soreness, with reddening of the skin at the surface of any joint, and tenderness in the soft tissues surrounding the joint.
• Complaints about "sore muscles."
• A mysterious high fever that comes and goes, accompanied by weakness, fatigue, weight loss, and, in some instances, the appearance of a rash that doesn't itch.

WARNING SIGNS OF JUVENILE RHEUMATOID ARTHRITIS

- Joint pain, particularly of the small joints
- Swelling, reddening, and soreness in the joint area
- Pain and swelling that travels from one joint to another
- Recurrent high fever
- Weight loss
- Fatigue
- Muscle weakness
- Rash
- Nodules under the skin at elbows, knees, and other bony prominences
- Eye inflammation

- Pains that seem to migrate from one joint to another.
- The development of nodules under the skin at the site of the bony prominences.

DIAGNOSIS

It is not unusual for a correct diagnosis to require careful study of the child over the course of several weeks. In some cases, hospitalization may be recommended for observation and special tests. Following a complete physical examination, the procedures that may be used to confirm a tentative diagnosis of juvenile rheumatoid arthritis are X-rays, blood tests, and tissue biopsy.

EYE INVOLVEMENT

A specific complication involving the eyes may occur in some cases. Technically called iridocyclitis, it is an inflammation of the iris and surrounding structures that can lead to cataracts and irreversible damage if untreated. The condition is thought to result from the same disturbance in autoimmune responses that causes the arthritis itself—that is, the formation of antibodies that attack healthy eye tissue in the same unexpected way that antibodies attack healthy synovial tissue.

Iridocyclitis causes considerable pain over and in the eye, and the inflammation produces redness and heavy watering. In its initial stages, this inflammation may be detected by an eye doctor, and it may be pointed out as a first sign of the onset of the child's rheumatoid arthritis. On the other hand, where the arthritis is known to exist in no matter how mild a form and with no other complications, a semiannual visit to an ophthalmologist is important.

TREATMENT OF JRA

The basic treatment for juvenile rheumatoid arthritis is a combination of drugs, rest, and exercise. It should begin immediately following diagnosis so that tissue destruction is halted and mobility of affected joints is maintained. While each case differs in intensity, children are usually started on aspirin in increasing doses until a satisfactory level of tolerance has been achieved. Aspirin not only relieves pain but also is a highly effective anti-inflammatory agent. Where it causes unpleasant gastrointestinal problems, the doctor may prescribe an alternative medicine, usually one of several nonsteroidal anti-inflammatory drugs.

Exercise is also an important part of treating juvenile rheumatoid arthritis. Specific exercises are usually scheduled and supervised by a physical therapist, especially in the most active phase of the disease. Swimming in a heated pool can be especially helpful in maintaining muscular mobility. A pattern of rest periods alternating with exercise is usually tailored to suit the individual needs of the child. In more acute cases, splinting of affected parts may be a necessary measure to prevent disabling contractures. Surgery is considered only if joints have been so badly damaged by unabated inflammation that less drastic treatment is ineffective.

Most children respond well to the combined therapy, especially when parents are active participants and a relationship of trust is established with the doctor and other members of the treatment team.

In January 1975, Congress unanimously approved the National Arthritis Act, which, among other stipulations, continues to provide federal funds for the establishment and maintenance of comprehensive treatment centers. Families may be referred to the local arthritis center where doctors, nurses, and physical therapists work together not only to improve the child's condition but also to provide family counseling and vocational guidance where such guidance becomes necessary.

Whenever possible, the young patient should be encouraged to maintain normal activities and normal relationships with peers. While it is usually advisable to inform the school about unavoidable absences and "morning stiffness," it is in the child's best interests to maintain an opti-mistic attitude about what is likely to prove to be a temporary disability. It can be permanently disabling emotionally for a youngster to have been saddled with a self-image of invalidism long after the disease itself has disappeared or is so intermittent as to be scarcely troubling.

SUMMING UP

Juvenile rheumatoid arthritis may be mild or acute, but in most instances a combined treatment of medication, exercise, and rest inaugurated promptly brings about a full recovery. Young patients are most cooperative as active participants in the regimen when they know that the treatment team involves not only professional specialists but their parents, too.

38. Systemic Lupus Erythematosus

COMMON CHARACTERISTICS

Systemic lupus erythematosus is, like rheumatoid arthritis, an autoimmune disease in which the body's disease-fighting mechanisms have somehow gone awry. In lupus, antibodies that should attack disease-causing agents such as viruses, bacteria, and allergens instead attack the body's own tissues, causing a wide variety of signs and symptoms. The disease occurs mostly in women of childbearing age, leading some scientists to suspect that it may be related to the levels of estrogens—female sex hormones—in the body. Other theories suggest that heredity may play an important role in the development of lupus or that a virus may cause the disease. While no theory about the cause of lupus has been confirmed, great strides have been made in the diagnosis and treatment of the disease.

SYMPTOMS

The symptoms of lupus vary greatly from patient to patient. The most common symptom, reported in 80 percent of cases, is joint inflammation (arthritis), usually occurring in the knuckles, wrists, and knees. The arthritis of lupus is less severe than rheumatoid arthritis, however, and it seldom produces joint damage or deformity. Skin rashes also occur in a majority of patients; the "butterfly" rash, which covers the nose and cheeks, is a particularly distinguishing sign, but both rashes and joint inflammation may appear in any part of the body.

Other signs and symptoms include low-grade fever, fatigue, persistent swollen lymph nodes, unusual sensitivity to sunlight, loss of weight and appetite, hair loss, and ulceration in the mouth and nose. The kidneys are affected in the majority of cases, but the severity of kidney involvement varies widely, from mild dysfunction apparent only in laboratory tests to complete kidney failure requiring dialysis or

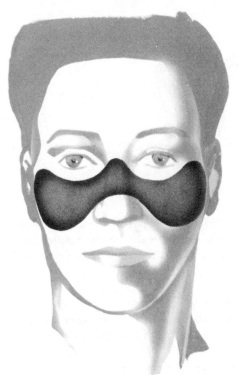

The butterfly rash, extending across the cheeks and over the bridge of the nose, is a common manifestation of lupus.

transplant of a healthy kidney. Lupus also causes pleurisy (inflammation of the pleura, the membrane that covers the lungs) and inflammation of both the inner and outer membranes of the heart (endocarditis and pericarditis). Occasionally, lupus affects the central nervous system, causing seizures and psychotic symptoms.

Because the most common symptoms of lupus are similar to those of rheumatic fever or rheumatoid arthritis, it is sometimes misdiagnosed. Doctors usually look for a cluster of four or more of the above signs and symptoms to make a diagnosis of lupus. Laboratory tests are also used to detect signs of immune system dysfunction characteristic of the disease.

THE COURSE OF THE DISEASE

Lupus runs an unpredictable course. In most patients, symptom-free periods (remissions) alternate with periods when symptoms flare. The symptoms are often mild enough that many patients experience them for years without detecting a pattern or discovering their cause. In a few cases, however, the disease is progressively debilitating, causing chronic kidney failure, severe heart involvement, and major central nervous system effects. Because lupus is a chronic disease—and because it is potentially severe—patients should keep in close touch with their physicians. If any unusual symptoms occur, medical attention should be sought at once. Fever, fainting, headaches, infections, decrease in urine output, swelling or appearance of rashlike spots on the legs, or any unusual bleeding are signals of impending flare-ups and should be brought to the physician's attention.

It is particularly important for lupus patients to maintain healthful living habits. Eating properly and avoiding overexertion and emotional stress may well help forestall or limit the severity of flare-ups. Infections and physical injuries, both of which lower the overall resistance, should be scrupulously avoided. Because sun sensitivity frequently accompanies lupus, patients should limit their sun exposure and use sunscreens liberally. Finally, patients should take no drugs—including nonprescription medications—without first consulting the physician; in some people, certain drugs can precipitate lupus.

TREATMENT

Because lupus is different in each patient, the course of treatment chosen varies depending on the severity and type of symptoms. For mild symptoms, anti-inflammatory drugs—including aspirin—are the first choice. Those who find aspirin hard to tolerate may take other nonsteroidal anti-inflammatory drugs. Both are highly effective in reducing inflammation and easing joint pain.

If anti-inflammatory drugs fail to relieve symptoms, or if the symptoms are unusually severe, corticosteroids may be used. These powerful drugs not only reduce inflammation but also modify the abnormal immune response at the root of the disease. Oral corticosteroids are effective against arthritis and kidney problems, while corticosteroid ointments may be used on rashes. These medications have serious side effects, however, so they are rarely used for more than a short period and are always discontinued gradually.

Antimalarial drugs, derived from quinine, are an alternative to steroids in patients who cannot tolerate or benefit from other anti-inflammatory drugs. Antimalarials are particularly effective against skin rashes, although they also relieve arthritis. Like steroids, antimalarial drugs have serious side effects and so are reserved for more difficult cases.

Also, immunosuppressant drugs, which inhibit the immune response, are helpful in some patients. These drugs, which carry a risk of dangerous side effects, are commonly used to prevent rejection of transplanted organs; usually, they are reserved for patients who have failed to respond to other treatments or who are experiencing intolerable steroid side effects.

SUMMING UP

Systemic lupus erythematosus is an autoimmune disease in which the malfunctioning immune system, for unknown reasons, attacks body tissues. It occurs most frequently in women of childbearing age, and its most common symptoms are joint inflammation, skin rashes, pleurisy, and kidney problems. Although lupus cannot be cured, thousands of patients experience long periods of remission and require treatment only when the disease flares up.

Anyone in whom lupus has been diagnosed should maintain close contact with his or her physician so that if symptoms appear or worsen appropriate care can be given immediately.

39. Bursitis and Tendonitis

COMMON CHARACTERISTICS

Bursitis and tendonitis are rather common inflammatory disorders of the body's musculoskeletal system that can flare up suddenly causing pain, swelling, feverishness, and stiffness. Bursitis and tendonitis are usually not major problems. They may lead to brief periods of disability, but these are usually temporary and rarely become serious or prolonged.

In some instances, an attack can be the result of infection, trauma, or chronic irritation; in others, there may be no obvious cause. Symptoms can be acute, subacute, or chronic and are usually related to a certain body movement or position. Although bursitis and tendonitis are often spoken of together and treated similarly, the two disorders occur in completely different structures of the body.

BURSITIS

A bursa is a sac or pouch filled with a lubricating fluid that overlies and protects bony structures such as the shoulder. The bursa cushions the motion that takes place between muscles, tendons, and other surfaces, allowing them smooth functioning, free from friction. When a bursa develops an inflammation, the disorder is known as bursitis.

There are seventy or eighty bursae on each side of the body—all vulnerable to inflammation. But the most common sites, in addition to the shoulder, are the tip of the elbow, outer side of the elbow (tennis elbow), knee (housemaid's knee), hip, and ankle.

The involved area becomes tender, hot, red, and swollen and sometimes so painful

that it is almost impossible to move the affected joint because the pain generates spasms in nearby muscles. Acute inflammation of a bursa must be differentiated from other types of joint disease before a course of treatment begins.

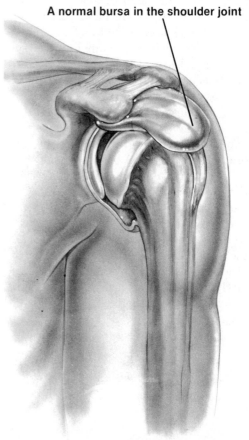

A normal bursa in the shoulder joint

Bursitis is an inflammation of the bursa, the sac that serves as a cushion over the joint space. Muscles and tendons ride over the bursa, which protects the joint from excessive wear and tear. Treatment of bursitis involves rest and, in severe cases, cortisone injections directly into the bursa.

TENDONITIS

A tendon is a band of tough, white, fibrous tissue that connects muscle to bone. Muscle fibers merge into one end of a tendon while the opposite end is attached to bone. The tendon conveys the action of muscles (sometimes over long distances) to bone.

Most tendons are encased in a sheath of synovial membrane that secretes lubricating fluid for easy sliding. Both tendons and their sheaths are vulnerable to injury and inflammation from overexertion, tearing, stretching, twisting, and other trauma. A disorder that causes swelling, soreness, and impaired motion of the tendon alone is tendonitis; if the problem involves both the sheath and the tendon, it is tenosynovitis.

With tenosynovitis, since both tendon and sheath are swollen, motion causes friction, making it extremely painful to move the affected limb. When the wrist is the site of the problem, for example, and the patient flexes or extends the fingers, the moving tendon may emit a squeaking sound as it tries to slide through the sheath.

It is unwise to ignore tendonitis or to keep using a painful limb. Instead, one should allow enough time for the tendon to rest until it heals.

Another somewhat common disorder of the tendon sheath is the formation of a ganglion, a ballooning out of the sheath to form a lump that fills with fluid. Common sites of ganglia are the wrist, upper surface of the foot, and back of the knee. Ganglia are harmless, far more a nuisance than anything serious. Their size may vary, but they are usually no larger than a pea. A ganglion may be hard or soft, and most often is painless. After a doctor determines the lump is a ganglion, it may be drained with a needle, although it may recur and disappear without treatment. In rare instances, the lump may be removed surgically.

TREATMENT

If there is any suggestion of infection as a cause of bursitis or tendonitis, the doctor will take a culture and prescribe an antibiotic appropriate to the identified organism. Clearing up infection is first priority because, if not treated, the infecting organism can cause the tendon to rupture.

If bursitis or tendonitis is mild or chronic and not the result of infection, home treatments such as rest for the painful joint, soaking in hot water to reduce swelling, and taking aspirin, other analgesics, or nonsteroidal anti-inflammatory drugs for pain are helpful. The doctor may inject a steroid preparation at the site of tenderness, which should provide relief. Most attacks are complicated by limitation of motion; it is wise to avoid motion for a few days until healing begins.

When pain subsides, carefully supervised broad range-of-motion exercises should begin. Applying heat before beginning may be helpful. However, mild pain at the time of exercising is to be expected, especially after the area has been at rest for some time. Acute pain that lasts more than half an hour signals excessive exercise.

For the shoulder, two effective exercises for maintaining full range of motion are worth trying: (1) letting fingers crawl slowly up a wall, reaching a little higher each time; and (2) swinging the arm like a pendulum, slowly and gently at first, then gradually with more vigor in ever-increasing circles. Ease of motion should increase gradually, and full flexibility should be regained in a few weeks to months.

If the bursitis or tendonitis is acute and is not caused by disease, there are a number of useful treatment methods that can be used. These include:

• *Rest and protection.* Keep the area as motionless as possible and avoid painful positions; use a splint or sling, if comfortable.
• *Cold compresses.* These lessen pain.
• *Anti-inflammatory drugs.* In the acute

stage aspirin or a nonsteroidal, anti-inflammatory agent may be prescribed.

• *Prescription analgesics.* When severe pain prevents sleep or rest, a prescription analgesic, such as codeine, may be needed temporarily until other measures begin to work.

• *Draining and steroid therapy.* Sometimes needle aspiration of the swollen bursa will relieve pain and pressure. Injection of a steroid drug directly into the inflamed area often brings dramatic relief in eight to twenty-four hours.

• *Reactivation.* When pain subsides, carefully start passive, then active range-of-motion exercises to prevent stiffness. Heat can be especially helpful at this stage.

SUMMING UP

From time to time, many people suffer painful bouts of bursitis and/or tendonitis. They are not a cause for alarm but should be identified by a doctor to rule out more serious bone, muscle, or other diseases. Successful treatments can vary for individuals, but most involve rest for the affected area, moist heat, and painkillers, followed by a period of gradual, careful reactivation of the limb. Although most often there is no permanent damage from bursitis or tendonitis, once an attack has occurred in a specific area, the patient should take care not to overuse the joint, as recurrent attacks can be common.

40. Common Foot Problems

A number of common problems affect the feet. Some cause minor discomfort; others produce pain sufficient to warrant surgical intervention.

CORNS AND CALLUSES

Corns and calluses are areas of skin that have become thickened as a result of constant pressure, usually from too-tight or ill-fitting shoes that cramp the toes. Hard corns form on the tops and on the tips of the toes, soft corns between the toes. Calluses are larger than corns and usually form on the soles of the feet. In themselves, corns and calluses do not hurt; rather, pressure on the hardened area causes pain in the underlying soft tissue.

Soft, well-fitting shoes and padding over hard corns (or between the toes for soft corns) will help reduce or redistribute the pressure and thus relieve the pain of a corn. Most over-the-counter corn preparations contain salicylic acid, which can harm normal skin but are safe when used as directed. The preparations should be used only on the corn itself; only five applications should be made; and the treatment should not be continued for more than two weeks.

Calluses can be reduced in size by gentle rubbing with a pumice stone after a hot shower or bath. The feet should then be thoroughly dried and a moisturizing lotion applied. No attempt should ever be made to pare corns or calluses with razor blades or scissors. This invites infection.

BUNIONS

A bunion is an inflamed bursa overlying the bony protrusion at the base of the big toe. (A bursa is a fluid-filled sac that minimizes friction between tissues that move constantly against one another, for example, the skin and the underlying bone.)

Bunions are usually caused by a foot disorder known as hallux valgus (*hallux* is the medical term for the big toe; *valgus* means "bent or twisted outward"). The toe is twisted, with the top bending toward the other toes and the large joint (metatarsal-phalangeal) protruding beyond the normal outline of the foot. Bursitis (inflammation of the bursa) makes the affected joint painful, and friction from footwear causes the overlying skin to become thickened and callused. In addition, the joint may be afflicted with osteoarthritis, occurring much earlier than it normally would. Bunions affect women more frequently than they do men; they tend to run in families. The condition is aggravated by wearing tight shoes, especially shoes with high heels.

Comfortable shoes with plenty of toeroom are helpful. Sometimes it may be advisable to relieve pressure on the bunion completely (by cutting a hole in the upper of an old shoe, or by going barefoot), so that the inflammation can subside. If the hallux valgus is severe, an operation to straighten the big toe may be required. However, the operation is both painful and inconvenient—the foot must be kept in a cast for up to two months after surgery —and is seldom recommended unless the pain is severe and the patient relatively young.

HAMMERTOE

This clawlike deformity usually affects the second toe. Pain is due to malalignment of the surfaces of the toe joints, and in severe cases surgery is necessary to correct the problem. Hammertoe is usually the result of wearing too small a shoe. In some cases, however, it results from muscle imbalance.

INGROWN TOENAIL

In this condition, which usually affects the big toe, the edge of the nail grows into the soft tissue next to it. The side edge is generally affected, but the forward edge may also become ingrown if the nail is trimmed too short.

If the area is not infected, it may be possible to pull the overgrown tissue gently away from the nail. This should be done after the foot has been soaked in warm water for twenty to thirty minutes; a small piece of cotton should then be placed under the nail to hold it away from the skin. This treatment should be repeated daily, until the corner of the nail has grown beyond the

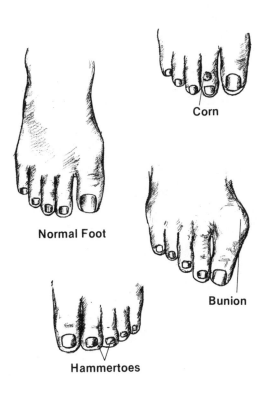

Corn

Normal Foot

Bunion

Hammertoes

point where it can cut into the flesh. If infection occurs and much soft tissue has grown over the nail, surgical removal of part of the nail is usually necessary.

Tight or pointed-toed shoes can aggravate or even cause ingrown toenails. For most people, the problem can be prevented by choosing shoes wisely and by cutting the toenails straight across.

PLANTAR WARTS

Plantar warts are common warts (verrucae vulgaris) occurring on the sole of the foot. The growth is small, hard, and usually whitish in color; in the center are small clotted blood vessels that resemble splinters. Where other common warts are slightly elevated mounds of skin, however, plantar warts are pushed into the surrounding soft tissues by the pressure of the body's weight so that the skin surface is level. They can be distinguished from corns and calluses by their tendency to pinpoint bleeding when their surface is pared away. Clusters of these warts, very small

and set closely together, are called mosaic warts. Plantar and mosaic warts are frequently very painful.

Unlike warts in other areas of the body, for which the best treatment may be no treatment, plantar warts should be removed. They may be treated with a destructive preparation such as salicylic acid plaster, used over a number of weeks. Alternatively, they may be cauterized electrically or frozen with liquid nitrogen. The latter is an effective treatment but may be painful enough to make walking impossible for two to three days.

SUMMING UP

Many of the problems that commonly affect the feet are either caused or exacerbated by ill-fitting shoes, in particular, pointed shoes that cramp the toes and high-heeled shoes that concentrate weight-bearing on the ball of the foot. Similarly, a change of shoes, in style or fit, can often do much to relieve common foot discomforts.

Gastrointestinal Disorders

---

41. Ulcers

COMMON CHARACTERISTICS

Peptic ulcers—small, open breaks or craters in the lining of the upper gastrointestinal tract—develop in one of three sites. The most common form in the upper portion of the small intestine and are known as duodenal ulcers; less common are those in the stomach itself, which are gastric ulcers. Ulcers also may develop in the esophagus, the canal that transports food from the back of the throat to the stomach. Surprisingly, 15 to 20 percent of bleeding ulcers occur initially without pain.

ORIGINS

In general, ulcers are caused by an imbalance in the stomach, either too much stomach acid or pepsin, the major digestive enzyme and the source of the term *peptic ulcers,* or too little protective mucous and protein secretions. This imbalance allows the stomach acids and enzymes to turn on the digestive tract itself, in effect, producing small ulcers. But there is not, as is commonly thought, a direct relationship between *excessive* acid secretion and ulcers. Many people with duodenal ulcers, for example, secrete large amounts of acid, but others do not. This has led many experts to suspect that poor tissue resistance and other factors, particularly cigarette smoking, that interfere with the flow of neutralizing secretions may contribute to ulcer development. Stress and emotional pressure are also frequently cited as causes of duodenal ulcers.

In the case of gastric ulcers, excessive acid secretion appears to be even less of a factor than in other forms of ulcer, since many patients have normal and even low levels of stomach acid. Again, external factors or substances have been implicated in the origin of gastric ulcers, the two major ones being alcohol and aspirin. Both are known to injure the stomach lining, and it is thought they increase the stomach's vulnerability to the acid that is present.

SYMPTOMS

Pain—centered in the pit of the stomach, just below the rib cage—is the most characteristic ulcer symptom, and it usually follows a distinct pattern. It normally begins several hours after eating or during the night, developing when the stomach is empty. The pain can manifest itself as a chronic gnawing or aching; it may grow worse during or immediately after meals; or there may be no pain at all, just belching. Any ongoing stomach discomfort should be called to a doctor's attention.

COMPLICATIONS

Gastrointestinal bleeding is one of the most common complications of ulcers.

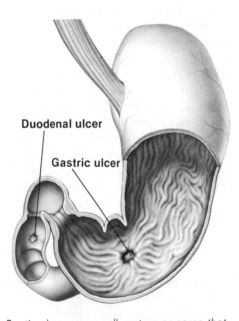

Duodenal ulcer

Gastric ulcer

Peptic ulcers are small craters or sores that form in the lining of the upper gastrointestinal tract, with the duodenum the most common site. The above cross section shows an ulcer crater in the lining of the duodenum and a gastric ulcer.

This may manifest itself as vomiting fresh, bright red blood or passing bloody or tarry stools. Weakness, fatigue, or, in the case of severe hemorrhage, loss of consciousness and shock also may result from bleeding ulcers. Ulcers always should be suspected when gastrointestinal bleeding occurs, even if there is no pain or other symptoms.

One serious complication is a perforated ulcer, which develops as acid deepens the ulcer and goes through the intestinal wall, spilling acid and bacteria into the abdominal cavity. This is always a medical emergency requiring immediate treatment, usually surgical. The pain is sudden, intense, and steady, and even the slightest movement seems to increase it. The major danger is peritonitis, a severe infection of the abdominal cavity. A second danger is caused by excessive scarring or adhesions. Usually, however, this only occurs in older ulcers where several layers of scar tissue have had a chance to accumulate. Piled on one another, these may block the digestive tract.

TREATMENT

While some ulcers heal on their own, most patients require some sort of treatment. But recent important changes in the three major areas of ulcer therapy—diet, drugs, and surgery—allow today's patients a freedom that would have been unimaginable to earlier generations of ulcer victims. In any case, ulcer patients who smoke should make every effort to stop. Avoidance of alcohol and aspirin, especially during a flare-up, also is recommended.

DIET

Milk and cream diets are still prescribed, as are small, frequent feedings of up to six meals a day. But today, these mainstays of dietary therapy are used much more judiciously than in the past. Since both seem to relieve ulcer pain effectively, they are routinely prescribed during flare-ups. But because there is no evidence that either actually promotes healing, once the pain has been relieved, patients are usually allowed to resume their normal diets.

DRUGS

The discovery of a new drug (cimetidine) that inhibits the flow of digestive acids and enzymes and thereby permits ulcers to heal has markedly changed ulcer therapy. Blocking drugs are now widely used in treating ulcers.

Another new approach is to administer drugs (e.g., sucralfate) that actually form a protective coating over the ulcer, giving it a chance to heal without disrupting the flow of gastric acids. Until the introduction of these new drugs, the approach had been to give drugs that neutralize acids already present rather than block acid secretion.

Many older drugs remain an important and valuable part of ulcer therapy, particularly the antacids. As acid neutralizers, they not only relieve discomfort but actively promote duodenal ulcer healing. Selected patients also may be treated with other agents, such as anticholinergics, drugs that slow down stimulation of secretions and other involuntary functions. In

any instance, treatment should be tailored to the needs of an individual patient—something only your physician is equipped to do.

SURGERY

For the majority of ulcer patients, the success of dietary therapy, drug therapy, or a combination of the two makes surgery unnecessary. But an estimated 10 to 15 percent of ulcer patients do eventually require surgery. Indications for surgery usually include perforation, obstruction due to scarring, and bleeding. Intractable pain also may justify surgical intervention, but usually only after other treatment alternatives have been tried.

SUMMING UP

While the causes of ulcers are still not completely understood, new therapies have dramatically improved the outlook for most ulcer patients. These include a more liberal attitude toward diet, new drugs, and improved diagnostic procedures. Stopping smoking and attempting to avoid undue stress also are recommended for ulcer patients.

42. Heartburn and Indigestion

COMMON CHARACTERISTICS

Indigestion and heartburn are popular terms used by patients to describe a large number of common digestive problems. Most of us have experienced many of these problems at one time or another, particularly after eating or drinking too much or as a result of stress. Indigestion refers to any disturbance of the digestive process; heartburn is one of its most common symptoms. Both indicate some difficulty in the upper part of the gastrointestinal tract, which includes the esophagus (the tube that leads from the throat to the stomach) and the stomach.

HEARTBURN

Heartburn, also frequently referred to as acid indigestion, is a burning sensation in the lower-middle chest that sometimes spreads to the neck, throat, and face. It often occurs after eating or lying down and frequently is accompanied by the reflux of stomach contents into the mouth.

Despite its name and the location of its discomfort, heartburn is *not* related to the heart. It is produced by the backward flow of irritating stomach acids into the esophagus. This condition, known as gastroesophageal reflux, is usually caused by a malfunctioning of the sphincter muscle at the lower end of the esophagus, which normally opens to let food pass into the stomach and closes to keep the stomach contents in place.

The gastroesophageal muscles may not work properly for any of several reasons. There may be a congenital defect; the muscle may not close properly because of disordered nerve action brought on by emotional disturbances; or conditions such as pregnancy, excessive air swallowing, or fluid retention may increase the pressure in the abdominal cavity and thus interfere with muscle function.

Sometimes, heartburn is associated with a hiatus hernia—the bulging of a portion of the stomach above the diaphragm. This condition may be caused by a stretching of the diaphragm muscle, which normally fits snugly enough around the esophagus to keep the stomach from pushing up into the chest cavity.

Repeated episodes of acidic reflux may lead to certain complications, including esophagitis (the inflammation of the esophagus), esophageal ulcers, and a narrowing of the esophagus. For this reason, diagnostic tests, such as X-rays or more technical procedures, may be required by the doctor to help determine the extent of the problem and the appropriate treatment.

PREVENTION AND TREATMENT

Heartburn can usually be prevented by alterations in diet and life style. Occasional attacks may be relieved by the use of antacids. In severe or complicated cases, or in cases associated with a hiatus hernia, surgery may be recommended.

Modifications in diet are likely to include the avoidance of foods and beverages commonly associated with heartburn. Among them are caffeine (contained in coffee, tea, cola, and chocolate), fatty foods, and alcoholic and carbonated beverages. By keeping a record of the particular foods that consistently bring on discomfort, other problem foods may be identified. These may include highly spicy foods, acidic fruits and juices, and foods that produce excessive amounts of gas during digestion, such as onions, cabbage, brussels sprouts, and beans. Eating too much and too quickly also should be avoided. Drinking skimmed milk before meals may be helpful because milk is known to buffer stomach acids and temporarily coat the lining of the esophagus.

Because gravity helps keep the stomach and its contents in place, even in patients with a hiatus hernia, lying down just after eating should be avoided. For the same reason, it may be helpful to sleep with the head of the bed elevated by about six inches, to bend at the knees rather than at the waist and to try to stand and sit as straight as possible. The pressure caused by tight

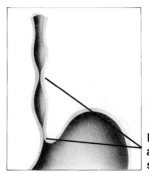

Normal pyloric and esophageal sphincters

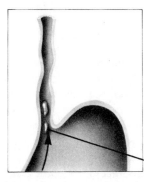

Malfunctioning sphincter

Normally, the esophageal sphincter at the entrance to the stomach opens to admit food and then closes to prevent backflow. But when the sphincter muscle is weak or malfunctioning, as shown in the lower drawing, gastric juices can move back into the esophagus, causing the burning sensation of heartburn.

belts, girdles or other constricting clothing should be avoided, as should smoking, which both weakens the esophageal muscle and leads to the swallowing of air.

Taking an antacid to relieve an occasional attack of heartburn is likely to be safe and effective, but more regular usage should be discussed with a doctor. Similarly, home remedies, such as baking soda, which has short-lived effects, should not be taken without consulting a doctor. When symptoms are severe or persistent despite sensible precautions, a doctor should be consulted.

INDIGESTION

Indigestion, also called dyspepsia, is a popular term that refers to a large number of symptoms related to the digestive process. These may include heartburn, nausea, vomiting, stomach cramps, bloating, belching, and diarrhea. A number of diseases involving every area of the gastrointestinal tract may bring on these symptoms. Listing the symptoms alone will not lead to accurate diagnosis of the underlying cause.

Some of the symptoms, such as nausea, vomiting, and diarrhea, may be caused by certain diseases, including viral and bacterial infections, gallbladder inflammation, and liver disease. Medications, ranging from aspirin to antibiotics, also may cause these symptoms.

The bloated feeling that often accompanies indigestion is usually caused by the excessive swallowing of air. Although small amounts of air are normally swallowed when a person eats or drinks, too much air may be swallowed as the result of eating too quickly, smoking, chewing gum, talking with a full mouth, or drinking carbonated beverages. Belching may provide temporary relief from the discomfort, but it eventually exacerbates the problem by allowing even more air to be swallowed. Bloating may also be caused by an excessive accumulation of gas in the stomach. Although gas is normally produced during the digestive process, some foods cause more gas to be produced than others. Among them are cabbage, broccoli, brussels sprouts, onions, beans, wheat germ, and bran.

PREVENTION AND TREATMENT

Like heartburn, the other symptoms of indigestion can usually be prevented by modifications in diet and life style your physician may recommend. Smoking, carbonated beverages, fatty foods, and caffeine-containing foods and beverages should be avoided or at least limited. Cooking fruits and vegetables may reduce the likelihood of their causing indigestion. The reduction of stress at mealtime may also be helpful. When symptoms of indi-

gestion are severe or persistent, they should be brought to a doctor's attention.

SUMMING UP

Heartburn and indigestion are common digestive problems that can usually be prevented by modifying diet, reducing emotional stress, and stopping or cutting down on smoking. Sometimes the control of heartburn, which occurs when the acidic contents of the stomach back up into the esophagus, may require additional measures, such as attention to posture and the avoidance of tight-fitting clothing. Chronic indigestion and heartburn require the attention of a doctor, who may tailor an appropriate treatment plan to the individual patient's needs.

43. Nausea and Vomiting

COMMON CHARACTERISTICS

Nausea is characterized by an unpleasant sensation or queasiness in the stomach area, often accompanied by an aversion to food and the tendency to vomit. Even small infants can communicate this sensation, and almost everyone experiences it at some point. Nausea generally precedes vomiting, or accompanies it, but the two may occur independently.

In vomiting, the lower region of the stomach contracts strongly and suddenly while the pyloric sphincter (the valve that opens into the uppermost section of the intestines) closes, forcing the contents of

the stomach up through the esophagus and out the mouth. The signal that produces vomiting is transmitted through an area of the brain called the true vomiting center. Stimuli originating in the gastrointestinal tract, the heart, the brain, the inner ear, the eyes and nose, and a center in the brain known as the chemoreceptor trigger zone all may produce vomiting. The exact mechanisms, however, are not known.

If nausea is mild or short-lived, or if there are only one or two episodes of vomiting, there is usually no cause for concern. If the sensation persists, however, or if vomiting is recurrent and is accompanied by other symptoms such as fever, pain, or faintness—if the vomit is stained with green bile or is very dark in color—you should contact your doctor or health center as soon as possible.

SOME CAUSES OF NAUSEA AND VOMITING

A number of chemical and physical stimulants may induce nausea and vomiting. Powerful painkillers such as morphine can cause vomiting, and nausea is a potential side effect of numerous drugs. Nausea and vomiting are frequent but not invariable side effects of drug and radiation therapy for cancer. If your doctor has prescribed a drug that you suspect is nauseating you, do not hesitate to report this. Often, modifications can be made that will relieve this distressing side effect.

Nausea and pain in young children sometimes indicate accidental poisoning. A doctor and/or a poison control center should be called at once if poisoning is suspected.

Greasy, fatty foods—or foods with an unpleasant association—may provoke queasiness and nausea and, occasionally, vomiting. Vomiting after the consumption of poisonous foods (mushrooms, berries, and seeds, for example) or food contaminated by such bacteria as salmonella or staphylococcus is a protective response on the part of the body, enabling the stomach to get rid of the poisons quickly. If nausea and vomiting are related to diet, substituting cereals, dry crackers, skimmed milk, lean meat, fish, and hard-boiled eggs for foods high in fats and spices is often helpful.

Nausea and Vomiting

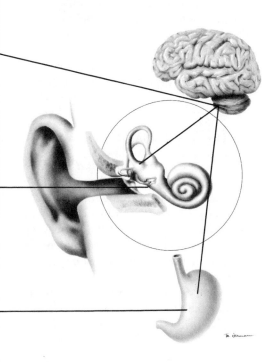

The feeling of nausea and the vomiting reflex are controlled at two sites of the brain stem.

The Chemoreceptor Zone detects toxic substances and triggers the *Vomiting Center,* which also can be activated by signals from the balance mechanism of the ear (motion sickness), the brain (sights, smells, thoughts), and the gut (infections, irritants).

The *Vomiting Center* sets up a sequence of responses:
- Stomach outlet to esophagus relaxes
- Abdominal muscles and diaphragm contract
- Windpipe closes
- Stomach is squeezed and the gastric contents are expelled

MOTION SICKNESS

Motion sickness may be brought on by travel in any moving vehicle—car, train, boat, plane, or an amusement park ride such as a Ferris wheel. The discomfort is a result of a disturbance of the three semicircular canals in the inner ear that control equilibrium.

The nausea of motion sickness, which may precede vomiting, often begins with a feeling of fatigue and is accompanied by pallor and chill. It is often intensified if visual contact with the horizon is lost and is aggravated by certain odors.

Travelers who are susceptible to motion sickness should sit where there is the least motion (in the front seat of a car, over the wings of a plane, amidships in a boat) and should avoid exhaust fumes and other odors. Other preventive measures include avoiding reading, keeping the horizon forty-five degrees below the line of vision, and keeping food and fluids to a minimum. Several effective nonprescription drugs are available to counter motion sickness. Typically, the initial dose is taken one-half to one hour before traveling and then once or twice a day during the journey. (See Chapter 84, "Vertigo and Motion Sickness," for more details.)

NAUSEA IN PREGNANCY

Nausea is common during the first three months of pregnancy and in some women precedes vomiting. Although it is called "morning sickness," it can occur at any time of day. Self-medication should be avoided. A doctor should recommend or approve any medication taken during pregnancy.

Fatty or fried foods tend to aggravate nausea and should be avoided. Large amounts of fluids, especially with meals, are known to contribute to the problem. Avoiding fluids one or two hours before and after meals and eating dry bread or crackers at two-hour intervals brings relief to many women. (See Chapter 161, "Morning Sickness," for more details.)

EMOTIONAL DISTRESS

Nausea may accompany emotional distress about such problems as marital difficulties, the loss of a job, or the ill health or loss of a spouse or close relative. Vomiting may express hostility, as when a child vomits during a temper tantrum, or it may be a response to general stress.

CHILDHOOD NAUSEA AND VOMITING

Vomiting is common in infants and young children. It may be associated with a great many conditions, including respiratory and gastrointestinal infections, allergy to foods, intestinal obstruction and an abnormal blood sugar level. If an infant seems sick, vomits more than once or twice, or has a fever of over 101°F, the doctor should be called.

Vomiting should not be confused with regurgitation, the spitting up of small amounts of milk or formula after feeding. This is generally of no significance and usually stops after the age of six months or so.

Occasionally a baby vomits with great force (projectively), so that the food lands at a distance from the mouth. Generally, this is nothing to worry about, but frequent projective vomiting, occurring within two weeks of birth, may indicate the condition known as pyloric stenosis, an obstruction of the pyloric valve, which prevents the stomach contents from moving normally into the small intestine. The problem can be corrected by surgery. Vomiting that comes on suddenly in infancy, especially if there is pain or if the vomit is tinged with green bile, may indicate an obstruction of the intestines. Such cases should receive prompt medical attention.

NAUSEA AND VOMITING AS SYMPTOMS

Nausea and vomiting are among the early or prominent symptoms of a large number of diseases, including disorders of the central nervous system, heart, kidneys, and liver. Acute infectious diseases, abdominal emergencies such as appendicitis and peritonitis, and some cancers are also associated with these symptoms. If there is prolonged nausea or persistent vomiting, a doctor should always be consulted.

DRUG TREATMENT

In most cases, nausea and vomiting are self-limiting and need not be treated. If nausea is prolonged, however, the reduced food intake leads to weight loss and debilitation; persistent vomiting also results in severe dehydration and a disturbance of the body's chemical balance. In such cases, drugs to prevent vomiting (antiemetics) are prescribed. These drugs are also sometimes given with presurgical anesthesia to reduce vomiting after an operation.

Medications can be given by mouth to counteract nausea, but once vomiting has begun they must be given by suppository or by means of an injection or intravenous drip.

SUMMING UP

Nausea and vomiting are symptoms of a wide range of conditions, from the simple and relatively benign to the potentially serious. In most cases, nausea and vomiting are short-lived and no treatment is needed other than to make the individual as comfortable as possible. Lying perfectly still, either on the stomach or on the back with a pillow under the knees, may be comforting, as may a heating pad on the abdomen.

It is usually not difficult to distinguish between mild cases and those that require professional help. Nausea in infants and young children, however, should be observed carefully. The nausea and vomiting associated with certain illnesses, surgery, some drugs, and radiation therapy can usually be controlled with the use of antiemetic drugs.

44. Diverticular Disease

COMMON CHARACTERISTICS

Diverticular disease—one of our most common gastrointestinal problems—is characterized by the formation of small, balloon-like sacs called diverticula in weakened segments of the large intestine (colon) wall. The outpouchings are usually one-fourth to one-half inch long and many may be present. About thirty million people in the United States have diverticular disease; it is estimated that a third of all Americans over age forty-five have some diverticula, and by age sixty or older the figure rises to two-thirds. For unexplained reasons, the disorder is somewhat more common in women than in men.

Most people with diverticular disease are unaware of the condition, since it usually does not produce symptoms. In about 10 to 25 percent of all cases, however, the diverticula become filled with feces, causing the outpouchings to become inflamed. This results in abdominal pain, nausea, vomiting, and diarrhea, often alternating with constipation. There also may be blood in the stools.

CAUSES

A number of researchers have noted that diverticular disease is very common among people who consume the highly processed, low-fiber diets typical of industrialized Western nations but is seldom seen among people in developing countries or in groups that consume a high-fiber diet. For this reason, the disease has been

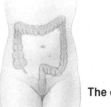

The colon

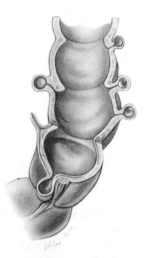

Cross section of a segment of the colon with diverticula

associated with the consumption of a diet high in fats, meat, sugar, and processed foods but low in dietary fiber or roughage, the nondigestible, fibrous parts of fruits, vegetables, cereal grains, seeds, and nuts. Although this association has not been proved, there is increasing evidence that eating a high-fiber diet is an effective approach to managing diverticular disease.

The actual outpouchings or diverticula are thought to be caused by excessive pressure within the colon. This pressure may result from the increased effort required to propel a hard, compacted stool through the large intestine. The condition is more common in people who suffer chronic constipation, for example. Dietary fiber eases this problem by producing bulkier and softer stools that move more easily through the digestive tract.

DIAGNOSIS

Any unexplained change in bowel habits, blood in the stool, recurring abdominal pain, nausea, or vomiting are signs that you should see a doctor. Since these symptoms may be caused by a number of disorders, one of two specific tests may be performed to diagnose diverticular disease. One is called colonoscopy and involves inserting a flexible hollow tube equipped with fiberoptics through the rectum and into the colon. (If only the lower portion of the colon is to be examined, a shorter instrument called a sigmoidoscope is used.) This enables the doctor to examine the inner wall of the colon. The examination is usually performed in a doctor's office or outpatient clinic and is preceded by special enemas to clean out the colon.

Diverticular disease also may be diagnosed by a barium enema examination. This involves flooding the colon with barium—a thick, chalk-like opaque liquid—which will fill any diverticula that may be present and make them visible on X-ray films.

TREATMENT

Most cases of diverticular disease are treated by prescribing a diet that is high in fiber. This represents a marked departure from the past, when patients were advised to avoid high-fiber foods in favor of a low-residue diet. Foods that may be recommended include whole grain cereals and breads, green leafy vegetables that are lightly processed, and fresh fruits. Patients also may be advised to add a small amount of bran to their diet. It is best, however, to follow a diet prescribed by your doctor. Too much fiber also can be harmful or may produce excessive intestinal gas and cramps. Your doctor can guide you in how much fiber you should consume and in what form.

For some patients, bulk-producing laxatives may be prescribed. These act by producing bulkier and softer stools that move more easily through the colon.

If excessive intestinal activity or motility is a problem, drugs may be prescribed to reduce this. For flare-ups of diverticulitis, antibiotics will be prescribed. Complications, such as the formation of abscesses, perforation, intestinal obstruction, and significant bleeding may require surgery.

SUMMING UP

Diverticular disease is a very common gastrointestinal disorder among Americans, particularly those over the age of forty years. Most people are unaware they have diverticulosis, unless the outpouchings become inflamed and result in symptoms. A high-fiber diet is the most common form of treatment, and some studies have indicated that consuming such a diet from an early age may also have a preventive effect. Drugs may be prescribed to overcome chronic symptoms such as pain and altered bowel function. Symptoms of diverticulitis should be checked by a physician and treatment instituted.

45. Gallstones

COMMON CHARACTERISTICS

Gallstones, technically called cholelithiasis, are a relatively common cause of abdominal pain, particularly in women over age forty. About sixteen million Americans are thought to have gallstones, three-fourths of whom are women. Many of these people are not aware that they have gallstones because they do not experience discomfort or other symptoms. These are referred to as silent stones and are usually detected during examination for some other problem.

The gallbladder is a small, sac-like organ that lies along the back of the liver. It collects bile, which is produced by the liver, and concentrates it for later use in digesting fats. Gallstones are, as their name implies, stone-like formations that collect in the gallbladder. Some are as small as grains of sand; others are the size of walnuts.

They may be smooth and round or irregular and multifaceted.

The most common type of gallstones are composed largely of cholesterol crystals; less common are those made up of bile salts or the products of worn-out red blood cells. It is not known why so many people, particularly those who live in developed countries such as the United States, develop gallstones, although the disorder is commonly associated with excessively high levels of cholesterol in the bile when it is secreted from the liver. The amount of cholesterol and fat in the diet, however, does not seem to be directly related to the formation of gallstones. On the other hand, overweight people who have a pattern of repeated dieting and weight gain seem to be particularly prone to developing gallstones. Estrogen has also been implicated as a triggering factor, which may explain why more women than men suffer from gallstones.

Gallstone attacks are caused by the passage of a gallstone into the cystic duct, the tube that carries the bile from the gallbladder to the common duct, which carries bile from both the liver and gallbladder to the small intestine, where fats are digested. The attack lasts until the stone passes through these narrow passages and into the small intestine.

In the most serious cases, a stone becomes wedged in the common duct, stopping the flow of all bile from both the liver and gallbladder. This may result in jaundice (the skin and eyes taking on a yellowish hue), infection, and potential harm to the liver. In some cases, the pancreas also may become inflamed.

DIAGNOSIS

About 800,000 new cases of gallbladder diseases are diagnosed each year, and practically all of them begin with gallstones.

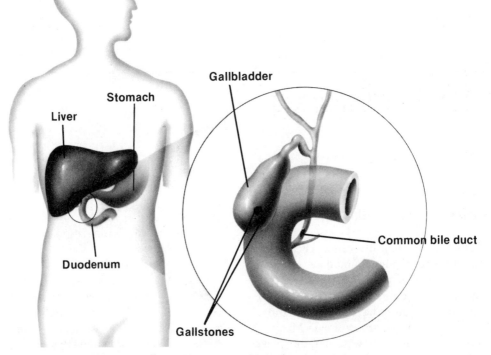

Liver Stomach Gallbladder Duodenum Common bile duct Gallstones

This detail shows the gallbladder, which shows two stones.

Although many people confuse indigestion, belching, and gas with gallstones, indigestion is not a characteristic symptom of gallstones; when the two occur together, it is a coincidence. Therefore, it is important to make sure that the symptoms are, indeed, caused by gallstones, before embarking on treatment. Since most gallstones do not show up on a regular X-ray film, other diagnostic tests are usually required. These include ultrasound, a test that uses soundwaves to map internal organs, and X-ray films taken after the injection of a dye directly into the bile duct system or, alternatively, after swallowing pills that contain a dye.

SYMPTOMS AND COMPLICATIONS

Although gallstones may be present for years without causing trouble, an attack can occur without warning. Typically, a gallbladder attack comes on suddenly with severe knife-like pain in the upper right abdomen that often spreads to the back and right shoulder blade. Attacks often come on after a heavy meal, and they may last for several hours. In some cases, the gallbladder becomes swollen and inflamed, and the pain may be accompanied by fever and vomiting.

TREATMENT

Surgical removal of the gallbladder remains the major treatment of gallstones; about 500,000 such operations (known as cholecystectomies) are performed in the United States each year. Surgery is usually reserved for those cases in which there are symptoms; most experts advise seeking a second opinion before undergoing surgery for asymptomatic or "silent" gallstones. Patients for whom surgery may pose special risks—for example, people with chronic lung disease—may be advised to try a low-fat, low-calorie diet.

A newer treatment involves the use of drugs to reduce the tendency to form gallstones and to even dissolve small cholesterol stones that are not calcified. The stones usually recur, however, when the medication is stopped. Still another new alternative to surgical removal of the gallbladder involves removing the obstructive stones from the bile duct by means of fiberoptic instruments, which are long, flexible tubes with special attachments to locate, grasp, and remove the stones. This operation can be done with a local anesthetic and does not require more than a day or so of hospitalization. In any instance, your doctor is the best judge of what treatment is best for your particular case.

SUMMING UP

Millions of Americans suffer from gallstones, one of the most common causes of acute abdominal pain. Millions of others harbor silent gallstones that cause no symptoms but are often considered a potential source of trouble. And many others who think they have gallstones have, instead, frequent bouts of indigestion. Once gallstones have been diagnosed, most experts recommend that they be treated, which may involve altering your diet, using drugs, surgical removal of the gallbladder, or an endoscopic procedure to remove the obstructive stones.

46. Hiatus Hernia

COMMON CHARACTERISTICS

Contrary to popular belief, a hernia is not necessarily a tear or a rupture, but a condition in which part of an organ protrudes in an abnormal way through a weak wall in the body cavity, or through a preexisting opening in an adjacent organ. The most common hernia (inguinal) occurs in the groin. While it may be present at birth, it is usually acquired by middle-aged men during the act of lifting. Umbilical hernia occurs in infancy and is likely to be self-healing. An incisional hernia results from the weakening of the abdominal wall by surgery.

A hiatus hernia—also called esophageal hernia—involves three organs and occurs in the following way: The diaphragm is the large shelf-like muscle that separates the abdominal cavity from the chest cavity. The esophagus is the ten- to twelve-inch tube that carries food from the throat into the stomach. This digestive transport is made possible by an opening, or hiatus, in the diaphragm. Ordinarily, the stomach remains anchored in the abdomen and is prevented from ascending into the chest because the muscular structure of the opening is a close fit. But if the hiatus is too wide, or when obesity, pregnancy, or a tight girdle cause unusual pressure against the stomach, it will ascend partially into the chest.

A hiatus hernia may exist without causing any problems at all. In fact, in examining the results of barium X-ray series, doctors find that it is one of the most common structural anomalies found in normal people.

On the other hand, this condition, and an associated condition in which the muscular ring or sphincter at the lower end of the esophagus becomes weakened, are responsible not only for many cases of heartburn but also for the reflux or backflow of some of the acid contents of the stomach up through the esophagus and into the mouth.

HEARTBURN AND OTHER DISCOMFORTS

Heartburn is a common form of indigestion unrelated to the heart. It is usually described as a burning sensation that starts below the breastbone and travels upward toward the neck. In more distressing cases, it is combined with an acid taste in the mouth caused by the reflux or regurgitation of some of the stomach contents.

The vagus nerves send the brain information on acidity, movement, and pressure in the stomach.

The esophageal sphincter

The diaphragm

Heartburn typically follows a heavy and especially a fatty and spicy meal and is most often triggered by bending over or lying down. Other symptoms associated with hiatus hernia and/or weakness of the lower esophageal sphincter may include breathing difficulties and flatulence. Breathing difficulties are most often observable during pregnancy or because of obesity. (See Chapter 42, "Heartburn/Indigestion.")

DIAGNOSIS OF HIATUS HERNIA

In some instances, the doctor may make a diagnosis of hiatus hernia based only on the patient's description of symptoms, and practical measures will be recommended to alleviate them. Where the symptoms persist in spite of self-treatment, the doctor is likely to schedule a series of barium X-rays as well as a direct examination of the lower esophagus with a flexible optical instrument, an endoscope, which may reveal abnormalities not detectable in X-ray pictures.

Careful diagnosis is especially important when acidy regurgitation is accompanied by a sharp pain that spreads as far as the jaw, since this combination of symptoms may be produced by the heart rather than the gastrointestinal tract.

A diagnosis of congenital hiatus hernia may be made when an infant keeps spitting up milk that is slightly blood-streaked. The condition often corrects itself when the baby's stomach moves down into the upper abdominal cavity. Until this occurs, the baby should be supported in an upright position so that food is retained. However, when it becomes obvious that the disability persists, the hernia may be surgically corrected.

PREVENTING DISCOMFORTS OF HIATUS HERNIA

The following measures usually minimize or eliminate most of the symptoms attributable to hiatus hernia:

- Avoid eating too much at one sitting; try to eat slowly and chew thoroughly.
- If obesity is an obvious factor, make an effort to lose the extra weight.
- Don't wear tight belts, girdles, pants or other constraining clothes.
- Try to change your eating habits so that you don't have your heaviest meal at night. If this isn't easy to manage, postpone bedtime for at least three hours after eating.
- Reduce the amount of air that's swallowed by giving up carbonated beverages and chewing gum.
- Since lying down increases the likelihood that stomach juices will flow upward, raise the head of the bed by inserting four-to-six-inch wood blocks under the two legs. This is a more practical and permanent solution than sleeping propped up with extra pillows.
- A mild antacid is likely to be most effective if taken about an hour after a meal.
- If a medication prescribed for some other condition seems to be causing symptoms associated with hiatus hernia, discuss possible alternatives with the doctor.

One especially compelling reason for reducing and if possible eliminating the chronic reflux of stomach acid into the esophagus is that the acid has a corrosive effect on the esophageal lining. In some cases, this constant irritant may cause bleeding or even scarring that might eventually interfere with swallowing.

SURGERY FOR HIATUS HERNIA

When all practical measures fail to relieve chronic acid reflux and a hiatus hernia is unambiguously established as the cause, surgical repair may be inevitable. However, if surgery is recommended before all other methods of treatment have been tried, a second opinion is desirable. It has recently been estimated that less than 5 percent of all symptomatic hiatus hernia cases require an operation.

SUMMING UP

Hiatus hernia is a common structural abnormality in which a portion of the stomach rises above the diaphragm. Many people experience no symptoms, while others are troubled by heartburn and indigestion, especially when they are lying down. Most cases can be controlled by changes in eating habits and other life-style changes. In a small minority of cases, surgical correction may be required.

47. Irritable Bowel Syndrome and Colitis

COMMON CHARACTERISTICS

Diarrhea and abdominal cramps are the major symptoms of both irritable bowel syndrome and colitis, but the two conditions are distinctly different diseases. Irritable bowel syndrome, which is also called spastic colon, nervous bowel, and irritable colon, is caused by excessive spasms of the large intestine. It is much more common than colitis; indeed, it is probably the most common abdominal complaint brought to the attention of doctors. It usually begins during late adolescence or early adulthood and, for unknown reasons, women are affected twice as often as men.

Colitis is a more rare and potentially serious disorder characterized by an inflammation of the innermost lining of the colon. Sometimes the entire length of the large intestine is involved; but more often, the inflammation occurs in the lower portion, in which case the disease is called proctitis. Colitis tends to come and go, with alternating periods of acute flare-ups and quiescence. In a large number of cases, the disorder progresses to ulcerative colitis, in which the lining of the colon becomes thickened and bleeds, resulting in blood and mucus mixed with diarrhea.

DIAGNOSIS OF IRRITABLE BOWEL

Diagnosis of the irritable bowel syndrome is often based on a review of the symptoms and a process of elimination of other disorders. The major symptoms—abdominal cramping, gassiness, bloating, and diarrhea, sometimes alternating with constipation—are characteristic of a number of other intestinal disorders, such as colitis, diverticulitis (the inflammation of pockets that form in weakened segments of the intestinal wall), and cancer. The diarrhea is somewhat distinctive in that it often occurs shortly after eating and sometimes immediately after getting up in the morning. The excessive intestinal spasms causing this syndrome may be detected during a barium enema—a test in which a chalky liquid substance is infused into the colon and X-ray films are taken—or during a sigmoidoscopic examination—a test in which a hollow tube with fiberoptics is inserted through the anus and into the colon. More often, however, these examinations are performed to rule out other colon disorders that may produce similar symptoms; after these other possibilities are eliminated, a presumptive diagnosis of irritable bowel syndrome is made.

CAUSES OF IRRITABLE BOWEL

After the digestion and absorption of nutrients by the small intestine, the waste matter is propelled into the large intestine for eventual elimination. Under normal circumstances, regular muscular contractions (intestinal motility) move this waste matter along the five-foot length of the colon and into the rectum for comfortable evacuation. However, when irritable bowel syndrome is present, the pattern of motility becomes disordered because of excessive muscular contractions, resulting in cramping and diarrhea.

There is no clear explanation for this intestinal overactivity, although a number of factors such as emotional stress, diet, and an allergic response to particular foods all have been implicated. Heavy cigarette smoking also seems to aggravate the problem.

TREATMENT OF IRRITABLE BOWEL

While psychological factors may play some role in this condition, there is no doubt that the patient is suffering from distressing physical manifestations that may themselves produce anxiety. It is important to understand that the condition, although distressing, is not medically serious. In many instances, consuming a diet that contains adequate fiber, or roughage, will help. Proper functioning of the lower intestine requires a minimal amount of bulk composed of the various kinds of fruit and vegetable fibers that go through the upper intestine virtually intact because they are not digested by humans. This fiber retains water and makes the stool bulky and soft, thus aiding in intestinal motility. Fiber can easily be added to the diet in the form of salads, raw or lightly processed fruits and vegetables, and whole grain cereals and breads.

For patients who do not respond to dietary and other life-style changes, such as reduced stress, drugs may be prescribed. These may include an anticholinergic agent to reduce the intestinal activity, a mild tranquilizer, or a sedative.

DIAGNOSIS OF COLITIS

There are several inflammatory bowel conditions called colitis, and the most common is ulcerative colitis. The major symptom is diarrhea containing blood and mucus, often accompanied by severe abdominal pain and cramping. Fever, loss of appetite, anemia, and weight loss may

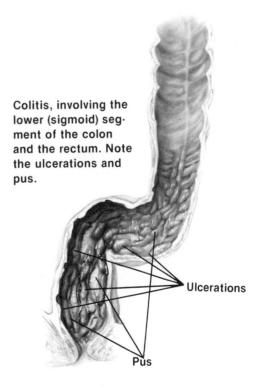

Colitis, involving the lower (sigmoid) segment of the colon and the rectum. Note the ulcerations and pus.

Ulcerations

Pus

occur, especially if the attack is prolonged or recurrent. The entire colon may be involved, but the disease usually begins in the rectum and lower portion of the colon. Some mild cases may be confined to this area, in which case the stools may be normal or even hard but contain blood and mucus.

Ulcerative colitis can be readily diagnosed by sigmoidoscopy, an examination allowing visual inspection of the lower portion of the colon. A barium enema and X-ray study also may be performed but usually not during an acute flare-up. Studies also may be indicated to determine whether the colitis is caused by an infection, such as amebiasis or salmonellosis.

COMPLICATIONS OF COLITIS

Hemorrhage is the most common complication of ulcerative colitis. In some cases, the bowel also may be perforated, leading to severe infection. This is always considered a medical emergency requiring immediate surgery.

Colon cancer is much more frequent in patients with ulcerative colitis, especially those with a family history of the two diseases and in whom the colitis begins in childhood. Cancer is also more common if the entire colon is involved. Therefore, patients with ulcerative colitis should be closely monitored for colon cancer.

TREATMENT OF COLITIS

Mild to moderate ulcerative colitis usually can be treated with drugs and a special diet. Medications, such as anticholinergics, may be prescribed to reduce colon motility. A normal diet usually can be consumed, but foods that cause diarrhea or irritate the colon should be avoided. Some patients may be advised to avoid raw fruits and vegetables. Antidiarrheal drugs also may be prescribed. More severe disease may require treatment with corticosteroid drugs. Surgery to remove all or most of the colon may be required in severe cases or those that are considered very likely to progress to cancer.

SUMMING UP

Irritable bowel syndrome is a common intestinal disorder characterized by diarrhea and abdominal cramps. Ulcerative colitis is a less common and more severe inflammatory disease that may involve the entire large intestine. Colitis tends to recur, but in most cases, a remission can be achieved through drug therapy. Since colon cancer occurs more frequently in ulcerative colitis patients, periodic cancer screening is recommended.

48. Diarrhea

COMMON CHARACTERISTICS

Diarrhea, which is the abnormally frequent passage of watery stools, is a symptom rather than a disease in itself. Depending on the cause, it may or may not be accompanied by fever, cramps, and vomiting. The stools are always excessively loose and, in some cases, may contain blood and mucus.

Most instances of diarrhea occur when the intestines have been unduly irritated by a foreign substance, causing secretion or excretion rather than the absorption of water and electrolytes (the chemicals in body fluids). Such irritants include bacterial toxins, parasitic infestation, and certain drugs.

Diarrhea may also be a consequence of a food allergy, overindulgence in foods of unaccustomed richness, or sudden introduction into the diet of too many high-fiber foods. It may also be one of the accompaniments of a hangover, and it is a rather common response to too much stress. For example, diarrhea often precedes an exam or follows a job interview.

Diarrhea ascribed to intestinal flu is usually the result of a viral infection of the lower intestinal tract. (The virus is not the same one that causes flu affecting the respiratory tract.) This condition may affect a whole family or population group, is typically self-limiting, and is also referred to as viral dysentery. (The term *dysentery* is used to describe any inflammatory intestinal disorder, usually of the colon.)

FOOD POISONING

Food poisoning is a relatively common cause of diarrhea. It was formerly referred to as ptomaine poisoning, but this vague designation has been dropped because of current knowledge about the specific bacteria and bacterial toxins responsible for diarrhea as a symptom of food poisoning. These include *Salmonella* bacteria, which may contaminate improperly refrigerated foods containing eggs (such as custards and salads made with mayonnaise), raw or smoked fish (including shellfish), poultry, pork and pork products. The toxins produced by *Staphylococcus* bacteria, transmitted by people who harbor the staph microorganism and are handling food, are another source of food poisoning. This is characterized by severe cramps, headache, fever, and an almost uninterrupted elimination of watery blood and mucus-streaked stools.

One of the most common causes of food poisoning has only recently been identified: the toxins produced by the microorganism Clostridium perfringens, whose spores are destroyed only by thorough cooking with high heat followed by prompt refrigeration. Roasts taken from the oven when they are "rare" and allowed to cool at room temperature are likely sources of the problem. Diarrhea caused by this agent usually occurs within twelve hours. It is not likely to be complicated by fever or severe cramps and lasts for no more than twenty-four hours in typical cases.

TRAVELERS' DIARRHEA

Diarrhea is endemic in those parts of the world where public sanitation and personal hygiene are minimal. (In Latin America alone, 150,000 deaths occur each year because of diarrheal illnesses.) The infectious agents are found in human

TRACKING DOWN THE CAUSE OF DIARRHEA

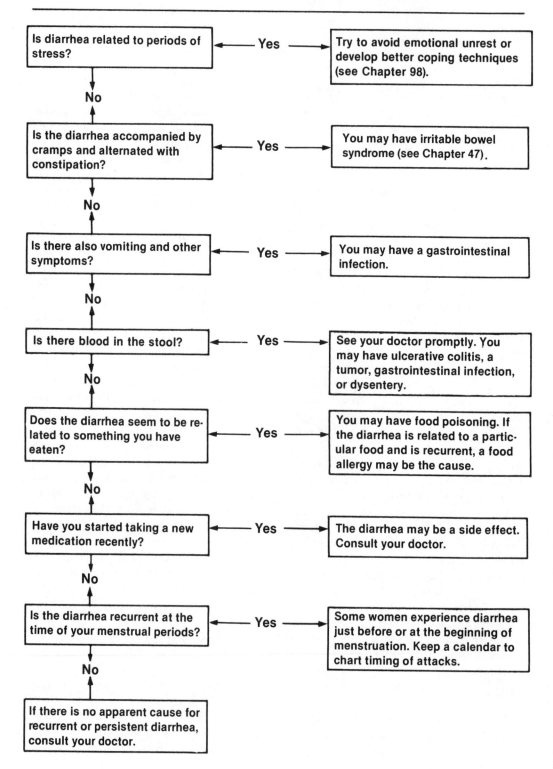

Is diarrhea related to periods of stress? — Yes → Try to avoid emotional unrest or develop better coping techniques (see Chapter 98).

No

Is the diarrhea accompanied by cramps and alternated with constipation? — Yes → You may have irritable bowel syndrome (see Chapter 47).

No

Is there also vomiting and other symptoms? — Yes → You may have a gastrointestinal infection.

No

Is there blood in the stool? — Yes → See your doctor promptly. You may have ulcerative colitis, a tumor, gastrointestinal infection, or dysentery.

No

Does the diarrhea seem to be related to something you have eaten? — Yes → You may have food poisoning. If the diarrhea is related to a particular food and is recurrent, a food allergy may be the cause.

No

Have you started taking a new medication recently? — Yes → The diarrhea may be a side effect. Consult your doctor.

No

Is the diarrhea recurrent at the time of your menstrual periods? — Yes → Some women experience diarrhea just before or at the beginning of menstruation. Keep a calendar to chart timing of attacks.

No

If there is no apparent cause for recurrent or persistent diarrhea, consult your doctor.

feces and are spread by flies, by the un-washed hands of food handlers, and by the seepage from plumbing that carries human wastes into the plumbing that carries the drinking water. Among the most serious diseases transmitted in this way are amebiasis (amebic dysentery), shigellosis (bacillary dysentery), and giardiasis (an infestation by protozoa). Fortunately, when stool samples are examined and the particular causative agent identified, prompt treatment with antibiotics of the tetracycline family usually is effective.

Most cases of travelers' diarrhea are traced to the less virulent *Escherichia coli,* a bacterial organism normally found in the intestines. It has been discovered that one strain of *E. coli* produces toxins responsible not only for the usual bout of travelers' diarrhea but also for life-threatening epidemics among infants and children. As a preventive measure against *E. coli,* some specialists recommend that doxycycline, a prescription antibiotic of the tetracycline family, be taken for a week before traveling. Others suggest the routine use of non-prescription liquid bismuth (Pepto-Bismol) even when there are no symptoms. However, the most effective precaution may well be discretion about food and drink: no salads or other uncooked vegetables, no raw, unpeeled fruit, no ice cream or other diary products—and for beverages, only those that are commercially bottled (even for brushing teeth), no water unless previously boiled, and absolutely no ice cubes.

People who frequently travel to areas in which travelers' diarrhea is common can obtain more information about local health conditions in the publication "Health Information for International Travel," available through the U.S. Government Printing Office Bookstore, 26 Federal Plaza, New York, NY 10278. The price is $4.75.

INTESTINAL DISORDERS

Intestinal disorders such as ulcerative colitis, regional enteritis (Crohn's disease), and irritable bowel syndrome also are characterized by diarrhea accompanied with cramps and often alternating with constipation. These disorders require diagnostic differentiation from each other and from the more typical causes so that the patient can be suitably treated.

TREATMENTS FOR DIARRHEA

For mild and uncomplicated diarrhea, home care consists in compensating fluid loss with clear soups, fruit juice, tea, and ginger ale. Frequent diarrhea may require even more fluid replacement to prevent dehydration. This is particularly true if a fever accompanies the diarrhea or if the weather is hot, resulting in added fluid loss from perspiration.

A diet of soft, cooked foods—boiled eggs, puddings, and the like—is soothing. Toast and crackers also can be included. Nonprescription antidiarrheal agents may help ease the symptoms, but a doctor should be consulted first. In any case, if symptoms persist for more than forty-eight hours, a doctor should be consulted. Professional diagnosis is especially important when travelers' diarrhea continues intermittently for a week or more after returning home. Laboratory tests of stool samples will indicate the nature of the infectious organism so that the right medication can be prescribed.

Diarrhea combined with flatulence and alternating with constipation may well be a symptom of an organic problem that also requires a doctor's evaluation and treatment.

SUMMING UP

Many cases of diarrhea subside within twenty-four hours without medical treatment, and others respond favorably in less than two days to simple home remedies. However, when the condition is accompanied by high fever and vomiting and the stools contain blood and mucus, or when the condition is chronic without traceable cause, a doctor should be consulted. Prompt professional guidance is especially critical in cases involving infants, the elderly, and diabetics.

49. Travelers' Diarrhea

COMMON CHARACTERISTICS

Travelers' diarrhea ("turista," "Montezuma's revenge") can spoil the best-planned vacation. This debilitating disease may affect any tourist, rich or not-so-rich, young or old. It strikes quickly and forcefully with loose, watery stools, and, in addition, such symptoms as abdominal cramps and rumblings, nausea, vomiting, chills, and a low fever. The symptoms vary in combination and in degree of severity; the disease runs its course in three to seven days.

The likelihood of getting travelers' diarrhea is determined to a major extent by one's destination. Of travelers in Mexico and other Latin American countries, Africa, the Mediterranean countries, and the Middle and Far East, up to 50 percent come down with the disease. Of these, 30 percent will be ill enough to be confined to bed, and 40 percent will have to change their planned activities.

CAUSES

Contrary to what was previously believed, travelers' diarrhea is not caused by a general change in the bacteria inhabiting the intestines or by the anxiety that may be occasioned by travel, or by the consumption of highly seasoned, unfamiliar foods. Rather, most cases of travelers' diarrhea are caused by strains of *Escherichia coli* bacteria (these organisms have been found in up to 70 percent of people suffering from the disease), other bacteria including shigella, and sometimes by viruses. In some cases, more than one agent is involved; in others, the exact cause cannot be determined.

When a person consumes food or water contaminated by *E. coli* (or any of the other diarrhea-producing organisms), the small intestine may become infected. Diarrhea

TO AVOID TRAVELERS' DIARRHEA

DO NOT CONSUME:

- Raw unpeeled fruits and vegetables
- Water, ice cubes, or other liquids that are not carbonated or have not been boiled for 15 minutes

OTHER PRECAUTIONS

- Do not use tap water to brush your teeth
- Do not swim in lakes or other waters that might be contaminated
- Do not buy food from street vendors or other sources that may not follow sanitary practices

and its associated symptoms are the inevitable result of this infection.

The name *travelers' diarrhea* is in fact something of a misnomer. The disease affects not only visitors but also people living in the region, especially young children. However, visitors are more susceptible to the disease since they have not been in the area long enough to build up an immunity to the organisms that infect the intestine.

PRECAUTIONS

Since travelers' diarrhea is caused by the consumption of contaminated food and/or water, a sensible precaution is not to drink the local water and not to eat foods that are likely to harbor live bacteria. Raw vegetables and unpeeled raw fruits should not be eaten, since the leaves, stems, and skins of these foods are frequently contaminated. Peeled fruit, cooked vegetables, and cooked fruit are usually safe.

Contaminated water is a common cause of travelers' diarrhea. To be safe to drink, water must be boiled for fifteen minutes. Ice that may have been made from contaminated water should be avoided, and tap water should not be used to brush the teeth. (These are two commonly overlooked ways in which bacteria can gain entry to the body.) Carbonated beverages are safe to drink because the carbonation makes the water too acidic for bacteria to survive. Water that has been bottled "at the source" may or may not be contaminated; it is advisable to drink only those bottled waters that have a good reputation for safety.

PREVENTION

Common sense about eating and drinking can do a great deal to decrease the risk of developing travelers' diarrhea but cannot completely eliminate the possibility. To further decrease the risk, doctors sometimes recommend certain drugs that have proven to be effective preventatives. One such drug is the nonprescription product liquid Pepto-Bismol (generic name, bismuth subsalicylate), which has been shown to reduce the rate of travelers' diarrhea by about 60 percent. However, large doses— a bottle a day—must be taken to prevent the disease. For this reason, the method is impractical for most travelers. A further cautionary note: Pepto-Bismol can cause a toxic reaction if taken in extremely large doses, so the bottle-a-day regimen should not be exceeded.

Another drug that is safe and effective against travelers' diarrhea is the antibiotic doxycycline. While this drug provides protection 60 to 90 percent of the time, there are some limitations to its use. The side effects include the possibility of gastrointestinal upset and extreme sensitivity to the sun (skin photosensitivity), a reaction that may be upsetting to those traveling in search of the sun. Further, there is concern that widespread use of antibiotic drugs of this kind will lead to the bacteria becoming resistant. Certain areas of the world already have a high incidence of resistance among strains of *E. coli.* For these reasons, doctors do not routinely prescribe doxycycline; rather, your doctor will decide whether you should receive it, based on your individual situation. Business travelers in a developing country for only a few days might benefit from the drug, for example, as would elderly travelers likely to develop serious complications from the diarrhea.

WHAT TO DO

If, despite efforts at prevention, you come down with travelers' diarrhea, there is comfort in the knowledge that the loose stools and other symptoms are most intense on the first day and that the disease usually runs its course within three to seven days. Many people find that resting in bed lessens the abdominal cramping.

RECIPE FOR FLUID REPLACEMENT SOLUTION

½ teaspoon table salt
½ teaspoon baking soda (sodium bicarbonate)
4 tablespoons table sugar
1 liter water (slightly more than 1 quart) that is carbonated or has been boiled for 15 minutes
Mix well and drink 8 ounces for each stool to prevent dehydration.

Continued severe symptoms may warrant medical attention. Since the main danger of travelers' diarrhea is dehydration, the doctor may prescribe a solution to replenish the fluid and electrolytes the body has lost to frequent bowel movements. This solution is sold in many countries under the brand name ORS or Oralyte. If the solution is not available, you can make a facsimile by following the accompanying recipe. Also, drink orange juice (not orange drink) or eat bananas to help replace lost potassium.

Although medications that slow the movement of the intestines help to curb loose stools, doctors usually do not prescribe these drugs for travelers' diarrhea since they may prolong the attack. Antibiotics are not generally prescribed, except in severe cases.

If you develop a fever of over 101° F or notice blood in your stools, consult a doctor immediately. These are the symptoms of dysentery, a diarrheal disease that is both more serious than common travelers' diarrhea and requires different treatment.

Infants and older people are more vulnerable to the complications of diarrheal disease. For this reason, travelers in these age groups who develop diarrhea should receive medical attention earlier than healthy young adults.

SUMMING UP

Travelers' diarrhea is a common, debilitating, but self-limiting disease to which tourists in developing countries are particularly vulnerable. Preventive measures include the avoidance of foods and water that may be contaminated with the bacteria and viruses responsible for the disease. In some cases, preventive medication may be advisable.

Researchers are working on the development of a vaccine against this disease, which would be of great benefit not only to travelers but also to local populations, especially children. These studies, however, are still in their preliminary stages.

50. Pancreatitis

COMMON CHARACTERISTICS

Pancreatitis—inflammation of the pancreas—is not a common condition. It affects about 27 of every 100,000 adults and occurs only very rarely in children. Pancreatitis may be acute—meaning that it comes on abruptly with severe pain and clears up completely and relatively quickly —or it may be chronic. The chronic form of the condition develops gradually over a number of years; the pain may be constant or intermittent, and there is a progressive loss of pancreatic function.

THE PANCREAS

The pancreas is a long, thin gland lying crosswise in the abdomen, behind the stomach and close to it. The gland is about eight inches long, with a broad head fitting into the curve of the duodenum (the first

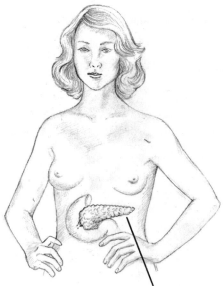

Position of normal pancreas

part of the small intestine). It is joined to the duodenum by the pancreatic duct.

The pancreas is a double-purpose gland, producing both the hormone insulin and a number of digestive enzymes. Insulin is essential for the utilization of sugars in the body; without it, diabetes may develop. It is produced in the islets of Langerhans, tiny islets of tissue scattered throughout the gland. The bulk of the pancreas (about 98 percent) is concerned with the production of enzymes that aid in the digestion of protein, fat, and carbohydrates, breaking them down into simpler substances that can be absorbed in the small intestine. These enzymes reach the duodenum through the pancreatic duct, which shares a narrow opening in the intestinal wall with the common bile duct leading from the gallbladder. The gallbladder stores and concentrates bile, releasing it when necessary into the small intestine to aid in the digestion of fats. Both the pancreatic enzymes and bile, in appropriate quantities, are essential for the proper digestion of the food we eat.

ACUTE PANCREATITIS

In acute pancreatitis, the powerful pancreatic digestive enzymes, instead of passing down the duct into the duodenum, build up locally, causing inflammation and destruction of tissue within the gland itself. The process starts suddenly, and it is not fully understood why it occurs.

Among the factors that contribute to the development of acute pancreatitis are gallstones, which, passing to the end of the common bile duct, may block the narrow opening to the duodenum and cause the pancreatic enzymes to back up. Other common contributory factors are alcoholism, surgery, particularly of the stomach or the biliary tract, and trauma to the abdomen—as, for example, a blow from the steering wheel of a car or a knife or a bullet wound. Occasionally acute pancreatitis occurs as a complication of pregnancy or of mumps or is associated with certain drugs. For reasons that are not known, acute pancreatitis is likely to occur more frequently among people with hyperparathyroidism, in which an abnormally high level of parathyroid hormones results in a high level of calcium in the blood. But in about 20 percent of cases of acute pancreatitis, there is apparently no underlying disease or predisposing cause.

SYMPTOMS OF ACUTE PANCREATITIS

The first symptom of acute pancreatitis is the sudden onset of excruciating pain. Typically, it comes on within twelve to twenty-four hours after a drinking bout or a heavy meal. Centered at first in the upper abdomen, the pain spreads to the back, the chest, and the lower abdomen. In an attempt to relieve the pain, the individual sits in a characteristic position: the body bent, the knees drawn up, and the arms folded across and pressing on the abdomen. The pain increases rapidly, reaching a maximum within a few minutes or hours, and remains steady until it gradually diminishes as the inflammation subsides over the next few days. Nausea, vomiting, and a very tender abdomen accompany the pain. In severe cases, the sufferer may also have the symptoms of shock: cold, clammy skin, racing pulse, and lowered blood pressure. Shock, if untreated, may prove fatal.

DIAGNOSIS AND TREATMENT

Someone with the symptoms of acute pancreatitis should be taken immediately to a hospital. The diagnosis will be established by tests of the blood and urine for the pancreatic enzyme amylase, which may be present in excessive amounts.

The immediate treatment consists of injecting analgesics to relieve pain and giving fluids and nutrients by intravenous drip. Gradually the individual will be able to return to a normal diet; however, alcohol will be forbidden thereafter. Most people who have an attack of acute pancreatitis recover completely with medical treatment. Occasionally, however, surgery may be necessary, particularly if the individual also suffers from gallbladder disease.

CHRONIC PANCREATITIS

This rare condition develops over a number of years. Sometimes a person with chronic pancreatitis has a history of recurrent subacute attacks, from which he or she never fully recovered. However, most sufferers have not previously had an acute attack; they generally consume excessive alcohol, or suffer from gallstones, or both.

Whatever the cause, in chronic pancreatitis the inflamed gland gradually becomes less capable of producing digestive enzymes. The digestion of fat in the small intestine is affected, and the stools become fatty and foul-smelling. In addition, insulin production may be affected, and the individual may develop diabetes mellitus.

SYMPTOMS OF CHRONIC PANCREATITIS

Pain is the chief symptom. It may be a dull, cramping pain that is made worse by food or alcohol and can be relieved somewhat by bending the torso forward, or it may be severe and gnawing. Often lasting for days or weeks at a time, the pain recurs more frequently as the condition worsens. (In about 10 percent of cases, however, there is no pain at all.) Nausea and vomiting occur frequently and there may be additional symptoms: indigestion between meals, mild jaundice, or weight loss.

TREATMENT OF CHRONIC PANCREATITIS

Frequently, chronic pancreatitis can be treated successfully with a no-alcohol, low-fat diet, together with medication that provides the digestive enzymes that the inflamed pancreas is no longer producing. Analgesic drugs are commonly prescribed for pain relief; severe unremitting pain may require strong painkillers, and there is a danger of drug addiction. Occasionally, bouts of abdominal pain become almost unbearable, and X-rays may show stones within the pancreas. In such cases, surgery may be necessary to remove a large part of the damaged pancreas.

SUMMING UP

Pancreatitis is, fortunately, a rare condition. In its acute form it is excruciatingly painful; in its chronic form it leads to gradual loss of functioning in the gland.

Many acute cases are associated with gallstones, excessive consumption of alcohol, or trauma (including surgical trauma). In about 20 percent of those affected, however, the cause is unknown. The chronic form develops insidiously over a number of years and occurs most frequently in alcoholics and those suffering from gallbladder problems.

51. Celiac Disease and Other Malabsorption Problems

COMMON CHARACTERISTICS

The body requires a constant supply of nutrients, both for its daily energy needs and for building and maintaining body tissues. The major site for the absorption of these nutrients into the bloodstream is the small intestine, a sixteen-foot length of gut lying between the stomach and the colon. If the structure of the intestine is abnormal as the result of disease or in reaction to certain elements in the diet, or if there is a deficiency or malfunction of the enzymes that normally aid in the digestive process, essential nutrients may not be absorbed properly. Malabsorption, therefore, is fundamentally a sign of some disease or condition that affects the function of the small intestine.

The most common and general symptoms of malabsorption are abdominal discomfort, diarrhea, and steatorrhea (pale, foul-smelling stools that tend to float in water because of their high fat content). If malabsorption goes unchecked over a period of months or years, there will be weight loss (or, in a child, failure to thrive), diminished energy, and breathlessness. Signs and symptoms of particular vitamin or mineral deficiencies may also develop, such as a sore tongue, anemia, bone pain, or numbness in the limbs.

Various diseases that affect the structure of the lining of the small intestine (the intestinal mucosa) may cause malabsorption. These include *celiac disease, tropical sprue,* and *Whipple's disease.* Malabsorption may also be associated with pernicious anemia, iron-deficiency anemia, and the rare hereditary disease cystic fibrosis. It may result from a lack or insufficiency of an intestinal enzyme, as in chronic pancreatitis or *lactose intolerance,* or from surgery on the stomach (gastrectomy) that changes the climate of the small intestine.

CELIAC DISEASE

Celiac disease affects both children and adults, but it is nearly always discovered and diagnosed in childhood. It is a congenital, hereditary disorder caused by an allergy to gluten, a cereal protein found in wheat and rye and, to a lesser degree, in barley and oats. When the lining of the small intestine comes into contact with gluten, it reacts by thinning out and becoming smooth (it is normally covered with villi, small finger-like projections through which nutrients are absorbed into the bloodstream). As a result of the allergic reaction, absorption is affected, sometimes very severely.

The symptoms of celiac disease usually begin to appear a few weeks after cereals are first introduced into a baby's diet (generally at about six months of age). The baby fails to thrive and may even lose weight. He or she is fretful and pale because of a lack of iron. The stools are loose, light-colored, bulky, and foul-smelling, and there is painful abdominal bloating. A swollen stomach contrasts with an otherwise undernourished appearance.

Celiac disease is treated by completely excluding wheat, rye, and other grain gluten from the diet. Advice from a dietician will be needed to identify the foods that must be avoided since gluten is widely used in many commercially prepared products—not only bread and cookies but soups, gravies, hot dogs, ice cream, and many other foods. Within a few weeks of starting on the diet, the symptoms will disappear and the baby will begin to gain weight and thrive.

When the child reaches adulthood, it may be possible for him or her to eat foods containing gluten without ill effects. However, most doctors advise against taking the risk of bringing on a relapse by abandoning a strict gluten-free diet.

It is very rare for celiac disease to appear for the first time in adulthood. When it does, the symptoms are abdominal pain and swelling, weight loss, diarrhea, and a loss of energy. The treatment, as for children, is dietary.

TROPICAL SPRUE

This disease is related in some way that is not fully understood to environmental and nutritional conditions. It affects both the indigenous population and newcomers in the Caribbean, south India, and Southeast Asia. Changes occur in the structure of the intestinal mucosa, and there is malabsorption of a number of vitamins and minerals, notably folic acid.

Individuals with tropical sprue usually have a three-part symptom: a sore tongue, weight loss, and diarrhea. The disease is treated by replacement of folic acid (and other vitamins and minerals as necessary), together with antibiotics. Treatment may take up to six months, depending on the severity of the disease.

WHIPPLE'S DISEASE

This rare disease occurs mainly in men between the ages of thirty and sixty. Its symptoms include anemia, weight loss, joint pain, diarrhea, and severe malabsorption. Untreated, Whipple's disease may prove fatal. Fortunately, it responds to a variety of antibiotics.

LACTOSE INTOLERANCE

In the condition known as lactose intolerance (or lactase deficiency), malabsorption results from a lack or insufficiency of the enzyme lactase. Secreted in the lining of the small intestine, lactase normally functions to break down lactose (one of the sugars in cow's milk) into simpler substances that can be absorbed into the bloodstream.

Some degree of lactase deficiency is normal in about 75 percent of adults of all ethnic groups except those from northwestern Europe. In these, 20 percent have some deficiency. The symptoms of the deficiency may be quite mild—a rumbling stomach, queaziness, abdominal cramps—or they may be severe. As to malabsorption, not only may lactose itself remain completely unabsorbed, but diarrhea may be severe enough to purge other important nutrients before they have passed into the bloodstream. Lactose intolerance, once it is recognized, is easily controlled by a diet that is free of dairy products.

In many people, a severe attack of gastroenteritis may produce a temporary lactase deficiency. The damaged intestinal lining fails to secrete lactase (or sufficient lactase); consequently lactose is not broken down but remains in the digestive tract, causing vomiting and explosive diarrhea. Until lactase secretion returns to normal, as it eventually does, children must be fed some lactose-free substitute for cow's milk, and adults avoid milk products.

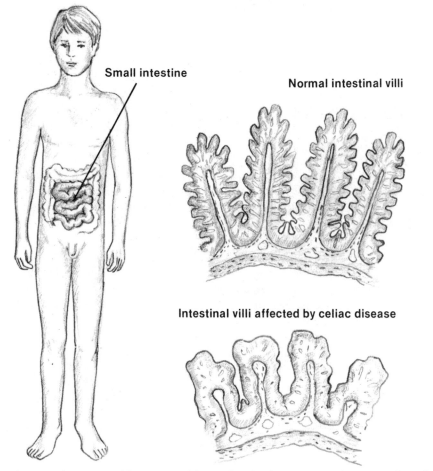

Small intestine

Normal intestinal villi

Intestinal villi affected by celiac disease

In celiac disease, the intestinal lining is unable to absorb gluten, a cereal protein. The villi—small, finger-like projections that cover the intestinal walls and absorb nutrients—react to gluten by flattening and smoothing.

SUMMING UP

Malabsorption is a sign that some disease or condition is affecting the small intestine to the extent that it is not performing its proper function: the absorption of nutrients. In some cases, changes in the actual structure of the intestinal mucosa affect absorption. In others, it is a lack of one or another of the enzymes that promote normal digestion that is responsible. In yet others, the cause of malabsorption may be surgery performed on the stomach or the intestines, or an infection of the intestinal lining.

Once the cause is indentified, it is generally possible to restore proper function to the small intestine—and thus correct malabsorption—by changes in the diet or by medication.

52. Constipation

COMMON CHARACTERISTICS

Constipation is the infrequent and often difficult passage of dry, hard stools. Almost everyone has experienced it at some point, but "being constipated" is a somewhat subjective condition that can mean different things to different people. To allay undue anxiety, it should be pointed out that the *daily* bowel movement ritual that is normal for many people is absent in others who also are perfectly healthy with normal bowel function. Many factors, including overall health, amount of exercise, type of diet, even available time, can help determine an individual's bowel movement pattern. For some people, two, even three movements a day can be normal; for others, two or three times a week is normal.

CAUSES

Still, there are occasions when one's "normal" bowel routine is interrupted and constipation does occur. In rare instances, constipation may signal a tumor in the colon or an intestinal obstruction or other organic cause. Most often, however, there is no single serious cause.

Prolonged inactivity, for example, confinement to bed, can weaken the abdominal wall muscles whose propulsive contribution helps move the stool through the intestines. Other causes of constipation include overdependence on laxatives, inadequate roughage in the diet, frequent postponement of bowel movements despite the body's urgings, insufficient intake of fluids, and drugs such as certain painkillers and antacids.

An active, fast-paced life in addition to a stressful job and family pressures also can interfere with digestion and "regularity." Since bowel movements are sensitive to timing, you can help break a constipation cycle—or prevent one—by setting aside a specific time each day for a relaxed, unhurried visit in the bathroom.

TREATMENT

A diet that emphasizes adequate helpings of foods high in fiber will resolve most cases of constipation. In general, this means eating servings of whole grain cereal and breads, fibrous and leafy vegetables, and raw and cooked fruits. Some fruits, such as prunes, rhubarb, figs, and dates, are natural laxatives in addition to being good sources of fiber. Fiber, which is the undigestible portion of fruits, vegetables, and cereals, absorbs water, making the stools soft and bulky and easier to move through the intestines. A small amount of bran cereal can be added by those who need extra roughage.

Drinking plenty of fluids is also essential. Six to eight glasses of water or other liquids, which may include tea, juice, or coffee, should be consumed every day. Exercise is also important in preventing and treating constipation.

USE OF LAXATIVES

For people whose constipation is not adequately controlled by diet and exercise, careful use of a laxative can resolve the immediate problem. However, laxatives should not be used over long periods because they can induce a "laxative habit," meaning that the body's natural reflexes will become sluggish from lack of activity, thus setting off a cycle of chronic constipation and laxative use. *Note:* Do not take a laxative when you have stomach pain, nausea, or vomiting. These could be symptoms of appendicitis or other serious intestinal disease, and the use of laxatives could worsen the problem.

There are five general types of laxatives, each with different actions. Most are over-the-counter medications that can be purchased without a doctor's prescription, although it's a good idea to ask a doctor's advice.

Bulk Producers

Laxatives that create bulk include products made of psyllium, malt soup extract, or fiber, such as methylcellulose. They work on the principle that a bulkier stool more easily stimulates the body's elimination mechanism. When mixed with fluids in the intestinal tract, these products swell and form a mass that is neither digestible nor able to be absorbed and must be expelled. Filling the bowel with this material triggers the reflex action that moves the stool through the intestine. Bulk-forming laxatives should be taken with a large amount of fluid. They should not be used by patients with an intestinal obstruction or fecal impaction. For others, they are safe and do not promote a laxative habit.

Stool Softeners

People who should avoid straining at stool elimination—for example, the bedridden and post surgery and myocardial infarction patients—can benefit from this type of laxative, which softens fecal matter, making it easier to pass. Preparations containing mineral oil "coat" the stool so it is more easily expelled. Mineral oil alone is also effective but should not be taken over long periods, as it can interfere with the intestines' absorption of fat-soluble vitamins.

Other stool softeners are dioctyl sodium sulfosuccinate and dioctyl calcium sulfosuccinate, which break down surface barriers and allow water and fats to penetrate the stool, softening it and adding to its bulk. When taking these products, drink several glasses of water each day.

Stimulant Laxatives

These preparations work by irritating the intestines so that the muscles begin the peristaltic activity that is part of the process of elimination. They are especially useful for the elderly and people whose intestinal muscles are sluggish or impaired but should not be used by nursing mothers (as they could cause diarrhea in the baby). Because they do irritate the bowel, these laxatives may cause cramps.

Stimulant laxatives usually contain at least one of the following substances: bisacodyl, casanthranol, cascara sagrada, castor oil, danthron, phenolphthalein (yellow or white), or senna. Castor oil works fastest—within three to four hours—and

can be made a bit more palatable if taken in fruit juice. Phenolphthalein (yellow) takes about six to eight hours and is generally thought to be nontoxic, but in rare instances it may cause a rash. Bisacodyl acts in six to eight hours. Cascara sagrada, danthron, and senna preparations move the bowels within six to twenty-four hours. Laxatives containing danthron or senna

Constipation and the Laxative Habit

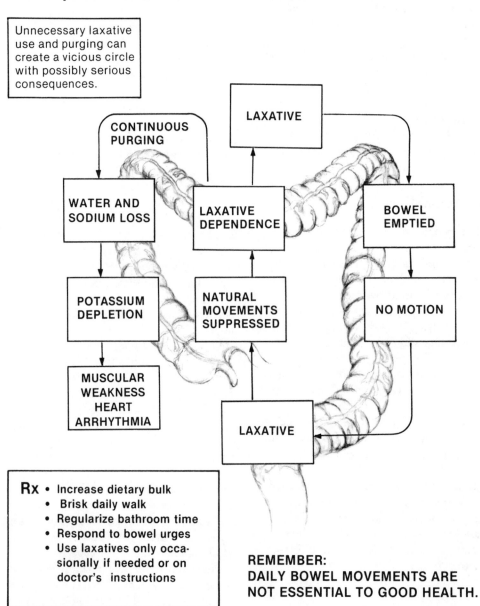

Unnecessary laxative use and purging can create a vicious circle with possibly serious consequences.

CONTINUOUS PURGING

LAXATIVE

WATER AND SODIUM LOSS

LAXATIVE DEPENDENCE

BOWEL EMPTIED

POTASSIUM DEPLETION

NATURAL MOVEMENTS SUPPRESSED

NO MOTION

MUSCULAR WEAKNESS HEART ARRHYTHMIA

LAXATIVE

Rx
• Increase dietary bulk
• Brisk daily walk
• Regularize bathroom time
• Respond to bowel urges
• Use laxatives only occasionally if needed or on doctor's instructions

REMEMBER:
DAILY BOWEL MOVEMENTS ARE
NOT ESSENTIAL TO GOOD HEALTH.

may turn the urine slightly pink, but this is a harmless reaction.

Saline Laxatives

Saline or salt-containing laxatives prevent the intestine from absorbing water. Therefore, the bowel fills with fluid, which in turn triggers peristalsis and evacuation in about three hours. Stools are bulkier than with stimulating laxatives, but most of the contents are fluids. These laxatives contain magnesium sulfate, citrate of magnesium solution, or sodium sulfate. Since the body absorbs some of the salt, people on diets that restrict their salt intake should not use a saline laxative. Of this type, magnesium hydroxide or milk of magnesia usually works less vigorously and somewhat more slowly than the others.

Lactulose Syrup

A relatively new type of laxative, lactulose syrup, can only be obtained with a doctor's prescription. Its mechanism of action is similar to that of the saline laxatives. It restores normal bowel function within twenty-four to forty-eight hours, thereby ruling out prolonged laxative use.

SUMMING UP

Although constipation is a common complaint, it can often be eradicated or controlled by simple life-style changes: exercise more, eat sensibly, drink more water, develop regular but relaxed bowel habits. Remember, "normal" bowel patterns vary in different individuals. If a laxative is needed, take one for only a short time.

53. Hemorrhoids

COMMON CHARACTERISTICS

Hemorrhoids are clusters of varicose veins in the area of the anus or rectum. These swollen veins, which are also known as piles, may be either external (located just outside the anus and covered with skin) or internal (located inside the rectum and covered with mucous membrane). Both may cause bleeding, although the external ones are more likely to produce symptoms, such as pain, burning, and itching.

Hemorrhoids are very common, especially among people in Western industrialized societies. For example, it is estimated that more than half of all Americans over the age of forty have hemorrhoids. In contrast, the condition is very rare among Africans, Asians, and others living in agricultural or developing nations where the diets include more roughage (fiber) and less of the processed foods consumed by Americans.

SYMPTOMS

Blood in the stools is the most common symptom of hemorrhoids. Since this is also an early warning sign of colon or rectal cancer and other potentially serious gastrointestinal disorders, blood in the stool should *always* be checked by a doctor. The

vast majority of cases, however, will turn out to be hemorrhoids.

External hemorrhoids sometimes become enlarged and filled with clots, a condition known as thrombosis. This may cause pain, itching, and burning, as well as some bleeding. In most instances, the clots will be absorbed in a few days, ending the symptoms and leaving harmless little flaps called skin tags.

Internal hemorrhoids are usually painless, but they may bleed enough to cause anemia. Internal hemorrhoids also may be forced downward through the anus during a bowel movement, especially if straining is involved. If they remain outside the anus, they are called prolapsed hemorrhoids and may cause the itching, burning, and pain associated with external hemorrhoids.

CAUSES

The underlying cause of hemorrhoids is excessive pressure placed upon particular veins in the abdominal cavity, especially those into which the rectal veins drain. Chronic constipation is the most common cause of this excessive pressure. Habitual straining during bowel movements is another cause and one that is often related to constipation. Obesity is still another source of abdominal pressure leading to hemorrhoids. Many women develop hemorrhoids during pregnancy; however, these often heal and disappear following childbirth. Still other precipitating factors include liver disorders, intestinal or rectal tumors, and habitual use of strong laxatives.

THE ROLE OF DIET

In recent years, a number of studies have linked low-fiber diets—those high in meats and highly processed or refined flours and cereals and low in whole fruits and vegetables—with an increased incidence of hemorrhoids. This may explain why hemorrhoids are so common in industrialized societies in which highly processed foods are commonplace. Therefore, a diet high in fiber and low in sugar, cholesterol, and other fats and red meats is now considered a sound preventive measure against constipation, hemorrhoids, and possibly other more serious intestinal disorders.

Fiber is the portion of plants that is not digested by the human enzyme system that transforms foods into their basic nutritional constituents. Some forms of fiber, such as bran, are made up mostly of cellulose and can be obtained by eating whole grain breads and cereals. Pectin, another important form of fiber, is found in fruits such as apples, oranges, pears, and grapes. Dried beans and peas, raw carrots, leafy greens, potatoes, and other raw or lightly processed fruits and vegetables are still other excellent sources of fiber. A diet that includes an assortment of whole grain products, fruits, and vegetables will provide ample fiber for most diets.

The abrupt addition of large amounts of fiber—for example, adding miller's bran to foods—should be avoided; otherwise stomach rumbling, gas, and a bloated feeling will result. Also, large amounts of bran may rob the body of niacin and other important nutrients. In short, common sense and moderation should be the rule in adding fiber—or any other element—to the diet. Remember, a doctor's guidance should be sought before making any major dietary change.

LAXATIVE EFFECT OF FIBER

Fiber absorbs a large amount of water as it moves through the digestive tract. This added bulk hastens its passage through the intestines and also produces a softer and bulkier stool that is easier to eliminate than a hard, compacted one.

TREATMENT OF HEMORRHOIDS

Hemorrhoids that cause only occasional minor discomfort can be treated with warm sitz baths. If constipation is a prob-

lem, a bulk stool softener may be recommended. However, suppositories and strong laxatives should be avoided unless specifically recommended by your doctor.

NONPRESCRIPTION PREPARATIONS

A wide variety of nonprescription ointments, creams, and other preparations are available. Many contain a local anesthetic to relieve pain as well as soothing oils, glycerin, starch, or calamine to relieve itching and protect the tissue. These preparations provide temporary relief from the symptoms, but if the symptoms persist or if there is continued bleeding, a doctor should be consulted.

OTHER TREATMENTS

In refractory cases, surgery may be recommended. This may involve surgical removal of the hemorrhoidal tissue, an operation performed in a hospital under general anesthesia. A new procedure called cryosurgery utilizes liquid nitrogen to freeze the tissue. This painless procedure can be done in a qualified doctor's office or a hospital outpatient department. Within a few days, the frozen tissue will slough off, leaving only small skin tabs. External hemorrhoids also may be treated by ligation, which involves applying a rubber band around the hemorrhoid. Within a few days, the tissue will shrivel and slough off. Still another treatment involves injecting the hemorrhoidal tissue with a chemical irritant to promote the body's healing of the swollen veins. Finally, spontaneous healing without treatment often takes place after the precipitating cause is removed. This is particularly true of the hemorrhoids that develop during pregnancy.

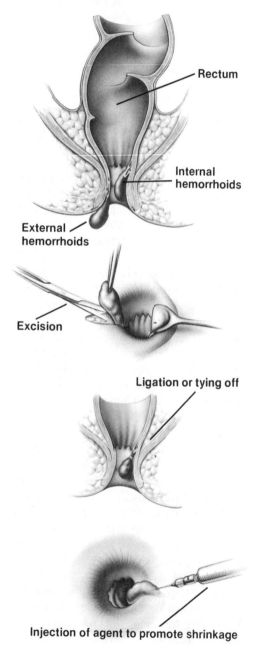

Rectum

Internal hemorrhoids

External hemorrhoids

Excision

Ligation or tying off

Injection of agent to promote shrinkage

SUMMING UP

Millions of Americans have hemorrhoids. Most cases produce few or no symptoms and can be controlled through diet and judicious self-medication. More refractory cases may require removal through surgery, cryosurgery, ligation, or injection. A diet that provides adequate fiber will help prevent constipation, the major underlying cause of hemorrhoids.

54. Intestinal Gas

COMMON CHARACTERISTICS

Although intestinal gas problems have long been a favorite target for jokes and off-color remarks, these problems are no laughing matter to the many people who have them. Symptoms of "too much gas" range in intensity from mild discomfort to severe pain that may interfere with normal activities. Most often, gas problems are chronic, and all too commonly, people who have these complaints try one remedy after another or go from doctor to doctor searching for lasting relief.

There are three basic types of gas problems: excessive belching, abdominal bloating and pain, and excessive rectal gas. Each of these problems has a different cause (or causes), and, for the most part, an individual will have only one of these complaints. Certain steps can be taken to avoid each of these problems, and there are specific medications your doctor may prescribe to treat bloating and excessive rectal gas. Further, it is important to remember that gas

SOURCES OF INTESTINAL GAS

BELCHING
Swallowing air
  - Mouth breathing
  - Chewing with mouth open
  - Talking while chewing
Carbonated beverages

ABDOMINAL BLOATING
Sluggish intestinal muscles
Spasm in intestinal muscles
Starchy foods, beer, alcoholic beverages
Certain digestive disorders

RECTAL GAS
Foods high in carbohydrates or fiber

problems—even those that produce severe, persistent pain—are usually harmless and are only rarely caused by any serious disease.

EXCESSIVE BELCHING

Most people belch once or twice after eating a large meal or drinking a carbonated beverage. This type of belching is the body's normal response to abdominal distress. Some people, however, belch frequently while they are talking, in the pauses between every phrase. Although these chronic belchers may experience a few seconds of relief after a belch, their feeling of discomfort comes back shortly afterward.

Contrary to popular belief, excessive belching is not the result of too much gas being produced in the stomach. Moreover, it is only very rarely a symptom of any serious disease of the stomach or intestines. Rather, belching is caused simply by swallowing too much air. Studies have shown that people who have belching problems swallow a gulp of air immediately before each belch. Chewing gum, chewing with your mouth open, and talking while chewing also promote air swallowing. Most of this swallowed air travels only part of the way down the esophagus; it is then forced back up and out of the body with the noticeable sound we call a belch. The small amount of air that is not expelled passes into the stomach and forms an air bubble, which grows larger with each swallow.

For many people, belching appears to be a nervous habit. Some chronic belchers believe that belching will relieve various forms of abdominal discomfort. However,

belching may actually worsen rather than relieve abdominal distress.

Many people find that once they are aware of the cause of their excessive belching—swallowing too much air—they are able to change the habit. It should be pointed out that medications such as antacids, anticholinergics, and antifoaming agents are of little use in treating excessive belching because they have no effect on its root cause.

ABDOMINAL BLOATING AND PAIN

Abdominal bloating and pain are seldom signs of a serious disease. Nor is this problem due to too much gas in the intestines, as many people believe. Studies have shown that people who suffer from abdominal bloating and discomfort have no more gas in their intestines than others. However, it appears that "bloaters" experience even normal amounts of gas as being painful. Other research has indicated that gas is not propelled through the intestines of people with bloating problems in a normal fashion, either because the intestinal muscles are sluggish or because of a muscle spasm. The spasm may cause gas to be trapped in the loops of the intestines, producing the sensation of bloating.

Because abdominal bloating and pain appear to be due primarily to a problem in moving gas through the intestinal tract, your doctor may prescribe a medication to combat this problem. Antacids, which neutralize stomach acid, have been found to be useful in treating people who have bloating and pain in the upper abdomen. Anticholinergics, prescription drugs that prevent spasms of the digestive tract, provide relief for some who have fullness and discomfort of the lower abdomen.

Several preventive measures can also be taken. Since bloaters find even normal amounts of gas uncomfortable, it is a good idea to avoid frequent belching. Foods that commonly cause gas should be eliminated from the diet. Among these are beans, peas, peanuts, white wheat flour, oats, bran, milk and milk products, raw apples, prunes, and beer and other alcoholic beverages. Walking briskly or jogging after a meal may lessen bloating and pain, since exercise stimulates gas to move through the digestive tract. Lying down after eating, on the other hand, should be avoided. In this position, digestive fluid covers the opening between the esophagus and the stomach, trapping swallowed air in the stomach.

EXCESSIVE RECTAL GAS

Rectal gas problems appear to be produced by eating foods containing carbohydrates that cannot be broken down by enzymes and absorbed into the bloodstream in the small intestine. These undigested and unabsorbed carbohydrates pass into the large intestine, where they are fermented by bacteria—a process that releases gas.

Excessive rectal gas is common in people with various diseases of the stomach and intestines, who may have problems in absorbing carbohydrates that healthy people can digest completely. However, people who are otherwise healthy can also have rectal gas problems. Many individuals have a deficiency of lactase, an enzyme that breaks down lactose, a sugar found in milk and milk products. Because they cannot completely digest lactose, they pass excessive amounts of rectal gas when they have consumed milk or milk products. Lastly, various foods, especially legumes (beans are the most notorious of these vegetables) and certain grains, cannot be fully absorbed, even in normal people, and therefore produce gassiness.

The most effective way to prevent rectal gas problems is to avoid completely, or greatly reduce your consumption of, foods known to cause gas. For this reason, your doctor will probably put you on a diet that is free of foods containing nonabsorbable carbohydrates, milk, and milk products. If the problem does not improve, white wheat flour (which is poorly absorbed) may be eliminated from the diet, or your doctor may advise a diet low in all carbohydrates. Those who have a lactase deficiency may also be given a preparation containing lactase that, when taken with milk, will lessen gassiness.

SUMMING UP

Intestinal gas problems are among the complaints most commonly brought by people to their doctors. Gas problems are of three types: belching, abdominal pain and bloating, and rectal gas. All are commonly thought of as being caused by "too much gas," but in fact only in rectal problems is excessive gassiness responsible. Care in avoiding foods that are known to produce gassiness, and the use of appropriate medications, are helpful in relieving abdominal bloating and pain and excessive rectal gas. Belching can often be minimized by changing the habit that is responsible for this condition: excessive swallowing of air.

It is important to remember that gas problems are only very rarely symptoms of any serious medical disorder.

Respiratory Disorders

---

55. Colds and Flu

COMMON CHARACTERISTICS

Colds and flu—by far our most common viral infections—are often mistakenly thought of as being variations of the same disease. In reality, they are distinctly different disorders caused by different organisms. They are similar, however, in that both are more common during the late fall, winter, and early spring, attack primarily the upper respiratory or airway tract, and have somewhat similar symptoms—runny nose, scratchy or sore throat, feverishness, nasal and sinus congestion, and general malaise. Flu—the popular term for influenza—is distinguished from the common cold by its more severe and generalized symptoms—the "ache all over" feeling, high temperatures, and tiredness, which may persist for several weeks after a bout.

COLDS

More than one hundred microorganisms called rhinoviruses can cause the common cold, which is defined as an infection of the upper respiratory system, primarily the membranes lining the nose, throat, and larynx. Sneezing, tearing eyes, runny nose, and a scratchy throat are common early signs of a cold. In some instances, the infection spreads into the lower respiratory tract, affecting the bronchial tree, the major breathing tubes leading from the windpipe to the lungs. This may develop into bronchitis, which is characterized by wheezing, a deep cough, and difficulty in breathing. These symptoms, especially when they occur in young children, the aged, or people who are debilitated by chronic disease, warrant calling a doctor immediately.

Since a cold is a viral infection, there usually is no point in taking an antibiotic, which is used against bacterial infections. There are some exceptions, however, such as a cold in patients with chronic bronchitis, emphysema, or other pulmonary diseases. In these instances, an antibiotic may be prescribed to prevent an overlying bacterial infection. But these cases are the exception rather than the rule.

Most colds are self-limited and will run their course in five days to a week. The viruses that cause colds are almost always present and are passed from person to person. However, since the germs are so prevalent, avoiding crowds and other preventive measures do little or no good. Similarly, there is no evidence that taking large amounts of vitamin C will prevent a cold, although some studies have found that vitamin C taken at the first sign of one coming on may lessen its severity and duration.

Many other myths regarding colds persist. Contrary to popular belief, getting

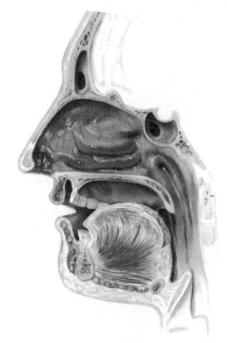

The effect of an upper respiratory infection (a cold) on the nasal passage. Inflammation of the mucosa leads to oversecretion of mucus—a runny nose. Other effects include feverishness, teary eyes, and a scratchy throat.

your feet wet, going outdoors with wet hair, and being chilled do not lead to your getting a cold. In contrast, lowered resistance, such as not getting enough sleep or being generally run down or emotionally "low," may make a person more susceptible to a cold.

FLU

Three different classes of influenza viruses, types A, B, and C, are responsible for flu. Flu, also called the grippe, tends to come in epidemics and, periodically, worldwide pandemics, which occur mostly from November through April. Type A flu is the most common, with widespread epidemics occurring about every three years. Outbreaks of type B flu occur every five years or so, while type C flu viruses are localized and cause only sporadic outbreaks of mild illness.

Flu viruses, particularly type A, are constantly undergoing change, with an entirely new strain appearing every decade or so. These new strains result in the worldwide flu pandemics, which cause thousands and even millions of deaths, as was the case with the Great Flu Epidemic of 1917–18. Other more recent examples include the outbreaks of Asian and Hong Kong flu. Type B flu viruses are also capable of genetic transformation into new strains, but to a lesser extent than type A. When a new strain of flu virus emerges, epidemics are likely to follow because the antibodies that make people immune to the earlier varieties do not protect against the new one. However, killer pandemics such as that of 1917–18 are highly unlikely because scientists constantly monitor the viruses and when a new strain appears in the offing, vaccines against it are quickly developed.

Flu vaccines are now recommended annually for people who are at special risk from flu complications. These include people with heart disease, chronic lung disorders, diabetes, kidney disease, severe anemia, and conditions that lower resistance to infections. Annual flu shots also are recommended for people over age sixty-five. The vaccines are changed every year or two to keep up with changes in the flu viruses, and antigens to protect against several strains of flu viruses are used to give as broad a protection as possible. There is also an oral medication, amantadine, which also can be used in both the prevention and treatment of type A influenza.

TREATMENT

As noted earlier, our major anti-infective agents, antibiotics, are ineffective against colds and flu. There are scores of cold remedies—most of them available without a prescription—that may ease some of the symptoms. But there is as yet no quick cure. Mild analgesics such as aspirin or acetaminophen will relieve the fever and aching symptoms. Bed rest, plenty of fluids (especially when a fever is present), and a vaporizer to keep the air moist are also helpful.

As for specific cold remedies, most of these contain a combination of ingredients to relieve symptoms. Common ingredients and their functions include:

• Decongestants. Most of these work by constricting the blood vessels and are found in both nose sprays and drops and oral medications.
• Antihistamines. These are included in cold preparations to help dry up the nasal secretions, thereby relieving the tearing eyes and runny nose.
• Expectorants. These are in many cough medications and are intended to help loosen the sputum. They are best used with productive coughs because they help liquefy the secretions.
• Antitussives. These are cough suppressants and help stop a dry, hacking cough that may interfere with sleep or normal activities. They should not be used with a cough that produces sputum, however, in which case the objective is to help the cough bring up the secretions, not suppress it.
• Anticholinergics. These agents are included in some cold medicines to help dry the nasal secretions.

SUMMING UP

From time to time, almost everyone suffers a cold or, less frequently, the flu. Although both diseases can make their victims feel miserable and miss school or work, the vast majority of people recover without complications. The exceptions are usually the very young, the very old, or people who are weakened by other serious or chronic diseases. Any sign of breathing difficulty during a cold should receive prompt medical attention; otherwise, rest and increased fluid intake are the best treatments. A number of nonprescription drugs are available to ease the symptoms, but as yet there is no fast cure for either colds or flu.

56. Asthma

Asthma is a chronic condition in which the upper airways become obstructed, resulting in wheezing and, at times, severe difficulty in breathing. It may be triggered by an allergic response to a particular environmental substance or circumstance—at home, at work, indoors or out—resulting in spasms that obstruct the breathing apparatus. Allergic asthma is presumed to be an inherited tendency, but the mechanisms involved are not fully understood. Onset may begin in early childhood, but in many people asthma starts in adulthood.

Asthma also may be caused by hypersensitive bronchi or chronic lung disease resulting from smoking. Attacks in this type of asthma also may be triggered by environmental factors or other causes such as bacterial infections. Asthma also may occur in people with congestive heart failure or pulmonary edema (fluid in the lungs).

Attacks vary widely in duration, intensity, and frequency. While milder cases are often more of a nuisance than a threat to health, prompt investigation and treatment are advisable if future complications are to be avoided. In typical cases, an attack comes on suddenly and is characterized by distressful efforts to exhale, and as air is taken in, there are spells of coughing and wheezing.

These attacks occur because of the abnormal reaction of the windpipe (trachea) and the bronchial tree to a precipitating stimulus, which constricts the airway passages in the following way: The smooth muscles go into spasmodic contractions; there is a swelling of the membranes that line the bronchioles; and the secretion of

mucus increases. Because this bronchial mucus is abnormally sticky, coughing does not expel it, and it therefore plugs up the smaller air passages.

Since greater difficulty is experienced in breathing out than in breathing in, increas-

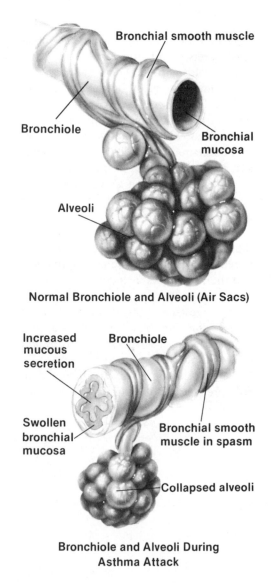

Normal Bronchiole and Alveoli (Air Sacs)

Bronchiole and Alveoli During Asthma Attack

ing amounts of stale air are retained as new breaths are taken. In a severe attack, this leads to a feeling of near suffocation. An attack may be brief, or it may last long enough to demand emergency measures.

CAUSES OF ASTHMA

Well over half a million people suffer from allergic asthma, and in a majority of cases, the specific and immediate cause cannot be identified. Where the disorder runs in the family, and especially when onset occurs in childhood, a particular allergen may be identified as the cause, thus simplifying and hastening treatment. Among the more common offenders are house dust, mold spores, dander from the hair or feathers of house pets, and dairy products, especially eggs and milk.

At any age, a first attack may occur as a result of a respiratory infection, strenuous exercise, or other nonallergenic factors such as sensitivity to cold air. For a significant number of adults, onset may occur because of exposure to occupational hazards, such as chemical fumes or other industrial air pollutants. Sensitivity to tobacco smoke is another major precipitating factor.

Much has been made of the role of emotional stress as a prime cause of the disorder, but most specialists now agree that in both children and adults emotional complications are likelier to be a result of the condition rather than the cause.

TREATMENT

While there is not yet a cure for asthma, more effective medications have recently become available that help control symptoms. When a particular substance has been identified as the cause of the disorder, treatment may involve desensitization by injection. Avoidance of the offending allergen is also recommended but is often difficult, especially when a beloved pet, on-the-job pollution, or very common substances, such as house dust, are involved. In these instances, drug therapy may be recommended as an alternative to life-style change. For all asthma patients, smoking should be avoided.

DRUGS TO TREAT ASTHMA

The most widely used preparations contain ingredients that act as bronchodilators, meaning they relax and widen the airways that link the windpipe and lungs. To treat severe attacks known to originate in an allergic response, an inhalant may be prescribed.

When these medications, separately or in combination, fail to produce the desired results of relaxing bronchiolar muscles, reducing inflammation and swelling of mucous membranes and loosening the obstructive plugs of viscous mucus, a corticosteroid may be prescribed in aerosol form, so that it can be inhaled directly to the airways instead of being absorbed into the body, as would be the case with cortisone preparations taken by mouth or by injection. Steroid drugs should be used under close medical supervision and are usually reserved to treat the more severe asthmatics.

Breathing exercises and biofeedback techniques are among the more unconventional methods now being used to forestall attacks, minimize their unpleasantness, and shorten their duration. However, to avoid falling victim to quackery, make sure these approaches are taught by recognized medical authorities.

COMPLICATIONS AND PRECAUTIONS

Untreated asthma can lead to emphysema because the continued stretching of the bronchial sacs during attacks by accumulations of stale air can eventually enlarge the delicate tissues to the point where they lose their elasticity and cease to function. However, self-treatment is inadvisable and especially dangerous for older people who attribute their chronic shortness of breath to asthma when, in fact, they may be suffering from progressive heart failure. Anyone who experiences breathing difficulty should consult a doctor.

SUMMING UP

Asthma, especially if untreated, can be a disabling disease that afflicts both children and adults. Efforts should be made to identify precipitating causes, especially in children, because effective treatment is then easier to prescribe.

A variety of therapeutic approaches may be tried to control asthma; effective therapy usually involves combinations of treatments that may include drugs, avoidance of precipitating causes, and desensitization shots. Although many people have the mistaken notion that asthma is an emotional disorder, this does not seem to be the case. However, asthma—like any chronic disease—can produce emotional problems that involve not only the victim but other family members as well. Emotional support, for both the patient and family members, is an important element in the overall treatment of asthma.

57. Bronchitis

COMMON CHARACTERISTICS

Bronchitis is an inflammation of the bronchial tubes, or bronchi, the air passages that go from the windpipe into the lungs. The inflammation may be caused by a virus, bacteria, smoking, or inhalation of chemical pollutants or dust. When the cells of the bronchial-lining tissue are irritated beyond a certain point, the tiny hairs (cilia) within them that cleanse the air become immobilized. Thus, as the air passages are additionally clogged by debris, irritation increases. In response, there is a heavier secretion of mucus, which in turn causes the cough characteristic of bronchitis.

ACUTE BRONCHITIS

When a "head cold" becomes a "chest cold," the condition is accurately described as acute bronchitis. This disorder may also follow or accompany the flu, or its onset may occur without prior infection. Acute bronchitis usually runs its course in about ten days. At its most distressing, it can cause general malaise, chest pains, fever, and a hacking, dry cough that eventually produces the obstructive mucus.

Prompt treatment is advisable to prevent serious complications. If, for example, the inflammation should extend downward to the farther reaches of the bronchial tree into the small bronchi (bronchioles) and then into the air sacs, bronchopneumonia results. The most effective way to deal with acute bronchitis consists of the following regimen: Avoid fatigue, stay indoors when the weather is cold and windy, and drink large amounts of fluid to help keep the chest mucus liquefied.

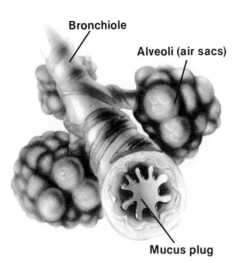

Bronchiole

Alveoli (air sacs)

Mucus plug

Cross section showing mucus plug blocking one of the bronchial tubes.

Self-medication with cough suppressants is inadvisable, since the congestive mucus should be coughed up. However, a doctor may recommend an expectorant to help loosen the mucus. Older people should consult a doctor about whether to take antibiotics to eliminate the risk of serious bacterial infection due to lowered resistance. A doctor should also be consulted when the sputum produced by the coughing is greenish-yellow and thick rather than gray and watery, or when fever goes up and chest pains become severe.

CHRONIC BRONCHITIS

Chronic bronchitis is defined as excessive mucus secretion in the bronchi and a chronic or recurrent mucus-producing cough that lasts three or more months and recurs year after year. In diagnosing chronic bronchitis, it is important to rule out heart disease, lung infections, cancer, and other disorders that may produce bronchitis-like symptoms. Chronic bronchitis may result from a series of attacks of acute bronchitis, or it may evolve gradually because of heavy smoking or the inhalation of air contaminated with other pollutants in the environment.

When the so-called smoker's cough is constant rather than occasional, the likelihood exists that the mucus-producing layer of the bronchial lining has thickened, narrowing the airways to the point where breathing becomes increasingly labored. With the immobilization of the cilia that sweep the air clean of foreign irritants, the bronchial passages become more vulnerable to further infection and an extension of tissue damage.

SMOKING

There is no doubt that smoking is the chief cause of chronic bronchitis, and recent studies indicate that smoking marijuana causes similar damage. Thus, unless some other factor can be isolated as the irritant that produces the symptoms, the first step in dealing with this disorder is to stop smoking altogether. To alleviate symptoms, the doctor may prescribe a combination of medications that will dilate the obstructed bronchial airways and thin the obstructive mucus so that it can be coughed up more easily. A steam vaporizer near the bed can also be helpful in easing chest congestion at night.

EARLY DETECTION OF TISSUE DAMAGE

Insidious and progressive damage of bronchial tissue cannot be detected by chest X-rays. However, screening tests have been developed recently for measuring the early changes in respiratory function that eventually lead to chronic bronchitis and other respiratory disorders. According to these tests, a high incidence of disease of the smaller airways already exists among young people who have smoked for one to five years and seem completely free of symptoms making them highly likely candidates for future respiratory diseases.

HELP FROM THE DOCTOR

For the heavy smoker suffering from chronic bronchitis, self-treatment is inadvisable. Use of over-the-counter medicated inhalers and cough medications, unless specifically recommended by a doctor, may produce undesirable results in dealing with bronchitis. Also, there is no conclusive evidence that massive doses of vitamin C are effective in preventing bronchitis. If smoking is at the root of the problem and you have difficulty in stopping, ask your doctor for guidance. There are numerous stop-smoking programs, ranging from peer-support groups to hypnosis and behavior modification.

SUMMING UP

Bronchitis—an inflammation of the bronchial tubes—may be caused by smoking, air pollution, or viral or bacterial organisms. Complications of a cold or flu may lead to acute bronchitis, which can be treated by bed rest, drinking plenty of fluids, and staying indoors in inclement weather. A series of attacks of acute bronchitis, heavy smoking, or prolonged inhalation of contaminated air may result in chronic bronchitis. Since chronic bronchitis can in fact be life-threatening, it should receive professional attention, no matter what its underlying cause.

58. Pneumonia

COMMON CHARACTERISTICS

While antibiotics have helped to conquer a wide range of infectious diseases, pneumonia continues to rank among the top ten killers in our country. Even so, this common lung ailment can often be prevented or effectively treated with proper medical care.

The lungs consist of a spongy mass of air-filled sacs called alveoli. Air entering through the nose or mouth passes down the bronchial tubes and into the alveoli, where oxygen is extracted and passed into the bloodstream. Simultaneously, carbon dioxide is extracted from the blood, passes up through the air passages, and is exhaled.

When the lungs become infected and inflamed, the alveolar sacs fill up with fluid

and cells and are unable to perform their job. Breathing becomes difficult, and a variety of complications may ensue. Such infection, whatever the source, is called pneumonia.

The most frequent causes of pneumonia are bacterial infections, which can easily be treated with antibiotics, and viral infections, against which antibiotics are powerless. However, distinguishing between bacterial and viral infections may be difficult. Pneumococcal pneumonia is the most common form of bacterial pneumonia, while more severe cases may involve the staphylococcal bacterium.

Pneumonia may also be caused by chemical damage to the delicate lung structures from inhaling a poisonous liquid or gas such as chlorine. Or it may follow blockage of a section of the lung caused by inhaling a tiny bit of food or vomit.

WHO GETS PNEUMONIA

Pneumonia can strike at any time from infancy through old age. Those with chronic lung, heart, or kidney disease or diabetes; the elderly; people who smoke cigarettes; alcoholics; and those who are severely overweight are particularly prone to the disease. Pneumonia may be contracted year-round but tends to be more common during the winter months.

SYMPTOMS

Pneumonia may follow an upper respiratory infection or may begin with cold symptoms. Chills and fever then develop, with temperature rising as high as 105°. The patient feels weak and experiences muscle aches and appetite loss, often with stomach distress. Breathing becomes difficult and is complicated by a cough. As the illness progresses, the cough produces sputum, ranging from green to yellow or rusty in color—the latter indicating bleeding.

Not all of these symptoms will necessarily appear in everyone, but the presence of breathing difficulty without exertion should always serve as a warning sign.

If left untreated, the lung infection can spread to other parts of the body, including the joints, ear, heart, bloodstream, and even the brain, where it leads to meningitis. The more severe complications may cause death.

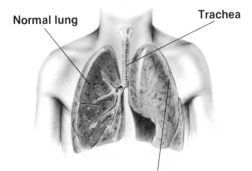

Normal lung

Trachea

Pneumococcal pneumonia of the upper lobe of the right lung. The air sacs (alveoli) are filled with fluid, causing the lung to solidify into a firm, dense mass.

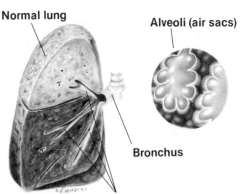

Normal lung

Alveoli (air sacs)

Bronchus

Bronchial tubes

TREATMENT

Before beginning treatment, the doctor will use a stethoscope to listen for abnormal sounds in the lungs and will conduct blood and other tests. Sometimes a chest X-ray may be necessary. Bacterial pneumonia is usually treated effectively with antibiotics. The choice of antibiotic is based on identification of the causative bacterium by means of a culture. Bed rest is essential. To help reduce fever, aspirin and cool sponge baths may be recommended. Plenty of fluids should be consumed. The patient with pneumonia must be monitored carefully because the disease can become severe in just a few hours, often warranting hospitalization and oxygen to facilitate breathing.

Recovery may take ten days to three weeks, depending on the general health of the patient. Those who have complicating illnesses may require an extended period of convalescence.

PREVENTION

Prompt treatment of any upper respiratory infection can help prevent pneumonia. Additionally, a new vaccine against pneumonia is now available to help protect those at special risk. The vaccine only provides protection against pneumococcal pneumonia, and it is not recommended for everyone. However, those who have a chronic disease or who are fifty years of age or older should discuss the option of vaccination with their physicians.

SUMMING UP

Pneumonia is characterized by infected and inflamed lungs, breathing difficulties, chills, and fever. It is usually caused by a bacterial or viral infection and is more common in the winter months. People of all ages are susceptible, with the elderly and the chronically ill being particularly at risk. Pneumonia can be life-threatening if not treated properly.

59. Emphysema

COMMON CHARACTERISTICS

Emphysema is a pulmonary disease in which progressive damage to the millions of tiny air sacs in the lungs makes breathing increasingly difficult. It is often, but not always, accompanied by chronic bronchitis. Together, these conditions are sometimes referred to as chronic obstructive lung diseases, or C.O.L.D.

The chief symptom of the disease, described as air hunger, is typically manifested between the ages of fifty and sixty, and, in more than 80 percent of all cases, is a direct consequence of smoking. While men are about eight times more susceptible than women to emphysema, this ratio, like that for lung cancer and other diseases related to smoking, shows female cases on the rise.

During the respiratory process, the tiny grape-like clusters of air sacs called alveoli expand and contract in unison as air is inhaled and exhaled. As emphysema develops, these chambers lose their elasticity, becoming more and more like a balloon that is flabby from overuse. To compensate for their inefficiency, the air sacs overexpand and then may rupture and form cysts.

Under normal conditions, there is an efficient exchange of oxygen and carbon dioxide in the alveoli. But when the chambers become damaged, the carbon dioxide cannot be expelled completely. It therefore accumulates as stagnant air, interfering with the ability of the lungs to achieve a full intake of oxygen. Shortness of breath results, and as breathing requires more effort, the muscles of the neck, chest, and abdomen have to work much harder to get enough oxygen into the bloodstream. The overdevelopment of these muscles results in the "barrel-chested" look of the emphysema patient. Shortness of breath also leads to a speeding up of respiration, during which inhalation occurs about twenty-five times a minute instead of the normal fifteen.

CAUSES OF EMPHYSEMA

By far the leading cause of emphysema is smoking, particularly over a long period. Heavy smokers exposed to industrial pollutants on the job or environmental pollutants in their community are at considerably higher risk. However, even in light smokers, studies show that emphysema and destruction of lung tissue are not uncommon.

Emphysema may also be hereditary. In 1977 a National Institutes of Health report estimated that perhaps as many as one-third of all cases have a genetic tendency for the disease. When the genetic fault is inherited from both parents, onset of a severe form of emphysema occurs in early adulthood.

DIAGNOSIS OF EMPHYSEMA

While emphysema in its early stages is impossible to detect by X-ray, airway obstruction can be measured by a test where labored breathing is present. The diagnostic test, called spirometry, is done in the doctor's office. The spirometer measures the amount of air that the patient can expel from the lungs as a result of maximum effort. Where measurements indicate that residues of carbon dioxide remain in the lungs, there is reason to believe that the cause is impairment of the air sacs.

Researchers have developed a screening test that identifies the genetic enzyme deficiency before the onset of symptoms. When such potential emphysema victims are identified, they can receive preventive counseling through their private doctor or through the outpatient services of a general hospital.

TREATMENT OF EMPHYSEMA

It is mandatory that all patients stop smoking completely if any improvement is to be achieved. In all cases, close medical supervision and the informed cooperation of the patient are essential. If occupational

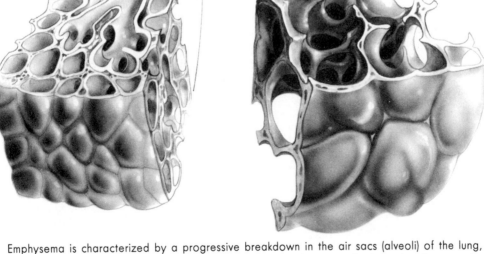

Normal

Emphysema

Emphysema is characterized by a progressive breakdown in the air sacs (alveoli) of the lung, making it impossible to fully exhale. Normal alveoli are shown on the left; alveoli ruptured from emphysema are on the right.

pollutants are a proven cause of the disease, a change of job or early retirement with compensation for the disability are possible options.

While there is no medication that will rehabilitate damaged tissues, a greater degree of comfort and prevention of further damage can be achieved in various ways. For example, when clogged bronchial tubes are an additional cause of obstructed breathing, the doctor can prescribe bronchodilator medicines. Doctors may also prescribe broad-spectrum antibiotics at the first sign of bronchitis or other lung infection that aggravates emphysema. Pocket flasks of oxygen are available for averting emergencies, and oxygen tanks can be provided for bedside use. Portable machines that supply a steady stream of oxygen through a nasal tube can be used to facilitate the performance of routine tasks. All these devices require cautious use and professional supervision.

Self-treatment should also include avoiding exposure to wet and windy weather; keeping respiratory infections to a minimum by flu shots and pneumonia immunization; and losing weight if necessary. Patients also should drink lots of liquid to keep sputum loose and learn how to rid the lungs of accumulated mucus through postural drainage. This is done by lying down with the head lower than the chest so that the force of gravity clears the air passages.

HELPFUL BREATHING TECHNIQUES

Outpatient clinics or a specialist can teach emphysema patients to make maximum use of impaired lung capacity through breathing retraining. Exercises, which make more effective use of abdominal muscles, consist of breathing in slowly at the same time that the abdomen is made to protrude, and then breathing out slowly through pursed lips at the same time that the hands press down on the lower abdomen.

After learning this technique, the patient can practice it while sitting and standing until it becomes more or less habitual. During sleep, respiration is less labored if the foot of the bed is raised.

SUMMING UP

Not smoking is the most effective way to reduce the risk of emphysema. Even patients who have been hospitalized show improvement when they give up cigarettes. For milder cases, medical supervision combined with good health habits and regular checkups will keep symptoms from interfering with most activities. Exercises that improve breathing capacity, instruction in postural drainage, and self-administration of oxygen during emergencies are among the outpatient hospital services available to emphysema patients through their doctor. Medication to widen the bronchial tubes (bronchodilators) may be prescribed to ease breathing. Community social services can be consulted when family counseling is advisable for the patient's well-being and the informed cooperation of other members of the household.

60. Pleurisy

COMMON CHARACTERISTICS

Pleurisy is an inflammation of the pleura, the double-layered membrane that encases the lungs and lines the cavity of the chest. There are two pleurae, one for each lung, and under normal conditions this protective membrane enfolds the lungs so snugly that there is practically no space between its two layers. However, a thin lubricating fluid flows between the inner and outer lining, thus facilitating the free movement of the pleurae as the lungs expand during respiration.

In typical cases of pleurisy, the two sheath-like surfaces roughen and scrape against each other each time the lungs expand. When inflammation causes this roughening, a deep breath produces a stabbing pain that may go from the chest to the neck. In diagnosing this illness with the use of a stethoscope, the doctor hears a sandpapery sound called a friction rub, one of the characteristics of "dry" pleurisy.

Sometimes "dry" pleurisy turns into "wet" pleurisy, commonly called water on the lung and technically known as pleural effusion, indicating that fluid has seeped into the space between the two pleural layers. Small amounts of fluid cause no special problems and may drain off naturally, but a large accumulation is likely to interfere with normal breathing.

CAUSES OF PLEURISY

Pleurisy is said to be *primary* when the cause is a viral or bacterial attack on the tissues themselves or when the inflammation is the result of a growth or chest injury that traumatizes the membranes. When the inflammation is a consequence of pneumonia, tuberculosis, or some other condition originating in the lungs, such as an abscess or tumor, then *secondary* pleurisy is said to exist. While the symptoms in both primary and secondary pleurisy may be the same, the diagnostic differentiation may be essential for correct treatment.

SYMPTOMS OF PLEURISY

Acute onset of dry pleurisy is too painful to ignore, since any attempt at normal breathing produces sharp pain. Efforts to avoid the pain may lead to shallow breathing, which in turn may be accompanied by a dry cough. Headache, rapid pulse, and loss of appetite are not uncommon, and when symptoms are neglected, chills and fever may occur.

When wet pleurisy develops, there may be no pain at all because the membranes are not rubbing against the chest wall. But with the increase in fluid accumulation, greater pressure on the lungs makes it almost impossible for them to expand fully when a deep breath is taken.

Chronic pleurisy, which may be either wet or dry, painful or painless, can be a troublesome aftermath of pneumonia, or it may recur again and again because of low resistance or neglect in pursuing diagnosis and treatment of an underlying lung disorder.

COMPLICATIONS OF PLEURISY

In some cases of dry pleurisy, inflammation and pain will subside following treatment, but breathing will continue to feel "raspy" for some time afterward. Where the inflammation has been prolonged and the healing slow, threads of dry tissue called adhesions may have developed, and here and there they may have tied some areas of the pleural lining to the chest wall. But only rarely are the adhesions extensive enough to impede lung movement. Usually, when the pleurisy has been promptly treated and normal breathing resumed, the adhesions are negligible and those that might exist become so elastic that they offer no discernible impediment to respiratory function.

The complications of wet pleurisy depend on the amount and nature of the fluid. When the accumulation of clear fluid is not absorbed back into the tissues and increases to the point where it compresses the lungs and pushes against the heart, it may have to be withdrawn by needle aspiration. Before this is done, however, the doctor may wish to explore the reason for the fluid accumulation. If, for instance, the cause is a simple virus infection, it is more than likely that the fluid will recede when the inflammation recedes. If the presence of the fluid can be ascribed to heart failure, treatment of this underlying condition with a diuretic and other suitable medication will diminish the fluid.

Sometimes the effusion is caused by a tumor rather than by an infection. If a tumor is suspected, large amounts of pleural fluid are withdrawn from the lung and examined in the laboratory for tumor cells.

The most serious complication of wet pleurisy occurs when the fluid becomes infected and filled with pus. This condition, called empyema, rarely occurs now because of the effectiveness of antibiotics prescribed in the early stages of pleurisy. However, when empyema has set in, the pus may find its way into the air passages, causing the patient to cough up thick, foul-smelling, yellow-green mucus. The pus requires surgical drainage in a hospital.

TREATMENT OF PLEURISY

Pleurisy in and of itself is not a serious disease with dire consequences. When the inflammation is primary and localized and can be ascribed to viral or bacterial infection, it usually clears up without further complications when antibiotics are taken.

Aspirin or some other analgesic is usually recommended to ease discomfort, and bed rest may be considered advisable, especially when fever is present. The doctor may also suggest particular changes in sleeping surface and modifications of sleeping posture to help alleviate respiratory pain.

When the pleurisy is secondary to an underlying lung disorder such as tuberculosis or cancer, treatment is directed at the previous condition.

SUMMING UP

Most cases of pleurisy are effectively treated with antibiotics, and when complications occur, they can be brought under control when promptly diagnosed.

DISTINGUISHING FEATURES OF PLEURISY

CHARACTERISTICS	DRY PLEURISY	WET PLEURISY
Pain	Sharp stabbing pain when breathing	Little or no pain; feeling of pressure in chest
Breathing	Shallow breathing to avoid pain	Difficulty in taking deep breath
Other symptoms	Fever; rapid pulse; headache; dry cough	
Possible complications	Adhesions impeding lung movement; risk of recurrence; chronic pleurisy	Empyema (infection of pleural fluid)

The American Lung Association advises the following: A persistent cough that lasts for more than two weeks, especially when accompanied by painful breathing, should be brought to a doctor's attention without further delay. If you think you have pleu-risy, remember that early diagnosis and treatment are important. Follow the doctor's advice about all aspects of treatment, and if you're told to stay at home, or in bed, or in the hospital, stay there until the return of normal good health.

61. Occupational Lung Disorders

COMMON CHARACTERISTICS

Respiratory disease is one of the most serious health problems originating in the work place. Some occupational lung disorders, such as silicosis caused by inhaling silica (or quartz) dust and black lung common among coal miners, were brought to public attention in the nineteenth century. But not until well into the twentieth century has there been an accumulation of sufficient evidence of cause and effect to identify the common factor in a variety of occupational lung disabilities. This common factor is long-term exposure to various microscopic and submicroscopic dusts, whether the source is inorganic (minerals and metals) or organic (cotton, moldy hay, mushroom spores).

Although some occupational lung disorders may take the form of chronic bronchitis, emphysema, or cancer, most are now grouped under the single heading of dust diseases, technically *pneumoconioses* (from the Greek *pneumo,* or lung, plus *konis,* dust).

While the development of pneumoconiosis depends on the type of dust and the extent (both in time and daily intensity) of exposure, the process by which the disease occurs is the same in most cases.

VULNERABILITY TO DUST DISEASE

The respiratory organs are provided with efficient cleansing devices for eliminating foreign matter that might cause eventual injury to the lungs. Even as far down as the bronchioles—the small air tubes that branch off the bronchial tree—large particles are driven back toward the throat by the movement of hairlike cilia whose vibrations also stimulate the secretion of mucus that carries the offending material upward to be expectorated, or coughed up.

But because this defense mechanism is not sufficiently refined to entrap microscopically fine dust particles, they make their way from the bronchioles downward into the airways of the lungs. Thus the particles, ranging in diameter from one-fifty thousandth to one-five thousandth of an inch, eventually reach the alveoli (air sacs), and there they remain, accumulating over the years of occupational exposure. In many instances, the insidious effects of these dusts may take several decades to manifest themselves, thus postponing recognition of the ongoing progress of damage to tissues. The increase in dust concentration leads to scarring of the lungs (fibrosis) and eventual disablement of lung function.

THE DUST DISEASES

Silicosis

Caused by the inhalation of silica dust, silicosis has traditionally been one of the most widespread of the pneumoconioses because of the number of industries that place workers at high risk. In its pure form, silica is quartz, and where particles are as large as beach sand (also silica), they never reach the lower airway passages of the lungs. However, various aspects of mining (other than coal), as well as pottery making, sandblasting, and work in quarries and foundries, produce a dust fine enough to be deadly. Continued exposure causes fibrous nodules to develop, resulting in shortness of breath as lung function is impaired. Many doctors believe that the dust dissolves within the lungs, producing a chemical poison. More recently, the theory has been proposed that the dust triggers a destructive autoimmune process. Silicosis is often complicated by tuberculosis and is also a leading cause of chronic bronchitis and emphysema. Diagnosis is based on symptoms, occupational history, X-rays, and lung function tests.

Black Lung

Officially known as coal workers' pneumoconiosis, black lung results from the inhalation of coal dust without silica. Miners of both hard (anthracite) and soft (bituminous) coal are at high risk, with official estimates at over 100,000 active and retired coal miners suffering from the disease. The death rate from respiratory disease in this group is placed at five times that of the general working population. Simple coal workers' pneumoconiosis may be characterized by slight impairment of

ventilation lung function. If the condition worsens, it is known as progressive massive fibrosis, in which respiratory disability is likely to lead to premature death. Diagnosis usually requires pulmonary function tests, which are considered a more reliable indicator of damage than X-rays alone. Symptoms and occupational history are the doctor's first clue to the nature of the disease.

Brown Lung

Byssinosis, or brown lung, is a progressively debilitating disease caused by an allergy-like response to inhaled cotton dusts as well as dusts from hemp and flax. It was described as a disease entity as early as 1930 in Great Britain. Eventually byssinosis was recognized in the United States as an occupational disease originating in the textile mills.

Unlike some of the other dust diseases, byssinosis cannot be identified by changes in lung tissue, nor does it show up on X-rays. What happens is this: A particular portion of the cotton boll (the bract) contains an agent that produces an organic dust during an early stage of cotton processing. The susceptibility of the individual worker to the allergy-producing properties of the dust determines the acuteness of the reaction. When the dust triggers a release of histamine in the lungs, the result is broncho-constriction, usually described as a feeling of "tightness" in the chest. Because the reaction typically occurs after a dust-free weekend, the early stages of brown lung have been called "Monday fever." However, the condition worsens over the years, with symptoms becoming increasingly debilitating.

The disease pattern starts with something like an asthma attack: acute air hunger, shortness of breath, and a cough caused by the accumulation of abnormal amounts of thick mucus in the bronchial tubes and the consequent narrowing of the airways. Because the air has difficulty moving out of the mucus-clogged passages, a wheezing sound is produced. As such attacks become more frequent and repeated exposure causes unremitting inflammation of the bronchial passages, chronic bronchitis sets in, and eventually, with the rupture of the air sac walls, emphysema is inevitable.

What is not yet understood is the mechanism of byssinosis: why a histamine-producing broncho-constricting agent in cotton dust results in irreversible loss of lung function. Diagnosis is based on occupational history, symptoms, and lung function tests. Chest X-rays are not a reliable source of information about the progress of this disease.

Farmer's Lung

Farmer's lung is the best known of a group of occupational lung disorders caused by the inhalation of vegetable dusts (usually dust spores). Farmer's lung is directly traceable to exposure to moldy hay. Similar pulmonary disorders of the workers in fields and woods are bagassosis, traceable to the moldy fibers of sugar cane after the extraction of the juice; maple bark stripper's pneumonitis; and mushroom picker's lung. Of these farmer's lung has been most closely studied, but the pattern for the others is similar. They are all grouped together as hypersensitivity diseases involving immunologic (allergic) response. Typical symptoms are shortness of breath, chills and fever, and a cough. Continued exposure to the offending spores leads to chronic attacks, with spreading inflammation of the alveoli and a marked interference in lung function. In the United States, farmer's lung has been recognized as a distinct disease entity in the pneumoconiosis category since 1957, when a group of Wisconsin scientists maintained that, on the basis of laboratory tests, clinical observation, and occupational and medical history, the farmers' affliction had uniform clinical features that differentiated it from bronchial asthma and emphysema. Technically known as granulomatous in-

terstitial pneumonitis, it is diagnosed on the basis of occupational history, symptoms, X-ray findings, and lung function tests.

Asbestosis and Asbestos-Induced Cancers (Mesotheliomas)

These are caused by the inhalation of asbestos fibers. The material itself has become an especially sinister health hazard precisely because of its uniquely versatile qualities: It is a fibrous mineral that can be made into thread and cloth, but unlike cotton it is heat-proof, fireproof, and resistant to chemical action and therefore practically indestructible. Until the mounting disability claims on various industries, it has been found everywhere—homes, school, and the work place—and in more than three thousand products ranging from the insulation that lines the air ducts of air-conditioning systems to children's toys. As early as 1975, a publication of the American Lung Association on occupational respiratory diseases pointed out the following:

> Approximately 200,000 workers in this country are directly involved in the production and installation of asbestos products, and another 3 million to 5 million are secondarily involved in the handling of products made from the basic materials, according to an estimate of the National Institute for Occupational Safety and Health.

Why is this material so lethal? Its structure is a partial explanation. Asbestos fibers, visible under an ordinary microscope, are composed of thousands of fibrils so infinitesimally small that there are one million to the inch. These fibrils can be seen only with the help of a powerful electron microscope, and they settle in the lungs without any interference from upper airway deterrents.

Some of the most definitive ongoing studies of asbestos workers and their families have been conducted by Dr. Irving Selikoff, Chief of Environmental Medicine at Mount Sinai Hospital in New York City. He has estimated that 27.5 million workers were exposed to asbestos from 1940 to 1980, and this number does not include their families—the wives who washed the workers' clothes, the children who hugged the workers when they came home from work. Noting that lung cancer is seven times more common in asbestos workers than in the general population, Dr. Selikoff estimates that exposure to asbestos has resulted in 8,000 to 10,000 deaths per year over normal cancer rates.

In spite of the fact that as early as the 1930s industry leaders were keeping files labeled "Dust" in their personal safes, the real extent of the hazard has only recently come to light. It now appears that in addition to causing asbestosis, which with continued exposure leads to lung cancer, another kind of cancer, formerly extremely rare, mesothelioma, can be caused by levels of asbestos so minimal that they do not even cause asbestosis. Mesothelioma is a cancer of the pleural linings of the lungs and chest (a similar membrane, the peritoneum, lines the abdominal cavity and is vulnerable to the same cancer from the same source). It is inoperable and always fatal. Smoking among workers exposed to asbestos seems to compound the cancer risk.

THE OCCUPATIONAL SAFETY AND HEALTH ACT

In 1970, Congress passed legislation that led to the creation the following year of the National Institute for Occupational Safety and Health. It is generally agreed that the increase in disabling occupational lung diseases was one of the prime movers of the legislation. The institute's program includes applied research projects, especially in the area of dose effect studies; hazard evaluations and toxicity determinations when such studies are requested by

workers and/or employers; an annual compilation of a list of toxic substances; and the training of occupational safety and health professionals. (The politics of health and safety, whether on the job or in the environment, continue to be a source of front-page news.)

PREVENTION OF OCCUPATIONAL LUNG DISEASE

The bottom line in the prevention of the dust diseases that have been disabling and killing hundreds of thousands of workers each year is money—money for the improvement of safety measures and of equipment, for the introduction of new processes, and for regularly scheduled on-the-job lung function tests and chest X-rays. The federal benefits received by totally disabled miners and miners' widows run to about $600 million a year. As disabled workers in other high-risk industries and their families press their claims, the figures continue to skyrocket. The flood of claims focuses attention on the fact that environmentally and occupationally related illness is a national problem of potentially vast magnitude.

Individual workers can help protect

A tight-fitting mask should be worn for protection from all substances that can be aspirated, such as spray paint or coal dust.

themselves in several ways. It is important to know what the risks are and to take measures to protect oneself from them. This includes wearing proper masks and other protective equipment; removing all work clothes and showering thoroughly before leaving the work place; and following all regulations intended to reduce the hazards of dust or other hazardous material.

Not smoking is also important. Studies have found that smoking compounds the risk of lung cancer among workers exposed to asbestos. It also exacerbates other chronic lung problems, such as emphysema and bronchitis.

SUMMING UP

Occupational lung problems continue to be a major cause of disability and premature death among workers exposed to various types of dust and other work-place pollutants. Strengthened regulations to reduce the hazards, as well as increased medical surveillance of workers who are at risk, are among the preventive measures now being undertaken. Individuals can help protect themselves by wearing protective masks and making sure that safety standards are observed at all times.

62. Cystic Fibrosis

COMMON CHARACTERISTICS

Cystic fibrosis is a relatively rare inherited disease that affects nearly all of the body's exocrine glands, although with differing degrees of severity. (The exocrine glands—examples are the pancreas and the sweat glands—are those that deliver their secretions through ducts to various organs and surfaces of the body rather than pouring them directly into the bloodstream.) The disease is characterized by persistent, serious lung infections; loose, pale stools that are foul-smelling and float in water; and a failure to gain weight.

Cystic fibrosis is usually first recognized in infancy or early childhood; in about 10 percent of cases, however, it escapes detection until the teens. Among whites, the incidence is about one in two thousand children. In blacks, it is much lower: about one in seventeen thousand. There is no known cure for cystic fibrosis; however, proper treatment can improve life expectancy and maintain health.

GENETIC DISORDER

Although the underlying metabolic defect in cystic fibrosis is not known, doctors have established the pattern of its inheritance. The disease is caused by a single defective gene, which is recessive. That is to say, it will occur only if *both* parents contribute the gene that determines the disease to the fertilized ovum.

About one person in twenty is a carrier for cystic fibrosis, usually without knowing it. These people are free of the disease themselves, yet, since they carry the recessive gene responsible, are capable of transmitting it to future generations. If two carriers have a child, there are a number of different possible outcomes: the child may inherit a normal gene from both parents and so be neither diseased nor a carrier; the child may inherit one normal and one defective gene and thus be a carrier; or the child may inherit a defective gene from both parents, in which case he or she will have cystic fibrosis.

The chances that a child born to two carriers of cystic fibrosis will be born with the disease are one in four. Unfortunately, there is no reliable test for identifying carriers. There is often, however, a family history of the disease. People who have close relatives with cystic fibrosis have the option of seeking genetic counseling before having children.

SYMPTOMS

The first symptom may occur shortly after birth, when the baby is unable to move his bowels because they are obstructed with excessively sticky meconium (this is the pasty, greenish material that fills the fetus's intestines and normally forms a newborn's first bowel movement). The obstruction may be dislodged by an enema, but in some cases surgery may be necessary. This condition—meconium ileus—occurs because the baby's pancreas fails to produce the digestive enzyme that normally breaks up the meconium, making it soft and easily passed out of the bowel.

Only one in four babies with cystic fibrosis has meconium ileus. In the others, the first symptoms may be foul-smelling stools and a failure to put on weight despite a good appetite, or the development of pneumonia in the first few weeks of life. The digestive symptoms are the result of abnormalities in the pancreas: the gland does not produce sufficient quantities of the enzymes that normally break down proteins, fats, and carbohydrates so that they can be absorbed into the bloodstream. Thus fats and other nutrients pass out of the body largely unabsorbed. The respiratory symptoms are due to malfunctioning of the exocrine glands that line the bronchial tubes. These glands usually produce a thin mucus that is easily coughed up, together with any bacteria that may have been trapped in it. In cystic fibrosis, however, the mucus is thick and sticky and tends to clog the tubes. Bacteria multiply readily in the choked airways, causing chronic bronchitis and numerous attacks of pneumonia. As the child gets older, he or she may develop shortness of breath and difficulty breathing because the thick mucus secretions hamper the exchange of oxygen and carbon dioxide in the lungs.

Among the other exocrine glands affected by cystic fibrosis are the sweat glands, which produce excessive amounts of salt. (This can be tasted on the baby's skin.) In hot weather, or when a child has

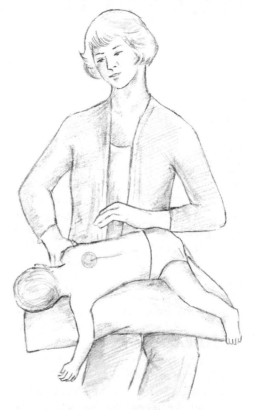

The proper position for postural drainage of babies with cystic fibrosis.

a fever, heavy sweating may result in a serious loss of salt.

DIAGNOSIS AND TREATMENT

The earlier the disease is diagnosed and treatment started, the better the outlook for the child. In those cases where the first signs of the disease are meconium ileus, or foul-smelling stools and failure to gain weight soon after birth, the doctor will follow up on the symptoms. However, when the predominant problem is respiratory infection and this does not develop until the child is several weeks old, the parents may be the first to be aware that anything is wrong. The diagnosis of cystic fibrosis can be made with certainty on the basis of tests showing elevated levels of sodium and chloride in the child's sweat and tests that measure the secretion of digestive enzymes from the pancreas.

Treatment involves giving extracts of animal pancreas—in the form of powder, tablets, or capsules—to replace the missing or insufficient pancreatic enzymes. A diet low in fat and high in protein will be prescribed, and the child will be given multivitamins and additional amounts of vitamins A, D, and E—the fat-soluble vitamins.

To keep the lungs as free of mucus as possible, the child will need regular physiotherapy, which can be learned by parents and done at home. The basic technique is postural drainage, which involves placing the body in such a position that fluid drains from the lungs by force of gravity and can then be coughed up. Cold-mist (aerosol) humidifiers are also used to keep the bronchial tubes clear. When respiratory infections occur, they should be treated with appropriate antibiotics.

SUMMING UP

Modern treatment has improved the life expectancy for many children with cystic fibrosis. Of those diagnosed in infancy and treated in centers that specialize in the disease, more than half live to young adulthood. Many are able to marry and earn their own living. In other cases, although the life expectancy is not long, health can be maintained to a great extent by preventing pulmonary complications or by treating them promptly when they do occur.

Section Six:
Urological Problems

---

63. Urinary Tract Infections

COMMON CHARACTERISTICS

Infections of various types are among the most common disorders affecting the urinary tract, with the kidney, bladder, and prostate being the most frequent sites. Although the onset of a urinary tract infection may be insidious and silent, more typically, the infection announces itself by one, two, or a combination of these symptoms: fever, back or groin pain, and painful, frequent, or bloody urination. In most cases, diagnosis is easily established by microscopic examination of the urine and by identification of the causative microorganism.

CYSTITIS

Cystitis, which is an infection or inflammation of the urinary bladder, can occur at any age and in either sex but strikes women more often than men and adults more frequently than children. The most common source of infection is a bacterium called *Escherichia coli,* although other bacteria as well as viruses and fungi may be involved. *E. coli* normally resides in the colon, but it can migrate to the urinary tract, where it multiplies. Gonorrhea also may manifest itself as urinary tract infection. Still another common bladder infection in women is the so-called honeymoon cystitis, which most often occurs among sexually inexperienced women and is related to beginning sexual intercourse. In most women, the problem subsides with time, but there are others who frequently experience cystitis following sex.

In men and children, the leading causes of cystitis are obstructions or structural defects in the urinary tract. A common example—at least among men over fifty—is an enlarged prostate, which impedes the outflow of urine. The urine collects in the bladder and promotes the proliferation of bacteria, leading to infection. If onset of cystitis is gradual, the first symptom is usually an increase in the nocturnal urge to urinate; the victim may find himself getting up three or four times a night, and this frequent urge may persist during the day. In the case of acute onset, there is often a painful, burning sensation during urination, and, not infrequently, the urine itself contains blood and is foul-smelling. A fever or general malaise may also be present. The ureter—the tubes that carry the urine from the kidney to the bladder—also may become infected, a condition known as ureteritis.

DIAGNOSIS

Cystitis is usually diagnosed by observing the presence of bacteria in the urine. Blood in the urine, a symptom that often accompanies urinary tract infections, is not, in itself, proof of infection. Other conditions, such as tumors and injuries, may cause blood in the urine. Long-distance runners, for example, may have a temporary show of bloody urine following a long race—a condition that usually clears up in a few days. In any instance, blood in the urine always should be investigated by a doctor to rule out a serious cause.

It is also important to determine whether the urinary infection is the result of gonorrhea or some other sexually transmitted disease. If untreated, gonorrhea can lead to serious consequences, especially in women, who may develop inflammatory disease of the pelvic organs and sterility.

TREATMENT

Generally, a week to ten days of antibiotic therapy will bring cystitis and/or ureteritis under control. During this time, your physician will probably advise you to drink plenty of water and to avoid alcoholic beverages. If an obstruction is causing the cystitis, once the infectious phase subsides, it will also have to be dealt with, usually by surgery. If the cystitis is related to sexual intercourse, the woman may be advised not to use a diaphragm, which seems to increase the problem. She also should void before and after intercourse. Applying an antibiotic ointment to the perineal area after voiding following intercourse, and again after voiding in the morning, also may help prevent recurrence. If these measures fail, she may be advised to take an antibiotic following sex as a preventive measure.

Although cystitis usually is not a serious disorder, if it is not treated promptly, it may lead to a chronic, smoldering infection that can persist with periodic flare-ups for months or even years. Chronic urinary tract infections are often difficult to treat and may require prolonged therapy with low doses of sulfa drugs.

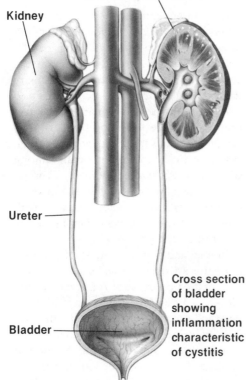

Cross section of kidney showing a pus characteristic of a kidney infection

Kidney

Ureter

Bladder

Cross section of bladder showing inflammation characteristic of cystitis

PYELITIS AND PYELONEPHRITIS

Pyelitis is a bacterial infection of the outer midsection of the kidney known as the kidney pelvis and the tubules that collect the urine. It strikes men and women in about equal numbers. Pyelonephritis involves both the kidney pelvis and the nephron, the part of the kidney that filters wastes from the blood. The latter condition is far more common among women than men and is a frequent complication of pregnancy, labor, and delivery.

Initial symptoms, such as difficulty in urination, foul-smelling or bloody urine, general malaise, headache, and other signs of infection, may be similar to those of cystitis. But pyelitis and pyelonephritis often are also accompanied by a characteristic pain that begins as a dull ache in the small of the back which grows progressively worse as the inflammation and swelling increase. The pain is steady and may radiate to the groin and lower abdomen. Spiking fever, chills, and generalized weakness may occur as the condition worsens.

Pyelonephritis may be caused by bacteria carried to the kidney from some other infection in the body. In contrast, pyelitis is usually caused by an infection arising from the lower urinary tract, particularly in women. Obstructions and structural defects also may be a contributing factor.

DIAGNOSIS AND TREATMENT

Diagnosis should include careful identification of the causative bacteria. This is done by examining an uncontaminated urine specimen. In some rare instances, the infection may be caused by the tubercle bacillus, which leads to a serious condition known as tuberculous pyelonephritis. Once the bacterium has been identified, the proper antibiotics to eliminate it can be prescribed. It should be emphasized that these kidney infections require prompt treatment; if either becomes chronic, permanent kidney damage—or, in extreme cases, kidney destruction—may result.

If a structural problem or obstruction, such as kidney stones, is involved, it should be treated to prevent recurrence. This may involve surgery or other appropriate treatment. In the case of tuberculous pyelonephritis, drugs used to treat pulmonary tuberculosis may be administered. If the kidney is severely and irreparably damaged, surgical removal may be necessary, particularly to prevent spread to the remaining kidney.

SUMMING UP

Urinary tract infections, particularly those involving the bladder and urethra, are common, highly treatable disorders. They do not pose a serious threat to the kidneys and other urinary tract organs when diagnosed and treated in an early stage. However, chronic infections may result in permanent damage as well as difficult treatment. When obstruction or structural abnormalities are contributing factors, these may require treatment to prevent recurrence.

64. Kidney Stones

COMMON CHARACTERISTICS

One of the diverse functions the kidneys perform is to regulate the concentrations of many important chemical substances—calcium, sodium, potassium, and phosphate, for example—in the blood and urine. Under a number of circumstances, this function may be impaired, causing abnormal quantities of minerals and salts to accumulate within the kidneys and form deposits known as stones.

In the United States, 200,000 people are hospitalized annually because of problems associated with kidney stones, and it is estimated that 5 percent of the population suffers from them. Nevertheless, the incidence of kidney stones in the Western world is declining, perhaps because of changes in diet and life style. The condition remains very prevalent in tropical countries.

Stone formation has a tendency to run in families and is more common among men than women. People over thirty years of age are more susceptible than younger individuals; children are rarely affected. Kidney stones are likely to become a recurring problem among those who have suffered one or more attacks in the past.

STONE FORMATION

Kidney stones, technically known as renal calculi, generally form in the middle region of the kidney, the area known as the kidney pelvis. Here urine collects before entering the ureter, the narrow duct connecting the kidney with the bladder. Typically, a stone begins as a tiny speck of solid matter—a bacterium, for example, or a bit of mucus—and grows continually larger as chemical crystals precipitated out of the urine adhere to it. Over a period of years, it may increase to as much as an inch in diameter, although most stones remain less than a quarter that size, and some are even smaller. There may be single or multiple stones in either kidney or in both.

Stones vary in chemical composition as well as in size. A very large proportion (88 percent) have calcium as their principal component, but there are also stones that are composed mainly of oxalate, uric acid, or, much more rarely, cystine. The chemical composition of a stone can often give the doctor a clue to the reasons for its formation and suggest what measures should be taken to prevent recurrence. For example, the presence of calcium stones indicates a possible excess of calcium in the urine, due to insufficient water intake or an excessive consumption of milk or alkaline substances. Uric acid stones are often seen in gout patients. Other precipitating factors include urinary tract infections, urinary obstruction, prolonged bed rest, inherited abnormalities, and certain rare metabolic disorders. A tumor of the parathyroid gland sometimes results in increased excretion of calcium and phosphorus and therefore makes it likely that calcium phosphate stones will form.

SYMPTOMS

Very small stones are passed out of the kidney along the ureter to the bladder and are then excreted with the urine, causing little or no discomfort. A larger stone, moving along the urinary tract, may cause excruciating pain. The pain, referred to as renal colic, strikes in waves every few minutes. It may start on either side of the small of the back and then shift over a period of hours or days to the groin area, indicating that the stone is descending through the ureter. The pain is caused by a spasm of the muscle of the ureter and it recurs with every attempt made by the muscle to force the stone down toward the bladder. Renal colic is often accompanied by blood in the urine, nausea, chills, feverishness, and pain on urination. Once the stone reaches the bladder, its passage through the rest of the urinary tract is usually painless.

Occasionally, a stone will stick in the ureter, blocking the flow of urine and producing back-pressure on the kidney. When this happens, surgery is usually necessary.

A stone with a diameter of one-fifth of an inch or more is likely to remain trapped in the kidney. Unless several are formed, such stones seldom cause problems. Sometimes, however, a stone too large to be passed may obstruct the outlet to the ureter from the kidney. Pressure builds up behind the obstruction, and the kidney itself becomes distended, causing severe pain and increasing the likelihood of infection. Surgery is indicated for this condition.

Some stones that are too large to enter or obstruct the ureter may move about in the kidney and damage the renal tissues. Occasionally, these stones practically fill the kidney pelvis and take on the irregular shape of that cavity. These are known as staghorn calculi.

DIAGNOSIS

The diagnostic tests usually performed to confirm the presence of kidney stones include X-ray films, intravenous pyelogram (X-rays taken after the injection of an opaque dye), blood analysis, and urinalysis. These tests establish the size and exact location of a kidney stone, help determine its effect on normal kidney function, and aid in identifying its chemical composition. An instrument called a cystoscope may also be employed in diagnosis. The cystoscope is a flexible tube with a fiberoptic device. It is passed directly into the urinary tract, without a surgical incision and permits direct visual inspection of the area.

TREATMENT

Treatment may begin with an adjustment of the diet. The intake of calories, calcium, and sodium will all be reduced. Water consumption will be increased, perhaps to as much as eight pints a day, to help flush the stone through the urinary tract. An additional—or alternative—treatment involves the use of medications containing thiazine and phosphates to prevent further stone formation. Medication and dietary therapy combined may succeed in flushing out the stones and halting their further development within three to twelve months.

If kidney stones do not respond to conservative treatment, or if more immediate results are sought, a cystoscopic procedure may be performed under general anesthesia. A small, basket-shaped instrument is inserted in the cystoscope and used either to remove or to crush the stone. In complicated cases, the stone may have to be removed by abdominal surgery.

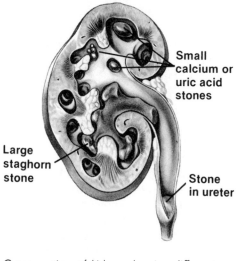

Small calcium or uric acid stones

Large staghorn stone

Stone in ureter

Cross section of kidney showing different types of kidney stones.

PREVENTION

Preventive therapy is advisable for those who have already suffered from kidney stones or who have a family history of stones or other kidney disorders. It usually involves the regular use of medication and the consumption of large amounts of fluid and a controlled diet.

SUMMING UP

Kidney stones are relatively common, affecting about 5 percent of the popula-tion. Most stones either remain in the kidney causing no harm or are passed in the urine with little pain. Sometimes, however, there is renal colic—a severe, spasmodic pain—when a stone is passed. Occasionally a cystoscopic procedure or abdominal surgery is necessary to remove a stone.

65. Kidney Failure

COMMON CHARACTERISTICS

Kidney failure (or renal failure, to use the correct medical term) occurs when the kidneys can no longer clear from the bloodstream the chemical products of normal organ function. Renal failure is not in itself a disease. Rather, it may occur as the result of a wide variety of disorders of the urinary or cardiovascular systems or of several generalized diseases that ultimately affect kidney function.

Kidney failure may be complete or only partial, temporary or permanent. It may begin suddenly (acute failure) or develop slowly over a long period of time (chronic failure). The failure may progress to the point where the kidneys work so poorly that modern technology must take over their function if the individual is to survive (end-stage renal failure).

About thirteen million Americans have potentially life-threatening kidney disease. Many of them have enough remaining kidney function to live near-normal lives for a number of years. Unfortunately, however, for some seventeen thousand people each year, kidney disease progresses to end-stage failure.

THE KIDNEYS

The kidneys, two bean-shaped organs, each weighing about five ounces, are situated just above the waist in the back of the body. They filter the bloodstream twenty-five times a day, removing the chemical products of tissue function and maintaining the proper balance of salts, acids, and water in the blood. Waste materials and excess water move through the tubular system of the kidneys and then to the bladder

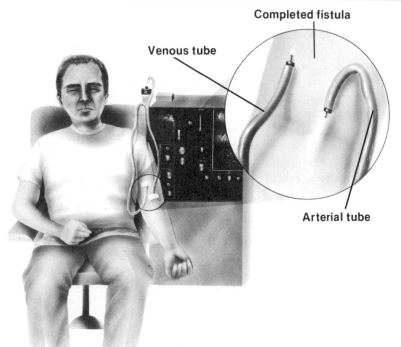

Completed fistula

Venous tube

Arterial tube

During kidney dialysis, two tubes are attached to a fistula in the patient's arm. One draws blood from an artery and passes it into the dialysis machine, where impurities are filtered out. The filtered blood is then returned into a vein through the second tube.

to be excreted as urine. In addition, the kidneys manufacture hormones that help to regulate the blood pressure and the rate of production of red blood cells.

If one kidney is damaged or destroyed, the remaining organ is usually able to perform the necessary functions. The same is often the case if both kidneys are partially damaged—in fact, kidney function can be adequate with as little as 20 to 25 percent of the renal mass. When, however, the kidneys can no longer function adequately— as in end-stage failure—insufficient water is excreted, the balance of chemicals in the blood is upset, and toxic metabolic products accumulate. Life is threatened.

TRANSPLANTATION

The replacement of a severely diseased kidney with a healthy one is the ideal treatment of end-stage renal failure. Kidney transplantation is increasingly common—

more than ten thousand Americans have undergone the operation successfully. Because of the shortage of donated kidneys, however, and difficulties in matching the tissues of donor and recipient, many of those who could benefit from the operation must avail themselves of alternative treatment. Fortunately, medical researchers have succeeded in designing a machine that comes close to replacing the natural function of the living kidney.

HEMODIALYSIS

The word *hemodialysis* comes from the Greek words *hemo* (blood) and *dialyo* (to separate). Hemodialysis machines (sometimes called artificial kidneys) rely on the same principles as does the living kidney— diffusion and filtration of the blood to cleanse it of impurities.

A hollow tube (cannula) is placed in an artery in the patient's arm or leg. The blood is then filtered through the machine, a process during which waste products are filtered out. The purified blood is then returned to the body through a vein. The blood supply is kept moving safely by means of pumps, flow meters, and devices that can trap any bubbles or clots.

Most patients on hemodialysis attend a hospital or dialysis center three times a week. A typical treatment takes from four to six hours. Some patients participate actively in the procedure, with professional supervision; others rely on the staff. About 10 percent of dialysis patients are treated at home, with the help of a family member or some other person who has been trained in the use of the machine. Home dialysis is considerably less expensive than in-center treatment and gives the patient greater independence. Hemodialysis, either in-center or at home, can be continued safely for many years.

A diet that is low in protein, fluids, and salt is prescribed for patients who have end-stage renal failure. It must be carefully followed in order to obtain maximal benefit from the dialysis.

Many patients on dialysis are able to lead full and rewarding lives, normal in every way except for the regular appointments with the kidney machine. In general, the more independent the patient is able to be, the better the outcome—socially, psychologically, and medically. In any instance, problems associated with dialysis, including emotional ones, should be discussed with your doctor.

CONTINUOUS PERITONEAL DIALYSIS

Continuous ambulatory peritoneal dialysis (CAPD) is a new, alternative technique which does not require elaborate machinery, is relatively easy to learn, and may give patients much greater mobility and independence. The technique is now being used successfully by more than a thousand patients and may soon be available to more.

In CAPD, the peritoneum (the lining of the abdominal cavity) acts as the dialysis membrane. Waste material passes across it into a filtering solution, similar to that used in dialysis machines, in the abdominal cavity. This sterile solution is supplied in a collapsible plastic container and emptied directly into the abdominal cavity by means of an in-dwelling tube. Four or five times a day the solution, now containing waste materials, is drained back into the container and replaced with a fresh supply. Again, your doctor can tell you if CAPD might be suitable for you.

SUMMING UP

In the past, individuals with advanced kidney disease had little hope of survival, but in the last two decades great advances have been made in the management of end-stage renal failure. Transplantation, hemodialysis, and continuous ambulatory peritoneal dialysis now enable many thousands of Americans whose kidneys have ceased to function to live normal and productive lives.

66. Prostate Gland Disorders

COMMON CHARACTERISTICS

The prostate gland is a walnut-sized structure, present only in males, situated deep in the lower abdomen beneath the bladder and surrounding the urethra, the passage through which urine passes from the bladder. During ejaculation, it secretes a substance into the seminal fluid that is thought to stimulate the activity of the sperm.

The prostate may become a site of growths or infections, and because of its immediate proximity to the bladder and the urethra, any prostate disorder is likely to interfere with the normal flow of urine.

PROSTATE ENLARGEMENT

Enlargement of the prostate is one of the most common disorders affecting the gland. The enlargement is due to the enlargement of the cells of the gland (called hypertrophy) and the connecting tissue around the cells. By the age of forty-five most men are in some degree affected, and by age sixty the condition is virtually universal. Often, enlargement occurs without causing troublesome symptoms and requires no treatment. Problems may result when the swollen prostate also becomes rigid, constricting the urethra, and thus impairing the flow of urine. Complete emptying of the bladder may then be prevented, greatly increasing the likelihood of infection.

SYMPTOMS

The symptoms of prostate enlargement may include involuntary urination in minute quantities, difficulty starting urination, increased frequency of the urge to urinate, and an abnormally weak stream of urine, especially at the start of the day. Except in extreme cases there is no severe pain. Occasionally, blood may be present in the urine.

DIAGNOSIS AND TREATMENT

An enlarged prostate is diagnosed by a rectal examination during which the doctor gently probes the gland to ascertain its size and consistency. Treatment of prostate enlargement is not always necessary, but when the condition persists, or when the degree of urinary obstruction is severe, a portion of the gland may have to be removed during a surgical procedure called prostatectomy. There is at present

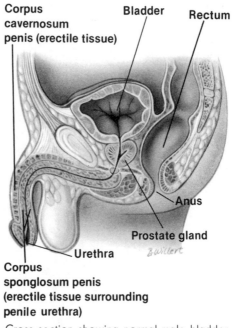

Cross section showing normal male bladder, prostate gland, and ureter.

no proven drug medication for reducing an enlarged gland.

PROSTATE INFECTION

Prostate infection, also called prostatitis, is another common disorder. It may occur as an accompaniment of a urinary tract infection that has spread to the prostate or to a venereal disease. Prostatitis occurs most commonly in men over thirty-five. It may develop gradually over a long period with no symptoms beyond a slight fever, vague fatigue, and an increase in the frequency of urination. It may also manifest itself suddenly in an attack involving severe swelling of the gland, pain at the base of the penis, difficulty passing urine, chills, and fever.

DIAGNOSIS AND TREATMENT

Diagnosis is usually based on rectal examination and a urine sample to identify the infectious agent.

Treatment commonly entails a course of antibiotics. Where the infection does not respond to antibiotics, a minor surgical procedure may be necessary to drain the prostate.

CANCER OF THE PROSTATE

Of the three major types of prostate disease, cancer of the prostate is by far the most serious and one of the most common cancers seen in older men. However, if prostatic cancer is detected in its early

stages, it is highly curable, and because of its slow rate of growth and its tendency to remain localized, it often requires no treatment at all. In fact, nearly all males who have reached the age of eighty have small amounts of this cancer in their prostate.

SYMPTOMS AND TREATMENT

Symptoms may include difficulty urinating or traces of blood in the urine, as well as other symptoms characteristic of prostate enlargement. But there may be no symptoms at all of the early development of the cancer.

Treatment depends upon the state of development of the disease, as well as on the age of the patient and his medical history. Where the cancer shows signs of having spread to other areas, the prostate gland may have to be removed surgically, followed by medication with the female sex hormone estrogen, which discourages further growths. The treatment may then be completed with radiation therapy to prevent further spreading.

SUMMING UP

The most important key to treating disorders of the prostate is early diagnosis. Therefore, an annual rectal examination is recommended for all men over the age of forty-five. This allows the doctor to discover any abnormal growth in its early stages and to make a proper diagnosis. In addition, any changes in urinary function should be investigated by a doctor.

Liver Diseases

---

67. Viral Hepatitis

COMMON CHARACTERISTICS

Viral hepatitis is an infectious disease that causes acute inflammation of the liver. Recognized since early Greek and Roman times, it has become a major public health concern throughout the modern world. Several varieties of viral hepatitis are known to exist today, and although they share similar signs and symptoms, including jaundice—a yellowing of the skin and the whites of the eyes—they are caused by different viruses.

HEPATITIS A

Hepatitis A is transmitted via food, water, milk, clothing, eating utensils, and other objects contaminated by feces. Raw shellfish from sewage-contaminated water is a common source of the disease. It passes easily from person to person, often in epidemics in areas with poor sanitary facilities or overcrowding.

Hepatitis A typically starts with intestinal flu-like symptoms: fever, headache, aching muscles, loss of appetite, nausea, and vomiting. These symptoms do not appear until two to six weeks after exposure to the virus. The virus travels through the bloodstream and lodges in the liver. There it multiplies rapidly, causing infection and, ultimately, swelling, tenderness, and often sharp pain in the upper right abdomen. Bile formed by the liver backs up into the bloodstream, causing the patient's skin and eye-whites to turn yellowish. The breath develops a sickly sweet odor, and the urine turns brown because abnormally high amounts of bile are being excreted through the kidneys. The patient's stools may become much lighter colored because very little bile is reaching the intestinal tract; fever and loss of appetite continue, and even the slightest physical effort may cause exhaustion.

Treatment

Since antibiotics and other drugs are not effective against the hepatitis virus, treatment is largely to ease the symptoms and promote self-healing. This includes a period of complete bed rest, careful attention to diet (no fatty foods, for example), no alcohol for at least six months, and care not to take drugs that may affect the liver. Even in relatively mild cases, hepatitis saps one's energy tremendously, and a lengthy convalescence may be necessary while the damaged liver repairs itself. A complete recovery usually can be expected within three to six months.

Because hepatitis A is so highly contagious, a patient must be relatively isolated from other family members during the acute phase of the disease. The patient should use separate dishes, cutlery, towels, and, if possible, separate, disinfected bathing and toilet facilities. Unfortunately, hepatitis A is also contagious before symptoms appear; thus, these precautions should be taken as soon as the patient suspects that he may have been exposed to hepatitis. Family members can be immunized against hepatitis A for a short time by having gamma globulin injections.

Recovery is a virtual certainty for the hepatitis A patient. In addition, hepatitis A patients develop antibodies that confer permanent immunity to the hepatitis A virus.

Preventive Measures

Both the drinking and the bathing water at camp and beach areas should be checked for purity. Public health departments usually have information on the safety of the water in recreation areas; many newspapers publish such information during the summer months.

The toilet facilities at schools and camps should be carefully examined. Inadequate sewage disposal and unsanitary latrines may contaminate water used for bathing; dirty bathrooms and improperly laundered towels are possible sources of contamination.

Strict personal hygiene should be practiced. In particular, the hands should be thoroughly washed after using the toilet and before preparing or eating food.

Gamma globulin injections should be obtained if it is necessary to spend time in an area where hepatitis is widespread.

HEPATITIS B

Hepatitis B is a more serious form of viral liver disease. It produces virtually the same symptoms as hepatitis A but is caused by a different virus, has potentially more serious consequences, and has a longer incubation period, from six weeks to six months. Hepatitis B, also known as serum hepatitis, is transmitted by contaminated blood or by intimate or sexual contact with an infected partner, as the virus can be present in saliva and seminal or vaginal fluids.

The disease spreads in a number of ways: use of infected needles, for example, for ear piercing, tattooing, acupuncture, or any medical or dental procedures that cut or puncture the skin. Drug addicts who use each other's paraphernalia are at high risk of hepatitis B. It is also spread by carriers who, having failed to develop antibodies after having the disease, are symptomless and do not know they pose a danger to others. There are thought to be about 200 million such carriers around the world.

Treatment

Treatment of hepatitis B is the same as for hepatitis A: bed rest, attention to diet, no alcohol, and no drugs that affect the liver. As the disease wanes and the jaundice subsides, most patients will gradually begin to become active and return to normal routines. The majority will have no long-term effects, but regular checkups may be advised because a small number of patients develop chronic persistent hepatitis, which heals slowly, with recovery sometimes lasting over a year. A more severe variant, chronic active hepatitis, may

DIFFERENT TYPES OF VIRAL HEPATITIS

CHARACTERISTIC	HEPATITIS A	HEPATITIS B
Route of transmission	Fecal contamination	Direct contact with body fluid
Common sources	Food, water, milk, clothing, eating utensils, raw shellfish	Blood transfusions, sexual contact, infected needles, saliva
Symptoms	Fever, headache, muscular aches, fatigue, nausea, vomiting, loss of appetite; later symptoms include yellowing of skin and eye whites (jaundice), abdominal swelling, brown urine, light feces, sweet odor to breath	Same as for hepatitis A, but may last longer and be more severe
Treatment	Bed rest, low-fat diet, no alcohol or drugs that affect liver	Same as for hepatitis A
Long-term consequences	No serious long-term effects; patients develop immunity to hepatitis A virus	May develop chronic hepatitis, cirrhosis or liver cancer; virus remains in bloodstream for long periods or life
Prevention	Follow strict sanitary practices; gamma-globulin injections if exposure is suspected	Immunization for at-risk groups

also develop, leading to cirrhosis of the liver. Hepatitis B also is closely associated with liver cancer.

Former hepatitis B patients may carry the virus in their bloodstream for long periods, even a lifetime. Therefore, it is extremely important that they never become blood donors.

Prevention Through Immunization

One of the most promising advances against hepatitis B is the development of a vaccine, recently approved by the Food and Drug Administration, that may eventually suppress the disease. The vaccine, given in three shots over a six-month period, was made available initially to those most at risk of contracting hepatitis B: surgeons, lab technicians who work with blood products, dentists, dialysis personnel. Thus far, it has proved about 90 percent effective, with protection lasting about five years.

NON-A, NON-B HEPATITIS

There are cases of viral hepatitis that cannot be traced to the A or B virus. They are caused by one or possibly several other viruses and like B can be transmitted by complications of blood transfusion or kidney dialysis. This form of hepatitis can be severe, with considerable yellowing of the skin. There is also evidence of prolonged presence of virus in the blood, and in some patients chronic liver damage may occur.

SUMMING UP

Viral hepatitis may be caused by several different viruses that invade the liver, causing illnesses characterized by flu-like symptoms, yellowing of the skin, and severe debilitation and exhaustion, which may persist even after the symptoms have subsided. In most patients, there will be no permanent liver damage or other lasting effects. Some, however, will become carriers of the disease; others will develop chronic liver disease and, in very rare instances, liver cancer. An important weapon against the most serious form, hepatitis B, is a newly developed vaccine that has thus far proved about 90 percent effective.

68. Cirrhosis

COMMON CHARACTERISTICS

The liver is the largest organ in the body and the most complicated, performing about five hundred different vital functions. It is about one-fortieth of the body's weight and is located in the upper right portion of the abdomen. Because it has the capability of regenerating its own damaged tissue, it is less vulnerable than other organs. However, when damage proceeds to the point of destruction and irreversible scarring, as it does in cirrhosis, liver function becomes increasingly impaired.

The onset of many liver diseases, including the most common—infectious hepatitis—is signaled by the yellowing of skin and eye-whites characteristic of jaundice. Other disorders may be insidiously asymptomatic until they become critically serious. In most cases, however, there is enough evidence of trouble to demand investigation by a doctor. Typical indications include tar-like stools, a swelling of the abdomen, and tenderness and enlargement of the liver itself.

CAUSES OF CIRRHOSIS

Hepatitis—the term for any form of liver inflammation—may progress to cirrhosis. Liver inflammation resulting from chronic alcoholism is the most common cause of cirrhosis; other forms of hepatitis leading to cirrhosis include those caused by bacteria, parasites, protein deficiency, congenital faults in metabolism, and toxic chemicals, including certain drugs.

In the process of unabated inflammation, healthy cells are transformed into fibrous tissue (fibrosis), and unless the condition is reversed by proper treatment, the fibrous tissue turns into the scar tissue of cirrhosis. This scarring obstructs circulation, causing the blood to look for alternate passageways and increasing the pressure in the vessels of adjacent organs, especially in the stomach and lower esophagus.

Liver disease is the seventh leading cause of death in the United States, with mortality rising, not only because of the increase in alcoholism but also because of occupational and environmental exposure to toxic substances in amounts beyond the liver's ability to detoxify them.

An estimated 15 percent of all alcoholics have a cirrhotic liver, but if the cirrhosis is mild enough to have left the major part of the liver unscarred, function may continue to be normal. But as deterioration continues, the patient has a general feeling of weakness and malaise usually attributable to anemia, a loss of weight, and a dimin-

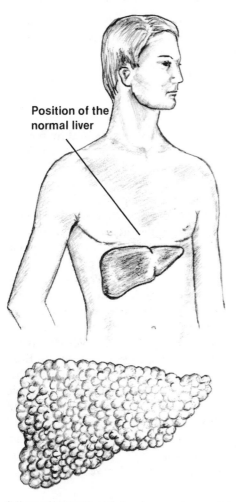

Position of the normal liver

A liver affected by cirrhosis, causing nodules of scar tissue that obstruct circulation

ished sex drive. Swelling of the ankles occurs, and sensitivity to drugs and toxins goes up as the liver's ability to inactivate or detoxify them goes down.

DIAGNOSIS OF CIRRHOSIS

Cirrhosis of the liver is verified by blood and urine tests as well as laboratory tests of liver function. A biopsy may also be performed by obtaining a tissue sample. This is accomplished in a few minutes by inserting a small needle through the skin into the liver. Other diagnostic procedures may include scanning with computerized tomography and ultrasound.

TREATMENT OF CIRRHOSIS

When alcoholism is the cause and damage is not too far advanced, the patient is usually hospitalized to accomplish alcohol withdrawal and to be given a special diet. Blood transfusions may be necessary, and during withdrawal from alcohol, tranquilizers may be given to ease the detoxification. Follow-up counseling for both the patient and family also may be recommended.

When the cirrhosis is the result of continued exposure to toxic substances, rehabilitation efforts must be preceded by a change in occupation or environment. Prognosis for arresting liver damage is good in cases where the cirrhosis has been limited and the cooperation of the patient can be depended on.

FATTY LIVER

Fatty liver is a condition in which the liver cells contain an unusually high level of fat. The condition, which is said to be present in one out of every four individuals, has various causes: injury to the liver by chemicals and drugs, including alcohol, corticosteroids, and industrial toxins; a protein-deficient diet or one too rich in fats; a genetic fault in metabolism. Many people have a fatty liver without being aware of it.

In some cases, a fatty liver becomes swollen and tender, and while it may lead to jaundice, it is rarely the cause of cirrhosis. When the underlying cause is defined, the condition can be reversed.

OTHER LIVER DISEASES

Wilson's Disease
This is a hereditary disorder of metabolism in which there is a progressive accumulation of copper in the liver and other organs. When the copper is released from the liver into the red blood cells, it produces anemia, and as it keeps accumulating in the liver, it produces cirrhosis. Diagno-

sis is based on liver biopsy and blood tests. If untreated, this disease can result in fatal liver failure; therefore, therapy should begin promptly to reduce the accumulation of copper. This is accomplished by a special diet that eliminates all foods high in copper and the prescription of penacillamine (a drug that removes copper from the tissues and blood to be eliminated through the kidneys). Constant monitoring of the patient is indicated and the treatment may have to continue over a lifetime.

Schistosomiasis

Also called bilharzia, this is a disease in which parasites that originate in freshwater snails infect humans bathing in infested waters by penetrating their skin. The adult worm develops in the liver, travels through the viscera, where it produces eggs, and the eggs return to the liver to repeat the cycle. In addition to cystitis and severe diarrhea, this parasitic life cycle results in a cirrhotic liver and an enlarged spleen. The disease is diagnosed by examining the stool and urine for living eggs. Treatment depends on the extent of the infestation. Schistosomiasis is endemic in parts of China, Japan, the West Indies, Africa, the Middle East, and large parts of South America. Travelers should avoid swimming the lakes, ponds, and rivers in these parts of the world.

SUMMING UP

The liver in a normally healthy body is a sturdy and efficient organ that needs no special attention. In a routine checkup, the doctor will be able to tell when the liver is larger than it should be, and the patient will be able to tell when it is tender to the touch. When the health of the liver is threatened by alcoholism or damaging exposure to chemicals, the problem should be dealt with promptly. People on special medications (methotrexate for psoriasis, thorazine or stelazine for severe emotional disturbance, isoniazid for tuberculosis) should undergo periodic liver checks for the possibility of adverse side effects. Even when a certain amount of liver tissue has been damaged, regeneration is possible when the cause has been discovered and dealt with.

Additional information is available from the American Liver Foundation, 30 Sunrise Terrace, Cedar Grove, NJ 07009.

Blood and Circulatory Disorders

69. Anemia

COMMON CHARACTERISTICS

Anemia (the word literally means lack of blood) is not a specific disease. Rather, it is a physical state—a lack of adequate hemoglobin in the blood—for which there are a number of possible causes, some of them potentially serious.

Among the symptoms of anemia are pallor, fatigue, weakness and even fainting, shortness of breath, lack of appetite, and palpitations. While these symptoms are characteristic, anemia can be diagnosed accurately only by blood tests (the color of the lining of the lower eyelid is not a reliable guide). Moreover, anemia should be treated only by a doctor. Taking over-the-counter medications for self-diagnosed "tired blood" may mask the symptoms of a serious but treatable underlying disease.

THE RED BLOOD CELLS

Red blood cells (erythrocytes) account for almost half the blood volume. Their most important component is hemoglobin, a red pigment which combines with oxygen in the lungs and carries it through the circulatory system to all the tissues in the body.

Red blood cells are formed continuously in the marrow of the bones. The mature cells do not divide but exist in the circulation, as simple receptacles for oxygen, for about four months. They are then destroyed by specialized white blood cells. (In a healthy person, there is an exact balance of cells produced and destroyed each day—about 1 percent of the total blood volume, or 250 billion.) The main site for the destruction of old red blood cells is the bone marrow, although the spleen is also involved. When a red blood cell is broken down, one part of the hemoglobin molecule forms bilirubin, the yellow substance that colors bile and the stools; the other, iron-containing part is largely recycled.

Anemia occurs when there is a decrease in the number of red blood cells (or in the amount of hemoglobin they contain) and, as a result, a reduction in the transport of oxygen to the body tissues. There are numerous possible causes, among them insufficient iron in the body (resulting in iron-deficiency anemia); lack of vitamin B_{12} (pernicious anemia) or of folic acid (folic acid deficiency); too rapid destruction of the red blood cells (hemolytic anemia); hemoglobin that is defective because of a congenital disorder (sickle cell anemia, thalassemia); and bleeding that exceeds the bone marrow's ability to release new erythrocytes.

IRON-DEFICIENCY ANEMIA

The body requires a daily supply of iron for the manufacture of new hemoglobin, replacing that lost in the destruction of old red blood cells. In most people, this iron is obtained from reserves (mainly in the bone marrow, liver, and spleen), which are in turn replenished with iron released during the breakdown of cells and iron absorbed from the diet. When these reserves are lost because there is insufficient iron in the diet, or because the iron is not properly absorbed, or because there is chronic or intermittent loss of blood, anemia results.

Iron deficiency anemia due to lack of nutritional iron is most common in children and adolescents who are growing rapidly and in pregnant women (the volume of circulating blood doubles during pregnancy). Premature infants are almost invariably iron deficient since they lack the reserves built up by full-term babies during the last weeks in the uterus. Elderly people who eat a diet of the tea-and-toast type may also suffer from iron deficiency anemia due to nutritional causes.

In other cases of iron deficiency anemia, there is enough iron in the diet but the digestive system is unable to absorb it. The most common cause for this absorption failure is the lack of part of the stomach as a result of surgery done for the relief of a gastric ulcer or a tumor. Another possible cause is celiac disease, an allergic condition of the small intestine in which the intestinal walls are incapable of absorbing nutrients properly (see Chapter 51, "Celiac Disease and Other Malabsorption Problems").

Loss of blood is responsible for the majority of cases of iron deficiency anemia since, when blood is lost, the iron it contains is also lost. If the blood lost is due to an injury, both the blood supply and the iron reserves will be rebuilt quickly. But in women who have heavy menstrual periods —the largest group of anemia sufferers— the iron reserves may become exhausted over time. The same is true in those who have intestinal blood loss (often unnoticed) due to ulcers, tumors, or hemorrhoids. In the elderly, intestinal blood loss, rather than dietary iron deficiency, is the usual cause of anemia.

Iron deficiency anemia often comes on insidiously and almost without symptoms; many women, adjusting to a lowered hemoglobin level, attribute their fatigue to the demands of home and job, or to aging. On the other hand, the symptoms may be easily noticeable and sometimes so severe as to be incapacitating. For example, angina pectoris, severe chest pains that are usually due to a disorder of the blood vessels of the heart, may also be caused by anemia, in which the heart muscle also is deprived of adequate oxygen.

Treatment must be overseen by a doctor since it is possible to accumulate iron to toxic levels, damaging the liver, pancreas, and heart. Iron supplements—in liquid form for children, in tablet form or as injections for adults—should be augmented by a diet high in iron-rich foods. Beef, liver, fish, poultry, whole grain cereals, and dried fruits are rich in easily absorbable iron; the iron present in milk and milk products, eggs, and such vegetables as spinach is less readily taken up by the body. Vitamin C—present in citrus fruits, tomatoes, green peppers, and other vegetables—enhances iron absorption when taken at the same meal with iron.

PERNICIOUS ANEMIA AND FOLIC ACID DEFICIENCY

The production of red blood cells requires two vitamins, B_{12} and folic acid, which are normally absorbed from the diet. If the supply of either is inadequate, the production of erythrocytes falls. Moreover, those that are produced are defective: overlarge and misshapen.

Vitamin B_{12} is derived exclusively from animal products and is present in adequate quantities in most Western diets, with the exception of extremely strict vegetarian diets. A deficiency of vitamin B_{12}, therefore, is usually caused by problems with absorption, typically by the absence of the "intrinsic factor." This is a chemical that is excreted by the lining of the stomach wall and is essential for the absorption of vitamin B_{12}. In some cases, abdominal surgery that removes part of the stomach is responsible for poor secretion, or nonsecretion, of the intrinsic factor—and hence for poor absorption or nonabsorption of vitamin B_{12}. In other cases, the reasons are poorly understood.

The anemia that results from a deficiency of vitamin B_{12} is known as pernicious anemia. In addition to the symptoms common to all the anemias—pallor, fatigue, shortness of breath, palpitations—pernicious anemia is characterized by a smooth, red, sore tongue, indigestion, and a lemon-yellow color to the skin. (This last symptom is due to rapid breakdown of the red blood cells and a consequent increase of bilirubin levels in the blood.) The most serious symptoms of pernicious anemia, however, are neurological: a staggering gait, numbness and tingling in the hands

DIFFERENT TYPES OF ANEMIA

TYPE	USUAL PATIENT	DISTINGUISHING CHARACTERISTICS
Iron deficiency	Pregnant or menstruating women; newborn infants; accident or surgery patients; patients with intestinal bleeding	Fatigue, pallor, shortness of breath, chest pains, palpitations
Pernicious	People who lack vitamin B_{12}	All symptoms listed above plus smooth, reddened, and sore tongue; indigestion; yellowish skin; staggering gait, memory loss; numbness
Folic acid deficiency	Poorly nourished elderly; pregnant women; people who don't eat fresh vegetables; chronic alcoholics	Same as for iron deficiency anemia
Hemolytic	May be inherited or result from adverse drug reaction	Same as for iron deficiency anemia; jaundice
Sickle-cell	Blacks with inherited disorder	Same as iron deficiency anemia; impaired circulation, fever, pain in long bones, abdomen, chest
Thalassemia	People of Mediterranean origin with inherited disorder	Same as for severe iron deficiency anemia

and feet, loss of memory, and confusion. If pernicious anemia is recognized early and is properly treated, these nervous system symptoms can be reversed; delaying treatment can cause permanent damage to the nerves of the spinal cord.

Pernicious anemia, once diagnosed, is easily treated. For most people with this condition, a monthly maintenance dose of vitamin B_{12}—given by injection since it cannot be absorbed through the intestine —is sufficient to ensure normal red cell production. Treatment must be lifelong since the injected B_{12} replaces a deficiency, rather than righting a biochemical defect.

Pernicious anemia is a relatively rare disease, affecting about 1 in 2,500 people. It is a disease of middle and later life, uncommon before the age of forty and most common in those fifty years old or older. People with close relatives who have had the problem are more likely to develop it than is the general population.

Anemia caused by folic acid deficiency occurs more frequently than that resulting from a deficiency of vitamin B_{12}. Folic acid is present in green vegetables but is inactivated by overcooking. People whose diets are low in fresh vegetables frequently suffer from this type of anemia —it is found, for example, in about 10 percent of elderly persons admitted to the hospital. It also commonly affects pregnant women, who need extra supplies of folic acid for the developing fetus and for their own increased blood volume. Up to 10 percent of women carrying twins suffer from a mild deficiency of folic acid and 3 percent of those who are having one child.

When the deficiency is caused by a poor diet, a short course of folic acid tablets and a diet containing adequate fresh vegetables can clear up the anemia completely. In those cases where the problem is one of absorption, folic acid tablets may have to be taken indefinitely.

HEMOLYTIC ANEMIA

Hemolysis (literally, "blood destruction") is the shortening of the normal life span of the red blood cells. Hemolytic anemia occurs when production in the bone marrow cannot keep up with an accelerated destruction of red cells. The problem may be congenital, involving an inherited fault in red cell production, or it may be acquired. In all hemolytic anemias, there is an increased production of bilirubin and an increase in the number of immature red blood cells. The symptoms are those of the other anemias, with the addition of jaundice and sometimes fever, weakness, and vomiting. All forms of hemolytic anemia are rare. Only about one person in fifteen thousand is affected.

One of the common inherited hemolytic disorders among whites is hereditary spherocytosis, in which the marrow produces small, fragile red blood cells. From birth, the balance between the production and the destruction of cells is precarious; a mild infection or a fracture may precipitate a hemolytic crisis, increasing the jaundice and pallor that are the disease's most prominent signs. An acute crisis may be life-threatening. Since the spleen is the main site of red blood cell destruction in this condition, treatment often consists in the surgical removal of the organ (splenectomy).

Acquired hemolytic anemia is frequently due to drugs taken for some other condition which damage the red blood cells and shorten their life span. Alternatively, there may a breakdown in the body's ability to distinguish its own cells from foreign ones, resulting in the formation of antibodies (an autoimmune disorder). Specific antibodies to the red blood cells are found in the blood of many people with acquired hemolytic anemia.

A hemolytic anemia caused by drugs is treated simply by discontinuing the drugs. If the cause is an autoimmune disorder, steroids may be prescribed to lessen symptoms and to speed up the natural recovery that usually takes place over time.

SICKLE-CELL ANEMIA

In sickle-cell anemia, an inherited disease that occurs almost exclusively among blacks, the hemoglobin is abnormal. This defective hemoglobin (hemoglobin S) causes the red blood cells to take on sickle- or oat-shaped forms, especially when short of oxygen. As the sickling worsens, the blood becomes thicker and the red cells more fragile; hemolytic anemia develops; and the blood supply to many organs, including the central nervous system and the lungs, is impaired. Characteristic "crises," with fever and pain in the long bones of the arms and legs, the abdomen, or the heart, mark the course of the disease.

The most important factors in avoiding painful crises and the cumulative damage they cause are good nutrition, prompt treatment of any infection, and the avoidance of dehydration. In addition, people with sickle-cell anemia should avoid flying and high altitudes because crises are precipitated by a lack of available oxygen. Crises are treated by relieving the symptoms—usually with painkillers, oxygen, or blood transfusion—but there is no known cure for the basic inherited defect.

Sickle-cell anemia is inherited recessively. If both parents carry the symptomless sickling "trait" (it is present in up to 13 percent of the black population), each child born to them has a 50 percent chance of inheriting the trait and thus being a carrier, a 25 percent chance of having the disease, and a 25 percent chance of being neither diseased nor a carrier. If only one parent has the trait, there is an even chance that each child will inherit the trait; none, however, will have anemia. The presence of the sickle-cell trait can be determined by a simple blood-screening test. It is possible to diagnose the disease itself prenatally, but only by the specialized technique of fetoscopy,

in which a blood sample is taken directly from the fetus in the uterus.

THALASSEMIA

Thalassemia, or Mediterranean anemia, occurs mainly in people who live in countries bordering the Mediterranean, or in their descendants in other parts of the world. It may occur in a mild or even asymptomatic form, thalassemia minor, or as a severe anemia, thalassemia major.

In this condition, an inherited defect prevents the formation of normal hemoglobin (hemoglobin A); instead, the cells contain hemoglobin F, which is usually found only in newborns. In adults, however, only small amounts of hemoglobin F are produced, and the red blood cells are few in number and have a shorter than normal life span; as a result, people with thalassemia tend to be profoundly anemic.

The only effective treatment is blood transfusion, given regularly on a lifetime basis. This, however, leads to an overload of iron, which may damage the liver and the heart and prove fatal. If the spleen is found to be destroying excessive red cells, a splenectomy may be beneficial. But the underlying defect is incurable, and the disease is often fatal in childhood.

A diagnosis of thalassemia can be made prenatally, by fetoscopy. The parents then have the option of terminating the pregnancy.

SUMMING UP

Anemia is a clinical sign or symptom, not a particular disease. It occurs when the number of red blood cells, or the hemoglobin they contain, or both, fall below the level necessary to carry adequate oxygen to the tissues of the body. The causes of anemia are quite various, ranging from a deficiency of iron, which is easily treated and rarely serious, to inherited defects of the hemoglobin for which no cure is as yet known.

70. Edema

Edema is the abnormal swelling of some part of the body due to the retention of fluid in body tissues. Most often, when physicians refer to edema, they are talking about swelling of the lower legs or ankles. Edema is not a disease itself. Rather, it is a sign that may be related to illness or injury or may simply be related to an inappropriate life style. To treat edema, the underlying cause should be identified; appropriate treatment can then be initiated. While some of the causes of edema are minor, others may be life-threatening; therefore, any unusual swelling should be investigated by a doctor.

SIMPLE CAUSES

Swollen feet and ankles are quite common in people who are on their feet a lot, such as dentists, cashiers, and barbers. The problem usually disappears with rest and an appropriate change in daily habits. If a job requires a good deal of standing, the employee should take hourly breaks to sit down and, if possible, raise the feet for a few minutes. This edema occurs when the veins in the lower extremities fail to keep pace with the arteries, the outward flow of blood lagging behind the inward flow. If the large veins of the lower extremities are actually diseased, the edema brought on by standing is likely to be very noticeable.

Swollen ankles also may be caused by tightness around the upper legs, such as that caused by garters, rolled stockings, or other constricting garments. In these instances, simply not wearing such garments should end the edema.

Weak leg muscles, particularly those in the calf, also cause edema. Older women, whose leg muscles may deteriorate with normal aging, are thus highly susceptible to edema. Deep varicose veins in the legs, another frequent complaint among older people, contribute to edema as well.

Many women experience some edema just before their menstrual periods, which may be noticeable in their breasts, legs, and abdominal areas. It should disappear with the onset of menstruation. Many of the hormonal changes surrounding menstruation, pregnancy, and contraception can contribute to edema. It has been a troublesome problem for many women taking birth control pills. The higher the estrogen content of the pill, the more likely it is that the woman will develop edema. Reducing salt intake may help. In fact, excessive salt consumption also may be responsible for edema in both healthy people and those with special health problems. Since salt tends to hold water in the body, restricting salt intake is frequently advised—and sometimes vital—for those with edema problems.

ORGANIC DISEASE

Edema also can be a sign of the onset of kidney, liver, or heart disease. Repeated episodes of leg or ankle swelling, or any unexplained episode that lasts more than a day or two, should be reported to a physician.

A frequent cause of edema is congestive heart failure, a condition in which the heart fails to pump as effectively as it should. When inadequate amounts of blood are circulating, salt and water are retained by the body in the legs and, sometimes, the abdomen. The result can be a

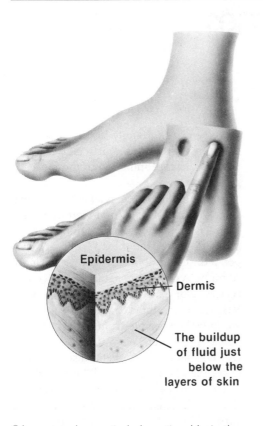

Epidermis

Dermis

The buildup
of fluid just
below the
layers of skin

Edema may be particularly noticeable in the
ankles and feet. Pressure, such as the
pressing of a finger into swollen tissue,
produces pitting, or indentation, that lasts
several minutes.

significant weight gain amounting to ten to
fifteen pounds or more.

Kidney and liver disorders are other
common causes of edema. If the kidneys
are unable to excrete the excess salt in the
diet from the body, a buildup of body fluid
may result. Edema associated with kidney
disease is often first noticed as a puffiness
in the face. Liver disorders, particularly
cirrhosis of the liver, may also lead to ex-

cess body fluids. Some drugs, such as the
beta-blockers used to treat high blood
pressure, also may cause sodium retention
and edema, unless they are given with a
diuretic.

Depending on the cause of edema, the
physician may recommend a variety of
treatments. Those most often recommended are the restriction of salt intake
and the use of diuretics. These are medications that prevent the reabsorption of salt
and water by the kidneys, thus decreasing
edema and diminishing some of the symptoms of congestive heart failure.

RESTRICTING SALT INTAKE

Salt is a natural component of most of
the foods we eat, so we cannot eliminate it
totally from our diet. However, careful
monitoring of food and its preparation can
eliminate much of the salt that is added
during the commercial processing and the
traditional cooking of foods. Remember,
high quantities of salt are hidden in many
foods, particularly canned soups and vegetables, TV dinners, preserved meats (such
as hot dogs, ham, bacon, and corned beef),
cheeses, and baked goods.

SUMMING UP

Edema is a warning sign that some normal body process has gone awry. Sometimes the problem may be localized, and a
simple change in life style may eliminate
the swelling. At other times, it is a symptom of a generalized disease that warrants
treatment. Any recurrent swelling of the
legs or generalized body puffiness or
unusual weight gain should be investigated by a physician.

71. Clotting Diseases

COMMON CHARACTERISTICS

In most people, minor bleeding because of a damaged or severed blood vessel does no harm because the body acts quickly to stop the blood loss. Three mechanisms working in conjunction with one another accomplish this. First, the larger affected blood vessels contract, restricting the blood flow. Second, platelets (one of the three types of cells found in the blood) gather at the site of the wound and form a plug. Third, clotting agents in the blood plasma combine to form a thread-like substance called fibrin, which contributes to the clot that seals the break in the vessel.

In the numerous rare bleeding disorders, of which hemophilia and thrombocytopenia are examples, part of the threefold mechanism for halting blood loss is faulty. Bleeding from a cut may last for hours or even days instead of stopping within a few minutes, as is normal. Minor injuries may result in major bruises (a bruise forms when blood from an internal injury oozes into nearby tissues). In hemophilia, bleeding may also occur in the joints, sometimes resulting in severe disability.

HEMOPHILIA

Of the bleeding disorders, hemophilia is the best known and the most common. It is, nevertheless, very rare, affecting only one in every ten thousand male babies. The disease is inherited in a complex way, being transmitted by women who are carriers and do not themselves have symptoms, to their male children (and, in extremely rare cases, to female children). In about 75 percent of cases of hemophilia, there is a strong family history of the disease; in the remainder, it seems to originate in a chance mutation in the mother's genes.

In hemophilia, there is an inherited deficiency in one of the blood-clotting factors found in the blood plasma, the yellowish fluid in which the blood cells are suspended. In hemophilia A—by far the more common type—the coagulation factor that is lacking or inadequate is known as factor VIII. In hemophilia B, whose symptoms are indistinguishable from those of hemophilia A, the deficient substance is factor IX. This latter form of the disease affects fewer than 20 percent of all hemophiliacs.

The signs of hemophilia begin early in childhood, often shortly after birth, and persist throughout life. The boy may bruise easily; cuts may bleed for a long time. Internal bleeding from a fall may leave the affected limb swollen and painful for several days. However, there is much variability in the bleeding tendency. For some hemophiliacs, the condition poses problems only when they have a tooth extracted or suffer a fairly severe cut. For others, even ordinary daily activities result in bleeding into the joints, with consequent crippling deformity.

Infants and young children should be protected against injury. The sharp edges of the crib and playpen should be padded, and toys should be soft. As the child grows, he will learn to avoid being bruised. While contact sports must be banned, the boy should be encouraged to engage in swimming, running, and similar activities.

Treatment should always be given for any cut or bruise, however minor, since delayed bleeding is a frequent occurrence and may be hard to control. Firm pressure should be applied to a bleeding wound; if the bleeding does not stop, the doctor should be called. A bruised joint should be treated with an ice pack and then firmly bandaged. Again, the doctor should be called because of the possibility of permanent damage to the joint.

The most effective therapy is the replacement of the deficient coagulating substance. Factor VIII is available in a concentrated form prepared from donated blood. When a bleeding episode starts, the factor can be given by injection directly into a vein—in many cases by the hemophiliac himself. Factor VIII disappears rapidly when stored. Hemophiliacs who treat themselves, or are treated by their families at home, must always have a very fresh supply on hand. (Factor IX, which is deficient in hemophilia B, is more stable and remains active for long periods of time.)

THROMBOCYTOPENIA

Blood platelets (thrombocytes) are essential in the blood-clotting process. When an injury to a blood vessel occurs, these cells stick to the walls of the injured vessel and to one another, forming a plug to stop the flow of blood; coagulating agents in the plasma then contribute to the sealing of the wound. In thrombocytopenia, the blood contains only a fraction of the normal number of platelets—and sometimes even fewer. As a result, any bleeding, internal or external, lasts much longer than normal.

The main symptom of thrombocytopenia is a rash of minute purple-red specks (purpura). The rash may be small or extensive and may appear on any part of the body. It is a sign that bleeding is occurring into the skin. There may also be bleeding from the gums, the nose, the gastrointestinal tract, and the genitourinary tract and abnormally heavy menstrual periods.

Thrombocytopenia is somewhat more common than hemophilia and affects both males and females. Its most usual form is idiopathic thrombocytopenia purpura (ITP), in which the body forms antibodies against its own platelets, damaging and destroying them at an excessive rate. In addition, although the platelet-producing cells

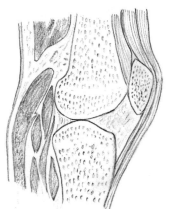

Normal knee joint

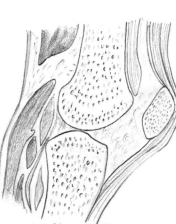

In some cases of hemophilia, the space between parts of the joint becomes enlarged and bleeding occurs within the joint. This condition, called hemarthrosis, may recur if not treated, eventually resulting in disability.

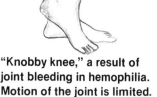

"Knobby knee," a result of joint bleeding in hemophilia. Motion of the joint is limited.

in the bone marrow (megarocytes) are plentiful, they are relatively inactive, contributing to a lowered platelet level. The trigger for the antibody formation in ITP is not known, but occasionally a severe viral infection precedes the appearance of the bleeding symptoms. ITP often occurs for the first time in early childhood. In children, it may be self-limited; in adults, it almost always requires treatment.

Thrombocytopenia may also be drug-induced. Certain antibiotics, diuretics, and anti-inflammatory drugs may damage the bone marrow, affecting platelet production, so that the number drops or the cells are defective. In addition to being a disease itself, thrombocytopenia may also occur as a symptom of other disorders of the blood, including leukemia.

When it is established that thrombocytopenia is caused by a drug and the drug is stopped, platelet levels return to normal within a few days or weeks. In ITP, steroids are usually prescribed to prevent antibodies from destroying the platelets and allow the count to rise. For those who do not respond to steroids, or who have a relapse when the steroids are discontinued, an operation to remove the spleen may be necessary. The spleen, which is not essential to life, is the main site of platelet destruction; the operation (a splenectomy) produces a cure in about 70 percent of cases and an improvement in the remainder. When platelet counts are low and bleeding is severe, platelet concentrates may be given to control bleeding until the more specific treatment—drugs or surgery—takes effect.

SUMMING UP

Bleeding disorders such as hemophilia and thrombocytopenia are rare diseases involving a fault in the three-part mechanism that checks bleeding from a cut or damaged blood vessel. The danger of these disorders lies in uncontrolled or uncontrollable bleeding.

In hemophilia, there is an inherited deficiency of one of the factors essential to the complex process of blood clotting. This is no longer the hopeless disease it once was, but the defect is permanent and the hemophiliac must learn to adjust to his handicap. In many cases, there is still progressive disability because of bleeding into the joints.

In thrombocytopenia, the deficiency is one of platelets, which normally act to form a plug where a blood vessel is damaged. Treatment for this disease, which has several forms, aims at restoring the platelet count to normal, whether by drugs or surgery.

72. Varicose Veins

COMMON CHARACTERISTICS

Varicose veins are veins that have become swollen and twisted because blood has collected or pooled in them. They are usually found in the legs. While most people simply lament the unsightly look of varicose veins, they also can be painful and lead to more serious health problems if they are not properly treated.

HOW BLOOD FLOWS

Blood that has circulated down into the legs and feet must return up to the heart. As the blood travels upward, it is moving against gravity. Several body actions contribute to this upward blood flow. Pressure from the pumping of the heart is the first. The contraction of your leg muscles as you walk or move around also helps the blood to move upward.

In addition, there is a series of one-way valves in the veins that helps the blood to flow toward the heart. These valves are flap-like curtains that lie flat against the wall of the vein when blood is going to the heart but billow out if the blood begins to flow backward. Thus, the valves allow blood to flow through them only in the direction toward the heart.

When varicose veins develop, some of these valves break down so that blood is allowed to seep back down toward the feet. The blood continues to seep backward until it encounters a valve that is functioning properly—one that won't let it seep backward any farther. At that spot, a buildup of blood begins to form. As a more than normal amount of blood accumulates in the area, internal pressure in the vein becomes higher than normal and the thin walls of the vein start to expand, resulting in a varicose vein, or varicosity.

PEOPLE AT RISK

A variety of factors may contribute to a breakdown in normal valve function. Some people are born with a tendency for weak veins and valves. People whose jobs require that they stand for long periods of time, such as department store salespeople, bank cashiers, dentists, and barbers, are also more susceptible. Varicose veins are twice as common among women, whose leg muscles may be underdeveloped, as among men. Further, they are more likely to develop with age or overweight.

There also is a connection between varicose veins and pregnancy. Many women develop them for the first time when they are pregnant. There is an increased amount of blood in a woman's body at this time and, particularly, an increased flow of blood to and from her pelvic area. This increases the pressure on the veins in the legs. The upward flow of blood is further hampered by the pressure exerted by the baby against the great veins in the pelvis. However, varicose veins that occur during pregnancy often clear up after the baby is born.

SYMPTOMS

Enlargement and darkening of the veins are the first symptoms of varicosity. There also may be feelings of tightness or congestion in the veins, tired leg muscles, tenderness in the areas of the veins, or muscular leg cramps. Some people also develop ankle swelling.

If varicose veins are not treated, inap-

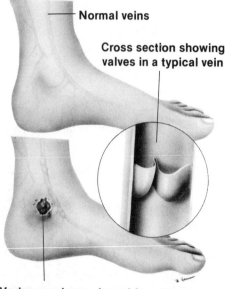

Normal veins

Cross section showing valves in a typical vein

Varicose veins and resulting ulceration

propriate bruising, infection, and even ulceration can develop. Phlebitis—an inflammation of the veins that can lead to blood clots—also is more common in people with varicose veins (see Chapter 73).

TREATMENT

The primary approach to treating varicose veins is self-care. Try to avoid either standing up or sitting down for long periods of time. Keep moving around. People whose jobs require remaining stationary should take frequent breaks to change position and, preferably, raise the legs every hour. This can be as simple as sitting down and placing the legs on a chair that is at least as high as the hips or, preferably, a few inches higher. Both movement and leg elevation help promote the emptying

of blood from the veins. Bicycling is a particularly good exercise for varicose veins. Avoid crossing the legs, which hinders circulation.

Wearing elasticized support stockings also can help relieve pressure. Prescription hose give better support to veins than those available without a prescription. Be careful not to wear tight shoes or garters that restrict circulation.

For cases that are not managed by these simple approaches, medical treatment may be advised. One approach involves injecting a special solution into the vein that causes it to harden and seal off further blood flow. The blood is then forced to reroute itself through healthier veins. While this is a simple office procedure, it rarely brings about a permanent cure.

Surgery may be recommended for severe varicosities. The veins lying just beneath the surface of the skin are tied off and removed. This forces the returning blood to use other veins deep inside the leg. The entire circulatory system of the leg tends to work better when the damaged veins are removed.

SUMMING UP

Varicose veins is a common problem that one can do a great deal to treat or even prevent by attention to daily activities. These include regular exercise such as walking or bicycling, use of support hose, avoiding standing or sitting in one position for long periods of time, and periodic elevation of the legs. Severe cases should be treated medically.

73. Phlebitis

COMMON CHARACTERISTICS

Phlebitis means the inflammation of a vein. It is a common disorder that may lead to the formation of a blood clot, also called a thrombus, that adheres to the wall of a vein and partially or completely blocks the flow of blood. Technically, this is called thrombophlebitis or venous thrombosis.

There are two types of thrombophlebitis. One is a superficial condition, which is painful but is not considered potentially life-threatening. The other, deep thrombophlebitis, warrants prompt medical attention because clots can break free (embolize) and travel through the circulatory system to areas where they can cause severe problems. For example, a complication of deep thrombophlebitis known as pulmonary embolism may occur, in which a clot may travel to tiny blood vessels in the lungs and lodge there. If a large pulmonary vessel is blocked, the result can be fatal. Deep thrombophlebitis and its complications are responsible for the hospitalization of over 300,000 Americans every year, and it is a significant contributing factor for death among people with chronic heart and lung disease. But if phlebitis is spotted and treated early, such complications usually can be prevented or controlled.

PEOPLE AT RISK

Those most likely to develop superficial phlebitis are people with varicose veins. It is also frequently seen in pregnant women, people who are bedridden for long periods, such as victims of stroke or arthritis or those in plaster casts for fractures, and surgery patients. In rare cases, it may strike apparently healthy, active people.

Physicians still do not fully understand why phlebitis occurs. However, it is known that three key factors can create a predisposition to the condition:

• Slowing of the blood flow due to bed rest or inactivity.
• Damage to the vein wall through injury, bacteria, or chemicals, such as certain irritating intravenous solutions used after surgery.
• Coagulation changes in the blood, such as those observed in some women using oral contraceptives.

DIAGNOSIS

Phlebitis most often occurs in the legs. If a superficial vein close to the skin surface is involved, the vein itself may swell and show through the skin resembling a cord-like bump. This may be the only sign, but other symptoms of inflammation could also occur. If deep vein thrombophlebitis

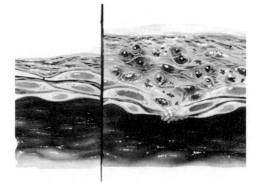

Cross section showing a normal vein (left) and a vein affected by phlebitis. The swelling and inflammation of the vein promote the breakdown of the vein lining, leading to clotting and possible blockage.

is involved, there usually is pain, tenderness, and swelling of the limb. The skin may become bluish in color and feel warm to the touch. You also may run a fever. If the condition is acute, a severe heaviness, aching, or pain in the leg may be felt. Pain probably will be worse when the leg is down and eased when it is elevated.

Sometimes the physician can make the diagnosis simply by observing the symptoms. However, a definitive diagnosis may be obtained by taking a special kind of X-ray photograph after injecting a dye into the bloodstream to show clearly where the flow of blood is stopped by the clot.

TREATMENT

The two types of thrombophlebitis require different approaches to treatment. In deep thrombophlebitis, anticoagulant medication may be prescribed to help reduce the likelihood of future blood clots. This medication may be either injected or taken in the form of pills, depending upon your condition and the drug prescribed. Frequent blood tests may be required to determine whether the blood is being thinned too much; if so, the dosage will be modified. Bed rest and the use of elastic stockings also may be indicated.

If pain is severe, additional medication may be prescribed. However, do not take any other medication—especially aspirin —while you are taking anticoagulants without informing your physician. Aspirin is not to be taken because it also decreases clotting and the combination of the two drugs may lead to excessive thinning of the blood.

Superficial thrombophlebitis may be treated with bed rest, nonsteroidal anti-inflammatory drugs, and, if needed, antibi-otics. In your daily activities, you should avoid staying in one position for long periods, either standing up or sitting down. The key is to keep moving around. Your physician also may recommend applying warm compresses to help ease inflammation and wearing elastic support stockings to help reduce swelling. If you smoke, it is advisable to quit promptly because cigarette smoking may further promote clotting.

While such self-care and medication usually clear phlebitis within a few weeks, persistent, severe cases may warrant more aggressive medical care, including bed rest, continuous warm packs, and leg elevation. If surgery is necessary, the surgeon opens the blocked vein and removes the clot and the inner lining of the blood vessel.

A FINAL CAUTION

If you are taking anticoagulants, you should alert your physician to any of the following symptoms: changes in the color of your urine and stool, prolonged or profuse menstrual flow, bleeding from your gums, abdominal pain, severe headache, diarrhea, weakness, or dizziness. These could be signs of internal bleeding or other problems.

SUMMING UP

While phlebitis may be present without symptoms, it is usually characterized by pain or tenderness and swelling in a particular area, most often the leg. The condition can be troublesome but usually is not serious if treated promptly. Even if treated successfully, phlebitis can recur, and symptoms should be reported promptly to a doctor.

74. Chronic Obstructive Arterial Disease

COMMON CHARACTERISTICS

The first symptom of chronic obstructive arterial disease is usually a cramp-like pain in the calf muscles which is triggered by exertion and quickly relieved by rest. This pain is due to an inadequate supply of blood to these muscles—although the supply is sufficient when the muscles are resting, it is not enough to meet the increased demands of physical activity.

In the vast majority of cases, the disorder underlying obstructive arterial disease is arteriosclerosis—hardening of the arteries. Almost all middle-aged and elderly people suffer from this degenerative condition to some degree. However, it seldom causes any symptoms until it is quite advanced.

ARTERIOSCLEROSIS

In arteriosclerosis, the lumen (the inner tube-like channel) of the artery is gradually narrowed by a buildup of yellowish fatty deposits containing cholesterol, other fibrous substances, and sometimes calcium. The artery, at first partially clogged by these deposits, may later become completely blocked (thrombosed) by a blood clot over a length varying from half an inch to six inches or more. Frequently, a new network of blood vessels develops around the blockage. This collateral circulation may provide enough blood to keep the tissues alive but does not supply adequate blood to the muscles during exercise.

RISK FACTORS

There are several risk factors that make some people more likely than others to develop arteriosclerosis:

- *Cigarette Smoking.* There is strong evidence that cigarette smoking not only helps cause arteriosclerosis but also makes it worse. Cigar and pipe smoking may also contribute, but the evidence is less clear.
- *Diabetes.* Regardless of sex, diabetics are more vulnerable to this disease than are nondiabetics.
- *Hypertension.* Especially after age forty-five, people with high blood pressure stand a greater chance of developing arteriosclerosis than do people with normal blood pressure.
- *Sex.* Men are much more susceptible than women until women reach the menopause. The risk then becomes even.
- *Age.* The older the person, the higher the risk.
- *Heredity.* People whose parents had the complications of arteriosclerosis (heart attack or stroke) at a young age have a greater risk of developing this disease.
- *High blood levels of cholesterol or triglycerides.* Whether caused by diet alone, or by genetic or other factors, those with high blood levels of cholesterol or other fats (lipids) are more likely than others to develop arteriosclerosis.

SYMPTOMS OF CHRONIC OBSTRUCTIVE ARTERIAL DISEASE

Usually, the first symptom is a cramp-like pain, or weakness, tiredness, or numbness, in one or both legs. This usually strikes in the calves, but some people may experience it in their thighs, feet, hips, or buttocks (or, less frequently, in the arms). The pain occurs after walking—especially walking fast or uphill. After a few minutes' rest, the individual can then walk the same distance again before the pain returns. The affected leg may feel cold; in severe cases, the foot may look pale or bluish-purple in color, or may tingle or burn. The pain is a signal from the muscle that the blood supply is inadequate.

Usually, the first symptom of chronic obstructive arterial disease is a cramplike pain in one or both legs, brought on by exertion and relieved by rest. The pain is a signal that the leg muscle is not getting enough oxygen because the artery that supplies blood to the muscle is clogged. The insert shows an artery that is partially obstructed by fatty plaque.

As the disease progresses, it becomes increasingly difficult to walk for any distance without pain. Although the pain is usually brought on by exertion, it may occur in the foot of some people even at rest. This type of pain is persistent and is usually worse at night. It can be eased by letting the leg hang down; it is aggravated by elevating the leg. Pain at rest is evidence that there is severe blockage of the blood flow in the artery.

DIAGNOSIS

Obstructive arterial disease can usually be diagnosed on the basis of a simple physical examination in which the pulses are checked and the leg examined for signs of reduced blood flow. Physical signs include hair loss from the extremities and shiny skin on the toes. Some laboratory tests may also be necessary. The doctor may want to confirm the diagnosis by checking the blood pressure in the leg. This is done by means of a painless procedure, ultrasound.

If the condition is advanced, and surgery is being considered, the doctor may have the arteries X-rayed to pinpoint the exact location and amount of obstruction. This type of X-ray is called an arteriogram.

TREATMENT

The only treatment that can completely relieve the symptoms of obstructive arterial disease is surgery to bypass or clean out the blocked artery. However, since the disease is not life-threatening, nonsurgical types of treatment are usually preferred, except in severe cases. Such nonsurgical approaches do not eradicate the disease but may well alleviate the symptoms and allow the individual to resume his or her normal daily activities without pain.

Exercise is very important; in this way, a compensatory circulation may be built up and improve blood flow to the affected leg. Many people with obstructive arterial disease find that within three months of starting to exercise they can walk much farther, and without pain or discomfort, than previously. Various types of exercise are suitable—jogging, dancing, brisk walking, jumping rope, climbing stairs. The only important criteria appear to be that the exercise be performed in an upright position and that it be performed regularly—every day for half an hour to an hour.

Tobacco use must be eliminated. One study has shown that cigarette smokers (both men and women) are twice as likely as nonsmokers to develop obstructive arterial disease. Another study found that 11 percent of patients with this disease who continued to smoke had to have a leg amputated within five years; in contrast, amputation was not required in any of the patients who stopped smoking.

Preventing infections in the feet and legs is particularly important, since infection (or injury) can easily lead to major problems when the disease is severe. The feet should be kept dry, clean, and warm and the toenails cut carefully and always horizontally. Corns and calluses should be treated by a podiatrist. Shoes should be comfortable and fit well. No medication should be applied to the skin of legs or feet without a doctor's approval, since some medications can cause chemical injury to the skin.

A diet to reduce weight, or lower the levels of cholesterol or fat in the blood, or both, may be recommended. Regardless of body weight, a person with obstructive arterial disease should avoid carrying heavy items.

It is also important to control diabetes and hypertension. Just what the link is between these two ailments and the development or worsening of obstructive arterial disease is open to question. However, it is known that diabetics and people with high blood pressure are more likely to have obstructed arteries than are those without these conditions. Therefore, treatment programs for these problems should be followed carefully.

DRUGS

Drug therapy is not the cornerstone of treatment. However, there are several types of drugs that have been used for patients with obstructive arterial disease. One type, the vasodilators, relaxes the blood vessels, allowing blood to flow through them more easily. There is, however, no proof that vasodilators are of any great benefit. Other drugs prevent blood from clotting or may dissolve blood clots already formed; these drugs are sometimes prescribed in chronic obstructive arterial disease.

SUMMING UP

Arteriosclerotic disease seldom causes any symptoms until it is quite advanced and an artery becomes clogged or completely blocked. Inadequate blood flow in the major vessels in the legs (a common site for arteriosclerosis) is almost always the cause of chronic arterial obstructive disease, a painful condition but not a life-threatening one.

If arterial obstructive disease becomes very severe, surgery to clean out or bypass the blocked artery may be necessary. However, nonsurgical treatments—exercise, eliminating tobacco, a change of diet, and great care in preventing infection or injury in the lower extremities—are usually very effective in relieving the symptoms and making it possible to resume normal daily activities.

75. Raynaud's Disease

Raynaud's disease is a disorder of the blood vessels that affects the fingers and sometimes the toes (and occasionally also the nose and the tongue). In response to cold, the small arteries (arterioles) that supply blood to these extremities go into spasm; with the supply of oxygenated blood restricted, the digits change color and become numb. Emotional factors such as anger and anxiety seem to increase the susceptibility to cold in people with Raynaud's disease.

The condition is far more common in women than in men. It is estimated that, in a mild form, it affects about 20 percent of the female population, almost always occurring for the first time in early adulthood.

The circulatory problem may also occur as a secondary effect of conditions other than cold (it is then known as Raynaud's phenomenon). The regular use of high-vibration machinery such as chain saws or pneumatic drills may damage the blood vessels of the hands and trigger the problem. It may also be caused by a disorder of the connective tissue such as scleroderma, a chronic disease that affects not only the skin but also the joints and many of the internal organs. Raynaud's phenomenon is also one of the common symptoms of Buerger's disease (an inflammatory condition of the small and medium-sized veins that mostly affects male cigarette smokers in their twenties, thirties, and forties) and may, in addition, be the result of emotional stress or a sensitivity to the beta-blocker drugs used in the treatment of cardiovascular diseases.

SYMPTOMS

The chief symptom of Raynaud's disease is a change in skin color of the fingers (or other affected areas). As the arterioles constrict in reaction to cold, the temperature of the fingertips drops quickly to that of the surrounding air and the skin turns color. It may become pale, indicating that arterial spasm is decreasing the blood supply, or bluish, indicating that the tissue is deprived of oxygen, and then red as the blood returns and becomes congested in the arteries. Or the pale stage may not occur and the change may have only two phases, bluish and red. There is seldom any pain, but while the attack lasts—which may be for minutes or for hours—there are usually sensations of numbness, tingling, or burning. Normal color and feeling return when the hands are warmed.

Raynaud's disease worsens only very slowly. In those who have had the problem over a long period of time, the skin on the fingers and toes may become smooth and tight; tissues may be lost subcutaneously because of the inadequate blood supply. Sometimes small, painful ulcers develop on the tips of the digits. In very severe cases, prolonged contraction of the arteries may reduce the blood supply to the point that ulcers on the fingertips, and ultimately, gangrene, develop. This, however, is rare. More commonly, the disabilities of Raynaud's disease are weakness and loss of the sense of touch.

TREATMENT

Keeping the hands and feet warm and dry can prevent many attacks of Raynaud's disease. People with this condition should wear gloves, mittens, thick socks, and lined, waterproof boots when outdoors in cold weather. (Gloves and socks may also be worn to bed.) In extremely low temperatures, it is advisable to stay indoors. Since both caffeine and nicotine constrict the blood vessels, further damaging an already inadequate circulation, coffee, tea, colas, and cigarettes should be avoided. Some doctors prescribe mild sedatives for those with this condition.

Medical treatment for more severe cases of Raynaud's disease aims at encouraging the expansion of the arterioles. Even when the arterial walls have been permanently damaged, vasodilator drugs (agents which dilate the small blood vessels so that more blood is able to flow through) can improve the circulation significantly. Although alcohol is a vasodilator, its use in Raynaud's disease is discouraged because it

PROGRESSION OF RAYNAUD'S DISEASE

PHASE 1—MOST COMMON SYMPTOMS
Constriction of arterioles causing:
1. Change in skin color of extremities
2. Sensation of numbness, tingling, or burning

PHASE 2—MAY TAKE YEARS TO DEVELOP
Progression of symptoms:
1. Skin on extremities becomes smooth and tight
2. Loss of tissue because of lack of blood
3. Diminished sense of touch

PHASE 3—SEEN ONLY RARELY
1. Ulcers on tips of fingers and/or toes
2. Gangrene

ultimately increases the effect of the cold.

When there is progressive disability as the result of the disease, surgery may be performed. The operation, a sympathectomy, severs the nerves that control the arteries' ability to contract. Surgery often abolishes the symptoms entirely, but relief may not last for more than a year or two.

Biofeedback is effective in many cases of Raynaud's disease, reducing the number of attacks in 60 percent of those trained to use the techniques and in some people causing the symptoms to disappear altogether. In biofeedback, patients learn to control what is normally an involuntary response—in the case of Raynaud's disease, the changing temperature of the fingers. With practice, those who have learned the techniques are able to raise finger temperature when they feel an attack coming on, or when they go out in cold weather.

Treatment of the disease when it is secondary to some other condition (Raynaud's phenomenon) depends on the nature of the underlying problem.

SUMMING UP

Most people with Raynaud's disease can learn to live with the condition. It is an annoyance but does not seriously disrupt their lives. Protecting the hands and feet against the cold and avoiding smoking and the consumption of beverages containing caffeine can do much to control the mild form of the disease. If it becomes severe, however, Raynaud's disease may cause serious disability, and surgery may be needed to relieve the symptoms. Unfortunately, the operation is not always of lasting benefit.

Section Nine:
Metabolic and Hormonal Diseases

76. Juvenile Diabetes

COMMON CHARACTERISTICS

Diabetes is a chronic disease in which, because of an insufficiency or total lack of the hormone insulin, the body cannot use the sugars and starches in the diet properly. The full name is diabetes mellitus, the latter word meaning honey-sweet. It is estimated that there are as many as ten million people in the United States today who suffer from the disease, four million of whom are unaware of their condition.

Diabetes takes two forms: insulin-dependent (juvenile onset) and non-insulin-dependent (maturity onset) diabetes. The former, which usually starts during childhood through young adulthood, is characterized by a failure to produce sufficient or any insulin, the hormone needed to regulate the body's use of glucose or sugar. To control the insulin-dependent form of the disease, diabetics must have injections of insulin on a regular—daily or more often—basis.

Insulin is produced by cells in the islets of Langerhans, which are located throughout the pancreas. In insulin-dependent diabetics, the islets produce little or no insulin. The reasons for this are not fully understood. Without insulin, or with insufficient insulin, glucose accumulates in the blood. There is normally some glucose in the blood (about one part in one thousand), but in diabetes the amount rises considerably to dangerously high levels and spills over into the urine.

SYMPTOMS AND DIAGNOSIS

The most common symptom of diabetes is thirst, accompanied by frequent urination (as often as once an hour). There is often marked weight loss, and there also may be repeated infections of the skin, gums, or urinary tract and fatigue, weakness, or apathy. Tingling sensations in the hands and feet, cramps in the legs, and blurred vision are further symptoms. The weight loss occurs because fat and muscle are being burned up to provide energy. In insulin-dependent diabetes, the symptoms usually develop rapidly.

Diabetes is usually diagnosed by a simple test in which the glucose level in the blood is measured; if it is persistently elevated, the patient has the disease.

TREATMENT

As of yet, there is no cure for diabetes, but the disease can be controlled by insulin injections, diet, and a program of physical exercise. The goals of treatment are to relieve the symptoms, reduce the amount of glucose in the blood and urine, and lower the risk of complications. For insulin-dependent diabetics, treatment consists of

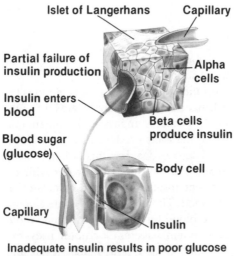

Islet of Langerhans   **Capillary**

Partial failure of insulin production

Alpha cells

Insulin enters blood

Blood sugar (glucose)

Beta cells produce insulin

Body cell

Capillary

Insulin

Inadequate insulin results in poor glucose metabolism, rise in blood sugar.

The hormone insulin—which is produced in the islets of Langerhans in the pancreas—regulates the body's use of sugar (glucose). In juvenile-onset diabetes, there is a total or partial failure of insulin production and glucose accumulates in the blood. This schematic drawing shows partial failure of insulin production.

injections of insulin, which may be required as seldom as once a day or as often as three times a day. Since insulin is a hormone that is digested if taken orally, it must be administered by injection. Therefore, it is important to learn to administer the injections yourself. This may seem difficult at first, but with proper instruction and practice, even a child can soon master injections. Your doctor will tell you where and how to give them.

Diet is also important in controlling diabetes. In a typical diabetic regimen, calories (800 to 1,500 daily, depending on the patient's weight) are distributed in small meals taken at regular intervals. Carbohydrates make up 50 to 60 percent of the total intake, with plenty of fibrous foods such as whole grain breads and cereals, fruits, and vegetables. Simple carbohydrates are restricted to 5 to 15 percent of all carbohydrate calories and should come from natural sources such as milk and fruit rather than from candies, cookies, and so on. Of the total calories, 30 to 35 percent come from fats, and 12 to 20 percent (depending on age and activity) from protein. Key factors are controlling the intake of simple carbohydrates (sugars), eating balanced meals, and maintaining an ideal body weight.

It is important to keep rigorously to the prescribed timetable of meals and snacks. The diet is designed to keep the blood glucose level steady so that each dose of insulin will have approximately the same amount of glucose to act upon.

TESTING

The effectiveness of the treatment in keeping blood glucose at an acceptable level must be checked frequently—in some cases, several times a day. You may be asked to test your urine, using specially prepared paper reagent strips.

Many doctors now prefer that their patients use the relatively new blood test rather than the urine test to monitor glucose levels. These self-monitoring kits are now widely available. A small needle or lancet is used to prick a finger, and a drop of blood is then squeezed onto a chemically treated strip. The strip is then either compared to color samples or inserted into a meter to identify the glucose level.

STRESS

Surgery, injuries, pregnancy, emotional upsets, any illness (from a cold to a heart attack), and even changes in the weather cause stress and thus increase the body's demand for insulin. Doctors and dentists should be told about your condition before starting treatment so that they can take proper precautions.

COMPLICATIONS

In spite of careful management of the diabetes, complications may occur. One of the most common (and one that family members should know how to treat) is hypoglycemia, a low level of blood glucose. It may result from taking too much insulin, failing to keep to the diet, or prolonged muscular exertion. The onset of hypoglycemia is usually fairly rapid, with symptoms that include sweating, nervous irritability, and a tingling tongue. There is time to counteract it by taking sugar or some other quick-energy food. Sometimes, however, a patient will become confused and even aggressive. Occasionally, the onset is sudden and the diabetic slips quickly into unconsciousness. In such cases, glucose should be quickly injected into a vein. Hypoglycemia may be life-threatening, but in most cases the patient will recover. Because of the possibility of an attack occurring when you are among strangers, you should carry a card explaining your condition and detailing what should be done in an emergency. Wearing a Medic-Alert bracelet is an additional safeguard.

Another common complication of dia-

betes is hyperglycemia, which is excessive sugar in the blood. Hyperglycemic coma comes on slowly, over several hours or even days. It occurs when the body uses fat as a substitute for glucose to provide energy; as a result, acidic compounds (ketones) are formed. Drowsiness, incessant urination, and intense thirst are early symptoms.

Arteriosclerosis, or hardening of the arteries, is also somewhat more common in diabetics than in others. There also may be some loss of sensation in the legs and feet, which can result in unperceived injury to the skin or joints. You should take good care of your feet, wear well-fitting shoes, and cut your toenails carefully.

The eyes may also be affected by diabetes. Diabetics often suffer repeated bleeding into the retina, leading to the formation of scar tissue. Diabetes also may

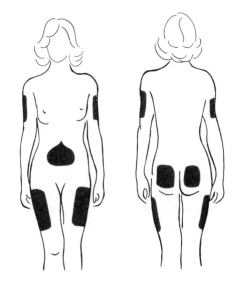

Since insulin must be taken by injection, it is vital that all diabetics, including children over the age of seven or eight, know how to give themselves injections. Skin should be sterilized with alcohol-moistened cotton and the sites varied according to doctor's instructions. The most common injection sites are shown here. Never make an injection less than a half-inch from a recently used site.

promote the formation of cataracts. All diabetics should have frequent eye examinations. New treatments, including the use of lasers, are reducing the incidence of blindness resulting from diabetes.

SUMMING UP

Once the diagnosis of insulin-dependent diabetes is confirmed and proper treatment is begun, most diabetics are able to lead normal, productive lives. Although regular insulin injections and self-discipline are vital in controlling the disease, diabetes should not be allowed to dominate day-to-day living.

77. Adult Diabetes

COMMON CHARACTERISTICS

Adult, or maturity-onset, diabetes is also referred to as non-insulin-dependent diabetes. It can usually be controlled without insulin (hence the name) and is less serious than juvenile, or insulin-dependent, diabetes. Non-insulin-dependent diabetes usually affects people forty years of age or older and is more common among women than among men. Many of those affected are overweight, some seriously so.

It seems probable that the condition is due to an inherited predisposition and that some external agent is required to convert the genetic tendency into the disease. What that external agent is, however, is not known.

SYMPTOMS AND DIAGNOSIS

The symptoms of adult diabetes are similar to those of juvenile diabetes; namely,

thirst, frequent urination, repeated infections of the skin, gums, or urinary tract, and fatigue, weakness, or apathy. Sometimes there are no apparent symptoms at all, and the condition is detected in the course of a routine medical checkup.

The presence of diabetes is confirmed by a simple test in which the fasting blood glucose level is measured; if it is persistently elevated, the patient has diabetes.

TREATMENT

The purpose of treatment is to relieve the symptoms, reduce the amount of glucose in the blood and urine, and lower the risk of complications. For almost a third of non-insulin-dependent diabetics, the disease can be controlled by diet alone. The diet must be designed by a doctor and carefully adhered to by the patient.

In a typical diabetic regimen, calories (800 to 1,500 daily, depending on the pa-

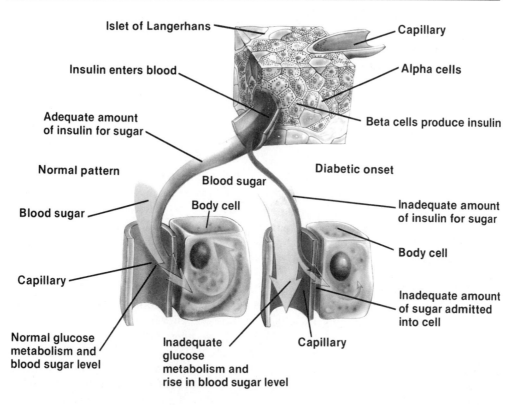

Islet of Langerhans

Capillary

Insulin enters blood

Alpha cells

Adequate amount
of insulin for sugar

Beta cells produce insulin

Normal pattern

Diabetic onset

Blood sugar

Blood sugar

Body cell

Inadequate amount
of insulin for sugar

Body cell

Capillary

Inadequate amount
of sugar admitted
into cell

Normal glucose
metabolism and
blood sugar level

Inadequate
glucose
metabolism and
rise in blood sugar level

Capillary

This schematic drawing shows both normal and insufficient insulin production and glucose metabolism. Note differences between this pattern and the one shown for juvenile diabetes in Chapter 76.

tient's excess weight) are distributed in small meals taken at regular intervals, keeping the blood glucose level as steady as possible. Carbohydrates make up 50 to 60 percent of the total intake, with plenty of fibrous foods such as whole grain breads and cereals, fruits, and vegetables. Simple carbohydrates are restricted to 5 to 15 percent of all carbohydrate calories and should come from natural sources such as milk and fruit rather than from candies, cookies, and so on. Of the total calories, 30 to 35 percent come from fats and 12 to 20 percent (depending on age and activity) from protein. Compared to the average American diet, the diabetic regimen requires reducing the intake of sugar, fat, protein, and salt and increasing the intake of complex carbohydrates and fiber. Key factors are controlling the intake of simple carbohydrates, particularly sugar, honey, and other sugars, eating balanced meals,

and achieving and maintaining an ideal body weight for the control of the disease.

MEDICATION

If diet alone is insufficient to manage the disease, medication will be prescribed to lower the blood glucose. These drugs, generally referred to as oral hypoglycemic agents, appear to work by stimulating the release of insulin and also by increasing its effects on blood sugar. In severe cases, insulin injections may be required, but this is unusual in maturity-onset diabetes, at least in the early stages of the disease.

Occasionally, when too high a dosage of medication is taken, hypoglycemia (a low level of blood glucose) will result. The onset of hypoglycemia is usually gradual, with symptoms that include sweating, nervous irritability, and a tingling tongue. In extreme cases, hypoglycemia may cause loss of consciousness. Sugar lumps or some other quick-energy food should always be carried when away from home and taken at the first symptoms. You should also carry a card explaining your condition and detailing what should be done in an emergency. A Medic-Alert bracelet is an additional safeguard.

TESTING

The effectiveness of the treatment in keeping blood glucose at an acceptable level must be checked regularly. You may be asked to test your urine daily or twice daily, using specially prepared paper reagent slips. (In the morning, perform the test on the second specimen that is voided; the first is always positive.) If the urine is free or almost free of glucose, the diabetes is under control.

Many doctors prefer that their patients monitor the glucose level in the blood rather than in the urine. Self-monitoring kits are now widely available. A small needle or lancet is used to prick a finger and a drop of blood is squeezed onto a chemically treated strip. The strip is then either compared to color samples or inserted into a meter to identify the glucose level.

STRESS

Surgery, trauma, or any illness (from a cold to a heart attack) may cause stress and thus increase the body's demand for insulin. Doctors and dentists should be told about your condition before starting treatment so that they can take proper precautions.

SUMMING UP

Once a diagnosis of diabetes is confirmed, and proper treatment is begun, most diabetics are able to lead normal, productive lives. Although self-discipline, especially in weight control, is vital in managing the disease, it is most important that the fact of having diabetes not be allowed to dominate day-to-day living.

78. Thyroid Disease

COMMON CHARACTERISTICS

The thyroid controls the body's rate of metabolism and, as such, is one of the body's most important regulators. When the thyroid produces too much of its hormones, the metabolic processes speed up; when it produces too little, the entire system slows down. Both types of malfunction can lead to serious, even life-threatening consequences if not detected and treated.

THE THYROID

The thyroid gland, weighing about an ounce, lies in the neck, just below the larynx. Its function is to produce the thyroid hormones, thyroxine and, its stronger form, triiodothyronine. The thyroid is unique among the endocrine glands in that it requires a substance taken directly from outside the body to manufacture its hormones. This substance is iodine, and it must be ingested in small quantities every day. The manufacture, storage, and release of the thyroid hormones are controlled by the pituitary gland's thyroid-stimulating hormone, which is in turn controlled by the hypothalamus portion of the brain. For good thyroid function, there must be an adequate daily intake of iodine, a normal pituitary gland, and a normal pattern of manufacture and release of the hormones from the thyroid.

The thyroid hormones control the body's rate of oxygen consumption (the metabolic rate), promote growth, and are necessary for proper brain development. Too much thyroid hormone speeds up the metabolic rate (hyperthyroidism); too little produces a low metabolic rate and slows all biochemical and metabolic processes (hypothyroidism). Both are charac-

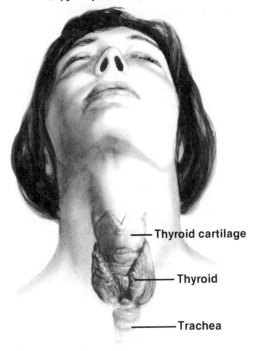

The thyroid gland partially surrounds the front side of the upper rings of the trachea (windpipe) and the thyroid cartilage, or Adam's apple.

terized by development of a goiter—a swelling in the neck area.

HYPERTHYROIDISM

Hyperthyroidism, also known as Graves' disease or thyrotoxicosis, is characterized by the overproduction of thyroid hormone. One of the most common early symptoms is an unexplained weight loss, despite increased hunger and food consumption. The disorder also produces irritability, heart palpitations, and insomnia. People with an overactive thyroid also tend to be very sensitive to heat. As the disease progresses, facial changes, most notably bulging eyes that give a person a startled appearance and an enlarged area of the neck (goiter), develop.

Diagnosis

Any enlargement in the neck or throat area is a sign of possible thyroid disease and should be investigated by a doctor. Final diagnosis, however, depends upon laboratory tests. These include a basal metabolism test, which measures the amount of oxygen consumed by the body. The amount of oxygen absorbed by a person with hyperthyroidism is increased; the opposite is true in hypothyroidism. Other diagnostic tests include the use of radioactive iodine. If the thyroid is producing too much hormone, it will consume more of the iodine. The amount of iodine in the blood also may be measured; if it is elevated, it is a sign of an overactive thyroid; if it is low, it is a sign of an underactive one.

Treatment of Hyperthyroidism

The most common treatment for hyperthyroidism involves the use of radioactive iodine to reduce the gland's activity. The radioactivity released by the substance in the thyroid cuts its functioning and thus reduces the amount of thyroid hormone produced by the gland. In the past, all or part of the gland was removed. This type of surgery is still employed if drug treatment does not adequately control the gland's overactivity.

HYPOTHYROIDISM

Underactivity of the thyroid can be the direct result of too little iodine in the diet. This is most likely to occur in geographic areas where the soil is iodine-depleted, as in some mountainous regions, or in inland areas where fish is rarely eaten (the oceans contain most of the earth's supply of iodine). Hypothyroidism can also be caused by thyroid failure due to problems in the pituitary gland or by atrophy of the thyroid as a result of inflammation and subsequent scarring. Overly vigorous treatment of the opposite condition, hyperthyroidism, is responsible in some cases. In adults, especially middle-aged women, a common cause is an autoimmune process (Hashimoto's struma) that gradually destroys the gland, producing an equally gradual drop in hormone production.

Congenital Hypothyroidism

The traditional term for a child born with a deficient thyroid is *cretin*. Cretinism is characterized by mental retardation, short stature, a puffy face, sparse hair, and a protruding tongue. One type of cretinism, which is now fortunately rare, occurs in regions where iodine-deficiency has been a problem for generations. In such places, hypothyroidism may develop in the womb. Sometimes a child is born without a thyroid, or with a partially developed one. Occasionally, the thyroid is present and, although enlarged, is incapable of producing sufficient hormone. The presence of any of these congenital thyroid disorders can be diagnosed as early as the fifth day of life; treatment should be started as soon as possible to prevent the development of cretinism.

Symptoms

No matter what the cause, the symptoms of hypothyroidism are always similar. The whole body slows down, from the pulse rate to the growth rate and the mental processes. Appetite drops off, but excessive weight is gained. In women, the complex hormonal regulation of the reproductive cycle is disturbed, and infertility may result. Lethargy, apathy, and fatigue overtake the individual insidiously; these symptoms may be mistaken for those of depression.

Body temperature drops and the individual becomes sensitive to cold. Hair grows thin, dry, and lifeless. The skin also becomes dry and puffy—hence the name *myxedema* (swelling of the tissues). The mucus-like substance collecting under the skin grows on the vocal chords as well, making the voice deep and hoarse. This substance may develop in the ears, causing hearing loss, and on the wrists, where it presses on the nerves and causes numbness and tingling in the hands. If hypothyroidism continues untreated, it can lead to rapidly developing arteriosclerosis and a greatly increased risk of coronary disease.

In very severe cases, especially among the elderly, the individual becomes very cold and drowsy and eventually loses consciousness. This myxedema coma is a medical emergency warranting immediate hospitalization.

Treatment

When the cause of the underactivity of the gland is lack of iodine in the diet, small quantities of iodized salt often produce a slow but steady reversal of symptoms. When the thyroid is incapable of producing enough hormone (whether or not an iodine deficiency is involved), a synthetic thyroid hormone is prescribed in pill form. Within days of beginning treatment, patients improve. Within a few months, their symptoms usually disappear.

For children born with a deficient or nonexistent thyroid, prompt treatment usually leads to normal or near-normal growth and development. Medication must continue to be taken daily, however, throughout life.

SUMMING UP

Thyroid disease may be characterized by either an overproduction or underproduction of thyroid hormones. Both are serious conditions that effect the body's metabolism and numerous other functions. Any swelling in the throat is a possible sign of thyroid disease and should be checked. Both hypothyroidism and hyperthyroidism are treatable. by drug therapy, although in some cases of an overactive thyroid, surgery may be used.

79. Addison's Disease

COMMON CHARACTERISTICS

Addison's disease, also known as adrenocortical insufficiency, was first recognized in the mid-1800s by the British doctor whose name it bears. His description of the condition is as accurate now as it was then: "Anemia, general langour or debility, remarkable feebleness of the heart's action, irritability of the stomach, and a peculiar change in the colour of the skin." The cause of Addison's disease is now known to be a glandular disorder in which there is an undersecretion (hypofunction) of hormones by the adrenal cortex.

The adrenals are part of the endocrine system of glands whose secretions go directly into the bloodstream. There are two adrenal glands, one above each kidney. The inner core, or medulla, produces adrenaline, the "fight or flight" hormone first isolated in 1901. The bark or cortex that covers the medulla (the adrenal cortex) is now known to produce about thirty different vital substances, of which the most important and versatile appears to be cortisone.

Just as the study of diabetes led to the discovery of insulin, so the research into the causes of Addison's disease led to the discovery in 1949 of cortisone, a breakthrough for which a team of three scientists (two Americans and one Swiss) received the Nobel Prize in 1950.

Since this hormone is critical to normal metabolic function, a deficiency results in the interrelated symptoms originally observed by Dr. Addison. In practically all cases, the clinical condition is now reversible by hormone replacement therapy.

CAUSES AND EFFECTS

Addison's disease is a comparatively uncommon disorder affecting about 1 person in 25,000, with no sexual difference in the statistics. Onset may occur at any age depending on the cause. In most cases, the condition is attributable to shrinking (atrophy) of the adrenal cortex, for which there is no discoverable cause, but which is generally believed to be an autoimmune disorder. In about one-fourth of all cases of *primary* adrenocortical insufficiency the cause is tissue destruction by tuberculosis or tumor. *Secondary* insufficiency is traceable to malfunction of the pituitary gland, which secretes the adrenocorticotrophic hormone, more commonly known as ACTH. Since ACTH is the stimulus for the hormone productions of the adrenal cortex, underproduction leads directly to underproduction of cortisone.

This hormone deficiency disturbs the metabolism of fats, proteins, and carbohydrates; blood pressure drops, and cardiac function diminishes. There is an imbalance in water and salt retention and elimination, and low blood sugar (hypoglycemia) is typical.

Manifestations of these disturbances include weakness and apathy, fatigue, loss of appetite (anorexia) resulting in weight loss and, in some instances, anemia; nausea with or without vomiting; and diarrhea. Tolerance to cold, resistance to infection, and ability to deal with stress are significantly diminished. Inevitably, the disturbance in body processes is accompanied by mental and emotional instability.

Characteristic and most conspicuous is the darkening or "bronzing" of the skin. Patches of dark skin (hyperpigmentation) and black freckles appear because the adrenal cortex is not producing enough cortisol to check the pituitary's production of ACTH and MSH (melanocyte-stimulating hormone), a hormone that causes the formation of pigment cells. These skin problems are not present in secondary adrenocortical insufficiency, since that condition arises from a malfunction in the pituitary and a consequent lack of ACTH.

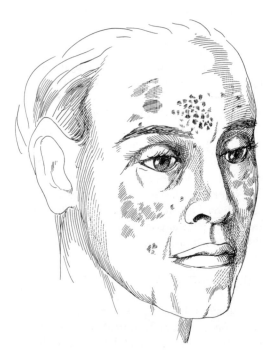

Brown patches and a general darkening of the skin are characteristic of Addison's disease. These changes in coloring are the result of low production of cortisol by the adrenal cortex. Cortisol checks the production of MSH (melanocyte-stimulating hormone, which produces pigment cells) by the pituitary; thus, when there is a low level of cortisol, there may be an overabundance of MSH.

DIAGNOSIS AND TREATMENT

Because of the comparative rareness of Addison's disease and the diversity of symptoms, a definitive diagnosis rests with blood and urine tests as well as X-rays. When it is clear that the adrenal glands are unable to produce appropriate amounts of cortisone either for primary or secondary reasons, hormone replacement therapy is undertaken, with doses monitored carefully until the proper therapeutic level is achieved without negative side effects. As in the case of insulin for diabetes, cortisone taken by mouth or by injection becomes a lifetime therapy. If tuberculosis is the cause of the insufficiency, appropriate TB therapy is initiated.

SUMMING UP

Addison's disease is a disorder in which underfunctioning of the adrenal cortex can result in a combination of serious physiological and psychological disturbances. If neglected, they can become increasingly life-threatening. However, the prognosis is excellent for patients on hormone replacement therapy with cortisone in monitored amounts. Unless there is a complica-

tion from some other source, there is no reason why normal activities cannot be pursued over a lifetime.

80. Hypoglycemia

COMMON CHARACTERISTICS

Hypoglycemia is the medical term for low blood sugar, and contrary to popular notions, it is *not* a common clinical condition in the general population. An abnormally low concentration of sugar in the blood is a circumstance that occurs mainly in diabetics as a result of taking too much insulin or too many antidiabetes pills.

One likely reason for the trendy use of the term is that many of the symptoms of an impending hypoglycemic crisis are the same as those of an acute anxiety attack: rapid pulse, palpitations, sweating, restlessness, apprehension, and an inability to concentrate. However, while an attack of anxiety or mental confusion caused by psychological stress is not potentially fatal, acute hypoglycemia requires emergency treatment.

CAUSES OF HYPOGLYCEMIA

Diabetes is characterized by the presence of abnormally high blood sugar levels (*hyper*glycemia), and therapy consists of normalizing the condition with insulin. The first obvious cause of *hypo*glycemia is overtreatment of diabetes. However, low blood sugar may also result from an oversecretion of insulin by the pancreas, liver

malfunction sometimes but not always associated with alcoholism, or underfunction of the thyroid or adrenal glands. Spontaneous (or functional) hypoglycemia may occur when the body produces too much insulin as an overreaction to glucose utilization. This combination of responses may occur during pregnancy, high fever, unusual physical stress, or unusual emotional stress.

HOW HYPOGLYCEMIA HAPPENS

In the normal nondiabetic individual, several metabolic processes monitored chiefly by the endocrine glands maintain glucose (sugar) levels in the blood that prevent the occurrence of adverse symptoms. When, for whatever reason, the level drops and is not properly compensated, the most important organ to suffer is the brain. Unlike other parts of the body, the brain does not readily break down fats or protein for use as fuel, and it therefore depends on sugar for proper functioning. When deprivation occurs, mental confusion, dizziness, fainting, and eventually coma may occur. (It is for this reason that standard emergency treatment for a person found unconscious is likely to be an intravenous injection of glucose solution.)

When the body attempts to meet the

CONDITIONS PRODUCING HYPOGLYCEMIA

1. Overtreatment of diabetes
2. Oversecretion of insulin
3. Underactive thyroid
4. Addison's disease
5. Liver disease
6. Excessive stress

challenge of low blood sugar, the hormones respond by stimulating an outpouring of adrenaline into the bloodstream. This in turn activates the liver into releasing some of its stored sugar as a corrective. It is the flow of adrenaline that is responsible for many of the manifestations of a hypoglycemic attack. Adrenaline not only causes palpitations but, by closing the small blood vessels in the skin, produces the profuse cold sweat that is often an early clue of hypoglycemia onset.

Everyone who has fasted for twenty-four hours has experienced a giddiness or slight disorientation that is promptly corrected with the intake of carbohydrates. All diabetics are told that they must carry a candy or lump of sugar as emergency treatment in case of insulin shock. A spoonful of honey or a glass of orange juice will also quickly relieve an insulin reaction.

Hypoglycemia onset may also occur following the ingestion of a meal heavy in carbohydrates, causing the body to produce too much insulin in an effort to *reduce* the blood sugar level. In this process, a reactive hypoglycemia may result.

DIAGNOSIS

Since blood sugar imbalance may be the first sign of diabetes, where any uncertainty exists, accurate diagnosis is based on a procedure called the three-hour oral glucose tolerance test for *hyper*glycemia. The same test, extended over five hours, is given for *hypo*glycemia. Following an overnight fast and the giving of a blood sample, the patient drinks a measured amount of glucose (dissolved in tea or water) sufficient to cause an immediate rise in blood sugar levels. The extent of the rise and the time involved are measured by a check of blood samples every half-hour. As the body's insulin is secreted, the levels begin to equalize. However, if there has been an oversupply of insulin in response to the heavy carbohydrate load, the patient will begin to show signs of hypoglycemia as the blood sugar levels drop—dizziness, sweating, palpitations. This oversupply of insulin is an indication of the presence of hypoglycemia, in this case, the body's inability to deal with a heavy carbohydrate load.

In recent years, many individuals have been told that they are clinically hypoglycemic, not on the basis of a glucose tolerance test and other laboratory investigations, but rather on the basis of symptoms alone. Since many conditions can cause symptoms similar to those of hypoglycemia, a review of symptoms alone is not sufficient for an accurate diagnosis.

TREATMENT

The treatment for low blood sugar depends on the cause. The most common set of causes (ruling out an insulin overdose for diabetes) for "reactive" hypoglycemia can be effectively treated by cutting down on carbohydrates and in many cases alcohol, by eating regular meals high in protein rather than alternately feasting and fasting, and by eating smaller meals more often than the usually spaced three a day.

So-called fasting hypoglycemia checked out by the glucose tolerance test may require thyroid injections or other drug therapy to compensate for excessive insulin effect. It is especially important before embarking on treatment for such cases to rule out liver dysfunction and tumors of the pancreas. Where the tumors exist, surgical correction may be indicated. If they are inoperable, they may be treated medically in a way that will lower insulin production.

SUMMING UP

Where recurrent symptoms of palpitations, dizziness, and cold sweat are relieved or aborted by eating a piece of fudge or drinking warm milk heavily laced with honey, it would be difficult to say whether the problem is anxiety or hypoglycemia. However, where mental functioning becomes impaired or physical manifestations interfere with normal activity, or where there is an increase in the frequency or intensity of symptoms, a doctor should be consulted for diagnostic tests. In the majority of cases, a modification of eating and drinking habits offers an effective solution. When more serious organic causes are involved, treatment may be based on hormone pills or other medication. All patients with diabetes taking insulin or oral equivalents are always instructed in the emergency procedures that will prevent an acute hypoglycemic attack.

Neurological Disorders

81. Headaches

TYPES OF HEADACHES

All of us suffer from an occasional headache; in fact, twenty million Americans see their doctors each year because of headaches. Although headaches can be very uncomfortable and temporarily disabling, most are not associated with serious illness and can be relieved by resting in a quiet room or by taking a nonprescription painkiller, such as aspirin or acetaminophen. Others, however, may require stronger prescription medications, and a few are warning signs to seek immediate medical attention. These warning signs include:

• Severe, sudden headaches that seem to come on like a "bolt out of the blue."
• Headaches accompanied by confusion, visual blurring, loss of consciousness, alertness, sensation, or other neurological changes.
• Recurrent headaches affecting one particular area, such as an eye, temple, etc.
• Recurrent headaches of increasing intensity or frequency.
• Headaches accompanied by neck stiffness and fever.
• Headaches that wake you up.
• Any unexplained change in the nature or frequency of headaches.

TENSION HEADACHES

The most common headaches are those associated with tension or muscle contractions and are directly related to stress. The pain tends to be steady and dull, rather than throbbing. It is usually felt in the temples, forehead, neck, or back of the head. Sometimes the pain seems to encircle the head like a tight band. Tension headaches may occur at any time but are most commonly associated with periods of stress or worry.

Treatment involves relieving the tension through massage, heat, a hot shower, relaxation techniques—in short, putting aside the worries of the moment. Nonprescription painkillers, such as aspirin or acetaminophen, also may help. For severe muscle tension headaches, other slightly more potent drugs may be prescribed. These drugs may cause drowsiness and slow reflexes and should be taken with caution by people who work with machinery or drive. Most doctors also recommend that they be used for only short periods (not more than a few days at a time).

MIGRAINE HEADACHES

Migraines vary from person to person, but typically they are throbbing headaches affecting one side of the head. They are

The major blood vessels on the surface of the brain. The enlargement shows an expanded vessel typical of a migraine or vascular headache.

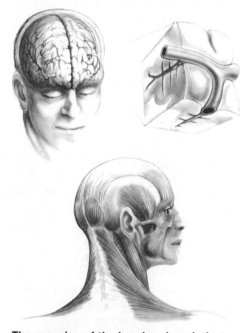

The muscles of the head and neck that are most commonly the cause of tension headaches

often accompanied by a number of other symptoms, which also vary. Some people have very little head pain but suffer from distorted vision and hearing, or feelings of intense anxiety. Others may suffer from incapacitating pain lasting for several days. Most fall between these two extremes.

Many people are warned of an impending migraine attack by bizarre distortions of size, position, time, and place—the so-called Alice-in-Wonderland syndrome. Others see flashing lights or bright colors in unusual shapes. Nausea, vomiting, chills, fever, dizziness, diarrhea; abdominal, arm, or leg pain; and sensitivity to light are still other symptoms that may accompany a migraine.

Regardless of the differing symptoms, all migraines are related to changes in the blood vessels of the head and neck. This is why migraines are often referred to as vascular headaches. Early warning symptoms of a migraine are thought to be caused by a narrowing of these blood vessels, while the head pain is a result of the subsequent expanding or dilating of the vessels. What causes these changes is unknown, although many researchers now believe that chemicals produced in the body that act on the blood vessels may be responsible.

TRIGGERING FACTORS

Dozens of factors appear to trigger migraines in susceptible individuals, but again, these vary from person to person. Common precipitating factors include hormonal changes, particularly those associated with menstruation or use of birth control pills; sudden changes in weather or temperature; emotional factors; certain foods or additives, especially the preservatives in cured meats, monosodium glutamate (MSG), or caffeine, chocolate, cheese, and corn products; drugs; glaring lights; strong odors; and cigarette smoke. Avoiding these triggering factors can solve the problem for many people. Others, however, may require treatment.

TREATING MIGRAINE

Unfortunately, there is no cure for migraines, although most can be controlled through a combination of avoiding precipitating factors, drugs, and other therapies. Aspirin may help some migraine patients, especially children, but most adult sufferers require additional or alternative medications. The most successful treatments are those that either prevent an attack or stop it in its earliest stages. Ergotamine or drugs related to ergot derivatives may be prescribed to be taken at the first warning signs of a migraine. These drugs constrict or narrow the arteries, thus relieving the pain from the expanded cranial vessels. These drugs should not be taken by people who have hardening of the arteries, high blood pressure, angina, coronary disease, or other circulatory problems; severe infection; or disorders of the kidney or liver. And since they narrow the blood vessels, they should be used with caution by anyone who will be exposed to the cold, which further reduces blood flow to the arms and legs.

Another treatment involves giving a beta-blocking drug, which prevents the expanding of the cerebral arteries and thus prevents migraine attacks. Since these drugs slow the rate of heartbeats, they are often contraindicated for heart patients. They also should not be used by people with asthma or diabetes.

Only your doctor, who knows your particular medical needs, can determine whether a prescription drug is indicated, and if so, which one is best for you. If a prescription is given, it is important to use the drug only as directed.

CLUSTER HEADACHES

Cluster headaches are a rare variant of migraine which, as the name implies, strike several times in rapid succession. They are seen most often in men and are extremely painful. The drugs used to treat migraine are often prescribed but must be given early in an attack and are therefore often administered by injection or suppository to allow the medication to enter the bloodstream rapidly.

SINUS HEADACHES

Sinus headaches are associated with a swelling of the membranes lining the sinuses of the nasal passages. The pain tends to be dull and may shift if you move your head in a certain way. Sinus headaches may be relieved by simple painkillers or, in some cases, a decongestant to relieve the swelling.

SUMMING UP

The vast majority of headaches are not cause for alarm. Most can be controlled by the use of simple medications and by altering habits or life style, as in the case of frequent tension headaches.

82. Pain

Millions of Americans suffer from chronic pain, one of the nation's most serious and baffling health problems. While many people focus on their back, or their head, or some other localized source of pain, there are specialists who have come to believe that pain is not always a symptom but rather a disease in itself, requiring concen-

trated study. The scope of the problem was summarized by a special conference sponsored by the Federal Interagency Committee on New Therapies for Pain and Discomfort: every year 40 percent of Americans have acute or chronic pain problems requiring treatment; many millions of dollars are spent annually in the search for pain relief; and 700 million workdays are lost. Pain sufferers also

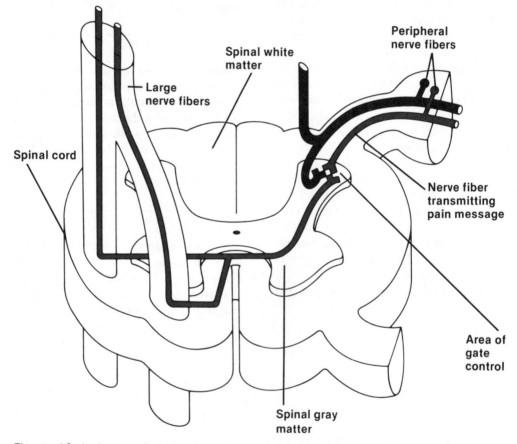

This simplified schematic illustrates the pain gate control theory. The smaller nerve fibers transmit pain impulses and meet with the larger nerve fibers that conduct sensation to the brain in the spinal cord. By overloading the large fibers, the gate can be shut to the pain impulses being transmitted by the small fibers.

spend millions on quack treatments each year.

All pain, whether acute or chronic, is a message carried to the brain by nerves near the surface of the skin or deep in the body's interior. The message is usually a warning—of injury, organic disorder, or the effects of stress on body function. Acute pain—sudden in onset and brief in duration—may be caused by an infection, accident, or surgery and is rarely baffling either to doctor or to patient. But chronic pain which may be attributable to a particular condition does not diminish with treatment and does not go away with the passage of time. As the pain continues, it affects the personal relationships, professional commitments, and self-image, inevitably developing a psychological component to the basic problem.

A PAIN THEORY

An understanding of precisely how pain happens is basic to finding more effective ways to deal with it. In the mid-1960s, two researchers at M.I.T.—Dr. Ronald Melzack and Dr. Patrick Wall—formulated the "gate theory," which can be summarized as follows: There are millions of sensory receptors on the surface of the body and within it that keep the brain constantly informed about temperature, condition of organs, unusual changes, and the like. These receptors and the brain communicate in a complicated neural code through a network of nerves spread throughout the body. Every nerve consists of bundles of fibers that vary in thickness. The larger fibers carry impulses relating to touch. The smaller fibers send their messages much more slowly, and it is these fibers that transmit pain impulses. Both sets meet in the spinal cord. These scientists believe that there is a gate-like mechanism in the spinal cord that can be shut against pain messages, opening them only sometimes to admit them.

This theory may account for the relief associated with electrical stimulation or acupuncture, in both cases sending counterimpulses through the large fibers to the brain that trigger the release of endorphins—natural body chemicals which in turn cause the pain gate to be closed.

PAIN CATEGORIES

Pain specialists have separated pain sources into six categories, each presenting somewhat different problems:

• Joint and muscle pain, which accounts for the majority of patients attending pain clinics.
• Causalgia, the burning pain that follows a bullet wound or some other sudden shock to the peripheral nervous system. This type of pain is likely to go away within a few months, but in some cases it continues for years.
• Neuralgia, especially trigeminal neuralgia (a very painful facial tic), originating in the peripheral nerves and unaccountably triggered by cold air, chewing, or stress.
• Phantom limb pain, which may originate sometime *after* an amputation, with mild sensations of "pins and needles" that turn into shooting pains that continue to be agonizing for years.
• Vascular pain, associated with the dilated blood vessels around the brain that cause migraine headaches.
• Cancer pain, resulting from the destruction of tissue or blockage of major organs by a growing tumor, or the metastases of certain cancers that reach the spine and press on nerves.

PERCEPTION OF PAIN

Some people seem to be more sensitive to pain than others, and different people respond differently to different kinds of pain. In almost all cases, however, distracting circumstances such as loud music or intense physical effort can send messages to the brain that override the pain messages. On the other hand, the intensity of pain can increase during fatigue, depression, or anxiety. Experiments have shown that the pain threshold (the point at which the pain stimulus is perceived or at which it produces a reaction) can be raised significantly not only by distractions but by such techniques as hypnosis or meditation. A study on the chemistry of pain indicates that men are less sensitive to pain than women, and older people are less sensitive than the young. Many responses to pain are learned through cultural or parental patterns, and individual character traits have a great deal to do with susceptibility to what is sometimes called the chronic pain syndrome.

METHODS OF PAIN RELIEF

For some individuals, one of the most critical aspects of a reduction in pain consists in their total desire to feel better and their belief that their chosen method can accomplish this. The methods below are listed alphabetically, not in the order of their popularity or effectiveness.

Acupuncture

While many Western scientists remain skeptical about the validity of acupuncture as a therapeutic discipline, there is some evidence to indicate that the technique stimulates the release by the brain of endorphins, naturally occurring painkilling chemicals, into the bloodstream. Acupuncturists use stainless steel fine-gauge needles inserted and rapidly rotated and sometimes combined with electrical stimulation at particular "pressure points" in the body determined by the whereabouts of the pain but usually remote from it. Further details may be obtained about licensed practitioners in various parts of the United States by writing to the Acupuncture Information Center of New York, 57 East Seventy-second Street, New York, NY 10021.

Anesthesia

Literally, "loss of feeling," local anesthesia in the form of cocaine derivatives (procaine and lidocaine) to deaden sensation. It is most frequently employed in dentistry, although it also may be used on a short-term basis in back pain and to treat accident patients. It has limited long-term application, but it may be practical for alleviating the acute pain of certain neuralgias or bursitis.

Behavior Modification

A form of therapy that has its uses with people for whom chronic pain has become a way of life and for those who use their pain as a way of gaining control over others. It is based on the assumption that many symptoms that began as authentic responses have hardened into habits that have to be unlearned. People whose lives are closely involved with the patient are usually asked to participate in the therapy. Behavior modification is usually one of the many-faceted approaches used in pain clinics.

Biofeedback

A technique requiring intensive practice in concentration in which patients learn how to control certain involuntary body processes such as constriction of blood vessels. By mastering this method, patients can reduce the chronic discomfort of vascular headaches and some types of stress-induced muscle tension.

Chiropractic

A treatment based on the theory (never scientifically validated) that most disorders result from pressure on the nerves caused by the faulty alignment of the spinal vertebrae. Manipulation is the main technique. However, where problems of the spine itself are not the source of the chronic pain, chiropractic treatment has not proved relevant. Chiropractors are licensed to practice in most (but not in all) states.

Electrotherapy

Also called transcutaneous nerve stimulation, electrotherapy appears to have an effect on the larger nerve fibers that either short circuits messages of pain or that stimulates the release of endorphins. The compact easy-to-use equipment can be operated by the patient as necessary. It is reported to be helpful in reducing chronic neck, shoulder, and lower back pain.

Exercise

Most chronic lower back pain is alleviated by strengthening particular muscles. Exercise such as swimming that induces relaxation can be helpful in alleviating stress-induced pain such as headaches, and regularly scheduled running is known to stimulate endorphin production in the brain responsible for a gratifying "high." The very fact that exercise provides distraction, and in some cases acute discomfort, increases its effectiveness as an antidote to certain kinds of pain.

Hypnosis

While there is no general agreement about how or why it works, hypnosis is now generally accepted as a way of controlling and reducing pain. All hypnosis is self-hypnosis in the sense that the subject has decided to concentrate on producing a mental state that will diminish anxiety and suffering. When it does work (many people are incapable of the necessary concentration) it has the advantage of being free of unpleasant side effects no matter how often it is used.

Massage

Because many people who suffer from acute pain are rarely free of anxiety, they benefit from the relaxing results achieved by a competent manipulation of tight muscles. One technical explanation for the effectiveness of massage is offered by Dr. Louis Lasagna, a clinical pharmacologist at the University of Rochester Medical Center: "If you bombard the nervous system with impulses from the periphery, you interfere with other impulses." Masseurs must be licensed in most states, and referral by a doctor or hospital clinic insures reliability.

Medication

Painkilling drugs range from over-the-counter medications such as aspirin and acetaminophen to powerful narcotic analgesics. Some painkilling drugs work through the central nervous system to alter local pain perception. Others act as muscle relaxants, and still others alter a body process. Examples of the latter are drugs that inhibit the body's release of prostaglandins —hormone-like substances that are thought to contribute to certain types of pain. These drugs, commonly called nonsteroidal anti-inflammatory agents, are now prescribed to treat arthritis and other musculoskeletal pain, menstrual cramps, and certain inflammatory disorders.

Doctors have long been aware of the placebo effect—the beneficial results to many patients of providing the equivalent of sugar water or "pink pill" as "medication." It has recently been discovered that when a placebo is taken by a patient with the anticipation of benefit, this state of mind in itself triggers the release of endorphins. Some specialists go so far as to say that discreetly administered placebos provide pain relief to about one-third of the population.

Meditation

One of the most popular self-help techniques of recent years for the alleviation of pain is meditation, which, like biofeedback, enables people to gain control over body states once they have mastered the discipline. The positive results of diminishing pain and pain perception through this altered state of consciousness—the opposite of setting out to "fight" the pain through the exercise of one's will—are yet another indication of the relationship between brain/mind and body.

Psychiatry

Pain presumed to originate in the stress of emotional conflicts is called *functional* or *psychogenic* pain, and it is just as real and distressing as pain that has an obvious cause. More often, psychogenic pain has a component of anxiety or suppressed anger that leads to constant and immobilizing headaches or tight muscles causing neck and shoulder problems.

Surgery

One of the oldest procedures for surgical relief of intractable pain is a chordotomy, in which certain nerve pathways are cut or sectioned off. This is now considered the treatment of last resort and is usually reserved for certain types of neuralgia, or the burning pain that follows a shock to the peripheral nervous system.

PAIN CLINICS

Since 1960, when the first pain clinic was established at the University of Washington in Seattle, similar comprehensive treatment centers have been organized all over the country. Most of them are attached to hospitals and call on the services of many specialists. Seattle's Dr. John Loeser has pointed out that "the overwhelming majority of chronic pain patients need to have their whole lives examined." To accomplish this may require the combined expertise not only of particular medical doctors but also of neurologists, orthopedists, psychiatrists, physical therapists, and psychologists skilled in training the patient in techniques of self-help. Anyone wishing to investigate the services of a pain clinic should ask the family physician for a referral or contact the director of the department of anesthesiology at a hospital attached to a university medical school. While many specialists have come to think of chronic pain as a disease in its own right requiring treatment, patients who wish to attend a pain clinic should find out if the costs—which may be considerable—are covered by the terms of their health insurance policies.

SUMMING UP

During the past twenty years, pain as a problem in its own right has received a great deal of attention from the scientific community, with promising results for the millions of people whose lives are dominated by chronic discomfort. Many pain-causing problems are better understood, and therefore they are more effectively treated. Among these are various kinds of chronic headaches, premenstrual pain, lower back pain, and the neck, shoulder, and face pain resulting from misalignment of the temporomandibular joint that connects the lower jaw to the upper part of the skull. Progress in understanding the neurochemistry of the brain's own pain-killers—the endorphins—has spurred research and production of new categories of medication, and various forms of self-help have become an important part of effective pain control. Thanks to these developments, many people whose pain problems seemed insurmountable in the past have been successful in finding a combination of treatments that has reduced their suffering and transformed their lives.

83. Epilepsy

COMMON CHARACTERISTICS

Epilepsy, also referred to as spells, fits, or seizures, has long mystified the medical community. At one time in history, its trance-like effects were considered so awesome that epileptics were taken for holy people and thought to be in direct communication with the gods. The name of the disease, derived from Old French, means falling sickness and refers to the fact that a seemingly well person suddenly falls to the floor. Today, epilepsy is known to be caused by a defect in the transmission of motor impulses in the brain. In almost all cases, it can be controlled, enabling the patient to live a normal life.

TYPES OF EPILEPSY

There are several categories of epilepsy that are differentiated by the type of seizures involved. These are described in the following sections.

Grand Mal Seizures

This type of epilepsy is also called tonic-clonic contractions. Attacks sometimes start with a warning sensation of queasiness or a mood change. (These warning signals may give a patient a chance to sit or lie down and thus avoid an injurious fall.) The seizure itself usually involves a loss of consciousness, falling, and convulsive movements of the arms, legs, and head lasting two to five minutes. When patients regain consciousness, they may feel tired and fall into a deep sleep. Others may suffer from a headache or muscle soreness. Grand mal epilepsy can start at any age, and attacks occur at unpredictable intervals.

Petit Mal Epilepsy or Absence Seizures

These attacks, which mainly afflict children and rarely recur after age twenty, usually last only ten to thirty seconds and are characterized by sudden loss of consciousness and fluttering of the eyelids. They may occur quite frequently—even several times a day. The disease seems to be genetically transmitted. Children are also the exclusive victims of akinetic seizures, in which there is a slowness of movement (akinesia) and which often involve abrupt falls.

Focal Seizures

As their name implies, focal seizures are disruptions in a specific portion of the brain, sometimes characterized by twitching muscles, chewing, or smacking of the lips and sensory hallucinations. The term *Jacksonian seizures* refers to focal seizures that commence in one locale—such as a foot or hand or the corner of the mouth—and then spread to another region or throughout the entire body.

Psychomotor or Complex Partial Seizures

These are commonly associated with brain damage and involve severe disorientation and mental confusion, lasting up to three or four minutes.

Simple-Partial or Sensory Motor Seizures

These attacks are characterized by brief disturbances of sensory perception, combined with regional muscle convulsions.

Considerable overlap exists among the various types of epilepsy, and many patients suffer from what is commonly referred to as "mixed seizures."

DIAGNOSIS

Identifying the cause (if any) and the type of epilepsy is crucial to proper treatment. An account of the disease (history taking) is the first step. Be sure to tell your doctor about any injury (birth trauma, car accident, fall) suffered, as well as all major infectious diseases, strokes, episodes of high fever, poisonings, and drugs taken regularly. Witnesses to seizures may provide helpful details, and family medical histories are always useful.

Diagnostic tests may include an electroencephalogram (EEG), which is a recording of the electric brain waves that helps identify the affected areas of the brain; a skull X-ray; and computerized (CAT) brain scan. The spinal fluid also may be examined to determine whether the seizure is caused by an infection.

DRUG THERAPY

Successful treatment of seizure disorders may involve several drugs; a suitable regimen is often established by trial and error. Drugs should be taken precisely according to your doctor's instructions since any deviation may result in a flare up of the seizures. The type of drug prescribed depends upon the type of seizure involved.

The incidence of seizures increases during certain types of stress, such as fever, infections, and surgery. Your physician should be informed of any of these conditions so that your medication dosage may be altered accordingly.

FIRST-AID MEASURES

• Protect epileptic patients from injury during a seizure by helping them lie down, loosening their clothes, and moving furniture and other objects out of the way.
• A person undergoing a seizure should be turned to his or her side, with the head turned sideways to prevent secretions from clogging the throat.

TYPES OF EPILEPTIC SEIZURES

Epilepsy is classified according to severity of attacks

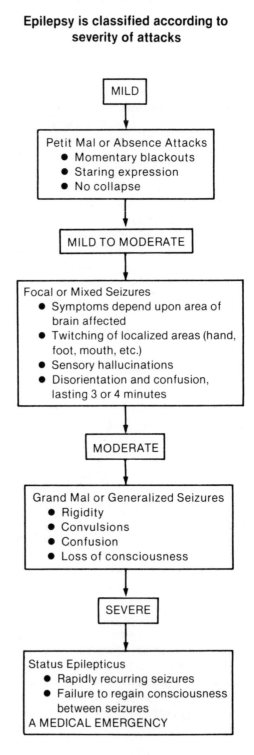

• A smooth, nonbreakable object should be inserted into the patient's mouth so that the tongue will not be chewed or swallowed. Make sure the air passage is clear.
• Many epileptics carry medical identification tags or cards; contact the indicated party for help.

SUMMING UP

Epileptic seizures can usually be controlled through drug therapy. Persons who achieve seizure-free status can expect to live normal lives, often including participation in sports and other demanding activities. Your doctor will tell you what, if any, restrictions should be observed.

84. Vertigo and Motion Sickness

COMMON CHARACTERISTICS

Dizziness—the major symptom associated with vertigo and motion sickness—is not a specific disease but, instead, a result of a problem involving sense of balance. Organs that are involved include the inner ear, eye muscles, brain, and body muscles. When these organs are working in harmony, all is well with the sense of balance. But when something goes awry, dizziness results. The explanations range from something as simple and benign as motion sickness to severe brain disease. Therefore, anything more than transient occasional dizziness should be reported to a doctor.

What people call dizziness varies considerably from person to person. It is a term used to describe a wide range of feelings —from a vague floating or swimming sensation in the head to severe vertigo, in which a person experiences extreme whirling sensations in the head. Between these extremes are feelings of lightheadedness such as might be experienced before fainting, giddiness, or a general sense of unsteadiness or confusion.

MOTION SICKNESS

Many people experience severe discomfort when riding in cars, trains, boats, or planes. This discomfort may include faintness, dizziness, nausea, cold sweats, stomach aches, and even vomiting. It is caused by a disturbance in the balancing mechanism of the inner ear, as a result of continuing irregular motion of the body. It may be intensified by reading in a moving vehicle because both the eyes and the body are moving at the same time, making it more difficult for the brain and inner ear to achieve equilibrium.

While motion sickness usually disappears as soon as the motion stops, it can make any travel a miserable experience. Children are more likely to be afflicted than adults and tend to grow out of the problem. Sometimes, simple preventive measures can avoid motion sickness. These include not eating a large meal before traveling and sitting where the motion is least marked—in the front seat when traveling by car or in a middle seat or cabin when flying or sailing. If motion sickness does occur, try to keep the head still and focus on a stationary object. Lying down may help, and many people avoid the problem by sleeping through a trip.

If you are commonly afflicted by motion sickness, a dose of a drug to impede disequilibrium taken before the trip may help prevent the problem. Most are taken orally, but some are now available in a new form that is simply absorbed through your skin from a patch that looks like a small, round, plastic bandage that is placed behind the ear.

LIGHTHEADEDNESS

A sense of lightheadedness together with mild unsteadiness may occur when suddenly rising from a sitting or lying position or when straightening up from a bent-over position. It is believed to be due to a sudden, but very temporary, reduction in the flow of blood to the brain at that particular moment. This type of dizziness is a sign to rise more slowly. Sometimes this response, known as orthostatic hypotension, may be part of a reaction to a medication, especially some of the drugs used to treat high blood pressure. At one time or another, however, most people experience such sensations, and they are not serious.

Low blood pressure also can lessen blood flow to the brain, causing lightheadedness or giddiness. Other symptoms include seeing spots before your eyes, experiencing overall weakness, and feeling as if you are going to faint. Lying down with the legs and feet elevated helps fairly quickly. Certain situations, such as the sight of blood, emotional tension, physical and nervous exhaustion, or even an overheated room, may stimulate the vagus nerve, causing the heart rate to slow and the blood pressure to drop sud-

denly. Although the resulting dizziness may frighten you, it is not serious. However, if the problem is recurrent, a consultation with your physician is warranted.

MODERATE DIZZINESS

A number of conditions affecting the ear produce dizziness. Cold water in the outer ear, for example, may affect the neighboring inner ear, resulting in dizziness. A head cold may extend into the ear, producing the sensation of disturbed balance.

Sometimes injuries to the head upset the delicate workings of the inner ear and cause a loss of balance. Low blood sugar, sometimes called hypoglycemia, is another possible cause.

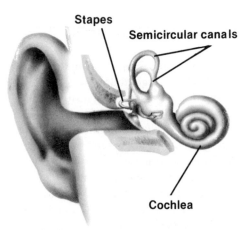

Stapes

Semicircular canals

Cochlea

The labyrinth, or semicircular canals of the inner ear, is usually the root of vertigo and motion sickness. These canals are filled with fluid, and they control the sense of balance by detecting the movements and position of the head and relaying the information to the brain. The brain coordinates information from the inner ear with stimuli from the eyes and muscles, thus maintaining a sense of balance. Dizziness and other symptoms of motion sickness are likely to appear when the brain's perceptions and the messages from the inner ear differ.

VERTIGO

True vertigo, probably the most troublesome form of dizziness, can be caused by an irritation of the inner ear or of the nerves that are connected to the inner ear. The irritation can result from an infection or from the excessive use of a wide variety of substances, such as alcohol, nicotine, or even aspirin. People with vertigo experience a very unpleasant, often frightening sensation of moving or spinning around. Nausea and vomiting often accompany vertigo. One common form of vertigo, known as Ménière's disease, has no apparent cause but is often accompanied by ringing in the ears (tinnitus) and hearing loss. In this disorder, the vertigo attacks come on suddenly and may last up to twenty-four hours. Antivertigo medications usually can relieve the symptoms.

Heart disease, anemia, hardening of the arteries in the brain, and high blood pressure all interfere with the blood supply to the inner ear and can lead to vertigo. Repeated occurrences of severe dizziness in the elderly may be an indication of a more serious medical problem. In these cases, treating the underlying cause may resolve the problem.

SUMMING UP

Generally speaking, occasional dizziness without any other symptoms is not serious. If the dizziness becomes chronic or there is no obvious cause of the problem, a physician should be consulted. Vertigo that recurs or lasts for a prolonged period definitely should be investigated by a physician. In most instances, relief can be obtained, either through antivertigo medication or by identifying and treating the underlying cause.

85. Parkinson's Disease

COMMON CHARACTERISTICS

Parkinson's disease, sometimes referred to as shaking palsy, affects approximately half a million people in the United States, or about 1 percent of persons over fifty. It is a disorder that results from the degeneration of certain brain cells, and its most characteristic feature is defective message transmission from the brain to various portions of the body. This results in uncontrollable movement, which may be manifested as tremor, muscular rigidity, or sluggishness.

CAUSE AND TYPES OF PARKINSONISM

The most common form of the disease is called idiopathic parkinsonism and has no known cause. It has no known hereditary component, nor is it contagious. Parkinsonism affects women and men in equal proportions.

There is also drug-induced parkinsonism, which is caused mostly by drugs to treat severe mental illness. This form of parkinsonism is usually reversed when the drug is discontinued or its dosage de-

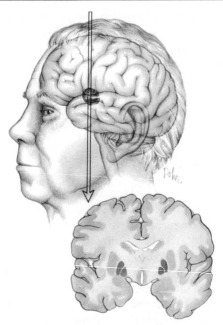

Cross section of the brain showing the area of disturbance, the motor control and reflex centers.

creased. Parkinsonism also may be caused by disorders such as encephalitis and hardening of the arteries (arteriosclerosis), or following certain brain injuries, including those caused by a stroke.

MECHANISM OF PARKINSONISM

Parkinsonism is believed to be related to the *substantia nigra* (black substance) of the nerve cells, which produce and store a chemical substance called dopamine—one of several neurotransmitters. (A neurotransmitter relays messages from the brain across a small open space—or synapse—at the junction of the nerves.) Parkinson's disease apparently interferes with dopamine storage and/or production, which causes disturbances in nerve message transmission. This, in turn, leads to shaking or other defective motor responses. In addition to dopamine depletion, parkinsonism also seems to involve an excess of cholinergic activity. Treatment, therefore, entails either increasing the concentration of dopamine or de-

creasing the concentration of acetylcholine, another neurotransmitter that causes symptoms of Parkinson's disease when dopamine levels are reduced. Both treatments are often used.

SYMPTOMS

Parkinson's disease usually starts very gradually. Early symptoms, which may go unnoticed for years, include stiffness of the hands, fatigue or weakness, depression, and a slight limp or changes in posture. The symptoms increase and eventually may develop into full-blown parkinsonism, exhibiting muscular rigidity, tremor, and slowness of movement. Other symptoms vary from patient to patient and may include soft, monotonous, or slow speech, difficulty in swallowing, trouble in walking, shuffling, a change in bowel habits, slow urination, excessive sweating, and drooling. Symptoms often are limited to one side of the body. Diagnosis is sometimes assisted by analysis of the patient's handwriting, which may show evidence of tremor, is typically small, and tends to decrease in size with the passage of time.

TREATMENT

A short while ago, a diagnosis of parkinsonism was a lifelong condemnation. But parkinsonism has become a very treatable condition, and many patients are able to function normally for many years.

Since the cause of the disease is still unknown, therapy is aimed at relieving symptoms. Treatment usually consists of drug therapy, physical therapy, and the use of devices (such as a typewriter, instead of writing by hand, or a speech amplifier) that permit patients to lead productive lives. Treatment does involve trial and error, and both doctor and patient must persevere in an attempt to find the best individual combination of drugs and dosages. Drug treatment usually entails supplying the brain with the missing neurotransmitter, dopamine. These drugs are called dopamine precursors. Some patients react best when the excessive acetylcholine is inhibited through the use of anticholinergic drugs.

EXERCISES

Exercises are usually prescribed by the doctor, who may refer the patient to a physical therapist.

• Patients who stoop are taught to line up their spine against a wall or door jamb several times each day.
• Patients who shuffle are taught to raise their feet over books placed at regular intervals along the floor.
• Patients who have trouble getting out of chairs are taught to stand up by leaning forward 45 degrees and pushing up with their hands.
• Patients who have trouble speaking may benefit from reading aloud.

General physical condition is also important, and patients are encouraged to develop general exercise routines for home practice.

GENERAL TIPS

• Good, comfortable shoes and a cane, if the patient is unsteady, will make walking easier.

• Patients who have trouble getting out of chairs should avoid deep, upholstered furniture. A chair whose back legs are two inches higher than the front legs may prove helpful.
• Handbars and rails in the bathroom and/or a raised toilet seat will assist disabled victims.

SUMMING UP

Parkinsonism is a serious but treatable disease. As with most chronic illnesses, patients may be depressed, anxious and fearful. Parkinson's disease patients and their families may contact a voluntary health agency for support and information. Major organizations are:

• The American Parkinson's Disease Association, 116 John Street, New York, NY 10038 Tel.: 212/732-9550
• The Parkinson's Disease Foundation, Columbia-Presbyterian Medical Center, 640 West 168th Street, New York, NY 10032 Tel.: 212/923-4700
• The National Parkinson's Foundation, 111 Park Place, New York, NY 10007 Tel.: 212/374-1741, and 1501 Northwest Ninth Avenue, Miami, FL 33136 Tel.: 800/327-4545
• The United Parkinson's Foundation, 220 South State Street, Chicago, IL 60604 Tel.: 312/922-9734.

86. Multiple Sclerosis

COMMON CHARACTERISTICS

Multiple sclerosis (MS) is a chronic, slowly progressing disease of the brain, the spinal cord, and the optic nerves. It is one of a group of disorders known to doctors as demyelinating diseases. MS may manifest itself in a wide variety of recurrent mental and physical problems, with periods of complete remission, during which all symptoms disappear, in the early stages of the disease. The condition may be very mild, with many years (sometimes as many as twenty) intervening between attacks. On the other hand, after a few years of recurrent attacks, the disease may lead to partial or total disability.

In the United States, about one person in two thousand suffers from this disease. (In the tropics, MS is much less common: only one person in ten thousand is affected.) Women are affected somewhat more often than men. In two-thirds of cases, attacks start to occur between ages twenty and forty. They virtually never begin in childhood or in later middle age.

DEMYELINATION

Many of the nerves in the brain and the spinal cord (the central nervous system) are enclosed in a protective covering of white, fatty material called myelin. The myelin sheath provides nourishment to the delicate nerve fibers within; it is also essential to the normal conduction of electrical impulses along the nerve fibers. When the myelin sheath is defective—as in MS—the nerve fibers lose their ability to conduct messages from the brain to the muscles and their ability to conduct such messages as pain, sight, hearing, and touch to the brain. Demyelination (loss of myelin) may affect any part of the brain or spinal cord that contains myelin-sheathed nerves. It is generally patchy, with different parts of the central nervous system being affected in succession.

Despite many years of active research, it is not known what causes the loss of myelin. The research suggests, however, that MS may be an autoimmune disease. The term *autoimmune* means that the body, for an unknown reason, does not recognize its own cells and sends out antibodies against them. In MS, such antibodies may be attacking the myelin covering of nerve fibers. Other possibilities are that the damage may be due to a virus, or to a deficiency or abnormality of the fatty substance that composes myelin. MS seems to run in families, suggesting that genetic factors may increase a person's susceptibility to the disease.

SYMPTOMS

Myelin is widespread in the central nervous system; thus, MS may manifest itself in many different ways. Often the first symptom is a tingling or feeling of numbness in an arm or leg. Weakness in the limb may cause fumbling, or an unsteady gait. There may be general physical unsteadiness (ataxia), slurred speech, mental changes, a sudden loss of vision in one eye, or difficulties with bladder control. Usually the first symptoms disappear within a few weeks or months. In some cases, there are no further problems. Other individuals, however, suffer recurrent attacks, with the appearance of the same symptoms or others in other parts of the body, over a period of five, ten, or more years.

CHARACTERISTICS OF MULTIPLE SCLEROSIS

Symptoms correspond to the area of the central nervous system in which the nerve fibers are affected by demyelination—loss of the protective myelin sheaths surrounding the nerves.

SITE OF DEMYELINATION	SYMPTOMS
Optic nerve	Pain in one eye; total or partial loss of vision
Posterior (back) of spinal cord	Tingling in fingers or toes; sensation of tightness around trunk or limbs
Brain stem (all of the brain except the cerebrum and cerebellum)	Double vision; paralysis of eye muscles; numbness of the face; dizziness, nausea, and vomiting
Cerebellum, corticospinal tracts (outer layer of gray matter in the cerebral cortex, spinal cord)	Involuntary eye movement; muscular incoordination; slow, hesitant speech; weakness and numbness in the limbs
Spinal cord	Bladder dysfunction (urinary urgency, frequency, incontinence); sexual dysfunction; weakness and numbness in the limbs; paralysis
Beneath the cerebral cortex	Seizures
Cerebrum (largest part of the brain, separated into two hemispheres)	Euphoria, loss of memory, depression

In the later stages of the disease, recovery after each episode becomes less complete.

Only a limited number of people with MS are crippled by the disease. In many people, the symptoms are mild and leave no ill effects. Others are left with minor disabilities but succeed in leading essentially normal lives.

DIAGNOSIS

A tentative diagnosis of MS is usually made after several attacks and remissions characteristic of the disease occur. Laboratory examination of cerebrospinal fluid (the clear fluid that surrounds the brain and the spinal cord) will be performed to strengthen the diagnosis, but there is no clear-cut diagnostic test for MS. If MS is present, the cerebrospinal fluid is likely to contain elevated levels of protein and antibodies, particularly one called immunoglobulin.

COPING WITH MS

Frank open communication between the MS patient, physician, and family members is important. Multiple sclerosis may entail a number of disabling conditions; it is important to make life-style adjustments because of these limitations. On the other hand, the MS patient should not fall into the trap of being overly babied. Every effort should be made to lead as full and normal a life as possible. Activities should be paced to avoid overexertion. Situations that provoke tension and anxiety should be avoided since these tend to aggravate MS.

Massage often helps weakened arms and legs, and exercises involving passive movement help keep muscles in tone. Physical therapy is an important factor in adapting to MS.

Loss of bladder control (urinary incontinence), with a resulting increased risk of urinary tract infections, is another complication of multiple sclerosis. Such problems should be reported to the treating physician promptly. If the incontinence becomes particularly troublesome, a catheter may be inserted into the bladder so that the urine can drain away into a bag.

TREATMENT OF MS

Several drugs are helpful in the treatment of multiple sclerosis and its complications. Short-term therapy with a substance called ACTH (adrenocorticotropic hormone), which stimulates the natural production of cortisone, is effective in lessening the severity of the attacks. Other drugs may be prescribed to treat muscle spasms and urinary tract problems. When using these drugs, it is important to follow instructions carefully. Other drugs, including over-the-counter medications, should not be used without first consulting a physician.

A number of experimental treatments are also showing promise. Doctors are testing a treatment that combines corticosteroids and immunosuppressive agents, which block the immune system's production of antibodies. It should be noted, however, that these regimens are still in the experimental stage and available only at certain medical centers.

Perhaps the most important thing that someone with MS can do is try to come to terms with the disease. Although it is difficult not to be anxious, those who can approach the problem optimistically and constructively have the best success in making satisfactory adjustments to their condition. More information and guidance can be obtained from the National Multiple Sclerosis Society, 205 East 42nd Street, New York, NY 10017 Tel.: 212/986-3240.

SUMMING UP

Multiple sclerosis is a chronic disease for which there is as yet no cure, although there is much research currently being done. It is impossible to predict the outlook for all patients, since the severity of the disease varies so widely. While a small percentage of sufferers are crippled by the disease, many are completely well for varying periods of time, and some have gone as long as twenty years between attacks.

A person with multiple sclerosis should follow the normal routines necessary for good health—getting enough sleep and exercise, eating well-balanced meals—and in addition should maintain as normal and active a life as possible.

87. Spinal Cord Injuries

COMMON CHARACTERISTICS

The spinal cord runs through the hollow of the vertebrae from the brain to the lower back. It is about eighteen inches long and

a little more than half an inch in diameter at its widest portion and resembles a cable that tapers at both ends. It is surrounded by three membranes continuous with the meningeal membranes that surround the brain, and like the brain, the spinal cord is composed of both gray and white matter. The gray matter consists of nerve cells that form an H-shaped column in the center of the cord. The outer white sheath is composed of bundles of nerve fibers.

Cerebrospinal fluid is contained in the space between two of the meningeal membranes. The front (anterior) "horns" of the H contain the nerve roots that control muscle function; the back (posterior) nerve roots carry sensory messages to the brain. From the brain, nerve fibers connect to create the twelve pairs of cranial nerves that serve the head, ears, eyes, throat, and some organs of the chest and abdomen.

Along the length of the spinal cord and through the openings of the spinal vertebrae at various levels run thirty-one pairs of nerves that supply all the muscles of the body (except those of the head and neck) and bring sensory messages back to the brain. The nerves from the upper part of the cord branch out and group into nerve trunks that lead to the upper torso, arms, and hands. From the lower portion of the cord, the nerve branches form the trunks that connect with the pelvis, thighs, legs, and feet. The spinal cord is also connected to the autonomic or self-regulating nervous system that controls the involuntary body processes such as breathing, digestion, bowel and bladder continence, the function of erectile tissue, and reflex withdrawal from pain-producing stimuli.

The degree of disability from a spinal cord injury depends upon the location of the injury. A broken neck, for example, may cause paralysis and/or total loss of sensation in all areas below the neck, whereas severe injury to the lower back (lumbar) region need not affect the nervous system at all.

TYPES OF SPINAL CORD INJURIES

The spinal cord is vulnerable to a number of diseases, such as poliomyelitis, in which destruction of the anterior motor nerve roots results in muscle paralysis; multiple sclerosis, a neuromuscular disorder in which patches of scar tissue that develop in areas of the brain and spinal cord cause impairment of motion; and transverse myelitis, in which inflammation of parts of the cord may cause irreversible damage. Inoperable tumors of the spine, or metastases from elsewhere in the body, may also injure the cord.

However, most injuries to the spinal cord originate in car, industrial, and athletic accidents and in bullet wounds incurred during war. Severe fractures of the spinal vertebrae may damage the cord either because of compression or because splinters of bone have lodged in it. A heavy blow to the back, or the strain of lifting a heavy object, may cause the prolapse of one of the discs between the vertebrae. These discs are pads of cartilage that

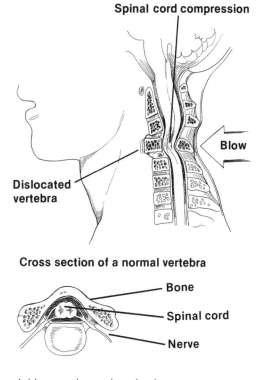

Spinal cord compression

Blow

Dislocated vertebra

Cross section of a normal vertebra

Bone

Spinal cord

Nerve

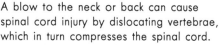

A blow to the neck or back can cause spinal cord injury by dislocating vertebrae, which in turn compresses the spinal cord.

function as shock absorbers. If their inner spongy tissue is forced to protrude at the back of a vertebra, the spinal cord may be affected. Dislocation of the spine as an aftermath of wrestling or an improperly executed high dive may also involve damage to the spinal cord.

RESULTS OF INJURY

Because the spinal cord is considerably shorter than the spinal column, many of the nerves that serve the lower half of the body emerge at a higher point—that is, there is an increasing misalignment between portions of the cord and levels of the vertebrae. Thus, a severing of the cord above the fifth cervical vertebra (as occurs in a broken neck) is usually fatal because of paralysis of the respiratory muscles. Injury to the spinal cord between the fourth and fifth cervical vertebrae results in quadriplegia—loss of movement in both arms and both legs. If damage has occurred between the fifth and sixth cervical vertebrae, the arms can move; between the sixth and seventh, shoulder movement and elbow flexion remain unimpaired, but legs, wrists, and hands are paralyzed. Moving down to the thoracic vertebrae, damage to the cord between the eleventh and twelfth affect sensation and function of the legs above and below the knee, and between the twelfth thoracic and the first lumbar vertebrae, only the area below the knee is paralyzed.

In assessing damage following an injury, the patient's inability to move arms and legs which themselves show no sign of injury should be ascribed to spinal cord damage. Spinal fracture will cause severe pain not only of the back but also along the course of the spinal nerves that extend into the chest and abdomen and down the legs. If the spinal cord is involved, paralysis and disordered sensation will affect areas below the level of the injury.

TREATMENT

Injury to the spinal cord is diagnosed by X-ray, computerized axial tomography (CAT) scans, and neurological examination. The site of injury may be located by electrical stimulation of muscles, and where sensation has been lost, it becomes possible to outline an area of damage. When a spinal fracture has caused bone fragments to lodge in the spinal cord, impairment may be temporary thanks to neurosurgical techniques for removing them without further damage to cord tissue. Spontaneous improvement is likely after several days.

Rehabilitation of the victims of spinal cord injury has made great progress since World War II thanks in part to increased research and special facilities to aid injured veterans. Where once the paralyzed patient deteriorated from inaction and inattention, professionally trained therapists and ingenious mechanical devices now help the patient move around to prevent muscle atrophy. Artificial limbs, wheelchairs designed for easy control by the user, a regimen of exercises, psychiatric counseling—all are aspects of treatment that restore the patient's self-confidence and morale to the point where independent activities can be undertaken in spite of handicaps.

PREVENTION

Since most spinal cord injuries are caused by accidents, awareness of potential dangers and precautionary rules is indispensable to avoiding them. Thanks to continuing pressure from safety groups, automobile manufacturers redesigned front seats so that neck support significantly reduces whiplash injuries and their frequently tragic consequences. Every car passenger should wear a seat belt. Safety seats should be provided for children. "Daredevil" attitudes of motorcyclists, high divers, wrestlers, and active sports enthusiasts should be reexamined in terms of their possible results. Spinal cord injuries incurred at the work place could be significantly reduced (with a consequent reduction in the cost of worker's compensation and workdays lost) if rules governing heavy lifting and other hazardous endeavors were rigorously obeyed and enforced.

SUMMING UP

While the seriousness of injury to the spinal cord cannot be minimized, the outlook for rehabilitation and recovery of patients is much more optimistic than it used to be. Advances in neurosurgery have made it possible to perform operations that were once unthinkable; multiple therapies, technological advances in artificial limbs, and a more sophisticated understanding of patient needs have enabled many paraplegics and other victims of paralysis to lead useful and satisfying lives that transcend their disabilities.

88. Myasthenia Gravis

COMMON CHARACTERISTICS

Myasthenia gravis is a chronic neuromuscular disease characterized by weakness and abnormal fatigue of the voluntary muscles. While any group of muscles may be affected, the most vulnerable are those of the eyes, neck, and throat. Less frequently, the arms and legs may be affected. Symptoms may come and go, varying in severity in different cases and in the same person at different times.

While mild cases may recover completely, people with myasthenia gravis are more likely than the general population to develop other ailments regarded as disorders of the autoimmune system, especially diabetes and rheumatoid arthritis. Estimates of the number of people affected vary broadly, ranging from 11,000 to 100,000.

A clearer understanding of the nature of the disease has led to improved methods of treatment. In recent years, there has been a dramatic decline in long-term death rates and a significant increase in the number of patients whose conditions improve with surgery or medical therapy.

CAUSES OF MYASTHENIA GRAVIS

Under normal circumstances, the neuromuscular transmission system depends on the release of the chemical acetylcholine at the junction between the nerve ending and the adjacent muscle fiber. This junction is known as the cholinergic receptor. When the acetylcholine reaches muscle fibers, they contract so that the muscle can perform its task effectively. In myasthenia gravis, however, an unknown mechanism triggers an antibody reaction to the cholinergic receptors, thereby immobilizing them. (A clue to this unwanted antibody substance in the blood is the fact that mothers with MG sometimes give birth to babies with a transient form of the disorder which disappears within the first six weeks, never to return. The presence of the anomalous antibodies does not mean that the disease is inherited. However, like rheumatoid arthritis and some of the other autoimmune disorders, myasthenia gravis tends to run in families.)

In 1976, the antibody was identified by a biochemist, Dr. Jon Lindstrom at the Salk Institute in California, and since that time it has been found to be present in the blood serum in all but 10 percent of patients.

NATURAL COURSE OF THE DISEASE

This is an erratic disease, and symptoms vary widely, depending on which muscles are affected. In many cases, eyelids droop

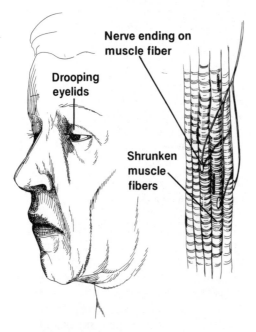

Myasthenia gravis usually affects the facial muscles, causing weakness and muscle fatigue. Drooping eyelids (ptosis) are a common manifestation. A dysfunction at the junction of the nerve ending and muscle fiber—the cholinergic receptor—causes myasthenia gravis. Muscle fibers eventually shrink (atrophy) from disuse.

as the muscles around the eyes weaken. This disability may be followed quickly by a weakening of the voice, slurred speech, and an inability to chew and swallow properly as muscle weakness advances through the neck and throat. When this occurs, the patient runs a risk of choking if food is trapped in the windpipe. More serious still is the possibility of a *myasthenic crisis,* a life-threatening circumstance which may occur if the respiratory muscles collapse. This complication may be precipitated by a high fever accompanying an infectious disease, by the hormonal changes of menstruation or pregnancy, or by a stressful situation such as a death in the family or a serious accident. Exacerbation of symptoms short of a crisis may result from the effects of Novocaine (procaine), the local anesthetic widely used by dentists, from a high intake of quinine (as in tonic water), and from certain antibiotics (but not penicillin).

DIAGNOSIS OF MYASTHENIA GRAVIS

The patient's history of inexplicable fatigue combined with obvious changes in appearance or speech are usually the first indications of myasthenia gravis. Most often, the tensilon test is used to reach a diagnosis. Tensilon (edrophonium) inhibits acetylcholinesterase (AChE), a substance that in turn limits the action of acetylcholine. The inhibition of AChE causes brief improvement in the strength of muscles affected by myasthenia gravis. In the tensilon test, the patient performs an action involving a weakened muscle group before and after intravenous administration of two milligrams of tensilon. If improvement occurs after the tensilon is administered, the test is positive, indicating that myasthenia gravis is present.

Tests of muscle responses to electrical stimuli are also used to confirm the diagnosis. With a diagnostic tool known as electromyography, the doctor receives information (similar to that provided by an electrocardiograph about heart performance) about the extent of impairment of muscle performance. Chest X-rays may also be scheduled in order to evaluate the health of the thymus gland. This organ, situated behind the breastbone, plays a not yet precisely defined role in the working of the body's immune system. Where thymus enlargement is detectable, or where a tumor is present, surgical removal (thymectomy) may be recommended. According to some authorities, 25 to 75 percent of myasthenia patients experience a remission of symptoms following this operation.

DRUG THERAPY

Medical treatment involves chemical compounds (acetylcholinesterases) that prevent the breakdown of acetylcholine so that it can do the necessary job of triggering muscular response. Among these drugs are pyridostigmine (Mestinon) and neostigmine (Prostigmin). Since these medicines may have undesirable side effects, they are prescribed in small doses and monitored carefully until maximum benefit is achieved with minimum amounts. Where they prove ineffective, other suppressors of immune response, such as corticosteroids, may be prescribed.

NEW PLASMA TECHNIQUE

A recent treatment for myasthenia gravis and some other blood serum diseases is *plasmaperesis,* in which the patient's blood is slowly pumped out, the abnormal antibodies removed, and the cleansed blood replaced. Pioneered in the late 1970s after the identification of the antibody, the technique takes from three to five hours, but because it is costly and somewhat hazardous, it has not been used routinely. It may, however, be a lifesaving measure in a crisis.

ONGOING RESEARCH

Since its establishment in 1950, the National Institute of Neurological and Communicative Disorders and Stroke has conducted basic research into the cause of myasthenia gravis in the hope that the defect can be corrected at the level of cellular function. This government agency cooperates with the voluntary organization, the Myasthenia Gravis Foundation, which has more than fifty chapters throughout the United States. The national office, located at 15 East Twenty-sixth Street, New York, NY 10010, will supply information about family counseling, support groups, publications, drug discounts, and other services to members. The request should be accompanied by a stamped self-addressed envelope.

SUMMING UP

A clearer understanding of some of the aspects of myasthenia gravis has resulted in improved patient care through proper medication and, in some cases, effective surgery. Except in extreme instances, most people with this disorder can look forward to an optimistic prognosis. A significant number experience remission of symptoms, and even where there is a pattern of recurrence, patients who cooperate with their doctors find that their activities are not restricted and they can lead normal lives without ill effect.

Psychological Problems

---

89. Depression

COMMON CHARACTERISTICS

Depression is our most common mental disorder. It afflicts an estimated 50 million Americans at some point in their lives, 35 million of whom receive some form of treatment. All of us can be affected, regardless of age and social or economic status. Although it is generally assumed that the disorder is more prevalent among women than men, it may well be that men are equally affected but that women are more likely to seek help.

Now and then, everyone feels down; differentiating normal sadness from clinical depression is sometimes difficult. In response to life circumstances—for example, the loss of a loved one or job, or an illness —all of us become sad, and some of us become depressed—a condition commonly referred to as reactive depression. Others, particularly people with a family history of depression, seem to have an inherited tendency for depression and may become depressed in the absence of obvious external distress or upset.

DIAGNOSIS OF DEPRESSION

The American Psychiatric Association has defined depression, in part, as "loss of interest or pleasure in all or almost all usual activities and pastimes." As a clinical condition, depression is usually identified by the extent to which its symptoms interfere with normal functioning. In contrast, the feelings of melancholy that are a natural consequence of stressful or sorrowful life events are more transitory. Grief is dealt with more or less philosophically, the sense of self remains intact, and the daily round of involvements is resumed.

Stressful circumstances that can result in depression may occur at any age from infancy through old age. Hereditary depression also may occur at any age, and it tends to recur. Very often, it alternates with periods of extreme euphoria—a condi-

Diagnosis of Depression

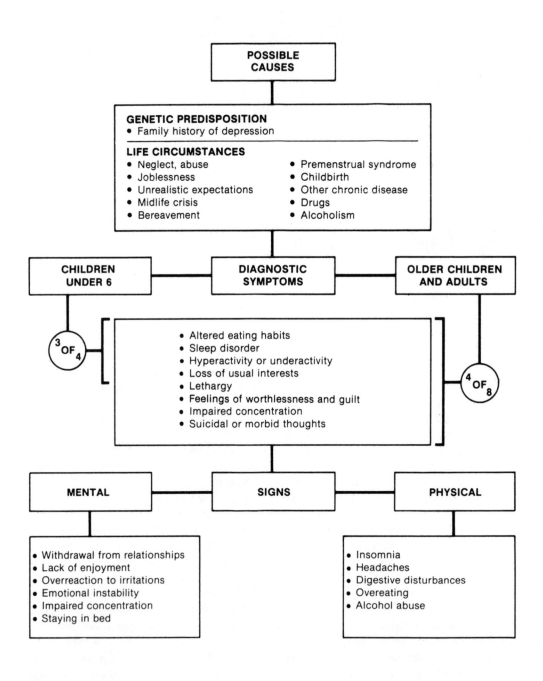

tion often referred to as manic-depression.

In diagnosing depression, at least four of the following symptoms must be present most of the time for a minimum of two weeks (except in children under six years of age, in which case at least three of the first four must be noted): (1) altered eating habits, manifested by marked increase or decrease in appetite and significant change in weight; (2) insomnia or excessive sleepiness; (3) hyperactivity or slowed movement; (4) loss of interest or pleasure in usual activities or decrease in sexual drive; (5) loss of energy or fatigue; (6) feelings of worthlessness, guilt, or self-reproach; (7) reduced ability to concentrate or think, and (8) recurrent thoughts of death or suicide or attempted suicide.

Some symptoms of depression, such as feelings of guilt or inadequacy, may be apparent only to the person experiencing them. But these feelings in turn bring about changes in attitudes and behavior that are noticeable to friends, family, colleagues: a withdrawal from the usual relationships; an inability to find pleasure in the normal joys of living; overreacting to the minor irritations of daily life; emotional instability and inexplicable mood swings; impaired concentration; crying spells, anxiety attacks, and an increasing inability to get out of bed in the morning to face the day's responsibilities.

Physical symptoms also may appear—insomnia, headaches, gastrointestinal disturbances, and, in some cases, a change in appetite or sexual function.

A child of any age may be sending out signals for help in dealing with a depression when he or she complains of headaches and cramps with no physical cause, refuses to see friends, has raging tantrums for no reason, neglects schoolwork, and is self-destructive.

A transitory postpartum depression—also known as after-the-baby blues—is a common and normal condition that may affect both parents. However, if the new mother's feelings of helplessness or entrap-ment and resentment persist to the point where she keeps losing sleep or is afraid to handle the baby because she thinks she might harm it, professional help is needed.

Depression may also manifest itself as a reaction—probably biochemical—to such infectious diseases as hepatitis, mononucleosis, and tuberculosis. A number of drugs, particularly central nervous system depressants, or "downers," especially alcohol and barbituates, also may be responsible for feelings of depression.

TREATMENT

Some people with a genetic tendency to recurrent sieges of mild depression are able to deal with the problem without medication. They find relief in working at meaningful and productive tasks, in spending time with friends who enhance their self-esteem, or in regularly scheduling strenuous exercise, which may be alternated with periods of relaxation or meditation.

In many patients, antidepressant drugs along with or followed by counseling may be required. Most studies have shown that psychotherapy and medication are complementary and additive in value. The medication seems to affect the specific symptoms and the psychotherapy affects the problems of living. The most commonly prescribed types of drugs are:

Tricyclic Antidepressants

These drugs work through the central nervous system to relieve the symptoms. Most take several days or even up to four to six weeks to have their full effect. Some tricyclic antidepressants are combined with antianxiety agents if anxiety is present.

Monoamine Oxidase (MAO) Inhibitors

These drugs block the action of an enzyme that aids in the breakdown of certain chemicals in the brain. They are faster acting than the tricyclic antidepressants, usually working within several days. People taking MAO inhibitors must be careful not to eat foods containing tyramine—for example, certain types of ripe cheese or red wine—because the combination may lead to dangerously elevated blood pressure. They should obtain a diet sheet from their physician with details of foods to be avoided.

Lithium Salts

These are naturally occurring crystalline salts, used to treat manic-depression, a disorder marked by extreme mood swings from exhilaration to deep depression. They may be given in combination with an antidepressive drug during the acute phase and then be taken alone to prevent the mood swings. The lithium dosage should be carefully monitored by a doctor, since even a slight overdose may have toxic effects.

Other nondrug treatments are also available and may be recommended, depending upon the severity and duration of the depression.

SUMMING UP

Depression can be a serious illness that interferes with one's ability to function and cope with life's adversities. Fortunately, a number of effective treatments for depression have been developed, and most people now recognize that telling a depressed person to "buck up" is not likely to do any good. Most cases of depression improve within a few months of treatment. Even when symptoms continue beyond that time, they are likely to be sufficiently alleviated so that the patient can resume most normal activities; at the same time, he can learn how to avoid unnecessarily stressful situations and achieve an increasing level of equanimity through an individually prescribed combination of self-awareness, suitable medication, and—where indicated—a program of counseling, psychotherapy, or other treatments.

90. Anxiety

COMMON CHARACTERISTICS

Medically, anxiety is defined as a state of apprehension, fear, or uneasiness about some impending or anticipated event. It is a specific emotional reaction which may be accompanied by a variety of physical symptoms, such as difficulty in swallowing, diarrhea, muscle tension, or irregular heartbeats.

Anxiety is one of the most common of all emotions. In some situations, such as one involving physical danger, anxiety is an appropriate response. In others, either the degree of anxiety or the apprehensive response itself is not warranted by the situation.

APPROPRIATE AND INAPPROPRIATE ANXIETY

Anxiety is a natural response to something that threatens health or well-being. Throughout life, most of us are subjected to many stressful situations that provoke anxiety. However, if the degree of anxiety

Characteristics of Anxiety

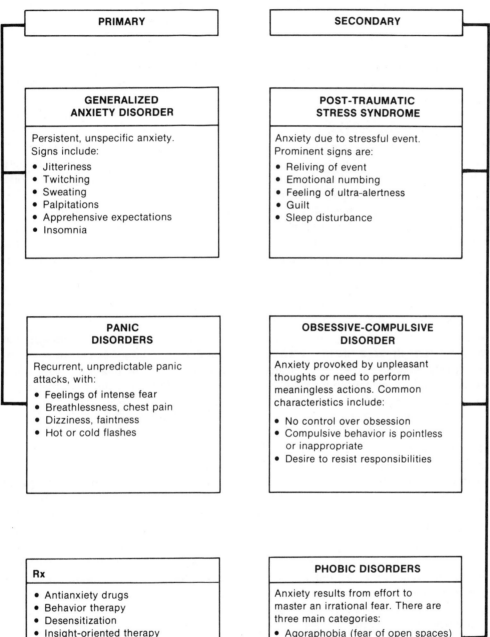

PRIMARY

SECONDARY

GENERALIZED ANXIETY DISORDER

Persistent, unspecific anxiety.
Signs include:
- Jitteriness
- Twitching
- Sweating
- Palpitations
- Apprehensive expectations
- Insomnia

POST-TRAUMATIC STRESS SYNDROME

Anxiety due to stressful event.
Prominent signs are:
- Reliving of event
- Emotional numbing
- Feeling of ultra-alertness
- Guilt
- Sleep disturbance

PANIC DISORDERS

Recurrent, unpredictable panic
attacks, with:
- Feelings of intense fear
- Breathlessness, chest pain
- Dizziness, faintness
- Hot or cold flashes

OBSESSIVE-COMPULSIVE DISORDER

Anxiety provoked by unpleasant
thoughts or need to perform
meaningless actions. Common
characteristics include:

- No control over obsession
- Compulsive behavior is pointless
  or inappropriate
- Desire to resist responsibilities

Rx

- Antianxiety drugs
- Behavior therapy
- Desensitization
- Insight-oriented therapy
- Relaxation training

PHOBIC DISORDERS

Anxiety results from effort to
master an irrational fear. There are
three main categories:
- Agoraphobia (fear of open spaces)
- Social phobia (fear of being with
  people)
- Simple specific phobias, such as
  water or certain animals

is inappropriate to its cause, is exaggerated beyond reason, or is brought on by unlikely events, the response is usually considered abnormal and may require treatment.

Appropriate anxiety is chiefly characterized by worry. For example, if your job is threatened, you might be constantly thinking of where else you might find employment and be planning steps for obtaining a new position. In this situation, the anxiety serves a useful purpose: It causes enough stress to send you in search of a constructive solution to the problem.

If, however, the dread of job loss is not realistic, then the anxiety breeds more anxiety. This type of anxiousness that has no identifiable cause very often impairs the individual's ability to function.

The origins of such internal emotional problems are still not fully understood. In some instances, they may be traced to childhood experiences. This is often true of phobias, such as a fear of dogs that can be traced to a childhood dog bite. Another common example of a phobia is agoraphobia (fear of open spaces), in which anxiety is aroused when a person tries to leave the familiar setting of the home (see Chapter 91, "Phobias"). Certain organic illnesses, such as low blood sugar (hypoglycemia), also may produce feelings of anxiety. In about half of all cases of clinical anxiety, however, there is no discernible cause.

ANXIETY STATES

In most people, anxiety is a temporary feeling. In some, however, anxious feelings and thoughts are almost constantly present in what is called an anxiety state. This chronic state occasionally peaks in a "panic attack," which can occur without any apparent reason at any time. The physical symptoms of fear increase to such a frightening extent that the victim may, in fact, think that he or she is suffering a heart attack. Hyperventilation, or overbreath-

ing, is common during panic attacks and may lead to lightheadedness and even to fainting.

PHYSICAL SYMPTOMS

When an individual is anxious, certain body processes speed up. These are the normal "fight or flight" reactions that help us cope with emergencies. The physical symptoms include breathing irregularities, particularly hyperventilation, muscle tension, sweating, and an increased pulse rate. Other manifestations of severe anxiety may include gastrointestinal symptoms such as diarrhea and symptoms related to the cardiovascular or the pulmonary system: vague chest pains, irregular heartbeats, fatigue, or dizziness. Any of these symptoms should be reported to a physician and carefully evaluated.

TREATMENT

There are a number of approaches to consider in treating anxiety. In some instances, practicing relaxation techniques such as meditation, taking a warm bath, or exercising may help in overcoming mild anxiety. If hyperventilation is a problem, breathing into a paper bag will help overcome the overbreathing and feelings of lightheadedness.

Medication may also be recommended to help the patient cope more effectively with anxiety, particularly the unwarranted anxiety that has no apparent cause. Most commonly, the medication prescribed is one of the tranquilizing drugs. These drugs, like any medication, should be taken only according to your doctor's instructions. They should not be taken in combination with alcohol, and your doctor should be aware of any other medication you may be taking.

Behavior modification therapy, including desensitization, is often helpful in treating phobic anxiety states. For example, an agoraphobic undergoing desensitization would be helped, in a series of graduated steps, to encounter the crowds and public spaces that cause anxiety. A number of other therapies, including psychotherapy, are used in treating anxiety. Your doctor is the best judge of which ones are most appropriate for your type of anxiety.

SUMMING UP

Most anxiety is normal, and most emotional conflicts can be discussed with family or friends with good results. However, if these usual means of dealing with problems do not prove adequate and if anxiety produces undue distress, professional help is advisable. A number of effective treatments, which may include the use of tranquilizing drugs, can help those who suffer anxiety to live more comfortable and productive lives. Remember, no one is immune from anxiety. The important thing is to recognize anxiety as a medical problem and to work with your doctor or counselor to relieve it entirely or, at least, to reduce it to manageable levels.

91. Phobias

COMMON CHARACTERISTICS

Everyone has fears, and in many situations fear is an appropriate response. Phobia (the word is derived from the Greek *phobos,* meaning flight, panic, or fear) differs from normal, appropriate fear in that it is persistent, irrational, and completely out of proportion to the object or situation that gives rise to it. Fear of this kind, and a compelling desire to avoid the object or situation that provokes it, are the main characteristics of all phobic disorders.

It is estimated that as many as twenty million Americans (about 1 percent of the population) suffer from a phobic disorder. For about half a million, the condition is serious enough to disrupt normal living severely. Women are affected far more frequently than men, although it is not clear why this is so. There is often a family history of anxiety disorders in people who are affected by phobias.

COURSE

Typically, a phobic disorder begins in late adolescence or early adulthood with a sudden, unexpected attack of anxiety, which may mount to panic. The attack may occur in response to a particular anxiety-provoking event or may come with no warning and for no apparent reason. Commonly, people describe these spontaneous attacks as being entirely unlike any other anxiety or fear they may have experienced, even under stress. Many feel disoriented, depersonalized, out of control, and fearful of dying or becoming insane. Accompanying physical symptoms may include a rapid pulse, a pounding heart, and chest pain; hyperventilation leading to lightheadedness and faintness; and nausea and dizziness. There may also be strange sensations: the feeling that the ground is moving, or that objects are shrinking. The episode —and subsequent ones—may last anywhere

TYPES OF PHOBIAS

CLASSIFICATION	MANIFESTATIONS
Agoraphobia	Fear of being alone, or in public place; avoids crowds, stores, elevators, public transportation. Often becomes home-bound.
Social phobia	Fear of public speaking, eating, using public lavatories.
Simple phobia	Fear of specific object or situation; most common are fears of animals, snakes, insects, mice, closed spaces (claustrophobia), and heights (acrophobia).

from several minutes to several hours.

The circumstances of this first anxiety attack often determine what will be in future that individual's phobic stimulus—the object or situation that is so feared that it provokes an anxiety or panic attack (phobic response). If the first attack takes place on suddenly coming on a snake, for example, snakes may in future provoke a phobic response. The object thus becomes a conditioned stimulus, and the phobic response is, in effect, a conditioned response.

Because of their association with the original phobic stimulus, other objects and situations may also become capable of provoking a phobic response. Fear of one bus, for example, may extend to encompass fear of all forms of public transportation, and the thought of taking a train ride may be enough to provoke a phobic response.

Anticipatory anxiety about having a panic attack causes the phobic individual to do everything possible to avoid the phobic stimulus—including everything that has come, by association, to be part of it—even if avoiding it means never leaving the house. Thus fear of the object or situation and fear of the possibility of an attack, together with the compulsion to avoid the phobic stimulus, come to dominate the phobic's life.

TYPES OF PHOBIC DISORDER

Doctors divide phobic disorders into three types: agoraphobia (or phobia of situations), social phobia (or phobia of function), and simple phobia (or phobia of objects). All types tend to be chronic, waxing and waning in severity and sometimes going into remission completely for a while. Occasionally a phobic disorder disappears spontaneously, but this is unlikely to happen if the symptoms have persisted for more than a year.

Agoraphobia

This is the most severe and pervasive phobic disorder. It is relatively common, affecting 0.5 percent of the population at some time in their lives. It is popularly thought of as being a fear of open spaces (*agora* is the Greek word for marketplace), but in fact the fear is far more complex. The individual with agoraphobia is threatened not only by open, public places but by being alone in places away from home and by being in places and situations where there is no easy way of escape or of getting help in case of sudden incapacitation—crowded streets and stores, tunnels, bridges, elevators, buses, and trains. The individual may be able to cope with the phobia by having a friend or family member (the so-called obligatory companion) always with him when away from home. In other cases, the agoraphobic progressively restricts his or her activities until completely housebound.

Social Phobia

Here, the phobic stimulus is a social situation that involves the possibility of embarrassment or humiliation. Among the more common social phobias are fears of speaking in public, of using public restrooms, of eating in public, and of writing while others are present. Usually, the phobic individual is aware that his basic fear is that other people will detect signs of his anxiety. For example, someone with a fear of writing in public may be concerned that other people will see a hand tremor. This fear generates anxiety, causing the hand to shake and so providing a justification for avoiding the phobic situation—a vicious cycle. Social phobia is relatively rare and, in itself, seldom incapacitating. However, the need to avoid the phobic situation may cause considerable inconvenience.

Simple Phobias

Sometimes referred to as specific phobias, simple phobias are very common. Many involve animals (dogs, snakes, mice, spiders and other insects, mice, and rats are the most usual phobic stimuli). Animal phobias usually begin in childhood. Other common simple phobias are acrophobia (fear of heights) and claustrophobia (fear of enclosed spaces). If the phobic object is rare and easily avoidable—for example, fear of snakes in a person living in the city —it is easy for the individual to "live with" the disorder. Sometimes, however, when the phobic object is common and unavoidable—for example, fear of elevators in a person who lives and works in high-rise buildings—the individual's life style may be severely affected.

TREATMENT

The goal of any treatment plan for a phobic disorder must be twofold: first, to control the anxiety underlying the disorder; and, second, to overcome the individual's avoidance of the objects and situations that provoke the phobic response. Only by reversing the pattern of avoidance can treatment successfully overcome the self-perpetuating symptoms of phobic disorders. Current treatment programs involve a combination of medication and behavior therapy.

Tranquilizers such as diazepam (Valium) are useful in reducing anticipatory anxiety. The eruption of panic attacks can often be entirely prevented by appropriate dosages of MAO inhibitors (notably phenelzine) or tricyclic antidepressants (imipramine and desipramine). Usually there is a delay of three to four weeks before the effect of either of the latter type of drug is apparent.

Behavior therapy focuses on overcoming avoidance behaviors by making the phobic individual confront the stimulus and overcome the panic. The most common technique is desensitization. The patient is exposed, serially, to anxiety-provoking stimuli, beginning with the least frightening and gradually proceeding to the most frightening. An agoraphobic, for example, might start by confronting the sidewalk outside the building, proceed to the main street, and eventually reach the station platform, the most frightening place for him. At each step, the patient learns how to induce in himself a positive feeling strong enough to suppress the anxiety, usually through the use of drugs, hypnosis, or relaxation techniques. In this way, he gradually becomes sensitized so that the stimulus which was previously the most anxiety-provoking no longer elicits any painful feeling.

Another behavioral technique that may be used is flooding (implosion therapy). The patient is forced to experience the phobic anxiety vividly and for as long as it can be tolerated. Eventually he will reach a point when fear is no longer felt. In the technique known as modeling, the patient observes another person undergoing the phobic situation without fear and may then find it possible to copy that person.

In general, simple and social phobias respond best to behavioral techniques. For agoraphobics, especially those with whom panic attacks are a severe and continuous problem, the therapies are not always successful. Much depends on attitude: treatment can be successful even in severe cases if the phobic individual is determined to overcome the problem.

SUMMING UP

Phobic disorders may produce only minor inconveniences in an individual's life—or they may come completely to dominate it. With treatment that combines drug therapy and behavioral techniques, however, the great majority of those who suffer from these conditions are able to lead active lives, beset only by such anxieties as are experienced by everyone.

92. Psychotic Disorders

COMMON CHARACTERISTICS

Mental illness in its most severe form is technically called psychosis. It is qualitatively different from the emotional disturbances that take the form of anxiety, minor or reactive depression, or phobias. There are two main types of psychosis —schizophrenia and manic-depression— both of which are characterized by profound, pervasive, and unpredictable mood changes, disorganized thought, and withdrawal into a world of fantasy.

Until comparatively recently, people suffering from mental illness were doomed to live useless lives under restraint, heavy sedation, or impenetrable clouds of imagined dangers. Many withdrew further and further into their fantasies or permanently regressed into infantilism—unreachable and incurable. Now, however, thanks to medications developed in the last thirty years, increasing numbers of mental patients, while not "cured," can again function in the everyday world. But in order for patients to live productive lives, community cooperation on every level and in terms of supportive facilities, job opportunities, and living quarters are essential aspects of ongoing treatment and recovery.

SCHIZOPHRENIA

The term *schizophrenia* literally means split mind, but in strict clinical usage, schizophrenia has become a designation for a grouping of severe mental disorders. These are characterized by a split between emotions and intellect, between feelings and thought, so profound that the patient is prevented from functioning as an integrated human being.

Schizophrenia is said to affect 1 percent of all populations—in societies ranging from the most primitive and preindustrial to the most advanced, cutting across racial, ethnic, social, and economic groups. In 1982, the National Institute of Mental Health estimated that in the United States there were two million schizophrenics being treated as inpatients or outpatients in psychiatric facilities. Unlike some stress-induced disturbances, this psychotic disorder is not primarily attributable to the culture, but at different times and in different cultures the hallucinations and delusions have different content.

CHARACTERISTICS OF SCHIZOPHRENIA

SYMPTOM	RESULTS
Thought disturbances	Various types of delusions, often persecutory or negative in nature; jumbled thoughts and incoherence also may occur.
Altered perception	Hallucinations, such as hearing voices or sounds; other senses, such as sight, taste, smell, and touch, also may be involved.
Change in affect	Dull or blunted expression; monotonous voice, inappropriate responses, grimaces, or other mannerisms.
Loss of ego	Confusion over identity or sense of self.
Movement disorders	Inability to react to environment; may assume rigid posture or repetitive, purposeless movements, such as rocking or chewing movements.

According to the Diagnostic and Statistical Manual of the American Psychiatric Association, a diagnosis of schizophrenia is made on the basis of the following manifestations:

• Delusions of control—thinking that one's brain is all-powerful and can manipulate future events.
• Thought broadcasting—hearing one's thoughts as though they were spoken aloud and thinking that others hear them, too.
• Thought insertion—believing that Martians or the Devil are putting thoughts in one's head.
• Thought withdrawal—believing that one's thoughts are being stolen.
• Hearing voices—hallucinated arguments or voices commenting on one's behavior.
• Incoherent speech accompanied by inappropriate expressions of emotion, e.g., laughing when announcing a death.
• Impairment of routine daily functioning.
• Catatonic behavior—holding the body in the same rigid position for several hours.
• Persistence of symptoms for at least six months.

CAUSES OF SCHIZOPHRENIA

Although the precise causes of schizophrenia are unknown, most experts now agree that biochemical and other biological factors are probably involved. If environmental stress plays a role in triggering onset of the illness, it is likely to do so only in the presence of genetic predisposition. However, it is unlikely that psychosis is entirely a matter of heredity because in identical twins, if one develops schizophrenia, the other will too in only 50 percent of all cases. If the disorder were entirely attributable to genetic anomaly, there would be 100 percent concordance. (In fraternal twins, when one develops the disorder, 10 percent of the other twins will, too. This figure is about the same in siblings of different ages.)

MANIC-DEPRESSIVE PSYCHOSIS

This psychotic disorder, also called bipolar depression, is characterized by profound disturbances in mood that occur in cycles of a "high" or manic phase inevitably followed by a "low" or depressed phase. Of the seven million Americans who experience immobilizing depression in any given year, only a fraction suffer from the bipolar form of the illness. Although the depressive aspects are similar, the manic phase is typically part of the psychotic illness. The manic phase is characterized by extreme elation, hyperactivity, rapid speech, and a quick flight of ideas. It should be noted, however, that psychotic episodes sometimes occur with other forms of depression.

TREATMENT OF PSYCHOTIC DISORDERS

Treatment of severe mental illness has been revolutionized by the introduction of antipsychotic drugs, sometimes referred to as major tranquilizers, and antidepressant agents, which are described in Chapter 89, "Depression."

More than twenty antipsychotic drugs are now available in the United States. The first of these, chlorpromazine (brand name, Thorazine), was developed in the early 1950s, and it is still considered the prototype drug. Although the drugs are of varying potency and have different secondary pharmacological properties and side effects, all have the ability to reverse the schizophrenic thought process. While these drugs do not actually cure the disease, they are capable of producing a complete remission in most patients.

Treatment with antipsychotic drugs is usually divided into three phases. The first is an initial or "loading" phase, which generally is carried out in a hospital setting. Relatively high doses of the drug are given until symptoms are controlled and improvement occurs. This is followed by an early maintenance phase, in which the dosage is lowered gradually to the point where the symptoms are controlled on the lowest possible dosage. This phase usually is carried out in the hospital and may take up to two or three weeks to complete. Other treatment, such as psychotherapy or counseling, may be started at this time.

The third phase involves long-term maintenance therapy and usually takes place on an outpatient basis. Unfortunately, much remains to be learned about the dosage and duration of long-term maintenance for psychotic disorders. Frequent followup is desirable but is often difficult to maintain given the nature of the illness and the mobility of our society. Thus, relapses are not uncommon.

Antipsychotic drugs tend to have a number of adverse effects involving nearly every major organ system in the body. Sedation or drowsiness is very common, especially during the initial phases of treatment. Movement disorders, usually taking the form of uncontrollable twitches, tremors, and muscle spasms of the eye, face, tongue, and neck, also are common. Some of these movement disorders disappear when the drugs are stopped or the dosage is lowered. However, long-term therapy sometimes produces Parkinson-like tremors and tardive dyskinesia, characterized by involuntary movements of the face and tongue. Other potential adverse effects include dizziness or fainting when standing (postural hypotension), impotence, and heart rhythm disturbances, among others. Given the broad spectrum of potential adverse effects, careful monitoring and dosage adjustment is important. Serious side effects usually can be avoided or minimized, and when one considers that the alternative is often a life spent in a mental institution, the benefits outweigh the risks.

SUMMING UP

Most patients suffering from psychotic disorders can resume a normal life if they receive appropriate treatment early in the course of their illness. Hospitalization may be required during the acute phase, but once the symptoms are controlled and the thought processes returned to normal, most patients can be treated on an outpatient basis. Although there is a greater acceptance and understanding of mental illness on the part of the general public than in the past, problems remain for both patients and family members. In recent years, a number of organizations and self-help groups have been formed to help mental patients. More information about these may be obtained from Friends and Advocates of the Mentally Ill, PO Box 157, Cathedral Station, New York, NY 10029, and the National Alliance for the Mentally Ill, 1234 Massachusetts Avenue, NW, Washington, DC 20005. Both provide information about referrals, patient rights, self-help groups, and other problem areas.

93. Insomnia and Other Sleep Problems

COMMON CHARACTERISTICS

Insomnia—the inability to sleep, or to sleep satisfactorily—is the most common sleep disorder. It may vary from restless or disturbed sleep to a reduction in the usual time spent sleeping or, in the extreme, complete wakefulness.

Requirements for sleep vary widely. Most adults need the traditional seven or eight hours of sleep a night, but some adults are "short sleepers" and do well on only three or four hours. Many people overestimate the amount of sleep they need and underestimate the amount they actually get during a restless night. Generally, there is no need for concern, even if an unbroken night's sleep is a rarity. An indication of whether loss of sleep is a problem is if it impairs your ability to function well during the day.

ROLE OF SLEEP

It is not known exactly what mechanism induces sleep or precisely what happens to mind and body during sleep that makes it necessary to good health and efficient mental functioning. What *is* known about sleep is that it consists of two very different states. In one state, rapid-eye-movement (REM) sleep, the eyelids move under the closed lids, the heartbeat quickens, and all body processes speed up. Dreams occur during REM sleep and sexual arousal is common, even if the dreams themselves are not sexual in content. Periods of REM sleep last about twenty minutes and occur four or five times during the night. They alternate with longer periods of non-REM sleep, during which the body functions slow down. Non-REM sleep has four stages, of which stages 3 and 4 are the deepest. In these deep stages, it is hard to arouse a sleeper. As the night goes on, the periods of non-REM sleep become progressively shallower.

SLEEPING PATTERNS

Insomnia can take a variety of forms: difficulty falling asleep (initial insomnia); difficulty staying asleep; and early wakening. Sleeplessness is also common in pregnancy, especially in the later weeks. The elderly typically sleep lightly (stage 4 sleep tends to be absent) and fitfully.

Some people are kept awake by painful conditions such as arthritis; others are disturbed by the need to urinate frequently or by leg cramps. People with serious conditions such as asthma are unable to sleep because of the fear of dying in their sleep. For still others, the cause of insomnia may be attributed to their social environment. Arguing with family members; watching exciting programs on television late at night; and consuming caffeine (found in tea, coffee, or cola drinks), heavy alcohol, or a large meal close to bedtime, all may interfere with sleep.

In the majority of cases, however, the core problem is emotional. Anxiety and internalized, unexpressed anger are common causes of sleeplessness. Depression is also implicated in producing some forms of insomnia; waking in the early morning is common in some depressed individuals.

Paradoxically, insomnia may result from the use of a sedative prescribed to relieve it. Especially in elderly people, an inverted sleep rhythm may develop: drowsiness in the morning, sleep during the day, and wakefulness at night.

TREATMENT FOR INSOMNIA

There are a number of ways in which you may be able to help yourself fall asleep more easily. These include exercising during the day, going for a stroll an hour or so before bedtime, taking a warm bath, or drinking a glass of warm milk (milk contains an amino acid that is converted to a sleep-enhancing compound in the brain). Sexual intercourse has a relaxing effect for many people. Relaxation techniques, including muscle-relaxation exercises and meditation, may be useful. If these or similar tension-reducing exercises fail, it is often possible to break the cycle of insomnia by deliberately staying awake for an entire night.

If insomnia is persistent, a doctor should be consulted. Often the reassurance that the problem is the result of normal anxieties or of a treatable physical disorder will relieve distress and help to restore a normal sleeping pattern. A similar reassurance may be helpful for elderly people who are experiencing the change in sleeping patterns normal with advancing years. Treatment of any underlying emotional problem or alteration of living habits is necessary if one or the other is causing chronic insomnia; it is important to create a situation that is conducive to sound sleep.

When the cause of insomnia includes a particularly stressful situation (a bereavement or the loss of a job, for example) or a pain from some physical condition, or if a person's efficiency and sense of well-being are seriously impaired by sleeplessness, drugs may be prescribed. Hypnotic drugs should never be combined with even a small amount of alcohol, which is also a sedative and enhances gastrointestinal absorption of the drugs, compounding their effects. In any instance, you should follow your doctor's specific instructions for treating insomnia.

SLEEP APNEA

People with sleep apnea suffer repeated cessations of breathing during sleep—sometimes hundreds of times a night. The breathlessness, of which they are unaware, is usually interspersed with periods of difficult breathing characterized by loud snoring, gasping, or choking. Apnea sufferers often awaken with a headache and, because of lack of sleep at night, are apt to fall asleep at inopportune or even dangerous times during the day. The disorder is relatively rare but can be serious if the breathing halts for more than a few seconds. Treatment, when required, involves making a permanent opening in the windpipe to ensure continued passage of air to the lungs, even when breathing is halted.

Overcoming Insomnia

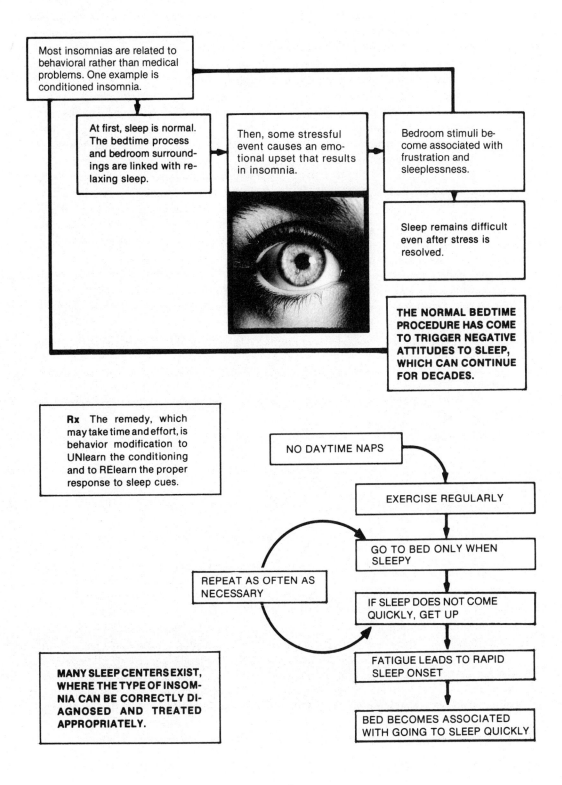

Most insomnias are related to behavioral rather than medical problems. One example is conditioned insomnia.

At first, sleep is normal. The bedtime process and bedroom surroundings are linked with relaxing sleep.

Then, some stressful event causes an emotional upset that results in insomnia.

Bedroom stimuli become associated with frustration and sleeplessness.

Sleep remains difficult even after stress is resolved.

THE NORMAL BEDTIME PROCEDURE HAS COME TO TRIGGER NEGATIVE ATTITUDES TO SLEEP, WHICH CAN CONTINUE FOR DECADES.

Rx The remedy, which may take time and effort, is behavior modification to UNlearn the conditioning and to RElearn the proper response to sleep cues.

NO DAYTIME NAPS

EXERCISE REGULARLY

GO TO BED ONLY WHEN SLEEPY

REPEAT AS OFTEN AS NECESSARY

IF SLEEP DOES NOT COME QUICKLY, GET UP

FATIGUE LEADS TO RAPID SLEEP ONSET

MANY SLEEP CENTERS EXIST, WHERE THE TYPE OF INSOMNIA CAN BE CORRECTLY DIAGNOSED AND TREATED APPROPRIATELY.

BED BECOMES ASSOCIATED WITH GOING TO SLEEP QUICKLY

NARCOLEPSY

Often referred to as "sleeping sickness," narcolepsy is defined as sleep attacks during which a person falls asleep without warning in the daytime. The attacks cannot be resisted and are usually associated with a complete loss of muscle tone (cataplexy). Sleep paralysis—the inability to control one's movements during the twilight stage between sleep and wakefulness—and vivid auditory or visual hallucinations are other components of the syndrome.

HYPERSOMNIA

An excessive need for sleep is the hallmark of hypersomnia. Victims usually sleep much longer than is normal—from many hours to several days. Hypersomniacs often overeat to a serious extent and suffer from obesity accompanied by breathing problems (Pickwickian syndrome).

SUMMING UP

Nearly half of all Americans have some kind of sleep disorder, usually insomnia to a greater or lesser degree. Worry, anxiety, unconscious tensions, and health problems —both major and minor—can all affect the quality of sleep.

Simple tension-reducing measures, such as a warm bath or moderate exercise, often help restore normal sleeping patterns. If they do not and insomnia becomes a chronic problem, medical help should be sought. Sleep-inducing medications should be considered temporary solutions, useful when there is great emotional stress or considerable physical pain, or when sleeplessness is seriously affecting the quality of a person's life. In cases of sleep apnea and other more serious sleep disturbances, medical help should be sought.

94. Senility

COMMON CHARACTERISTICS

Senility and senile dementia are terms often used with negative connotations and misunderstanding. For years they were mistakenly used to mean progressive and incurable mental impairment in the aged. Precisely defined, however, dementia is an impairment of intellectual abilities severe enough to interfere with daily functioning. When it occurs in persons over age sixty-five, it is known as senile dementia. It does not imply irreversibility. Instead, its potential for treatment and cure depends upon its cause. Although most cases of senile dementia are associated with Alzheimer's disease, a condition that is currently irreversible, some cases are caused by disorders that may be cured, improved, or arrested.

Another myth surrounding senility is the long-standing belief that dementia is the inevitable outcome of aging. In reality, although some changes in intellectual (and physical) ability are common among the elderly, the gross mental impairment and confusion of dementia are not produced by the normal aging process. Instead, they are manifestations of disease, affecting an estimated 10 percent of Americans over sixty-five.

SYMPTOMS

The symptoms of dementia include deficits in at least three of the following intellectual functions: memory, cognition (the manipulation or use of knowledge), visual-spatial discrimination, language, and personality.

Usually, loss of memory is the first and most noticeable symptom. Events from the past may be remembered with relative ease, while recent events—even something as simple as a task performed a few hours earlier—may not be remembered at all. The patient may be disoriented and confused about his or her surroundings and the time of day. The severity of this deficit helps distinguish it from the minor forgetfulness that afflicts all of us but that does not interfere with daily functioning.

Frequently, the symptoms of dementia are difficult to distinguish from those of other mental disorders, particularly depression and delirium. For this reason, extensive laboratory tests, as well as physical, neurologic, and mental status examinations, may be required by the doctor to confirm the presence of dementia and to identify its cause.

CAUSES

Senile dementia may be caused by a number of disorders. The most common is a progressive neurologic disease known as Alzheimer's disease. Currently, this condition can be neither cured nor arrested. It may, however, be managed so that symptoms are relieved and behavior enhanced.

Multi-infarct dementia, thought to be the second most common type of senile dementia, is caused by blood clots or other obstructions that interfere with the brain's blood supply and cause scars in the brain (infarcts), usually the result of repeated strokes. Frequently associated with hypertension or cardiac arrhythmias (irregularities of the heartbeat), multi-infarct dementia may be arrested and improved if the underlying cardiovascular problems are treated effectively and rehabilitative measures undertaken.

Less frequently, dementia occurs as a secondary complication of any of a wide variety of illnesses. Among them are metabolic disorders, such as diabetes and thyroid dysfunction; viral and bacterial infections; vitamin deficiencies; brain disorders, including tumors; toxic disorders, caused by alcoholism, industrial chemicals, or therapeutic drugs; and many others. Most of these conditions are readily responsive to treatment. When they are cured, the dementia is also reversed.

Psychological stress, resulting from such traumas as the loss of a mate or hospitalization, may also bring on the symptoms of dementia in the aged. Elderly persons who have learned to compensate for mild intellectual deficiencies are particularly sensitive to any change in their surroundings or daily routine. Depression is still another treatable disorder that is frequently misdiagnosed as dementia in the elderly.

TREATMENT

Multi-infarct dementia and secondary dementia may be arrested or reversed, respectively, by appropriate treatment of the underlying disease.

Treatment of dementia caused by Alzheimer's disease focuses on relieving its symptoms and improving certain aspects of behavior. Although the use of many drugs may exacerbate dementia in the elderly, certain medications, such as psychotropic drugs, may be prescribed to help alleviate

Senility

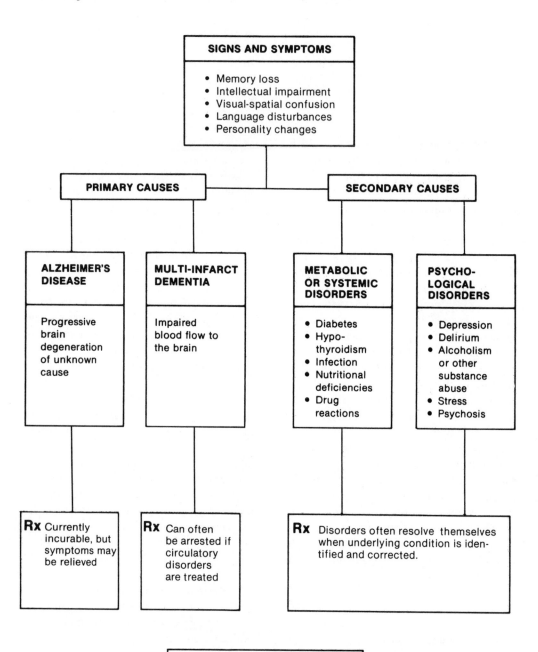

SIGNS AND SYMPTOMS

- Memory loss
- Intellectual impairment
- Visual-spatial confusion
- Language disturbances
- Personality changes

PRIMARY CAUSES

SECONDARY CAUSES

ALZHEIMER'S DISEASE

Progressive brain degeneration of unknown cause

MULTI-INFARCT DEMENTIA

Impaired blood flow to the brain

METABOLIC OR SYSTEMIC DISORDERS

- Diabetes
- Hypo-thyroidism
- Infection
- Nutritional deficiencies
- Drug reactions

PSYCHO-LOGICAL DISORDERS

- Depression
- Delirium
- Alcoholism or other substance abuse
- Stress
- Psychosis

Rx Currently incurable, but symptoms may be relieved

Rx Can often be arrested if circulatory disorders are treated

Rx Disorders often resolve themselves when underlying condition is iden-tified and corrected.

REMEMBER—DEMENTIA IS NOT AN INEVITABLE PART OF AGING. MOST PEOPLE RETAIN MENTAL ALERTNESS THROUGHOUT LIFE.

emotional and behavioral difficulties. Such medications are usually introduced gradually and prescribed in as low a dose as is effective and well tolerated.

It is generally agreed that home care is better for the patient than institutionalization as long as it is practical. Care provided by familiar persons in familiar surroundings may help to minimize the fear, confusion and discomfort accompanying the loss of intellectual abilities. Family members participating in the patient's care may benefit from the following guidelines:

• *Adaption should be encouraged.* An effort should be made to reduce the patient's need for lost functions, while encouraging the fullest possible use of his or her preserved abilities.

• *Avoid stressful situations and reinforce current reality.* These include unfamiliar places, persons, and circumstances. Appropriate interests and social stimuli, such as listening to music and visiting with old friends, should be maintained. A calendar, an easy-to-read clock, and the daily newspaper can be helpful.

• *Treat medical problems promptly.* Because any illness may exacerbate a dementia, the doctor should be informed of all physical and emotional problems at the onset of symptoms. Early treatment may prevent complications. Poor eyesight and hearing loss should be corrected if at all possible.

• *Meals should be monitored.* Because the patient may neglect to eat, and poor nutrition may compound the symptoms of dementia, it is important to provide regular nourishing meals daily.

• *Regulate sleeping patterns.* Patients should be encouraged to be active during the day and to go to sleep at an appropriate hour.

• *Monitor medications carefully.* No drugs should be taken without the doctor's knowledge. All prescription drugs should be taken exactly as directed.

When home care is not practical, the patient may need to move to a nursing home. This transition may sometimes be eased by having the patient take along some familiar objects from home.

SUMMING UP

Senile dementia refers to an extensive deterioration of mental abilities in the aged. It may be caused by a number of disorders, some of which may be cured, arrested, or improved. When Alzheimer's disease is the underlying cause, steps can be taken to avoid exacerbating the dementia. Appropriate medications and practical living arrangements may help the patient to live more comfortably. Organizations have been established to provide support for the families of these patients in a number of cities. Information about these groups is available from the Alzheimer's Disease Association, 292 Madison Avenue, New York, NY 10017.

95. Anorexia Nervosa

COMMON CHARACTERISTICS

Anorexia nervosa is a serious emotional disorder most often found in adolescent girls. (Boys and adult women who have had children also develop it, but this is very rare.) Patients display an abnormal preoccupation with, and fear of, getting fat. They exercise obsessively, eat minute portions of food, and, though they deny they are hungry, spend inordinate amounts of time shopping for food, collecting recipes, preparing meals for others, and learning calorie counts.

The onset of anorexia nervosa can be sudden. An ordinarily active, seemingly well-adjusted teenager, who may or may not be a bit chubby, simply begins to diet to improve her appearance. She then goes on to eat less and less and continues to drop pounds to the point where she becomes emaciated.

This disorder has serious emotional, educational, social, as well as physical implications during an important period of an adolescent's development. Although it is a rare disease, it is becoming more prevalent and mortality rates are high—according to some, as high as 30 percent.

SIGNS OF ANOREXIA NERVOSA

Most often young women with anorexia are children of industrious, middle- or upper middle-income parents who have high performance standards. She is usually a model daughter, a perfectionist about herself and her schoolwork, obedient, and eager to please. The disease may occur after a critical life event such as losing a friend, changing schools, or beginning to menstruate. Visible signs include marked weight loss, voluntary restriction or refusal of food, and obsessive exercising and physical activity aimed at keeping thin. The cessation of menstrual periods is often a first symptom. So fearful is she of getting fat that she denies she is ill or behaving oddly and becomes deceitful about her eating habits. Many patients go on secret food binges, followed by sessions of self-induced vomiting and abuse of diuretics or laxatives. She will withdraw from friends, school activities, even from her usual family involvements.

As more time elapses, the patient's skin becomes dry, scaly, and dirty-looking and covered with excessive hair, although scalp hair begins to thin out. Patients complain of being cold, become constipated, and experience lowered blood pressure, heart rate, and respiratory rate.

CAUSES

The precise cause of anorexia nervosa is unknown, but a number of factors seem to play a role. The disease appears to stem from multiple interacting causes including genetics, physiology, culture, education, nutrition, and even childhood experiences. But large gaps in present knowledge persist.

By some mechanism still to be identified, the cumulative effect of these factors triggers dieting, which leads to loss of weight, and eventually to malnutrition, which in turn causes mental and physical changes in the patient. Thus a vicious cycle is set up in which mental changes foster further dieting, yet the patient stubbornly denies she has a problem and therefore is not receptive to suggestions of help. Changes in the body caused by depriving it of the necessary nutrients lead to loss of appetite, and the cycle becomes self-perpetuating.

These patients suffer from a loss of self-esteem and self-confidence and have an inordinate need to be in total control of their lives. They actually see themselves as fat, when in truth they are very thin.

From a psychological perspective, some observers theorize that a core problem is the patient's fear of becoming an adult woman. She rejects her sexuality, is terrified of pregnancy, and even fantasizes oral impregnation. Cessation of menstruation satisfies her wish to stay a child, unthreatened by adult sexuality.

TREATMENT

Treatment is a long-term proposition that most commonly involves psychotherapy or behavior modification, or a combination of the two, and very often, family therapy. Although psychotherapy is a long, difficult process, it has been successful in many cases. Under this approach, the

Cycle of Anorexia Nervosa

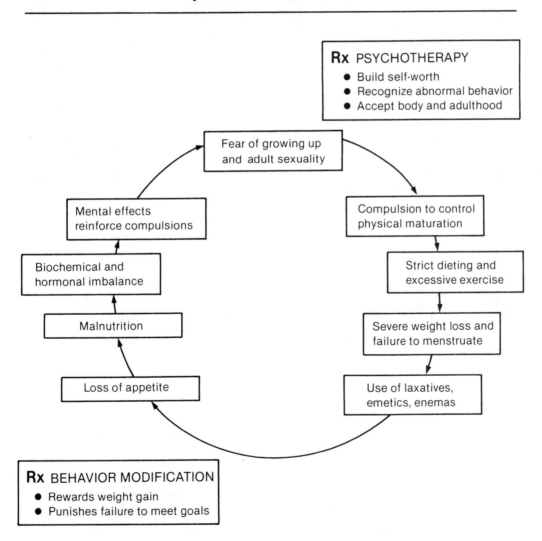

Rx PSYCHOTHERAPY
- Build self-worth
- Recognize abnormal behavior
- Accept body and adulthood

Fear of growing up and adult sexuality

Mental effects reinforce compulsions

Biochemical and hormonal imbalance

Malnutrition

Loss of appetite

Compulsion to control physical maturation

Strict dieting and excessive exercise

Severe weight loss and failure to menstruate

Use of laxatives, emetics, enemas

Rx BEHAVIOR MODIFICATION
- Rewards weight gain
- Punishes failure to meet goals

patient's malnutrition, if not too severe, will have to be borne until she is persuaded to give up her rigid control system voluntarily for a more flexible, mature way of thinking and acting. Forcing the patient in any respect has proved counterproductive, since she equates any such measures with taking away her control. However, in cases of severe malnutrition, hospitalization may be necessary to prevent death by starvation. Success rates with psychotherapy alone, without hospitalization, are considered comparable to other forms of treatment.

A quite different approach is behavior modification therapy. It is usually conducted in the hospital, where supportive medical facilities are easily available. The immediate goal in this instance is weight gain which will reduce the short-term risk of death. At the start, the patient is put to bed, has no bathroom privileges, and is strictly supervised at mealtime. A system of positive or negative reinforcements is set up: the patient gains more privileges if she gains weight, they are removed if she loses. Sometimes psychotherapy or sessions with family members are held in conjunction with the behavior modification therapy. Discharge from the hospital depends on the patient's achieving a certain weight agreed upon at the beginning of treatment. The behavior modification approach shortens the period of malnutrition, but the relapse rate also is known to be high. Medication may be helpful in some cases.

SUMMING UP

Anorexia nervosa is a potentially fatal disorder, still very poorly understood, which involves adolescent girls in a cycle of dieting and weight loss. It may have its beginnings in psychological and social conflicts, but much more research is needed before its cause or causes will be clearly identified. Current treatments are psychotherapy, behavior modification therapy, or combinations of both, with or without medication. Relapses are common, and the treatment period is long and often difficult for patient, physician, and family. Early recognition of the problem and seeking professional help are crucial in increasing the chances of controlling the disorder.

96. Effects of Stress on Health

COMMON CHARACTERISTICS

Stress occurs when the body does not adjust properly to stimuli, whether of internal or external origin. In 1915, the physiologist Walter Cannon described the body's reaction to highly stressful situa-

tions as a "fight-or-flight" response. Under these circumstances, quantities of epinephrine, or adrenaline, a hormone produced by the adrenal glands, are released into the blood, stimulating the liver to provide the body with stored carbohydrates for extra energy. Other changes include quickened

Effects of Stress on Health

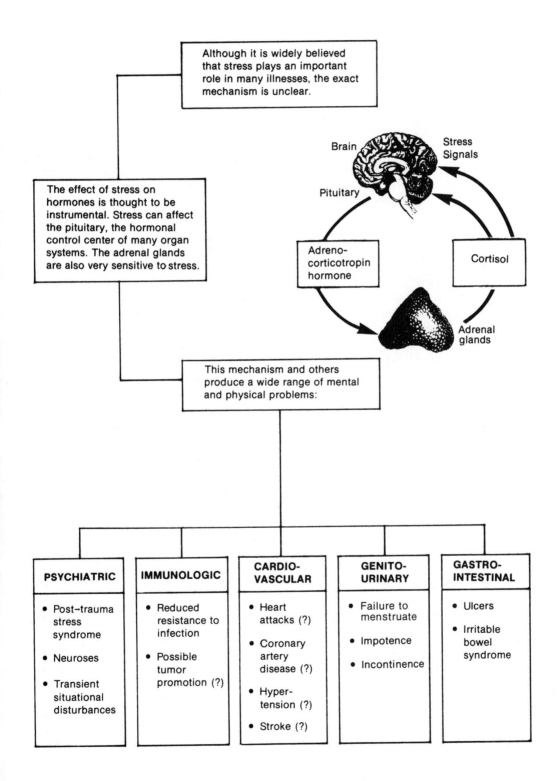

Although it is widely believed that stress plays an important role in many illnesses, the exact mechanism is unclear.

The effect of stress on hormones is thought to be instrumental. Stress can affect the pituitary, the hormonal control center of many organ systems. The adrenal glands are also very sensitive to stress.

Brain

Stress Signals

Pituitary

Adreno-corticotropin hormone

Cortisol

Adrenal glands

This mechanism and others produce a wide range of mental and physical problems:

PSYCHIATRIC	IMMUNOLOGIC	CARDIO-VASCULAR	GENITO-URINARY	GASTRO-INTESTINAL
• Post–trauma stress syndrome • Neuroses • Transient situational disturbances	• Reduced resistance to infection • Possible tumor promotion (?)	• Heart attacks (?) • Coronary artery disease (?) • Hyper-tension (?) • Stroke (?)	• Failure to menstruate • Impotence • Incontinence	• Ulcers • Irritable bowel syndrome

heartbeat and respiration and increased blood pressure and muscle tension. The body is prepared for extraordinary physical exertion, and, if none is forthcoming, this frustrated readiness may exact a toll in headaches, upset stomachs, irritability, and a host of other symptoms.

While stress in and of itself probably does not cause illness, it does contribute to the circumstances in which disease may take hold and flourish. Stress weakens and disturbs the body's defense mechanisms and may play a role in the development of hypertension, ulcers, cardiovascular disease, and—as recent research has indicated —possibly cancer.

In most cases, we cannot do much to alter the stressful conditions in which we live. We can, however, improve the ways we react to potentially stressful stimuli— through exercise, caution, and a better understanding of our external and emotional environments—and thus preclude some of the harmful effects. Some people have a stronger reaction to stress than others; little problems become major ones until life is a series of crises. Some diseases—for example, arthritis or other painful conditions —also may aggravate stress.

STRESS AND SICKNESS

In today's fast-paced, clamoring world, the body may find itself in frequent fight-or-flight responses to work pressures, noise pollution, overcrowding, and other stressful situations where direct, physical outlet would not be appropriate. Under prolonged stress, the body's adaptive and resistance mechanism may become exhausted, and hormonal changes may take place that weaken the body's defenses against disease. A link between emotional stress and certain types of cancer has been suspected for more than a century; recent animal tests have suggested that cancer-susceptible mice are much more likely to contract the disease when exposed to constant stress. Stress also has been linked to

illnesses characterized by an immune-system defect, but so far theories along this line have not been proved.

One of the most impressive and useful studies of stress and sickness had its origins at the turn of the century in the work of Dr. Adolf Meyer, a Johns Hopkins professor who kept "life charts" on his patients. These charts indicated that illness usually occurred around the time that major events took place in the patients' lives. Later researchers Holmes and Rane at the University of Washington refined and systematized these findings, specifying the most stressful life events and assigning them differential point values. In examining the chart, we can see that the life events may be either tragic or joyful; the common denominator among them is change. The more changes an individual undergoes during a given time span, and the more points he or she accumulates, the greater the likelihood of a serious illness or accident. For example, statistics indicate that a person who scores between 150 and 300 points during a particular period runs a fifty-fifty risk of falling seriously ill within two years. If the score exceeds 300, the likelihood shoots up to 80 percent.

CONTROLLING STRESS

One of the most important findings of these studies is that most people can exercise a degree of life-style restraint to control the number of stress-inducing changes. The lesson is not that all change is bad but that there are recognizable thresholds beyond which additional change becomes health-threatening.

Other research points toward the benefits of regulating emotional and physiological response to stressful events; thus, many people are learning to counteract life's pressures through breathing exercises, meditation techniques, and regular participation in sports. In medical studies conducted at Harvard and elsewhere, it was found that these relaxation techniques

THE SOCIAL READJUSTMENT RATING SCALE

Life Event	Mean Value	Life Event	Mean Value
1. Death of spouse	100	22. Change in responsibilities at work	29
2. Divorce	73	23. Son or daughter leaving home	29
3. Marital separation	65	24. Trouble with in-laws	29
4. Jail term	63	25. Outstanding personal achievement	28
5. Death of close family member	63	26. Spouse begins or stops work	26
6. Personal injury or illness	53	27. Begin or end school	26
7. Marriage	50	28. Change in living conditions	25
8. Fired at work	47	29. Revision of personal habits	24
9. Marital reconciliation	45	30. Trouble with boss	23
10. Retirement	45	31. Change in work hours or conditions	20
11. Change in health of family member	44	32. Change in residence	20
12. Pregnancy	40	33. Change in schools	20
13. Sex difficulties	39	34. Change in recreation	19
14. Gain of new family member	39	35. Change in church activities	19
15. Business readjustment	39	36. Change in social activities	18
16. Change in financial state	38	37. Mortgage or loan for a lesser purpose	17
17. Death of close friend	37	38. Change in sleeping habits	16
18. Change to different line of work	36	39. Change in number of family get-togethers	17
19. Change in number of arguments with spouse	35	40. Change in eating habits	15
20. Mortgage or loan for a major purpose	31	41. Vacation	13
21. Foreclosure of mortgage or loan	30	42. Christmas	12
		43. Minor violations of the law	11

can block the action of epinephrine and norepinephrine, the adrenal hormones directly responsible for stress-induced changes.

SUMMING UP

Environmental stress factors may be unavoidable, but it is possible to establish patterns of coping that will minimize their adverse effects. A significant way to reduce stress and stress-related illness is to control, where possible, the number of major life changes that occur within a limited time span. Finding outlets, such as regular sports activity, to counter the buildup of tensions associated with stress also may help in coping with stress.

Allergies

97. Hay Fever

COMMON CHARACTERISTICS

Hay fever is the common term for a seasonal allergic response to a particular airborne substance, especially to ragweed pollen, but also to pollen from other plants, flowers, and grasses or to molds or spores generated in dead or dying organic matter. It is an irritating and debilitating condition, but it is not usually life-threatening. Technically called allergic rhinitis, hay fever affects some fifteen million Americans with signs and symptoms of varying degrees of intensity.

The fact that ragweed pollen, the chief offender, is most abundant in late summer led to the confusion with harvesting or haying time. But the onset of characteristic discomforts—itching, teary eyes, running nose, uncontrollable sneezing, a scratchy soreness in the throat—may occur earlier in the year, at the beginning of a particular pollen season. "Rose fever," for example, usually begins in June. Onset does not include fever, nor is the condition contagious.

For most people, atmospheric pollens, dusts, animal danders, and the like present no threat to well-being. When they breathe in these substances, their immunological system automatically neutralizes whatever harmful effect they might have. But in about 10 percent of the population, the immunological defense has a fault that results in allergic hypersensitivity, or atopy. This hypersensitivity seems to run in families: Some members may be allergic to particular foods, others to cats and still others to a tree pollen, but the tendency to atopic response is shared by all.

BODY MECHANISMS

The symptomatic overreaction that occurs in typical cases of seasonal allergy is a result of a chain of circumstances. First, pollen granules with a particular molecular structure reach the membranes of the

Mechanism of Allergic Response

Individuals inherit a predisposition to allergies. The development of specific allergies depends on exposure to particular substances or allergens.

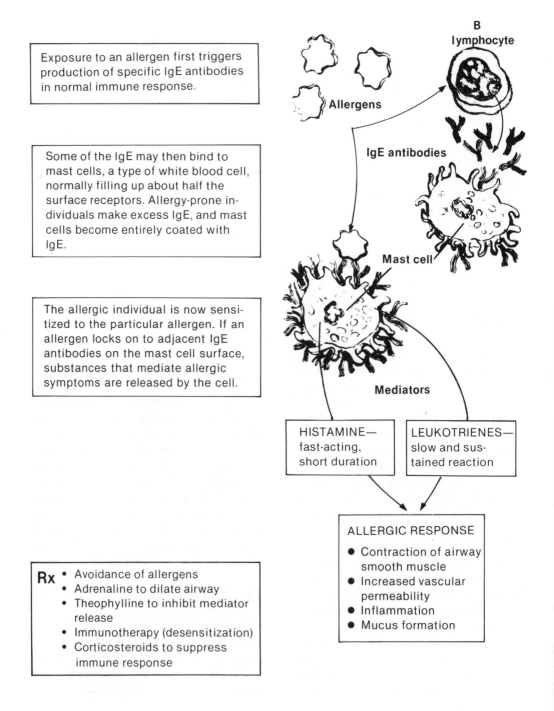

Exposure to an allergen first triggers production of specific IgE antibodies in normal immune response.

Some of the IgE may then bind to mast cells, a type of white blood cell, normally filling up about half the surface receptors. Allergy-prone individuals make excess IgE, and mast cells become entirely coated with IgE.

The allergic individual is now sensitized to the particular allergen. If an allergen locks on to adjacent IgE antibodies on the mast cell surface, substances that mediate allergic symptoms are released by the cell.

B lymphocyte

Allergens

IgE antibodies

Mast cell

Mediators

HISTAMINE—
fast-acting,
short duration

LEUKOTRIENES—
slow and sustained reaction

ALLERGIC RESPONSE

• Contraction of airway smooth muscle
• Increased vascular permeability
• Inflammation
• Mucus formation

Rx
• Avoidance of allergens
• Adrenaline to dilate airway
• Theophylline to inhibit mediator release
• Immunotherapy (desensitization)
• Corticosteroids to suppress immune response

nose. Antibodies, alerted to the presence of a foreign substance, are then synthesized by special cells and begin to hook onto the pollen granules. Hypersensitive individuals manufacture an excessive amount of these antibodies, known as immunoglobulin-E (or abbreviated as IgE). As the immunoglobulin-E and the pollen granules combine, histamines and other chemicals are released. When these substances enter the bloodstream, they cause a dilation of the capillaries, leading to itching, reddening, swelling, and oversecretion from the mucous membranes.

MEDICATIONS FOR HAY FEVER

Antihistamine medications effectively reduce and, in some cases, practically eliminate symptoms for most hay fever sufferers. There are now at least four different categories of such drugs. It is therefore possible to try more than one to see which gives the best results for a particular individual. Drowsiness is a typical undesirable side effect. Since these medicines work best when they are taken at four- to six-hour intervals, activities requiring alertness and concentration—especially driving—should be suspended if at all possible. Alcoholic beverages and tranquilizers should be eliminated altogether, since they intensify the effects of the antihistamines on the central nervous system.

Some over-the-counter allergy pills combine an antihistamine with a decongestant. However, this combination may be counterproductive, since the decongestant may increase the flow of histamine. Professionally supervised use of nose drops may be advisable when symptoms interfere with sleep, and prescription eye drops can be used when itching, burning, and weeping eyes interfere with normal activities.

Seasonal allergies that go untreated may cause vulnerability to secondary infections, particularly of the sinuses. Although effective medication may produce drowsi-ness, untreated symptoms can produce not only an out-of-focus feeling but also general malaise, upset stomach, headaches, and fatigue from lack of sleep.

IMMUNOTHERAPY FOR HAY FEVER

Immunotherapy may be proposed as an alternative when antihistamines provide insufficient relief or when many pollens are involved, spread over a long season. Formerly known as "desensitization," immunotherapy is particularly effective against ragweed pollen, with a reported one-third of patients relieved of their symptoms.

Immunotherapy consists of injecting the patient with increasingly stronger extracts of the allergen on a regular weekly or biweekly schedule before the pollen season starts. These allergen extracts produce immunoglobulin-G (IgG) antibodies, which block the action of the IgE antibodies, thus preventing an allergic reaction. Booster shots are given at longer intervals throughout the season. Because the procedure is costly and inconvenient and must be maintained uninterruptedly, it is usually undertaken only by those people with a prior condition that precludes antihistamine medication or those whose symptoms are too severe to be alleviated in any other way.

SKIN TESTS

When the cause of the allergic reaction eludes easy identification and there are compelling reasons for relieving the symptoms, skin tests are the quickest way to find out what substances are responsible. Most often, more than one substance is implicated. In these tests, a minuscule amount of the suspected allergen in very weak and highly purified form is injected under the skin. When a particular substance causes the skin to become red and itchy at the site of injection, the allergen probably has been identified. The patient can then embark on immunotherapy if so desired or can make the necessary efforts to avoid exposure to the allergen whenever possible.

SELF-HELP FOR HAY FEVER VICTIMS

Severity of symptoms often is directly related to the weather. The pollen count is highest when summer days are sunny and breezy; it goes down dramatically when the weather is rainy and cool. Whatever the climate, the hay fever victim is almost sure to be more comfortable in the city than in the country and will also be more comfortable indoors, especially if the interior is air-conditioned.

If the cause of the symptoms is known to be mold spores, damp woods should be avoided, newspapers should be discarded promptly, and bed pillows (avoid feather pillows) should be aired regularly in the sun.

SUMMING UP

Medical science has known for some time that the molecules of immunoglobulin-E antibodies behave in a way that triggers the release of histamine and other chemicals in patients with allergic hypersensitivity. What has been ascertained more recently is that such patients have ten times more immunoglobulin-E in their blood than other people. Research is now concentrating on creating substances that will suppress this blood component or reduce its potency. Until such medications are available, hypersensitive patients, in consultation with their doctors, can choose from a large variety of antihistamines in order to reduce their symptoms to a minimum or can embark on immunotherapy with the likelihood that, when the pollen season begins, their usual hay fever attacks will not occur.

98. Food Allergies

COMMON CHARACTERISTICS

All true allergies, whether to pollen, animal dander, or particular foods, are a result of a defect in the body's immune system in which normally protective antibodies attack harmless substances as though they were dangerous foreign invaders. Once the antibodies, or immunoglobulins, form, they circulate in the bloodstream, eventually causing the release of histamines and other powerful chemicals that alter the normal condition of body tissues, constricting bronchial passages or dilating blood vessels.

The immunoglobulin involved in practically all allergic responses has been designated immunoglobulin-E (IgE), and it appears that allergy victims have ten times more of this antibody in their blood than most people. Thus while food allergies are not hereditary, there is a genetic tendency to create the IgE antibodies responsible for the adverse reactions. If there is a history of one or another type of allergy on one side of the family, the offspring has a 50 percent likelihood of being allergic to something, and a 75 percent likelihood if allergies are present on both sides. Where the tendency does exist, the antibodies will become activated against the first allergens they are exposed to—which is why some babies are prone to milk and egg allergies.

However, neither heredity nor diet are the only factors in food allergies. It is presumed that an allergic response to a particular food may occur when other circumstances cause a tolerance overload: an especially high pollen count, an infection, a prolonged period of stress.

It is also possible for a food allergy to arise at any time of life, since the amounts eaten and the frequency of intake, plus one or another relevant variable, can lead to unexpected sensitization. Fad diets, addiction to chocolate, gorging on a particular food during its limited season (soft shell crabs or strawberries, for example, can trigger the histamine-induced changes responsible for hives, headaches, or respiratory discomfort). While it is possible to be allergic to almost any food, the typical offenders are shellfish, nuts, eggs, tomatoes, milk, wheat, corn, and various legumes, including soy beans.

In spite of the many people who insist they are allergic to a food or food category, they are a small minority compared with sufferers from hay fever, asthma, and other types of sensitivity. Among children, about 7 percent have a food allergy, and the condition is rare after age three. What does happen is that the food allergies of infancy and early childhood are likely to be transformed into asthma or hay fever, and even these conditions are likely to be outgrown.

SYMPTOMS

Many food allergies strike the skin in the form of an itchy rash that turns into oozing blisters, or an eruption of itchy welts commonly called hives and technically urticaria. In children, symptoms may cover a wide range of complaints: rashes, wheezing and sneezing, and in some cases, severe cramps, vomiting, and diarrhea.

Although the occurrence is very rare, a food allergy may cause the hypersensitive person to go into a state of anaphylactic shock. This acute systemic reaction can occur at any age to the unwary victim. It appears that in cases where a penicillin injection or a wasp sting might be deadly, a similar response can be triggered by shellfish or peanuts. A shock response is preceded by cramps, vomiting, swelling of the air passages causing respiratory distress, and a sudden drop in blood pressure. Emergency treatment consists of prompt injection of epinephrine (adrenaline) for the restoration of normal function. Epinephrine relieves the breathing problems by relaxing the bronchial smooth muscle, as well as increasing cardiac output to raise the blood pressure.

In infants it is suggested by some specialists that colic is the typical symptom of food allergy, and in older children, itchy rashes either wet or dry.

FINDING THE OFFENDER

People with a food allergy who are fortunate enough to be able to say precisely what causes their problem can avoid the offending substance without further ado. In some instances, it is even possible to have it in small doses from time to time without dire consequences. But where the allergic response has a less obvious source, other methods are necessary for identifying it.

Skin tests

It is possible to pinpoint the problem by injection, minute amounts of a series of suspected allergens under the skin. If the patient is lucky, one of the tests will produce the red-ringed welt that identifies the troublemaker.

Radioallergosorbent test

Another test, RAST, uses blood samples to identify allergens. An extract of a suspected allergen, in insoluble form, is mixed with a blood sample. IgE with a specific sensitivity to the allergen attaches to the insoluble extract, and further testing

TYPICAL ELIMINATION DIETS

ALLOWED FOODS	SUSPECTED ALLERGEN: BEEF, PORK, FOWL, MILK, RYE, CORN	SUSPECTED ALLERGEN: BEEF, LAMB, MILK, RICE, WHEAT	SUSPECTED ALLERGEN: LAMB, FOWL, RYE, RICE, CORN, MILK, WHEAT
Cereal	Rice products	Corn products	None
Vegetable	Lettuce, spinach, carrots, beets, artichokes	Corn, tomatoes, peas, asparagus, squash, string beans	Lima beans, beets, potatoes (white and sweet), string beans, tomatoes
Meat	Lamb	Chicken, pork	Beef, pork
Flour (bread or biscuits)	Rice	Corn, 100% rye ("ordinary" rye bread contains wheat)	Lima beans, soybeans, potatoes
Fruit	Lemons, pears, grapefruit	Peaches, apricots, prunes, pineapple	Grapefruit, lemons, peaches, apricot
Fat	Cottonseed oil, olive oil	Corn oil, cottonseed oil	Cottonseed oil, olive oil
Beverage	Tea, coffee (black)	Tea, coffee (black)	Tea, coffee (black), juice from approved fruit
Miscellaneous	Gelatin (non-corn sweetners), cane sugar, maple sugar, salt, olives	Cane sugar, gelatin, corn syrup, salt	Gelatin, cane sugar, maple sugar, salt, olives

measures the amount of this antigen-specific IgE in the bloodstream, indicating the severity of the allergy. RAST may be used in patients whose allergies are so severe that introducing the allergen into the body, even under the skin, could cause a serious reaction.

Elimination diets

These are the practical course of action when the allergen eludes discovery in any other way. Such diets consist in the orderly elimination of particular foods. It is easy enough to find out that tomatoes or soybeans are causing the problem, but when the allergen is a particular grain, meat, or vegetable, detection becomes more difficult. The following elimination diets can be followed over a monitored period, with notes kept of negative responses, until the offending substance can be identified. During the testing period, restaurant dining and dinner parties should be avoided, and the labels on all processed foods should be carefully examined so that the eliminated food is not eaten inadvertently during the test period. There are many cookbooks available in local bookstores and public libraries that contain tasty and ingenious recipes for people who have to forgo a basic food once it has been isolated.

Children's diets

Where there is a family history of food allergy, pediatricians often advise that an infant be breast-fed for as long as possible. Other recommendations include postponing cow's milk and cow's milk products until the baby is six months old and waiting for the first birthday before introducing eggs, citrus fruit, berries, and legumes. Typical allergic responses in older children are likely to take the following form: citrus fruit may produce hives; a wheat allergy may cause asthma; chocolate may be responsible for headaches. Since a young child's diet can be supervised, elimination of suspected allergens should extend over a two-week period, after which the eliminated foods can be reintroduced one at a time at five-day intervals in order to zero in on the problem. It should not be overlooked that infants may have dietary difficulties that have nothing to do with allergy but are caused by certain enzyme deficiencies that are due to metabolic anomalies.

And no matter at what age, it is possible that a negative reaction to a particular food is environmentally or culturally determined and is not a true allergy at all. People who always heard a parent say, "Eggs don't agree with me," or "Oranges give me an upset stomach," may have a body response that originates in the psyche rather than in the immune system. Similarly, incidents of vomiting and gasping for air may occur when Jews or Moslems who observe the dietary laws of their faith discover that they have unknowingly eaten a food containing pork.

SUMMING UP

While food allergies can cause considerable discomfort, they are much easier to deal with than those that cause hay fever and asthma. In most cases where the source of the problem is not easily identified and thereby easily avoided, it is usually possible to discover the offending food by a process of elimination, after which effective self-treatment is based on self-discipline rather than medication. New parents with allergy problems should inform the baby's doctor about the family's history so that new foods can be introduced one at a time on a conservative schedule.

99. Allergic Skin Rashes

COMMON CHARACTERISTICS

Dermatitis means inflammation of the skin; its most common manifestation is a rash. One type of rash, allergic contact dermatitis, is characterized by itching blistered skin and is the result of direct skin contact with an irritating substance. The classic example of such an irritant is poison ivy, but there are literally thousands of substances, natural and manmade, to which an individual's skin may be sensitive. A similar dermatitis, photoallergic contact dermatitis, requires two factors for its development: exposure to sunlight, and the presence of certain chemicals on the skin. A different, although equally irritating, type of rash is urticaria (hives). This rash is the manifestation on the skin of an allergy to something that has been ingested—a food or a drug.

ALLERGIC CONTACT DERMATITIS

Allergic contact dermatitis is due to a delayed hypersensitivity. The allergic reaction does not occur at the first exposure to an irritating substance (allergen). Between the time of the first exposure and the particular reexposure that triggers the dermatitis, there is a latency period during which hypersensitivity develops. This may be as short as five or six days (with poison ivy) or as long as several years (with gold). Numerous exposures to the allergen may take place during the latency period with no ill effect, but eventually a threshold stage is reached. Reintroduction of the allergen at this point results in the release of histamine into the bloodstream. The chemical dilates the small blood vessels and brings on the itchy rash typical of allergic contact dermatitis: reddened skin and a sharply delineated wheal filled with fluid. In severe allergic reactions, there may also be considerable swelling.

Among the substances commonly responsible for allergic contact dermatitis are plants, including poison ivy, to which about 80 percent of the population is sensitive, poison oak, poison sumac, tulip bulbs, geraniums, gladiolus, and chrysanthemums; chemicals used in cosmetics, insecticides, solvents, and dyes; topical antibiotics; and agents used in the manufacture or processing of rubber, leather, and various fabrics. In a practical sense, the worst allergens are those that are an inseparable part of a person's occupational environment, such as petroleum products, greases, and alkalis. However, most people who have to use these substances at work experience a reaction only after thousands of exposures.

Often it is possible to identify the irritant by the location of the rash. Sometimes, however, this may be misleading. An allergic reaction on the eyelids or mouth, for example, may be due to a product used on the fingers that touch those areas, such as a nail polish or hand lotion ingredient. If the offending substance is air-borne—a pollen or an insecticide spray—any part of the exposed skin that comes in contact with it may be affected. When identification is difficult, the doctor will attempt to track down the allergen by careful questioning and by doing patch tests. (In this proce-

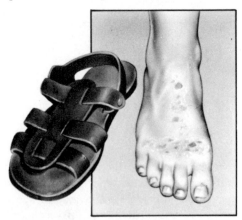

In allergic dermatitis, the location and pattern of the rash often point to the cause. In this drawing, the pattern follows that of the leather sandal and indicates an allergic response to something in the leather.

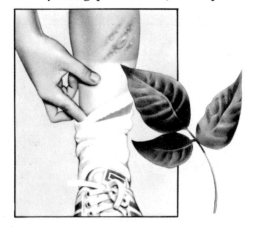

Poison ivy is a common cause of contact dermatitis, with the rash and blisters appearing where the skin has come in contact with oil from the plant's leaves.

dure, possible allergens are left in contact with the skin for twenty-four hours to see if a reaction occurs.)

The extent of the rash is usually determined by the extent of the contact. Poison ivy blisters, for example, erupt only where the plant has touched the skin; even if the blisters are broken by scratching and the fluid they contain is released, the rash does not spread further. Swelling, however, may be more generalized.

The treatment of allergic contact dermatitis depends on the extent of the rash and the accompanying swelling. In mild cases, topical ointments—either prescription or over-the-counter—may be used to reduce itching and dry the blisters before they rupture. Severe flare-ups may require prescription medication (steroids) taken by mouth. The allergic reaction to poison ivy and similar plants can be kept to a minimum if the skin is washed thoroughly with laundry soap as soon after contact as possible. Antihistamines have no effect on this condition, except insofar as they are sedative. Desensitization, which is helpful in other allergic conditions such as hay fever, is not effective.

The best treatment is avoidance of the irritant, if possible. People who have identified the source of their discomfort—as may be the case with sensitivity to wool or a particular cosmetic—need only find a satisfactory substitute. Irritant dermatitis on the hands is best avoided by wearing suitably protective gloves. Poison ivy can be identified and avoided, although it should be remembered that clothes—and animals —that have been in contact with the plant may be contaminating. If the cumulative effects of the allergen become an occupational hazard (as is known to be the case with painters whose hands develop rashes because of contact with turpentine), the use of alternative materials should be investigated.

PHOTOALLERGIC CONTACT DERMATITIS

In some hypersensitive people, the combination of sunlight and the presence of certain chemicals on the skin gives rise to the symptoms of a sudden, severe sunburn: redness, inflammation, and swelling. A brief exposure to the sun may be all that is needed to set off the reaction. Among the agents commonly involved are aftershave lotions, sunscreens, topical antibiotics, perfumes, and coal tar preparations. A variety of drugs can produce similar photosensitive reactions. They include certain antibiotics, tranquilizers, sedatives, and diuretics.

Treatment involves identifying the responsible chemical or drug and finding a suitable substitute. In addition, people prone to photosensitivity should avoid the sun, wearing hats and long-sleeved shirts and using sun-blocking preparations on all exposed areas of the skin.

URTICARIA

Acute hives (urticaria) is usually a reaction to something taken internally—a drug, a food, or a food additive—but the problem can also arise as a result of exposure of the skin to cold, sunlight, heat, or even water. Itching is generally the first symptom. It is followed by the appearance of red, swollen, itching wheals. The outbreak comes and goes, with a given lesion remaining in one place for up to twenty-four hours, disappearing, and then reappearing elsewhere. Generally, urticaria subsides on its own within a week. The itching may be relieved by using cold compresses or calamine lotion on the skin, or by taking an oral histamine, or both. If the causative agent can be identified, as it usually can, it should clearly be avoided to prevent future attacks.

SUMMING UP

People often find it hard to believe that they have suddenly become allergic to substances that they have used for years with no ill effects. However, allergic contact dermatitis always involves a latency period between the first exposure to an allergen and the subsequent reexposure that results in the rash. Sometimes this latency period is several years long, but with one of the most common allergens, poison ivy, it can be less than a week.

If a rash develops in the course of drug treatment, a doctor should be consulted. Sometimes what appears to be an allergic contact dermatitis is in fact an adverse reaction to a drug. Drugs are also a common cause of hives (urticaria) and, in addition, may interact with sunlight to produce an acute photosensitive reaction.

100. Insect Stings

COMMON CHARACTERISTICS

For most people, a bee sting is unpleasant, producing an itchy, somewhat painful wheal, but is not likely to be dangerous. Even multiple stings may produce only temporary discomfort. However, in someone who is hypersensitive to the venom in the stings of wasps, bees, and hornets *(Hymenoptera),* a single sting can cause a sudden, life-threatening allergic (anaphylactic) reaction. Death may occur within five to thirty minutes if the necessary medication is not available.

In the United States, hymenopterons are responsible for more deaths than all other poisonous creatures combined (the list includes snakes, spiders, and scorpions). If you are allergic to the stings of these insects, one defense is to avoid being stung. This requires some knowledge about the appearance and habitat of the various hymenopterons.

AVOIDING THE STING

Most stinging hymenopterons are fairly large; many are highly colored, with elaborate yellow and black or white and black markings. Wasps, yellow jackets, and hornets appear smooth; bees look fuzzy.

The hymenopterons are true insects, which means that their bodies are divided into three specialized regions: head, thorax, and abdomen. The term *wasp waist* describes by analogy the extreme constriction in wasps at the point where the thorax joins the abdomen. All stinging hymenopterons share this type of waist, although in bees it is not as exaggerated.

Many of these insects live in colonies. Perhaps the most familiar of these are the plate-like nests of the *Polistes* (wasps), which are commonly found hanging from the eaves of buildings and in other similar locations. Each colony contains only a few dozen members. In contrast, colonies of the bald-faced hornet, *Vespa maculata,* contain up to ten thousand members, which will attack at the slightest provocation. The paper-like nests, most often attached to tree branches, are oval in shape and open at the bottom—the point from which the hornets will attack.

Yellow jackets are smaller and more brightly colored than hornets. Like hornets, they build nests of pulp by masticating wood fiber. These nests are built in hollow trees, under the eaves of houses, and in holes in the ground. The somewhat elongated aerial nest may reach nine to ten inches in diameter.

Solitary wasps build a series of mud cells on stones or walls, or excavate a nest in pith, wood, or soil. The most familiar of the solitary wasps are the thread-waisted mud daubers, whose nests are common under bridges, in the eaves of houses, and in other sheltered places.

Most of our thousand or so species of bees are solitary in habit, making their nests in burrows or cavities like the solitary wasps. The only social bees in North America are the bumblebee, which usually nests in the ground, and the honeybee, *Apis mellifera*.

In addition to avoiding the habitats of hymenopterons during the warm weather, individuals who are allergic to insect venom should keep away from flowers and should not use scented preparations while outdoors. Bees and wasps are attracted by various scents, including those used in many deodorants and hairsprays. You should keep an insecticide spray with you at all times.

IF YOU ARE STUNG

The stinger looks like a small splinter. If it remains in the skin, it should be removed. Teasing or scraping it out is better than attempting to pull it free. When the venom sac has been left in the skin, as is usually the case with a bee sting, it can continue to contract and exude venom for as long as three minutes. Take care that you do not squeeze any additional venom

into the skin when removing the stinger. To minimize the spread of the venom, and to relieve pain, ice can be applied to the skin.

The symptoms of impending anaphylaxis are shortness of breath, generalized or severe swelling, wheezing, abdominal pain, uterine cramps, and faintness. If

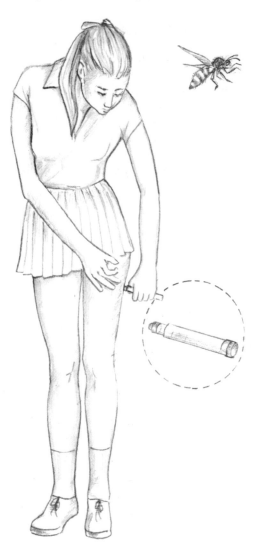

Anyone who is allergic to insect stings should carry a pen-sized, self-injectable dose of epinephrine when outdoors. The device (shown in the inset) is in ready-to-use form; the premeasured dose is injected when the top of the cylinder is pressed.

you develop any of these symptoms after being stung by a hymenopteron, you should go directly to an emergency room for proper information and medical care. People who are hypersensitive to insect stings should carry a special bee-sting kit whenever they are likely to be exposed to bees.

FURTHER PRECAUTIONS

People with known sensitivity to the stings of bees, wasps, and hornets should carry a kit containing a fast-acting antihistamine and epinephrine when they are outside during the warm months. It is important that the medication be instantly available.

The long-term treatment for anaphylactic reaction to insect venom is desensitiza-tion. This can be carried out using extracts of whole bees or wasps, or whole-venom antigens. Your doctor can advise you on the relative value of this procedure for your individual problem.

SUMMING UP

While for most people a bee sting is merely an unpleasant experience, for those who are hypersensitive to insect venom it can be life-threatening. Knowledge of the appearance and habitat of the stinging hymenopterons can aid in preventing a sting. Those who know they are hypersensitive should always carry a kit containing an antihistamine and epinephrine when there is any chance that they might be stung. Desensitization is an effective, long-term treatment.

Nutrition

---

101. Basics of Good Nutrition

GENERAL CONSIDERATIONS

Toward the end of the eighteenth century, the father of modern chemistry, Lavoisier, observed that "life is a chemical process." More than one hundred years later, thanks to advances in chemistry and laboratory technology, the science of nutrition was born. This science is based on the realization that in order for food to sustain human life, two needs must be fulfilled: a quantity sufficient for growth and activity, and a quality providing specific chemical ingredients. With the understanding that illness and abnormality resulted not necessarily from something eaten, but from something *not* eaten, modern nutritional science took an enormous step forward.

Early in the twentieth century, an international group of food chemists and physiologists presented definitive proof that good-quality protein was indispensable to animal growth and development. Soon after, "other substances" that were neither carbohydrates, fats, nor protein, but that seemed to play a vital role in nutrition, were identified as "vitamins." To this list of nutrients was added a group of essential minerals and the so-called trace elements.

In order to define the role of some of these more recently identified nutritional components, the most refined research techniques were required. Essential though they are, the amounts are almost unimaginably microscopic—as little as a few millionths of an ounce daily.

THE ESSENTIAL NUTRIENTS

Nutritionists generally agree that there are about forty-five known essential nutrients, including oxygen, which is needed for the combustion of food into energy, and water, which is needed to transport nutrients throughout the body. The essential nutrients are classified under five main categories:

1. Carbohydrates (sugars and starches) which, no matter what their source, are converted into the type of sugar called glucose, regarded as the body's principal source of fuel.

2. Fats, which can be stored in the body for eventual energy supply.

3. Proteins, called the body's building blocks because they provide the substances that build and repair the body's tissues. In addition to carbon, hydrogen, and oxygen, proteins contain nitrogen as well as varying amounts and varieties of the twenty-two amino acids, many of which must be obtained from food, since the body cannot manufacture them.

4. Seventeen essential minerals in amounts ranging from one-thirtieth to one-thirty thousandth of an ounce per day; these include calcium, chloride, iron, mag-

MAJOR ESSENTIAL NUTRIENTS AND THEIR SOURCES

NUTRIENT	SOURCES
Vitamin A (retinal)	Liver, egg yolk, butter, fortified margarine, whole milk, dark leafy vegetables, deep yellow vegetables and fruits, tomatoes
Vitamin D	Liver, fortified milk, oily saltwater fish, sunlight exposure
Vitamin E	Whole grain cereals, wheat germ, eggs, fish, meats, liver
Vitamin K	Green leafy vegetables, pork, liver, eggs
Vitamin C (ascorbic acid)	Citrus fruits, melons, strawberries, raw or minimally cooked broccoli, peppers, cabbage, tomatoes, potatoes, brussels sprouts, other greens, strawberries, melons
Vitamin B_1 (thiamin)	Pork, organ meats, yeast, eggs, green leafy vegetables, whole or enriched cereals and breads, nuts, legumes, and berries
Vitamin B_2 (riboflavin)	Organ meats, milk, cheese, meats, eggs, whole grains, legumes, leafy vegetables
Niacin	Liver, meats, fish, whole grain and enriched cereals and breads, nuts, peanut butter, dried peas and beans
Vitamin B_6 (pyridoxine hydrochloride)	Liver, meats, whole grain cereals, soybeans, peanuts, corn, bananas, potatoes, avocados
Vitamin B_{12} (cyanocobalamin)	Organ meats, fish, meat, whole milk
Folic acid	Liver, dark green leafy vegetables, lima beans, whole grain cereals, lentils, oranges, asparagus
Pantothenic acid	Organ meats, egg yolk, peanuts, cereal brans, peanuts, cabbage, broccoli, many other plant and animal sources
Biotin	Organ meats, peanuts, egg yolk, mushrooms, chocolate; also produced in intestines

(Continued)

NUTRIENT	SOURCES
Calcium	Milk and other dairy products, egg yolk, shellfish, canned sardines and salmon (with bones), soybeans, dark green vegetables
Phosphorus	Meats, fish, poultry, eggs, milk, cheese, legumes and other high-protein foods
Iron	Liver and other organ meats, red meat, shellfish, egg yolk, dried beans and other legumes, dried fruits, nuts, green leafy vegetables, dark molasses, whole grain and enriched cereals and bread
Potassium	Oranges, tomatoes, bananas, peanuts, legumes, dried apricots, and other dried fruits
Zinc	Eggs, herring, liver, meats, fish, nuts, legumes, whole grain breads and cereals, yeast, oysters

Other trace elements are widely distributed in foods, and deficiencies are rare.

nesium, phosphorus, potassium, sodium, and sulfur, plus the nine so-called trace elements, some in amounts as small as a few millionths of an ounce daily—chromium, cobalt, copper, fluorine, iodine, manganese, molybdenum, selenium, and zinc.

5. Vitamins, some in amounts measured in billionths of an ounce, play an indispensable role in maintaining normal health. At present, there are thirteen: vitamins A, C, D, E, and K, and the eight vitamins originally grouped together as B complex and now known as thiamin, riboflavin, niacin, pyridoxine, cobalamin, folic acid, pantothenic acid, and biotin.

A BALANCED DIET

In 1980, the National Academy of Sciences updated its nutritional standards and recommendations to conform with the latest findings relative to dietary requirements of healthy individuals in all stages of life. These recommendations are the guidelines for school lunches, meals served in the armed forces, and the like. The basic concept is contained in the letters RDA, which stand for recommended dietary allowances (see chart). Although

these are expressed as daily amounts, it is generally agreed that requirements can be balanced out over a week. Deprivation of an essential nutrient over a period much longer than that is likely to impair the body's effectiveness in dealing with illness, accident, or stress.

The most important shift in the balance of nutrients is the endorsement of a higher proportion of complex carbohydrates (in foods such as whole grains, legumes, vegetables, and fruits), as well as a reduction of animal fats and refined sugars. Specialists in the relationship between diet and disease stress the fact that a diet that depends on carbohydrates as a source of energy rather than on fats is typical in countries where there is a lower incidence of heart disease and certain cancers.

In general, a healthy balance is achieved by apportioning nutrients in the following way: 30 percent of the daily caloric intake should come from fats, with animal fats making up about a third of this; 20 percent from protein; and 50 percent from carbohydrates.

A few guidelines make it easier to get maximum nutritional value from meals without eating too much (see Chapter 102,

"Weight Control"), and without having to rely on dietary supplements:

• Eat a wide variety of foods rather than a few that have been "fortified" with extra nutrients.

• An occasional "fast food" hamburger may be an inevitable convenience, but its high-fat, high-salt content is unsuitable for regular purposes. Lean meat, chicken, and fish are best for high-quality protein, interspersed with meatless meals high in protein from lentils, beans, milk, and eggs.

• Keep fat intake within bounds by steaming and broiling instead of frying. Use a small amount of margarine instead of a lot of butter, and use other low-fat sub-stitutes, such as low-fat yogurt for sour cream.

• Don't lose the minerals in vegetables by boiling them. Steam them briefly and eat them raw from time to time.

• Spread calories throughout the day, and avoid cakes, cookies, candy, and low-calorie soft drinks in favor of fruit, fruit juice, and skimmed or low-fat milk.

VEGETARIAN NUTRITION

According to the National Academy of Sciences, even strict vegetarians—those who derive all their nourishment from plant sources—have little difficulty consuming the daily requirement of 1.4 ounces (40 grams) of complete protein es-

REVISED RECOMMENDED DIETARY ALLOWANCES

	Age years	Weight kg	lbs	Vitamin A IU	Vitamin D IU	Vitamin E IU	Ascorbic Acid (C) mg	Folacin µg	Niacin (B_3) mg	Riboflavin (B_2) mg	Thiamine (B_1) mg	Pyridoxine HCl (B_6) mg	Cyanocobalamin (B_{12}) µg	Calcium mg	Phosphorus mg	Iodine µg	Iron mg	Magnesium mg	Zinc mg
Infants	0.0–0.5	6	13	2,100	400	4	35	30	6	0.4	0.3	0.3	0.5	360	240	40	10	50	3
	0.5–1.0	9	20	2,000	400	6	35	45	8	0.6	0.5	0.6	1.5	540	360	50	15	70	5
Children	1–3	13	29	2,000	400	7	45	100	9	0.8	0.7	0.9	2.0	800	800	70	15	150	10
	4–6	20	44	2,500	400	9	45	200	11	1.0	0.9	1.3	2.5	800	800	90	10	200	10
	7–10	28	62	3,500	400	10	45	300	16	1.4	1.2	1.6	3.0	800	800	120	10	250	10
Males	11–14	45	99	5,000	400	12	50	400	18	1.6	1.4	1.8	3.0	1,200	1,200	150	18	350	15
	15–18	66	145	5,000	400	15	60	400	18	1.7	1.4	2.0	3.0	1,200	1,200	150	18	400	15
	19–22	70	154	5,000	300	15	60	400	19	1.7	1.5	2.2	3.0	800	800	150	10	350	15
	23–50	70	154	5,000	200	15	60	400	18	1.6	1.4	2.2	3.0	800	800	150	10	350	15
	51+	70	154	5,000	200	15	60	400	16	1.4	1.2	2.2	3.0	800	800	150	10	350	15
Females	11–14	46	101	4,000	400	12	50	400	15	1.3	1.1	1.8	3.0	1,200	1,200	150	18	300	15
	15–18	55	120	4,000	400	12	60	400	14	1.3	1.1	2.0	3.0	1,200	1,200	150	18	300	15
	19–22	55	120	4,000	300	12	60	400	14	1.3	1.1	2.0	3.0	800	800	150	18	300	15
	23–50	55	120	4,000	200	12	60	400	13	1.2	1.0	2.0	3.0	800	800	150	18	300	15
	51+	55	120	4,000	200	12	60	400	13	1.2	1.0	2.0	3.0	800	800	150	10	300	15
	Pregnancy			+1,000	+200	+3	+20	+400	+2	+0.3	+0.4	+0.6	+1.0	+400	+400	+25	†	+150	+5
	Lactation			+2,000	+200	+4	+40	+100	+5	+0.5	+0.5	+0.5	+1.0	+400	+400	+50	‡	+150	+10

†This increased requirement cannot be met by ordinary diets; therefore, the use of 30–60 mg of supplemental iron is recommended.

‡Same requirement as for nonpregnant women, but continue supplementation for two to three months after parturition.

Source: Reproduced from Recommended Dietary Allowances, 9th ed., with the permission of the National Academy of Sciences, Washington, D.C., 1980.

sential for good nutrition. Complete proteins, containing all of the essential amino acids in the right proportions, are found in meat, eggs, and dairy products. When these are eliminated from the diet, it is still possible to obtain complete proteins by combining plant proteins in such a way that the essential amino acids lacking in one food are present in another. One such combination is brown rice and beans; another is lentils and whole grain bread. Other high protein sources are nuts (including peanut butter) and various seeds, which also contain vegetable fat, iron, and B vitamins. Fruits and vegetables provide most other essential nutrients. But for the "strict" vegetarian, a daily supplement of vitamin B_{12} is necessary, since it is found only in such foods as meat, fish, milk, eggs, and oysters.

VITAMIN AND MINERAL SUPPLEMENTS

About 100 million Americans, or about 44 percent of the population, use vitamin or mineral supplements regularly. According to the National Academy of Science's Committee on Dietary Allowances, most people can obtain all of the essential nutrients by eating a balanced diet. Exceptions might be women who are pregnant and breast-feeding, or people with certain diseases that interfere with normal metabolism. For those people who still feel that they want to take a daily vitamin and mineral supplement, the committee urges that they select one that does not exceed the RDAs for the various nutrients. Excessive amounts of vitamins and minerals are of no nutritional benefit and may, in fact, be detrimental.

NUTRITION FADS

Americans spend millions of dollars each year on so-called health foods and nutritional fads that are of little or no benefit. A fairly recent development in this area is the proliferation of self-styled nutrition specialists who have no valid credentials yet establish flourishing practices as nutritional consultants. Some sell diagnostic services, while others promote megavitamins, trace minerals, and other dubious supplements. While many people can benefit from legitimate nutritional counseling, before engaging the services of a specialist it is well to check his or her credentials. Good sources of expert counseling include hospital dieticians, physician referrals, or university departments of nutrition or dietetics.

SUMMING UP

The basics of good nutrition consist in following a few simple rules: Instead of depending on pills and "fortified" foods, get essential nutrients from varied and balanced meals. Total caloric intake should be about 20 percent protein, 30 percent fat, and 50 percent carbohydrates. Avoid indulging in "empty" calories that are mostly sugar. Cut down on animal fats, cholesterol, sugar, salt, and alcohol. Eat more foods high in fiber, vitamins, and minerals, such as fruits, vegetables, and grains. Preserve nutrients by steaming vegetables. Read labels on processed foods for recommended dietary allowances. And before going on any low-calorie diet, consult a doctor.

102. Weight Control

In a world in which the majority of people do not get enough to eat, it is somewhat ironic that being overweight is the number one nutritional problem in the United States today. An estimated 25 million Americans are considered obese, meaning that they are 20 percent or more above the ideal weight for their height, build, age, and sex.

CAUSES OF OVERWEIGHT

Why some people become overweight and others remain slim, even while appearing to eat more than their obese peers, is not fully understood. It would seem that weight gain and loss are matters of simple addition and subtraction: When more calories are consumed than the body requires, weight goes up; when more are burned than consumed, weight goes down.

Unfortunately, however, weight control is more complex than simple arithmetic. Genetics, metabolism, socioeconomic status, and modern technology all are important factors. Studies have found that the average American today actually eats less than his or her counterpart in 1900 but is more apt to be overweight thanks to modern technology and work-saving devices that not only save human labor but also reduce our calorie requirements.

Moreover, such inactivity compounds the problem of weight control, because people tend to eat more when they are sedentary. Recent studies suggest that exercise helps regulate the brain's appetite control center, which means an inactive person may have more trouble controlling his appetite than someone who adheres to even a moderate exercise program.

Although inactivity and overeating ac-count for most weight problems, biology also seems to create a predisposition in some people. New research, for example, has confirmed what many obese individuals have long claimed: They do not necessarily eat more food than slim people, they just burn it up more slowly. This is particularly true of people who go on crash or semi-starvation diets—they may lose weight at first, but the body adjusts by lowering its metabolism. As a result, they actually require fewer calories to maintain normal weight than before. This phenomenon is even more apparent in repeat dieters, which explains why many dieters tend to regain some weight even if they stay within normal caloric consumption.

HAZARDS OF OBESITY

An extra four or five pounds has no effect on health. But an extra twenty, thirty, or forty pounds poses numerous and well-documented dangers. Obese people have higher rates of diabetes, high blood pressure, arteriosclerosis, heart attacks, kidney disorders, and gallbladder disease. Not coincidentally, they also have a higher premature death rate. Because of the added burden that excess weight puts on the musculoskeletal frame, arthritis, gout, and back disorders are also more common among the obese.

DIAGNOSIS

At any given point in time, millions, perhaps tens of millions, of Americans are dieting. And while most of them will be healthier and happier without the extra pounds they are trying to shed, America's obsession with slimness also has produced

Weight Control

BALANCING THE EQUATION

$$\text{CALORIE INTAKE} \quad = \quad \text{ENERGY OUTPUT} \quad + \quad \text{ENERGY STORAGE}$$

In the Western world, food is abundant, but it is still linked to emotional gratification.	Most jobs are sedentary, and labor-saving devices reduce physical activity.	Historically, efficient fat storage was an important survival factor.

These factors all tend to favor the development of obesity, which is defined as being 20 percent or more over ideal weight.

OBESITY IS A PRIMARY FACTOR IN:

- Adult diabetes
- Menstrual disorders
- Reproductive problems
- Heart failure
- Arthritis
- Gout
- Hypertension
- Back pain and other musculo-skeletal disorders

OBESITY IS ALSO ASSOCIATED WITH:

- Uterine cancer
- Atherosclerosis
- Gallbladder disease
- Premature death

DESIRABLE WEIGHT FOR HEIGHT

Height (in shoes)		Small frame	Medium frame	Large frame
MEN				
5 ft.	2 in.	112–120	118–129	126–141
5	3	115–123	121–133	129–144
5	4	118–126	124–136	132–148
5	5	121–129	127–139	135–152
5	6	124–133	130–143	138–156
5	7	128–137	134–147	142–161
5	8	132–141	138–152	147–166
5	9	136–145	142–156	151–170
5	10	140–150	146–160	155–174
5	11	144–154	150–165	159–179
6		148–158	154–170	164–184
6	1	152–162	158–175	168–189
6	2	156–167	162–180	173–194
6	3	160–171	167–185	178–199
6	4	164–175	172–190	182–204
WOMEN				
4 ft.	10 in.	92–98	96–107	104–119
4	11	94–101	98–110	106–122
5		96–104	101–113	109–125
5	1	99–107	104–116	112–128
5	2	102–110	107–119	115–131
5	3	105–113	110–122	118–134
5	4	108–116	113–126	121–138
5	5	111–119	116–130	125–142
5	6	114–123	120–135	129–146
5	7	118–127	124–139	133–150
5	8	122–131	128–143	137–154
5	9	126–135	132–147	141–158
5	10	130–140	136–151	145–163
5	11	134–144	140–155	149–168
6		138–148	144–159	153–173

$$\text{LESS FOOD} \quad + \quad \text{MORE EXERCISE} \quad = \quad \text{WEIGHT LOSS}$$

a troubling paradox. Even people who don't need to diet often do. Usually, although not always, the chief victims of this mania are women and, more often than not, they are endomorphic. Naturally round, with a higher fat-to-muscle ratio, even at their ideal weights endomorphs tend to look slightly pear-shaped. No amount of weight reduction can change that basic shape. But since the current ideal is to look like Vogue models (who, as ectomorphs, tend to be tall and thin), many endomorphs spend a great deal of time and energy trying to diet themselves into a different body type, which is impossible.

How can you tell if you are overweight? In most instances, an honest look at your unclothed body in a full-length mirror will give the answer. Insurance weight tables, which give the ideal weight adjusted for age, sex, build, and height, are a further checkpoint. However, the true test lies in the ratio of body fat to lean (muscle and bone) tissue. A heavy-boned, very muscular person (for example, a professional football player) may weigh far more than the ideal weight listed on an insurance table yet not be overweight because he has relatively little body fat. The amount of body fat can be determined most accurately by weighing a person while submerged in water; the use of a special caliper to measure the layer of fat just below the skin is still another way to estimate the amount of body fat.

TREATMENT

For people who need to lose weight, there are literally hundreds of diet plans available. *No one should undertake a drastic diet that markedly changes food consumption or eating habits without first consulting a doctor.* The most successful and medically sound diets are those that reduce caloric intake but still allow a healthy variety of foods and at the same time alter eating habits and exercise levels to help ensure that the weight is not regained. Fad or crash diets

that specify eating a very limited number of foods (the rice, grapefruit, or liquid protein diets are recent examples) may help shed pounds quickly but are likely to fail because they don't help people alter long-term eating habits.

Some diets are built on gimmicks, many of which are health hazards. Diet pills that contain amphetamines or other stimulants, liquid protein and other food substitutes, and thyroid are but a few examples of diet gimmicks that may be dangerous to health. One of the latest, starch blockers, has been banned by the Food and Drug Administration.

BEHAVIORAL MODIFICATION

Whatever the cause of obesity, the way to lose weight is to modify one's eating habits. Modifying or altering eating habits into new, learned patterns is, therefore, an essential factor in maintaining normal weight. Behavioral modification includes learning to eat slowly and only at definite times during the day. Portion sizes are scaled down, and alternate ways of dealing with stress are devised. However, behavioral programs are also complicated and often require the assistance of a therapist.

EXERCISE

Many people have the notion that moderate exercise is of little value in weight loss, but this has been disproved by a number of studies. In addition to helping control the appetite, exercise does consume calories that, over a period of time, will result in a loss of weight. For example, there are 3,500 calories in a pound of subcutaneous fat. A brisk twelve- to thirteen-minute walk burns 100 calories, meaning that if a dieter—who normally burns 2,500 calories a day and keeps his caloric intake at that level—begins walking twelve minutes a day, he will lose a pound a month, or twelve pounds in the course of a year. Walking twenty-four minutes a day will increase the loss to more than two pounds a month, or twenty-six pounds in a year. What's more, weight loss is accompanied by a decrease in caloric output that hinders further weight loss and the maintenance of normal weight. Exercise is the way to conquer this effect.

Also important is the rate at which pounds come off. Weight that is lost slowly is likely to stay off, while quick dramatic weight losses are likely to be regained. For most dieters, two to three pounds a week is a realistic goal. Those who seek to lose more should do so only under a doctor's supervision.

SUMMING UP

Millions of Americans are overweight, and millions of others are constantly trying to lose five or ten pounds, even if they don't really need to. Dieting without the guidance of a physician or other qualified health professional can be both futile and hazardous to your health. By the same token, chronic overweight also can lead to serious health problems and premature death. The goal of any dieter should be a gradual loss of weight and changes in eating habits that will help maintain normal weight throughout life.

103. Teenage Dieting

COMMON CHARACTERISTICS

Dieting is a common practice in adolescence, both among those whose weight is normal and among those who are overweight. Like other eating habits associated with the teenage years—skipped meals and empty-calorie snacks, for example—dieting may interfere with good nutrition at a time when this is of the greatest importance for proper growth and development. A weight reduction diet necessarily involves a lowered consumption of calories but adolescents require large numbers of calories simply for growth. If a low-calorie diet is maintained over a period of time, the growth spurt may be delayed or may fail to reach its full potential.

CALORIES AND GROWTH

The recommended dietary allowances (RDAs) for calories in adolescence reflect the timing of the growth spurt, which in girls usually occurs between the ages of eleven and thirteen and in boys an average of two years later. The RDA for boys between the ages of eleven and fourteen is 2,700 calories daily; for boys between ages fifteen and eighteen, the allowance is 2,800—or 20 calories per pound of body weight. For girls, the RDA is somewhat lower. Girls store more weight as fat, which uses fewer calories than does the muscle that boys are developing at this time. Adolescent girls between ages eleven and fourteen should consume 2,200 calories a day, those between fifteen and eighteen need

2,100—or 17 calories per pound of body weight.

Calorie consumption must be sufficient to promote a proper gain in body weight. If calories are insufficient, protein will be used for energy rather than for growth. A difference of as few as five calories per pound of body weight daily is enough to retard growth.

During adolescence, carbohydrates should provide approximately 58 percent of the daily total calories, protein approximately 12 percent, and fats approximately 30 percent. (Of the fats, only 10 percent should be saturated fats.) It is not of great importance from a nutritional standpoint if the carbohydrates are simple (sugars) or complex (starches). However, sucrose, the most common of the sugars, promotes dental caries and is best limited for this reason.

NORMAL-WEIGHT ADOLESCENTS AND DIETING

Preoccupation with appearance is greater during adolescence than at any other time in the life cycle, especially among girls. Many girls of normal weight and with normal fat distribution have an exaggerated concern with overweight, basing the conception of their "ideal" weight on photographs of models in fashion and beauty magazines. This measure of thinness is both unrealistic and unhealthy for a girl of normal build.

Dieting with the object of becoming fashionably slender should not be confused with dieting that reflects a distorted body image, as is often the case with adolescent girls suffering from anorexia nervosa (see Chapter 95).

OBESITY

An estimated 20 to 30 percent of American adolescents are overweight, many to the extent that they can be classed as obese. (Overweight is generally considered to be a weight 10 percent or more above the "ideal" range of weight for height; obesity is a weight of 20 percent more than the "ideal.") Girls are particularly vulnerable to being overweight and malnourished since they must obtain necessary nutrients in fewer calories if they are to maintain their weight but are exposed as regularly as boys to low-nutrition, high-calorie foods.

Only in a very few cases is obesity due to an endocrinological (hormonal) imbalance. Rather, it is the result of a pattern of eating too much, or exercising too little, or both, that can usually be traced to childhood. The children of overweight parents are more likely to become overweight than those of slim ones, not so much because of hereditary factors—although these may play a role—but more likely because they are inevitably exposed from infancy to poor eating habits, such as using food to deal with boredom or tension.

FUNDAMENTALS OF A TEENAGE WEIGHT-REDUCTION PROGRAM

For adolescents, the ideal weight-reduction regimen comprises a moderately restricted, well-balanced diet, increased physical activity, a behavior modification plan, and psychological support from family and friends. In some cases, especially where obesity is massive and is resulting in social and emotional problems, it may be helpful for an adolescent to join an organized weight-reduction program. If a weight loss of more than a few pounds is contemplated, a doctor or qualified dietician should be consulted.

Diet

In any teenage diet, it is important that the balance of carbohydrate, protein, and fat required for diet be maintained. Rather than eliminating any one major food group, the goal should be to eat a balanced diet while reducing the quantities of all meals and snacks. Cutting out all favorite foods (which tend to be high-calorie foods) is unnecessary and unduly burden-

CALORIE CONTENT OF
TEENAGE FAVORITES

FOOD	AVERAGE CALORIES
Typical fast-food hamburger	550
French fries, medium serving	220
Milkshake made with ice cream	520
Hot dog with chili sauce	325
Pizza, half of 15″ pie	1,200
Whole milk (cup)	150
Nondiet soft drinks (8 oz.)	170
Danish pastry, with nuts	325
Doughnuts (cake type, 2½″)	100
Apple pie (1 average piece)	350
Brownie (1½″ × 1½″)	100
Frozen custard (1 cup)	375
Ice cream (1 cup)	270
Yogurt (fruit, 8 oz.)	230

some. The diet should include no fewer than 1,200 calories a day, resulting in a gradual loss of weight without loss of body tone.

Low-calorie "crash" diets and fasting should be avoided. These compromise health and growth, do nothing to change the eating habits that have produced the overweight, and do not promote lasting weight loss. A period of crash dieting or fasting is usually followed by a return to normal eating habits and food preferences and a quick return to the previous weight.

Contrary to the claims made by many quick weight-loss diets and products, losing weight is a simple matter of arithmetic, of balancing the number of calories consumed against those expended. For example, a person whose ideal weight would be maintained on a 2,200-calorie-per-day diet can, on a 1,200-calorie diet, lose about two pounds per week; the 7,000-calorie-per-week reduction equals two pounds of body fat burned off. (A pound of fat equals 3,500 calories.) If the dieter's activity level increases at the same time that his calorie total decreases, weight loss will occur more rapidly.

Exercise

Provided that it is regular and is sustained over a period of time, exercise is extremely beneficial as part of a weight-reduction plan. Even a moderately demanding exercise program, such as walking briskly or cycling at ten to twelve miles an hour for half an hour a day, results in the loss of a pound a month when the food intake remains constant.

Behavior modification

A behavior modification plan, whose object is to correct the faulty attitudes toward food that have caused the weight problem, is an essential part of the regimen, for adolescents as for adults. Studies have shown that obese people, rather than eating when they are hungry, are often prompted to eat solely by the sight or availability of food. In addition, many eat out of boredom, or when tense or angry, or to comfort or reward themselves. Obese teenagers may also overeat in unconscious rebellion against parental emphasis on self-control. It is important to distinguish between these false stimuli to eating and true hunger. Keeping a food diary which records accurately what is eaten, and the circumstances (including the emotional circumstances) under which it is eaten, is helpful in detecting the role played by external cues or inappropriate emotional stimuli in the eating pattern.

Practical steps that can be taken to change eating behaviors include, most importantly, making a conscious effort to eat more slowly. Obese people eat about 40 percent faster than those of normal weight, finishing a meal in considerably less than the twenty minutes needed for the satiety signal from the brain to reach consciousness.

Other helpful ways of changing eating behaviors that may contribute to overweight are altering routines in order to avoid places and situations where food is a known temptation; establishing a time schedule for meals and snacks; avoiding distracting activities and arguments while eating; eating only when seated and only in one specific room; and reserving low-calorie foods for snacks.

Support

Parents should attempt to motivate an overweight adolescent to take primary responsibility for his or her diet, providing all possible support but avoiding prodding, which is usually counterproductive. It is unwise to attempt to impose a rigid dietary regimen on adolescents, since this accentuates social pressures for immediate results and may create a risk of anorexia nervosa.

SUMMING UP

Many teenagers diet in pursuit of an "ideal" weight that is unrealistic and unhealthy. (Usually, such diets are dropped long before they result in any harm.) For others, however, some weight loss is medically advisable. Any diet that involves the loss of more than a few pounds should be designed in consultation with a physician or nutritionist.

Losing weight in adolescence is complicated by the fact that a considerable intake of calories is required for growth. Adolescent weight-loss regimens, therefore, should emphasize a moderately restricted and well-balanced diet, in conjunction with exercise and a behavior modification plan.

104. Salt in the Diet

GENERAL CONSIDERATIONS

Next to sugar, salt is by far the most common substance we add to our food. In addition to being sprinkled on foods at the table, salt and other sodium compounds are found in most processed foods, including those that do not taste particularly salty —like baked goods, ice cream, cereals, soft drinks, and gelatin desserts. It's even found in many drugs, particularly antacids.

Salt and other sodium compounds are added to foods not only to make them taste better but also to improve color and texture, to preserve, and, in the case of fermented foods such as pickles and sauerkraut, to act as the curing agent.

Before modern times, salt was a highly valued luxury. It was one of our first medicines; the Roman god of health, Salus, derived his name from the Latin word for salt—the same derivation for the words *salubrious* (healthful), *safe,* and *salary* (because Roman soldiers were partly paid in salt). The situation is much different today, however. In about one-sixth of the population, overuse of salt poses a major health risk. For these people, who are unable to excrete sodium efficiently, salt is a possible contributing cause of high blood pressure, a disease that affects about 34 million Americans and is a major factor in strokes, heart attacks, and kidney failure. Research suggests that those susceptible to salt-related health problems have family histories of high blood pressure, but the predisposing factors are still unknown.

Salt is made up of sodium and chloride, two minerals that are essential to maintain the body's balance of fluids. When salt intake is increased, we feel thirsty because extra fluid is needed to dilute it. The kidneys help maintain the fluid–sodium balance by excreting extra sodium in the urine or, when the body needs salt, reabsorbing it from the urine. If the kidneys cannot excrete the salt load, the volume of body fluid gradually increases. The blood vessels, in effect, become fluid-filled and overloaded, causing the heart to work harder and blood pressure to increase. Over a period of time, this conceivably could lead to chronic high blood pressure, or hypertension.

In addition to raising blood volume and pressure, excessive sodium also causes swelling of body tissues, a condition known as edema. The legs are often first affected, causing difficulty in circulation and walking. Many women experience a swelling of the legs and pelvic region just before menstruation or during pregnancy. This is believed to be due to the extra retention of sodium and water in the body by the kidneys. Interestingly, many women crave salt during these times, but increasing salt intake only makes the problem worse.

HOW MUCH SALT IS NEEDED

As noted, both of the components of common table salt, sodium and chloride, are essential to maintaining life. But they need to be consumed in only a small amount to satisfy this requirement—as little as 220 milligrams, or about one-tenth of a teaspoon of salt, is all that is needed per day. To be on the safe side, the recommended dietary allowance (RDA) for adults calls for three to eight grams of salt a day. (About five grams equals one teaspoon.) The RDA for children is much less than this, ranging from as little as one-third of a gram to about six grams, depending on age. The average American, however, consumes about eighteen grams of salt a day—many times what is actually needed. Studies have found that most population groups that consume a high-salt diet also have a high incidence of hypertension, heart disease, and strokes. In contrast, populations that traditionally have consumed very little salt—desert nomads, certain jungle tribes in South America and Africa, and Eskimos—also have little or no hypertension and related diseases.

CUTTING DOWN ON SALT

Many foods, such as dairy products, vegetables such as celery, beets, and artichokes, and even drinking water in some parts of the country, are naturally high in salt. In fact, most people can get all of the sodium they need by simply eating a varied diet without any added salt. Still, many people have acquired the salt habit and automatically reach for the salt shaker before even tasting their food. In addition, salt is added to most processed food (see accompanying chart for examples).

The first step in cutting down on salt consumption is removing the salt shaker from the table. Secondly, learn to cook without salt, using herbs and other flavorings instead. Many people find that they actually enjoy the natural taste of foods once they get used to cooking and eating without salt. Learn to read labels, and watch for phosphates, baking soda, baking powder, MSG, soy, nitrates, nitrites, and hydrolyzed vegetable protein—all sources

Food Item	Amount	Sodium (mg)
Chicken noodle soup (canned)	1 cup	1,107
Macaroni with cheese	1 cup	1,086
Instant vegetable soup	1 cup	1,058
Onion soup (canned)	1 cup	1,051
Soy sauce	1 tbsp.	1,029
Vegetable beef soup	1 cup	957
Spaghetti, with tomato sauce and cheese	1 cup	955
Beef, corned	2 slices	802
Sauerkraut	½ cup	777
Tomato juice	6 fl. oz.	659
Frankfurter, all meat	1 frankfurter	639
Instant chocolate pudding	½ cup	480
Cheese, cottage	½ cup	457
Cheese, American	1 oz.	406
Pizza with cheese	1 slice	380
Cornflakes	1 oz.	350
Corn, canned or creamed	½ cup	336
Tuna, chunk, canned in oil, drained	1(3¼-oz.) can	328
Potato chips	1 oz.	285
Bacon, regular	2 slices	274
Pickles, dill	1 spear	232
Bread, rye	1 slice	139
Bread, white	1 slice	114

of sodium. Learning to spot foods that are high in sodium and cutting back on them is another obvious way to cut down on salt consumption. There are also a number of good cookbooks featuring low-salt recipes. These include *Craig Claiborne's Gourmet Diet* by Craig Claiborne (New York Times Books, 1980), and *Cooking Without Your Salt Shaker* by the American Heart Association, which can be obtained from local AHA chapters.

EFFECTS OF SALT REDUCTION

While most doctors agree that reducing salt consumption is a good idea, the precise health benefits have yet to be proved. There is some evidence that children whose blood pressures are in the high-normal range are less likely to develop hypertension if they consume low to moderate amounts of salt. In some people with moderate hypertension, salt reduction may be adequate treatment, at least for a period of time. But the large majority of people with high blood pressure require drug therapy in addition to reducing their total salt intake.

People with edema also may benefit from reducing salt intake, but again, diuretics (drugs to reduce the fluid volume and increase excretion of sodium) also may be needed. Women who suffer from swelling, temporary weight gain, and pelvic congestion in their premenstrual week may find some relief in reducing salt intake at this time.

SUMMING UP

The high salt consumption of the average American has been associated with high blood pressure and other health problems, such as edema. By not using table salt and avoiding processed foods that are particularly high in sodium, most people can markedly reduce overall salt intake. For people with high blood pressure, however, this should not be considered an alternative to drug therapy unless the doctor finds salt reduction is an adequate treatment. A significant number of people, though not everyone, can expect to lower their risk of high blood pressure by reducing their intake of salt. Furthermore, consuming less salt is not likely to harm anyone. Until research explains exactly who is at risk from overconsumption of salt, moderation may be the safest course for everyone.

105. Cholesterol and Other Fats

COMMON CHARACTERISTICS

High levels of cholesterol, a fatty compound found in the blood, is considered one of the leading risk factors in hardening of the arteries (arteriosclerosis) and heart attacks. Consequently, doctors now advise patients with elevated cholesterol and other blood fats (lipids) to decrease their intake of dietary fats. Losing excess weight and increasing physical exercise also seem to lower cholesterol levels. In some instances, cholesterol-lowering drugs also may be recommended.

WHAT IS CHOLESTEROL?

Cholesterol is one of several fatty compounds manufactured by the body. It is essential for a number of vital body functions, including the manufacture of cell membranes and the protective sheaths for nerve fibers and the production of sex hormones, vitamin D, and bile. Although cholesterol is essential to maintain life, it is not necessary to consume any in the diet—the body manufactures all that it needs from carbohydrates and other fats.

Cholesterol is found in all fat of animal origin, which includes not only the fats in meat but also the fat in egg yolks, milk, and other dairy products. About 95 percent of all dietary fat—the fat consumed in food as opposed to the fat that is stored in the body —is made up of triglycerides, which is in turn made up of fatty acids.

In general, the more saturated a fatty acid, the harder or more solid it is at room temperature. Thus, the highly saturated animal and butter fats are solid at room temperature, while the monounsaturated and polyunsaturated fats, which are found in various vegetable, nut, and seed oils, are liquid. Saturated fats tend to raise the level of blood cholesterol, monounsaturated fats —for example, olive or peanut oil—do not alter it one way or the other, and polyunsaturated fats—the oils found in corn, sunflower and safflower seeds, and many fish —lower blood cholesterol.

Recent studies have found that cholesterol circulates in the blood in several different ways. Since cholesterol is a fatty substance and the blood is made up mostly of water—and water and fat don't mix—the cholesterol must be carried by another substance, in this instance a protein which can associate with fats, a lipoprotein. These are manufactured in the liver, and three types are instrumental in transporting cholesterol in the body. One type, high-density lipoproteins, or HDL cholesterol, is often referred to as the "good cholesterol" since it seems to protect against the buildup of fatty deposits in the artery walls (atherosclerosis). The other two types, low-density and very-low-density lipoproteins (LDL and VLDL cholesterol), are thought to play a role in the development of atherosclerosis. Therefore, the higher the ratio of HDL to LDL and VLDL cholesterol, the better.

Some people seem to have a genetic predisposition to high levels of HDL. Others, also on a hereditary basis, have high LDL; such people may die at an early age of heart attack. Vegetarians or people who consume a low-fat diet tend to have high levels of HDL cholesterol. The effect on HDL of adding unsaturated fats or oils to the diet remains uncertain. Athletes, particularly long-distance runners and others who regularly participate in very vigorous exercise, also tend to have high HDL cho-

A Lipid Primer

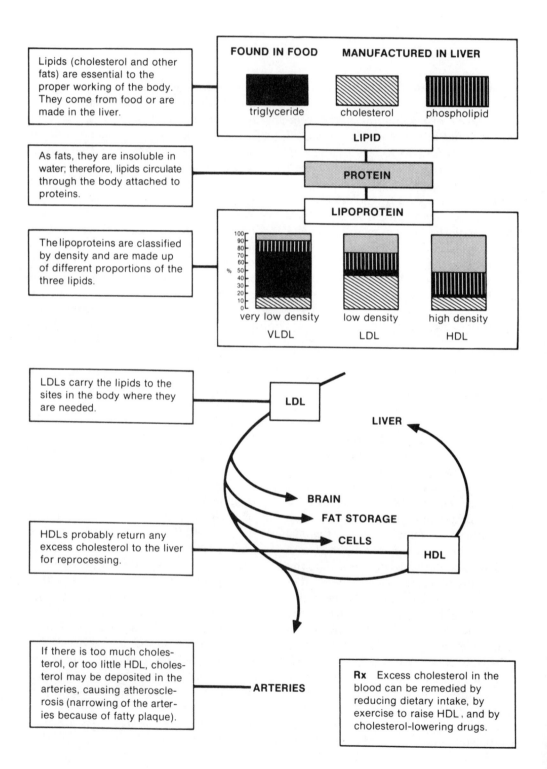

Lipids (cholesterol and other fats) are essential to the proper working of the body. They come from food or are made in the liver.

FOUND IN FOOD   MANUFACTURED IN LIVER

triglyceride   cholesterol   phospholipid

LIPID

As fats, they are insoluble in water; therefore, lipids circulate through the body attached to proteins.

PROTEIN

LIPOPROTEIN

The lipoproteins are classified by density and are made up of different proportions of the three lipids.

very low density   low density   high density
VLDL   LDL   HDL

LDLs carry the lipids to the sites in the body where they are needed.

LDL

LIVER

BRAIN

FAT STORAGE

CELLS

HDL

HDLs probably return any excess cholesterol to the liver for reprocessing.

If there is too much cholesterol, or too little HDL, cholesterol may be deposited in the arteries, causing atherosclerosis (narrowing of the arteries because of fatty plaque).

ARTERIES

Rx Excess cholesterol in the blood can be remedied by reducing dietary intake, by exercise to raise HDL, and by cholesterol-lowering drugs.

lesterol, as do women before menopause, which may explain the low incidence of heart disease in women before age fifty.

ROLE OF CHOLESTEROL IN HEART DISEASE

Exactly how a high level of blood cholesterol leads to heart disease is unknown, but a high-fat diet can raise blood cholesterol and other lipids. The typical American diet provides six to eight tablespoons of fat a day—many times what is required to maintain health. Since Americans tend to eat large quantities of red meat and dairy products, much of this fat is high in cholesterol. As noted earlier, the body also manufactures its own cholesterol. The body can thus contain more cholesterol than it needs, and this can result in the formation of deposits along the artery walls. If the coronary arteries that nourish the heart muscle are involved, the result is increasingly narrowed vessels that may lead to angina or a heart attack.

HOW MUCH IS TOO MUCH?

Most experts agree that a cholesterol level greater than 250 milligrams of cholesterol in 100 milliliters of blood is too high, and certainly anyone whose cholesterol is over 300 milligrams should make an effort to reduce it. In the United States, a cholesterol level of 200 is considered normal, but this is still higher than in many parts of the world, such as Greece, Italy, or Japan, where people consume low-fat, high-carbohydrate diets and have low cholesterol levels and very little heart disease. Many doctors in the United States now recommend that people strive for levels between 175 and 200.

LOWERING CHOLESTEROL

Diet is considered the most effective means of lowering blood cholesterol. Reducing total fat consumption and emphasizing the use of unhydrogenated vegetable oils in preference to animal fats will, for most people, result in lowered cholesterol. Increased exercise also helps lower total cholesterol and increase the level of protective HDL cholesterol. There are also drugs that help lower cholesterol, either by increasing the excretion of lipids from the body or reducing cholesterol production in the liver. These are often prescribed for people who have a hereditary trait for very high cholesterol—a condition known as familial hypercholesterolemia.

SUMMING UP

High cholesterol is considered a risk factor for heart disease in this country. The high-fat diet consumed by most Americans may provoke high levels of cholesterol. Reducing consumption of animal fats, increasing exercise, and losing excess weight can lower the level of cholesterol.

106. The Role of Fiber

COMMON CHARACTERISTICS

The word *fiber* suggests a solid, thread-like substance. In fact, however, much of the fiber in the diet resembles a gelatin or mucilage.

Fiber makes up the cell walls of plants, giving these structures elasticity and strength. Often referred to as roughage, it is resistant to the digestive enzymes in the stomach but can be partially broken down by the bacteria that inhabit the lower digestive tract. Fiber is a nonnutrient (it is not absorbed by the body). Nevertheless, it is an essential part of a well-balanced diet, providing the bulk necessary for the proper elimination of waste products. In addition, an elevated fiber intake is important in the treatment of a variety of medical conditions.

TYPES OF FIBER

Different plants contain different types of fiber, among them cellulose, hemicellulose, lignin, pectin, and gums. Within a plant species, the fiber content depends on such factors as the variety, growing conditions, maturity at harvest, and type of processing that has taken place. In general, cereals and grains are high in non-watersoluble fibers (notably cellulose and hemicellulose), and fruits and vegetables are high in pectin and gums, which are soluble in water.

Because different fibers have different properties, the diet should include a variety of plant foods: fruits, vegetables, cereals, legumes, seeds, and nuts. Bran is the substance that is most commonly associated with fiber and is indeed the richest in cellulose. However, cellulose is not the only fiber needed by the body, and bran is not the only valuable source of dietary fiber.

MEASUREMENTS OF FIBER

The fiber content of foods is often expressed in terms of "crude fiber," a measurement of the organic material that remains after food has been "digested" chemically in a laboratory. This chemical process, however, is far more thorough than the human digestive process, and nutritionists generally prefer the more accurate measurement "total dietary fiber," where this has been calculated for a given food. The total dietary fiber content of a food is usually two to three times higher than the crude fiber content.

Any food that contains 6 percent dietary fiber or more is considered to be a high-fiber food. Examples are 100 percent bran cereals (30 percent dietary fiber), oatmeal (14 percent), kidney beans (10.4 percent), dried figs (18.5 percent), and almonds (14.3 percent).

HEALTH BENEFITS OF FIBER

It is well established that fiber is valuable in treating constipation and in helping the bowels function regularly. Fiber absorbs moisture—some types can absorb many times their weight in water—and in doing so increases the volume and softness of food materials passing through the digestive tract. The muscles of the intestines are stimulated by the bulk, speeding elimination and reducing strain on the lower bowel.

Bran, which is almost entirely cellulose, is the best source of fiber for the relief of constipation. Raw fruits and vegetables and the so-called bulk laxatives (which contain hemicellulose and gum) are useful in keeping elimination regular.

It has not been established that a high-fiber diet can *prevent* hemorrhoids, but such a diet is helpful to those who have the condition. The passage of soft stools requires less stretching of the rectal tissues—including the blood vessels that have varicosed to become hemorrhoids.

Fiber delays digestion and therefore slows the conversion of starches into the blood sugar glucose. A gradual conversion reduces the need for a heavy output of insulin, the hormone that is lacking (or insufficient) in people with diabetes. Diabetics on a diet high in fiber-rich carbohydrates—and low in sugar and fat—can greatly improve their control of their blood sugar levels, some to the point that they are able to stop using insulin or drugs. Pectin and gums, the soluble fibers found mainly in fruits and vegetables, have the greatest immediate effect on blood sugar levels. The fiber-rich foods must be eaten as part of a meal rather than as a between-meal snack to be of benefit.

Some types of fiber have the capacity to bind dietary cholesterol and triglycerides, thus reducing the amounts of these fatty substances that are absorbed from the intestinal tract. The soluble fibers, pectin and gums, are most effective in lowering cholesterol; cellulose is of no benefit. (It should be noted that, although high levels of blood cholesterol are associated with cardiovascular disease, it has not been proved that lowering the cholesterol level by using fiber can actually prevent heart disease.)

FIBER AND WEIGHT CONTROL

A high level of fiber in the diet makes it easier to cut down on the amount of food consumed and to increase the length of time between meals. Fiber-rich foods swell in the digestive tract, creating a feeling of fullness. They also generally need thorough chewing—and a small amount of food eaten slowly prompts the brain to register satisfaction before too many calories have been consumed.

RISKS AND DRAWBACKS OF HIGH-FIBER DIETS

The most common undesirable effect of the introduction of a high-fiber diet is a temporary increase in "gassiness." Sometimes bloating and flatulence are severe, are accompanied by nausea and vomiting, and last for as long as two months or more.

Fiber may aggravate digestive tract conditions such as ulcerative colitis and regional ileitis (Crohn's disease). People with these problems should consult their doctors about the advisability of increasing their fiber intake.

In addition, fiber appears to reduce the absorption of zinc and iron. This, however, should cause no problems if the diet is a well-balanced one.

INTRODUCING FIBER INTO THE DIET

The average American daily diet contains about four grams of crude fiber, as against the six to eight grams considered optimal for a healthy adult. Extra fiber should be introduced gradually, to avoid problems with bloating and "gas."

Because of the different properties of different fibers, a variety of plant foods should be eaten, with more emphasis placed on fruits and vegetables (raw and unpeeled, if possible) than on grains. Products made from refined flours should be replaced with whole grain breads, crackers, and cereals. Bran should always be taken with a liquid, since dry bran, particularly if it is finely ground, may clog the intestine.

Fine fibers such as wood cellulose also tend to induce constipation. Wood cellulose is an ingredient in commercial high-fiber breads. Although its constipating

HIGH FIBER FOODS

FOOD	SERVING SIZE	FIBER (GRAMS)
All Bran cereal	1 cup	23
Bran Buds cereal	¾ cup	18
Bulgur, dry	⅓ cup	5.6
Grapenuts cereal	⅓ cup	5.0
Shredded Wheat	2 biscuits	6.1
Whole wheat bread	1 slice	2.4
Apple	1 small	3.1
Grapefruit	½	2.6
Pear, raw	1 medium	2.8
Strawberries	½ cup	2.6
Cabbage, cooked	¾ cup	2.2
Carrots, raw	1 medium	3.7
Celery, raw	2½ stalks	3.0
Corn kernels	⅔ cup	4.2
Lentils, cooked	½ cup	4.0
Parsnips, cooked	½ cup	5.9
Peas, cooked	½ cup	3.8
Potatoes, cooked	⅔ cup	3.1
Summer squash, raw	1 5-inch	3.0

effect is offset by the presence of other ingredients such as wheat bran and other fibers, it is not considered advisable to allow high-fiber commercial breads to take the place of more nutritious cereals.

Fiber should be taken as an integral part of foods rather than as a supplement. Fiber "pills" have not been shown to be beneficial.

SUMMING UP

Fiber is an important part of the normal, well-balanced diet, promoting regular elimination of waste products. Diets high in fiber can be helpful in the relief of constipation, in the reduction of cholesterol levels, and, for those with diabetes, in the control of blood sugar levels. However, fiber is not a cure-all, and many of the claims that have been made for it—for example, that it prevents heart disease, colon cancer, and appendicitis—are unproven.

Extra fiber should be added to the diet gradually and in moderation. People with gastrointestinal disorders should not attempt self-treatment with fiber and should consult their doctors before increasing their fiber intake.

Eye, Ear, Nose, and Throat

107. Sight Disorders

COMMON CHARACTERISTICS

Sight disorders are most easily understood through some knowledge of the structure and function of the normally healthy eye.

The eyeball itself is a sphere filled with a viscous fluid and covered with a tough protective layer called the sclera, which makes up the "white" of the eye. This outer coat is continuous with the translucent cornea in front of the eye. Behind the cornea, which has a slight bulge, and in front of the lens, is the iris, the colored part of the eye. The pupil, the hole in the center of the iris, enables it to function like the diaphragm of a camera, adjusting to varying conditions of light by narrowing or widening the opening through which the light passes. After passing through the pupil, the light is focused onto the retina, the inner coat of the eye, by the lens. The lens focuses light by a process called accommodation: when the eye sees distant objects, the lens is stretched thin and almost flat by tiny muscles so that light rays are hardly bent at all. When the perceived object is nearby, the pull on the lens relaxes, the distance between front and back surfaces increases, and the light rays must be bent more sharply to bring them into focus on the retina.

Practically all common defects of vision result from errors of refraction (malfunction in the bending of incoming light rays). It is these errors that are corrected by individually prescribed lenses (see Chapter 108, "Why You Need Glasses").

TESTING EYESIGHT

Visual acuity is assessed in a series of tests. A projected chart with standardized letters ranging in size from very large to practically microscopic is placed at a distance equivalent to 20 feet from the viewer. The chart is designed so that the topmost letter, usually an E, can be read at

200 feet by the normal eye. Each successive row is sized for normal reading at 100, 70, 40, 30, 20, 15, and 10 feet, respectively.

When normal eyesight for each eye is 20/20, it means that the viewer can stand at a 20-foot distance and see what should normally be seen at that distance. When the viewer must stay at a distance of 20 feet to see what should normally be seen at a distance of 40 feet, the visual acuity is designated as 20/40. When the viewer can see at 20 feet what the normal eye can see only by coming as close as 15 feet, the designation is 20/15.

Near vision is usually tested by a standard typeface card. The tester records the smallest size of type that can be read and the distance at which the card is held when reading it. The ability to read the smallest type at a distance of 14 inches (14/14) is equivalent to 20/20 on the big chart.

Errors in refraction are tested by the use of a retinoscope equipped with a reflecting mirror in which the doctor can observe the light reflexes projected back from the patient's eyes as the patient responds positively or negatively to the effectiveness of a series of different lenses placed in a frame before each eye. After determining the degree of near- or farsightedness in this way, the doctor evaluates possible astigmatism by presenting the patient with an image of black spokes radiating from a center. If all the lines are not perceived as uniformly black, cylindrical lenses are inserted in the frames until all the lines are seen as equally black.

A complete eye checkup always includes an examination with an ophthalmoscope—the lighted instrument a doctor uses to look into the eyes—to determine the general health of the retina, anterior chamber, and the optic disk, as well as the blood vessels and nerves of the eye. Such an examination is usually part of a complete medical checkup. Since the eye is an open window into the body—and the only place in which a doctor can look directly at blood vessels—damage to the blood vessels and the retina seen through the ophthalmoscope may be an early indication of arteriosclerosis, diabetes, kidney disease, or hypertension.

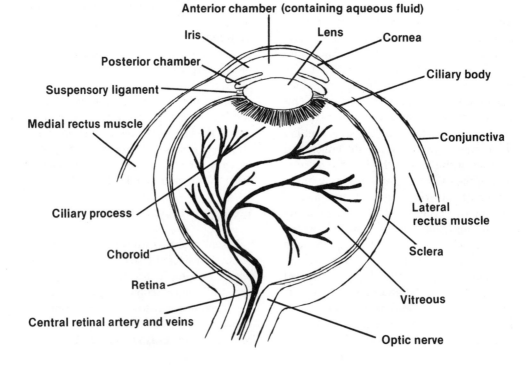

MISCELLANEOUS SIGHT DISORDERS

Diplopia

Diplopia, or double vision, is usually caused by poor coordination or weakness of the muscles that control eyeball movement. The condition may be observable as walleye or crossed eyes and can be corrected by surgery. However, the sudden onset of double vision may be the first indication of damage to the optic nerve by a head injury, a brain tumor, or chronic alcoholism.

Night Blindness

This is an inability to see in dim light even though vision is normal in bright light or daylight. It is a specific symptom of a deficiency of vitamin A (also called retinol) and can be corrected by therapeutic doses of this vitamin as well as long-term changes in the diet so that it contains adequate amounts of butter, egg yolk, and vegetables such as carrots, sweet potatoes, and tomatoes, which are rich in carotene, the pigment converted by the body into vitamin A. (However, vitamin A should *never* be self-prescribed in large doses since it can have extremely dangerous consequences in excessive amounts.) Night blindness may also be an early indication of the onset of glaucoma in people over age forty. When night blindness occurs in childhood or early adolescence, it may be the first sign of the hereditary disease retinitis pigmentosa, discussed below.

Color Blindness

This is almost always an inherited and incurable defect rare in women and present in about 8 percent of all men. It is unrelated to other aspects of sight. The cause is a genetic fault in the behavior of the protein molecules in the cone cells of the retina which differentiate the color signals to be sent to the brain. The typical manifestation of color blindness is confusion between red and green. (Blue-violet confusion is unusual.) Drivers, bicycle riders, and people whose livelihood depends on making accurate color distinctions should be aware of their disability so that they can work out practical ways of dealing with it.

Retinitis Pigmentosa

This is a comparatively rare hereditary disease of the retina affecting approximately 100,000 people in the United States, practically all males. Onset of the disorder, which is incurable, usually occurs in childhood, with such signs as stumbling over furniture in an unlighted room because of night blindness. The deterioration of eyesight is due to a scattering of black pigmented matter at the sides of the retina to the point where the range of vision is so narrow that nothing can be seen above, below, or to the sides of the perceived object. The disease therefore creates what is known as "tunnel" or "telescopic" vision, and although it proceeds at a different rate in each case, most victims are legally blind by the time they are forty years old. Highly publicized "cures" claimed by Russian doctors remain unsubstantiated. Information about the disease, progress reports on research, and the value of genetic counseling will be supplied on request by the National Retinitis Pigmentosa Foundation, Rolling Park Building, 8331 Mindale Circle, Baltimore, MD 21207.

SUMMING UP

Most common eye problems can be corrected, but proper testing is an essential first step. Parents should be particularly aware of any visual problems in their children, especially when there is a problem reading or there are complaints about headaches. Since the eyes provide important information about other body functions and organ systems, a medical examination should include a careful examination of the eyes.

108. Why You Need Glasses

COMMON CHARACTERISTICS

The most common problems with vision—nearsightedness (myopia), farsightedness (hyperopia), the change in vision caused by aging (presbyopia), and the distortion of vision known as astigmatism—are problems of focusing. These errors of focus or refraction can be corrected by the use of glasses or, in most cases, contact lenses.

The right glasses or contact lenses make it possible to see more clearly. The structure of the eye itself, however, remains unchanged. The wrong glasses can blur the vision and cause eyestrain and headaches but cannot damage the eye. Badly fitted or badly handled contact lenses, however, may scratch the cornea, leading to discomfort or even serious problems.

THE FOCUSING POWER OF THE EYE

The eye is a receiving organ. Its function is to bring the reflected light from an object into focus on the retina (the light-sensitive tissue that lines the back of the eye) and to convert the stimuli of light into nerve impulses. These are then carried to the brain for interpretation, and the image is then "seen."

The cornea of the eye, part of its outermost layer, plays a major part in the focusing of light. It is similar to a fixed lens and does not change its shape. The crystalline lens within the eye, made of transparent modified skin cells and capable of changing shape, is responsible for the fine focusing of nearby objects.

At rest, the normal eye is focused for distant vision. Rays of light from objects twenty feet or more away are nearly parallel; they are correctly focused onto the retina by the cornea and the lens in a "resting" state. Rays of light from objects nearer than twenty feet, however, are slightly divergent. For correct focusing they must be deflected inward. When it is necessary to see clearly objects at a distance of twenty feet or less, the ligaments and muscles (the ciliary body) to which the lens is attached cause the lens to change its thickness and curvature. It becomes more convex, deflecting the rays of light so that a sharp focus is obtained. This process is called accommodation.

MYOPIA

In myopia, or nearsightedness, images of distant objects are focused not on the retina but slightly in front of it. Such images are therefore blurred, but near objects are seen clearly. Myopia is usually the result of an eyeball that is too long from front to back. Less commonly, it results from excessive focusing power in the cornea and lens.

Nearsightedness is a very common problem, affecting one in every six people and often running in families. It usually develops in late childhood, between the ages of six and ten, and may come on quickly. The child will have difficulty seeing the blackboard at school and, when reading, will hold the book very close to the eyes. Myopia may worsen during the teenage years, becoming stable in the twenties.

The refractive error that results in myopia is corrected by concave lenses. These move the images of distant objects back onto the retina and thus bring them into sharp focus.

How the Eye Sees

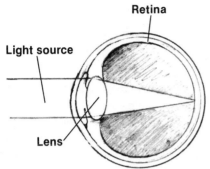

Normal Eye
In normal vision, parallel light rays focus exactly on the retina. The ciliary muscle changes the curve of the lens to compensate for different distances. With age, this flexibility lessens; this is why many middle-aged people need glasses.

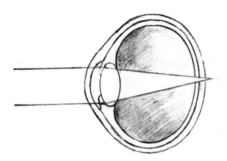

Farsighted (Hypertropic) Eye
Farsightedness occurs when the axial length of the eyeball is too short and light comes to a focal point beyond the retina.

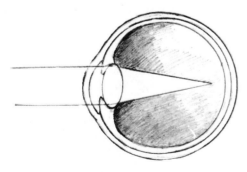

Nearsighted (Myopic) Eye
Nearsightedness occurs when the axial length of the eyeball is too long and light comes to a focal point short of the retina.

HYPEROPIA

For someone with severe hyperopia, or farsightedness, the images of all objects are blurred, and those of near objects especially so. In hyperopia, the point of focus is (theoretically) behind the retina, usually because the eyeball is too short from front to back, sometimes because of weakness in focusing on the part of the cornea and lens. Farsighted people may be able to bring near objects into focus by means of accommodation, but this involves overuse of the ciliary muscles and may result in chronic eyestrain. Hyperopia often runs in families and is usually present at birth. A child who is farsighted may complain of aching, tired, or sore eyes.

The refractive error in hyperopia is corrected by convex lenses, which reinforce the focusing power of the cornea and lens, moving the point of focus forward onto the retina. As an individual ages, the ciliary muscles that are involved in accommodation for near vision tend to become weaker; progressively stronger lenses will be needed.

ASTIGMATISM

In astigmatism, the curvature of the cornea is uneven. Depending on which rays of light are affected by the irregular curvature, horizontal lines will be in focus and vertical ones blurred, or vice versa. Diagonal lines may also be unevenly focused. The distortion in vision is somewhat like that produced by an old, uneven windowpane.

Astigmatism can usually be corrected by the use of a lens that refracts the light in only one plane—either vertical or horizontal. Such lenses are known as cylindrical lenses.

PRESBYOPIA

With age, the lens of the eye gradually hardens and becomes less plastic. Thus its ability to accommodate for near vision gradually diminishes. This condition, presbyopia (from the Greek, "old eye"), usually becomes evident in the mid-forties and worsens with increasing age. Unlike other disorders of refraction, presbyopia usually affects both eyes equally.

If presbyopia is not corrected, it becomes possible to read only when the printed page is held at some distance from the eyes. As the condition worsens, the distance needed increases, and eventually the page appears blurred even at arm's length. With age, people with myopia and increasing presbyopia find that they must remove their glasses in order to see near images clearly.

Convex lenses that reinforce the power of the lens of the eye are used to correct presbyopia. Every few years, as the power of the natural lenses gradually decreases, increasingly stronger corrective lenses will be needed.

CONTACT LENSES

For many people, contact lenses offer an alternative to eyeglasses for the correction of errors of refraction. When properly fitted, and when the wearer has good motivation, contact lenses provide freedom from the drawbacks of glasses (fogging, poor peripheral vision, breakage, misplacement) and may also provide superior vision.

All contact lenses are made of plastic and fit on the cornea. They are shaped to correct errors of refraction much as glasses are. Unlike glasses, however, contact lenses may interfere with the supply of oxygen to the cornea. (The cornea has no blood supply and depends for oxygen on exposure to the air and to the tears that constantly wash the eye.) For this reason, most contact lenses must be removed at night.

A variety of lens types is now available. Each type has both advantages and drawbacks.

Hard lenses generally provide excellent vision correction and are the only ones suitable for people with severe astigmatism. They are the least expensive and the most durable and require the least care. However, a long breaking-in period is necessary, and the lenses cannot be worn on an off-and-on basis—after a few days, a new breaking-in period is required.

Gas-permeable lenses are hard lenses that allow some oxygen and carbon dioxide to reach the cornea. They are more comfortable and easier to adjust to than conventional hard lenses. They are also more expensive.

Soft lenses are made of water-absorbent plastic and fit snugly against the cornea, taking on its shape. For this reason they are not suitable for people with astigmatism. They are more comfortable than hard lenses, require less breaking in, and can be worn intermittently. However, they are more expensive and less durable and need meticulous cleaning.

Extended-wear soft lenses, recently available, are particularily useful for people with disabilities that make the daily insertion and removal of contact lenses difficult.

SUMMING UP

Glasses or contact lenses can correct the most common problems that interfere with clear vision, those in which errors of refraction or focusing are involved. Both glasses and contact lenses have drawbacks in use, and in some cases contact lenses are medically unsuitable.

If you think that you are having trouble seeing as clearly as you should—or, most importantly, if you suspect that a child is having difficulties with vision—you should arrange for an eye examination by a qualified professional (an ophthalmologist or an optometrist) without delay. Sight is too precious a sense to be neglected.

109. Conjunctivitis

COMMON CHARACTERISTICS

Conjunctivitis, sometimes called "pink eye," is an inflammation of the conjunctiva, the thin mucous membrane that lines the eyelids and covers the surface of the eyeball, or cornea. In typical cases, the blood vessels of the affected areas become visibly red; the eyelids may be puffy, and the secretion from the irritated membrane gets thick enough to cause the eyelids to become stuck together during sleep.

Conjunctivitis rarely presents a threat to vision, except in those cases where untreated infection or ongoing irritation from an object embedded under the eyelid leads to ulceration of the cornea and possible irreversible scarring.

Conjunctivitis caused by bacterial infection is a common disorder of childhood because of the widespread practice of rubbing the eyes with dirty hands. This practice may also produce a stye, a pimple-like infection of the oil-producing sebaceous gland at the root of an eyelash. The combination of conjunctivitis and stye may also occur in adults during periods of low resistance to infection.

Depending on the cause, the inflammation may occur in both eyes simultaneously. When styes are present, efforts should be made to keep the infection from spreading to others. One of the most effective ways to do this is to use only disposable tissues and towels until the condition has been cleared up by medication.

CAUSES OF CONJUNCTIVITIS

Conjunctivitis is caused by both bacterial and viral infection: The measles virus and *Staphylococcus aureus* bacteria are examples of such infectious agents. Various allergic, chemical, and physical factors are also causes, including sensitivity to pollen during the hay fever season or to other airborne allergens, such as mold spores or animal dander. Allergic conjunctivitis is almost always accompanied by the characteristic symptoms of burning and itching eyes.

The inflammation may be a recurring occupational problem originating in exposure to various chemicals in liquid, powder, or spray. The careless use of aerosol hair sprays, or a change in the brand of eye makeup, may also cause conjunctivitis.

Among the more common physical causes are friction from an inward-growing eyelash or from a sharp particle that becomes embedded under the eyelid. Without dark goggles, sunlamp enthusiasts are as vulnerable as welders to actinic conjunctivitis, which is caused by exposure to ultraviolet light. People who swim frequently may have intermittent conjunctivitis caused by the chemicals used in pools or by infectious bacteria that infest untreated water.

TREATMENT OF CONJUNCTIVITIS

Conjunctivitis should be investigated by a doctor without delay. If the irritant is an eyelash or a dust particle, only a professionally trained person should attempt to remove it. If the condition is clearly traceable to an allergy, an oral antihistamine may be prescribed. If bacterial infection is the likely cause, an antibiotic ophthalmic preparation containing chloramphenicol may be prescribed. If the infection persists, an erythromycin ointment or one containing bacitracin and neomycin may be indicated. These medications are usually ap-

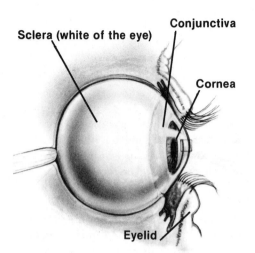

Sclera (white of the eye)
Conjunctiva
Cornea
Eyelid

Conjunctivitis affects the transparent membrane covering the outer eyeball, giving the white of the eye a pinkish color.

plied in the morning and at bedtime, and in most cases, the condition clears up within a week.

When on-the-job exposure causes frequent problems with conjunctivitis, either because of allergens or chemical irritants, goggles should be worn.

PREVENTION OF CONJUNCTIVITIS

Children should be encouraged to wash their hands at specified times and discouraged from rubbing their eyes. When using hair sprays, one should keep the eyes closed. Women who use eye makeup should never borrow or lend mascara brushes or liner applicators. People swimming in public pools or in those operated by private clubs should concern themselves with the enforcement of health regulations. Ponds or other such waters should be tested by health authorities for possible pollution.

SUMMING UP

Conjunctivitis is a condition that can occur at any age, though it is most common among children. Rarely are there complications that affect eyesight. In some cases, the condition is self-limiting, lasting no more than a day or so. However, it is usually advisable to see a doctor for correct diagnosis and prompt treatment, especially in those circumstances where the spread of infection—to the other eye and to other people—can be prevented by proper medication. Sensible precautions involving routine cleanliness, care in the use of aerosol sprays, and the wearing of protective glasses will further reduce the likelihood of eye inflammation. When conjunctivitis is known to be allergen-related, the discomfort can usually be reduced to a minimum with antihistamines; when the cause is a bacterial infection, antibiotic eyedrops or ointment may be used.

110. Glaucoma

COMMON CHARACTERISTICS

Glaucoma is a disease of the eye marked by increased pressure within the eyeball. The pressure may cause impaired vision, ranging from slight loss of sight to total blindness. About two million Americans have glaucoma, and it is the cause of one out of seven new cases of blindness.

The disease has two main forms. Chronic (open-angle) glaucoma, which is by far the more prevalent, progresses slowly and painlessly and may result in significant loss of vision before the individual is aware of it. Acute (closed-angle) glaucoma is less common, accounting for less than 20 percent of cases. It is characterized by recurrent attacks of blurred vision and pain in, around, and behind the eyeball.

The risk of developing glaucoma, both acute and chronic, increases with age. Those with a family history of the disease have an increased risk, as do individuals suffering from diabetes. In some cases, glaucoma occurs as the result of other eye disease, an injury to the eye, or prolonged treatment with corticosteroid drugs. However, in the majority of cases the cause is not known.

THE MECHANISM OF GLAUCOMA

A watery fluid known as the aqueous humor is produced by cells behind the lens of the eye. This fluid bathes and nourishes the interior of the eye and then flows forward into the space between the cornea and the lens (the anterior chamber). It is drained from the eye through a minute channel in the angle of the anterior chamber, the canal of Schlemm. Normally the rate of production and the outflow of aqueous humor are in balance. If, however, the outflow channels become blocked or narrowed for any reason, fluid accumulates in the anterior chamber. The resulting pressure within the eyeball reduces the blood supply to the retina and the optic nerve. Nerve fibers die, producing permanent loss of vision. This usually occurs first in the outer edges (the periphery) of the visual field, creating a "tunnel" of vision that becomes increasingly narrow. Eventually, the optic nerve becomes irreparably damaged and blindness is total.

SYMPTOMS

Chronic (Open-Angle) Glaucoma

In this form of glaucoma, the blocking of the drainage channels occurs gradually. The eyes appear to be normal and there is no pain. The disease is insidious: many

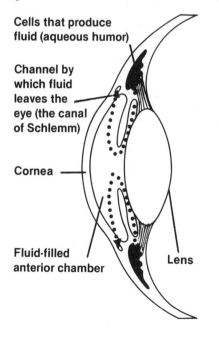

Cells that produce fluid (aqueous humor)

Channel by which fluid leaves the eye (the canal of Schlemm)

Cornea

Fluid-filled anterior chamber

Lens

people have no symptoms at all until much of their peripheral vision has been lost. Often the first symptom is a blurring of vision on the side toward the nose. Unless recognized and treated, this may spread to involve other areas in the field of vision. In chronic glaucoma, both eyes are usually affected.

Acute (Closed-Angle) Glaucoma

Acute glaucoma is the result of a sudden blocking of the canal of Schlemm. The first symptoms are usually a reddened eye, blurred vision, headache, and eyeache. Often, but not invariably, the individual sees brightly colored rings (halos) around lights. The acute attack may subside with rest. However, it may become more severe, with fading or even absent vision, and acute pain. The victim may go into a kind of shock, with pallor, nausea, and faintness. Attacks are always recurrent, and each one produces increasing damage. Thus even a mild attack requires immediate medical attention. With surgical treatment, further damaging attacks can be prevented.

TESTING FOR GLAUCOMA

Because glaucoma so often develops insidiously, regular eye testing—at least every two years; more frequently for those at high risk—is important.

In the course of the examination, intraocular pressure is measured with an instrument known as a tonometer. The eye is anesthetized with a drop of local anesthetic and the tonometer is placed directly on the cornea. The amount of force that is required to flatten a known area of the cornea provides for a good evaluation of the intraocular pressure. A recent innovation in tonometry is the noncontact tonometer, which requires no anesthetic and measures pressure with an air jet.

In addition to measurement of pressure, the eye test includes an examination of the interior of the eye (behind the lens) with an ophthalmoscope to determine whether there is any damage to internal structures. Further necessary tests are gonioscopy, the examination of the anterior chamber and the angle where the canal of Schlemm is located, and perimetry. This latter test reveals how much sight has been lost on the periphery of the field of vision.

Testing for glaucoma may be done either by an ophthalmologist (a medical doctor who specializes in the eye) or by an optometrist (a specialist in problems of vision but who does not have a medical degree). However, treatment can be given only by an ophthalmologist.

TREATMENT

The preferred treatment for chronic glaucoma is the use of drugs to lower the intraocular pressure. The goal is to avoid damage, or to prevent further deterioration if damage has already occurred.

Drugs with two kinds of action are used. One action is to remove the obstruction to the outflow channel and thereby facilitate the elimination of fluid. The other action is to inhibit the formation of the aqueous humor itself. Given in the form of eye drops, the drugs must be used three or four times a day to keep the intraocular pressure down.

Successful outcome depends greatly on the proper and continued use of the medications. Unfortunately, many patients do not follow their doctors' instructions. Some may be discouraged by occasional discomfort from the use of the drugs; others, who are without apparent symptoms, see no reason why they should continue to use expensive (and inconvenient) medications. As a result of noncompliance with drug therapy, vision is often irreversibly impaired.

Surgery is usually reserved for those with chronic glaucoma in whom drug treatment is ineffective or poorly tolerated and for individuals with the acute form of the disease. There are several surgical procedures for the control of glaucoma, all of which have the object of providing improved drainage of aqueous humor. Surgery cannot restore vision that has been lost. If successful, however, as it is in the majority of cases, it checks the progress of the disease.

Not all of those with increased intraocular pressure require treatment. If there is no damage to vital parts of the eye and no sign of early visual impairment, someone with mildly increased pressure may need only periodic followup examinations to detect any damage that may occur.

SUMMING UP

Glaucoma, which is more common among people forty years of age and older, is one of the leading causes of blindness in the United States. Increased pressure of fluid within the eyeball leads first to loss of peripheral vision and then, if the disease is not recognized and treated, to irreversible, total blindness.

There is at present no cure for glaucoma. However, permanent visual damage can be prevented with proper treatment. Regular eye testing is the best defense against this crippling disease.

111. Cataracts

COMMON CHARACTERISTICS

Cataract is the term used to describe an opacity, or clouding, of the normally transparent lens of the eye. The opacity may obstruct clear vision by blocking the passage of light through the eye and making it difficult for the eye to focus properly.

If untreated, the condition may gradually worsen, causing severe impairment of vision. Although cataracts are rarely painful and are not life-threatening, they can pose a serious threat to eyesight, and once their presence has been diagnosed, their development should be monitored periodically by an ophthalmologist.

CAUSES OF CATARACTS

The lens of the eye is normally a crystal clear, flexible, bloodless structure located near the back of the eyeball and composed mainly of soluble protein and water. In conjunction with the cornea (another lens located at the front of the eyeball), it serves to screen and refract light rays and to keep what you see in focus. In order to function well, it must be continually supplied with nutrients from the watery substance which surrounds it. If there is a decrease in nutrient uptake by the lens, as often occurs in the elderly, then the lens may lose its transparency and flexibility and cataracts may result.

Most commonly, then, cataracts occur in the elderly as a natural consequence of aging. Other possible causes include any injury to the eye where it is actually penetrated, illnesses associated with high blood sugar, such as diabetes, and an inflammation of the eyes known as uveitis. Drugs such as cortisone and its derivatives have also been implicated as causal agents, as well as exposure to X-rays, microwaves, and infrared radiation.

There are two causes of cataracts in newborn infants; both are preventable. If a pregnant woman contracts rubella (German measles) early in her pregnancy, there is a risk that her baby may be born with cataracts. This can be prevented by her either receiving the rubella vaccine before she becomes pregnant or actually having rubella before pregnancy. Secondly, infants afflicted with the hereditary metabolic disease galactosemia may develop cataracts shortly after birth. This may be prevented by placing the newborn on a diet that excludes galactose, a sugar found in milk.

INCIDENCE

Cataracts are one of the most common eye ailments. It is estimated that well over three million Americans have cataracts. However, the majority of these have only mild forms of the disease and do not require surgery. Nonetheless, over 200,000 cataract operations are performed in the United States each year, and many more cases go untreated. Three-fourths of those affected are sixty-five years of age or older, and only one in five is between the ages of forty-five and sixty-five.

NATURAL COURSE

A cataract usually begins as a small opacity in the lens of the eye and may at first have no noticeable effect on vision. As the cataract grows, blurring of vision occurs, occasionally accompanied by double vision (diplopia). The blurring may be particularly noticeable while driving at night, when the clouded lens may cause the light from oncoming headlights to seem dispersed or "scattered." Frequent changes of eyeglasses may be necessary as the cataract develops, but eventually new eye-

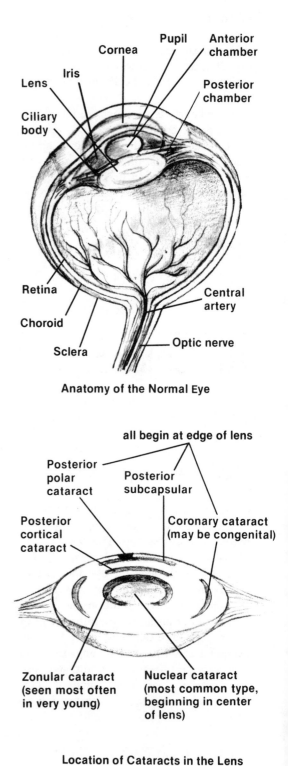

Anatomy of the Normal Eye

Location of Cataracts in the Lens

glasses may no longer help. Cataracts may form in one eye only, or simultaneously in both eyes. They may grow gradually, as is typically the case, and never require surgical intervention, or they may enlarge rapidly. If present in both eyes, their rate of growth in each eye may be different.

Normally, cataracts will not take any sudden turns for better or for worse during their development but will change gradually over a span of months or years, and usually there are no accompanying symptoms other than blurring of vision. However, it may be a symptom of other illnesses besides cataracts, and the best policy is always to consult a physician promptly for any visual abnormality.

TREATMENT

Once a cataract has been diagnosed, a course of treatment can be planned. Often, particularly if the cataract is still in the early stages, nothing will be done except to check it periodically. If, however, it reaches a point where it significantly interferes with sight, then surgery, which remains the only definitive treatment for cataracts, may be recommended. Fortunately, surgical treatment of cataracts is highly successful, resulting in marked improvement in 95 percent to 98 percent of all cases.

The three most common types of surgical treatment are *intracapsular extraction, extracapsular extraction,* and *phacoemulsification.*

In intracapsular extraction, the most common surgical method used today, an incision is made into the eye near the edge of the iris, often by means of a freezing probe, and the entire lens is removed.

In extracapsular extraction, only the central portion of the lens is removed, by means of a suction device. If, subse-

quently, the remaining portion of the lens develops a cataract, a minor second operation may be required.

Finally, in phacoemulsification, the third most common method of removing cataracts, the cataract is extracted through a special needle whose tip vibrates at high frequency, fragmenting the cataract and then removing it through the needle's hollow core.

Whichever type of surgery is elected, several weeks must pass for complete healing. The choice of which procedure is best suited to a particular patient depends on the type and severity of the cataract and the presence, if any, of coexisting eye diseases.

Once the lens has been partially or completely removed, a substitute must be provided to restore the eye's ability to focus. This may be accomplished by glasses, contact lenses, or an intraocular lens implant directly within the eye.

Glasses, the traditional approach, are losing favor today because they require the highest amount of magnification and therefore require the greatest amount of visual adjustment. Contact lenses are recommended with increasing frequency and have been greatly improved in recent years. The new intraocular lens implants, in many ways the best approach, have a higher risk of complications and cannot be used by everyone.

SUMMING UP

Cataracts are a very common eye disorder, particularly in older people. Once one of the leading causes of blindness, cataracts today can be effectively treated by surgery in most people. In many people, the cataracts never advance to the stage where special treatment is required. Any changes in vision should be checked by a doctor, however. If a cataract is diagnosed, it should be followed periodically to ensure that appropriate treatment is undertaken at the proper time.

112. Hearing Loss

Deafness, whether it is complete or partial, is not in itself an illness. Rather, it is a symptom of some injury or disorder in the complex structure of the ear or the nerves that carry impulses to the brain, where sound is heard.

THE EAR

The ear has three parts, each with its special function in hearing. The visible external ear gathers vibrations in the air and funnels them down the auditory canal to the eardrum, one and one-half inches within, making it vibrate.

Immediately behind the eardrum is the middle ear, an air-filled cavity surrounded by bone and connected with the throat by a tubular passage, the Eustachian tube. In the middle ear, the vibrations of the eardrum are amplified, passing through a chain of tiny bones or ossicles, the malleus (hammer), incus (anvil), and stapes (stirrup). The handle of the hammer is attached to the eardrum, and the footplate of the stirrup is in contact with a membrane-covered opening into the inner ear, known as the oval window.

The inner ear is a complex bony structure which contains the central organ of hearing, the cochlea (the name is from the Latin word for snail shell) and the structure that governs balance, the labyrinth. Sound waves reaching the oval window

Structure of the Normal Ear

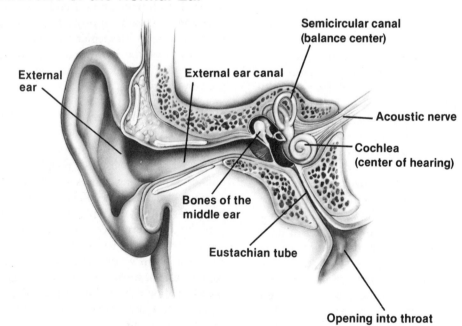

External ear

External ear canal

Semicircular canal (balance center)

Acoustic nerve

Cochlea (center of hearing)

Bones of the middle ear

Eustachian tube

Opening into throat

cause the fluid that fills the inner ear to vibrate. Tiny hair-covered cells in the cochlea transform these vibrations into nerve impulses; these are ultimately transmitted by the acoustic nerve to the auditory centers of the brain. Here the sound is heard.

All sound vibrations that stimulate the acoustic nerve become audible. In addition to the airborne vibrations that strike the eardrum, vibrations can reach the nerve endings through the bones of the skull. This secondary form of hearing, bone conduction, plays a large part in the way one hears one's own voice.

SOUND

Sound can be described in terms of pitch (cycles, or wave frequencies, per second) and in terms of volume (decibels). For example, the pitch of ordinary human conversation ranges between 300 and 4,000 cycles per second and registers about 60 decibels.

The normal young ear can hear tones within the range of 16 cycles per second (the lowest note on a church organ) to 20,000 cycles per second or more (high-pitched sounds such as a bat squeaking). As a person ages, there is a steady and completely normal loss of hearing in the high-frequency range. In their sixties, few people can hear sounds of 12,000 cycles per second.

In most people, sound at 90 decibels or above causes pain in the ears. The pain is a warning that there is a likelihood of damage if exposure continues. Regular exposure to sound at or above 90 decibels may in time lead to hearing loss, especially in the higher frequencies.

TESTS OF HEARING

Standardized techniques make it possible to measure loss of hearing in terms of loss of decibels. In testing hearing, doctors use an instrument called an audiometer, which emits pure tones that can be am-

plified decibel by decibel, making it possible to determine how well an individual hears at different sound frequencies. If a sound of a particular frequency must be made 20 decibels louder than standard for an individual to hear it, he or she is said to have a 20-decibel hearing loss for that frequency. (A 30-decibel hearing loss generally means that a hearing aid is necessary if ordinary conversation is to be heard clearly; if the loss is 50 decibels or more, it is difficult to hear over the telephone.)

Other testing devices may be used by hearing specialists. Some are simple—a watch or a tuning fork, for example; others are highly sophisticated. Various techniques have been devised to test hearing in children, including those too young to understand and cooperate with a doctor.

TYPES OF HEARING LOSS

There are two types of hearing loss: conductive deafness and sensorineural (or perceptive) deafness. In conductive deafness, airborne sounds are not conducted properly through the external and middle ears, so that the inner ear receives an inadequate message or no message at all. In sensorineural deafness, sounds reach the inner ear but are not transmitted to the brain. In individual cases, there may be mixed impairment, involving both the conductive and the perceptive aspects of hearing.

Conductive Deafness

Conduction of sound may be impaired by something as simple as a lump of wax in the external canal. However, most defects in conduction are located in the middle ear. Hearing may be impaired because of infection, congenital malformation of the middle ear, skull fracture, a blow to the ear, otosclerosis, or other problems.

Middle ear infections. A common cause of a defect in the middle ear is infection spreading up through the Eustachian tube from the throat (this is particularly the case with children, in whom the tube is short and comparatively wide). A middle ear infection causes pain and deafness because the membranes lining the middle ear swell and the cavity fills with fluid, obstructing movement in the eardrum and ossicles. If severe and untreated, a middle ear infection can lead to a perforated eardrum that fails to heal, or to the erosion of the ossicles, and permanent deafness. Antibiotic treatment, however, is usually very effective, when begun promptly (see Chapter 113, "Ear Infections").

Repeated middle ear infections may lead to the filling of the cavity with sterile fluid that is not cleared by drainage down the Eustachian tube. This condition (recurrent *otitis media*) is often painless, with deafness as its only symptom. It may be necessary to drain the ear for weeks or even months by means of a tiny plastic tube inserted through the eardrum.

Otosclerosis. This is a common cause of conductive deafness, and in over half the cases there is a family history of the condition. A painless abnormal growth of bone forms inside the oval window of the inner ear, gradually immobilizing the stapes so that airborne vibrations no longer reach the middle ear.

The first symptom, which usually occurs in the late teens or early adult years, may be difficulty in hearing faint or distant sounds. The individual generally hears his or her own voice quite well through bone conduction—it may, in fact, seem overloud. Bone conduction also exaggerates the noise of chewing.

Hearing loss caused by otosclerosis can usually be compensated for by the use of a hearing aid (see below). However, this is an aid, not a cure. To restore the conduction of sound, a operation called a stapedectomy can be performed (it is successful in 90 percent of cases). The fixed stapes is removed and replaced by a metal or plastic substitute, allowing movement to occur again. If otosclerosis is not treated, there is usually a slow progression to complete deafness over ten to fifteen years, although sometimes a degree of hearing is retained.

Sensorineural Deafness

Sensorineural deafness is due to a disorder in the inner ear or in the nerves leading to the auditory centers in the brain. The cause may be a congenital malformation, an injury such as a fractured skull, or poisons, viruses, or drugs (among them, quinine, nicotine, and some antibiotics). Infections may spread from the middle to the inner ear and damage the organs involved in both hearing and balance, causing deafness, tinnitus (noises in the head that have no apparent acoustic stimulus), and dizziness. Rhesus-factor incompatibilities, jaundice, and complications of labor may be associated with inner ear defects in an infant.

Prolonged exposure to excessive noise damages the sensitive hair cells lining the cochlea and is a frequent cause of sensorineural deafness. Since the inner ear has little power of recovery, prevention is all-important. People exposed to dangerous levels of noise should wear suitable ear protectors and have regular tests so that possible loss of hearing can be detected early.

Ménière's Disease

This disorder of the labyrinth affects both hearing and balance. It is not uncommon in middle age. The main symptoms are attacks of dizziness (vertigo), which may last for several hours and are accompanied by nausea, vomiting, tinnitus, and distorted hearing. The hearing problems frequently continue between the attacks of vertigo. In most cases, only one ear is affected, with hearing becoming progressively worse over the years.

No single treatment is successful in all cases of Ménière's disease. A variety of drugs is used: antihistamines, motion sickness medication, tranquilizers, diuretics, and vasodilators to reduce the excess fluid in the labyrinth. If drug treatment is unsuccessful, surgery may be performed to drain the labyrinth. In severe cases, the organ of balance may be destroyed by surgery or ultrasound, curing the vertigo but resulting in complete deafness in the affected ear.

DEAFNESS IN INFANTS AND CHILDREN

It is extremely important to recognize deafness early in a child's life. Even a minor hearing problem, if not treated, may interfere with normal development. Parents should be alert to any sign that a baby or child does not hear clearly and should inform the doctor promptly.

Lack of hearing is likely if an infant is born with an abnormality of the external ear, since this indicates a defect in other aural structures. A congenital defect may be due to the mother having had rubella or some other viral infection or having taken certain drugs during the first three months of pregnancy.

If there is no malformation, the earliest obvious sign of profound deafness is that the "startle reflex" is absent—a sudden loud noise provokes no response from the baby. This sign can be detected at about six months of age. Another important sign is absence of speech: a deaf child does not begin to talk at the usual age (one year to eighteen months). It should be remembered that a child born with normal hearing may lose it after an attack of mumps, measles, or some other infection, or as a result of an injury.

Conductive deafness in children can often be corrected surgically, or by the use of a hearing aid. Sensorineural deafness, if it is total or almost total, presents a far more difficult problem. Special speech training techniques are needed for a child who has never heard, and therefore cannot imitate, sound. It is important that training programs be started in infancy, when children are adaptable and eager to learn.

HEARING AIDS

Modern hearing aids are highly compact electronic amplifying devices. They should be selected with the advice of a specialist who is aware of the individual's problem. Sometimes, even with a well-fitted and well-made hearing aid, the return of sounds that have not been heard for years is disconcerting, even alarming. Patience and a period of training in discriminating overlapping sounds may be necessary.

Hearing aids are usually very beneficial in cases of simple conductive deafness. Air-conduction devices are worn in the ear, bone-conduction types in contact with the bone behind it. Since sensorineural deafness may involve loss of hearing in certain frequencies only, the hearing aid must be designed to compensate for lost frequencies while not overamplifying those that are still audible.

PSYCHOLOGICAL FACTORS

Finding normal conversation difficult, the hard of hearing often become withdrawn and depressed. If they are unable to discriminate the source of sound, they may become suspicious, thinking that people are whispering behind their backs. If they do not hear a question, and therefore do not answer it, they may be branded as rude or ill-tempered. And even when the family is understanding and helpful, a degree of social isolation is almost inevitable.

SUMMING UP

Loss of hearing is a symptom of a defect or disorder in the ear or the auditory nerves. The causes are numerous, ranging from injury to structural changes to prolonged exposure to loud sound.

When deafness is the result of a defect in the outer or middle ear, the problem can usually be corrected surgically or compensated for by the use of a hearing aid. Damage to the inner ear or the auditory nerves, however, is very often irreversible, leading to permanent impairment of hearing.

113. Ear Infections

Earache may have a number of causes. It is a warning that something is wrong, although usually the problem is not a serious one. It can mean that a fungus or bacteria has invaded the ear canal or that an infection has erupted behind the eardrum in the middle ear and is causing pain. Whatever the cause, home remedies—such as putting a few drops of warm olive oil in the ear—should not be used. Such remedies may temporarily ease discomfort but usually cannot correct the underlying problem; they may, in fact, make diagnosis more difficult by obscuring the doctor's view of the ear canal and eardrum. If an earache does not subside within twenty-four hours, a doctor should be seen. Of course, a doctor should be called immediately if the situation is obviously serious and there is extreme pain.

OUTER EAR DISORDERS

The outer ear is made up of the visible folds of cartilage and skin that serve to collect sound, and a canal through which the sound travels to the eardrum. Glands in the canal produce wax, which has lubricating, protective, and cleansing functions. If the ears are not washed properly, wax can accumulate and harden to the extent that sound waves are prevented from passing through the canal and hearing is impaired. This condition can sometimes be corrected by softening the wax with a few drops of 3 percent hydrogen peroxide in an equal amount of warm water and rotating a cotton swab against it. However, since some of the wax can be pushed back into the canal and become impacted, it is usually better to let the doctor flush out the ear. One should never try to scrape wax out with a hairpin, pencil, toothpick, or any other sharp instrument. Youngsters between the ages of two and six frequently insert beads, bugs, erasers, pebbles, and the like into their ears. Debris of this kind should be extracted by a doctor before infection sets in.

Sometimes the canal develops a painful boil, which may have to be drained by a physician. The canal is also the site of a fungal or bacterial infection called "swimmer's ear," caused by water remaining overlong in the ear after a swim, bath, or shampoo. Fungi or bacteria settle in the ear canal, multiply rapidly, and cause an itchy, crusted condition that "weeps" fluid. A physician should be consulted to prescribe appropriate medication. Using earplugs and drying ear canals carefully after swimming can prevent this painful ailment.

Air travel can cause ear discomfort, ranging from feelings of pressure to sharp pain, particularly if one has a cold and/or nasal or sinus congestion. Pain—and, in more severe cases, symptoms of deafness—can last several days. For some, the discomfort can be minimized by chewing gum or by frequent swallowing and yawning while the plane is ascending and descending. These symptoms are due to changes in the relative air pressure in the middle ear and its environment.

MIDDLE EAR INFECTIONS

The middle ear lies behind the eardrum and contains three minute bones that transmit eardrum vibrations to the organs of hearing located in the inner ear. The middle ear is directly connected to the back of the throat by the Eustachian tube. The Eustachian tube is surrounded by the adenoids.

Middle ear infections (otitis media) are common complications of colds or respiratory infections in children. A child's Eustachian tube is straighter and shorter than that of an adult, making it easier for the viruses or bacteria from the nose and throat to reach the middle ear and cause infection. Middle ear infections in children may also be the result of measles, mumps, or diseased tonsils or adenoids.

Acute middle ear infection can be extremely painful and may be accompanied by ringing in the ear and fever—even by hearing loss in some instances. Sometimes a sticky, yellow pus will flow from the infected ear, indicating that pus buildup behind the eardrum has burst the drum, relieving the painful pressure. The eardrum will heal over fairly rapidly once the infection is controlled, however, and usually is not permanently damaged.

Prompt treatment with antibiotics is mandatory for middle ear conditions. One of the penicillins is usually given or if penicillin sensitivity is a concern, erythromycin and sulfa may be prescribed. Because of the danger of reinfection, it is vital that the patient receive the entire course of medication prescribed, even though he or she may feel better and be without fever within a day or two. If treatment for serious middle ear infection is neglected, or even unduly postponed, some loss of hearing may result. Untreated ear infection may also lead to mastoiditis, an inflammation of the mastoid bone located behind the ear, which may require surgical treatment.

Another middle ear disorder, serous otitis media, frequently follows otitis media. In this condition fluid accumulates behind the eardrum. Since antibiotics have been given for the otitis media, the fluid is usually sterile, but it is trapped by a blocked Eustachian tube and may thicken and cause hearing problems. A child may complain of the sensation of "hearing under water." The doctor will often prescribe a decongestant to help shrink the nasal mucosa and open the Eustachian tube. In severe cases, the child may be referred to a specialist, who will drain the fluid and then insert a tiny plastic tube, which may remain in place for several months, allowing air into the middle ear. Physician followup is important to prevent permanent hearing loss.

INNER EAR DISORDERS

The inner ear is made up of coiled, fluid-filled chambers called the cochlea, which house thousands of hair-like nerve endings. These pick up vibrations traveling

What Happens During an Ear Infection

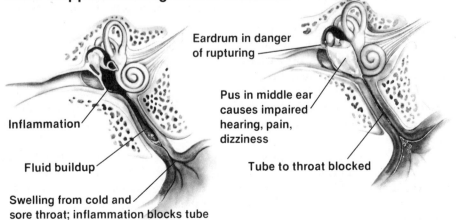

Eardrum in danger of rupturing

Pus in middle ear causes impaired hearing, pain, dizziness

Tube to throat blocked

Inflammation

Fluid buildup

Swelling from cold and sore throat; inflammation blocks tube

through the fluid of the cochlea and transmit them to the auditory nerve, which, in turn, sends the information to the brain. The inner ear also contains the organs of balance—three semicircular tubes, or canals. Sensory receptors in the canals detect movements of the head and relay the information to the brain, which delivers appropriate signals to the muscles for maintaining the body's balance. Thus, if the inner ear is inflamed or impaired, the brain is likely to receive faulty information, and the result can be a case of vertigo, or dizziness. Vertigo, however, is rare among children, and the dizziness usually disappears promptly with antibiotic treatment. Allergic disturbances also may cause vertigo. These usually respond to antihistamines.

SUMMING UP

Mild ear infections are common in young children and can have a variety of causes. Most frequently they are associated with colds or respiratory problems when viruses or bacteria pass freely from the throat to the middle ear through the Eustachian tube. With prompt, proper drug treatment, few ear infections develop into a major illness for the child.

114. Sinusitis

COMMON CHARACTERISTICS

Sinusitis is an inflammation of delicate membranes in the sinuses, or air cavities, in the skull. Symptoms of sinusitis include a stuffy nose, pain above or below the eyes or over the cheeks, and possibly a headache.

Sinusitis is most likely to develop after a cold or during or after an allergy attack. An infection—viral or bacterial —or an allergic reaction may start an inflammatory process in the nose. Then the inflammation spreads into the sinus through those continuous mucous membranes.

Some people seem to be more prone to sinusitis than others, and many factors may be involved. Irritation of the nasal passages from allergies, smoking, or other causes can predispose a person to sinus aggravation. (Occasionally, sinusitis may follow dental treatment when infection from the root of a tooth spreads through the bone and up into the sinus.) Even where you live can have an effect—sinusitis is more common among those who live in temperate or cold climates, where the typical cold and other respiratory infections are more frequent.

THE SINUSES

The sinuses are cavities in the facial and head bones. They are lined with membranes similar to those lining the nose and are connected to them. There are four "groups" of sinuses with matching cavities on both sides of the head; these are called the frontal, maxillary, sphenoidal, and ethmoidal sinuses. Sinusitis most frequently occurs in the frontal and maxillary sinuses, resulting in pain just above the eyes and on both sides of the nose from the eye level down, spreading out to the cheeks. These empty cavities act as resonators for the voice, and when they are inflamed or filled with fluid the resonance of the voice is lost. Because the tissue that lines the nose continues into the sinuses, there is a direct connection. Therefore, bacteria or viruses that invade the nose can travel deeper into the head to infect the sinuses.

SYMPTOMS

Sinusitis can be distinguished from the nasal and head symptoms of a cold by the fact that instead of getting better after a few days, the nasal blockage worsens. The discharge may be clear but is often yellow or greenish because of the breakdown of white blood cells from inflammation. The discharge may cease altogether if the mucous membranes become so swollen that

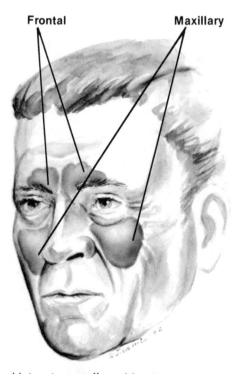

Frontal **Maxillary**

Major sinuses affected by sinusitis.

the passageways between the nose and the sinuses become blocked. There is often a feeling of difficulty in breathing through the nose, but perhaps the most troublesome symptom is pain and pressure around the eyes, cheeks, and forehead.

SELF-HELP

Unlike a cold, sinusitis usually should be brought to the attention of a physician because, if untreated, it can lead to a chronic condition or a spread of the infection deeper into the head. Until the doctor is seen, however, or until the symptoms can be distinguished from those of a cold, a number of steps can be taken to gain relief. The first steps for treating sinusitis are similar to those of treating a cold: using mild nose drops that contain a mucosal-constricting substance and avoiding an overly dry environment. A humidifier or vaporizer may be needed to keep the air moist. If these are not available, inhaling steam from a sink, hot shower, or tea kettle may be an alternative. Avoid blowing your nose hard; aspirin or acetaminophen may be used to relieve pain. If an allergic reaction is responsible, nonprescription sinus medication that contains antihistamines to help shrink swollen membranes also may be used. These drugs may produce drowsiness; follow instructions on the label and do not use for more than a few days at a time. When an allergic reaction is not present, drugs containing pseudoephedrine may be preferable.

WHEN TO SEE A DOCTOR

If self-help does not produce significant improvement within a few days, one should consult a physician. If a bacterial infection is the cause of the sinusitis, antibiotics may be prescribed. If the problem is related to an allergy, an antihistamine may be indicated.

There is also prescription and nonprescription medication available to help reestablish drainage, which will make you more comfortable. Such medication can be oral—pills to be taken by mouth—or topical—drops or sprays to be applied to the nasal cavity. As with all medication, make sure to tell your physician about any other drugs you are taking. Never take anyone else's prescription sinus medication.

Usually, medication will clear an attack of acute sinusitis. In some cases, chronic sinusitis develops, sometimes aggravated by the growth of polyps in the nasal tract that further block breathing and normal discharge. After diagnosis by special examination of the internal air passages of the nose and, possibly, X-rays, minor surgery may be required to drain the sinuses or remove the polyps.

SUMMING UP

Sinusitis is a fairly common problem, especially after a cold. Proper home care can often relieve its symptoms until the doctor is seen. However, prompt consultation with a physician is necessary to prevent further infection and chronic illness.

115. Strep and Other Sore Throats

COMMON CHARACTERISTICS

One of the most common physical complaints is a sore or scratchy throat. This soreness can range from mild to severe, and it often accompanies or follows a cold. It may indicate a localized irritation or infection, or it may be the first warning of a wider-scale viral or bacterial disease. A sore throat accompanied by fever should be called to a doctor's attention, especially if it persists for more than one day.

CAUSES OF SORE THROAT

A runny nose accompanied by a slightly sore throat is usually no more than a common cold. A person with a mild viral infection tends to tire easily, and it may be advisable to stay at home. If there is no improvement after a few days of limited activity and simple home treatment, a more serious illness may be present.

Laryngitis—inflammation of the larynx or voice box—may occur with or without a sore throat, and hoarseness is always evident. Laryngitis may also produce a "tickle" in the throat that leads to a dry cough, in which case a vaporizer may be helpful. The best treatment for laryngitis that is unaccompanied by other symptoms is a day or so of silence and whispering, which gives the vocal cords an opportunity to heal.

Sore throat may also occur in the pharynx, the passageway at the back of the tongue. Pharyngitis, like other infections of the upper respiratory tract, frequently results from a viral infection. Such infections usually originate as a common cold and clear up without treatment after a few days. Aspirin or acetaminophen may be taken to relieve fever and other symptoms.

Mouth breathers may suffer from chronic sore throat because the air they breathe does not get humidified or filtered through the fine hairs in the nose. Drying and environmental pollutants may thus cause irritation. Mouth breathers may have increased susceptibility to upper respiratory infections as well.

An allergic response to ragweed pollen or the spring pollens of trees and grasses or to mold spores may produce a sore throat as well as watery eyes, runny nose, sneezing, and itching of the palate. Collectively called hay fever, such responses are rarely seen before the age of three or four. When allergy is diagnosed as the cause of sore throat, an air-conditioned, dust-free room may alleviate the more troublesome symptoms.

THE SPECIAL CASE OF STREP THROAT

The possibility of streptococcal throat infection ("strep throat") is the compelling reason for consulting a doctor whenever a sore throat is severe or is accompanied by high fever. This condition is an acute and contagious infection of the throat or tonsils by a strain of streptococcus bacteria *(Streptococcus pyogenes)*. Prompt and complete treatment is essential if severe complications are to be avoided, particularly in children.

Although in some cases symptoms are minimal, many patients with a strep throat will complain of intense pain when trying to swallow. On inspection, the back of the throat and the tonsils are beefy red and swollen. The uvula—the fleshy mass that hangs down from the back of the mouth above the roof of the tongue—may also be conspicuously inflamed. A yellowish secretion of pus may be visible on the tonsils. Lymph nodes

at the sides of the neck become swollen and sore. Body temperature often rises to 102°F or more, although sometimes there may be very little fever.

DIAGNOSIS AND TREATMENT OF STREP THROAT

Persons exhibiting any of the above symptoms should be examined by a doctor. Diagnosis of the disease can be confirmed by a culture of swabbings taken from the back of the throat.

Treatment consists of a full and uninterrupted course of antibiotics (usually penicillin) administered by a single injection or given orally for ten days. Other medications are available if the patient is allergic to penicillin. It is important that the medication be given precisely according to the doctor's instructions; it must not be stopped before the prescribed number of days are up, even if the throat is no longer sore and the patient feels well. This will ensure that all of the bacteria have been killed. Other recommendations include bed rest, aspirin, adequate fluid intake, and light meals as soon as swallowing is more comfortable and fever subsides.

The uvula, the fleshy mass at the back of the mouth, may be swollen and red.

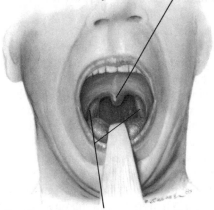

A yellowish pus may appear on the tonsils.

In strep throat, the back of the throat and the tonsils are beefy red and inflamed.

During the course of the disease, other family members—especially those with histories of strep infections—will be at risk. It is advisable to have the doctor examine them, too.

COMPLICATIONS OF STREP THROAT

The bacterial agent that causes strep throat is also responsible for scarlet fever (strep throat plus a rash), rheumatic fever (a disease that attacks the connective tissue and causes pains in the joints, and may also cause severe heart damage), and a type of kidney disease called glomerulonephritis.

Only rarely do streptococcal throat infections, treated or untreated, result in rheumatic fever or kidney disease. Nonetheless, prompt treatment with antibiotics reduces the risk of rheumatic fever and may help prevent the onset of glomerulonephritis.

SUMMING UP

Most sore throats are minor illnesses due to viral infections that clear up spontaneously and whose symptoms may be treated with aspirin or acetaminophen and gargling. When high fever and/or severe throat pain are present, a doctor should be consulted to rule out the possibility of a streptococcal infection. If strep throat is diagnosed, a complete course of antibiotics is needed.

116. Tonsillitis

COMMON CHARACTERISTICS

Tonsillitis is an inflammation of the tonsils, which are made up of clusters of lymph tissue located on either side of the throat, directly behind the back teeth. The tonsils are closely related to the adenoids, which are composed of similar tissue and situated at the back of the upper part of the throat, near the opening to the nose. Both the tonsils and adenoids play an important part in helping the body fight off infection.

At one time, a tonsillectomy (removal of the tonsils), usually accompanied by removal of the adenoids, too, was almost routine in childhood. Today, because of the development of antibiotics and other means of preventing and controlling infections, that situation has changed.

Tonsils enlarge as a natural part of a child's growth. Each year, until the age of nine or ten, they gradually become larger. Then, the process reverses itself. Before this natural process was properly recognized, enlarged tonsils were considered diseased and were usually removed.

THE LYMPHATIC SYSTEM

The tonsils and adenoids are part of the lymphatic system, which is important in helping the body defend itself against infection. This system consists of the lymph glands, which are found mostly in the neck, the armpits, and the groin; the lymph tissue of the tonsils and adenoids; and a

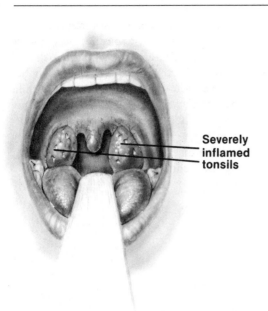

Severely inflamed tonsils

vast network of tiny transparent vessels, the lymphatics. The lymph glands and lymph tissues produce large numbers of white blood cells and antibodies, which together are capable of recognizing and destroying foreign organisms such as invading bacteria and viruses. Thus, when you suffer from an infection, microorganisms traveling along the lymphatics are trapped and destroyed by the lymph glands. In the process, the glands and tissues often become swollen, those near the surface noticeably so.

Because of their position, the tonsils and adenoids are the body's first line of defense against invading organisms in the throat and nose. Germs that get into the mouth are also likely to be identified and destroyed by the tonsils—and young children frequently place germ-laden objects in their mouths. Redness and swelling of the tonsils indicate that they are functioning properly in responding to infection and preventing its spread.

WHEN INFECTION STRIKES

Inflammation of the tonsils may be caused either by viruses or bacteria. The most common bacterial infection of tonsils is due to streptococcus. When a physician identifies a particular form of bacteria as the cause of tonsillitis, an antibiotic usually is prescribed that can promptly clear up the infection and help prevent complications. However, it has been found that the majority of tonsillitis cases are caused by viral infections, which the standard antibiotics do not help. Instead, one must wait for the normal process of recovery to occur on its own.

Initially, home care is the best approach when a youngster develops a sore throat, even with a low fever. Bed rest, plenty of fluids, and aspirin to reduce the fever and ease the pain are a standard, traditional approach for two or three days.

If the illness persists for more than two days—or if glands in the neck swell, the fever becomes high or the child develops a rash—a physician should be contacted.

THE QUESTION OF TONSILLECTOMIES

Surgical removal of the tonsils dates back centuries. In the early 1900s, family tonsillectomies were popular; that is, when the procedure was recommended for one child, all the siblings underwent it as well "to get it over with." Fortunately, this practice has been abandoned today.

Clearly, size alone should never warrant a tonsillectomy. Of course, if tonsils are so large that they make it difficult to swallow or breathe, they should be removed. Also, if they are enlarged because of chronic infection they should be removed.

Another myth is that tonsils cause frequent colds and sore throats. It has been found that these illnesses are just as common in children after the removal of tonsils as before. Similarly, recurrent ear infections, tonsillitis, and even rheumatic fever are not adequate reasons for tonsillectomy in and of themselves. Neither are stuttering or other speech problems, which have been found to be totally unrelated to the tonsils.

The old notion that a tonsillectomy is a

minor operation involving no risk also is not true. All surgical procedures involve a degree of risk, such as that related to anesthesia and uncontrollable bleeding. The psychological trauma involved in surgery for a young child can also be significant. No operation, no matter how minor, should be undertaken unless the expected benefits clearly outweigh the risks.

SUMMING UP

Tonsillitis is a relatively common childhood illness involving inflammation of the tonsils. Most cases do not require treatment. The need for tonsillectomy is now relatively rare, and the operation should be performed only after a physician has made a thorough examination of the child and monitored his or her health for a period of time. Parents should not urge surgery at the first sign of tonsillitis simply because that was the medical practice during their childhood.

Section Fifteen:
Skin Problems

117. Acne

COMMON CHARACTERISTICS

Acne is one of the most common skin complaints. Although it occurs most often during the teenage years, many acne sufferers are in their twenties, thirties, and older. In fact, it can develop at any age.

Acne is not a single disease but rather a group of skin conditions characterized by the development of blackheads, whiteheads, pimples, cysts, and boil-like lumps. They appear primarily on the face, chest, shoulders, and back—areas where most of the body's sebaceous (oil-producing) glands are located. Acne is a chronic ailment that erupts and subsides erratically. To some patients, it is more nuisance than disease; it is relatively mild and disappears as adolescence wanes. But to others, it can be a prolonged, disfiguring experience, which is not only damaging physically but can be psychologically troubling as well. Teenagers, especially, can suffer emotional distress, embarrassment, and negative self-image from a long battle with unsightly acne.

HOW ACNE DEVELOPS

Acne occurs when the sebaceous glands produce too much sebum, an oily, waxy substance. Located in the skin layer di-

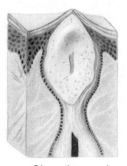

Closed comedo

Dead skin cells and excessive sebum clog the hair follicle, producing a pimple or comedo. This may be closed (whitehead) or open (blackhead).

Typical facial distribution of severe acne

rectly under the epidermis, sebaceous glands empty into the hair follicle canal opening on the surface as a pore. Normally, the sebum carries dead cells lining the hair follicle canal up to the skin surface. But overproduction of sebum traps the cells in the sticky substance, and they remain in the hair follicle. As the passageway narrows, the sebum and cells back up and eventually clog the pore, producing a visible lump (comedo).

This process creates two distinct types of comedo. If the duct is closed at the skin surface, the comedo remains whitish or skin-colored and is called a whitehead. If it has an opening on the surface, the substance turns dark and is called a blackhead. The discoloration is not caused by dirt, as is often supposed, but by an accumulation of pigment made by adjacent pigment cells.

Acne falls into two categories—noninflammatory and inflammatory. The latter type is more serious and more likely to cause permanent scarring. The buildup of sebum, cast-off cells, and bacteria, formed usually in a closed comedo, can cause such pressure within the follicle that the matter breaks out into the surrounding tissue, causing inflammatory acne in the form of disfiguring abscesses and cysts.

MAJOR CONTRIBUTING FACTORS

Despite scientific knowledge about how acne develops, its various manifestations, and the courses they follow, what actually triggers the acne process is still largely unknown. However, two important factors believed to contribute to its onset are hormones and bacteria.

Hormones

Acne almost never occurs before the age of puberty, at which time an increase in the levels of male hormones (androgens) stimulates overproduction by the sebaceous glands. Although girls also suffer from acne, it is usually less severe than in boys, since adolescent girls produce far less of these hormones than boys do.

Bacteria

Again, the exact role is not clear, but evidence shows that certain bacteria contribute to inflammation by breaking down fats into chemicals that irritate the follicle walls.

OTHER FACTORS

Additional factors that may contribute to the acne process include exposure to oils and grease, which plug pores; excessive humidity; various cosmetics and greasy hair tonics; and picking or squeezing blemishes, which aggravates the condition. Old wives' tales to the contrary, the following do *not* cause acne:

- *Diet.* No scientific evidence exists proving that chocolate, greasy foods, pizza, cola, ice cream, or any other foods are related to acne development.
- *Sex.* Sexual activity does not prevent or clear up acne; nor does masturbation cause it.
- *Dirt.* Since acne starts deep in the pore, surface grime is not a cause. But once acne is present, gentle washings with a mild soap can help control it by removing excess sebum and causing some drying of the area. Don't scrub too vigorously; it can make acne worse.

TREATMENT

As adolescence eventually passes, so do many cases of· noninflammatory acne. However there are many ointments, gels, soaps, and medicated pads available for treatment of minor acne, as well as a variety of stronger measures that can control serious, inflammatory forms of the disease.

One treatment for noninflammatory acne is removal of blackheads and whiteheads by a physician using a simple loop device, which expresses the blemish. Nonprescription drugs are also frequently used:

Exfoliants

These contain sulfur, resorcinol, or salicylic acid and do the job by causing the skin to dry out and peel. They are the mildest type of anti-acne drug, and some contain coloring ingredients that help mask skin eruptions. A few people may develop dermatitis after long-term use; therefore, fair, sensitive-skinned patients should begin with the weakest preparation to minimize irritation.

Benzoyl Peroxide Products

This group of agents (some of which do require a prescription) reduce bacterial activity in addition to promoting healing. In many cases, benzoyl peroxides will be the only treatment method necessary, but they can be highly irritating and must be kept away from eyes and lips. Initial applications may produce burning and stinging. If skin is extra-sensitive, start with a mild solution and gradually use higher concentrations.

Prescription drugs can help control inflammatory acne and reduce residual scarring that may result from the disease.

Antibiotics

Both topical (applied to the skin) and systemic (taken orally or injected) forms are proving useful, especially when administered with benzoyl peroxides. The primary role of antibiotics is to prevent new comedones; they cannot clear up existing lesions but do reduce bacteria and act against a possible outbreak of secondary infections. The most commonly used antibiotics for treating serious acne are the tetracyclines and erythromycins, both topical and systemic. Derivatives of these drugs are available in creams and lotions. Long-term use of systemic tetracyclines may cause gastrointestinal symptoms in some patients; they should not be used in pregnancy because of possible harm to the fetus.

Retinoic Acid or Tretinoin

Derivatives of vitamin A, these can be used effectively in extreme cases and work best in conjunction with benzoyl peroxide. Such treatment should be very carefully controlled by a physician because of the potential for excessive irritation. Patients using these agents should avoid overexposure to the sun. If benzoyl peroxide is also being used, one product should be applied in the morning, the other in the evening— never together.

13-cis-retinoic Acid

A synthetic member of the vitamin A family, this promising new agent has shown good results in studies. Only now becoming available by prescription for carefully supervised use, the drug inhibits sebum production. One of a number of other retinoic acid analogs currently being developed, it should not be taken during pregnancy.

SUMMING UP

Although no single treatment or combination of agents will completely cure all types of acne at the present time, the variety of topical and systemic measures available can bring about remarkable improvement for most patients, with minimal risks.

118. Athlete's Foot and Jock Itch

COMMON CHARACTERISTICS

Athlete's foot (tinea pedis) and jock itch (tinea cruris) are among the most prevalent of contagious skin diseases. They are caused by a group of fungi called dermatophytes, which invade only nonliving tissue, the outer layer of the skin (the epidermis), the hair, and the nails. They belong to the group of conditions classified by physicians as ringworm infections.

Athlete's foot and jock itch are irritating and occasionally painful but harmless. They are, however, hard to eradicate. Symptoms of infection may last for weeks, despite treatment. Even after the infection subsides and there are no apparent symptoms, the fungus may still be present, greatly increasing the chances for recurrence. Both conditions are quite infectious; entire families are often affected, as are groups of people who share bathroom or gymnasium facilities. Once infected by either condition, a person stands a greater chance of being infected by the other, and it is not uncommon for athlete's foot and jock itch to occur simultaneously.

ATHLETE'S FOOT

The fungi causing athlete's foot generally grow in or around the moist areas between and under the toes, particularly between the fourth and little toes. The infection may spread to the soles of the feet, causing small blisters, and can also affect the upper surface of the feet, the palms of the hands, and the area between the fingers. The skin in the affected area becomes red, flaky, and itchy; water and sweat may make the outer layer white and soft. If the nails are affected, they become

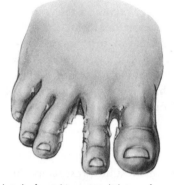

Athlete's foot (tinea pedis) is a fungal infection that usually occurs on the skin between and under the toes. Less frequently, the sole and upper part of the foot, as well as the hands and nails, also may be affected.

thickened and yellowed. Severe inflammation can lead to painful cracking and peeling of the skin, and infections with other, potentially more harmful, organisms may follow.

Athlete's foot may affect persons of either sex, but it is nearly six times more prevalent in men than in women. Adults are more susceptible than children. And some people are practically immune to infection by these fungi.

Most commonly, athlete's foot is contracted from infected scales of skin that have fallen onto the floor, typically in a bathroom or locker room. Tightly fitting socks and shoes, and hot, humid weather increase susceptibility. If the condition is already present, these factors tend to exacerbate it.

Successful self-treatment of athlete's foot is usually possible with the use of nonprescription antifungal powders or creams. However, it is important that hygiene be meticulous and that the medication be applied regularly. Perseverance is essential.

The affected area must be kept clean and dry at all times, and socks should be changed frequently. Lightweight, well-ventilated shoes or sandals are helpful, as is going barefoot. The antifungal medication should be applied two or three times daily for several weeks. Infections between the toes may require a month or more of diligent applications. The medication should be continued for a month after the symptoms have subsided to prevent recurrence.

If a nonprescription medication has been used appropriately for several weeks and there has been no relief, a physician should be consulted. A disease other than athlete's foot, or secondary to it, may be involved. In any instance, certain symptoms of athlete's foot should be brought to a physician's attention. These include infection of the toenail itself, eruptions that exude a pus-like liquid, infection of areas other than those around the toes, and swelling or inflammation of the entire foot. In these cases, a topical antifungal medication may be prescribed, one that is more powerful than nonprescription preparations. The doctor may also prescribe an oral antifungal agent, which is very effective in treating superficial fungal infections and is the only agent effective for fungal conditions of the nails.

JOCK ITCH

Jock itch may be caused by a number of different organisms, including bacteria and yeasts as well as fungi. Most commonly, however, it is the result of infection by dermatophytes. It usually begins as a slightly inflamed, moist, itchy patch on the inner upper thigh, especially where there is contact with the scrotum. As the infection develops, small blisters may appear, and the affected area may spread and begin to "weep," or sweat profusely. An unpleasant odor may be present.

Factors that may increase susceptibility to jock itch include tightly fitting underpants, lack of good hygiene, hot or humid

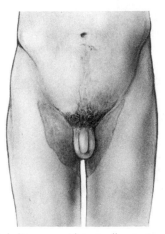

Jock itch (tinea cruris) typically starts as a tender, moist, itchy patch on the upper inner thighs. The rash often spreads to the buttocks and groin. Tight clothing and obesity promote the growth of the responsible fungi, particularly during hot weather.

weather, and obesity. As with athlete's foot, jock itch is not limited to any particular gender or age group, although adult males are most often affected.

Self-treatment of jock itch is often possible with conscientious use of topical nonprescription powders, creams, or lotions. For treatment to be effective, however, it is necessary that the groin area be kept clean and dry. This must be done without excessive bathing, which may actually prevent healing by causing excessive abrasion. Underwear should be made of cotton and fit loosely. If the condition persists after several weeks of self-treatment with a nonprescription preparation, a doctor should be consulted so that a more effective antifungal agent may be selected and to rule out the possibility that some other cause may be responsible. Oral antifungal medications may also be prescribed, and drying solutions and sitz baths may be recommended.

SUMMING UP

In most mild cases, athlete's foot and jock itch can be successfully treated with over-the-counter preparations, provided that good hygiene is observed and the medication applied regularly and over an extended period of time. In more severe cases and in those where the nails are in-volved, a physician should be consulted. Prescription oral antifungal medications are extremely effective in treating superficial ringworm infections such as athlete's foot and jock itch.

119. Eczema

COMMON CHARACTERISTICS

Eczema—or atopic dermatitis, to give it its correct medical name—is a skin rash characterized by itching, blistering, and scaling. It is a common condition, affecting about one in ten young babies to some degree or another. Eczema usually begins in the first few months of life and tends to subside by the age of three or four years. In some children, however, it may come and go for several years, eventually disappearing around the age of puberty. For a minority, eczema becomes a lifelong problem.

FAMILY HISTORY

The cause of eczema is not known, but a tendency to the condition seems to be inherited. In most cases, there is a family history of such allergic disorders as asthma, hives, and hay fever, and it seems likely that children affected by this condition inherit a very reactive skin. Allergies to food (eggs, wheat, fish, oranges, and especially milk) or to irritating substances such as soap, pollen, and animal dander may play a part. Some babies have eczema only when the skin is irritated by cold weather, others only when it is irritated by perspiration, others only in the diaper area. Often, a baby with eczema suffers also from asthma.

SYMPTOMS

When it is mild, or in its early stages, the rash of eczema is usually light red or a brownish pink. As it gets worse, the color darkens and the rash becomes intensely itchy. Usually, it evolves into oozing, "weeping" blisters. These eventually form crusts which, if not removed by scratching, cause the affected area to become scaly. Changes in pigmentation may occur as the blisters dry. Even when the rash has healed, a roughening and thickening of the skin can still be felt.

In babies, the rash usually begins on the cheeks or forehead; it may then spread to the neck and the arms and legs. In older children and adults, it generally appears in the crook of the elbows or behind the knees, or on the wrists, the neck, and the eyelids. In severe cases, the blisters may cover the entire body, including the soles of the feet.

COMPLICATIONS

The intense itching of eczema makes scratching almost inevitable, especially in a young child. The lesions that result provide easy access for bacterial and viral infections, which are common complications of eczema. In addition, ingredients in creams and salves used to ease the itching may set up an allergic reaction, making the condition worse. Eczema may also be aggravated by an overall dryness of the skin, which is common in people with this condition, by changes in temperature and humidity, by emotional stress, and by wearing wool next to the skin or using feather pillows.

A person with eczema should not be vaccinated against smallpox or exposed to anyone who has recently been vaccinated, since the skin has no innate immunity to the vaccine and a serious feverish illness (Kaposi's varicelliform eruption) may result. For the same reason, he or she should not be in contact with anyone who has cold sores, the active stage of infection by the herpes simplex virus (see Chapter 131, "Cold Sores and Canker Sores").

TREATMENT

Although its cause is not known, eczema can be controlled to some extent. Treatment is aimed at suppressing the symptoms and keeping the patient comfortable.

As far as possible, anything that seems to intensify the eczema—foods, pollens, danders, wool fibers, and so on—should be avoided. Also to be avoided are faddish diets and the unsupervised use of "miracle" creams and ointments that may, in fact, make the condition worse. Bathing with soap and water should be kept to a minimum, as this can dry and irritate the skin. Instead, mineral oil can be used to clean the skin.

Creams or ointments containing corticosteroids may be recommended to reduce the inflammation and itching of eczema. However, continued use over a long period of time, or on extensive areas of the body, is not generally advised, especially in the case of infants. Bath oils and moisturizing creams help reduce scaliness and prevent the skin from developing fissures. For children, an antihistamine may be given as a sedative at bedtime, when the

Typical eczema rash, showing oozing blisters that become crusty and scaly

itching is at its worst. Corticosteroids taken by mouth may be prescribed, but only as a last resort; these medications have many undesirable side effects, including a stunting of growth, if taken over a long period of time.

SUMMING UP

Parents of children with severe eczema understand the need to try to keep them from scratching and may therefore be reluctant to cuddle their babies for fear of irritating the skin. They should be aware,

however, that these children need physical closeness as much as all children do—possibly even more. Parents should also remember that most eczemas that start in the early months clear up completely within the following two years, or at least become much less severe.

As an adult, the victim of childhood eczema will still have an overreactive skin. For this reason, he or she should avoid those professions and occupations where contact with common skin irritants is likely —for example, nursing, hairdressing, and construction work.

120. Lice and Scabies

COMMON CHARACTERISTICS

Lice are small, visible insects that live in the hair and suck blood from underneath the skin. Certain kinds of lice, popularly known as crabs, live almost entirely in the pubic hair and are transmitted through sexual contact. Head and other body lice can be transmitted through any kind of

Nits (eggs) of hair lice, attached firmly to the hair shaft. The most likely site of infestation is the back of the head.

close contact, including an exchange of clothing.

Scabies is a disease that is caused by a nearly invisible mite that lays eggs under the skin. When these eggs hatch, the result is a harmless, but highly uncomfortable, itching. Scabies mites usually attack widely; they tend to burrow in around the buttocks, wrists, hands, and armpits. Scabies is easily curable, but it is important to remember that it can spread quickly among families or other groups of people who share the same living quarters.

Both lice and scabies may occur within any social or economic group. There is nothing "unclean" about either condition. Such infestations are usually communicated through casual, routine physical actions.

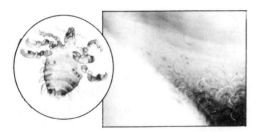

Pubic lice usually attach themselves to the pubic hair, but also may be found in beards and eyebrows.

DIAGNOSIS OF HEAD LICE

Head lice can usually be seen. If you suspect that you have been exposed to head lice, look carefully in a magnifying mirror. The lice will appear to the naked eye as minuscule grayish dots. The eggs, or nits, are white and can be found tightly attached to the hair shaft. Head lice cause intense itching within a short time of initial exposure.

Contact your doctor as soon as possible. There are effective medications for killing lice. Shampoos, creams, lotions, and soaps should be used carefully, according to a doctor's instructions. These medications usually relieve symptoms rapidly. A followup treatment may be needed, however, making it important that treatment not be discontinued until your doctor has examined you.

To prevent reinfestation, any clothing or bedding that has been used during the period of infestation should be thoroughly washed in hot, soapy water. Children with head lice should be kept home from school until treatment is completed. Practicing good hygiene is important, but once infestation has begun, it is very difficult to prevent the spread of lice within a group of individuals who live or work together closely. Health officials at camps, schools, and other institutions where people remain in constant close contact should provide education and widespread treatment programs.

PUBIC LICE

Pubic lice (crab lice) are almost always transmitted sexually. The lice, which can be found attached to the pubic hair, are yellow-gray in color, becoming dark after they are engorged with blood.

An infestation of crab lice causes intense itching in the pubic area as a reaction to the parasites' bites. It can be readily cured with the application of a prescription cream, lotion, or shampoo. To prevent reinfestation, the sexual partner(s) should also be treated, and clothes and bed linen should be washed.

RECOGNITION AND TREATMENT OF SCABIES

It is practically impossible to see the scabies mites themselves, and the symptoms they cause mimic those of other conditions. Their burrows, however, can be seen, as tiny dark lines on the skin, along with small reddish lumps. The lesions are intensely itchy, particularly when the individual is in bed. Scratching them may lead to a secondary, bacterial infection, more serious than the scabies infestation.

As with lice treatments, scabies medications should be prescribed or recommended by a doctor. An antiscabies medication should be applied to the entire body after careful bathing. Sometimes this treatment must be repeated, but a doctor should be consulted before this is done. Washing clothing, towels, or bedding in

Scabies mite and egg in burrow under the outermost layer of skin. Common sites of infestation include the webs of the fingers, the wrists, armpits, elbows, and belt line.

very hot water is highly recommended to prevent future attacks by the scabies mites. Family or group members who share the same clothing, towels, and linens should be treated simultaneously.

SUMMING UP

Both lice and scabies infestations are conditions that have held social stigmas for centuries. While it is true that poor personal hygiene and overcrowding may contribute to widespread infestations, small-scale breakouts of lice and scabies may occur in any community. The important fact to remember is that *anyone* can get lice or scabies, even if the most rigorous health habits are practiced. These attacks can be easily treated with the proper drugs and precautions. It is both sensible and thoughtful to let those around you know that they have been exposed.

121. Psoriasis

COMMON CHARACTERISTICS

In the normal growth process, the continuous loss of worn cells from the skin's surface is in balance with the continuous production of new cells in the basal layer of the epidermis (the outermost layer of the skin). On average, a cell passes from the basal layer to the surface in about two months, during which time it gradually forms an accumulation of keratin, the substance that gives the skin its firm texture. Sometimes, however, for reasons that are not understood, there is an abnormally fast rate of cell production; the new cells reach the surface in as little as six days and do not have time to accumulate keratin. The result is the unsightly flaking of the skin called psoriasis.

Psoriasis is a fairly common condition. Two to four percent of white Americans—far fewer blacks—suffer from it in varying degrees of intensity. It is unusual before puberty but thereafter can appear for the first time at any age. Almost 30 percent of those with psoriasis have a family history of the disease.

Psoriasis and arthritis sometimes occur together. It is not clear whether the arthritis is characteristic of psoriasis or whether psoriatic arthritis is a separate condition.

Psoriasis is a long-term problem. The disease flares up unpredictably and then subsides—often for long periods, even years—but never clears up completely. The condition can be annoying, even demoralizing, but it is not one that affects general health except in rare, unusually severe cases. Fortunately, psoriasis is not contagious.

SITES OF INVOLVEMENT

Psoriasis usually begins as a small red spot (or spots) with white scales. The lesion may be slightly itchy or sore. As the disease progresses, the small areas may merge together or form bright red patches covered with scales that resemble mica or the inside of an oyster shell. In some cases, the patches grow progressively larger and blend together, involving extensive areas of the skin. In one form of the disease known as exfoliative psoriatic dermatitis, the skin is red and covered with fine scales that often obscure the typical lesions. Sterile pustules, usually on the palms of the hands and the soles of the feet, are characteristic of another form called pustular psoriasis.

The most common sites are the scalp—especially the area behind the ears—the knees, elbows, back, and buttocks. Less frequently, patches may appear on the hands, under the breasts, in the genital region, or in the armpits. The face is usually spared. In some patients, the nails are affected, becoming thick and pitted.

TRIGGERING FACTORS

Despite a great deal of study and research, the precise cause of psoriasis is not known. The evidence, however, strongly suggests that a tendency toward the disease is inherited.

Many factors may trigger the condition, including stress, allergies, severe sunburn, throat infections, and exposure to excessive cold. Often a surgical incision or a cut or burn precipitates an eruption at the site of the wound. Sometimes localized psoriasis appears at pressure points—on the hands of mail carriers and golfers, for example. Once the condition has been established, it persists even when the triggering factor ceases.

TREATMENT

Although there is at present no treatment that can cure psoriasis, there are a number of medical approaches that, in most cases, are effective in controlling it. Usually, the simpler methods are tried first, with the more complex and stronger treatments kept in reserve.

In many cases, exposure to warm temperatures and moderate sunshine or another source of ultraviolet light can be helpful. (A sunburn, however, can worsen the condition.) Unfortunately, embarrass-

Overgrowth and shedding of epidermal cells

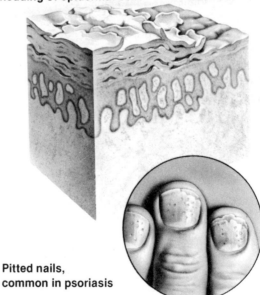

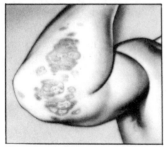

Common sites of involvement include the neck and scalp, arms, and legs.

Pitted nails, common in psoriasis

Psoriasis is caused by accelerated growth of the outer skin (epidermal) cells, resulting in scaling, itching, and other symptoms.

ment about their condition inhibits many patients from sunbathing.

For mild to moderate cases, creams, lotions, gels, bath additives, and shampoos are prescribed to reduce scaling and relieve the discomfort caused by excessive dryness. These products contain derivatives of coal tar, one of the oldest treatment agents for skin disorders still in use. Some combine the tar with salicylic acid or some other peeling agent. The preparations have a distinctive odor and can stain clothing, bedding and the skin itself. Tar, which is a photosensitizer, is also used in combination with ultraviolet light to help control scaling and acute flare-ups of the disease.

Topically applied corticosteroids may be used instead of the tar preparations, or in addition to them. These drugs produce dramatic initial results that unfortunately tend to be transitory. The treatment usually must be repeated at frequent intervals, and in many patients, the lesions become increasingly less responsive with repeated applications of corticosteroids.

An experimental treatment called PUVA (for psoralen plus ultraviolet A) is showing promise in cases of recalcitrant and extensive psoriasis. It involves the use of a compound (psoralen) that is activated by light, combined with carefully controlled exposure to high-intensity ultraviolet rays. This treatment often produces lengthy remissions. However, there is a risk of skin cancer, due to repeated exposure to intense light. The long-term benefits and risks of the treatment will not be known until further research is completed.

For severe, disabling psoriasis that is unresponsive to topical agents and to PUVA, the anticancer drug methotrexate, taken orally, is very effective. Methotrexate seems to act by interfering with the rapid growth of the skin cells. As with most anticancer drugs, it has a number of potentially serious side effects, and the benefits must therefore be carefully weighed against the long-term risks. Methotrexate doses should be kept as low as is feasible, and the drug should be given intermittently, if possible.

SUMMING UP

Psoriasis is a chronic and quite common condition. It can be unsightly, uncomfortable, annoying, and embarrassing—and may cause considerable emotional distress. However, it does not affect general health or become disabling unless intractable lesions develop or there is severe accompanying arthritis.

A number of treatments can help control psoriasis, but no permanent cure has yet been found. Experts have been unable to pinpoint a cause, although it appears that an inherited tendency is involved. Stress, throat infections, cuts, and burns are among the many factors that can trigger an outbreak. The condition is not contagious.

122. Itching

COMMON CHARACTERISTICS

Itching (pruritis) frequently accompanies skin disorders. It may also be a symptom—sometimes the only symptom—of a systemic disease (a disease affecting the body as a whole). It may occur as a side effect of numerous medications or as a reaction to stress and emotional disturbance. The skin may itch only in one particular place, or the itching may be generalized over a wide area of the body.

PRURITIS AND SKIN CONDITIONS

Severe localized itching is associated with the presence of parasites on or in the skin, most commonly lice, pubic lice or crabs, and the acarus mite that produces scabies. Itchy fungal infections include the ringworm disorders athlete's foot, jock itch, and ringworm of the skin and scalp.

Pruritis may also result from insect stings and from contact with allergens ranging from wool to poison ivy. Food allergies may cause excessive histamine to enter the bloodstream, producing itching hives and weals on the skin.

Eczema (atopic dermatitis), which affects mainly children, and lichen planus, which affects mainly the middle-aged, are among the specific skin disorders of which pruritis is a prominent symptom.

Dry skin may cause both localized itching and more generalized irritation. "Winter itch" is the result of excessive bathing that deprives the skin of its natural oils; of overexposure to dry, cold air outdoors, and dry, overheated air indoors; and of contact with clothing and bed linens laundered with strong detergents. In elderly people, severe pruritis may be caused by the gradual decrease in sebum production that occurs with aging.

PRURITIS AND SYSTEMIC CONDITIONS

Among the systemic conditions that cause generalized pruritis are Hodgkin's disease (a cancer of the lymph glands) and other lymphomas, leukemia, blockage of the bile duct, the blood disease polycemia rubra vera, and hepatitis and other liver disorders. Tumors of the thyroid cause alterations in hormone production and may produce pruritis; it may also be a symptom of internal cancers of other types.

Diabetes mellitis seldom produces generalized pruritis but may be the cause of localized itching, especially in the groin and the area of the rectum. The connection between diabetes and pruritis is not clear, but it is known that the skin of diabetics is normally dry and subject to inflammation.

Pregnancy is another condition that may cause pruritis. During the later months, a pregnant woman may have considerable itching without any outbreak on the skin.

PRURITIS AND DRUGS

Numerous commonly used medications may cause pruritis. Among them are antibiotics, sedatives, tranquilizers, oral contraceptives, and aspirin. If the itching is accompanied by hives, the drugs should be stopped and a doctor contacted as this may be a sign of a systemic allergic reaction.

PRURITIS AND THE EMOTIONS

Pruritis which cannot be attributed to any physical cause or condition, or to a drug reaction, may be the product of stress

Itching (Pruritis)

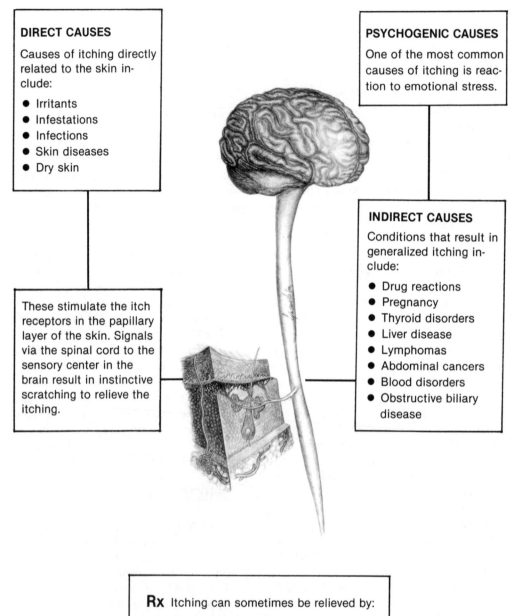

DIRECT CAUSES

Causes of itching directly related to the skin include:

- Irritants
- Infestations
- Infections
- Skin diseases
- Dry skin

PSYCHOGENIC CAUSES

One of the most common causes of itching is reaction to emotional stress.

These stimulate the itch receptors in the papillary layer of the skin. Signals via the spinal cord to the sensory center in the brain result in instinctive scratching to relieve the itching.

INDIRECT CAUSES

Conditions that result in generalized itching include:

- Drug reactions
- Pregnancy
- Thyroid disorders
- Liver disease
- Lymphomas
- Abdominal cancers
- Blood disorders
- Obstructive biliary disease

Rx Itching can sometimes be relieved by:

- Soothing emollients
- Minimal bathing
- Antihistamines
- Tranquilizers
- Sedatives (if sleep is disturbed)

or emotional factors. Although the symptoms can be relieved by medication, cure may depend on the underlying problem being resolved or at least understood.

SCRATCHING

Itching produces an almost uncontrollable desire to scratch. This damages the skin and results in a vicious cycle (irritation-scratching-damage-irritation) that may be difficult to break. Damage to the skin includes redness, weals, scrapes, and crusts along the scratch lines. Oddly enough, however, it is often the case that the skin of an individual complaining of generalized pruritis shows no sign of having been scratched or rubbed.

TREATMENT

The doctor's most important step in treating pruritis is to try to determine and correct its cause. If there is no apparent skin disease or infestation, he or she will investigate medications, systemic diseases, and possible emotional causes for the symptoms. A tranquilizer or antihistamine may be prescribed to make the sufferer more comfortable while the cause of the itching is sought. A sedative may be given if itching is disrupting sleep severely.

In cases of generalized pruritis, whatever the cause, bathing should be kept to a minimum since this may aggravate the condition. Irritating substances—woolen clothing, for example—should be avoided. Emollients such as white petrolatum or hydrogenated vegetable oil with menthol may be used to soothe the skin, or an antipruritic ointment may be prescribed to alleviate discomfort.

SUMMING UP

Pruritis or itching accompanies skin disorders of many kinds, including allergic reactions, fungal infections, and infestations. In addition, it may be caused by drugs or may be the product of emotional stress. Pruritis is also, and more gravely, a symptom of a variety of serious systemic diseases, including several different cancers.

123. Pigment Disorders

COMMON CHARACTERISTICS

Pigment-producing cells (melanocytes) are distributed evenly throughout the normal skin. The brown to black pigment they produce, melanin, determines the color of the skin: the denser the supply, the darker the skin.

Melanin production is stimulated by exposure to sunlight. The resulting darkening, a suntan, serves to give the skin some protection from some of the harmful effects of ultraviolet rays.

A number of different skin conditions reflect problems with the normal, regular production of melanin.

ALBINISM

This is a rare inherited condition in which the melanocytes, although present in the skin, do not produce any pigment. People with albinism, as a result, have pale skin, white hair, and pink or very pale blue eyes. They should avoid exposure to sunlight since their skin, unprotected by melanin, burns very easily and is prone to develop cancers. Sunblock preparations should be used on all exposed skin surfaces, and dark glasses should be worn to protect the eyes.

VITILIGO

In this condition there is an absence of melanocytes in certain areas of the skin. Patches where the skin is hypopigmented (lacking in pigment) are commonly found on the cheeks, at the hairline, on the backs of the hands, and around the eyes and nose. There may be only one or two such patches, or they may almost entirely cover the body. The lesions usually have sharply defined edges and are prone to sunburn.

Vitiligo occurs in people of all races, affecting about 2 percent of the population, but is naturally more conspicuous in those from dark-skinned ethnic groups. In many cases there is a family history of the condition—and in some, a history of injury to the head—but its cause is not known. Vitiligo is not a patchy variety of albinism; the eye color is not affected.

Drugs called psoralens are sometimes used to treat vitiligo, but the treatment is tedious and time-consuming, and for many patients the results are not satisfactory. Usually, doctors advise camouflaging the light patches, either with a natural or synthetic stain or with the special makeup that is used to cover birthmarks.

CHLOASMA

In some women, hormonal changes due to pregnancy or to the use of oral contraceptives result in irregular increases in melanin production in the skin of the face. A darkened (hyperpigmented) area—a chloasma or "mask of pregnancy"—appears, usually on the cheekbones, the forehead, or the temples. It is generally a dark, bluish-brown, with distinct margins. Exposure to sunlight makes the chloasma much more noticeable.

In pregnant women, the chloasma usually fades after childbirth; in other women, it lightens when oral contraceptives are discontinued, or simply disappears with time. A hydroquinone cream can be used to bleach the chloasma somewhat. It is important to test the cream on an inconspicuous patch of skin before applying it to the face, since it may cause an inflammation or may lighten the skin too much. A sunblocking preparation should be used on the hyperpigmented areas, and overexposure to the sun should be avoided.

"LIVER SPOTS"

These small, hyperpigmented patches have nothing to do with the liver or with a person's general state of health. They appear in the later years of life, generally on the face and hands, and, as with other hyperpigmentation conditions, darken in response to sunlight. No cream or lotion is effective in removing these melanin deposits, but chemical or mechanical peeling of the skin may be helpful. Many doctors, however, consider peeling techniques unsuitable for use on the thin skin of the back of the hands, a common site for liver spots.

BERLOCK DERMATITIS

Pigmentation changes on the neck and the wrists may result from regular use of perfumes containing oil of bergamot. Reacting with sunlight, this popular ingredient produces small brownish spots, which may be permanent.

KERATOSES

The two most common types of keratosis—an overgrowth of the horny layer of the epidermis—are seborrheic and actinic. It is important to distinguish between them since the latter are precancerous and some will become malignant if not treated.

Seborrheic keratoses usually appear on the back and chest, sometimes on the face and scalp. They vary greatly in size and color—some are pale, others black or almost black—but they are invariably raised above the surface of the skin, looking as if they had been stuck on. These keratoses tend to increase in number with age and do not need treatment unless they become irritated or are a cosmetic problem.

Actinic keratoses are one of the disturbing results of years of overexposure to sunlight, seldom appearing on parts of the body that are normally covered. Fair skins are particularly susceptible. The keratoses, which are usually hard, flat, and grayish-brown in color, should be treated by a doctor.

TINEA VERSICOLOR

Tinea versicolor is a fungus infection that is common in adolescence. White or tan spots, which are slightly scaly and tend to run together, appear on the back, chest, and upper arms, and occasionally on the face. These patches may spread to adjacent areas, involving a good part of the body. Often, it is in summer that this condition becomes apparent, as "sunpots" that fail to tan like the surrounding skin. The spots seldom itch except when the individual gets overheated—and not always then.

Treatment involves applying a medicated lotion to the affected areas at bedtime and washing it off in the morning. This usually clears the condition very quickly. However, it may be several months before the skin regains its normal pigmentation. Unfortunately, tinea versicolor has a tendency to recur, often within the year.

SUMMING UP

Most pigmentation disorders, while they may be more or less unsightly, are not

PIGMENT DISORDERS

DISORDER	CHARACTERISTICS	CAUSES
Albinism	Pale skin, white hair, pale blue or pink eyes	Genetic
Vitiligo	Patches of white skin	Unknown
Chloasma	Darkened patches on face	Hormonal changes of pregnancy or oral contraceptives
Liver spots	Small dark patches on face and hands	Age, exposure to sun
Berlock dermatitis	Brownish spots	Perfumes containing oil of bergamot combined with sun exposure
Keratosis	Horny overgrowth	Precancerous condition; overexposure to sun
Tinea versicolor	White or tan spots	Fungus

serious. They do not demand any great adjustment of the life style other than avoiding overexposure to sunlight.

Certain systemic diseases, such as Addison's disease, produce a generalized hyperpigmentation of the skin. Hyperpigmentation is also associated with hemochromatosis, a disease of older men, and with long-term use of silver, especially in nose drops and tranquilizers. Certain tumors of the pituitary gland also cause the skin to darken.

Any unexplained darkening of the skin, whether generalized or local (as in a keratosis), should be brought to a doctor's attention.

124. Skin Rashes (Nonallergic)

COMMON CHARACTERISTICS

Irritations and eruption of the skin can have a number of causes, among them bacteria, such as those that produce impetigo and cellulitis, and the fungus that is responsible for ringworm. Frequently, however, the cause is unknown or, though suspected, is unidentified.

SKIN RASHES WITH UNKNOWN OR UNIDENTIFIED CAUSES

Lichen Planus

The cause of lichen planus, a condition that affects mainly people in their middle years, is unknown. Sometimes, however, a period of stress precedes the eruption of the characteristic shiny, violet-colored, itchy pimples. These usually appear on the wrists, the bend of the knees, the torso, and the genitals—rarely on the face. In half of all cases, there are also blue-white, lacy lesions on the inside of the cheeks and the edges of the tongue.

The initial attack of lichen planus may persist for weeks or months; there may be recurrences over a period of years. Treatment includes the use of prescription medications and oral antihistamines to reduce the itching. Mouthwashes containing a local anesthetic and an antihistamine are helpful if the lesions in the mouth become ulcerated. Occasionally, the condition becomes widespread and the itching severe; an oral corticosteroid may then be prescribed.

Pityriasis Rosea

This mild skin disease may occur at any age and at any season, but it is most common in young adults in the spring and the fall. It is thought to be due to an as yet unidentified infectious agent, probably a virus.

The first sign of pityriasis rosea is a single, red, scaly area, usually on the torso, the "herald" or "mother" patch. Five to ten days later, there is a sudden, generalized eruption of scaly oval patches, rose or tan-colored, usually between the neck and the knees. Sometimes the lesions appear mainly on the arms, occasionally mainly on the face. In rare cases, the whole body is involved.

The suddenness with which the rash erupts is alarming, but pityriasis rosea is not contagious, and the skin usually clears up spontaneously within four to five weeks. Exposure to sunlight often hastens recovery. If the lesions become itchy and inflamed, the doctor may prescribe a medicated cream containing menthol.

SKIN RASHES CAUSED BY BACTERIA

Impetigo

Impetigo is one of the few contagious skin conditions and is far more common among children than among adults. This bacterial infection starts as a group of small blisters, usually around the nose or mouth. The blisters break, form a yellowish crust, and spread. Fresh infected areas may appear on other parts of the body, the bacteria being carried to new sites by the fingers.

The crusts of impetigo should be removed gently with warm, soapy water or Burow's solution three or four times a day. In addition, the doctor will prescribe an antibiotic ointment for use on the skin or antibiotics to be taken internally. To avoid spreading the infection, the washcloths and towels used by someone with impetigo should be kept separate from those of the rest of the family. School authorities may ask that an infected child stay home until the rash has cleared.

Cellulitis

This acute skin inflammation is usually caused by the bacterium *Streptococcus pyo-genes* invading the skin through a cut or rash, most often on the legs. The skin becomes tender, hot, and very swollen, with an "orange peel" appearance. Usually the edges of the rash are blurred, but in one type of the infection, erysipelas, the edges are raised and distinct. There may be blistering and oozing; sometimes abscesses form and have to be drained. In many people, a fever, chills, or a headache accompany cellulitis; others feel normal, apart from the affected area of the skin.

Cool, wet dressings help relieve the discomfort of cellulitis, and keeping the leg up helps prevent swelling. The doctor should be consulted since cellulitis, although it may clear up on its own, responds very quickly to antibiotic therapy.

SKIN RASH CAUSED BY FUNGI

Ringworm

Ringworm is highly contagious and can even be caught from household pets. It is not caused by a worm but by one of several dermatophytes, fungi that invade only the "dead" tissue of the skin, hair, and nails.

On the scalp, ringworm causes flaking, itching, and temporary bald patches. On the body, it starts as an itchy red, circular patch, which enlarges until it is about an inch across. As it grows, the center heals, leaving a slightly raised red ring on the skin. After a week or so, further patches may appear close to the original one.

TYPES OF NONALLERGIC SKIN RASHES

RASH	CHARACTERISTICS	CAUSES
Lichen planus	Shiny, violet itching eruptions; bluish mouth lesions	Stress(?)
Pityriasis rosa	Red scaly area that gives rise to widespread rose or tan itchy rash	Virus(?)
Impetigo	Yellowish, crusty blisters	Bacteria
Cellulitis	Tender, swollen "orange peel" rash	Bacteria
Ringworm	Flaking, itching rash	Fungus

Ringworm is treated with antifungal creams or lotions and, if it is severe or resistant, with the antifungal medication griseofulvin, taken orally. Griseofulvin does not kill the fungi directly; rather, it prevents further fungal invasion of the keratin tissues of the skin. As the old keratin grows out, the fungus is shed. The time needed for cure therefore depends on the rate of keratin turnover in the skin: about twenty-eight days. (A fungal infection of the nails, whose keratin turnover is much slower, may take up to four months to clear up, using griseofulvin.)

CONTACT DERMATITIS

Dermatitis—inflammation of the skin—may be caused by a delayed hypersensitivity reaction (see Chapter 99, "Allergic Skin Rashes"). Often, however, it is the result of direct irritation of the skin. Among the most common irritants that produce the blisters, redness, and swelling of contact dermatitis are detergents and household cleansers. Such products are so common a cause of skin irritation on the hands that doctors often use the term *housewives' dermatitis* to describe the rash. It usually occurs during the winter, when humidity is low and the skin more susceptible to irritation, and after repeated contact with the irritant substance or substances. Other, stronger irritants, which commonly cause more immediate skin reactions, include acids, alkalis, and phenol.

Usually, the redness disappears and the blisters dry up within a few days, when the irritant is removed. If it is not possible to avoid using the offending substance, protective clothing—lined rubber gloves, for example—should be worn.

SUMMING UP

A skin rash may have an easily identifiable cause, such as contact with an infected person, or it may appear "out of the blue." While few skin rashes are serious in themselves, some may be symptoms of systemic disease. Any suspicious rash should therefore receive medical attention.

125. Warts

COMMON CHARACTERISTICS

Warts are small benign skin growths that are almost invariably painless and harmless. However, a great many myths surround them, such as the belief that they are caused by handling toads or frogs. Just as many misconceptions abound on how to get rid of them. One approach to warts is to ignore them, and oftentimes they disappear as mysteriously as they appeared.

THE SOURCE

The medical term for warts is verrucae. Technically, warts are benign tumors. They may be caused by any one of a common group of viruses called the papovaviruses. They occur most often in children, decreasing in frequency with age, and are rare in the elderly. Indeed, anyone over age forty-five who develops what looks like a wart should see a physician promptly; rather than a harmless wart, it may be a serious skin problem.

When you develop one wart, you may infect yourself with the virus at other locations on your body and develop other warts or, more often, a cluster of warts at the original location. With or without treatment, the warts are apt to disappear after a few months or a few years. They may vanish forever or return years later at the same or a different location.

DIFFERENT TYPES OF WARTS

Common warts are slightly elevated mounds of bumpy skin, most often occurring on the hands, elbows, knees, face, and scalp. Their appearance is frequently compared to the bumpy surface of cauliflower. They usually range in size from about one-eighth to three-eighths of an inch. When they occur around the plate of the fingernail, they are called periungual warts.

Plantar warts are common warts that occur on the sole of the foot. They tend to become hard and flat due to the pressure of the body's weight. These are the only warts that are apt to become tender and painful. They can be differentiated from corns or calluses by their tendency to pinpoint bleeding when their surface is pared away. Clusters of these warts are called mosaic warts and may cover areas of an inch or more.

Filiform warts are long and narrow and most often develop on the eyelids, face, neck, or lips. Flat or plane warts are, as their name suggests, flat rather than raised; they, too, are usually seen on the face.

In contrast to these various dry skin warts are the so-called venereal warts, which are moist and tend to occur in the genital area. These warts, which may

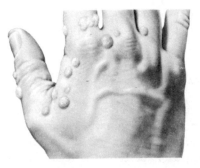

Common warts appear most frequently where the skin is subject to trauma.

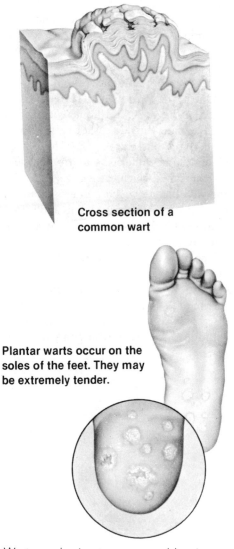

Cross section of a common wart

Plantar warts occur on the soles of the feet. They may be extremely tender.

Warts are benign tumors caused by viruses.

be transmitted to others through sexual contact, should be treated by a physician.

TREATMENT

As noted earlier, the best treatment may be none at all. Even when aggressive treatment to remove a wart is undertaken, as many as 35 percent may recur. However, if you or your youngster finds a facial wart embarrassing—and you have delayed as long as possible—there are steps your physician can take.

Certain "wart-dissolving" chemicals can be applied to the skin and covered with bandages. This leads to blister formation and eventual sloughing of the wart, but it is not a comfortable process.

One of the most successful treatments is freezing the wart with liquid nitrogen or solid carbon dioxide. Warts also can be burned off or scraped off. These techniques can be rather painful. In the case of plantar warts, which can cause severe pain and difficulty in walking unless removed, nonscarring treatments such as application of dissolving agents and paring by a physician are indicated.

The use of any nonprescription wart medications is discouraged. These are very strong chemicals that can damage surrounding skin. Never try to self-treat warts on your face or genitals, which could lead to severe pain and permanent scarring.

MIND OVER MATTER

Old wives' tales are filled with "hexes" to cure warts. The hexes themselves do nothing to remove the warts, but the power of suggestion seems to work, at least part of the time, particularly in young children. One physician's manual calls it "suggestion accompanied by an impressive manipulation," such as painting the wart with a fluorescent dye or warming it with a heat lamp. It is impossible to say whether the subsequent disappearance has to do with that all-important "stalling for time" element or whether it is another manifestation of the power of the mind to exercise some degree of control over supposedly involuntary functions of the body. Studies in biofeedback, for example, have demonstrated that we can change our body temperature, blood pressure, and heartbeat—all once considered totally involuntary functions—with our minds. Many parents have found that a very personal hex, such as covering the wart with a bandage, applying a "kiss to make it better," and not removing the bandage for at least a week often works.

SUMMING UP

Warts are rather harmless skin lesions that often get a lot more attention than they deserve. Patience is the best approach. However, if a wart is on the bottom of the foot or is a cause of concern, your physician can help.

126. Shingles

Shingles is a distressing and often painful viral infection affecting the nerve endings in the skin. Typically, the virus attacks one or more sensory nerves on one side of the body only, producing pain and tiny fluid-filled blisters along the pathway of the affected nerve or nerves.

Shingles may occur at any age but is most common in people fifty years of age and older. Old people are especially vulnerable to the disease: more than ten of every one thousand people eighty years of age or older contract shingles each year, compared with only three to five of every thousand under age eighty. The elderly are also more prone to develop the complications of the disease, persistent nerve pain (neuralgia) and widespread or disseminated shingles.

A "REACTIVATED" VIRUS

Shingles is caused by the virus varicella-zoster, which is virtually identical to the virus that produces chicken pox. Varicella-zoster belongs to the family of herpes viruses that is responsible for cold sores and genital herpes infections.

Like its fellow herpes viruses, the varicella-zoster virus has the ability to lie dormant for years in the body's nerve cells. Shingles occurs when the inactive varicella-zoster virus is "reactivated" and starts to multiply in the group of nerve cells on a sensory nerve root.

It is not known what factors cause the dormant virus to become active. However, since shingles often develops in people whose defenses against infection have recently been overtaxed (for example, as the result of injury, serious illness, or surgery), it is thought that a weakening of the body's immune system may allow the virus to become active. The vulnerability of the elderly to shingles may be due to the general lowered immunity to infection that occurs with aging. However, shingles may also develop in people who are otherwise in good health.

SYMPTOMS

Traveling along the nerve to the nerve endings in the skin, the varicella-zoster virus produces a sequence of symptoms. At first, the individual may feel pain and itching, burning, or tingling at the site of the future eruption. The skin may also be tender and highly sensitive to touch. Often there are accompanying symptoms such as fever, chills, and a general feeling of malaise. About a week later, painful fluid-filled blisters (vesicles) appear on the skin, following the path of the affected nerve. The vesicles tend to occur on one side of the body only. Over the next seven to ten days, these blisters dry out and become crusted. The crusts generally fall off two or three weeks later, in some cases leaving deep scars in the skin.

The searing or burning pain of shingles is felt right in the skin. Any movement or touching of the skin may stimulate the pain; some patients cannot even endure having clothing come into contact with the infected area. The pain (neuralgia) usually disappears within six weeks of the healing of the vesicles.

Shingles can affect any part of the body. The chest is involved in 55 percent of cases, the face and neck in 15 percent, the abdomen in 9 percent, and the groin in 3 percent. Less commonly, shingles develops on the arms and legs. If the eye is involved, blisters on the cornea may result in scarring and so interfere with vision.

Until the blisters have crusted over, an infected person is considered to be contagious. The varicella-zoster virus can be spread through direct contact and can also be transmitted through coughs and sneezes. One attack of shingles usually confers immunity for life.

TREATMENT

In a person who is young, generally healthy, and has only a mild case of shingles, symptoms can be controlled with rest, mild painkillers such as aspirin or acetaminophen, and medications to soothe the skin. The same is true for a person over fifty years of age who, after a few days, is experiencing only mild discomfort.

The type of topical medication prescribed depends on the stage of blistering. If the blisters are still filled with fluid, the doctor may recommend that cool compresses soaked with Burow's solution be applied and that these be followed with a soothing lotion. Ointments, creams, or gels containing steroids may be helpful in reducing inflammation at this stage. Once the blisters have become crusted, the doctor may recommend that, in addition to compresses, an antibiotic cream or ointment be applied alternately with one containing a local anesthetic.

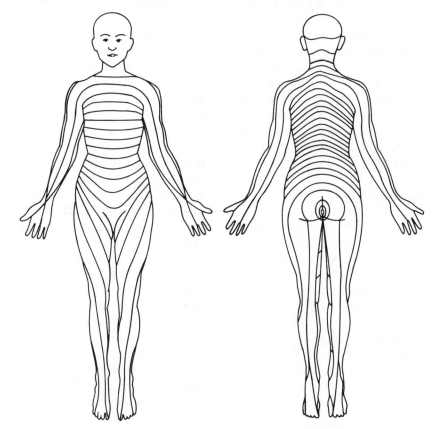

The "bands" indicate the pathways of various nerves in the body. In the viral infection shingles, painful vesicles follow the path of a nerve, usually occurring on one side of the body only. The chest is involved in 55 percent of cases, the face and neck in 15 percent, the abdomen in 9 percent, and the groin in 3 percent.

When there is considerable pain, a stronger painkiller may be needed. Morphine, codeine, or meperidine are frequently used. Many doctors treat severe cases of shingles by injecting a steroid drug in combination with a local anesthetic under the skin at the most painful sites, often called trigger points.

COMPLICATIONS

Persistent Neuralgia

In some people, particularly those over sixty years of age and those in whom facial areas are involved, neuralgia may persist for months or even years. The pain is sometimes intense. To prevent this complication of shingles in older people and susceptible individuals, doctors often prescribe oral steroids, to be taken for ten days to three weeks. This preventive therapy seems to be most effective if it is started within five to ten days after the symptoms of shingles appear.

If preventive measures are ineffective and persistent pain develops, there are several drugs which may help to alleviate it. A local anesthetic, either alone or in combination with a steroid drug, may be injected at the trigger points. Persistent neuralgia is often accompanied by severe depression. It has been found that treating the depression with mood-elevating drugs often helps to lessen the pain.

Disseminated Shingles

Especially when an individual's immune system has been weakened by serious in-

ternal disease, the vesicles may not be confined to one part of the body but may spread over large areas. This complication is called disseminated or generalized shingles.

Until recently, there was no drug effective in treating disseminated shingles. However, a new antiviral drug, adenine arabinoside, has produced good responses in people with this complication. Acyclovir, a drug that seems to be effective in treating genital herpes infections, may also be useful in combating disseminated shingles. Finally, it has been demonstrated that interferon, the substance produced in the body when the cells are exposed to viruses, prevents shingles from becoming generalized. Interferon, however, is not yet available commercially.

SUMMING UP

Shingles is an acute, often very painful, viral infection that affects the nerve endings in the skin. It is most common in people fifty years of age and older. The tiny blisters or vesicles of shingles usually appear on one side of the body only, and in a relatively confined area. The vesicles subside and disappear within a few weeks, but discomfort in the area may persist longer, in some cases for years.

A number of drugs are helpful in relieving the discomfort of the disease and in preventing complications from developing. It is extremely uncommon to have more than one attack of shingles.

127. The Sun's Effect on the Skin

A deep suntan is the hallmark of health and well-being, according to popular belief. Ironically, sun worshippers pay dearly for their bronzed complexions, not only with the stinging discomfort of sunburn but also with prematurely aging skin and a high risk of skin cancer. Repeated, prolonged overexposure to the sun's ultraviolet rays unquestionably causes the benign skin cancers basal and squamous cell carcinoma, and research indicates that the sun also plays a role in the development of melanoma, a more dangerous skin cancer. Additionally, even a mild sunburn can provoke a recurrence of a herpes simplex infection. The risks of sun damage are greatest for those with light skin, but even the darkest people are susceptible.

HOW SUN DAMAGE OCCURS

After years of too much sun, the elastic fibers in the skin break down, causing sagging and wrinkling, particularly around the neck. At the same time, the outer layers of skin cells thicken and develop a dry, leathery texture. The sun also damages the DNA in the skin; when this type of damage builds up, superficial skin cancers may develop. These lesions are generally curable, but they require surgical removal.

AVOIDING SUNBURN AND SUN DAMAGE

The tolerance for sun exposure depends on the amount of a pigment, melanin, present in the skin. Sunlight activates melanin, giving the skin its tan color and protecting against burning. Certain skin types, however, never produce enough melanin to prevent burning.

People whose skin is most sun-sensitive have what is known as type I skin. These fair-haired, fair-skinned individuals, often of northern European extraction, never get tanned and may burn after only ten to fifteen minutes in bright sunlight. Other light-skinned people belong to skin type II: they may, after repeated sunburns, become slightly tanned. Type III skin usually tans and sometimes burns, and type IV skin always tans and very rarely burns.

Many dermatologists advise those with skin types I and II not to try to tan at all. Avoiding the sun completely, however, is both impractical and unhealthful. By taking the following precautions, those with highly sensitive skin can prevent sunburn and skin damage and those who wish to tan can do so safely.

1. Avoid sunning between 11 A.M. and 3 P.M. During these hours, the sun's midrange light waves, those responsible for burning, are strongest.
2. Limit initial exposure to twenty or fewer minutes, depending on sun sensitivity. Build up to a longer exposure gradually over three to four weeks.
3. Use a sunscreen with a protection factor appropriate for the skin type. Most sunscreen packages display a number from 2 up to 15 indicating the strength of protection they provide. A screen with a protection factor of 4 allows wearers to stay in the sun four times longer without burning, a protection factor of 5 allows five times as much exposure, and so forth. Individuals with skin types I and II need a screen with a sun protection factor of 10 to 15. Sunscreens should be applied twenty-five to

forty minutes before going into the sun, followed by frequent reapplication, particularly after swimming or exercise. The best sunscreens contain PABA (para-aminobenzoic acid), which protects against the sun's burning rays, as well as agents such as benzophenones and cinnamates, which protect against longer wavelengths, thought to be responsible for wrinkling and aging the skin. Sunscreens slow the process of tanning, but they do not prevent it.

4. Use extra protection for the most sensitive areas of the body. Wear a wide-brimmed hat to shade the face, and, if a long exposure is anticipated, wear loose-fitting, tightly woven garments to protect the shoulders and the legs. (Light, loosely woven fabrics will not filter out all burning rays.) Apply extra-strength sunscreens or sun-blocking agents (zinc oxide or titanium dioxide) to the most vulnerable areas—nose, lips, chest, thighs, and backs of the knees.

5. Be on the lookout for photosensitivity reactions—increased susceptibility to sunburn—caused by certain drugs and cosmetics. Tetracycline, sulfa drugs, diuretics, antidepressants, antihistamines, and contraceptive pills all increase sun sensitivity, as do cosmetics containing bergamot oil and oils of citron, lime, sandalwood, and cedar.

TREATING SUNBURN

The sun can be deceptive. Burns often occur on moderately cloudy, brisk days, and, because sunburn doesn't become apparent until about four hours after exposure, people frequently burn without realizing it. A minor sunburn can be soothed with aspirin, cool compresses, and cool baths and showers. The physician may recommend a topical corticosteroid ointment for further pain relief. Topical anesthetics of the novocaine family should be used sparingly: they provide minimal relief and often provoke allergic reactions. Any sunburn that causes fever, nausea, severe blistering, and intense pain requires medical attention.

SUMMING UP

The sun's harmful rays toughen and wrinkle the skin prematurely and promote skin cancer, regardless of a person's skin type. Thus, a sensible approach to the sun is advisable for both light- and dark-skinned individuals. By using sunscreens, wearing appropriate clothing, and gradually extending the amount of time they spend in the sun, most people can avoid sunburn and long-term sun damage.

THE SUN'S EFFECT ON SKIN

SUN PROTECTION FACTOR	AMOUNT OF PROTECTION	WHO SHOULD USE
2–4	Minimal	People who rarely burn and tan easily
5–6	Moderate	People who tan well with minimal burning
7–8	High	People who burn moderately and tan gradually
9–14	Maximal	People who burn easily and tan minimally
15	Ultraprotection	People who burn easily and never tan

Section Sixteen:
Disorders of the Mouth and Teeth

128. Caries and Cavities

COMMON CHARACTERISTICS

Tooth decay (caries) is second only to the common cold as the world's most prevalent ailment. It is a progressively destructive disease that affects mainly children and young adults—the years of greatest decay activity are between three and ten and between thirteen and twenty-five—but may continue to be a problem throughout life.

Caries and the development of cavities are generally thought of as being one and the same. However, a cavity, the localized destruction of the enamel and underlying dentin of a tooth, is, in fact, a late manifestation of the disease.

CAUSES

Caries results from the interaction of three factors: specific bacteria in the mouth, carbohydrates in the diet, and a tooth surface that is susceptible to the disease. The bacteria are part of what is known as plaque, a gelatin-like mat that sticks to particular sites on the teeth, particularly the pits and cracks of the grinding surfaces of the molars and premolars, the area of contact between the teeth, and the gum line. Teeth that overlap one another in an irregular pattern are also hospitable to the buildup of plaque deposits. The bacteria—there may be hundreds of millions of them on a single tooth surface—use sugar as their source of energy and in the process liberate a variety of acids into the mouth. Some of these acids are powerful enough to dissolve the surface of a tooth whose enamel structure is less than optimal and so begin the process of decay.

Various kinds of sugar (sucrose, glucose, fructose, maltose, and lactose) and also starch, which is converted into sugars by enzymes in the mouth, are used by the plaque bacteria for their energy needs and therefore lead to the formation of acids. However, sucrose—by far the commonest sugar in the American diet, accounting for more than three-quarters of the total—has been shown to do the greatest damage. This is because this particular sugar is used by a strain of plaque bacteria, *Stretococcus mutans,* to manufacture a sticky substance called glucan, which enables these powerful decay-producing bacteria to build up on the tooth surfaces.

THE PROCESS OF DECAY

Each time that there is sugar or starch in the mouth, acid is produced by the plaque bacteria, most of it within the first twenty minutes after the food is eaten. Eventually, these cycles of acid production result in a small opaque brown or white spot on the tooth enamel, the first visible sign of caries. In time, the bacteria break through the weakened enamel and spread into the dentin, the sensitive tissue that makes up the bulk of the tooth. The undermined enamel cracks and breaks and the cavity becomes visible.

As the bacteria and their irritant products go deeper into the tooth through the tiny tubules in the dentin, there may be pain, especially when sweet foods or hot or cold liquids are consumed. More persistent pain is felt when the bacteria, penetrating further, reach the pulp tissue at the center of the tooth. Blood vessels in the pulp become infected and swell, but the pulp cannot expand to allow for the swelling (as would happen, for example, with an infection in the skin) because it is completely enclosed. Instead, the swelling blocks the tiny opening at the root of the tooth, reducing or cutting off the blood supply. This combination of infection and impaired blood supply causes the pulp to die—sometimes painlessly though usually not—unless dental help is obtained.

A "dead" tooth produces no problems until it abscesses, which it almost inevitably

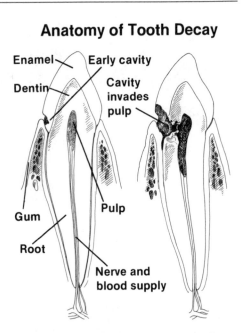

Anatomy of Tooth Decay

Enamel — Early cavity
Dentin — Cavity invades pulp
Gum — Pulp
Root — Nerve and blood supply

does within a few years. An abscess forms when the bacteria and their products, passing through the end of the root canal, infect the blood vessels in the surrounding bone and soft tissue. The tooth becomes very sensitive and "bites" ahead of the surrounding teeth because it is slightly elevated by the abscess at its root. An abscess usually produces a persistent, throbbing pain. It can lead to bacteremia (viable bacteria in the circulating blood) and, in susceptible people, to bacterial endocarditis—a serious heart infection (see Chapter 25, "Infective Endocarditis"). An abscess should be treated promptly with antibiotics and then "drained," either by extraction of the tooth or by root canal therapy.

PREVENTION

Just as there are several factors that interact to produce caries, prevention entails a combination of approaches: using good oral hygiene, modifying the diet, and increasing resistance to infection.

Oral Hygiene
Regular, thorough brushing and flossing are effective in removing plaque and

its decay-producing bacteria on some tooth surfaces. On the grinding surfaces of the back teeth, where a toothbrush is not effective, a plastic sealant applied shortly after the teeth come through the gums can reduce decay by about 50 percent. Sealants are long-lasting but not permanent; reapplication will be necessary within three to five years, on average.

Toothbrushing helps prevent caries only if it is done at frequent intervals. The teeth do not have to be brushed after every meal (that dictum dates from the time when the intent of oral hygiene was to remove fragments of food, rather than plaque) but should be cleaned thoroughly for five to ten minutes daily.

Diet

Where caries is concerned, the amount of sugar in the diet is less important than the form in which it is consumed and the frequency with which sweet foods are eaten. Sweet things eaten at mealtimes contribute little to tooth decay, largely because of the liquids that are consumed with them. Between-meal snacking is much more harmful, particularly when the foods are high in sucrose—soft drinks, cookies, pastries, candies. Especially damaging are sticky foods such as caramels and raisins, which remain in contact with the teeth for a comparatively long time, promoting bacterial activity.

Fibrous foods such as raw fruits and vegetables have value in preventing caries. While they do not remove plaque, they stimulate salivation, and saliva is a natural protective mouth rinse.

Increased Resistance

A proper intake of fluoride at the time the permanent teeth are forming is the most important factor in determining their resistance to later attack by plaque acids. Fluoride is incorporated into the enamel, making it harder and more resistant to decay.

For more than half the population of the United States, the water supply is either naturally high in fluoride or has been fluoridated to the appropriate level (one part fluoride per million parts water). In areas where the drinking water does not contain sufficient fluoride, children should be given supplements in the form of tablets or drops while their teeth are developing —that is, until about fourteen years of age. The supplements should be prescribed by a doctor or dentist and the dosage carefully followed. Too high a dosage can result in white spots or discolorations (fluorosis) appearing on the teeth when they erupt.

Further protection against decay can be provided by topical use of fluoride. For children, gels and solutions can be applied directly to the teeth. At any age, the regular use of fluoride toothpastes and mouthwashes helps build a protective level of fluoride on the surface enamel.

Studies have shown that the incidence of caries is reduced by as much as 65 percent when fluoride is present in the drinking water from birth and that an improved resistance to the disease continues throughout life. It has also been shown, conclusively, that there are no side effects to the proper use of fluoride, and that the only effect of an elevated level of this compound (such as occurs when the drinking water is naturally extremely high in fluoride) is the occurrence of fluorosis.

PROFESSIONAL TREATMENT

Fillings

Filling a cavity prevents further deterioration of the tooth. In preparing a cavity for a filling, the dentist carefully removes all traces of decay. He or she then shapes the space in such a way that the filling material will be retained. Local anesthetics are used for pain during this procedure.

Ideally, the filling material should match the tooth in strength, resistance to wear, reaction to changes in temperature, and, if possible, color also.

The most common filling material is an alloy of silver, copper, mercury, and other metals—the so-called silver or amalgam filling. Silver is the best material for small to moderate-sized fillings in the molar and premolar teeth. It is unsuitable for use in the front teeth because it is not attractive and tends to stain the surrounding enamel. Plastic composite materials can be matched very closely to the color of the teeth and are therefore used for fillings in the incisors and canines. These materials are currently not strong enough to be used where the biting forces are heavy. Composites have largely superseded silicates, which tend to dissolve in the mouth, for restorative work on the front teeth. Small cavities in the front teeth may also be filled with gold, but this material is more commonly used in the form of an inlay, where its benefits of strength and stability offset its cost.

Root Canal Therapy

When caries has caused the pulp of a tooth to die, root canal therapy may be done (the only feasible alternative is having the tooth extracted). All traces of pulp are removed from the pulp chamber and the root canals. The canals are then filed, reamed, sterilized, and sealed. The treatment usually takes at least three sessions. It is expensive but in almost every case results in a tooth that can be expected to be retained in the mouth for up to forty years. General practitioners may do root canal therapy on front teeth but usually refer the multiple-rooted back teeth to a specialist, an endodontist.

Extraction

If root canal therapy is not appropriate because the roots are narrow and twisted or the condition of the rest of the mouth is poor—or if the individual decides against it—a dead tooth will be extracted under local anesthetic. It may then be necessary to fill the gap with a fixed bridge or a partial denture.

Checkups and X-rays

Dental checkups should begin in early childhood, preferably when the child is two to three years old, by which time all the primary teeth will have come in. The frequency of visits should be determined on an individual basis, according to the amount of decay activity and other problems.

X-rays are no longer taken routinely on an annual basis by most dentists but are used when needed for diagnostic purposes. X-rays can show hidden cavities between the teeth and under the gum line; they can reveal the extent of decay or the presence of an abscess. As a general rule, a full-mouth X-ray should not be necessary more than once in five years.

SUMMING UP

Dental caries is an extraordinarily prevalent bacterial disease which principally affects children and young adults. Almost half of all American children have some tooth decay by the age of two; by the age of seventeen, the average youngster has eleven tooth surfaces that are decayed or filled. Decay activity tapers off in the mid-twenties but can continue to some extent throughout life.

Caries starts as a small opaque spot on the surface of the tooth enamel. If untreated, it may progress to the point that the tooth dies and eventually abscesses.

The saliva in the mouth provides some protection against caries, and the teeth themselves have an inherent resistance to the disease. This resistance can be bolstered by several preventive approaches: good oral hygiene, attention to the diet, and the use of fluoride.

129. Periodontal Disease

COMMON CHARACTERISTICS

Periodontal disease is the most common cause of loose and lost teeth in middle age and the later years of life (dental caries is responsible for most teeth lost before the age of thirty-five). The disease affects the supporting structures of the teeth, principally the gums (the gingivae) and the bone in which the roots of the teeth are embedded (the alveolar bone). Periodontal means, literally, around the tooth.

A majority of adolescents and almost all adults who have their own teeth suffer to some extent from the milder form of periodontal disease, gingivitis (inflammation of the gums). Of people forty-five years old and older, approximately 60 percent have the more severe form, periodontitis, in which bone is gradually lost and the teeth become loose and eventually fall out.

GINGIVITIS

Symptoms

The first symptom of the beginning stage of periodontal disease is usually a "pink toothbrush." The gums become red and swollen and bleed easily, especially when the teeth are brushed. There is seldom any pain, although the gums may be slightly tender.

Causes

The primary cause of gingival inflammation is the sticky film of bacteria and bacterial products called plaque that is constantly present in the mouth. Plaque tends to accumulate in areas of the mouth that are protected from the cleansing action of the tongue and the cheeks, principally between the teeth and along the gum mar-

Anatomy of Periodontal Disease

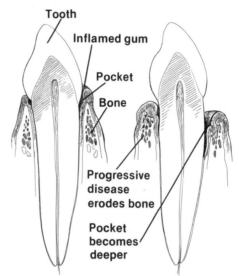

Tooth
Inflamed gum
Pocket
Bone
Progressive disease erodes bone
Pocket becomes deeper

gins. Here toxic products and enzymes produced by the bacteria inflame the nearby tissues. In addition, plaque may mineralize to form tartar (calculus), particularly in those parts of the mouth close to the salivary glands—the inside of the lower incisors and the outer surfaces of the molars. As this encrustation builds up in layers, it increases the irritation and inflammation of the gums.

Gingival inflammation is worsened by poor oral hygiene, misaligned teeth, overhanging or rough edges on bridges, crowns, or fillings. Inflamed gums are particularly noticeable during puberty and pregnancy, suggesting that hormonal changes affect the activity of the plaque bacteria. Pregnancy gingivitis usually clears up shortly after delivery.

Treatment

Thorough daily brushing and flossing will keep plaque and calculus formation to a minimum. Irrigating devices may be helpful in cleaning areas difficult to reach by other means. However, even with the best oral hygiene, professional scaling will be needed to remove calculus that has already formed and is firmly attached at and below the gum line. This should be done at least twice a year. Sharp instruments are usually used, but some dentists vibrate calculus off the teeth with an ultrasonic device.

This combination of good home care and regular professional treatment can prevent periodontal disease from progressing beyond the mild stage, gingivitis. It may even reverse the disease.

PERIODONTITIS

If gingivitis is not controlled, periodontal disease progresses to a more severe stage, periodontitis. (This condition used to be known as pyorrhea, from the Greek, "a flow of pus.") As the gingival inflammation continues, pockets form between the teeth and the gums. Plaque builds up in these pockets (they cannot be reached by a toothbrush), leading to further inflammation and a further deepening of the pockets—a vicious cycle. The gum margins detach from the teeth and pus may form in the pockets. The condition then spreads from the gums into deeper tissues, destroying the ligaments and bone that support the roots of the teeth and consequently producing the major symptom of advanced periodontal disease: loosened teeth. Other symptoms are changes in the bite and the development of gaps between the teeth. Even when the disease is far advanced, there is seldom any pain, unless an acute condition such as an abscess in a periodontal pocket is added to the chronic one.

The rate of bone loss is not related to the amount of plaque and calculus in the mouth but to what dentists call the bone factor. In people with a negative bone factor, the bone deteriorates very rapidly under very little stress; in those with a posi-

tive bone factor, it does so far more slowly. In general, however, the younger a person is when bone loss begins, the poorer the chances of saving the teeth.

Contributing Factors

Bone loss may be aggravated by the nervous habit of clenching the teeth in reaction to stress or the unconscious habit of grinding them during sleep. Individual teeth which carry an excessive burden in chewing, or a whole set that is habitually overloaded, are also susceptible to deterioration. Smoking and some drugs—including oral contraceptives and the antiseizure medication Dilantin—are aggravating factors in periodontal disease. In addition, diabetics and people with thyroid disease and various blood disorders have an increased risk of developing the advanced form of the disease.

Treatment

In the earlier stages of periodontitis, when the pockets are not deep, treatment usually involves removing plaque, calculus, and inflamed tissue from under the gum margins with a curved instrument known as a curet. The gums may then reattach to the teeth, or shrink and thus eliminate the pockets. This subgingival curettage, combined with good oral hygiene, may be all that is needed in many early cases.

If the disease is more advanced and the pockets are deeper (the dentist will measure their depth with a probe), a minor surgical procedure, a gingivectomy, may be done to eliminate the pockets. Or, in a similar procedure, excessive tissue may be removed to give the gums a shape that promotes better self-cleaning. Gum surgery should be done by a specialist, a periodontist. In very advanced cases, osseous surgery may be needed to correct bone defects, or plastic surgery techniques may be used to graft tissue flaps into areas where the gums have receded.

Other treatments may be needed, depending on the nature of the problem and the factors that aggravate it. The biting surfaces of the teeth may be filed or adjusted by orthodontic appliances so that the teeth and their supporting structures are evenly stressed during eating. If tooth grinding (bruxism) is a contributing factor, an appliance may be made to be worn at night.

An alternative approach which has yet to prove its long-term effectiveness and safety involves frequent professional cleanings and the daily use of salt, baking soda, and hydrogen peroxide to suppress the infection. The results of this home care are monitored by microscopic scrapings from under the gums. If necessary, antibiotics are prescribed.

SUMMING UP

The primary cause of periodontal disease is plaque, the sticky mat of bacteria and bacterial products that forms constantly in the mouth. (Plaque is also responsible for dental caries, but its mechanism in that disease is different.)

In the early stage of periodontal disease, known as gingivitis, deposits of plaque and calcified plaque (calculus) at the gum margins irritate the gums, which become red and puffy and bleed easily. If the disease is allowed to progress, continued inflammation leads to the formation of pockets between the teeth and the gums. As these pockets gradually deepen, the infection spreads to the underlying bone, progressively destroying it and loosening the teeth.

In its early stages, periodontal disease can be controlled or even reversed by good home care combined with semiannual professional scaling of calculus deposits. Treatment of more severe cases usually involves surgery on the diseased gum tissue. If the disease becomes very advanced, bone surgery or tissue grafts may be needed to repair the damage.

130. Temperomandibular (TMB) Joint Problems

COMMON CHARACTERISTICS

The temperomandibular joint, which connects the lower jaw (the mandible) to the temporal bones at the base of the skull, is vulnerable to the problems that affect all joints: fracture, dislocation, arthritis, rheumatoid arthritis, and stiffening with age. Displacement of the joint is relatively common, with the mandible too far forward and down for the mouth to be closed. In addition, the temperomandibular joint area is involved in a common but confusing muscular disorder, myofascial pain-dysfunction syndrome (MPD). (The word *myofascial* refers to the muscles of the face.) It is thought that at least half the general population has one of the symptoms

Structures Involved in Myofascial Pain-Dysfunction Syndrome

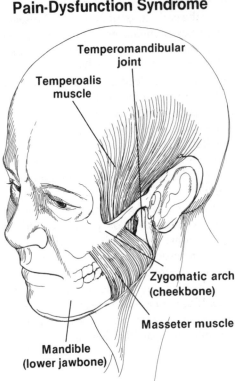

the jaws or grinding the teeth (bruxism), or the muscles involved in chewing may become generally tense in response to stress. The resulting muscle fatigue triggers the immediate cause of the syndrome: a spasm in the masticatory muscles. Sometimes a poor bite that puts the muscles under constant stress contributes to the problem. A badly fitting denture may also be implicated.

TREATMENT

Treatment aims at resting and relaxing the jaw. Someone with MPD will be advised to eat a soft, easily chewed diet and to limit the use of the jaw as much as possible. Hot moist packs, muscle relaxants, and tranquilizers may be prescribed to relieve tense muscles. Mild painkillers may also be helpful. In addition, the individual will be shown how to reduce tension in the jaw muscles by disengaging the teeth. While it may be possible to disengage the teeth voluntarily and consciously in the daytime, the habit of teeth grinding may persist at night. In this case, biteplates may be provided in an attempt to break the habit.

In addition to supportive therapy with heat and medication, the doctor or dentist may also suggest psychotherapy, with the object of uncovering life stresses that may be causative. This combination of treatments often has a notably beneficial effect. Biofeedback training, acupuncture, and hypnosis are other behavior modification techniques that have been used successfully with people suffering from MPD.

of MPD, and 30 percent report two or more.

SYMPTOMS OF MPD

The syndrome affects women more often than it does men. The most common symptoms are pain and tenderness in the jaw muscles; a dull pain that spreads from the area in front of the ears to the angle of the jaw and the back of the head; clicking or popping sounds in the joints of the jaw when chewing or opening the mouth; and limited or irregular movement of the lower jaw. In addition there may be ringing in the ears, dizziness, nausea, and episodes of blurred vision. The seeming unrelatedness of the symptoms frequently makes diagnosis difficult.

In the majority of cases, the root cause of MPD is tension. There may be specific tension-relieving habits such as clenching

SUMMING UP

Myofascial pain-dysfunction syndrome is a common syndrome that includes among its symptoms chronic headache and facial pain. While the immediate cause is a spasm in the muscles involved in chewing, there is almost always an underlying element of psychological and physical stress.

131. Cold Sores and Canker Sores

Both cold sores and canker sores are of frequent occurrence and both affect the mouth. However, they have little else in common. Cold sores, caused by a virus, almost always form on the *outside* of the mouth—on the lips and the skin around the lips. They are troublesome but seldom painful. Canker sores, on the other hand, are often acutely painful. When they are numerous, they may also be mildly disabling, preventing the sufferer from eating or talking. These sores form *inside* the mouth; their precise cause is unknown.

COLD SORES

Cold sores, also called fever blisters, are common infections. They are caused by a virus, herpes simplex 1, which is closely related to herpes simplex 2, the virus responsible for genital herpes.

The minute blisters, filled with clear fluid, form on a patch of red and slightly raised skin. They occur in small clusters, but often several groups merge together and cover an area of half an inch or more. Usually, before the blisters appear, there is a feeling of fullness, burning, or itching. A few days after they erupt, the blisters enlarge, burst, and begin to dry out. The sores usually heal on their own within two to three weeks and seldom leave a scar.

A major concern with herpes simplex 1 is that the virus may be transmitted to the eye. There it may ulcerate the cornea and even cause blindness.

Primary Infection and Recurrence

About three-quarters of the population is infected by herpes simplex 1 for the first time in early childhood. The incidence is particularly high among people living in crowded conditions and among those in the lower socioeconomic brackets. This primary infection often goes unnoticed because the blisters are so small. Sometimes, however, there is also loss of appetite, fever, and considerable ulceration in the mouth. If the primary infection occurs in late childhood or the teenage years, the virus may invade the bloodstream and cause severe systemic (bodywide) illness. In adults, in very rare cases, a primary systemic infection of herpes simplex 1 is fatal.

After the initial infection, whether it has been mild or severe, antibodies to the virus develop in the bloodstream. (These antibodies do not prevent recurrence of the infection, but they do make later attacks less severe.) The virus then lies dormant, presumably in the skin or in the nerve ganglia near the original site of the infection, sometimes for years, until something triggers another eruption. Often, the trigger is unknown, but in some people overexposure to sunlight, certain foods and drugs, or physical or emotional stress seem to be responsible. Some febrile diseases—pneumonia, for example—seem to stimulate a recurrence of cold sores.

While in the blister stage, the virus is highly contagious. During the "latent" stage between recurrences, however, it is not transmissible.

Treatment

Treatment is seldom necessary for cold sores, although an antibiotic may be prescribed if they become infected. A drying lotion such as camphor spirit can be applied to the sores if they are oozing. If sunlight is known to be a triggering agent, using a sunscreen containing amino benzoic acid can help reduce the frequency of the recurrences.

CANKER SORES

Canker sores, also called apthous ulcers, occur singly or in groups within the mouth —on the inside of the cheeks and lips, on the tongue, and on the soft palate. These sores, which are usually small but can be as much as an inch in diameter, begin as a shallow crater with a red, congested border. Within a week, the ulcers crust over and become acutely painful, remaining so for three or four days. They usually heal spontaneously—and, unless they are very large, without scarring—in seven to ten days.

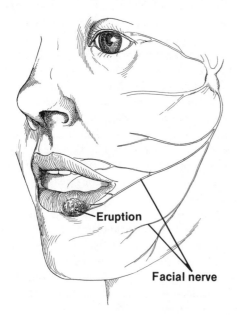

Between cold sore eruptions, the herpes simplex 1 virus lies dormant, presumably in the skin or in nearby nerve ganglia.

Canker sores can be mildly disabling as well as painful, especially when there are many of them and they interfere with talking and eating. Recurrent attacks are common, varying from one sore two or three times a year to a continuous series of many ulcers.

The precise cause of canker sores is unknown. Some people seem to be especially susceptible to them and may have an inherited predisposition. Deficiencies of iron, folic acid, or vitamin B_{12}—or a combination of these—increase susceptibility. In some people, recurrent sores are associated with injuries inside the mouth, such as pinpricks or scratches. In women, the onset of the menstrual period is often the trigger for an attack. Stress is frequently a precipitating factor—canker sores are common among students at examination time, for example.

Canker sores form quickly and generally heal quickly. If they are numerous, the antibiotic tetracycline may be given in a liquid form, to be held in the mouth for a few minutes and then swallowed. When started early, this treatment relieves the symptoms and prevents new ulcers from forming. If the ulcers are painful and prevent eating, a mouthwash containing a local anesthetic can be used before meals to provide relief.

SUMMING UP

Canker sores and cold sores are common, troublesome afflictions—and the former are frequently very painful. Both types of sores usually heal spontaneously and without leaving scars. Their causes, however, are different, and they affect different areas, with canker sores forming inside the mouth and cold sores on the lips and the adjacent skin.

Infectious Diseases

132. Gonorrhea and Other Sexually Transmitted Diseases

COMMON CHARACTERISTICS

Sexually transmitted diseases (venereal diseases) are infections that are contracted through intimate sexual contact. Once established, sexually transmitted diseases such as gonorrhea and syphilis can spread and cause extensive, serious physical damage. It is important to make a doctor's appointment immediately if you suspect that you have contracted—or have been exposed to—such an infection. If it is found that you have been infected, you should abstain from sexual contact until your doctor tells you that you are no longer contagious. You should also inform your sexual partners so that they can be examined and treated also, whether or not they have symptoms.

Although gonorrhea and syphilis are the most serious of the sexually transmitted diseases, there are a number of others that cause considerable discomfort or embarrassment. Venereal warts, for example, can be acutely painful. Pubic lice (crab lice) cause intense itching.

GONORRHEA

Gonorrhea is a bacterial infection, and an extremely contagious one. An estimated 2.5 million Americans contract this disease annually.

The symptoms of gonorrhea usually appear within one to three weeks after infection. In men, these symptoms include a white to yellow-green penile discharge, burning pain while urinating, and deep, aching pain or pressure in the genitals. In women, there may be painful and frequent urination, deep, aching pain in the lower abdomen, and, rarely, a vaginal discharge. Pharyngeal gonorrhea (in the mouth and throat) may produce a sore throat; rectal gonorrhea occasionally causes discomfort in the area around the anus and a slight discharge. However, in 10 to 20 percent of men and up to 80 percent of women, there are no perceived symptoms at all.

Untreated, gonorrhea commonly affects the urethra in men, making urination extremely painful and difficult; it may progress to chronic obstruction and infertility. In women, the disease can attack the fallopian tubes and other pelvic organs (pelvic inflammatory disease), causing pain, fever, and, very likely, infertility. The risk of infertility increases with each infection: 75 percent of women who have had three infections involving the pelvic organs are infertile. In both sexes, untreated gonorrhea may result in arthritis, or in a general-

ized bacterial infection affecting the heart and nervous system. If a woman has active gonorrhea at the time of delivery, her baby may develop permanent blindness.

Fortunately, once it is diagnosed, gonorrhea can be treated quickly and effectively with antibiotics.

A diagnosis of gonorrhea can be made by a microscopic examination of the discharge or a cervical smear; or, more reliably, by a culture that takes two days to incubate. The culture should be repeated one week after treatment.

SYPHILIS

Syphilis is caused by an organism called a spirochete that is spread through sexual

Sites Affected by Gonorrhea

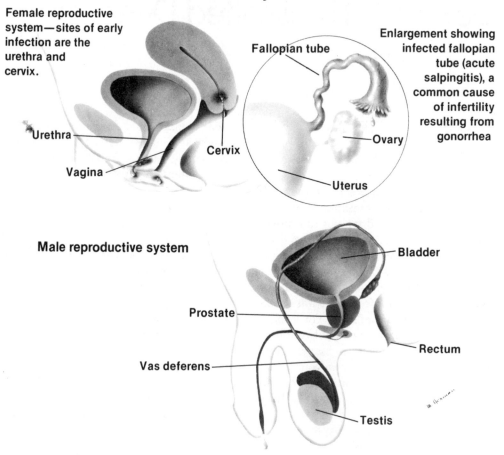

Female reproductive system—sites of early infection are the urethra and cervix.

Fallopian tube

Enlargement showing infected fallopian tube (acute salpingitis), a common cause of infertility resulting from gonorrhea

Urethra

Cervix

Vagina

Ovary

Uterus

Male reproductive system

Bladder

Prostate

Rectum

Vas deferens

Testis

contact. About twenty thousand cases a year are reported to United States health authorities, but it is highly probable that several thousand more are not reported.

The disease has three stages. First, skin ulcers (chancres), which are usually painless, appear in the genital area. The chancres may erupt anywhere from ten to ninety days after infection. Men may see them on the penis, but in women they usually form inside the vagina and may easily be missed. These sores heal in a few weeks, leaving little or no scarring. Meanwhile, the spirochetes circulate in the bloodstream and, in a few weeks, produce the symptoms of the second stage of the disease: fever, swollen glands, and reddish, scaly rash. These signs then also disappear, even without treatment, within ten days to two weeks; the disease becomes latent and, within two years, no longer infectious. The third stage may develop without warning, years later. In this final stage, there is tissue damage in the brain and the nervous system, heart, liver, bone, and skin. In as many as one-third of untreated individuals, this damage may result in death.

If a woman infected with syphilis becomes pregnant, or contracts the disease during pregnancy, there is a high risk that her baby will be stillborn or suffer from severe birth defects.

Syphilis is most accurately diagnosed by a blood test. It can be treated successfully with penicillin or other antibiotics. Periodic tests should be done for two years after treatment to make certain that the disease is cured. As is the case with all sexually transmitted diseases, sexual partners should be informed immediately and examined and treated.

VENEREAL WARTS

Venereal warts (condylomata acuminata), cauliflower-like and red, are caused by a virus and are thought to be almost exclusively sexually transmitted. In women, they appear around the vagina and rectum, growing more rapidly where they come in contact with any vaginal discharge and being greatly aggravated by pregnancy. In men, they appear on the penis and rectal area.

A wart-removing compound may be prescribed, although it is not recommended for use during pregnancy since it can be harmful to the fetus. The compound should be used with care and applied only to the surface of the warts. About six hours after its application, a sitz bath should be taken to remove any excess. Over-the-counter preparations should never be used; the genital tissues are too sensitive for such products. Occasionally it is necessary to remove veneral warts by electrocauterization (burning) or by surgery.

SUMMING UP

Sexually transmitted diseases such as gonorrhea and syphilis are highly contagious infections. If you are sexually active —other than with a single partner who is also monogamous—you risk exposure to these diseases; the more partners, the greater the risk. Sensible precautions that may be taken include urinating and washing the genitals after intercourse, using condoms and spermicidal vaginal foams, jellies, or creams, and being tested frequently for gonorrhea and syphilis if you have several sexual partners—or if your partner does.

If you suspect that you have a sexual infection, do not hesitate to tell your partner(s) and to visit your doctor or a clinic immediately. Sexually transmitted diseases can be cured only with prescribed courses of drug therapy. Never attempt to treat these diseases yourself. Above all, do not let fear or embarrassment stand in the way of receiving medical care.

133. Genital Herpes

COMMON CHARACTERISTICS

Genital herpes is among the many diseases caused by herpes virus, a family of viruses with five different strains afflicting humans with a variety of diseases that include chicken pox, shingles, and mononucleosis. The most common strain, herpes simplex, has two variations: type 1, which is usually associated with cold sores or fever blisters around the mouth; and type 2, which generally infects the genitalia, buttocks, and thighs with painful sores and blisters. The two types are not confined to these areas, however; studies have found type 1 herpes virus in genital sores and type 2 viruses in mouth and throat infections. Other parts of the body also may be affected, including the hands, eyes, brain, and spinal cord.

Although herpes viruses cause a wide variety of illnesses and have been studied extensively for the last few decades, they remain a medical enigma. Once they invade the body, herpes viruses remain for life, although they may be dormant most of the time. Some, such as the varicella-zoster strain, may have different manifestations. This variety causes chicken pox in children, after which the virus remains dormant in the nervous system. In most people, the virus never again becomes active, but for unknown reasons, in others it may erupt into painful attacks of herpes zoster, more commonly known as shingles. Similarly, herpes simplex also goes through recurring cycles of infectious activity and dormancy.

THE NEW "SCOURGE"

Genital herpes, although an ancient disease, was relatively uncommon in the United States until the late 1960s. Spread primarily through sexual contact, the disease has become the most common venereal disease in this country, afflicting an estimated 20 million Americans, with 500,000 new cases occurring each year.

The disease is spread most commonly by direct contact, meaning that to get herpes, uninfected skin must come in contact with an active herpes sore. Oral sex is believed to explain the presence of type 1 herpes sores in the genital areas or type 2 infections of the throat and mouth. Recent studies have found that the herpes simplex virus can survive for short periods on toilet seats, towels, and other such items, but most experts doubt that the disease is very likely to be contracted from these sources. It is highly contagious through direct contact, but in order to pass herpes to another person, there usually must be an active herpes sore or blister, although there may be a shedding of the virus without suffering symptoms of an attack. Also, since herpes sores may be hidden in the internal parts of the female genitalia or may not be painful, one may unwittingly infect others.

Typically, the herpes virus multiplies rapidly once it has penetrated the skin. The first symptoms are usually an itching or tingling sensation, followed by the eruption of sores or blisters that are unusually painful. In fact, the pain usually exceeds the actual medical seriousness of the disease. In the first attack, the sores customarily appear two days to two weeks after exposure and last two to three weeks. Subsequent attacks, which may occur in a few weeks or not for years, generally last about five days. Fever, general malaise, and headaches may accompany the first attack; these symptoms as well as the pain of the sores are usually milder in recurring attacks.

Once an attack subsides, the virus becomes dormant, traveling along the nerve fibers until it reaches a resting place. In rare cases, the herpes virus may travel to the brain, causing a serious, often fatal, form of encephalitis. More commonly than it infects the brain, herpes may infect the cornea of the eye; if untreated, a herpetic eye infection can lead to visual damage and even blindness. About 500,000 such eye infections occur each year in the United States. Type 2 virus may invade the spinal cord, causing a type of meningitis. None of these complications, however, is as common as recurrences at the original site of infection.

The blisterlike sores of herpes. In men, the most commonly infected sites are the penis and scrotum.

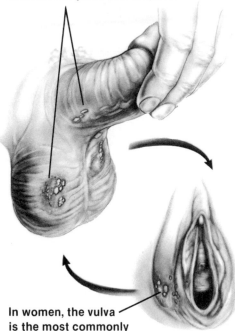

In women, the vulva is the most commonly infected site.

OTHER COMPLICATIONS

The most serious complications of genital herpes affect infants born to women who have active infections at the time of birth. About 50 to 60 percent of newborns who contract disseminated herpes infections die, and half of those who survive may suffer brain damage or blindness. Many doctors recommend that the baby be delivered by Caesarean if the mother has an active infection near the time of delivery. The decision of whether to have a Caesarean should be made early in labor, since Caesarean becomes a less effective preventive measure the longer the membranes have been ruptured. Women who have had genital herpes also are advised to have frequent examinations for active infection during the last three months of pregnancy.

There have been reports of an increased incidence of cervical cancer among women with genital herpes, but the evidence is not conclusive.

TREATMENT

As noted earlier, the herpes virus remains in the body, and as yet, there is no cure for genital herpes. However, a new drug, acyclovir, has been developed and recently approved for use in the United States, that will shorten the length of symptoms with the first attack, which is generally the most severe. The drug is available as a salve sold under the brand name Zovirax. It works by interfering with the replication of the virus, thus speeding the healing process in the first episode, but it does not prevent recurrence. Tests are now being conducted on an oral form of the drug. An intravenous form, recently approved for use in the United States, appears to be the most effective in severe cases.

Other types of treatment include the use of lasers to "vaporize" the herpes sores.

PREVENTION

The surest way to prevent herpes is avoiding all sexual contact with an infected person. Use of a condom and spermicidal agent will reduce the risk, but this is not absolutely foolproof, particularly when the lesions are on the skin of the perineum and not on the penis or in the vagina.

PSYCHOLOGICAL FACTORS

Although genital herpes itself is not usually a medically serious disease, it can lead to depression and other emotional problems. Many victims tend to resent the sex partner from whom they contracted the disease, leading to divorce or the breaking up of a relationship. Others consider themselves "unclean" or damaged for life, fearing that they are unfit for marriage or a lasting relationship. A number of herpes counseling centers and groups have been formed throughout the country to lend support and help to victims of the disease. Information about these groups can be obtained by contacting the Herpes Resource Center, 260 Sheridan Avenue, Suite 307, Palo Alto, CA 94306 Tel. 800/227-8922 or 415/328-7710.

SUMMING UP

Genital herpes has become the most widespread sexually transmitted disease in this country. While not as medically serious as syphilis or gonorrhea, it is very uncomfortable and can recur at any time. It also can be life-threatening to infants who are exposed to the herpes virus at the time of birth. A new drug has proven effective in easing the symptoms and speeding the healing in patients with the first episode. Although other treatments are in the experimental stage, no cure exists as yet.

134. AIDS

COMMON CHARACTERISTICS

AIDS (acquired immune deficiency syndrome) is a disorder characterized by severe and irreversible damage to the body's immune system, causing vulnerability to a variety of uncommon infections and a rare type of cancer. It appears to be a completely new disease with a high death rate.

First recognized in 1979 and established as a separate disease entity in 1981, its cause, natural course, and possible cure remain unknown. One of the reasons for the anxiety it has aroused is that no one yet knows how it is transmitted, if in fact it is transmissible. Its chief victims by far are homosexual men in urban areas, particularly New York and California. The disease has a high death rate, up to 70 percent within two years of diagnosis, according to the Centers for Disease Control in Atlanta.

Most of the deaths result from a rare pneumonia *(Pneumocystis carinii)* or from Kaposi's sarcoma, a rare cancer. It is not yet known whether people who seemingly "recover" from AIDS will ever regain their normal disease-fighting immune mechanisms.

While AIDS was first diagnosed among gay men, the second largest group consists of intravenous drug abusers. (In New York City, for instance, these two groups account for 91 percent of all cases.) Other groups at high risk are recently arrived Haitians and hemophiliacs who receive many blood transfusions. There is considerable uncertainty about whether Haitians should make up a separate category, since as illegal aliens they may have denied being homosexual or drug abusers. (There is also a strict taboo against homosexuality in Haitian culture.) In July 1983, health authorities in New York City removed them from the high-risk category, but they remain there in Miami. Of the reputed infant cases, ten occurred in New York City, and eight were the children of drug abusers, but the Centers for Disease Control has said that "infant cases are recorded separately because of the uncertainty in distinguishing their illnesses from previously described congenital immunodeficiency syndromes."

THE CLINICAL ASPECT OF AIDS

Although the cause of AIDS is still unknown, the effects of the disease are by now well known. The Centers for Disease Control uses the term *cellular immunodeficiency* to describe the seemingly irreversible imbalance in the categories of white blood cells (lymphocytes) that increase the immune system's efficiency in warding off infection. This imbalance in the "natural killer" cells leads to a pervasive and unmanageable vulnerability to so-called opportunistic infections that are almost always repelled when the body's immune system is intact. Until AIDS came on the scene, such vulnerability was limited to patients who were very old or whose immune system was genetically abnormal or

had been altered by cancer chemotherapy or for organ transplantation.

SIGNS AND SYMPTOMS OF AIDS

Most medical specialists agree that AIDS has a long incubation period, ranging from six months to two years, with about fourteen months the likeliest duration. One authority, Dr. Richard Krause, director of the National Institute of Allergy and Infectious Diseases, thinks that abnormalities of the immune system may develop weeks or even months before any symptoms show up, and if this is so, then many people may overcome the immunologic aberration without further consequences, leaving a small percentage in whom the abnormality takes over, with fatal consequences.

While other disorders begin with swollen lymph nodes, the AIDS patient experiences not only rapid swelling and soreness of the glands in the neck, armpit, and groin but also sudden weight loss and chronic fatigue, night sweats and/or fever, shortness of breath, a persistent cough, and reddish-purplish bumps on the skin. Any high-risk individual, or any individual in any way sexually involved with someone at high risk, who experiences any of these developments for more than a few days should see a doctor or hospital clinic familiar with AIDS.

HOW IS AIDS TRANSMITTED?

Most members of the scientific community who are concerned with disease control believe that AIDS is caused by a new virus (or a new virus in combination with a common one already known), but no such infectious agent or agents have yet been identified. These researchers also believe it unlikely that the viral agent is airborne and spread the way colds are spread, or transmitted through fecal contamination of food, as occurs in hepatitis A, or through insects, as occurs in malaria. They believe that the virus is transmitted like the hepatitis B virus, namely, that it is blood-borne. In the case of gay men, this may occur through anal intercourse, which often results in ruptures of the mucous membrane that lines the rectum. In the cases of drug abusers and hemophiliacs, transmission may be directly into the bloodstream.

Other researchers reject the idea that AIDS is caused by an infectious agent. Their hypothesis, known as immune overload, holds that gay men, drug abusers, and poorly nourished Haitians are typically victims of constant infection by viruses, parasites, and bacteria that undermine their immunity defenses and that their debilitated condition is further aggravated by inadequate diet, alcohol abuse, use of "poppers" in addition to antibiotic medication (taken for their many infections) that additionally undermines their body's immune processes. According to the "overload" theory, the cumulative effect of these factors, rather than a virus, is the cause of AIDS.

Charting the AIDS Epidemic

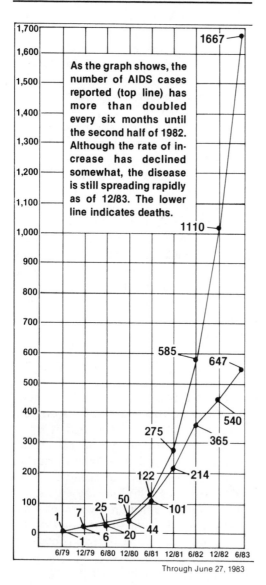

As the graph shows, the number of AIDS cases reported (top line) has more than doubled every six months until the second half of 1982. Although the rate of increase has declined somewhat, the disease is still spreading rapidly as of 12/83. The lower line indicates deaths.

Through June 27, 1983

SEARCHING FOR ANSWERS

Other than the fact that gay men are known to be the part of the population at highest risk, with intravenous drug abusers far behind and Haitians and hemophiliacs farther behind still, basic questions remain unanswered. What causes AIDS? What is the incubation period? How is it transmitted? Why have so few cases resulted from blood transfusions? Why have there been no Asians with AIDS? Why have practically no intravenous drug abusers in San Francisco become AIDS patients? Why is the twenty-five-to-fifty-year-old age group the most vulnerable? If a virus is the cause, is it related to the herpes virus? Extensive research is now underway to try to answer these questions.

Meanwhile experiments have gone forward on AIDS patients in tests involving two natural substances: interleukin-2, derived from a type of white blood cell (leukocyte); and interferon, also derived from white blood cells and known to combat certain virus invasions successfully.

Whatever the day-to-day outcome of research on all levels, public health officials feel that the hysteria largely engendered by misinformation and scare-mongering can best be dealt with by bringing the general population into the scientific information network.

HOT LINES

In July 1983, the government's Department of Health and Human Services opened a hot line that can be dialed free of charge from anywhere in the United States except Hawaii and Alaska. The number to call is 800/342-AIDS. From 8:30 A.M. to 5:30 P.M. EDT, questions can be asked and will be answered by a staff member; after these hours, information is provided by a three-minute tape recording. The same services are available to residents of Hawaii and Alaska by calling 1 202/245-6867, collect.

The National Gay Task Force has also established a toll-free hot line for calls from anywhere in the United States except New York State, Hawaii, and Alaska. The number is 1 800/221-7044. Residents of the other three states can call 212/807-6016. This number is staffed from 3 to 9 P.M. EDT.

USEFUL INFORMATION

Reports on various aspects of AIDS by a distinguished list of medical and health authorities have been collected in *The AIDS Epidemic,* edited by Dr. Kevin M. Cahill (St. Martin's Press, 1983).

PRACTICAL ADVICE

Public health authorities recommend that an individual at higher than normal risk should voluntarily refrain from being a blood donor. This category includes anyone with signs and symptoms suggestive of AIDS; anyone who is or has been a sexual partner of an AIDS patient; gay or bisexual men who are sexually active with many partners; Haitians recently arrived in the United States; intravenous drug users, both past and present. It is also recommended that gay men should discontinue "recreational" sex involving many partners, keeping in mind that there is no indication that the use of a condom provides reliable protection against infection.

If the prospect of AIDS is not a sufficient reason for drug abusers to abstain from their habit, they should not share needles or syringes and should *sterilize,* not just boil their equipment.

In addition, anyone who has a close but nonsexual relationship with an AIDS victim—a friend or family member—and who wishes to spend time with him at home or in the hospital, should speak to the patient's doctor about how best to arrange such visits so that they will do the patient the most good without causing anxiety to the visitor.

SUMMING UP

Latest figures from the Centers for Disease Control indicate that cases of AIDS have occurred in thirty-eight states, the District of Columbia, and Puerto Rico, and there have been cases in twenty-one other countries elsewhere in the world. Epidemiologists, immunologists, and other research scientists may solve the AIDS mystery within months, or perhaps not for years. Until a cause can be determined and a course of treatment pursued, all rational individuals—both those at high risk and the general population—would be well advised to avoid unnecessary anxiety by depending on reputable sources for information and guidance.

Anyone who has even the slightest suspicion that particular symptoms might be connected with AIDS should be checked by a doctor without further delay for his own peace of mind and for the well-being of his or her sexual partner.

135. Chlamydial Infections

COMMON CHARACTERISTICS

In recent years, the public has become more aware of the health hazards posed not only by syphilis and gonorrhea but also by "new" sexually transmitted diseases, such as genital herpes infections. Although less widely publicized than genital herpes infections, chlamydial infections are no less of a health problem.

Chlamydial infections are caused by the bacterium *Chlamydia trachomatis.* This organism is responsible for a variety of infections, most of which are spread through sexual contact. Some of these can cause serious complications if left untreated or if not treated properly. In addition, a pregnant woman who has a chlamydial infection can pass it on to her baby during delivery. Because of these potential dangers, it is important that chlamydial infections be diagnosed quickly and treated properly.

INFECTIONS IN MEN

Nongonococcal Urethritis

Nongonococcal urethritis (NGU) is an infection of the urethra. Sometimes called nonspecific urethritis, it is approximately twice as common as gonorrhea, and thus, though not reportable, may be the most common sexually transmitted disease in American men. *Chlamydia trachomatis* is responsible for 50 to 60 percent of all cases of nonspecific urethritis.

Some men with nongonococcal urethritis have no symptoms at all, while symptoms in others may be so mild that they go unnoticed. Most men with this infection, however, develop a watery pus-like discharge from the penis and experience a burning sensation when they urinate. These symptoms generally appear within seven to twenty-eight days after exposure to the infectious organism. They are often more marked in the early morning. If the sexual contact was rectal, there may be pain and soreness around the rectum, and often a discharge from the anus. Infection by *Chlamydia* as a result of oral–genital contact may result in an inflammation of the pharynx, the back of the throat.

The symptoms are very similar to those that appear in men who have gonorrhea, except that the discharge in nongonococcal urethritis may be less profuse and less thick than that in gonorrhea. For this reason, a laboratory test must be done on a sample of the discharge, to distinguish one infection from the other. It is in fact possible for a man to have both nonspecific urethritis and gonorrhea at the same time. This "double-barreled" infection often comes to light when a man continues to experience symptoms after being cured of gonorrhea.

Penicillin, which cures most cases of gonorrhea, is not effective in treating nongonococcal urethritis. Tetracycline and related antibiotics are used for this condition. To cure the infection completely, the antibiotics must be taken four times daily for seven days. Some patients develop complications and need longer courses of medication and bed rest. It is very important to take all doses of the medication for as long as prescribed, even if the symptoms clear up, in order to eradicate the organism.

Men with chlamydial infections are generally asked to see their doctors regularly for three months after treatment for physical examinations and bacteriologic and urine tests. During this period of time, about 20 percent have a recurrence of their symptoms and require retreatment. This is, naturally, worrisome; however, the medication is always effective eventually.

Since nongonococcal urethritis, like other chlamydial infections, spreads easily through sexual contact, it is essential to refrain from sexual activities until the infection is completely cured. The infection can be spread even if the infected person has no symptoms. In addition, all sexual partners of a person with nongonococcal urethritis must be checked for a chlamydial infection and treated if such is found. Contrary to what is popularly believed, one bout of a chlamydial infection—or any other sexually transmitted disease, for that matter—does not confer immunity.

Epididymitis

Chlamydia trachomatis may also cause epididymitis, an infection of the epididymis, the canal that transports mature sperm from the testicles to the penis. This type of chlamydial infection is most common in men under the age of thirty-five. The usual symptoms of this infection are fever and swelling and tenderness of the testicles. If untreated, epididymitis may cause infertility. Tetracycline antibiotics are used to treat this condition.

INFECTIONS IN WOMEN

Cervical Infections

In women, chlamydial infections most commonly affect the cervix; oral and rectal infections also occur quite frequently. Unfortunately, chlamydial cervical infections, like other sexually transmitted diseases, often produce no symptoms that might alert a woman to the need for treatment.

If left untreated, the chlamydial infection may spread to the uterus, the fallopian tubes, or the ovaries, where it can produce serious infection. Because of this, a woman whose sexual partner has been diagnosed as having nongonococcal urethritis should make an appointment with her doctor or a clinic as soon as possible. The infection can be diagnosed only by testing a cervical smear, which must be done in a specialized laboratory.

DISORDERS CAUSED BY CHLAMYDIA

DISORDER	CHARACTERISTICS	LIKELY VICTIM
Nongonococcal urethritis	Watery pus-like penile discharge; burning urination; no or mild symptoms	Sexually active male
Epididymitis	Fever, swelling and tenderness of testicles	Sexually active male under age of 35
Cervical infections	Slight vaginal discharge; no symptoms more likely	Sexually active women
Pelvic inflammatory disease	Lower abdominal pain, fever, nausea, painful intercourse, vaginal bleeding	Sexually active women, particularly those who use IUD
Chlamydial conjunctivitis	Inflammation of eye membrane	Newborn whose mother has chlamydia
Chlamydial pneumonia	Barking cough, lung congestion, rapid breathing, no fever	Newborn whose mother has chlamydia

Women who have chlamydial cervical infections are treated with tetracycline unless they are pregnant, in which case erythromycin will be prescribed. (Tetracycline taken during pregnancy may harm the fetus.) The antibiotics must be taken exactly as directed for as long as prescribed (seven days for tetracycline, fourteen days for erythromycin).

Pelvic Inflammatory Disease

Chlamydia is one of the most common causes of pelvic inflammatory disease (PID), a serious infection of the female reproductive organs. PID may cause permanent infertility if scar tissue forms and blocks the fallopian tubes. In extreme cases, it can be life-threatening.

The most common symptom of PID is pain in the lower abdomen, which may be mild or very severe. There may also be fever, nausea, vomiting, abnormal vaginal bleeding, and pain during sexual intercourse. Women who use intrauterine contraceptive devices have an increased risk of developing PID.

PID is usually treated with a combination of tetracycline and penicillin or a cephalosporin antibiotic. Although most women with PID can be treated at home, those with more severe cases may require hospitalization. As with other chlamydial infections, it is important that the sexual partners of women with PID be checked for infection and treated if necessary.

Chlamydial Infections During Pregnancy

Studies have shown that there is a 50 percent risk that a baby born to a woman with a chlamydial infection will contract the infection as it passes through the birth canal. (Babies delivered by Caesarean section are unlikely to become infected, unless the amniotic sac ruptures early in labor.) Accordingly, a woman who is pregnant and suspects she may have a chlamydial infection—or who has an infection and suspects she may be pregnant—should contact her doctor. These infections can be treated safely and effectively with erythromycin during pregnancy.

CHLAMYDIAL INFECTIONS IN INFANTS

Newborns exposed to *Chlamydia trachomatis* may develop conjunctivitis, an infection of the membrane lining the inner surface of the eye. This may develop at any time from five to fourteen days after birth. Chlamydial conjunctivitis is relatively benign and may disappear spontaneously within a few weeks or months. Erythromycin, either in ointment form or taken by mouth, is used to treat this condition.

Babies who have been exposed to *Chlamydia* may also develop pneumonia within four to twelve weeks after birth. The infant breathes rapidly and has a sharp, barking cough and lung congestion, but no fever. The infection may last for a month or more. Again, erythromycin is an effective drug.

SUMMING UP

Chlamydial infections are among the most common sexually transmitted diseases. In men, *Chlamydia trachomatis* is responsible for about half the cases of nongonococcal urethritis, probably the most common sexually transmitted disease among American males. The bacterium also causes epididymitis which, if untreated, may result in infertility. In women, *Chlamydia* commonly affects the cervix, usually without producing any symptoms. If unsuspected and untreated, a cervical chlamydial infection may spread to the reproductive organs, causing pelvic inflammatory disease and thus possible infertility.

As with other sexually transmitted diseases, it is of the greatest importance that the sexual partners of those with chlamydial infections be identified, and treated if necessary. Adolescents should be aware that, in most states, doctors do not need parental permission to treat a sexually transmitted disease in anyone over the age of 12.

136. Common Fungal Diseases

COMMON CHARACTERISTICS

A fungus is a form of plant life that includes mushrooms, molds, mildews, and yeasts. Fungi are not self-sustaining because they lack chloroyphyl, roots, and stems. They exist as parasites on live organic matter and feed on dead organic matter. Of the hundreds of thousands of different fungi found in nature, only about fifty are harmful to humans. Many antibiotics are derived from them, and many are highly prized by gourmets. Some are hallucinogenic, others poisonous, and the airborne spores and dusts of fungi are responsible for triggering the onset of asthma and hay fever in many individuals who are allergic to them.

The diseases caused by fungi are known collectively as mycoses. While the most common of these are confined to the skin and are more of a nuisance than a serious threat, others attack the mucous membranes and the lungs in a seemingly symptomless and insidious way. Mycotic invasions that proceed undetected and untreated to the vital organs, the bones, and the brain are rare but may be fatal.

Fungal diseases are classified under three headings: superficial (contagious infections localized on the body's surface); opportunistic (infections by usually harmless fungi that occur when the opportunity is present); and systemic (noncontagious diseases caused by airborne mycotic spores and dusts that reach the lungs through the respiratory tract).

SUPERFICIAL FUNGAL DISEASES

The superficial fungal diseases are collectively called tineas and are commonly known as ringworm. They are caused by about ten different fungal varieties whose favored targets are the skin, hair, and nails. Ringworm infections are highly contagious—from one person to another and from one part of the body surface to another. They flourish in a warm, damp environment and are difficult to get rid of. With patience and the right medication, they can be cured, but recurrences are not uncommon. Two of the most widespread ringworm infections are athlete's foot and jock itch (see Chapter 118). Others are described below.

Ringworm of the Scalp

Patches of the affected area are round, red at the edges where the disease is spreading, and pale and scaly at the center. The fungus also attacks the hair at the base, causing it to become dull and brittle and eventually to break off, thereby creating bald spots. When the scalp is examined with a special ultraviolet light for diagnosis, the infected patches have a distinctive fluorescence.

This condition is not responsive to local treatment. The only effective cure is the drug griseofulvin (Grifulvin, Grisactin) taken orally for three to six months. The course of medication should be supervised by a doctor since it may cause a rash, and patients should be cautioned about supersensitivity to sunlight during treatment. The doctor should also be consulted about negative interactions with medications taken for some other condition. The regular use of a medicated shampoo and a medicated salve can be helpful in preventing the spread of infection during the early period of griseofulvin therapy.

Ringworm of the Nails

This infection is usually associated with athlete's foot. The fungus is likely to spread to the base of the toenail and, in many cases, to the base of one or two fingernails as well. Topical medications such as haloprogin (Halotex) may control the spread of the infection but will not cure it. Treatment is the same as for ringworm of the scalp; griseofulvin over a course of many months, during which the patient should ascertain that the cure has been effected at the original site of infection.

OPPORTUNISTIC FUNGAL INFECTIONS

When the body's immune system is weakened and the ability to fight off invasion has been jeopardized by old age, chronic illness, or certain types of drug or radiation therapy, fungi that are otherwise harmless take hold with unpleasant and sometimes serious consequences. People with diabetes, kidney ailments, certain cancers, and AIDS are especially vulnerable. Opportunistic infections may also occur after treatment with broad spectrum antibiotics or prolonged steroid therapy and as the aftermath of a transplant that has undermined the patient's immune defenses. *Candidiasis* is the general classification for several opportunistic infections caused by the yeast-like fungus *Candida (Monilia) albicans.*

Vulvovaginal Candidiasis

This fungus may establish itself during pregnancy or following a course of antibiotics, or it may be transmitted sexually. It is characterized by intense itching and soreness in the affected area, accompanied by a yeasty white discharge. Treatment consists of vaginal suppositories containing clotrimazole (Lotrimin) or mystatin (Mycostatin). Creams containing these medications for direct application to the vagina, cervix, and vulva can cure the candidiasis but have a negative effect of destroying all the useful vaginal bacteria that

maintain a healthy acidic environment. The use of tampons should be discontinued during treatment, as should sexual intercourse.

Thrush

Thrush is caused by the same fungal agent, which produces patchy white areas on the mucous membranes inside the mouth and on the tongue, gums, and inside surface of the cheeks. It may be transmitted from mother to infant and may occur in a young child following the use of antibiotics. Treatment consists in rinsing the mouth several times a day with nystatin in oral suspension (in the case of infants, swabbing the affected area with the same medication). Gentian violet is also an effective swab.

Candidal Intertrigo

Obesity is usually the circumstance that encourages the spread of candidal intertrigo, in which the fungal infection is encouraged by the dampness and warmth under the breasts or between the buttocks. Formation of suppurating scaly sores that are itchy and painful can be discouraged only by keeping the affected areas thoroughly dry. Cool compresses followed by generous applications of nystatin powder are the most effective treatment short of losing weight.

The tissue at the base of the fingernail may become the site of a *Candida* infection if there is a break in the skin such as a hangnail, or because the area has been irritated by constant immersion in water and detergents. The technical term for this condition is paronychia, and unlike ringworm of the nails, it causes distortion and discoloration of the nail rather than disintegration. Recurrent or persistent inflammation can be controlled by keeping the hand dry, if necessary by wearing a watertight glove, and applying miconazole (Micatin) cream or lotion to the area. If medical history and/or examination indicates the presence of vulvovaginal candidiasis as a source of the infection, treatment with oral nystatin (Mycostatin) may be advisable.

When opportunistic fungal infections attack the very old or those who are vulnerable in other ways, they present the threat of becoming systemic diseases. When such is the case, drugs such as amphotericin B can be administered intravenously together with other oral drugs that control the spread of the fungi. Careful evaluation of possible negative side effects is essential.

SYSTEMIC FUNGAL DISEASES

There is a separate category of noncontagious fungal diseases caused by the inhalation of dusts containing microorganisms that produce a wide variety of symptoms, some indistinguishable from a mild case of flu and others having devastating consequences. These mycoses may be regional and/or occupational, and they are likely to be easier to prevent than to cure.

Histoplasmosis

This is caused by inhaling dust containing *Histoplasma capsulatum,* found in the soil and nurtured in the droppings of pigeons, starlings, chickens, and bats. While essentially a rural disease, the spores are also found on city rooftop pigeon cotes. Mild cases are self-limiting, with negligible symptoms, although subsequent chest X-rays may reveal calcified areas on the lungs similar to healed tuberculosis lesions. In severe cases, the liver, spleen, and lymphatics are involved, with increasingly damaging lung lesions causing respiratory impairment that may be fatal.

Treatment may involve prescribing amphotericin B, and a new antifungal medicine, ketoconazole, has been introduced recently. It is being used with positive results and very few negative consequences.

Ringworm of scalp

Thrush

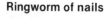

Ringworm of nails

Candidal intertrigo

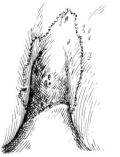

Paronychia

Fungal rash of chest and back

To prevent histoplasmosis, chicken farmers, pigeon fanciers, and children who help parents in these pursuits should wear protective gauze masks in the vicinity of accumulated dung. In city parks and playgrounds, mounds of pigeon and starling droppings should be cleaned up promptly.

Blastomycosis

Also called Gilchrist's disease, this involves the lungs, producing symptoms similar to tuberculosis. Thickly crusted ulcers also appear on areas of the face, neck, and arms, and if untreated, the disease spreads to bones and vital organs, inevitably leading to death. Correct diagnosis is based on identification of the fungus *Blastomyces dermatitidis* in culture samples of sputum or pus from abscesses. Treatment consists of prompt administration of amphotericin B, which results in early improvement. Combination therapy may include a drug specifically effective in this disease—hydroxystilbamidine isethionate.

Coccidioidomycosis

Valley fever, or, sometimes, "desert rheumatism," is caused by the airborne, spore-laden dust of the fungus *Coccidioides immitis.* In its primary form, infection may produce symptoms similar to those of a slight cold, acute bronchitis, or the chest pains and fever of pneumonia. If the primary infection is not self-limiting, it may slowly spread through the system, leading to critical weight loss, bloody sputum, and diminishing appetite and failing strength, eventually involving the bones, joints, and brain.

This systemic infection is insidious because significant symptoms may develop years after the exposure occurred and long after the patient, now mysteriously ill, has left the area where the disease is endemic. Diagnosis is based on establishing the presence of the microorganism in sputum, biopsy tissue specimens, and pus from skin abscesses. Treatment usually involves combined drug therapy based on amphotericin B and ketoconazole.

SUMMING UP

The superficial fungal diseases are not a threat to health but do cause considerable discomfort, and people who have ringworm in any of its manifestations are eager to be permanently rid of it. This can usually be accomplished with patience and the consistent use of medication. Opportunistic infections are relatively easy to deal with by following the doctor's instructions about medication. Where complicating factors involve impairment of the immune system, more elaborate measures are necessary. The much rarer and more serious systemic fungal diseases can be controlled and cured when they are correctly diagnosed before they can cause irreversible damage.

137. Mononucleosis

COMMON CHARACTERISTICS

Mononucleosis is an infectious disease caused by the Epstein-Barr virus, an organism in the herpes virus group. Because one of its characteristic symptoms is swelling of the lymph nodes, especially those in the neck, and because these nodes are popularly called glands, mononucleosis is sometimes referred to as glandular fever. And since it is often spread by oral contact, it also is widely known as the kissing disease.

Laboratory evidence indicates that 85 percent of preadolescent American children have been infected with the Epstein-Barr virus. During early childhood, symptoms may be so mild and the duration of the illness so brief that the infection is mistaken for a cold. But if infection occurs for the first time in the late teens, or early adulthood, mononucleosis can be a more serious and debilitating illness.

WHAT HAPPENS IN MONONUCLEOSIS

When the Epstein-Barr virus enters the body, it causes changes in a category of disease-fighting white blood cells known as B lymphocytes. These cells, which are crucial to the body's usual response to infection, react very vigorously to this direct infection, and the lymph glands throughout the body are greatly enlarged. It is generally assumed that one attack of mononucleosis confers immunity. However, the patient continues to carry the live virus in his or her throat for several months after recovery, which may conceivably lead to a recurrence of the disease. This continued viability of the virus also abets the spread of mononucleosis to other people.

THE CLASSIC SYMPTOMS

Onset of the illness becomes apparent within one week to two months following exposure. Symptoms vary in intensity, but typically the lymph nodes in the neck—and sometimes those in the armpit and groin—become swollen and sore. The patient may experience aching joints, fever, sore throat, difficulty in swallowing, fatigue, and, in some instances, a skin rash.

Since the symptoms may not be very specific, accurate diagnosis usually requires a blood test that confirms the high level and irregular appearance of B lymphocytes characteristic of the disease.

COMPLICATIONS

In a small percentage of cases, liver involvement may be considerable and thus jaundice occurs. Enlargement of the spleen is not uncommon. There is also a form of mononucleosis accompanied by prolonged fever, which is particularly troublesome.

While most people recover totally within a few weeks, others may continue to feel fatigued and ill for months after the acute symptoms have passed. Such extended convalescences may be accompanied by anxiety and depression due to the time lost from work or from other pursuits.

TREATMENT

Bed rest is mandatory for all forms of mononucleosis, mild or severe. Fluid intake should be increased, and a pleasant, nutritious diet is recommended. Intense physical and emotional demands should be kept to a minimum. Aspirin or other comparable analgesics may help reduce the discomfort of the sore throat (if it is present) or any other localized pains such as joint or muscle aches. Aspirin may also be used to control fever.

SUMMING UP

The Epstein-Barr virus, like other herpes viruses, usually infects people very early in life, causing mild symptoms or none at all, and conferring immunity against subsequent infection. When the disease occurs later on in early adulthood, it may be prolonged and immobilizing, but serious results may usually be avoided through a regimen of bed rest, aspirin, adequate fluid intake, simple and nourishing meals, and careful return to activity.

Mononucleosis

TYPICAL COURSE

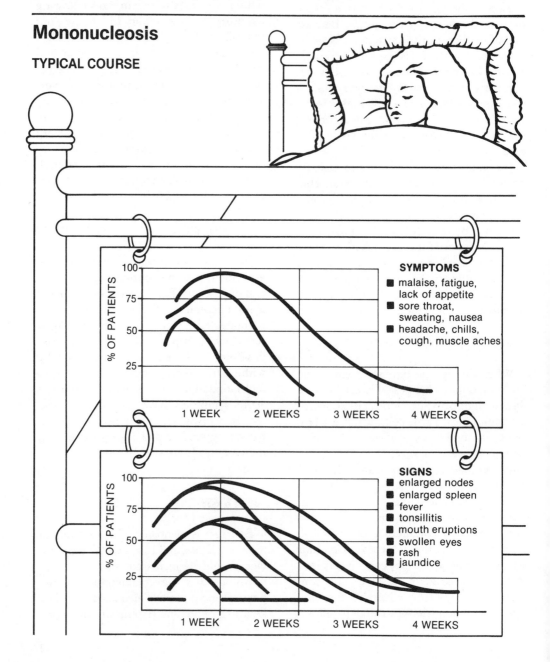

SYMPTOMS
- malaise, fatigue, lack of appetite
- sore throat, sweating, nausea
- headache, chills, cough, muscle aches

SIGNS
- enlarged nodes
- enlarged spleen
- fever
- tonsillitis
- mouth eruptions
- swollen eyes
- rash
- jaundice

Section Eighteen:
Problems Seen in Women

---

138. Menstrual Cramps

COMMON CHARACTERISTICS

Painful menstruation afflicts up to half of all menstruating women, making it the most common chronic health problem among women. Abdominal cramps, which may range from mild twinges to incapacitating spasms of pain that radiate through the lower abdomen to the back, are the most common symptom. Headaches, particularly migraines, nausea and vomiting, diarrhea, and other symptoms also may accompany menstruation.

In some women, the painful menstruation is caused by abdominal adhesions, fibroids or other tumors, or endometriosis (the abnormal growth of uterine tissue outside the uterus). More often, however, no specific cause can be identified; in these instances, the condition is known as primary dysmenorrhea.

Cramps and other symptoms are usually most severe on the first day or two of the period. In contrast, the cramps associated with endometriosis may increase in intensity as the period continues.

CAUSES OF DYSMENORRHEA

Until recently, there was a tendency to dismiss menstrual cramps as being "all in the head." Although psychological factors may be involved, research of the last few years has found that there is a link between the body's production of prostaglandins and menstrual cramps. Prostaglandins are hormone-like substances that are produced in cells throughout the body. There are many different types of prostaglandins, which are essential to numerous body functions, including the release of sex hormones, muscle contractions, and digestive processes. Researchers have found that some of these substances cause the uterus to contract—in fact, prostaglandins are instrumental in producing the uterine contractions necessary for childbirth.

Women who suffer from severe men-

Menstrual Cramps

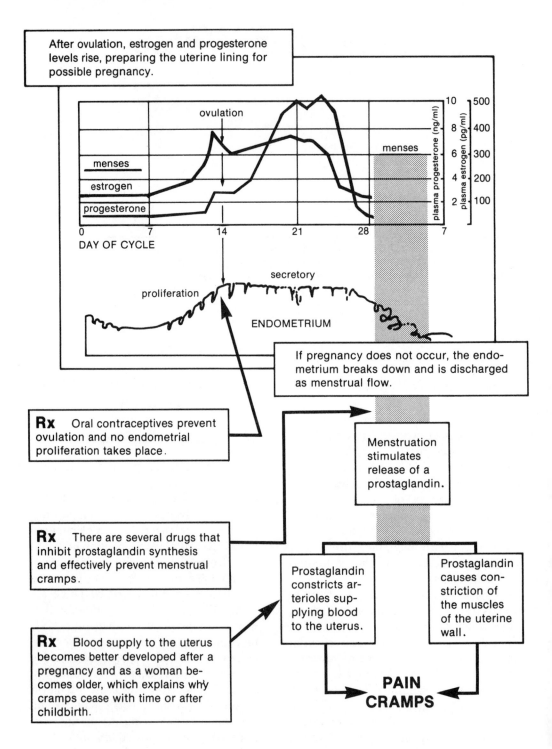

After ovulation, estrogen and progesterone levels rise, preparing the uterine lining for possible pregnancy.

ovulation

menses

menses

estrogen

progesterone

DAY OF CYCLE

plasma progesterone (ng/ml)

plasma estrogen (pg/ml)

secretory

proliferation

ENDOMETRIUM

If pregnancy does not occur, the endometrium breaks down and is discharged as menstrual flow.

Rx Oral contraceptives prevent ovulation and no endometrial proliferation takes place.

Menstruation stimulates release of a prostaglandin.

Rx There are several drugs that inhibit prostaglandin synthesis and effectively prevent menstrual cramps.

Prostaglandin constricts arterioles supplying blood to the uterus.

Prostaglandin causes constriction of the muscles of the uterine wall.

Rx Blood supply to the uterus becomes better developed after a pregnancy and as a woman becomes older, which explains why cramps cease with time or after childbirth.

PAIN CRAMPS

strual cramps seem to produce higher than normal amounts of uterine prostaglandins. Exactly how prostaglandins produce menstrual pain is not known, although several likely theories are being investigated. For example, it is known that prostaglandins cause an increase in uterine contractions, which in turn may reduce the flow of blood to the uterine muscle. When muscle tissue is deprived of oxygen, pain results. Other researchers have suggested that prostaglandins may increase the pain sensitivity or response in the uterine nerves; or the pain may be from some as yet unidentified response to prostaglandins.

TREATMENT

Regardless of the mechanism involved, the discovery that prostaglandins are, in some way, associated with menstrual cramps has led to an effective means of relieving the symptoms in most women who suffer from primary dysmenorrhea. This treatment involves prescribing drugs that block the synthesis and/or release of prostaglandins, particularly those produced by the uterus. Aspirin is one such drug, and many women who suffer mild menstrual cramps may obtain sufficient relief from this analgesic.

For women who do not get enough relief from aspirin, stronger antiprostaglandin drugs may be prescribed. These drugs are nonsteroidal anti-inflammatory agents, relatively new drugs that are commonly used to treat arthritis and other inflammatory or pain disorders. Studies have found that when these drugs are given at the first sign of a period or menstrual pain, they will prevent cramps in 90 percent or more of the women who regularly suffer from dysmenorrhea. These drugs are generally well tolerated in the relatively small doses required to prevent menstrual cramps. However, women with ulcers or bleeding problems should use these drugs with caution and under the close supervision of a doctor.

OTHER APPROACHES TO TREATMENT

Dysmenorrhea seems to occur mostly in women who ovulate. This explains why many adolescents may menstruate for a year or two without experiencing cramps and then suddenly start to have them; it may take that long to establish ovulation. Conversely, many women find that the cramps diminish in severity as they approach the end of the menstruating life (again, ovulation may cease before the end of menstruation). Women who take certain kinds of birth control pills also stop ovulating, which explains why oral contraceptives have sometimes been prescribed as a cure for menstrual cramps. For women who want to use this form of contraception, this remains an alternative to antiprostaglandin drugs.

COMMON MYTHS

As noted earlier, women have long been led to believe that menstrual cramps are of psychological origin; it is now quite clear that they are not. Over the years a number of folk remedies—everything from herbal teas to hot water bottles—have been recommended. However, few of these remedies bring relief, whereas the vast majority of women can be helped by taking drugs that block the production of the prostaglandins. Women who are not helped by these drugs probably should be carefully examined for a possible organic cause, such as endometriosis.

Women have also been led to believe that menstrual cramps will disappear after they marry or have a baby. Some women do, for some unexplained reason, experience less severe cramps following childbirth, but for others, having a baby has no effect. Still others who were not troubled by cramps before may actually begin to experience them after giving birth.

SUMMING UP

Millions of women from all cultural backgrounds and walks of life suffer from menstrual cramps. Contrary to popular beliefs of the past, the problem is not of psychological origin. Drugs that block the production of the prostaglandins will, in 90 percent or more of all cases, prevent the cramps from occurring. These drugs require a prescription, and people may respond differently to the various medications. Therefore, your doctor may prescribe one, and if it does not help, switch you to another. Women who do not obtain relief from the drugs may be investigated further for an organic cause or may be given an alternative treatment, such as birth control pills.

139. Facts About Menstruation for Teenagers

GENERAL CONSIDERATIONS

Of all the physical changes adolescent girls experience, perhaps the onset of menstruation is the most significant. Menstruation is the normal shedding of the uterine lining (endometrium) through the vagina that occurs approximately every twenty-eight days. It indicates that a woman's reproductive system has matured fully and is prepared for conception and pregnancy.

Despite today's greater openness about all matters relating to reproduction and modern women's deeper understanding of their bodies, myths persist about menstruation, and many adolescent girls are ill informed about exactly what it is. Menstruation is a healthy biological process—there is nothing unnatural or unclean about it. Furthermore, menstruation should not disrupt normal activities, including athletics and recreation, provided proper hygiene is observed.

THE MENSTRUAL CYCLE

The changes that take place during the menstrual cycle prepare the body every month for the possibility of pregnancy. During each cycle, one egg, or ovum (sometimes more than one, resulting in twins) is released from the ovary. This is called ovulation and in some women is heralded by a mild pain on one side of the lower abdomen, depending on which ovary has produced the egg. The inner lining of the uterus, known as the endometrium, also begins to grow and develop a network of blood vessels and glands to provide nourishment for the egg if it is fertilized. The proper sequence and timing of these changes are controlled by fluctuating levels of hormones produced by various glands and organs in the body and carried to other parts of the body in the blood. Estrogen and progesterone, which are produced by the ovaries, are important hormones in the menstrual cycle, as are hormones from the pituitary gland and the hypothalamus area of the brain which also play a role in endometrial changes (see chart).

If the egg is not fertilized by a male's sperm cell, the prepared endometrium is not needed. The blood supply to the en-dometrium is cut off, and pieces of the lining break off a little at a time and are shed, along with a small amount of blood, in a menstrual period. Although most of the endometrium is shed during menstruation, a thin layer remains, which begins to regrow as the next month's cycle begins.

Major Changes During Your Menstrual Cycle

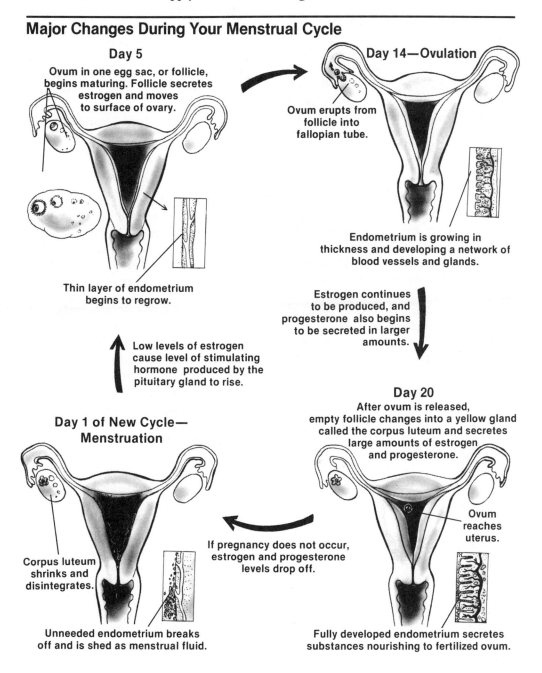

Day 5
Ovum in one egg sac, or follicle, begins maturing. Follicle secretes estrogen and moves to surface of ovary.

Thin layer of endometrium begins to regrow.

Day 14—Ovulation
Ovum erupts from follicle into fallopian tube.

Endometrium is growing in thickness and developing a network of blood vessels and glands.

Estrogen continues to be produced, and progesterone also begins to be secreted in larger amounts.

Low levels of estrogen cause level of stimulating hormone produced by the pituitary gland to rise.

Day 20
After ovum is released, empty follicle changes into a yellow gland called the corpus luteum and secretes large amounts of estrogen and progesterone.

Ovum reaches uterus.

Day 1 of New Cycle— Menstruation

Corpus luteum shrinks and disintegrates.

If pregnancy does not occur, estrogen and progesterone levels drop off.

Unneeded endometrium breaks off and is shed as menstrual fluid.

Fully developed endometrium secretes substances nourishing to fertilized ovum.

MENSTRUAL PROBLEMS

The age at which menstruation begins, the length of the cycle, the length of the period, and the amount of menstrual flow all vary from person to person. In the United States, the average age of onset of menstruation is twelve and a half. Most women's periods last from three to five days and occur every twenty-eight days, and usually one to three ounces of fluid are shed during a period. Variations from these averages are quite common among teenagers because their bodies have not established regular patterns of ovulation and endometrial growth. Problems sometimes do occur, however, in each of the areas listed below.

Regularity

Teenagers are particularly prone to menstrual irregularity for the first few years that they menstruate because the complex interactions among the hormones involved in the cycle do not become established immediately. The most frequent problem is lack of ovulation; the egg may not mature or burst from the follicle, although the endometrium develops and is eventually shed. Irregularity may be an inconvenience, but it seldom indicates a serious problem. Remember, though, that even very young women whose periods are not yet regular may ovulate at any time and become pregnant if they have sexual intercourse. Any sexually active teenager who misses a period should have a pregnancy test.

Missed periods may also be caused by stress, rapid weight loss, and strenuous exercise. As a rule, if pregnancy is not a possibility, medical attention should be sought when three consecutive periods are missed. The doctor may find a treatable hormonal problem and prescribe medication to restore menstrual regularity.

Age of Onset

It is perfectly normal for menstruation to begin at any time between ages ten and sixteen. Menstrual patterns tend to run in families, so girls whose mothers began menstruating in their late teens may follow suit. Rapid weight loss and strenuous activity may also delay the onset of menstruation. If a girl reaches the age of sixteen without having had a period, she should visit the doctor. If her breasts have matured to a level appropriate for her age, the problem may be that the hymen, a membrane that separates the internal from the external sexual organs, does not have a large enough opening to allow the menstrual fluid to pass through it. A more frequent reason for late onset of menstruation is absence of ovulation, caused by hormonal imbalance. Medical tests can pinpoint where the problem lies so that it can be treated.

Heavy, Long, or Frequent Periods

There is considerable variation among women in the length and frequency of their periods and in the amount of fluid shed. In teenagers, heavy or frequent periods are often due to lack of ovulation. The endometrium, in the absence of the proper hormonal signals to prompt shedding, continues to grow much longer than it normally would, so that when it is shed, there is more tissue to expel. Again, most women's systems will regulate themselves in time, but if frequent or heavy periods cause problems, three to six months of hormonal therapy may be prescribed to establish a normal cycle.

Menstrual Pain

Most women experience some type of discomfort during their menstrual period, ranging from a vague, heavy feeling in the abdomen to severe cramps accompanied by headache, backache, nausea, vomiting, and diarrhea. Although cramps are uncomfortable, they indicate that the menstrual cycle is normal—the powerful uterine contractions that expel the fully grown endometrium cause menstrual cramps. Scientists have discovered that these contractions are stimulated by hormone-like substances called prostaglandins. Drugs that limit the body's production of prostaglandins and interfere with their actions are highly effective in relieving menstrual cramps. Prostaglandin inhibitors are often prescribed for women whose menstrual cramps interfere with their normal routines. The drugs are usually taken only during the first two to three days of the period.

HYGIENE: SAFETY AND COMMON SENSE

The recent outbreak of toxic shock syndrome in women using superabsorbent tampons raised many questions about the safety of tampon use in general. Most doctors advise against using superabsorbent tampons, but other types of tampons appear to be harmless. Frequent changes of tampons—at least every six to eight hours —will also reduce the risk of toxic shock syndrome, as will alternating between tampons and pads during the day. If fever, diarrhea, or vomiting develop while tampons are in use, medical attention should be sought, since these are the early symptoms of toxic shock.

It is not necessary to use douches or special feminine hygiene deodorants at any time during the menstrual cycle. Some of these products actually do more harm than good by disrupting the normal chemical balance in the vagina. Daily washing with mild soap and water will control odors more effectively than any other regimen. If a foul-smelling discharge develops, visit the doctor; a discharge often signals an infection requiring medical treatment.

SUMMING UP

It may take teenagers a few years to establish a regular menstrual cycle. Irregularity and extremely heavy periods will usually correct themselves within a few years, but if they cause extreme difficulty, hormone therapy may be instituted. Menstrual cramps, common in teenagers, can be treated effectively with prostaglandin-inhibiting drugs.

Getting adjusted to the physical changes of adolescence is difficult for many teenagers. While some girls look forward to menstruating, others dread it and feel ashamed of their developing bodies. Understanding the reproductive system may help diminish these feelings.

140. Failure to Menstruate

COMMON CHARACTERISTICS

Amenorrhea is the term for the absence or cessation of menstrual periods, a normal occurrence during pregnancy or after menopause or a hysterectomy. The condition is called primary amenorrhea if the menstrual cycle has not begun by around age sixteen and secondary amenorrhea if the periods stop after a history of menstrual regularity. (Scanty or infrequent menstruation is known as oligomenorrhea.)

Normal menstruation is regulated by

the pituitary gland, which in turn is controlled by the hypothalamus and other higher brain centers. The hypothalamus is not only intimately related to the emotions; it also regulates the hormonal secretions that affect body growth and fat storage and trigger the secretions of the sex glands—which, in turn, affect the ovaries and the uterus. Thus abnormalities in the menstrual cycle are presumed to originate in some disturbance of these interrelated glandular functions. Whether the disturbance in an individual instance is attributable to psychological factors or to physical ones, or to a combination of both, is sometimes difficult to determine. (It is not unusual, for example, for amenorrhea to occur as the result of an intense fear of pregnancy, or as the result of an intense hope of pregnancy, as in the case of a "false" pregnancy.)

CAUSES OF PRIMARY AMENORRHEA

On the average, girls in the United States normally begin to menstruate at about age twelve and a half. Although recent studies of young ballet dancers and teenagers involved in competitive sports indicate a two- or three-year delay in the onset of their periods, it should not be assumed that strenuous physical activity is the explanation for the delay. A professional evaluation of primary amenorrhea is important in order to rule out other causes. For example, amenorrhea is often an early symptom of anorexia nervosa—a life-threatening illness that affects adolescent girls (rarely boys) during which they embark on an obsessional program of starvation. Periods often stop even before there has been any significant weight loss. (See Chapter 95, "Anorexia Nervosa.")

Other sources of emotional distress and clinical stress during adolescence—things like anxiety about going away to school, homosexual preference, making friends in a new neighborhood—may also cause primary amenorrhea. Other conditions that bear investigation include a thyroid disorder, glandular tumor, or a birth defect that affects ovarian function or genital tract development. In a few cases, primary amenorrhea is attributable to heavy use of illicit drugs.

It has been well known that malnutrition, or dramatic weight loss—whether self-inflicted or not—will delay the onset of menstruation. However, a recent study of teenage athletes who started rigorous training before beginning to menstruate indicates that the onset of their period was delayed at least two years beyond the normal. It is now assumed by some researchers on the basis of this and other accumulated evidence that the normal reproductive cycle will not begin unless body weight is 17 percent fat. However, while this assumption may be true statistically, it is by no means demonstrably true of all female athletes.

In a few cases, primary amenorrhea is related to a deficiency in the growth hormone secreted by the pituitary gland. The deficiency, which results in slower growth patterns but has no effect on mental development, is usually corrected by hormone replacement therapy.

CAUSES OF SECONDARY AMENORRHEA

With the growing popularity in exercise training among women, there has been an increase in menstrual cessation or irregularity among these women athletes. There is by no means universal agreement on the relationship between secondary amenorrhea and strenuous physical activity. Most women engaged in such activities report no changes in their menstrual cycle. However, the emotional stress of competition, possible nutritional factors, and the weight loss that brings body fat to less than 15 percent of the total may combine to cause the menstrual cycle to be interrupted. In addition, for some women, a critically low percentage of body fat leads to a reduction in estrogen production. Investigators are studying the prevalence of bone loss resulting from this hormonal deficiency in athletes. (The tapering off of estrogen production following menopause is presumed to be a factor in developing osteoporosis—the brittle bones of aging— but to date this has not been demonstrated in athletes.)

In addition to faulty nutrition, other causes of secondary amenorrhea include serious physical illness, a major accident, and an emotional trauma. Women who are extremely obese often experience menstrual interruption. The condition may also be ascribed to thyroid malfunction. Gynecological examination may indicate that scar tissue resulting from a faulty abor-

Failure to Menstruate

QUESTIONS TO ASK

Could you be pregnant?

No / Yes — Let's do a test to find out.

Have you ever had a period?

PRIMARY

Are you under 17?

No / Yes

No / Yes — Let's wait and see.

SECONDARY

Are you over 40?

Yes / No

Have you been ill or emotionally stressed?

No / Yes

Have you recently been very ill or had a lot of worry and anxiety?

Yes / No

Your body may need time to recover.

Have you been trying to lose weight?

No / Yes

Weight loss may be the reason.

Have you been on a crash diet?

Yes / No

Have you been using the Pill a long time?

Yes / No

Do you often skip meals or use laxatives, diuretics or emetics?

No / Yes

Your periods should resume in a few months.

An eating disorder called bulimarexia may be a factor.

Do you very much want to become pregnant?

Yes / No

Try to relax.

Are you sexually active and afraid of becoming pregnant?

No / Yes

Would pregnancy be a disaster?

Yes / No

Let's talk about a suitable method of contraception.

Do you take part in a lot of sports?

No / Yes

Do you engage in strenuous activity, sports, or athletics?

Yes / No

These may delay or interrupt menstruation.

Have you noticed any pelvic pain?

No / Yes

Have you had a pelvic exam recently?

Yes / No

There could be a structural problem.

Were you a "late grower"? Have you noticed any lack of energy?

No / Yes

Do you feel fatigued or depressed?

Yes / No

An endocrine or hormonal disorder may be a factor.

tion or cervical cauterization has caused cervical stenosis, a stoppage of the uterine opening. Women who have been on the contraceptive pill for several years also may experience prolonged amenorrhea when they discontinue its use.

TREATMENT

Treatment for amenorrhea, whether primary or secondary, depends on a correct diagnosis of the cause. In many instances, there is a spontaneous return or regular onset of the cycle through a properly balanced diet combined with a reduction in stress, whether physical or psychological in origin. Other cases require professional evaluation based on metabolism tests, X-rays, gynecological examination, and, for an increasing number of adolescents, an evaluation to investigate the possibility of anorexia nervosa.

There is no reason to believe that the delay in the onset of menstruation for teenage athletes has an adverse effect on later fertility. Nor does there appear to be any irreversible consequence of temporary amenorrhea for adult women athletes.

Where ovulation has been affected by long-term use of the pill or by factors involving strenuous athletic involvement, and a reestablishment of fertility is desirable in order to become pregnant without further delay, various drugs are available for hastening the return of the menstrual cycle.

SUMMING UP

While weight loss and athletic involvement may be explanations for both primary and secondary amenorrhea, they are by no means the only ones. Where the condition persists without an obvious explanation (crash dieting, serious illness, effects of the pill, and the like), evaluation by a doctor is recommended. In most cases, an accurate diagnosis and suitable treatment will bring about the normal onset or normal resumption of the menstrual cycle.

141. Premenstrual Syndrome (PMS)

COMMON CHARACTERISTICS

Many women experience psychological and physical changes during the week to ten days preceding the onset of the menstrual period. The psychological changes commonly include feelings of depression (the premenstrual "blues") which, as the start of menstrual bleeding approaches, give place to anxiety, restlessness, or irritability. These changes may be accompanied by such physical complaints as breast enlargement, abdominal bloating, constipation, and fatigue. Collectively, these psychological and physical changes are symptoms of what is called the premenstrual syndrome (PMS).

Until recently, many women—and their doctors—considered that premenstrual symptoms were "all in the head." (Alternatively, the complaints were dismissed as an inevitable part of being female and, as such, to be endured.) However, recent studies have established that premenstrual changes, both psychological and physical, are organically based. It is now clear, moreover, that the premenstrual syndrome is related to chemical changes that occur in the body just before the monthly period.

THREE-MONTH CHART SHOWING TIMING OF PREMENSTRUAL SYNDROME

	JANUARY		FEBRUARY		MARCH
1		1	BR W	1	
2	BR W	2	H CR BR W	2	BR W
3	BR W	3	HPH BR	3	M BR W
4	H BR W	4	M	4	M
5	H BR W	5	M	5	M
6	MP H BR W	6	M	6	M
7	MP BR W	7		7	M
8	M	8		8	
9	M	9		9	
10	M	10		10	
11		11		11	
12		12		12	
13		13		13	
14		14		14	
15		15		15	
16		16		16	
17		17		17	
18		18		18	
19		19		19	
20		20		20	
21		21		21	
22		22		22	
23		23		23	
24		24		24	
25		25		25	H
26		26		26	
27		27		27	
28		28		28	W
29				29	BR W
30	BR W			30	BR W CR
31	BR W			31	M BR W

To determine whether symptoms are due to premenstrual syndrome, try charting them on a calendar such as the one pictured here over the course of several months.
Symptoms that consistently appear at about the time of menstruation usually can be assumed to be related to the monthly cycle. The major symptoms experienced by the woman who completed this calendar are breast swelling (BR), crying spells (CR), headaches (H), and weight gain (W). Menstruation is indicated by an M and menstrual pain by an MP.

RANGE OF SYMPTOMS

Not all women experience PMS. In those who do, the symptoms and their severity vary widely. Some women experience only minor mood changes; in others, emotional fluctuations are severe. Feelings of nervousness, irritability, or hostility may become so intense that they affect performance at work, the ability to do household and other tasks, and relationships with others. Restlessness may make concentration difficult, and a woman may become temporarily absent-minded or accident-prone.

For some women, PMS is associated with very little physical discomfort. Many, however, experience breast tenderness and abdominal bloating or suffer from constipation. A small minority retain fluid and gain weight just before menstruation.

WHAT CAUSES PMS?

A number of theories have been put forward to explain the specific chemical changes responsible for PMS. Cyclical changes in the levels of the female hormones estrogen and progesterone have been implicated, but evidence to date suggests that they do not cause the symptoms directly. It is likely, however, that these hormonal changes trigger other chemical changes in the body that may be responsible for the various psychological and physical symptoms.

The premenstrual syndrome has also been attributed to such causes as a deficiency in vitamin B_6, low blood sugar, and a high level of prolactin, the hormone which governs milk production. None of these theories, however, accounts for all the various symptoms.

A gain in body fluids, widely suggested as a cause of PMS, appears rather to be a result. It may be due to increased intake of salt, which interacts with elevated estrogen levels.

A NEW THEORY

A recent promising theory holds that PMS is caused by sudden changes in the levels of naturally occurring morphine-like substances (endogenous opiates) in the brain. According to this theory, cyclical changes in female hormone levels produce fluctuations in the levels of these opiates. First, a surge in opiate levels during the week or ten days before menstruation causes "the blues" by blocking the nerve impulses in the brain that normally promote emotional equilibrium. Then, a sudden drop in opiate levels gives rise to the nervousness and irritability that many women experience just before a period. (It is known that opiates also may lead to constipation, another common premenstrual problem.)

This theory accounts for most of the symptoms that are part of PMS. However, further research remains to be done before it can be said conclusively that changes in opiate levels in fact cause PMS.

TREATMENTS

At present, there is no "cure" for PMS. There are, however, a number of treatments that relieve its symptoms. Since the symptoms are so various, and differ so greatly in severity, each woman must be treated individually. For those with relatively mild premenstrual symptoms, the best treatment may be simply to limit or restructure activity during this time of the month. For others, depending on the symptoms, one of a variety of drugs may be prescribed.

• Birth control pills containing combinations of synthetic estrogen and progesterone help relieve premenstrual symptoms in some women. In addition, birth control pills can be helpful in easing menstrual cramps and can thus serve a dual purpose in women who have both PMS and severe cramping. "The Pill" has both risks and benefits, and these should be discussed by a woman and her doctor before treatment begins.

• Mild painkillers such as aspirin or acetaminophen, either alone or in combination with codeine, may be helpful in relieving premenstrual headaches or muscle aches and pains.

• Diuretics ("water pills") may be prescribed if abdominal bloating is not alleviated by reducing consumption of foods high in salt or carbohydrates.

• Bromocriptine and danazol are effective in relieving breast swelling and tenderness. However, since these drugs have little effect on other symptoms of PMS and may produce troublesome side effects, they are of limited use.

• Tranquilizers are occasionally prescribed to reduce irritability, anxiety, and tension in the week before menstruation begins.

• Some researchers claim success in treating women with PMS with vitamin B_6 supplements or progesterone. These claims have not been definitely proved (or disproved). One of these supplements may be prescribed if all other medications have failed in alleviating the symptoms.

SUMMING UP

The psychological symptoms of PMS include abrupt mood swings and feelings of depression, anxiety, and irritability. Among the more common physical symptoms are swelling and tenderness of the breasts and bloating of the abdomen. Neither the psychological nor the physical symptoms are "all in the head." They are associated with the chemical changes that occur in a woman's body just before menstruation.

Recent studies have implicated changes in the levels of endogenous opiates in the brain as a possible cause of PMS. If this research is confirmed by additional stud-

ies, it may eventually lead to the development of new drugs to combat this complex disorder. Meanwhile, although there is no "cure" for PMS, a number of different medications may be helpful in relieving its symptoms.

142. Toxic Shock Syndrome

COMMON CHARACTERISTICS

Toxic shock syndrome is a form of blood poisoning, caused by a toxin produced by a common strain of bacteria, *Staphylococcus aureus*. The syndrome was first identified in 1978, in children between the ages of eight and seventeen, but little was known about it at that time. Two years later, however, a large number of cases began to be reported, most of them young women. In a majority of cases, a woman who developed toxic shock syndrome was menstruating at the time and was using tampons of the "superabsorbent" variety.

The body's reaction to the toxin is rapid (in a menstruating woman, it usually occurs on the third day of the menstrual period). The temperature rises suddenly to 102° to 105°F, there is vomiting and diarrhea, and a sunburn-like rash appears over most of the body (after three to seven days, the skin peels off in scales, particularly on the palms of the hands and the soles of the feet). In severe cases, there is a rapid drop in blood pressure, faintness, and shock. The illness usually lasts four or five days; in fatal cases, death occurs within a week.

The great majority of the victims of toxic shock syndrome are women; men ac-

WARNING SIGNS OF TOXIC SHOCK SYNDROME

The following warning signs require prompt medical attention:

* Sudden fever

* Vomiting

* Diarrhea

* Sunburn-like rash on hands and feet

* Numbness in fingers and toes

* Drop in blood pressure

* Fainting

* Shock

count for only about 2.5 percent of cases. Women who have been identified as having the syndrome have ranged in age from six to sixty-one. The disease is rare—it affects only 6 to 15 of 100,000 menstruating women a year—but the recurrence rate is as high as 25 to 30 percent. In about 10 percent of cases, toxic shock syndrome is fatal.

The importance of recognizing symptoms that may be those of toxic shock syndrome and getting immediate medical help cannot be overemphasized. The earlier the disease is recognized and treatment begun, the better the chances for recovery.

TAMPONS

In the first reports of the "new" disease in 1980, it appeared that the superabsorbent tampon "Rely" had been used by most of the victims. ("Rely" had recently been introduced with a promotional campaign that included the distribution of millions of free samples; it quickly captured a 20 percent share of the market.) The tampon was withdrawn, and, as a result of considerable publicity in the media, sales of other tampons declined by as much as 75 percent. By 1981, most observers, including epidemiologists at the Centers for Disease Control in Atlanta, concluded that the incidence of toxic shock syndrome in women had fallen precipitously. Other scientists, however, maintain that the incidence of the disease has remained fairly constant, with some twenty to thirty new cases a month.

It is clear that it is not tampon use in itself that causes toxic shock syndrome (among its victims have been men who have undergone surgery). Rather, tampons—especially if they are of the superabsorbent variety and are used exclusively throughout the menstrual period—in some way provide an environment that is conducive to the growth of the toxin-producing bacteria.

CAUSE OF TOXIC SHOCK

Millions of Americans of all ages and both sexes harbor S. aureus, the bacteria responsible for toxic shock syndrome, and are unaffected by the organism. The bacteria commonly inhabit the nose and throat, the skin, and the vagina (about 5 percent of menstruating women carry S. aureus vaginally). The bacteria are believed to enter the body through any type of open wound, producing a toxin which is carried by the blood from the site of the infection throughout the body. Nearly all of those who develop toxic shock syndrome appear to lack the antibodies that, in most people, provide protection against the effects of this toxin. Those toxic shock victims who develop mild cases appear to have some antibodies, although not enough for full protection; those who have a recurrence of the disease seemingly fail to develop immunity during the first attack.

It appears that the toxin produced by S. aureus suppresses the body's immune system, preventing it from defending itself against bacteria. With the immune system suppressed, bacteria in the body flourish unchecked. Many of them are producers of endotoxin. This bacterial product is extremely toxic: it can damage the liver and the kidneys, lower the blood pressure, destroy blood platelets, and produce diarrhea, vomiting, and shock—the symptoms of toxic shock syndrome.

Some scientists believe that the S. aureus that causes toxic shock syndrome is a new strain (this would explain the apparently sudden appearance of the disease). Deviant strains have in fact appeared in the past —for example, a strain of staphylococcus known as 80/81 that caused numerous outbreaks of infection in hospitals for about five years and then disappeared.

MODE OF ENTRY

Opinions differ as to how S. aureus enters the body of a menstruating woman, but experts generally agree that the use of superabsorbent tampons is somehow implicated. One study suggests that the tampons create a suitable environment for the growth of S. aureus by introducing air into the vagina, where there is normally little oxygen, and that the bacteria may then enter the body through some tiny vaginal lesion. The greater obstruction of the vagina provided by superabsorbent tampons is also thought to play a role.

Another theory notes that there is an association not only between superabsorbent tampons and toxic shock syndrome but also between these tampons and vaginal ulcers. It seems possible that the greater absorbency of these tampons may cause the vaginal membranes to become dry and easily irritated, providing an opportunity for the staphylococcal organisms to cause an ulcer and, in those who lack immunity to the toxin, toxic shock syndrome.

TREATMENT

In the acute phase of the illness, patients are usually treated in a hospital's intensive care unit. Treatment focuses on replacing fluids and electrolytes (dissolved salts in the body fluids) to prevent or treat low blood pressure and shock. Antibiotics are also given to eradicate *S. aureus*. In most cases, the organism is resistant to penicillin and ampicillin; therefore, other antibiotics, such as nafcillin and dicloxacillin, are administered. It is not clear whether these drugs have any effect on the acute course of the disease; however, they appear to be helpful in preventing recurrence.

COMMON-SENSE PREVENTIVE MEASURES

The great majority of women can continue to use tampons without incurring any major risk of toxic shock syndrome. However, doctors consider that it would be prudent not to use superabsorbent brands until more research has been conducted. To further reduce the risk associated with tampon use, the American College of Obstetricians and Gynecologists recommends that women alternate tampons with sanitary napkins or minipads—and when tampons are used, to change them every six to eight hours to reduce the risk of infection.

SUMMING UP

It appears that the strain of *S. aureus* that has been responsible for most cases of toxic shock syndrome is on the decline. However, experts on staphylococcal diseases believe that it is being replaced by a new strain that is also toxin-producing and that the incidence of toxic shock syndrome will remain as before.

Many questions about toxic shock syndrome remain unanswered, although it seems clear that those most at risk are menstruating women who carry *S. aureus* in the vagina and use tampons exclusively during their periods. Meanwhile, it seems only prudent for women to use common sense in their choice and use of tampons—and to be aware of the symptoms of this rare disease.

143. Excessive Menstrual Bleeding

COMMON CHARACTERISTICS

Menorrhagia is the technical term for excessively heavy or prolonged menstruation. It may be difficult to judge how much menstrual flow is too much menstrual flow. However, when more than eight tampons or sanitary napkins a day are needed, or when the menstrual discharge contains large blood clots, or when there is "flooding" (menstrual blood that issues in a gush), or when the period lasts for seven days or more, the condition should be evaluated by a doctor. Moreover, menorrhagia occurring over several months may result in anemia, which may also need to be treated.

CAUSES OF MENORRHAGIA

Approximately 10 percent of all menstruating women experience menorrhagia as an occasional or regular occurrence. Of these, the majority are either very young or are within a few years of menopause.

Menorrhagia sometimes is seen in girls who are just beginning to menstruate. Very often, these young women are having periods, but ovulation is not yet established. They may not ovulate regularly for a year or so after beginning to menstruate, and the resulting imbalance in the hormonal system may cause excessive or irregular shedding of the lining of the uterus. Various blood disorders; underactive thyroid (hypothyroidism); infections, especially pelvic inflammatory disease (PID) caused by the use of an intrauterine device (IUD) as a contraceptive;

and intense revulsion or emotional distress surrounding all aspects of sexuality can cause menorrhagia as well. Endometriosis —the abnormal growth of uterine tissue outside the uterus—is also sometimes associated with heavy bleeding.

Among older women, by far the most common cause of menorrhagia is the presence of benign tumors of the uterus known as myomas ("fibroids"). The hormonal changes that occur with the approach of menopause may also cause some monthly periods to be unusually heavy while others are unusually light.

TREATMENTS FOR MENORRHAGIA

An isolated instance of heavy menstrual flow unrelated to a possible miscarriage need not be cause for alarm. However, if during the next two or three periods the blood contains thick clots, or flooding occurs, a doctor should be consulted.

When a gynecological examination reveals no tumors or any sign of infection and an endometrial biopsy reveals no abnormalities, the treatment usually consists of synthetic hormone therapy to reduce the bleeding. If heavy bleeding is attributable to excessive shedding of the uterine lining (the endometrium) and hormone therapy over a few months is ineffective, a dilation and curettage (D&C) may be performed. In this procedure, the cervix is dilated and the lining of the uterus is scooped out with a spoon-like instrument called a curette. A D&C is usually done in a hospital, although increasing numbers are being done in outpatient settings; it is a quick, simple, and safe operation without painful aftermath.

If pelvic inflammatory disease (PID) is found to exist, broad spectrum antibiotics are prescribed for about ten days. When this infection is associated with the use of an IUD, the device is removed at once and other types of contraception are evaluated for future use.

ENDOMETRIOSIS

There has yet to be a scientific explanation as to why cells from the endometrium become embedded in other parts of the pelvic area—on the cervix or ovaries, for example. These wayward cells have the characteristics of their type rather than of their anomalous location and respond to hormonal stimulation during the monthly cycle just as if they were part of the uterus. They often cluster and multiply, forming benign tumors. This condition, known as endometriosis, sometimes exists with practically no symptoms, disappearing with pregnancy or during menopause. If a patient's history and a pelvic examination indicate that endometriosis is the cause of menstrual problems, hormone treatments are given to control it. In moderate to severe cases, surgery may be necessary to remove the tumors.

MYOMAS

Myomas ("fibroids") are found in one out of five women past the age of thirty-five. These benign growths usually produce no symptoms, but when they are discovered during the course of a pelvic examination, they are checked on subsequent occasions with regard to size and other developments. Should they become large enough or numerous enough to cause heavy menstrual bleeding, the patient should have a D&C for diagnosis and treatment. However, they may continue to grow in spite of hormone therapy, and symptoms of pressure on adjacent organs

(particularly the bladder and bowel) may appear, in addition to the excessive bleeding. Fibroids may grow so large that they prevent accurate examination of the ovaries. In all such cases, surgery is usually recommended.

When the problem exists in a woman of childbearing age, an operation known as a myomectomy can be performed. This procedure removes the fibroids without damaging the uterus. In an older woman, a hysterectomy may be indicated.

EMOTIONAL STRESS AND HEAVY PERIODS

Almost every woman has experienced an especially heavy or prolonged menstrual flow that can be related to a stressful circumstance. The delicate mechanism of the monthly cycle is regulated by hormones, and hormones and emotions seem to be interrelated. However, when the onset of menstruation causes so much deep conflict and anguish in a young girl as to lead either to the ongoing absence of normal periods or to abnormally prolonged ones, some form of psychotherapy or counseling may be indicated.

SUMMING UP

Menorrhagia may be so rare an occurrence as to require no more than a day or so of bed rest every few years during the

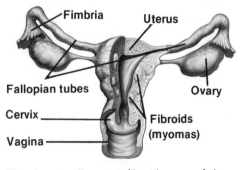

This drawing illustrates fibroids, one of the more common causes of excessive menstrual bleeding.

peak of the blood flow. However, when excessive blood loss, or the presence of blood clots in the menstrual flow, becomes a regular pattern, and especially when this is accompanied by such other symptoms as fever and pain, a doctor should be consulted. The possibility of anemia should be taken into account so that an iron deficiency does not become a complicating factor. Women who use an IUD should suspect this device as a prime cause of menorrhagia and proceed accordingly.

144. Menopause

COMMON CHARACTERISTICS

Menopause, also called the climacteric and familiarly known as the change, is the total cessation of the menstrual cycle and, consequently, the end of a woman's childbearing capacity. It is a natural physiological event—not an illness or an affliction. Its onset is gradual, generally occurring in American women between the ages of forty-eight and fifty-five, although it can start anytime from the late thirties to the late fifties.

The process is usually signaled by changes in the menstrual cycle: decreased bleeding, skipped periods, unusually heavy flow over a shorter than usual period, etc. The transition to menopause may take no more than six months or it may extend over two years. Since ovulation may still occur, even sporadically, contraception should be practiced until menstruation has stopped completely for four to six months, unless your doctor has determined there is no danger of an unwanted pregnancy.

HORMONAL CHANGES

During the years of fertility, either of the ovaries may produce an egg each month (ovulation) and supply the hormones—especially estrogen but also progesterone—to prepare for the development of the fertilized egg. As menopause approaches, these functions gradually taper off until egg production stops altogether and hormone production is insignificant.

The resulting changes in hormonal balance cause the characteristic symptoms of menopause—hot flashes and night sweats, which are experienced by up to 85 percent

CHANGES ASSOCIATED WITH MENOPAUSE

Premenopause
- Decline of ovarian function
- Irregular periods
- Lighter or heavier than normal menstrual flow
- Hot flashes
- Night sweats

Postmenopause
- Menstruation stops
- Thinning of vaginal tissue
- Vaginal itching and dryness
- Osteoporosis
- Weight gain
- Change in skin texture
- Possible increase in facial and body hair

of all women. Although the mechanism of these symptoms is not fully understood, they appear to result from a vasomotor (the body's temperature regulation system) instability related to changing hormonal levels. The hallmark is a sudden suffusion of heat affecting the face and upper part of the body. There may be a red blotching of the skin and excessive perspiration, followed by a chill. Their frequency and intensity varies considerably among women, ranging from the barely noticeable to the almost intolerable. Happily, the body almost always adjusts to the decreased levels of female hormones, and the flushes lessen and disappear.

The hot flashes usually occur without warning and may be over in a moment or may last for as long as a minute. Although many women experience discomfort from these flashes and are embarrassed because they fear they are obvious to those around them, the latter usually is not the case. Night sweats, another term for hot flashes that occur during sleep, are sometimes severe enough to disrupt sleep and, consequently, may give rise to the increased irritability, fatigue, or feelings of depression often associated with menopause. It should be emphasized that mood changes are *not* menopausal symptoms per se but instead may be consequences of concurrent factors in the woman's life, such as feeling unneeded as children move out on their own or as career and other roles change.

Vaginal dryness is another symptom directly related to the hormonal changes of menopause. This condition, which may lead to itching, infection, and discomfort during sexual intercourse, is relieved by the use of lubricating cream. Since many women experience a strong resurgence of sexual desire at menopause, problems in this area should be frankly discussed with your doctor so that they can be resolved promptly.

HORMONE REPLACEMENT

Hormone replacement therapy to make up for the body's diminished estrogen production will relieve the severity and frequency of hot flashes and the vaginal dryness. At one time, long-term estrogen replacement was widely recommended for all women. In recent years, however, there has been a shift in attitudes as more became known about possible risks of long-term estrogen therapy. Studies have linked estrogen replacement with an increased risk of gallbladder disease and cancer of the endometrium (the lining of the uterus). In the menstruating woman, fluctuating levels of estrogen and progesterone stimulate the endometrium to grow in readiness for a fertilized egg. If conception does not take place, the hormone levels drop and the lining is shed in the form of a menstrual period. During uninterrupted estrogen therapy, the endometrial tissue proliferates, but it is not shed. Some researchers feel this unopposed estrogen stimulation is a factor in the increased occurrence of endometrial cancer seen in women on long-term estrogen replacement. These risks can be minimized, many experts feel, by using the smallest possible dose of estrogen that effectively minimizes symptoms for as short a time as needed. Periodic endometrial biopsies also may be advised. Of course, the worry is moot for women who have undergone surgical removal of the uterus (hysterectomy), since they no longer have any risk of endometrial cancer.

In addition, a new approach has been developed that involves giving low doses of estrogen that are interrupted every month or two with a few days of progesterone. This, in effect, mimics the natural menstrual cycle and prevents the buildup of endometrial tissue. Women on this regimen will bleed as during a menstrual period, even though the ovaries have ceased to function.

In any event, your doctor is the best judge of whether estrogen replacement is indicated for you. There are some women, such as those who have an estrogen-sensitive breast cancer, in whom estrogens are contraindicated. There are others for whom they may be recommended not only to relieve menopausal symptoms but also to help prevent the loss of bone tissue (osteoporosis) that is common among older women. Estrogen is not indicated for depression or other mood problems or insomnia, despite popular reports to this effect.

SUMMING UP

Although many women regard menopause as "the beginning of the end," it should be noted that the average American woman lives a third of her life after menopause. While menopause may involve particular discomforts, these can be minimized until eliminated by time. Self-fulfillment and attractiveness are by no means limited to the young. Honest introspection about the pleasures and comforts of the later years, heart-to-heart talks with emotionally supportive family members or a respected friend, reaching out for new experiences, work in the community or a career, and common-sense counseling by your doctor are but a few of the avenues open to the woman experiencing menopause.

145. Benign Breast Disorders

COMMON CHARACTERISTICS

At one time or another, more than half of all women will discover an unusual lump in their breasts. Although breast cancer is the immediate fear upon finding such a lump, more than 80 percent turn out to be benign, or noncancerous. Variously called cystic breast disease, fibrocystic disease, or cystic mastitis, these noncancerous disorders are characterized by the development of lumpy breast tissue, which may or may not be painful. In some cases, the lumps may be large enough to distort the contour of the breasts; in others, they produce no symptoms other than a mild discomfort.

Such lumps are usually composed of fluid-filled sacs called cysts. These may be one large cyst or clusters of tiny cysts. Since cystic disease is typically related to the menstrual cycle, it usually becomes less severe with menopause.

CAUSE OF CYSTIC DISEASE

During a woman's fertile years, hormonal changes occur in the breasts each month in preparation for the possibility of pregnancy. At the time of ovulation, the milk-producing glands start to become distended with fluid, and the fibrous tissue around the glands increases in order to provide additional support for them. In some women, in the ensuing week to ten days, the breasts become swollen and tender; in others, the changes are barely noticeable. If the ovum (egg) is unfertilized and a pregnancy is not initiated, menstruation occurs and the breasts return to their usual size and condition as the additional fluid is lost and the supporting tissue returns to its postmenstrual state.

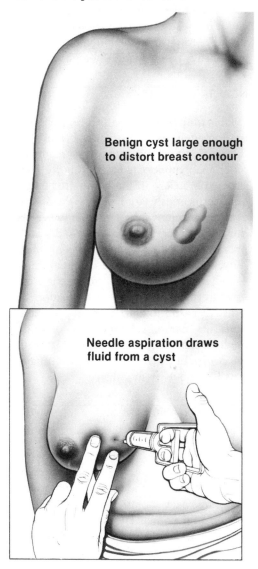

Benign cyst large enough to distort breast contour

Needle aspiration draws fluid from a cyst

When this monthly mechanism goes awry—either because of an overproduction of fluid and tissue or because of faulty reabsorption—the cysts develop, either in small clusters, or in groups of one or two large sacs.

DIAGNOSIS OF CYSTIC BREAST DISEASE

As women have become increasingly vigilant about the early signs of breast cancer, they have also become aware of changes in the consistency of breast tissue even when there are no other symptoms. Any unusual breast change should be seen by a doctor. Doubts about the nature of the disturbance are best resolved by breast X-ray (mammography) and biopsy, a microscopic examination of a tissue sample. Most of these benign breast lumps turn out to be cysts. If fluid can be aspirated from the cyst, no further tests are usually required. If not, a biopsy may be needed. A biopsy need not always involve hospitalization; it often may be accomplished in the doctor's office by aspiration—a technique in which a sample of the tissue is removed by inserting a hollow needle into the lump and removing a small amount of tissue. Since women with cystic breast disease have a higher than normal rate of breast cancer, they should undergo regular breast examination by a doctor.

OTHER BENIGN DISEASES OF THE BREAST

A fibroadenoma is a benign tumor that may be difficult to distinguish from a cyst. Whereas the cystic disorder involves fluid accumulation, fibroadenosis is a clumping of solid tissue. It is a solid mass that grows slowly, is not necessarily related to the menstrual cycle, and rarely causes pain. However, such lumps should also be examined by a doctor. In some cases, where the lump is large enough to deform the contour of the breast, surgical removal

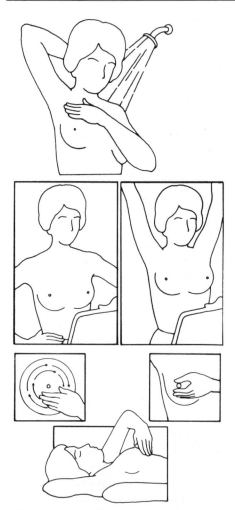

All women should examine their breasts each month. For menstruating women, this should be done mid-cycle; for others, at a specific time each month. The three-step examination, illustrated here, starts in the shower or tub, by carefully feeling each breast for any thickening or lumps. Then stand before a mirror and look for any changes, such as puckering of the skin. Next, lie down and place one arm under your head. Using the other hand, examine the entire breast, moving clockwise and from the outer portion toward the nipple. Repeat this procedure on the second breast, placing the opposite arm under your head. Finally, squeeze each nipple to see if there is a discharge. Any lump, change, discharge, or other unusual finding should be checked by a doctor.

may be desirable, both for aesthetic reasons and to make sure that there are no cancerous cells.

While there appears to be a higher incidence of breast cancer among women with cystic breasts, no similar relationship has been established between fibroadenomas and eventual malignancy.

Another circumstance that may produce a hard lump in the breast is a severe blow to the fatty tissue. (Women's breasts are one of the main storage areas of fat.) A solid lump of this kind is called fat necrosis. It may not form until long after the bruise, and it may cause a deformation of the skin surface. Any such development should also always be evaluated by a physician.

NEW TREATMENTS

Following a diagnosis of breast cystitis or fibroadenosis, some patients feel that their condition warrants no treatment other than support from a properly constructed brassiere. If the lumps are benign but conspicuously large, there is the option of surgical removal. Recently, however, a hormone preparation known as danazol, previously used for certain cases of infertility, has proved effective in diminishing —and in many instances suppressing for several years—the chronic formation of cysts. Danazol, like all hormone preparations, has marked side effects, so ongoing medical supervision is mandatory during the course of the treatment, which usually lasts for about six months.

THE IMPORTANCE OF SELF-EXAMINATION

Self-examination of the breasts should be a continuing routine for all women. The examination should be done at the same time each month, especially for premenopausal women. In such cases, the preferred time is a few days after menstruation, when hormonal processes are at a minimum and breasts are least full. Familiarity with lumps that come and go each month will make it possible to detect changes that persist through several monthly cycles and should therefore be called to a doctor's attention.

SUMMING UP

Lumpy breasts are a common condition before the onset of menopause because of fluid or tissue accumulation related to ovulation. Fibrocystic disorders are always benign, but if they cause pain or a disfiguring distortion of breast contour, they can be treated in various ways. Although the vast majority of breast lumps are benign, they always should be checked by a doctor to rule out the possibility of cancer. Self-examination of breasts should be a monthly routine, and any doubtful symptoms brought to a doctor's attention for prompt diagnosis.

146. After a Mastectomy

GENERAL CONSIDERATIONS

Until a few years ago, most women were reluctant to talk about breast cancer or its treatment. Our society tends to equate sexual attractiveness and feminity with the breasts. It is understandable that the standard treatment for breast cancer—a mastectomy, which entails removal of the breast and, depending on the type of operation, varying amounts of underlying and adjacent muscle and tissue—was often dreaded as much as the disease itself. More recently, however, as prominent women have begun to talk openly about their disease and treatment, others who also have breast cancer have gained new hope and understanding that make the disease more bearable.

In recent years, a number of studies have found that some women can be effectively treated for breast cancer without a mastectomy. Instead, the cancerous lump and surrounding tissue are removed (lumpectomy), and this is followed by radiation

therapy. In some cases, chemotherapy also may be given. This treatment is not suitable for all breast cancers, however. According to experts, the ideal candidate is a woman with a very small, localized tumor with no evidence of spread to other parts of the breast or the lymph nodes.

No one can deny that undergoing a mastectomy is a devastating experience, but it does not mean the end of a full and productive life. More than 60 percent of the women in the United States who are treated for breast cancer can expect to live at least another five years. If the mastectomy is performed before the cancer has spread beyond the breast, the five-year survival rate is more than 80 percent.

The *quality* of survival is also important. For many women who have had a mastectomy, the support of other women who have undergone the operation is of very great benefit. Such support is offered by the Reach to Recovery program of the American Cancer Society and by other rehabilitative services for breast cancer patients. In some cases, reconstructive surgery to minimize the deformity of a mastectomy is possible. These procedures may also greatly affect the quality of survival.

REACH TO RECOVERY

Thousands of women who have had mastectomies serve as volunteers in the Reach to Recovery program. They are carefully selected and trained by local Cancer Society chapters to visit mastectomy patients—after permission has been received from the woman's doctor. The first

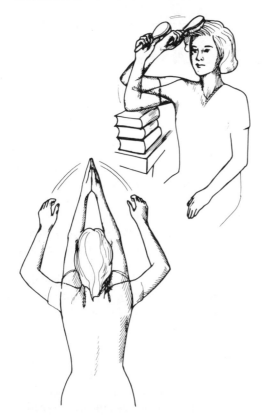

Rehabilitative exercises for mastectomy patients stress rebuilding and strengthening damaged underarm and chest muscles. Simple upward arm movements will speed healing and improve muscle tone. For movements severely limited by soreness, aids such as a pile of books placed beneath the elbow allow the patient independence while providing exercise.

visit is usually made a few days after the operation, while the patient is still in the hospital. The volunteer will bring with her a kit containing equipment and instructions for rehabilitative exercises, a temporary breast form, and informative literature not only for the patient herself but also for her husband and family. (In some areas, male volunteers are available to help a patient's husband adjust to his wife's surgery.)

With the consent of the patient's doctor, the volunteer will teach the exercises that are considered important in regaining strength, arm function, and self-confidence after a mastectomy. These vary from everyday movements—such as brushing the hair using the affected arm—to a variety of overhead reaching motions.

By virtue both of her training and of her own experience, the volunteer will be able to answer questions which may have to do with subjects that the patient is reluctant to discuss with her doctor or even a close friend. The volunteer will be able to reassure a woman who has just had a mastectomy that she will continue to be sexually responsive and attractive and that—in the vast majority of cases—she will be able to return to her job and to work and exercise as usual. Some modifications in clothing may have to be made—for example, a skimpy bikini may no longer be appropriate—but a mastectomy patient can easily find a wide variety of clothes that she can wear with ease and confidence. Talking with the Reach to Recovery volunteer, the patient will find that a shared experience, no matter how unhappy, is easier to bear.

RECONSTRUCTIVE BREAST SURGERY

Plastic surgery to minimize the deformity of a mastectomy is not possible for all patients, but it is at least technically feasible for most. The outcome depends a good deal on the type of mastectomy performed, the stage of cancer, overall health status, and certain psychological factors.

As would be expected, the more extensive the mastectomy, the more difficult the reconstruction. In the so-called radical mastectomy, there are four different deformities: the breast itself is gone; there is a hollow beneath the collarbone; the chest wall appears thin; and the skin and muscle forming the front part of the armpit are removed. Reconstruction after this type of mastectomy may entail several operations. Fortunately, because of the effectiveness of other therapies, radical mastectomies are performed infrequently today.

Reconstruction is easier and the results are better after a modified radical mastectomy, in which the underlying chest muscle is generally left in place, and after a simple mastectomy where only the breast and minimal adjacent tissue are removed. Radiation treatments may make reconstruction more complicated, but they do not necessarily rule it out.

The procedure usually involves inserting an implant similar to those used in plastic surgery to enlarge the breast. Rebuilding the nipple is also possible, using skin and tissues grafted from other parts of the body. Surgery on the remaining breast may be indicated, to provide greater symmetry. A reconstructed breast does not look or feel exactly like a natural one, but a plastic surgeon who is experienced in this type of operation can usually achieve acceptable cosmetic results.

In some medical centers, the mastectomy and reconstruction are done during the same operation. However, the usual procedure is to do the mastectomy first and the reconstruction several months later. In general, the reconstructive procedure is simpler and less painful and requires less rehabilitative effort than the mastectomy itself. In this regard, an important psychological factor is involved: the first operation was dreaded and unwanted; the second is a procedure that the patient has sought herself.

FOLLOWUP AFTER A MASTECTOMY

It is important for all women who have had a mastectomy to continue seeing their doctors for periodic checkups, for life. They are at risk of developing a new cancer in the second breast or a recurrence of the first. The latter may occur in the area of the removed breast or at a distant site. Women who have had reconstructive breast surgery should also see their surgeons periodically to make sure that all is well with the implant, the overlying skin, and the surrounding tissue.

In breast cancer, the chances of survival are greatest for those women whose cancers are small and localized in the breast. Early detection and treatment are therefore vital. Women who are in a high-risk group—those with a strong family history of breast cancer, those who have had an earlier breast cancer, or those who have a history of cystic (benign) breast disease—should be particularly diligent in examining their breasts for suspicious lumps, as well as in seeing their doctors regularly.

SUMMING UP

When breast cancer is treated early, the chances for survival are very encouraging. Moreover, new methods of diagnosis and treatment hold the promise of ever-increasing survival for breast cancer patients.

The standard treatment for breast cancer—a mastectomy, in which the affected breast and varying amounts of other tissue are removed—is a devastating experience, both physically and emotionally. However, it does not mean that a rich and fulfilling life is no longer possible, or signal the end of sexual activity. Support from such groups as the Reach to Recovery program of the American Cancer Society (and also, in some cases, reconstructive surgery) can help a woman cope successfully with life after a mastectomy.

147. Cervical Infections

Cervicitis is inflammation of the cervix, the lower portion of the uterus. The cervix, also called the "neck" of the uterus or womb, is a small, hollow cylinder about two inches long. Under normal circumstances, its diameter is about the size of a quarter; its opening (os) is the size of a drinking straw. The lower portion of the cervix protrudes into the vaginal canal.

Cervicitis, which may be acute or chronic, is perhaps the most common of all inflammatory conditions of the female reproductive tract. It may be caused by bacteria, viruses, fungi, or other organisms that are present in the genital tract or that enter the cervix from outside. Postpartum cervicitis commonly results from the infection of small cuts or tears (lacerations) of the cervix that occur during delivery. Similar lacerations and infection may follow an abortion. The use of birth control pills may be responsible for mild cervical inflammation. Another common cause is untreated gonorrhea. Users of intrauterine contraceptive devices (IUDs) are especially vulnerable to cervicitis and to pelvic inflammatory disease, a more serious and extensive infection that may involve the uterus, ovaries, and other reproductive organs.

Cervicitis may or may not be accompanied by cervical erosion. Cervical erosion occurs when some of the tissue forming the lining of the inner part of the cervix (columnar epithelium) spreads to cover the tip of the cervix, replacing the stronger tissue (squamous epithelium) that normally covers the outside of the cervix and lines the vagina. The word *erosion,* in this instance, does not refer to any wearing away but rather to the replacement of one kind of tissue by another. The columnar epithelium is very delicate, and once it has extended beyond the mouth of the cervix it is extremely susceptible to infection. The eroded area may bleed readily when touched; women with this condition, for example, occasionally notice spotting the day after intercourse.

Cervical erosion is very common; it is estimated that 95 percent of all women of childbearing age have the condition at some point. It is associated with the high rate of estrogen production characteristic of this period of a woman's life, which stimulates rapid growth of the cervical cells.

SYMPTOMS

Mild cervicitis is characterized by a white vaginal discharge—leukorrhea—which may have an unpleasant odor. If untreated, the condition may worsen to the

The Female Pelvic Organs

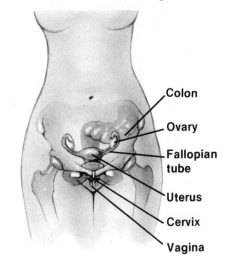

Colon

Ovary

Fallopian tube

Uterus

Cervix

Vagina

point where bleeding or spotting occurs between periods, and especially after intercourse. A burning sensation may accompany urination. Lower back pain and a low-grade fever—and also pain during intercourse—may indicate the spread of the infection.

Cervical erosion has few symptoms and causes little discomfort, although a bloody discharge may result if the erosion is irritated. Often, a cervical erosion goes unsuspected until the woman has a pelvic examination.

DIAGNOSIS

Examination of the cervix is accomplished by expanding the vaginal walls with an instrument called a speculum. A Pap smear, or sample of cervical cells, is taken for microscopic examination. If abnormal cells are found, a minute sample of cervical tissue is taken and is examined microscopically in order to distinguish cervical erosion from cervical cancer. Gynecological checkup may also reveal that the symptoms of cervicitis are being caused by cervical polyps or warts.

TREATMENT

If the suspected cause of the cervicitis is bacterial, it is treated with a medicated douche, or an antibiotic vaginal cream, which is applied well up inside the vagina for a period of a week or more, or by systemic antibiotics. A mild cervical erosion may be treated in the same way. When, however, the erosion is advanced, cauterization or cryosurgery may be recommended. Cauterization involves burning the erosion with an electrocautery or with silver nitrate. In cryosurgery, liquid nitrogen is used as a spray or to "freeze" instruments. Neither procedure is painful,

though there may be some momentary discomfort. Both can be done in the doctor's office. The purpose of both procedures is to destroy abnormal tissue and to promote the growth of normal tissue over the eroded area. Healing is painless, but the vaginal discharge may increase temporarily and take on a muddy color because of the presence of burned cervical cells. After the treatment, the patient should abstain from sexual intercourse for about two weeks.

If the erosion is very extensive, or is refractory to healing, or if there is recurrent abnormal bleeding, a surgical procedure called conization may be indicated. In this procedure, a circular cone-shaped section of the cervical tissue affected by the erosion is removed. Conization must be performed in a hospital; a local anesthetic, however, is almost always sufficient. When conization is performed in a young woman who has not yet had a child, there is a very small risk of future infertility.

Cervical polyps and warts are removed surgically. Where warts, a viral infection, exist, the sexual partner should also be examined and treated because of the possibility of contagion.

SUMMING UP

Cervicitis is a common inflammatory condition of the female reproductive tract. It has a variety of possible causes and may be acute or chronic, mild or severe. It responds readily to antibiotic treatment when its cause is bacterial. Cervical erosion may or may not accompany cervicitis. If an advanced case of cervical erosion is present, cauterization (burning) or cryosurgery (freezing) may be recommended. In some extreme cases, a cone-shaped portion of the affected tissue is excised in a surgical procedure known as conization.

148. Vaginitis

COMMON CHARACTERISTICS

The female reproductive tract, especially the lower portion, is particularly vulnerable to irritation and infection. The vagina—the passage between the uterus (womb) and vulva (the external "lips" covering the genitalia)—is frequently affected because of its anatomy, which provides a warm, moist environment ideal for many infecting microorganisms. Many of these organisms normally live in the vagina without causing problems; very frequently, however, an overgrowth of these organisms or invasions by other bacteria, yeast, or fungi can result in the itching, burning, discharge, and other symptoms characteristic of vaginitis.

In most instances, vaginitis is more annoying and uncomfortable than it is medically serious, although it may be a warning sign of diabetes or other disorders. It may also be associated with the use of oral contraceptives, a change in hormonal balance such as during pregnancy or menopause, the use of antibiotics that alter the normal bacterial flora of the vagina, the presence of foreign objects, or other factors. In any instance, successful treatment depends upon accurate identification of the cause and appropriate action to eliminate it. This often involves treating the sexual partner as well as the woman since a man may harbor the organism causing the vaginitis without suffering any symptoms himself.

Symptoms of vaginitis vary according to the cause. Itching, which may be so intense that it interferes with normal activities, is the most common symptom. Burning, soreness or pain during sexual intercourse or urination, a vaginal discharge, and, in some instances, an unpleasant odor are other common symptoms of vaginitis.

Many women are embarrassed by vaginitis and delay seeing a doctor, attempting instead to treat the problem with a variety of douches and other home remedies. These may provide temporary relief but are seldom successful in eliminating the problem. Many women will bathe or douche just before seeing a doctor, especially if there is an odor or discharge. Again, this can be self-defeating because it may hinder the doctor's ability to identify the cause of the problem. The most common types of vaginitis and their treatments are discussed in the following sections.

Normal Female Reproductive System

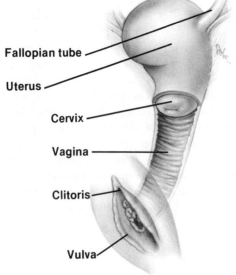

Fallopian tube

Uterus

Cervix

Vagina

Clitoris

Vulva

TRICHOMONIASIS

One of the most widespread forms of vaginitis is caused by *Trichomonas vaginalis,* which is a single-cell microorganism (protozoan). A few women may harbor the organism without suffering symptoms, but more commonly the infection is chronic with periodic acute flare-ups. Chronic trichomoniasis is characterized by itching, burning, and a heavy, greenish-yellow discharge with an unpleasant odor. In men, trichomonads can remain inactive, usually producing no symptoms at all, but occasionally may be associated with a slight burning sensation during urination.

Symptoms are relieved by eradication of the organisms in the vagina by the use of an oral drug, metronidazole. Male sexual partners also are treated with oral medication.

VAGINAL YEAST INFECTIONS

Another common form of vaginitis—especially during the childbearing years—is caused by an overgrowth of a yeast organism, *Candida albicans,* which thrives in the environment of the vagina. *Candida*—also referred to as monilia—are frequently found in the normal flora of the body, particularly in the mouth, intestinal tract, and rectum. (Candidiasis of the mouth is commonly referred to as thrush.) An overgrowth of these organisms often occurs when the body is weakened by some other illness such as diabetes or cancer, which is why they are referred to as opportunistic microorganisms. Vaginal candidal infections are particularly common during pregnancy, for reasons that are not well understood. The use of antibiotics also increases susceptibility to *Candida,* and there may be an increased risk with oral contraception. Symptoms also may increase in severity just before menstruation. In rare instances, *Candida* may cause a serious infection by invading the deeper tissues surrounding the vagina.

Candida can cause swelling of the vaginal tissues, an irritating discharge, severe itching, and a painful burning during urination or sexual intercourse. Treatment usually involves the use of vaginal creams or ointments, as well as oral medications prescribed to treat fungal infections (even though *Candida* is not a true fungus). Male sexual partners usually do not receive treatment. The male sexual partner of a woman with recurrent *Candida* infections should be given a medicated cream to apply to the penis before and after sexual intercourse. This is particularly important in the uncircumcised male. Candidal vaginitis during pregnancy should always be treated since exposure to it during birth may cause severe diaper rash or mouth thrush in infants.

Since *Candida* thrives in a warm, moist environment, wearing tight-fitting underclothes or jeans made of synthetic fabrics may exacerbate the problem. Wearing loose-fitting cotton clothes that allow air to circulate may help.

NONSPECIFIC VAGINITIS

Vaginitis with a foul odor that is not caused by *Trichomonas* or *Candida* is called nonspecific vaginitis. It is probably due to an overgrowth of anaerobic bacteria in the vagina. The metabolic products of these bacteria are responsible for the major symptom: heavy discharge with an unpleasant "fish-like" odor. (This type of vaginitis has been called *Hemophilus vaginitis,* but there is no evidence that the organism *Hemophilus vaginalis* causes the symptoms of the infection.) Some women can carry this organism in the vagina without having symptoms, and a clinical cure with metronidazole—the drug of choice for nonspecific vaginitis—does not eradicate it. In persistent cases, the male sexual partner should be treated.

OTHER TYPES OF VAGINITIS

In an older woman, vaginitis is often due to dryness and thinning of vaginal tissue following menopause. This condition, known as atrophic vaginitis, results in itching and painful intercourse. It is caused by the marked reduction in estrogen that occurs with menopause. Treatment involves using a lubricating cream or jelly. If this does not provide adequate relief, a cream containing estrogen or oral estrogen may be prescribed. Vaginitis may be one of the symptoms of gonorrhea. Since untreated gonorrhea may lead to severe infections, infertility, and other medical complications, it always should be ruled out as a possible cause of vaginitis. Still other possible causes of vaginitis include the presence of a foreign object, such as a forgotten tampon.

SUMMING UP

Vaginitis has many causes; effective treatment depends upon precise diagnosis to determine the appropriate therapy. Most types of vaginitis are not medically serious, but they can cause considerable discomfort and embarrassment. Although men may suffer no symptoms, they often harbor the causative microorganisms and should be treated along with their female sex partners.

149. Pelvic Inflammatory Disease

COMMON CHARACTERISTICS

Pelvic inflammatory disease, often referred to as PID, is perhaps the most common cause of pelvic pain seen in hospital emergency rooms. PID is not a single disease but rather a category of infections that includes parametritis (inflammation of the uterus), salpingitis (inflammation of the fallopian tubes), salpingo-oophoritis (inflammation of the fallopian tubes and the ovaries), and peritonitis (inflammation of the peritoneum, the membrane that lines the abdominopelvic cavity). PID is most common in young, sexually active women.

Pelvic inflammatory disease may be chronic or acute. The symptoms, varying in intensity, include generalized pain in the pelvic area, increasing pain during menstruation and especially during intercourse, irregular bleeding (including the discharge of blood clots between periods), profuse vaginal discharge, and general malaise with fever and chills. The acute

Inflamed fallopian tube

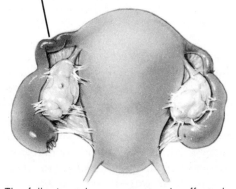

The fallopian tubes are commonly affected by PID. The drawing shows inflammation and pus from tubes.

symptoms of PID are such that it is difficult to differentiate it from acute kidney infection or appendicitis.

An acute attack of PID occurs most frequently immediately following a menstrual period, as infectious organisms spread up the uterus into the fallopian tubes. There is a fever in about one-half of the cases, lower back pain, and often an unpleasant-smelling vaginal discharge. In addition, walking—indeed, any motion at all—may be extremely painful. The woman will tend to shuffle along, hunched up, in an attempt to minimize the pain.

Left untreated, PID can eventually lead to infertility by causing scar tissue to form and block the fallopian tubes. In extreme cases, where abscesses continue to develop out of control, PID can become life-threatening.

CAUSES OF PID

The most common cause of PID—at least, of the first episode—is untreated gonorrhea. However, the intrauterine contraceptive device (IUD) is associated with an increasing number of cases. Other causes include the spread of bacteria, viruses, and fungi from untreated cervicitis (inflammation of the cervix), as well as infections resulting from a complicated delivery or abortion. A diagnostic dilation and curettage (D&C) can make a woman vulnerable to PID, since the infectious organisms are able to gain easy access to the uterus immediately following the procedure.

DIAGNOSIS

Following a consideration of the patient's history and symptoms, the doctor conducts a pelvic examination. Tissue and smear samples are taken for laboratory assessment. This can include the insertion of a hollow needle to obtain peritoneal fluid (culdocentesis). A laparoscopy may be done to rule out ectopic pregnancy, appendicitis, or some other emergency condition. (In this procedure, which is performed in a clinic or hospital under general anesthesia, a small incision is made just below the navel. A needle is inserted through this incision, and the abdominal cavity is carefully inflated with carbon dioxide gas. The laparoscope—a long, narrow, lighted tube—is then inserted so that the pelvic organs may be examined visually.)

TREATMENT

Promptly diagnosed, PID usually responds favorably to treatment with broad-spectrum antibiotics for about ten days. Complete bed rest for at least one week may be helpful, and the patient should abstain from sexual intercourse for at least two weeks to allow the infected area to heal. Where symptoms persist, the initial culture report will be evaluated to determine the precise infectious agent so that an antibiotic specific to that organism can be given. It is important that the drug treatment be continued for the prescribed length of time. Many women stop treatment as soon as the acute symptoms have disappeared but before the infection is eradicated completely. Treatment skimped in this fashion can lead to smoldering infection and progressive damage to the reproductive organs.

When the condition has reached a point where it is beyond the control of medication alone, hospitalization for surgery may be the only alternative. A hysterectomy and removal of ovaries and fallopian tubes can be performed for pain but is seldom necessary. New techniques to remove adhesions can be successfully employed in most cases.

SUMMING UP

Vaginal discharge, abnormal bleeding, urinary urgency, frequency, and pain, and discomfort during intercourse should be called promptly to a doctor's attention to avoid complications. Diagnosed early, many cases of PID can be treated successfully with antibiotics and rest. If treatment is neglected, the condition can progress to cause infertility and may even threaten life.

All women should schedule an annual

pelvic examination and Pap test—and a more frequent gynecological checkup if circumstances indicate such a need. A test to rule out the possibility of gonorrhea also may be recommended. Some women may be infected with gonorrhea without having any symptoms, but they may be "silent carriers" of the disease and capable of transmitting it to others.

150. Hysterectomy

COMMON CHARACTERISTICS

A hysterectomy is a surgical procedure in which a woman's uterus, usually including the attached cervix, is removed. The ovaries and fallopian tubes may also be removed, depending on their condition and the individual diagnosis. If the ovaries and tubes do remain, a woman will continue to ovulate, but her monthly periods will cease. Thus, whatever the extent of the operation, a hysterectomy marks the end of both childbearing and menstruation. A hysterectomy is rarely used now in this country as a means of sterilization, however. Tubal ligation is considered far more efficient and far more safe.

The hysterectomy has played a crucial part in reducing the incidence of deaths from cancer in women. Fifty years ago, cancer of the cervix was one of the most common forms of cancer in women (it still ranks high, along with cancers of the breast, lung, and colon); it was also almost invariably fatal. Today, when cervical cancer is recognized and treated early, the five-year survival rate is 91 percent. Although many cases of cervical cancer can now be treated without a hysterectomy, this operation remains an important approach to the disease. Survival rates from other forms of uterine and ovarian cancers following hysterectomy are similarly encouraging.

INDICATIONS FOR HYSTERECTOMY

Most doctors feel that a hysterectomy should be performed when there is a diagnosis of cancer or precancer of the uterus or ovarian tissues. (As with all cancers, early detection is the key to successful therapy.) A hysterectomy is also advised if there has been damage from severe pelvic or chronic infection, or in the presence of fibroids—large, usually benign, tumors. Another condition that in extreme cases may require a hysterectomy is advanced endometriosis. This is a displaced growth of the tissue that normally lines the uterus to other parts of the abdominal cavity. It can lead to menstrual pain, adhesions, and infertility. Often this condition can be treated successfully with medication or with less extensive surgery. However, especially in cases involving women past childbearing age, a hysterectomy and removal of the ovaries may be necessary to ensure complete removal of the tissue and to prevent its regrowth. Severe menstrual bleeding in an older woman approaching menopause is another indication for hysterectomy in some cases, especially when the bleeding results in anemia.

A hysterectomy is usually not performed as emergency surgery. You will generally have time to discuss your doctor's diagnosis and recommendations. Most doctors try to treat ovarian and uterine illnesses that are not life-threatening without having to resort to surgery. Even when surgery is necessary, a doctor will try to preserve as much ovarian tissue as possible in cases of women who are not yet past childbearing age.

THE PROCEDURE

A hysterectomy is done under general anesthesia and requires about a week's stay in the hospital, followed by several more weeks of restricted activity at home. The doctor removes the uterus and any other affected tissue through an incision in the

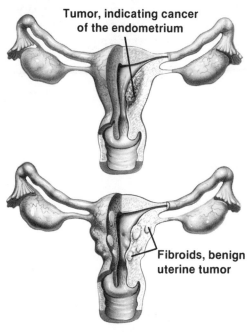

Tumor, indicating cancer of the endometrium

Fibroids, benign uterine tumor

Hysterectomy involves removal of the uterus and, in some cases, the ovaries as well. Indications for hysterectomy include cancer of the cervix, uterus, or ovaries; advanced endometriosis; fibroid tumors; and chronic and painful pelvic infections.

lower abdomen, or through the top of the vagina. The operation takes between one and two hours. There is very little scarring with modern hysterectomy surgery. The vaginal method leaves no external scarring.

After the operation, it is normal to have some vaginal bleeding and discharge. There also will be some soreness and the listlessness felt by anyone who has had general anesthesia. Some women take several months to recover completely. Others find that they can resume normal activities in a matter of weeks. General health as well as mental attitude are important factors in postoperative recovery.

AFTER SURGERY

If the operation has involved removal of the ovaries, hormone replacement therapy will often be necessary, especially for premenopausal women. If such therapy is not given, the woman will experience a premature menopause. The therapy consists of a regular series of hormone medication—usually some form of estrogen, along with progesterone—that replaces the natural hormones in the body. These hormones serve to stimulate secretions that lubricate the vaginal tissue. Some studies also show that they play an important role in curtailing osteoporosis, the loss of bone tissue that is common among older women, which may be accelerated when the ovaries are removed at a relatively early age. If the ovaries are left intact, they will continue to produce the female sex hormones, and any decision regarding hormone replacement therapy will not be needed until ovarian function ceases on its own.

CANCER AND HYSTERECTOMY

For many women, a hysterectomy means freedom from the threat of major, perhaps life-threatening disease. For those for whom intercourse has been painful and for those who have experienced embarrassing episodes of bleeding and discharge, the operation may bring relief and a more positive attitude about the body. However, the loss of her uterus may well affect a woman's body image and her feelings of self-worth. Young, childless women may find the adjustment particularly difficult to make. Some depression is natural. But attitudes about women's roles are changing, and women are coming to realize that their femininity has really very little to do with their ability to bear children.

After surgery, it may be helpful to talk with your doctor and with other women who have had the same operation. If you are generally healthy and have a rewarding life, any depression you may experience should be short-lived. Your response to your hysterectomy will depend largely on how you feel about yourself before the actual operation.

SUMMING UP

The hysterectomy is one of the most common surgical procedures performed in the United States today. Based on current data, nearly half of all American women will undergo this procedure by the time they are sixty-five. Despite this, doctors do not undertake this operation lightly. If your doctor wishes you to consent to a hysterectomy, he or she probably feels that there is no other therapeutic method of curing your disease or alleviating your symptoms. Any questions you might have about the surgery should be frankly discussed with your doctor.

While it is to be expected that you will experience a short period of depression and fatigue after surgery, there is no reason to be concerned about the long-term effects of the operation. The prognosis for women who have surgical removal of the uterus for cancer is generally good. A hysterectomy can mean freedom from pain and the threat of serious disease. Although the operation does signal the end of childbearing, women who undergo hysterectomies can usually look forward to many years of health, vitality, and sexual enjoyment.

151. Endometriosis

COMMON CHARACTERISTICS

Each month during a woman's childbearing years, hormonal changes prepare the womb lining (the endometrium) for a fertilized egg (ovum), thickening it and engorging it with blood. If pregnancy does not occur, the endometrium breaks down, and the tissue is sloughed off during menstruation.

Endometriosis is a condition in which, for reasons that are not known, some of the cells of the endometrium grow elsewhere in the body. Endometrial implants, as they are called, may develop on the uterine wall, the ovaries, and the fallopian tubes, or, less commonly, on the vagina, the intestine, the bladder, or other areas of the pelvic cavity. These aberrant cells respond to hormonal stimulation as if they were still part of the lining of the womb, undergoing the same cyclical congestion and bleeding. Since the cells are embedded in tissue, however, the blood cannot escape. Blisters form, scarring the surrounding tissue, and, over a period of time, small brown or purple cysts may develop. Adhesions also may develop, causing some of the pelvic organs to adhere to each other or to be twisted out of shape. When the ovaries and fallopian tubes are affected, even small areas of these endometrial growths can impair fertility.

Endometriosis is a common condition in women in their thirties and forties, particularly in those who have not borne children, and is responsible for many cases of infertility. Nevertheless, many women with the condition conceive in spite of it; the symptoms disappear during pregnancy. When the monthly stimulation of the endometrium ends with menopause, or with surgical removal of the ovaries, the disease ceases to progress or cause further symptoms.

SYMPTOMS

In many women, endometriosis produces little or no discomfort. Others, however, experience considerable pain. The pain is usually a dull aching or cramping felt in the lower abdomen or back during the few days before menstruation and continuing into the period. The pain tends to increase over time and to begin progressively earlier in the menstrual cycle. Depending on the location of the endometrial growths, there may also be pain with intercourse, in the rectum, or in the bladder, and blood may be present in the stool or urine during the menstrual period. Some women have unusually heavy menstrual bleeding; others have an occasional missed period, or a scanty or irregular one, with the pain occurring at its usual time.

In a young woman, the symptoms may be mild. However, the disease tends to progress steadily and to pose an ever-increasing threat to the normal functioning of the ovaries. Mild symptoms, therefore, should not be ignored.

DIAGNOSIS

During a pelvic examination, a doctor can often detect the small, tender nodules of endometriosis on the ligaments supporting the womb or in the cul-de-sac. The diagnosis is confirmed by a biopsy of the tissue or by direct examination of the uterus and internal structures by means of a laparoscope, a thin, flexible tube with fiberoptic devices that permits a doctor to view the inside of the pelvic cavity.

TREATMENT

What treatment is given depends on many factors, including the severity of symptoms, the extent to which the disease has spread, and the woman's age and her wishes about having children.

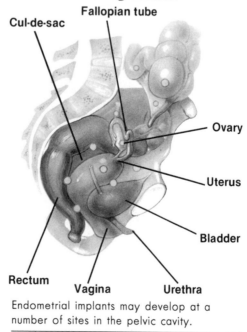

Endometrial implants may develop at a number of sites in the pelvic cavity.

In mild cases, hormone therapy is usually given. Female hormones—progesterone, or a combination of estrogen and progesterone—are prescribed in doses high enough to prevent menstruation entirely for a number of months, during which time the symptoms are relieved and the growth of endometrial implants is suppressed. Alternatively, the synthetic steroid, danazol, may be given to prevent menstrual bleeding. When the medication is withdrawn, the normal menstrual cycle resumes, and in many cases women who wish to become pregnant do so. The beneficial effects of hormone treatment often continue for months or even years, making it possible to delay surgery or even avoid it altogether.

If surgery is necessary to relieve the symptoms of endometriosis in a young woman who wishes to remain fertile, as many of the endometrial growths as can safely be removed will be excised. The surgeon will try to restore mobility to the fallopian tubes and the ovaries and will correct any misplacements that the growths and adhesions may have produced. Surgery of this kind frequently relieves the symptoms of the condition and restores fertility.

In women with severe symptoms who do not wish to have children—or who have completed their families or are nearing menopause—the entire uterus and the ovaries will be removed. This is done to remove the source of endometrial tissue and also to stop the natural production of estrogen, which stimulates the endometrium.

SUMMING UP

Endometriosis is a benign growth of uterine lining tissue in abdominal areas outside the uterus. The endometrial growths may cause discomfort or pain, in a cyclical pattern. They may also be responsible for infertility. Depending on the severity of the condition, and the woman's age and wishes about bearing children, endometriosis may be treated medically with hormones or by surgical methods.

Sexual Problems

---

152. Sexual Dysfunction

COMMON CHARACTERISTICS

The inability to experience sexual satisfaction or to provide it for one's partner is technically called sexual dysfunction. The cause may be physical, psychological, or cultural, or a combination of these factors. The most common forms of sexual dysfunction are impotence and premature ejaculation in the male and the inability to achieve orgasm in the female. More recently, sex therapists have reported an increase in a new category of sexual dysfunction, namely, a lack of interest in all sexual activity. Once considered a phenomenon limited to mostly older people, it is now estimated that about half of all patients seeking sex therapy do so because of what is called desire dysfunction. The problem seems to be particularly common among both men and women in their twenties and thirties.

Until comparatively recently, most people deprived of the satisfactions of a normal sex life had few options once any possible physical causes for their disability were ruled out. Either they learned to live with the problem, with increasing damage to their self-esteem and their love relationships, or they spent lots of time and money on what was likely to prove a fruitless exploration of their psyche.

MODERN SEX THERAPY

Human sexuality did not become an area of scientific study until a few decades ago. But it was not until the publication of pioneering work done by Dr. William Masters and Virginia Johnson that we began to gain a fuller understanding of the different types of sexual dysfunction and how they should be treated. Masters and Johnson evolved the theory that there are four major stages in which sexual dysfunction occurs: appetitive, excitement, orgasm, and resolution. Thus the first step in modern sex therapy is to rule out any organic cause, such as alcohol abuse, drug use, and other such causes. Next comes a careful evaluation to determine specifically the stage in which dysfunction occurs, and then working out step-by-step techniques for overcoming the problem.

TYPES OF DYSFUNCTION

Lack of Sexual Desire

Although this is considered a relatively new problem in sex therapy, experts are unsure whether there are now more people with little or no interest in sex or whether there are just more people who are willing to admit it. Two categories of desire dysfunction are recognized: those whose absence of appetite prevents their getting sexually interested in anyone at all, and those who are unresponsive only to their spouses. At Mount Sinai Medical Center in New York, Dr. Raul Schiavi, director of the human sexuality program, reported that every male patient who sought help for absence of desire was married.

However, many unmarried men and women who are capable of sexual gratification also report that they have more or less eliminated this activity from their lives.

Nonorgasmic Women

Ruling out problems of dyspareunia (painful intercourse) and related problems essentially physical, there are two main categories of nonorgasmic women. First, there are those women who have never been able to feel sexually aroused. Although they are capable of deep affection, at the same time they shrink from physical expression of it. Second, there are women capable of sexual excitement who cannot achieve an orgasm either through masturbation or during intercourse.

According to Dr. Lenny Myers, the physician in charge of sexual health services at the Midwest Population Center in Chicago, the main barrier to sexual fulfillment is early training in sexual restraint, in being "a good girl." This is borne out by the observation of Dr. Dagmar O'Connor, director of the sex therapy program at Roosevelt Hospital in New York. Of the more than six hundred nonorgasmic women treated, 88 percent described themselves as having been "good girls." For such patients, she has devised a program based on techniques to overcome inhibitions.

Premature Ejaculation

The occurrence of the male sexual climax in less than two minutes after the penis enters the vagina is technically called premature ejaculation. This sexual dysfunction, essentially a failure in control, typically leaves the female sexually aroused but unsatisfied and the male humiliated by feelings of sexual inadequacy.

STAGES IN SEXUAL RESPONSE CYCLE

STAGE	CHARACTERISTICS	TYPES OF DYSFUNCTION
Appetitive	Sexual fantasies; desire to engage in sex	Lack of sexual desire
Excitement	Growing sense of sexual pleasure; physiological changes (penile erection, vaginal lubrication, nipple erection, etc.)	Impotence; lack of vaginal secretions
Orgasm	Peaking of sexual pleasure; male ejaculation; vaginal contractions	Failure to achieve orgasm in women; failure to ejaculate in men
Resolution	State of general relaxation and well-being following orgasm	Feelings of unresolved arousal and failure

The condition is said to prevail in about 25 percent of all marriages. Since the cause is rarely organic, the problem usually can be successfully treated through a series of "stop-start" exercises, some masturbatory, others with the sexual partner. Sex therapists report that more than 90 percent of their patients eventually achieve satisfactory ejaculatory control for ten minutes or longer. Where the source of the problem is a deep-seated conflict about sexual activity as such, or about women as such, or about negative feelings for one's wife, psychological counseling may be included in the treatment.

Impotence

The inability to achieve and maintain an erection, and therefore to engage in sexual intercourse, is reported to be a problem experienced by some ten million men. Although there are a number of organic causes of impotence, including such things as diabetes and the use of certain drugs (see Chapter 154, "Effects of Drugs on Sexual Function"), most cases of impotence have a psychogenic basis. Personal background and attitudes play a critical role in sexual performance. The achievement of satisfactory sexual intercourse is closely related to a man's self-esteem and to his participation in lovemaking without anger, anxiety, or impersonal detachment.

A man who experiences chronic sexual failure (a few isolated incidents are no cause for alarm unless the anxiety factor begins to escalate) should have a complete physical examination. Organic factors, many of them previously overlooked, are now found to be the basic cause of impotence in about one-third of all cases, even though emotional factors may add to the problem. (For more specifics, see Chapter 153, "Impotence".)

SOME BASIC CONCEPTS OF SEX THERAPY

One of the most universally applied concepts of Masters and Johnson sex therapy is the importance of being at home in one's own body through touching and, as a consequence of touching exercises, of being able to touch one's sexual partner without anxiety or guilt, just for the pleasure of doing so, leaving out the eventuality of orgasm. Most sex therapists guide their patients slowly toward sexual fulfillment by telling them to forget about erections and orgasms and to learn how to enjoy sexual play.

Many therapists believe that in addition to essential physical exercises, nonorgasmic women make progress in group sessions where they feel free to discuss their bodies and their sexual desires and responses and to share their angers and resentments.

The length of therapy and the cost of the sessions vary with the problem and the cooperation of the participant. On the average, ten to fifteen sessions can produce good results.

HOW TO FIND HELP

Some family doctors have been trained in the techniques of sex therapy or can be depended on to make a suitable referral. Many hospitals now conduct sex therapy programs, increasingly under the supervision of the psychiatry department. In areas remote from such facilities, there may be properly trained sex therapists who are private practitioners. Under what circumstances medical insurance covers such treatment is a question that should be addressed to the insurance company's local representative. Names and addresses of professional practitioners of sex therapy are available through the American Association of Sex Educators, Counselors, and Therapists, 2000 N Street N.W., Washington, DC 20036 Tel.: 202/296-7205.

SUMMING UP

Researchers in human sexuality have found out that human sexuality begins in the womb and continues for a lifetime under optimal circumstances. If physical causes do not stand in the way of achieving sexual satisfaction, sex therapy is now an accepted method of dealing with the majority of problems that deprive people of a human birthright. Many of these treatment centers are affiliated with hospitals, and they combine structured exercises with supportive psychotherapy when there is a need for this double approach.

153. Impotence

COMMON CHARACTERISTICS

Impotence is the failure to attain or sustain an erection long enough to complete sexual intercourse. It is a very common, though usually temporary, occurrence among men of all ages. Occasional impotence may be brought on by a wide variety of emotional and physical problems. Chronic impotence may indicate more pervasive psychological or medical disorders.

If it is more than an occasional occurrence, impotence can be emotionally devastating, leading to feelings of shame, anxiety, guilt, or depression. These emotions, in turn, make recurrence more likely.

In the great majority of cases, impotence can be treated successfully. Depending on the cause, treatment may consist of some form of counseling aimed at improving communication between sexual partners, individual psychotherapy, or a specific medical therapy to correct an underlying physical problem.

CAUSES OF IMPOTENCE

When a full erection can sometimes be achieved—during masturbation, for example, or upon awakening in the morning—but there is failure during intercourse, the underlying problem is almost always psychological. Any number of factors may be involved, including fear of intimacy, guilt, depression due to marital difficulties or life circumstances, anxiety at the onset of a relationship, or anger at the deterioration of an old one.

In a smaller number of cases, the cause of impotence is a disease or a drug taken to counteract a disease. Diabetes is one such contributing disorder; others include pituitary and thyroid gland disturbances, certain cardiovascular conditions, inflammatory diseases of the genitals, and damage to the spinal cord. (When the cause is a physical condition of this kind, it is likely that there will also be psychological difficulties, often as the result of the impotence itself.)

Impotence has been found to be a side effect of some of the drugs prescribed to control high blood pressure. It may also result from mood-altering drugs such as tranquilizers, sedatives, and amphetamines. Alcohol consumption is one of the most common, and frequently overlooked, causes of sexual failure. Contrary to its image as an enhancer of romance, alcohol actually tends to reduce sexual response and effectiveness. Impotence and loss of sexual interest often accompany chronic alcoholism (see Chapter 154, "Effects of Drugs on Sexual Function").

In addition, impotence may stem from the abnormal functioning of the endocrine glands, which results in low production of the male hormone testosterone. Recent research has indicated that this condition may be more common than had previously been thought. Such endocrine abnormalities can be detected fairly simply through the screening of blood samples.

It should be noted that potency is not necessarily affected by aging. Some aspects of sexual function may decline, such as the amount and viability of sperm and the strength of ejaculation, but the ability to have an erection may continue into the seventies, eighties, and even later.

TREATMENT

If physical disorders or abnormalities are found, treatment is aimed at alleviating these underlying problems, if possible. Where hormone deficiencies can be conclusively demonstrated, for example, compensating treatment is in order. And if a specific drug can be isolated as the cause of the problem, then switching to another medication without the harmful side effects is an obvious course of action.

Otherwise, and in the majority of cases, impotence problems may be treated through counseling and sex therapy. It is usually strongly recommended that both sexual partners participate in the treatment. Its aim is to dispel myths and misinformation, promote mutual confidence and understanding, and help establish a situation which is undemanding for the male and pleasurable for both partners. Dr. William Masters and Virginia Johnson, who are pioneers in this field, have reported that therapy in their clinics, usually lasting from two to eight weeks, is successful in about 80 percent of cases. Consultation with a psychotherapist or marriage counselor may also be helpful for treating recurrent potency problems in cases where physical causes have been ruled out (see Chapter 152, "Sexual Dysfunction").

PREMATURE EJACULATION

Since the normal male biological response is ejaculation within two minutes of vaginal penetration, and since few women can reach orgasm in that time, most men must learn to retard ejaculation if their partners are to have satisfaction from inter-

COMMON CAUSES OF IMPOTENCE

Male sexual function requires the correct, interdependent functioning of four systems in the body: the brain, autonomic nervous system, hormones, and vascular system. Impotence may be due to a disturbance of one or more of these systems. Common causes include:

PSYCHOLOGICAL
- Guilt
- Fear of intimacy
- Depression
- Poor self-esteem
- Inadequate communication with partner

NEUROLOGICAL
- Diabetes
- Alcoholism
- Syphilis
- Prostatectomy
- Multiple sclerosis
- Spinal cord injury
- Stroke

- Sedative use

HORMONAL
- Low testosterone levels
- Pituitary tumor
- Hypothyroidism
- Some ulcer medications

VASCULAR
- Peripheral vascular disease
- Aortic aneurysm
- Congenital defects
- Pulmonary disease
- Use of antihypertensive drugs

course. Those who consistently reach orgasm before a normally responsive partner is satisfied are said to suffer from premature ejaculation. It is a common form of sexual dysfunction.

Premature ejaculation occurs frequently among adolescents, in whom it may be aggravated by fear of discovery or pregnancy, as well as anxiety about performance. It is also quite common among adults at the start of a relationship, but usually subsides as the relationship develops. Stress or tension of any kind may aggravate the problem. Occasionally premature ejaculation masks deep-seated psychological or interpersonal problems; in such cases psychotherapy may be needed. It may also result—but rarely—from an infection of the prostate gland or from diseases affecting the neural pathways.

Sexual control can be improved through training. One effective method is the "squeeze technique," in which ejaculation is forestalled by pressure on the penis just below the glans.

SUMMING UP

Most men experience impotence or premature ejaculation at some time in their lives. These problems may be due to emotional response to a particular partner or to sexuality in general, or to any number of other factors, both psychological and situational. Some diseases bring on impotence as a secondary effect, as do some medications. Alcohol is often a contributing factor.

Where disease does not contribute, as in the majority of cases, counseling and some form of sex therapy are generally effective in alleviating the problem.

154. Effects of Drugs on Sexual Function

COMMON CHARACTERISTICS

Doctors have become increasingly aware that many common prescription drugs produce undesirable side effects in male patients, causing potency problems or affecting other aspects of sexual functioning. These problems and difficulties are no longer dismissed with well-meaning words of reassurance, as was too often the case in the past. Rather, doctors are taking advantage of the wide variety of drugs now available to work out solutions that will benefit both their male patients' overall health and their sexual well-being.

SIDE EFFECTS

Proper male sexual functioning depends on a complex of psychological, emotional, neurologic, vascular, and hormonal factors. A medication that—as a side effect—inhibits a man's ability to become emotionally stimulated, or blocks the nerve pathways responsible for erection and ejaculation, or interferes with blood flow to the penis, or disturbs the natural hormonal balance, may well affect his sexual performance.

The chance of developing sexual side effects depends on the dose of the drug, how long the medication is taken, the general health of the person taking it, and, perhaps most important, the individual's sensitivity to the drug. Not all men taking the medications that have been reported to cause sexual side effects will develop problems. If that were the case, few doctors would prescribe these drugs and even fewer patients would take them.

Sexual side effects have been reported to occur with reserpine and related drugs prescribed for hypertension and with high doses of tranquilizers (both "minor" and "major" tranquilizers) prescribed for anxiety and depression. The side effects of these drugs include impotence, loss or diminution of sexual desire (libido), breast enlargement, and an inability to ejaculate. Similar side effects also occur with drugs commonly prescribed for irritable colon, colitis, diarrhea, and ulcers; with some drugs given to provide relief from muscle spasm, nausea, and vomiting; and with drugs taken to promote weight loss or to lower blood cholesterol levels. Swelling of the testicles and a reduced sperm count are less common side effects. It should be reemphasized, however, that all men taking such medications will not experience these problems.

UNDERREPORTING THE PROBLEM

A major obstacle to identifying and solving sexual problems arising from medication use is lack of awareness. Men may be more likely to attribute sexual difficulties to marital or interpersonal problems, stress, or aging than to link these problems with a drug that they are taking. Too often, failing to make the connection means that the problem is not brought to a doctor's attention. This creates a vicious cycle of underreporting in which doctors, drug companies, and the public alike remain uninformed about the true frequency of sexual side effects with various drugs. It is important to remember that knowledge about drug side effects depends largely on the willingness of patients to volunteer information about any problems they may be experiencing.

A second major obstacle is lack of frankness between patients and doctors. Many people who feel perfectly comfortable telling a doctor that a particular drug is upsetting their stomach or making them dizzy shy away from reporting a sexual side effect. Such uneasiness about sexuality is by no means limited to patients. Unfortunately, doctors sometimes do not probe as carefully for side effects on sexual function as they do for drug reactions affecting other functions or other parts of the body. Ideally, doctors should alert their patients to the possibility of side effects before drug therapy is begun and should ask about such reactions periodically during the course of treatment.

SOLVING THE PROBLEM

The first step toward alleviating the sexual difficulty is to determine whether it is actually related to the medication or not. If the problem started shortly after the course of medication was begun, it is probable that the drug is responsible.

Inability to have an erection *at any time* suggests that a medication or a physical illness is responsible for the trouble. However, if it is possible to become erect during masturbation or to achieve an erection with one partner but not with another, then the cause of impotence is probably psychological—worry, depression, the wrong partner, the wrong time, or the wrong place. Awakening with an erection, an event which does not depend on sexual stimulation, is reassuring evidence that the sexual function is not physically impaired.

DRUGS THAT AFFECT SEXUAL FUNCTION

DRUGS	LOSS IN LIBIDO	LOWER SPERM COUNT	IMPOTENCE	BREAST SWELLING IN MEN	TESTICULAR SWELLING	FAILURE TO EJACULATE
Antihypertensives						
Chlorthalidone (Hygroton)			X			
Clonidine (Catapres)			X			
Hydrochlorothiazide/reserpine (Hydropres)	X		X	X		
Methyldopa (Aldomet)	X		X	X		
Reserpine/chlorthalidone (Regroton)	X		X	X		
Reserpine/hydralazine/ hydrochlorothiazide (Ser-Ap-Es)	X		X	X		
Spironolactone (Aldactone)			X	X		
Spironolactone/hydro- chlorothiazide (Aldactazide)			X	X		
Antianxiety/antidepressants						
Amitriptyline (Elavil, Endep)	X			X	X	
Chlorpromazine (Thorazine)				X		
Diazepam (Valium)	X					
Doxiepine (Adapin, Sinequan)	X		X		X	
Imipramine (Tofranil)	X			X	X	
Lithium salts			X			
Perphenazine/amitriptyline (Etrafon, Triavil)	X		X	X	X	
Prochlorperazine (Compazine)				X		X
Thioridazine (Mellaril)	X			X		X
Trifluoperazine (Stelazine)				X		X
Gastrointestinal drugs						
Chlordiazepoxide/clidinium bromide (Librax)	X					
Cimetidine (Tagamet)		X		X		
Dicyclomine hydrochloride (Bentyl)			X			
Prochlorperazine maleate/ isopropamide iodide (Combid)				X		
Muscle relaxants						
Cyclobenzaprine (Flexeril)	X			X	X	
Antinauseants						
Prochlorperazine (Compazine)				X		X
Appetite suppressants						
Diethylpropion hydrochloride (Tenuate)	X		X	X		
Phentermine hydrochloride (Fastin)	X		X			
Phentermine resin (Ionamin)	X		X			

(Continued)

DRUGS	LOSS IN LIBIDO	LOWER SPERM COUNT	IMPOTENCE	BREAST SWELLING IN MEN	TESTICULAR SWELLING	FAILURE TO EJACULATE
Cholesterol-lowering drugs						
Clofibrate (Atromid-S)	X		X			
Antifungal drugs						
Metronidazole (Flagyl)	X					
Hormone agents						
Medroxyprogesterone (Provera)	X					
Other						
Alcohol	X					

OPTIONS

If it is determined that a medication is causing the sexual difficulty, several different options may be considered. If the problem is only mildly uncomfortable (breast enlargement, for example), or if the drug must be taken only for a short period of time (as might be the case with a drug prescribed for an ulcer), it may be reasonable to continue the medication. On the other hand, if normal sexual functioning is affected and the drug has been prescribed for a chronic condition, such as hypertension, the doctor will probably either reduce the dosage or change the medication. Once the dosage has been reduced or another drug has been substituted, the sexual difficulties should clear up.

SUMMING UP

A number of commonly prescribed drugs may affect normal male sexual functioning, producing impotence, loss of libido, inability to ejaculate, and other problems. These are, naturally, distressing side effects. However, provided the lines of communication between doctor and patient are kept open, it is usually possible to change or adjust medication in such a way that the patient's general health is maintained while his sexual functioning is not adversely affected.

155. Contraception

GENERAL CONSIDERATIONS

Contraception—any method used by one or both partners to prevent pregnancy—has been practiced in one form or another since ancient times. However, not until comparatively recently have techniques been devised that are statistically reliable and safe, as well as sufficiently varied to accommodate particular circumstances.

No single method of contraception is ideal from every point of view. Some methods are unquestionably more reliable than others, some are more suitable to one's particular sexual habits at a particular time of life, and some are more congenial to one's aesthetic sense or personal convictions.

"NATURAL" METHODS

Rhythm

This method entails abstention from sexual intercourse during that part of the menstrual cycle when ovulation occurs. Since very few women ovulate with exact regularity, the rhythm method is likely to have intrinsic inaccuracies. There are several ways of determining when ovulation is taking place; these include counting the number of days from the beginning of the last period, watching for the slight rise in temperature that usually accompanies ovulation, and noting a change in the vaginal secretion from a thick, white, sparse discharge to a thin, clear, profuse one, another herald of ovulation. None of these is foolproof, however.

Withdrawal

This is the oldest method of contraception and one that is still widely practiced in many parts of the world. It involves the withdrawal technique (coitus interruptus)—in which the penis is withdrawn just before orgasm and the semen is deposited outside the vagina. This method is generally considered unreliable and unsatisfactory and causes tensions to be built into the sex act.

THE PILL

Oral contraceptives are now available in two types: the combination pill, which contains synthetic estrogen and progestogen and which inhibits ovulation and alters the mucous secretions of the vagina, and the progestogen-only pill, which alters both the mucous secretions from the cervix so that sperm cannot penetrate the barrier and the lining of the uterus so that implantation of the fertilized egg becomes impossible. Of the two, the combination pill is considered the more reliable, although both enjoy a very high success rate. Most women, especially those under the age of thirty or thirty-five, can safely use the pill, although the combination pill is usually not recommended for women who smoke because of an increased risk of heart disease and blood clots.

INTRAUTERINE DEVICES

An intrauterine device (IUD), as its name implies, is a contraceptive device that is inserted into the uterus by a doctor. Once in place, no further contraceptive action is necessary. It may be left in place for at least a year if it has been properly fitted and there are no untoward results. It is considered almost as reliable as the pill.

IUDs come in several different types,

but all are supplied with a string that extends outward from the cervix into the vagina, so that the wearer can make sure that the device is in place. Correct fitting by a specialist is a critical aspect of the effectiveness of this device.

While IUDs are generally safe for most women, there are certain contraindications for their use. These include pregnancy, fibroid tumors, anemia, abnormal Pap smears, continuous treatment with cortisone-type drugs, previous ectopic pregnancy, and pelvic inflammatory disease. Recent studies also indicate that IUD users are more likely to develop severe pelvic inflammatory disease than those who use other methods.

BARRIER METHODS

The use of barrier methods of contraception—the condom, diaphragm, and spermicidal agents—has grown in recent years for a number of reasons. For example, with genital herpes and other sexually transmitted diseases reaching epidemic proportions, barrier methods probably lower the rate of spread of these diseases.

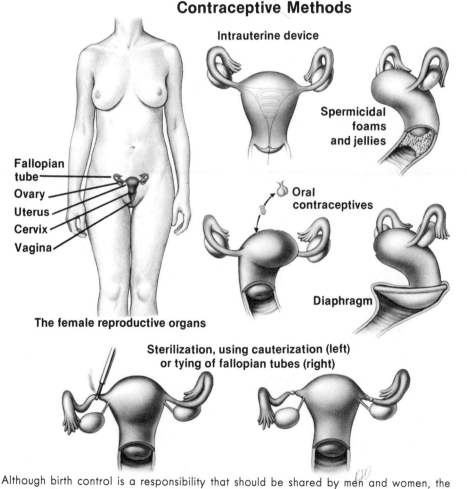

Contraceptive Methods

Intrauterine device

Spermicidal foams and jellies

Fallopian tube
Ovary
Uterus
Cervix
Vagina

Oral contraceptives

Diaphragm

The female reproductive organs

Sterilization, using cauterization (left) or tying of fallopian tubes (right)

Although birth control is a responsibility that should be shared by men and women, the methods illustrated here apply to women. When deciding on a method of contraception, questions of safety, reliability, suitability to particular circumstances, and the wishes of the sexual partner should be taken into consideration.

For women whose sex life is intermittent rather than regular, the day-in, day-out use of the pill or the wearing of an IUD seems out of proportion to their requirements.

Condom

The condom, or "rubber," is second only to the pill as the most popular form of contraception in the United States and remains the most widely used device throughout the world. In addition to providing protection against pregnancy and disease, condoms are easily available and are now being manufactured in materials so thin that interference with sensation has been almost entirely eliminated. Extra effectiveness and easier insertion are accomplished by the use of a spermicidal agent.

Diaphragm

The diaphragm is a soft, rubber cap surrounded by a flexible ring that is inserted into the vagina to cover the entrance to the cervix. Preceding intercourse, when the device is coated with spermicidal jelly, it provides both a chemical and mechanical barrier. A diaphragm must be individually fitted by a doctor and should be checked for proper fit about once a year, especially after pregnancy, abortion, or a significant change in weight. It should also be checked periodically for holes or other damage. Other advantages include possible protection against cervical infections and sexually transmitted diseases.

Spermicidal Agents

These chemicals—in the form of creams, jellies, suppositories, and foams—act in two ways when inserted into the vagina before intercourse: they kill sperm cells, and they create a barrier against their passage. When used alone, they are not totally reliable. However, in combination with a condom or a diaphragm, they provide an extremely high rate of effectiveness, with a failure rate of about 1 percent.

STERILIZATION

Both male and female sterilization have increased in popularity in recent years, and it is now the leading form of contraception among couples who have been married for more than ten years. The sterilization procedures for both sexes involve surgery and are considered permanent forms of contraception, although there have been a few instances in which reversal has been achieved. Vasectomy—the male sterilization procedure—involves making a small incision to sever the tubes through which the sperm travel. For women, sterilization may be achieved by severing or blocking the fallopian tubes to prevent the egg from reaching the uterus, or by removal of either the ovaries or uterus (hysterectomy). The latter are not recommended simply to achieve sterilization.

SUMMING UP

In choosing a contraceptive method, you should consider questions of safety, reliability, and suitability to particular circumstances. In the case of couples, the wishes of each partner should be spelled out so that a mutually agreeable decision is arrived at. For any given method, especially where new information becomes available regularly, you should feel free to ask your doctor about risks and benefits in order to make an informed choice. Whatever the decision at any given time, it need not be viewed as immutable. You should also clearly understand how long it takes for fertility to be reestablished after use of the pill or IUD. In any instance, contraception should be considered a mutual responsibility, and unless pregnancy is desired, it should be a conscious consideration before engaging in sexual relations.

156. Infertility

individual's general life style, are listed in the table on p. 435.

COMMON CHARACTERISTICS

Infertility, usually defined as the inability to conceive after at least one year of repeated attempts to achieve pregnancy, affects approximately 15 percent of all couples. Of these, about two-thirds will eventually become parents, but conceiving may require patience on the part of the future parents and their doctor. Often, the infertility problem can be traced to one partner or the other. Sometimes the infertility results from a combination of male and female factors. If both partners have a very low fertility, for example, it may take them unusually long to conceive. In such cases, patience may be the sole remedy. Whatever the cause of the infertility, the old medical truth that diagnosis must precede cure is particularly important.

Since infertility is a complex medical problem with many emotional overtones, it is especially important that the patients have good relations with the physician. Female infertility problems are usually handled by a gynecologist, often one who specializes in infertility. Male infertility problems usually are treated by urologists.

CAUSES OF INFERTILITY

The causes of infertility are complex. Among the most common are genetic disorders, sperm antibodies, vaginal mucus that is hostile to the sperm, impotence, premature ejaculation, and poor timing of intercourse. In about one-third of the cases, the infertility problem is traced to the man, and in two-thirds to the woman. Other causes, ranging from developmental and hormonal problems to aspects of an

DIAGNOSING MALE INFERTILITY

Since male infertility is easier to identify than female infertility, an examination of the sperm is usually the first diagnostic test. The ejaculate is measured, and the sperm are counted and examined for their shape and activity.

Some of the major causes of male infertility can be corrected surgically, and one in particular is varicocele—the presence of enlarged "varicose" veins in the scrotum —which interferes with the production of sperm cells. Other male infertility problems can be remedied by a change in habits, such as overeating and excessive smoking, or alcohol intake. Since sperm are sensitive to heat, sometimes the problem can be traced to something as simple as a preference for hot baths or saunas. If the problem of male infertility cannot be corrected, a couple may decide on artificial insemination, during which the woman is inseminated in a doctor's office with sperm from an unknown donor. About twenty-thousand babies are now fathered by artificial insemination in this country each year.

DIAGNOSING FEMALE INFERTILITY

Although the problems of female infertility are numerous and diverse, fortunately, many can be treated either surgically or by various drugs.

Female fertility is controlled by the monthly menstrual cycle, which is determined by the interrelationship of several hormones: the follicle-stimulating hormone (FSH), the luteinizing hormone

(LH) (these two hormones together are called the gonadotrophins and are identical with those found in the male), progesterone, and estrogen.

In diagnosing possible causes of female infertility, one of the important first steps is to determine whether the woman is producing an egg (ovum) monthly. Since the ovaries are located deep within the abdominal cavity, this is not easily determined. The hormones, however, slightly change the temperature of the body by about 1° C. There is a definite rise in temperature during ovulation, when progesterone production is at its maximum. Women who want to pinpoint their fertile period (for both contraceptive purposes [with the rhythm method] and infertility problems) often are instructed to take their temperature every morning, sometimes with a specially designed thermometer. Hormone studies

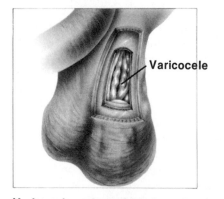

Varicocele

Varicocele, enlarged "varicose" veins in the scrotum, may lower the sperm count and sperm activity.

Obstruction

The fallopian tubes may become obstructed as a result of infections such as gonorrhea or pelvic inflammatory disease.

Infertility may be due to a large number of conditions both within and outside the male and female reproductive tracts. Two common ones are illustrated.

also are used to determine more precisely whether and when a woman ovulates.

If the woman is not ovulating but has intact ovaries and a normal reproductive system, hormones may be prescribed to stimulate ovulation. In some instances, the ovaries are overstimulated and release more than one egg, accounting for the increase in multiple births in women who take fertility drugs. Close medical supervision, however, minimizes the occurrence of such multiple births.

A diagnostic work-up to determine whether there are any structural or other defects affecting fertility will be performed in women who ovulate but are unable to conceive. Possibilities include blocked or poorly placed fallopian tubes, growths such as polyps, fibroids, and other tumors; and endometriosis, the growth of tissue that normally lines the uterus at other sites in the pelvic or abdominal cavity. Enormous progress has been made in the surgical treatment of many of these problems, thus restoring fertility to women who a few years ago would not have been able to conceive. With endometriosis, drug therapy, either with or without surgery to correct any adhesions or other deformities, can usually restore fertility.

More exciting still are the recent advances in the repair of the fallopian tubes, blocked most often because of infections, such as pelvic inflammatory disease or gonorrhea. Tubal repair is difficult, because the tubes are extremely narrow and are lined on the inside with cilia—hairlike projections that propel the egg downward to the uterus. Success rates for tubal repair now range from 20 to 70 percent, depending on the source of the blockage.

Simpler causes of infertility, such as hostile vaginal mucus, may be treated by various medications, including antibiotics and estrogens, to make the environment more viable for the sperm. Timing or position for intercourse or other corrective measures also may be suggested.

MALE	FEMALE
GENERAL	
Overweight or underweight; excessive use of alcohol; smoking	Overweight or underweight; anemia; excessive use of alcohol; smoking
DEVELOPMENTAL*	
Varicocele (enlarged veins in scrotum); undeveloped or undescended testicles; low sperm count; venereal disease; hydrocele (swelling in testis or spermatic cord); orchitis (inflammation of testicles); prostatitis; injury	Uterine malformations; polyps; fibroids; endometriosis; undeveloped ovaries; blocked fallopian tubes; venereal, tubercular, tubal, or fungal infections
HORMONAL	
Pituitary failure; thyroid disease; adrenal overdevelopment; low sperm count	Pituitary failure; thyroid disease; ovarian disorders; amenorrhea (no menses); post-pill amenorrhea

*Some of these changes may be caused by infectious diseases.

EXTRAUTERINE FERTILIZATION

A good deal of public attention has been focused on advances in extrauterine fertilization, or so-called test-tube babies. This is a complicated, still experimental procedure in which a mature egg is extracted from the woman at the time of ovulation and then fertilized in a test tube with sperm from the male partner. The fertilized egg is then introduced into the woman's uterus, where—if all goes well—it will become implanted in the lining and grow normally as in any pregnancy. Widespread use of this technique is still in the future, however.

SUMMING UP

Enormous strides have been made in the treatment of infertility, and most couples have a good chance of overcoming their problem with more progress still expected in the years to come. With couples for whom there is no hope of conceiving, adoption remains an alternative route to parenthood. Professional counseling to handle the often devastating emotional impact of infertility also may be recommended.

157. Adolescent Sexuality

GENERAL CONSIDERATIONS

Although sexual development begins in infancy, it seldom receives much attention from parents until adolescence, when changes in a youngster's body and behavior reflect the fact that the capability for reproduction is present. Parents who are concerned about a teenager's growing sexuality should remember that interest in sex is a normal part of the developmental process of adolescence and that sexual experimentation is a normal part of the experience of being an adolescent.

PETTING AND INTERCOURSE

The majority of adolescents in the United States engage in pre-intercourse activities (kissing, petting, touching, and being touched on the genitals), and about 30 percent of young people aged between ten and twenty have had intercourse at least once. Of girls aged fifteen, 14 percent have had intercourse; of girls aged nineteen, more than one-half are sexually experienced.

For girls, first intercourse is generally a negative experience; they describe it as being frightening, or uncomfortable, or painful. Boys, on the other hand, generally feel that the experience was a positive one, both for themselves and their partners.

Of the teenagers who have intercourse, the great majority form only a few (two or three) intimate sexual relationships during their adolescent years. Each relationship, in its turn, is exclusive—that is, neither of the pair has other sexual partners—and involves an emotional commitment over a period of time. It is usually tacitly understood that the relationship, although it may be long-lasting, is not a permanent one.

For a small percentage of adolescents, however, the pattern of relationships is markedly different. These youngsters have many sexual partners, and often two or more at the same time. Frequently, the pattern of sexual behavior is part of a generally "difficult" adolescence.

CONTRACEPTION

About half of all premarital first pregnancies occur in girls who have been sexually active for six months or less. This reflects the fact that many adolescents use no contraception at all in the first year of sexual activity. Overall, however, the use of contraceptives by adolescents has increased by 35 percent during the last decade. Many teenagers use over-the-counter methods (condoms and spermicidal creams or suppositories), but more than half of all sexually active adolescent girls have had contraceptives prescribed for them, either by private doctors or in family planning clinics.

A girl's choice among the various contraceptive methods available should depend, among other factors, on her personality and on the frequency with which she has intercourse. For example, oral contraceptives, which must be taken regularly to be effective, would be an unsuitable choice for a generally disorganized girl or one who has intercourse only once or twice a year. A diaphragm, if that is the method chosen, should be refitted if a girl gains or loses more than ten pounds.

PREGNANCY AND PARENTHOOD

The pregnancy rate among sexually active teenage girls has dropped by about 15 percent during the past decade. Nevertheless, approximately 1.2 million teenagers become pregnant every year. It is estimated that four of ten sexually active girls will become pregnant before they leave their teens, some intentionally, some through contraceptive failure, many because they are unprotected.

Only one-quarter of all teenage pregnancies are intended. Of the others, about 10 percent end in miscarriage and about 25 percent are terminated by induced abortion. Thus, approximately two-thirds of all unintended teenage pregnancies result in the birth of a child—about 560,000 live births a year. At least 80 percent of these are out-of-wedlock births. Some of the babies are given up for adoption, but the great majority (90 percent) remain with their mothers.

As a generalization, it is fair to say that the future does not hold much promise for a teenage mother. Youthful marriages have an extremely high rate of failure. Many young mothers drop out of school and, without training or an adequate education, find it hard to get work, becoming dependent on welfare for support. About half of the funds paid out by the Aid to Families with Dependent Children program goes to families in which the woman gave birth while still in her teens.

Teenage pregnancies have a higher than normal incidence of premature birth and low birthweight, which are often, but not invariably, related. Such babies have an increased mortality rate in the first year of life and an increased risk for cerebral palsy and mental retardation, among other medical problems. In addition, social problems may result in poor cognitive development.

VENEREAL DISEASE

Sexually active adolescents are, of course, at risk of contracting the venereal diseases that affect the population as a whole. Adolescent girls, however, seem to be at special risk of developing certain complications of these diseases. Some of

AREAS OF CONCERN TO ADOLESCENTS

FOR GIRLS

*Breast development
Slower than peers
Breasts too large or too small
Asymetrical breasts
Swelling and tenderness

*Menstruation
Failure to menstruate
Painful menstruation
Irregular periods

*Contraception
Unprotected intercourse
Ignorance
Fear of parental disapproval

*Pregnancy
Unplanned pregnancy
Health hazards to mother and fetus
Emotional and social problems

FOR BOYS

*Nocturnal emissions
Misplaced feelings of shame

*Contraception
Same as for girls

FOR BOTH SEXES

*Masturbation
Fear of parental disapproval
Misplaced feelings of shame
Misinformation regarding disease and
    possible harm

*Homosexuality
Worry about sexual identity
Feelings of shame
Emotional problems
Fear of parental and peer disapproval

the pubertal hormones appear to affect the transmission of such organisms as gonococci and chlamydia, making it more probable that the infection will spread from the initial site to the cervix and the fallopian tubes.

It is important that the sexual partners of anyone diagnosed as having a venereal disease be identified and treated. Adolescents may find it distasteful to "tell on" a partner but should realize that treating all known cases of venereal disease offers the only hope of controlling what is today an epidemic.

HOMOSEXUALITY

Fleeting homosexual fantasies and brief homosexual encounters are quite common among heterosexual adolescents. Although homosexuals make up only 10 percent of the adult male population, 17 percent of adolescent males have had one or more homosexual experiences. (Less is known about homosexuality in adult females, but 6 percent of adolescent females have had homosexual experiences.)

Although it is clear that homosexuality is normal for a minority of the population, an adolescent who is actively homosexual may find that family and community are unaccepting of the sexual preference. Professional counseling may be helpful.

MASTURBATION

Many adolescents half-believe the myths that abound about masturbation—that it makes the hair fall out, or causes pimples, for example. Many others feel guilty about the practice. It is, however, a natural and healthy activity which begins in childhood and is engaged in by the great majority of Americans of both sexes throughout their lives. Masturbation should, however, be restricted as to time and place.

PARENTS' ROLE

Parents often find it difficult to deal with their teenagers' sexual maturation and sexual activities straightforwardly. It is unfortunate that, as a result of parental inhibitions and anxieties, many adolescents do not know what they need to know about the bodily changes of adolescence, for example, or the mechanisms of intercourse and contraception, or the transmission of venereal disease. If parents are uncomfortable with discussion of explicitly sexual matters, they can give their children one of the numerous age-appropriate, factually accurate books on the subject.

Section Twenty:
Pregnancy and Childbirth

---

158. How to Tell If You're Pregnant

GENERAL CONSIDERATIONS

Even very early in pregnancy, before there are any obvious changes, many women can sense they have conceived. When pressed to reveal how they know, most cannot point to anything definite—they just know. For the majority, however, more definable signs are needed, and even then, the pregnancy often needs to be confirmed by blood or urine tests.

The most common sign of early pregnancy is a missed menstrual period. For women whose periods are irregular, or even absent, this may go unnoticed. Also, there are some rare instances in which women may menstruate during early pregnancy. In these unusual cases, the periods

SIGNS OF PREGNANCY

SIGN	STAGE WHEN FIRST NOTICED
PHYSICAL SIGNS	
Breast enlargement	4th week on
Darkening of nipples	4th–5th week on
Nausea	First trimester
Dizziness/fainting	First trimester
Change in sleep patterns	3d or 4th week on
Softening of cervical tissue	3d or 4th week on
Enlargement of uterus	9th week on
Presence of HCG in blood or urine	After 9–10 days

are usually lighter than normal. Other early signs of pregnancy may include a swelling of the breasts. They also may be tender, and the nipples and areola (the pigmented area surrounding the nipple) may become darker. Many women complain of feeling almost overwhelmingly sleepy; others find they are unable to sleep, especially in the early morning. Unusual dizziness and even fainting sometimes occur. Nausea, commonly referred to as morning sickness even though it can occur at any time of the day, often appears during the first few weeks of pregnancy. Some women experience an increased urge to urinate and describe a feeling of pressure in the bladder area.

Many women delay seeing a doctor until the second missed period, and by the ninth or tenth week of pregnancy, doctors usually can accurately diagnose pregnancy on the basis of the woman's description of her symptoms and physical observation of characteristic changes. The cervix will feel softer to the touch than usual, while the lining of the vagina may have a slightly bluish color. By pressing on the abdomen in the tenth week of pregnancy, the doctor can often feel that the uterus is enlarged.

TYPES OF TESTS

If there are doubts about whether or not a woman is pregnant, or if one wants to diagnose pregnancy in the early stages before other signs are apparent, a pregnancy test may be ordered. These tests are based on hormonal changes that take place in pregnancy. When the fertilized ovum (egg) has become implanted in the wall of the uterus, the outermost layer of tissue surrounding it (the chorion) begins to produce a hormone, human chorionic gonadotrophin (HCG). The precise function of HCG is not clear but it seems that this hormone is indirectly responsible for the increased production during the first trimester of other hormones—estrogen and progesterone—that are vital for a healthy pregnancy.

Human chorionic gonadotrophin secreted by the embryonic tissues passes into the mother's bloodstream and is excreted in her urine. Its presence is the basis for modern pregnancy testing.

Urine Tests

A test on the levels of HCG in the urine can detect pregnancy as early as ten days after the first missed menstrual period, or about three weeks after conception. A drop of urine is added to a slide whose contents include a drop of sensitized serum; if HCG is present, the mixture will not coagulate and the test is "positive." The process is very quick; the results will be known within a few minutes. However, especially when done early, the test is not completely reliable: false-positive and false-negative results occur in a small percentage of women.

Your doctor can order the test for you, or you yourself can arrange to have it done. Clinics where pregnancy testing is performed are listed in the Yellow Pages of the telephone directory, or you can ask your local Planned Parenthood office to recommend a medical laboratory.

If possible, the test should be done on a sample of the first-voided urine of the morning. Collect about half a cupful in a clean, dry, well-rinsed jar and refrigerate it until you take it to the clinic or laboratory. There is no need to restrict food or fluids beforehand.

Blood Tests

The blood test for the presence of HCG —commonly called the beta-subunit assay —is much more sensitive and reliable than the test for pregnancy using a urine specimen. (It is also more expensive.) This test, a specific assay for HCG, can detect pregnancy as early as nine days after conception, or approximately a week before the missed menstrual period.

The test is done on a sample of blood

taken from a vein in the arm. Collecting the sample takes a few minutes; the result of the test will be known in a few days. As with the urine test for pregnancy, the blood test may be ordered by a doctor or arranged for independently.

Home Pregnancy Tests

Some pregnancy tests are sold in kit form and use much the same hemagglutination inhibition technique that is the basis for standard urine tests. If a woman is pregnant, an indicator particle (the red blood cells of a sheep, coated with HCG) will react with her urine to produce a dark ring at the bottom of the test tube provided with the kit.

It is claimed for these testing kits that they are 96 to 99 percent accurate. However, such factors as sunlight, heat, vibra-

tion, and the presence of detergents and some medications can influence the results, producing both false-positives and false-negatives. It is therefore important that a woman have her condition confirmed with the more reliable urine or blood tests.

SUMMING UP

Some women know almost intuitively that they are pregnant, but most need to have the fact confirmed by a physician's diagnosis. This may involve simply noting characteristic changes. Very early pregnancies, however, must be confirmed by either a blood or urine test to detect hormonal changes. These tests, particularly the blood test, are now very accurate, and some can detect a pregnancy within nine or ten days of conception.

159. Diet in Pregnancy

GENERAL CONSIDERATIONS

An adequate diet is perhaps more important during pregnancy than at any other time in a woman's life. Because an expectant mother actually shares everything she consumes with her unborn baby, she must eat enough healthful foods to supply both herself and her child with the nutrients each needs. For this reason, most women are advised to eat an additional 200 to 300 calories a day during pregnancy and to gain at least twenty-five pounds. Usually, an expectant mother gains little or no weight during the early weeks of pregnancy. By the end of the third month, how-

ever, she is likely to gain at a steady rate of about one pound a week until term. Throughout pregnancy, weight reduction diets should be avoided.

NUTRITIONAL REQUIREMENTS

According to the recommended dietary allowances established by the National Academy of Sciences, pregnant women require considerably more protein than nonpregnant women. Women who normally consume about forty-five grams of protein a day are advised to increase their daily intake by thirty grams during pregnancy—the amount of protein in four cups of milk (whole or skimmed) or yogurt or four ounces of natural cheese, canned tuna, or chicken. A 25 to 50 percent increase in most vitamins and minerals is also recommended. To meet these nutritional requirements, pregnant women should eat a varied diet, including the daily consumption of foods from each of four basic food groups—high-protein foods, such as meat, poultry, fish, and legumes; dairy products, such as milk, cheese, and yogurt; grain products, such as breads, cereals, and rice; and fruits and vegetables.

Because a woman's blood volume doubles during pregnancy, extra iron is essential to produce healthy red blood cells. Since sufficient quantities of iron to meet this need are not obtained in an average

Diet and Weight Gain in Pregnancy

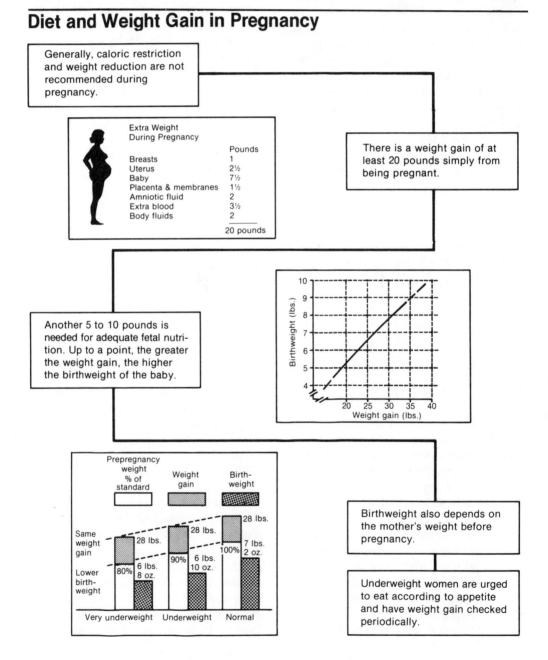

diet, doctors usually prescribe iron supplements during pregnancy in doses of thirty to sixty milligrams a day. Without supplementation, the woman risks becoming anemic, which increases susceptibility to infection and illness. In fact, most doctors advise expectant mothers to take multivitamin and mineral supplements during pregnancy to ensure an adequate supply of nutrients. The supplements generally include folic acid, and, in the last trimester, calcium. In some women, special vitamin and mineral supplementation may be necessary. Vegetarians, for example, may require supplementary zinc, chromium, and vitamin B_{12}.

Like drugs, vitamin and mineral supplements should not be taken without consulting a doctor. Similarly, pregnant women should not limit their consumption of specific foods, such as salt or fluids, unless so directed by their doctors.

SUBSTANCES TO AVOID

All drugs consumed by an expectant mother are carried to the fetus to some degree. Because many of them are known to be potentially harmful to an unborn child and others may be risky, self-medicating should be completely avoided. This means that any drug, prescription or nonprescription, should be taken only under a doctor's supervision as soon as pregnancy seems likely; the chances of a drug's damaging a fetus are greatest in the first ten weeks.

Among the currently available prescription drugs that have been found to be potentially harmful to the fetus are the steroidal hormones, estrogen and progestin (which were once used to prevent miscarriages) and barbiturates, amphetamines, and tranquilizers. Nonprescription drugs that may cause problems in expectant mothers and/or their babies include aspirin and drugs containing iodine. These drugs are contained in many over-the-counter products, including cold and cough remedies, sleeping aids, and medications that control nausea and vomiting. Many of these drugs also contain alcohol and caffeine, substances that can create adverse effects when large amounts are consumed during pregnancy.

Alcohol has been linked to physical deformities, brain damage, and growth problems among babies born to women who drink as little as two alcoholic beverages a day. For this reason, the National Institute on Alcohol Abuse and Alcoholism advises pregnant women to avoid alcohol completely.

The consumption of excessive quantities of caffeine, which is present in coffee, tea, cola, and chocolate, may be associated with increased risk to the fetus. It is wise, therefore, to limit its use during pregnancy.

Although studies of the effects of smoking during pregnancy have focused on only a few of the four thousand substances contained in cigarette smoke, smoking has been clearly linked to low birthweights and increased rates of infant death. Smoking also increases the risk of miscarriage and other complications. Women who smoke should, therefore, seriously consider stopping or, at least, cutting down during pregnancy. Smoking marijuana during pregnancy has not been extensively studied. The substance does, however, have proven effects on a number of body systems and therefore may present risks to the fetus.

COMMON PROBLEMS

A number of minor digestive problems may also occur during pregnancy. Often, simple modifications in diet can relieve them. Morning sickness, the nausea that frequently occurs during the early months of pregnancy, may be controlled by eating hard candy or crackers when arising or eating frequent small meals throughout the day. Constipation may be relieved by eating more fresh fruits and vegetables and drinking more fluids; diarrhea, an unusual complaint, may be aided by eating more binding foods, such as rice and dry toast. Heartburn, which occurs during the later stages of pregnancy, may be relieved by eating small meals frequently, drinking milk before eating, and sleeping with the head of the bed elevated. When symptoms are severe or persistent, the doctor should be consulted. If medications are prescribed, they should be taken only as directed.

SUMMING UP

Diet plays an important role in the health of pregnant women and their babies. To meet the increased demand for protein, vitamins, and minerals, most expectant mothers should eat an additional 200 to 300 calories of nutritious foods a day. Most doctors recommend a weight gain of at least twenty-five pounds by term. Vitamin and mineral supplements, particularly iron and folic acid, are commonly prescribed to help ensure satisfying the pregnant woman's increased nutritional needs. Pregnant women should avoid excessive smoking, regular use of alcohol, and excessive amounts of caffeine. Self-medicating should be avoided completely; instead, medical problems should be brought to the attention of a doctor, whose directions regarding medications should be followed carefully.

160. Exercise During Pregnancy

GENERAL CONSIDERATIONS

Pregnancy and childbirth are among the most thrilling and rewarding experiences in a woman's life. But they are also among the most physically stressful, which is why a woman should prepare for them as carefully as an athlete training for a particularly challenging contest. Obviously, muscles become stretched and weakened during pregnancy because of weight gain and lack of physical exercise. But with proper conditioning, both the short- and long-term negative consequences of these changes in the muscles can be prevented or minimized. These consequences include sagging abdominal muscles, chronic back problems, and urinary and sexual difficulties.

HOW TO PREPARE YOURSELF

The exercises recommended to prepare for childbirth and recovery are neither strenuous nor complicated. In fact, simple, easy-to-do exercises that involve repetitions of the same basic movements are better than strenuous ones that are repeated only a few times. It is also important to be selective about the muscle groups you exercise. Since the back, pelvis, and abdomen are subjected to the greatest stress during pregnancy, the muscles of these areas should be the focal points of exercise.

PRENATAL PROGRAM

Ideally, the best time to begin physical preparation for pregnancy is before it occurs or in its very early stages. Many women may delay exercising until the fourth or fifth month, but this is still not too late. In fact, most organized prenatal exercise programs focus on the last trimester, or three months, of pregnancy. Remember, however, that the sooner you begin exercising, the better you are likely to feel. For example, an early start in performing exercises that strengthen abdominal muscles makes it easier to support the increasing weight of the fetus. An early start in exercising the pelvic area also has many advantages. Strong, healthy pelvic

Pelvic tilts strengthen the muscles that support the back. Lie on your back with your head resting on crossed arms and your chin tucked in. Pull in your abdomen so that the small of your back is flat on the floor. Tighten buttocks and tilt hips upward. Hold for a count of 10 and relax.

Single-leg raises stretch the lower back and strengthen the abdominal muscles. Lie on your back, arms at your sides. Raise one leg as high as you can without straining. Keep the leg straight and the ankle and toes flexed. Lower slowly.

Double-leg raises strengthen abdominal muscles and stretch leg tendons. Lie on your back with your arms at your sides. Flex your ankles and toes and raise both legs together about 18 inches off the floor and then lower slowly.

Bent-leg sit-ups strengthen abdominal muscles. Lie on your back with knees bent, soles on the floor, chin tucked in and hands clasped behind your head. Raise your trunk about 30 degrees off the floor. Return slowly to starting position.

Deep knee-bends improve posture and balance. Stand with your feet together and your hands resting on a hip-level support. Rise to tiptoe, then lower gradually into deep knee-bend. Slowly return to standing. Keep your thigh muscles tense and your back straight throughout.

muscles permit the vagina to dilate, or widen, more easily during childbirth.

Lower back pain, poor posture, and fatigue are three other very common problems of pregnancy that can be helped by exercise, and all are less likely to be major problems in women who are physically fit. Pregnancy causes the center of gravity in a woman's body to shift forward. Back and postural exercises help strengthen the muscles and other supporting structures, thus minimizing the strain of pregnancy. In addition, they also help to prevent much of the discomfort of postural backache.

POSTPARTUM EXERCISE

In the days immediately following childbirth, stretched and strained muscles begin regaining their former shape and tone. But this is far from an automatic process. Flaccid abdominal, pelvic, and back muscles need activity to regain their original shape. Many experts feel a program of postpartum exercises should begin within twenty-four hours of childbirth; exercise is now a standard part of postoperative care in many hospitals. In general, postpartum exercises should be light—enabling a woman to repeat them many times—rather than strenuous—allowing only two or three repetitions.

The specific exercises depend upon individual needs and problems, but in general they are aimed at strengthening abdominal, back, and pelvic muscles. Because sagging abdominal muscles are so noticeable, many women are anxious to begin work on this area first and with the greatest effort. However, there are two important reasons why the pelvic muscles should receive top priority. First, the sooner they regain their former strength and tautness, the sooner sphincter, hence bladder control, will return to normal. And secondly, strengthening the abdominal muscles before the pelvic muscles increases the pressure on the pelvic floor, further weakening the pelvic muscles.

TIPS FOR EXERCISING

Start Slowly

A warm-up period is an important part of any exercise program. Start gradually and build up to the more demanding exercises. Toward the end of a session, taper off gradually. A good way to do this is to work back through the exercises in reverse order.

Don't Overdo

If you feel tired, breathless, or dizzy during an exercise, stop immediately.

Pay Particular Attention to the Back

Avoid positions and exercises that increase the hollow in the back, which puts extra stress on the stretched abdominal muscles and compresses the spinal joints. Exercise that involves a great amount of leverage also may unnecessarily strain recuperating muscles.

Make Exercise Enjoyable

Many exercise dropouts quit because of boredom. Exercising with a partner, child, or friend also adds variety. Many women find that joining or forming an exercise group not only provides the needed motivation to exercise but also gives them a much needed opportunity to get out of the house.

Incorporate Exercise Into Your Daily Routine

Many household chores or other tasks can double as exercise sessions. For example:

• Tighten the abdominal wall when standing or sitting.
• Get on all fours to wash floors or perform other household tasks.
• Squat to lift any object, light or heavy.
• Rotate ankles while feet are elevated.
• Rotate shoulders after feeding the baby.
• Check posture each time you pass a mirror.

JOGGING AND OTHER ACTIVITIES

Many of the old concepts about the hazards of strenuous exercise during pregnancy have been disproved in recent years. Women in large numbers have joined fitness movements and are jogging alongside men. If you jog, you probably can continue as long as you feel comfortable doing so. However, you should check with your doctor, who may advise you to substitute walking, swimming, or some other physical activity that will not place quite so much strain on the legs, back, and knees.

SUMMING UP

Exercise is important both during pregnancy and in the postpartum period. Exercises should be simple and of the kind that can be repeated many times without causing strain or fatigue, with emphasis on strengthening abdominal, back, and pelvic muscles.

161. Morning Sickness

COMMON CHARACTERISTICS

Nausea during early pregnancy, commonly called morning sickness, is experienced by about four out of five women. Although called morning sickness, it may occur at any time during the day or night. This kind of nausea is one of the earliest signs of pregnancy, and a perfectly normal, albeit unpleasant, condition during the first trimester (three months).

The nausea may be triggered by ordinarily innocuous odors or foods or may not have any immediate cause. Symptoms can be quite mild, passing in a few minutes, or so intense as to cause subsequent vomiting. This type of queasiness is not related to other, more serious gastrointestinal disorders.

CAUSES OF NAUSEA

The causes of morning sickness are not fully understood, although they are believed to be related to altered hormone levels. The increased levels of human chorionic gonadotrophin (HCG), a hormone associated with the formation of the placenta during early pregnancy, are believed to be implicating factors. Pregnancies with higher than the usual levels of HCG (i.e., multiple pregnancies) also have a higher than usual incidence of nausea and vomiting.

CONTROLLING NAUSEA

Most doctors feel that as little medication as possible should be given to pregnant women, especially during the early stages. Drugs cross the placental barrier, having some effect on the developing fetus. In extreme cases, when vomiting may threaten the health of the mother and the child, hospitalization may be required and small doses of antiemetic drugs may be administered. Since prolonged nausea also can result in dehydration, intravenous fluid replacement may be administered. However, this kind of severe vomiting, called hyperemesis, is rare.

The best way of controlling morning sickness is through moderate diet modification. Instead of eating a large breakfast upon awakening, many patients feel better eating only a piece of dry toast or a small serving of dry cereal. Some women find eating Saltines or drinking small amounts of soda effective. During the course of the day, it may be preferable to eat frequent, light meals rather than widely spaced, heavy ones. Consuming fewer fried, fatty, and greasy foods may help, too. It is, of course, essential for the patient to eat well-balanced and nutritious meals throughout pregnancy, whether or not there is nausea.

Morning sickness often vanishes as quickly as it appears. It may be experienced for only a week or so, or, in some cases, it may persist for several months. Usually, it is gone by the fourteenth week, but indigestion in some form is not uncommon in the later stages of pregnancy. If the patient is having a second or third pregnancy, the morning sickness may be more noticeable than it was during previous pregnancies. No two pregnancies are exactly alike, and many women who had no nausea during a first pregnancy have morning sickness the next time around and vice versa.

REMEDIES FOR MORNING SICKNESS

Nausea and vomiting associated with pregnancy usually pass by the end of the first trimester.

Following are treatments for both mild and severe morning sickness:

Mild nausea and vomiting

Eat little and often

Avoid fatty foods

Keep crackers by bedside and have one or two a few minutes before rising in the morning

Avoid very spicy foods

Do not attempt self-medication

Severe nausea and vomiting

Watch for signs of dehydration. If this occurs, hospitalization may be required to give:

Intravenous fluids

Antiemetic drugs

Gradual oral refeeding

SUMMING UP

For most women, the first trimester of pregnancy is an exciting and confusing time. The body undergoes a variety of changes to accommodate the growing fetus. During this time, it is normal to feel moody or cranky without a direct cause. You may also experience periods of enormous elation and well-being. Morning sickness is simply one of those symptoms that, like water retention, food cravings, and constipation, is annoying but neither serious nor permanent.

If the nausea does not stop by the fourth or fifth month, or if vomiting has become too frequent or has led to weight loss, a doctor should be seen as soon as possible. Medication for the nausea should not be taken without consulting a doctor. Even mild, over-the-counter remedies may have a serious effect on fetal development.

162. Diabetes and Pregnancy

GENERAL CONSIDERATIONS

If you have diabetes, your pregnancy will differ considerably from that of a woman without the disorder. It is important to be aware of these differences and the risks they may involve so that you and your doctor can work together toward a successful outcome.

Careful control of the diabetes throughout your pregnancy will help prevent the fetus from growing too large and will minimize the risk of dangerous complications, premature labor, and stillbirth. And after delivery your baby will need to be treated with special care, since infants born to diabetic mothers tend to be fragile.

Pregnancy puts strain on a woman's body and even a mild diabetes tends to become more severe during the course of the nine months.

INSULIN VARIABILITY

During the first trimester (the period from conception through the thirteenth week) the need for insulin often decreases. The reduced insulin requirements—and the increased need later in pregnancy—are related to the normal effects of pregnancy on the metabolism of the mother. Because of the decreased need for insulin, early pregnancy may be marked by episodes of hypoglycemia (a low level of blood glucose), especially if you are also suffering from morning sickness. The onset of hypoglycemia is usually fairly rapid, with sweating and symptoms that include irritability and a tingling tongue. There is generally time to counteract it by taking sugar or some quick energy food. Glucagon, which can quickly correct low blood sugar, is rarely used in pregnancy as it may cause severe nausea. It is best to have your doctor frequently adjust your dose of insulin to prevent any such hypoglycemic episodes. It is also important to have three meals and three snacks daily.

During pregnancy, urine tests sometimes show a large amount of sugar when the blood sugar is not alarmingly high. The increased flow of blood through the kidneys (a normal effect of pregnancy) results in more sugar than usual passing through the tubules without being reabsorbed. For this reason, insulin requirements in pregnancy are better monitored by periodic blood sugar tests than by urinary sugar levels.

During the second trimester (weeks 13 through 27) the diabetes may become more difficult to control. The need for insulin usually increases and continues as the pregnancy progresses toward term. Difficulty in control during the second trimester is due to insulin resistance—just like that of the nonpregnant obese patient. It is extremely important at this time to prevent excessively high blood sugar levels in the mother (and thereby in her fetus). With high blood sugar, the fetus may grow too big and may have breathing difficulties if early delivery becomes necessary.

Ketoacidosis, which occurs when the body uses fat as a substitute for glucose to provide energy, is a frequent complication of middle pregnancy. It may be dangerous to the fetus. Acetone in the urine, unquenchable thirst, nausea, and difficulty in breathing are danger signals and should be reported promptly to your doctor. If ketoacidosis occurs, greater quantities of insulin will be needed to restore acceptable blood sugar levels than are needed in a nonpregnant state.

Immediately after delivery, insulin requirements may be very low, so that there is almost a partial remission of the diabetes. At this time, insulin is usually started at one-third to two-thirds of the prepregnancy dose.

Your doctor will probably wish to examine you every week throughout your pregnancy to check on how your diabetes is being controlled. In addition to these weekly checkups, it is advised that pregnant women monitor their blood sugar frequently, using a home glucose-monitoring device, so that any difficulties in controlling the diabetes are quickly apparent.

PREGNANCY-ONSET DIABETES

It is not unusual for diabetes to appear for the first time during pregnancy. Often referred to as pregnancy-onset diabetes, it occurs most often in prospective mothers over age thirty-five. It is also more common in women who are overweight and who have a family history of the disease. Very often, the diabetes disappears after childbirth.

The diabetes is usually detected by routine urine testing for sugar during prenatal checkups. Diet may be recommended for mild cases, but increasingly, insulin is used to control the levels of blood sugar.

OTHER CONSIDERATIONS

During your checkups, your physician will look for certain factors that sometimes complicate a diabetic pregnancy.

Hydramnios (excessive amniotic fluid in the uterus) occurs in as many as one in five diabetic pregnancies. It is uncomfortable for the mother and has serious implications for the fetus. With hydramnios, there is a high frequency of premature labor and of congenital anomaly in the fetus. An indication of hydramnios is excessive weight gain, and an objective of treatment throughout pregnancy is to control weight.

Pre-eclampsia is another potentially serious complication of pregnancy. In its most severe form (eclampsia) it can result in seizures, which are dangerous to both mother and fetus. The early symptoms are edema, an abnormal rise in blood pressure, and the presence of protein in the urine. A carefully balanced, highly nutritious diet, together with adequate rest, may reduce the risk of pre-eclampsia. Late in pregnancy, bed rest may be advised.

A few women with diabetes develop pregnancy headaches. Several days of hospitalization are occasionally needed to relieve this problem. Anemia and urinary tract infections are common to all pregnant women; frequent examinations of blood and urine are done to determine whether treatment is needed.

WOMEN AT RISK TO DEVELOP DIABETES DURING PREGNANCY

RISK FACTOR	EXPLANATION
Age	Most common in women over age 35
Obesity	Adult diabetes more common in overweight people
Family history	Risk increases if close relatives have adult-onset diabetes
High blood pressure	Disease more common in hypertensives
History of big babies	Birthweight of 9½ pounds or more of earlier babies indicates possibility of diabetes
Sugar in urine	Common symptom of hyperglycemia (excessive blood sugar)

THE TIMING OF DELIVERY

The expected date of birth is usually calculated from the date of the last menstrual period, a full-term pregnancy being one of forty weeks' duration. (Additional information is provided by the initial pelvic examination, the size of the uterus, the time at which the fetal heart is first heard, and the size of the fetus's head as measured by ultrasound.) In diabetic women, however, irregular menses are common, and estimations based on the date of the last period may be incorrect.

It may be necessary for a woman with diabetes to be delivered before term, since there is a risk that the fetus may die in the uterus during the last few weeks of pregnancy. On the other hand, early delivery may result in the death of the newborn from respiratory distress syndrome if the baby's lungs are not sufficiently mature. The risk can be determined by measuring the amounts of two fatty substances (sphingomyelin and lecithin) in the amniotic fluid, which is obtained by inserting a needle into the uterus in a procedure called amniocentesis.

Other tests that may be performed toward the end of pregnancy to assess the fetus's health include hormone tests on blood or on twenty-four-hour collections of urine. Sonograms using ultrasound waves are helpful in estimating the growth of the fetus's head and thereby indicating maturity.

DELIVERY

If labor does not occur spontaneously, it can often be induced by rupture of the membranes enclosing the fetus (the amniotic sac), along with intravenous administration of the hormone oxytocin to stimulate contractions. If delivery is necessary to protect the baby and the uterus is not ready for induction of labor—or if there are other obstetrical indications—a Caesarean section will be done. The babies of diabetic women are often large, despite close control of the diabetes during pregnancy; the size of the fetus may determine the need for a Caesarean section.

The doctor will consider an emergency delivery for the sake of the fetus's health if pre-eclampsia worsens, if the requirement for insulin drops suddenly to prepregnancy levels, or if the fetus becomes inactive and tests show fetal distress. If, toward the end of pregnancy, you do not feel your fetus move for a period of eight hours, you should contact your doctor immediately.

THE NEWBORN'S HEALTH

All newborn babies have low blood sugars, but those whose mothers are diabetic have levels lower than normal and require glucose. Because they are often premature, the infants of diabetic mothers may have some respiratory distress that requires oxygen and intravenous treatment. They commonly develop jaundice and need special treatment for this condition in the neonatal nursery. Congenital anomalies occur with more than the usual frequency when the mother has diabetes. However, many of these anomalies are minor, and many can easily be corrected.

SUMMING UP

The pregnancy of a woman with diabetes differs in many ways from that of a woman who does not have the condition. In addition to being at a higher risk of several of the complications that may occur in any pregnancy, a diabetic woman has an increased risk of stillbirth and of having a very large baby or one with a congenital anomaly. In many diabetic pregnancies, it is necessary to deliver the baby before term, either by induction of labor or by Caesarean section.

It cannot be overemphasized that close control of diabetes during pregnancy will improve the chance for a happy, successful outcome. A simple blood test that diabetics can do daily themselves has markedly improved the ability to monitor the disease and prevent wide variations in blood sugar.

163. Amniocentesis

GENERAL CONSIDERATIONS

Great progress has been made in recent years toward identifying, early in pregnancy, fetuses affected by serious genetic diseases and conditions. The prenatal testing technique most commonly used is amniocentesis. It is a very important part of obstetrical care, especially since increasing numbers of women are becoming pregnant in their thirties and forties, a time when the fetus is more likely to be affected by a congenital defect.

Amniocentesis involves drawing and testing a sample of the amniotic fluid that surrounds the fetus in the uterus. Tests currently available are extremely accurate in detecting a large number of chromosomal abnormalities, congenital metabolic disorders, and spinal cord (neural tube) defects. In addition, tests can determine the sex of the fetus, a vital piece of information when there is a risk of inheriting a sex-linked disease such as hemophilia.

THE PROCEDURE

Amniotic fluid surrounds and protects the fetus in the uterus. The fluid begins to collect early in pregnancy, and by term as much as a quart has accumulated. Secretions from the fetus and cells shed by it are always present in the fluid; thus, analyzing it can provide information about the fetus's condition at a very early gestational stage.

In order to take a sample of the amniotic fluid, a long, fine needle is inserted through the abdominal and uterine walls and into the amniotic sac. (A local anesthetic is used during the procedure.) An ounce of fluid, or less, is then withdrawn through a syringe. Ultrasonography, a "sound wave" technique, is used to help guide the needle, preventing it from injuring either the fetus or the placenta.

Amniocentesis should be done between the fifteenth and the eighteenth weeks of pregnancy. At this stage, there is plenty of fluid available for testing, and if a defect is diagnosed and the couple decides not to continue with the pregnancy, there is time to terminate it before the legal limit of twenty-four weeks. There is a small risk of cramping, bleeding, or leakage of amniotic fluid, but these problems affect only two or three of one hundred women. The risk of miscarriage following amniocentesis is even smaller: about one in one hundred.

The sample of amniotic fluid is sent to a laboratory, where fluid and cells are separated. The fluid is tested for alpha-fetoprotein (AFP), which is produced in the fetal liver. High levels of AFP suggest a number of different abnormalities, including failure of the spine to close properly, failure of the abdomen to join, and an obstruction in the gastrointestinal or urinary tracts. The cells are cultured and, after several weeks, are examined under a microscope. This examination may reveal a chromosomal abnormality of one of the approximately seventy detectable metabolic disorders.

The accuracy of the testing in amniocentesis is very high—better than 99 percent. However, it is important to realize that, with one exception, tests are specific for a single condition. Each test, that is, can answer only one question. What question is asked will depend on the risk of a particular abnormality appearing in the offspring of a particular couple. A number of circumstances may suggest risk, among them the birth of a child with a defect or a family history of a particular disease or condition.

INDICATIONS FOR AMNIOCENTESIS

Because the procedure carries some risk, albeit a small one, and because it is expensive, amniocentesis is not a routine pregnancy test. It is, however, now done routinely in women over thirty-five, who have a significantly higher risk than younger women of bearing a child with a chromosomal defect. The most common defect of this type is Down's syndrome (trisomy 21), formerly known as mongolism. The risk of bearing a child with this incurable syndrome—it includes mental retardation and characteristic facial and bodily deformity—rises with age, from 1 in 300 at age thirty-five to 1 in 30 at age forty-five. The risk of other chromosomal abnormalities follows a similar pattern; a woman who is aged thirty-five to thirty-nine when she gives birth has a 1 in 70 risk of bearing a child with a chromosomal defect.

For pregnant women of any age, amniocentesis is recommended when a previous child has been born with a chromosomal defect or a neural tube defect. The test should also be done when either parent has a known risk of a disease that can be diagnosed prenatally or is known to have a translocation (abnormal arrangement) of the chromosomes. Further, it should be performed when both parents are known to be carriers of an autosomal disease such as Tay-Sachs disease.

Carriers of sex-linked diseases such as hemophilia should also be tested. Hemophilia itself cannot at present be safely diagnosed prenatally, but tests on the am-

Amniocentesis involves the insertion of a long needle into the uterus and withdrawing a small amount of the fluid surrounding the fetus. A local anesthetic is used to insert the needle, and an ultrasound monitor shows the doctor performing the test the exact location of the fetus to prevent any harm to the unborn baby.

niotic fluid can reveal the sex of the fetus. If the fetus is a male, there is an even chance that it will be affected by the disease.

Amniocentesis can be used to confirm the presence of Rh-disease in a fetus and to determine its seriousness. If the fetus's red blood cells are being destroyed rapidly by maternal antibodies, Rh-immune gamma globulin can be given to treat the condition *in utero.*

THE GOALS AND LIMITATIONS OF PRENATAL TESTING

The main goal of prenatal testing is to detect birth defects early in pregnancy so that an abortion can be performed if the parents so decide. (If they decide not to terminate the pregnancy, the diagnosis may be useful in helping them prepare for the care of a defective child.) However, in approximately 95 percent of cases, no abnormality is found. Thus, an important result of testing is that it provides reassurance to high-risk couples that a particular defect is not present.

It should be remembered that tests cannot cover all possible abnormalities and that, therefore, prenatal testing does not guarantee that a child will be born normal. A tested fetus which has been shown to be without one particular defect still runs the risk (4 percent) of being born defective that all babies do.

AMNIOCENTESIS IN LATE PREGNANCY

Premature infants have a high risk of respiratory problems at and shortly after birth, due to the immaturity of their lungs. The seriousness of the risk can be determined prenatally, by estimating the amount of two fatty substances—sphingomyelin and lecithin—in the amniotic fluid. The test can determine when it is safest to deliver the baby and how best to treat the infant once it is born.

SUMMING UP

Amniocentesis cannot guarantee a normal, healthy baby. It can, however—and in the great majority of cases, it does—reassure couples at high risk that their child will not be affected by a particular genetic disease. It is a test that should be performed on all pregnant women thirty-five years old or older since their age alone, regardless of other factors, puts these women at risk of bearing a congenitally defective child.

Amniocentesis is an extremely safe and virtually painless procedure. The test results are 99 percent accurate.

164. Normal Labor

COMMON CHARACTERISTICS

No labor is exactly like any other. There is, however, a sequence of events that is common to all normal or uncomplicated labors. When expectant women (and their partners) are aware of what can be expected to happen during labor—literally, the work of bringing a child into the world —there is less anxiety and tension, and consequently less pain.

Labor has three stages. The first lasts from the onset of labor to the time when the cervix at the base of the uterus is fully widened (dilated). In the second stage, the baby is pressed down through the birth canal; this stage culminates with the actual birth. In the third stage, the placenta and the fetal membranes are expelled. A normal labor may take up to twenty-four hours with a first baby; subsequent labors are shorter, lasting from three to twelve hours.

DUE DATE

The duration of a pregnancy is generally calculated as being forty weeks (280 days) from the first day of the last menstrual period. Only 5 percent of all babies, however, are born on the due date or expected date of confinement (EDC). Of the others, 90 percent are born within ten days either side of the EDC, the majority being "late."

ONSET OF LABOR

The first sign that labor is about to start may be a blood-stained discharge of mucus from the vagina, the so-called show. During pregnancy, this mucus has acted as a plug in the cervix, sealing off the uterus. Its appearance indicates that there are changes occurring in the area of the cervix. However, sometimes the show appears two or three weeks before labor begins; it should not be taken as a certain signal that labor is imminent.

Another sign that labor may be about to begin is the breaking of the bag of waters, the amniotic sac that surrounds the baby in the uterus. The sac may break suddenly, with a rush of fluid; more often, there is a slow leakage. In most cases, contractions start within a few hours of the breaking of the bag of waters. (If the sac breaks several weeks before the EDC, the doctor should be informed at once since there is a danger of infection to the baby in a long latent period.)

A third sign of labor is the beginning of contractions. The sensation is that of being gripped by a tightening muscular belt around the lower part of the abdomen and the small of the back. The sensation builds up, retreats, and is followed by a resting period. The contractions may be those of "false" labor, in which case they will taper off within a few hours. If, however, they are coming regularly, with increasing frequency, and are lasting for twenty seconds or more, labor can confidently be said to have begun.

During a contraction, the muscles at the top of the uterus tighten, pressing inward and downward and pulling the tissues of the cervix up into the lower part of the uterus. When the baby's presenting part (usually the head) is pressed down onto the cervix by a contraction, the tissues of the cervix stretch apart. The cervical area is the source of most of the sensations that are felt during a contraction, apart from the tightening of the muscles at the top of the uterus.

When contractions are regular and are coming at five-minute intervals, it is time to go to the hospital or birthing center.

ADMISSION

At the hospital, an internal examination will be done to determine the extent to which the cervix is dilated. An enema or suppository may be given to empty the lower bowel, and the hair surrounding the vagina may be shaved. However, this "prepping" is not done routinely on women in active labor, as was the case in the past.

If the bag of waters has not broken, and the cervix is three to four centimeters dilated, an amniotomy (artificial rupture of the membranes) may be done. This procedure is routine in many hospitals. Amniotomy speeds up labor since, once the cushioning fluid is released, the baby's head presses more firmly against the cervix and triggers stronger contractions.

In most hospitals today, an external electronic fetal monitor is put in place as a matter of course when a woman in labor is admitted. The device, held by straps

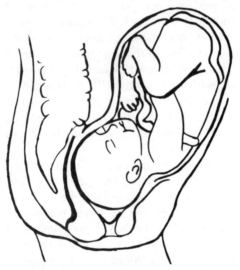

At the second stage of labor, pictured here, the cervix is fully dilated to 10 cm., and the uterus and vagina have joined to make a single birth canal.

around the abdomen, provides a continuous record of the fetal heart rate and the pressure of the uterine contractions—and thus early notice of fetal distress. Birthing centers, which emphasize a less technological approach, omit many of these preparatory procedures. A vaginal examination, however, will be performed by the midwife or doctor in attendance.

THE FIRST STAGE OF LABOR

The first stage of labor may take several hours, and occasionally more than a day. As it progresses, contractions become stronger and come increasingly closer together; they have a regular rhythm and a wavelike pattern, each building to a peak intensity before it subsides. By the end of the first stage, when the cervix is seven to eight centimeters dilated, contractions last for forty to fifty seconds and tend to become arrhythmic, with two or more sharp peaks occurring in each. For many women, this is the most difficult part of labor.

THE SECOND STAGE OF LABOR

The second stage of labor begins when the cervix is fully dilated (ten centimeters), making the uterus and the vagina into a single birth canal. Whereas in the first stage a woman is largely passive, the work being done by the uterine muscles, in the second stage the pressure of the baby's head creates a strong urge to push, or bear down, with each contraction. With a first baby, this stage takes one or two hours; with subsequent births, it may last as little as ten minutes.

Second-stage contractions come every two minutes and last a minute or more. With each, there may be as many as five separate brief urges to bear down, pressing the baby along the birth canal. When the baby "crowns"—that is, when the widest part of the head is at the vaginal opening and remains there between contractions—a woman will be asked *not* to bear down since doing so may tear the perineum (the area between the anus and the vagina). A surgical incision to enlarge the birth opening (episiotomy) may be done at this point, under local anesthesia, especially when a woman is having her first child. Only a few contractions separate crowning from delivery.

DELIVERY

At delivery, the baby's head usually faces downward. Once it is free, the head rotates to come into line with the shoulders, still turned sideways in the birth canal. The doctor or midwife presses the baby's head down, so that the upper shoulder can be delivered, then raises the head to free the lower one. The rest of the infant's body then quickly follows. The umbilical cord is then clamped and cut.

The infant may breathe and cry spontaneously and immediately. If not, he or she will be held with the head down and the back will be gently rubbed until a breath is taken. A suction tube may be used to clear any mucus out of the respiratory tract.

At birth, the baby may be covered with a fatty substance, vernix. The skull may be pointed or asymmetrical since the spaces between the skullbones, the fontanels, close up as the baby passes along the birth canal. The forehead may recede, and the infant may have only a very small chin. The nose may be flattened, and there may be red marks between the eyes and on the eyelids. All this is entirely normal.

THE THIRD STAGE OF LABOR

After the baby is born, contractions continue, separating the placenta from the lining of the uterus and then expelling both it and the fetal membranes. This third stage of labor usually takes five to ten minutes. Further uterine contractions, which are stimulated by the baby's sucking at the breast, prevent excessive bleeding from the raw surface where the placenta was attached.

After the placenta and membranes are delivered, the episiotomy—if this was done—will be sutured, a process that may take as long as an hour.

PAIN IN LABOR

Women who are physically well prepared for childbirth, who understand what is happening, and who have a supportive partner or relative with them during their labor, often find that they are able to deliver their babies with little pain and without requiring drugs. This is advantageous, since all drugs cross the placental barrier and affect the baby to a greater or lesser extent. However, if pain is experienced during labor, this should be freely acknowledged—labor is not a test of stoicism.

Medications for the relief of pain in childbirth range from analgesics (Demerol, for example) and tranquilizers to local anesthetics that numb the nerves covering large areas of the body (regional anesthetics). Epidural anesthesia, in which the anesthetic is injected in the middle of the back, blocking sensation from the waist down, is the form of regional anesthesia most commonly used. An anesthetic of this kind allows a woman to remain conscious, but her active participation in the second stage of labor will depend on coaching from her partner or attendants.

SUMMING UP

While every labor is unique, all labors follow the same sequence from onset through the delivery of the placenta. Those women who know what to expect during a normal labor, who are physically prepared for the hard work involved, and who have the emotional support of a partner or friend, are the most likely to find the experience of childbirth fulfilling and relatively pain-free.

165. Miscarriage and Premature Labor

Miscarriage, or spontaneous abortion, refers to the process by which a fetus is expelled from the womb at any time up to and including the twentieth week of pregnancy. Premature labor, on the other hand, refers to the onset of the labor—and the delivery of a child, frequently alive—between the twentieth and twenty-seventh weeks (the normal gestation period is thirty-eight weeks). Both are serious, or potentially serious, complications of pregnancy and demand immediate medical attention.

MISCARRIAGE

About one in ten pregnancies ends in miscarriage. Three-quarters of these spontaneous abortions occur in the first trimester, most of them between the sixth and the tenth weeks. The first warning sign is usually vaginal bleeding. If you have bleeding other than the slightest spotting early in your pregnancy, you should call your doctor; if the bleeding is heavy and associated with cramping, you should make arrangements to be taken to the hospital.

CATEGORIES OF MISCARRIAGE

Spontaneous abortions can be grouped into several categories. Many women experience a threatened abortion early in pregnancy. The usual signs are vaginal bleeding or spotting, often accompanied by cramping. With bed rest, the process may stop, and the pregnancy may proceed normally. However, the process may continue and become what is called an inevitable abortion: the fetus has died, and miscarriage cannot be prevented by medical means. Bleeding becomes profuse; there are strong uterine contractions and progressive cervical dilation. The fetus, amniotic sac, and placenta may be expelled entirely (a complete abortion). An incomplete abortion must be completed by a doctor, to protect against serious infection. Usually, a dilation and curettage (D & C) is done, cleaning the uterus so that it will heal.

Occasionally a fetus will die but be retained in the uterus. This is known as a missed abortion. The death of the fetus can be determined by ultrasound techniques. A dilation and curettage is usually performed as soon as the diagnosis is certain; alternatively, labor may be induced if the loss occurs later in pregnancy.

If a woman has several consecutive miscarriages, she is said to have habitual abortion. This condition may be due to hormonal imbalance or uterine or chromosomal abnormalities.

CAUSES

Possible causes of a miscarriage may include some form of fetal abnormality, a structural defect of the uterus, or a hormonal imbalance in the mother. (A fall or minor accident seldom results in miscarriage because the fetus is well protected in the uterus.)

In the great majority of cases, the fetus

is abnormal. Genetic defects, maternal syphilis, drugs, and emotional stress severe enough to effect hormonal imbalance are among the causes of the type of fetal abnormality that leads to miscarriage. Excessive caffeine and alcohol use, heavy smoking, and poor maternal nutrition also play a role. The high rate of abnormality among miscarried fetuses is in its way a

reassurance that a pregnancy reaching the sixth month will most likely result in a healthy baby.

AFTER A MISCARRIAGE

Intercourse can usually be resumed within two to four weeks after a miscarriage, or when the cervix has closed. An-

Premature Labor

If labor begins before term, the physician must decide what is likely to be best for the baby: to go ahead with delivery or to try to stop labor and delay the birth.

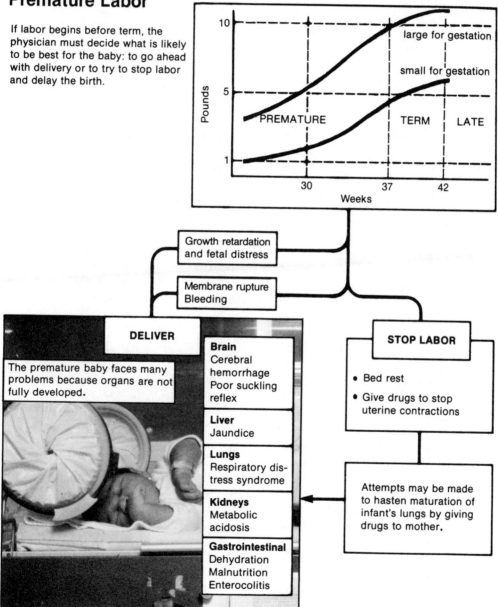

The premature baby faces many problems because organs are not fully developed.

DELIVER

Brain
Cerebral hemorrhage
Poor suckling reflex

Liver
Jaundice

Lungs
Respiratory distress syndrome

Kidneys
Metabolic acidosis

Gastrointestinal
Dehydration
Malnutrition
Enterocolitis

Growth retardation and fetal distress

Membrane rupture
Bleeding

STOP LABOR
• Bed rest
• Give drugs to stop uterine contractions

Attempts may be made to hasten maturation of infant's lungs by giving drugs to mother.

other pregnancy can be planned after one or two normal menstrual cycles.

Miscarriages come at what should be a joyful time: the beginning of a pregnancy. Grief and anger are common—and normal—emotional reactions. Feelings of grief are often complicated by guilt, causing tension between a woman and her sexual partner. They may, for example, needlessly reproach themselves and each other for having had intercourse too frequently. It is important to understand that such factors are not responsible for a miscarriage. Another common feeling is fear that the miscarriage may signal infertility, but in most cases, a subsequent pregnancy is normal.

PREMATURE LABOR

In about 5 percent of all pregnant women, labor begins before term, sometimes well before the expected date of delivery. The outcome for the infant depends greatly on how premature the labor is, what kind of neonatal care is available, and the infant's own weight and functional development. Every ounce can make a difference. Of babies who weigh two pounds at birth, about 50 percent can survive given appropriate medical treatment; at three pounds or more, a baby has a better than 90 percent chance of life.

Poor general health, heavy cigarette smoking, and inadequate nutrition increase the likelihood of premature labor. Specific causes include infectious diseases such as syphilis, pre-eclampsia (a disorder characterized by high blood pressure, edema, and protein in the urine), and eclampsia (similar to pre-eclampsia, with convulsions or coma), thyroid disturbances, diabetes, and placental abnormalities. Occasionally, premature labor is triggered by physical trauma, such as a bad fall. Even more rarely an emotional shock may be responsible. However, in nearly half the cases, there is no identifiable explanation.

SYMPTOMS AND MANAGEMENT

The first sign of premature labor is usually the beginning of regular uterine contractions. Sometimes there is vaginal bleeding, increased vaginal discharge, or vaginal pressure. Premature rupture of the membranes (the amniotic sac), which results in a flow of water (amniotic fluid) from the vagina, occurs in 20 to 25 percent of all premature deliveries.

Examination by your physician is imperative. He or she will probably recommend that you enter a medical center equipped for the care of preterm infants, if such a facility is available. The duration and frequency of the contractions will be observed, and the extent of cervical dilation and effacement (thinning) will be determined. In addition, the fetus's heartbeat will be monitored.

Depending on the circumstances, the doctor may decide to proceed with preterm delivery, or to administer a drug to suppress labor. (Only 25 percent of all cases of premature labor, however, are candidates for labor-suppression drug therapy.) It is almost impossible to stop premature labor that is associated with vaginal bleeding or rupture of the membranes.

CHANCES OF SURVIVAL

More than ever before, premature infants are surviving, and without the complications or permanent damage experienced in the past. Most large medical centers now have special facilities and teams to care for preterm babies; in other instances, the baby may be taken to a regional center that offers such facilities.

SUMMING UP

The birth of a premature infant often finds the parents emotionally unprepared. Feelings of guilt and anxiety about the baby are very frequently associated with a premature delivery. In many instances, the hospital's precautions add to the anxiety. For example, premature infants are particularly susceptible to infections—the more premature, the more susceptible. On the more positive side, premature babies today stand a much better chance of normal survival.

166. Abortion

GENERAL OVERVIEW

Abortion refers to the interruption of pregnancy before term. It can be either spontaneous, in which case it is usually referred to as a miscarriage (see Chapter 165, "Miscarriage and Premature Labor"); therapeutic, when the mother's life is threatened or the baby is likely to have a major genetic defect; or voluntary or elective.

Abortions or attempted abortions have been performed for thousands of years. The oldest known method was used some 4,600 years ago by the Chinese, who resorted to having the mother swallow mercury—a potentially lethal poison as dangerous for the mother as for the unborn child. The development of modern abortion techniques, however, has made the procedure relatively safe and simple, especially when it is done in the early stages of pregnancy.

Abortions, however, may still take a great emotional toll. No matter how valid the reasons for the abortion, many women experience guilt, depression, or anger. Emotional problems should be faced and dealt with by talking to a physician, social worker, friend, or other counselor as well as with the sex partner. The abortion technique used depends on the length of pregnancy and the preference of the physician and patient.

The most common methods involve the use of suction and/or curettage (scraping) to empty the uterus. These methods can be used only in early, usually first-trimester, abortions; later, or second-trimester, abortions may require inducing early labor with injections of saline or urea or administering prostaglandins to stimulate uterine contractions.

BEFORE THE ABORTION

Before any abortion procedure, the physician should examine the patient and perform tests to determine that she is, indeed, pregnant. Other standard tests, such as a blood count and urinalysis, also may be performed. The doctor should be informed of any medical problems, including chronic diseases, infections, use of any medications—both prescription and nonprescription—and whether there have been any prior abortions, miscarriages, or complications of pregnancy.

MENSTRUAL EXTRACTION

The earliest type of abortion, which must be performed within a few days of an overdue period, involves using a mini-suction procedure known as menstrual extraction. A soft plastic tube is inserted into the uterus, and the lining is gently vacuumed, causing it to slough off as in a regular period. When this procedure was first developed, it often was done before the period was overdue if there was a good chance of pregnancy. More recently, however, tests have been developed that can detect very early pregnancy, eliminating the need to perform menstrual extraction on nonpregnant women. Even so, there may be instances in which a woman would prefer to have a menstrual extraction without firmly establishing whether she is pregnant, thus avoiding difficult emotional decisions.

EARLY ABORTIONS

Early abortions are those performed in the first trimester or three months of pregnancy. Most involve using some sort of

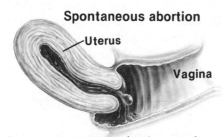

Spontaneous abortion

Uterus

Vagina

During a spontaneous abortion, or miscarriage, the embryo and the lining of the uterus are expelled into the vagina.

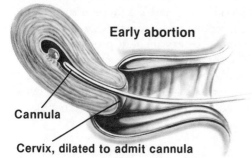

Early abortion

Cannula

Cervix, dilated to admit cannula

A cannula is threaded through the cervix, previously dilated, and into the uterus. The uterine contents are withdrawn by suction.

suction to empty the uterus. When the method was first developed, a syringe was used. Today, however, more sophisticated machines equipped with pressure gauges are used.

A flexible plastic tube, called a cannula, is threaded through the cervical canal and into the uterus. Before this can be done, the canal must be widened or dilated; the degree of dilation required will depend upon the length of the pregnancy. As would be expected, the degree of dilation increases with the duration of the pregnancy. Dilation may be accomplished by inserting a series of graduated metal rods, known as dilators, into the canal. The first one is about half the diameter of a pencil, with the size increasing until the needed cervical widening is accomplished. In general, dilation occurs more rapidly in women who have had children.

An alternative method of dilation involves using laminaria tents, commonly called Japanese seaweeds. These are organic reeds that swell when exposed to moisture and thus dilate the cervical canal gradually. They are usually inserted the day before the abortion because the dilation may take several hours to accomplish.

Once the cervical canal is sufficiently widened, the cannula is inserted and the suction machine withdraws the contents of the uterus. The suction may be followed by a curettage, in which the doctor gently scrapes the uterine lining with a surgical instrument called a curette. The entire suction procedure takes about ten minutes or less and is generally painless, although there may be some cramping and discomfort. If curettage is performed, a local anesthetic is used.

SECOND-TRIMESTER ABORTIONS

Abortions performed after the sixteenth week—or so—of pregnancy are referred to as instillation abortions and involve inducing labor to expel the uterine contents.

They are usually carried out in a hospital or special clinic and involve more risk than the earlier suction abortions.

Labor is induced by instilling saline or urea (a compound found in blood, lymph, and urine) into the amniotic sac, or by administering prostaglandins. These are hormonelike substances that, in this instance, cause the uterine muscles to contract. The prostaglandins may be administered by injection or by using a tampon containing the substance. Abortions accomplished by the saline or urea injections or by using prostaglandins may take twenty-four hours or a little longer to complete and usually entail a hospital stay of two or three days.

POSTABORTION CARE

Although abortion is now a relatively safe procedure, it is not entirely without risk. Any abnormal or very heavy bleeding is a warning sign to see a doctor immedi-ately. Infection, although not as common as in the past, is also a danger. To minimize the risk, antibiotics are sometimes given prophylactically after an abortion, especially if the woman has a history of vaginal or other infections. Women also are advised to refrain from having intercourse for a week or so and from using tampons immediately following an abortion.

SUMMING UP

Although abortion today is relatively painless and safe, it remains a highly controversial issue with moral, legal, ethical, and emotional overtones. The need for abortions should be minimized through the use of reliable contraception. If pregnancy is the result of a contraceptive failure, a doctor should be consulted to advise an alternative or more reliable contraceptive.

167. Breast Feeding Your Baby

GENERAL CONSIDERATIONS

Today, one new mother in four breast-feeds her baby, and the number seems to be increasing. With support and encouragement from her partner, her doctor and other medical professionals, and her family, almost every woman can nurse her baby successfully. The most important factor is that she really want to do so. She will then be willing to persevere when setbacks occur, as they almost invariably do.

REASONS FOR CHOOSING BREAST FEEDING

Many women choose to breast-feed primarily because this is the most natural and in many ways the simplest way of nourishing a baby. (Breast milk is always available, needs no preparation, and is always at the right temperature.) In addition, most women find breast feeding a physically pleasurable and emotionally satisfying experience.

A strong argument in favor of breast

feeding is the fact that the nutritional substances contained in human milk are ideal, both in quality and quantity, for the baby's growth and development. For example, the fat in human milk is easily absorbed by the infant, and its high content of lactose (a sugar) provides an excellent, readily available source of energy. Often infants who can tolerate no other food have no difficulty in digesting human milk.

Breast milk and colostrum (the substance secreted by the breasts before the milk "comes in") have the further advantage of providing immunity to disease for the first months of the baby's life. Colostrum is especially high in maternal antibodies, protecting the newborn against a number of bacterial and viral infections, including infant diarrhea. It is largely because of the immunity conferred by breast milk in the first few weeks that many doctors recommend that women nurse their babies for at least a month, even when they know that they will be unable to continue.

Breast feeding is better adapted than bottle feeding to satisfy the baby's sucking instinct. A breast-fed baby can suck for as long as he or she needs—there is always a little fresh milk being produced in the breast—without being overfed. Breast feeding also provides the close physical contact that has been shown to be of importance for the future emotional well-being of the child. While a bottle-fed baby may also experience this, if the person doing the feeding holds the infant closely, it is an integral part of breast feeding.

There are valid reasons for not nursing a baby—among them the wish that the father share in the infant's care. However, one reason that is sometimes given—fear of losing one's figure—is not supported by the facts. If care is taken to prevent stretching of the skin and the tissues of the breasts by wearing a well-fitting bra both during the latter part of pregnancy and during lactation, there is no reason to anticipate that nursing a baby will flatten the breasts.

Many women nurse several children with no ill effects.

THE BREASTS AND BREAST MILK

Within each breast, embedded in fatty tissue, are some fifteen to twenty groups of milk-producing glands. A milk duct runs from each group to a sinus or sac in the center of the breast behind the areola (the dark area of skin surrounding the nipple), and thence to a tiny opening in the nipple. The areola itself contains a number of small sebaceous glands, which function to keep the nipple from becoming stiff and dry.

During pregnancy, the milk-duct system of the breasts enlarges, as the result of an increased secretion of the ovarian hormone estrogen. Another hormone, pro-

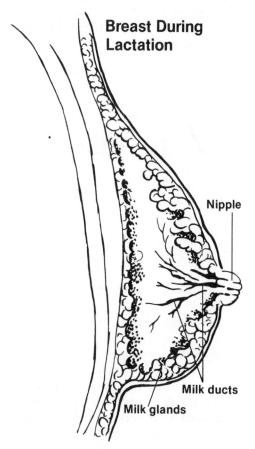

Breast During Lactation

Nipple

Milk ducts

Milk glands

gesterone, causes the milk-secreting tissues within the breast to proliferate. These changes account for the steady increase in size and weight of the breasts as pregnancy progresses.

Shortly after delivery, the breasts begin to secrete small quantities of the precursor substance, colostrum. Within three or four days—sometimes earlier in a woman who has a previous child—true milk appears. This may be a gradual process, but in many women the milk "comes in" so quickly and strongly that the breasts become engorged —swollen, hard, and sometimes very painful (see illustration, p. 464).

It takes about a week before the supply of milk is well established. During this time the baby will lose weight. It should be remembered, however, that all babies lose weight initially. Those who are bottle-fed regain their birthweight more rapidly simply because nourishment is immediately available.

Regular nursing helps establish the supply of milk. When a baby is nursing properly, as most instinctively do, not only the nipple but the entire areolar area is taken into the mouth. The sinuses, which lie directly behind the areola, are squeezed by the action of the baby's gums, and milk is forced out through the nipple. It is the regular emptying of the sinuses that stimulates the glands to produce milk. Supply keeps pace with demand: as the baby grows and nurses longer and more vigorously, more milk is produced.

FEEDINGS

At first, many women find it more comfortable to nurse lying down, because of soreness in the perineal area. Whatever the position, lying or sitting, it is important to be comfortable and relaxed. Tension, both physical and emotional, may interfere with the supply of milk. If sitting, the mother should not bend over the baby but rather should bring the baby to the level of her nipple, having some support under her arm. It is not necessary to put the nipple into the baby's mouth; if it is touched to the cheek, the baby will turn to find it.

Some doctors recommend that only one breast should be offered at a feeding, ensuring the complete emptying that stimulates further milk production. Others suggest that the infant nurse on one breast for about fifteen minutes and then be offered the other. (The breasts should be alternated at alternate feedings.) A baby nursing eagerly will take most of the milk in the first five or six minutes; from the point of view of nutrition, there is no need to prolong a feeding for more than twenty to thirty minutes.

After lactation is well established, giving an occasional bottle will not discourage milk production, but a woman should try not to miss two consecutive feedings. If both partners are playing a part in satisfying the baby's needs—the most prominent of which is for food—the father should give the single bottle feeding the same time each day. In part-time breast feeding, regularity is the key.

SOME COMMON PROBLEMS IN BREAST FEEDING

Engorgement

In the latter part of the first week, when the milk comes in, the breasts frequently become distended or engorged. The engorgement may affect only the areolar area, with the sinuses becoming overfull, or may involve the whole breast. In the latter case, the distended breast becomes firm and sore and sometimes very painful.

Engorgement can usually be relieved by having the baby nurse. However, because the areolar area will be too firm and swollen to be taken into the baby's mouth, it will be necessary to soften it by expressing the excess milk manually or with a breast pump. The breast, gently compressed from above and below, can then be offered to the baby. If the entire breast is involved and the baby cannot take enough milk to relieve the engorgement, it may be necessary to massage the breast, working from the outer edges toward the areola, and to express milk until the discomfort is eased.

The breasts seldom remain engorged for more than two or three days, and the problem seldom recurs after the first week.

Cracked Nipples

A cracked nipple produces pain that persists throughout the feeding (a passing twinge of pain at the beginning of a feeding is common and insignificant). When a nipple is cracked, it will be necessary to stop nursing on that breast until the sore heals. Milk should be expressed manually, to relieve fullness and give the breast some stimulation, two or three times daily. After a few days, the baby can be allowed to nurse briefly; if there is no pain, the time at that breast can be gradually extended.

A common cause for cracking and soreness in the nipples is dampness. After nursing, the nipple should be allowed to dry for fifteen minutes before the flaps of the nursing bra are closed.

A cracked nipple may also result from the baby nursing improperly, chewing on the nipple. If the baby starts to chew, he or she should be taken promptly from the breast—putting a finger in the corner of the baby's mouth reduces the suction—and should then be offered the entire areolar area, slightly flattened between thumb and forefinger.

Cramping

Particularly in the first few days after delivery, nursing is often accompanied by cramping, as the uterus contracts in response to the baby's sucking. This problem is more common in women who have had more than one child.

Insufficient Milk

Other than weighing the baby before and after every feeding, there is no way of knowing exactly how much breast milk he or she is getting. The question of whether there is enough milk for the baby's needs is decided by considering both the rate of weight gain and the baby's general satisfaction and behavior. If a mother is not producing sufficient milk, it is often helpful if she takes more rest, increases her consumption of fluids, and tries to be more relaxed. (In most instances, fatigue and emotional stress are responsible for a dwindling milk supply.) If it is essential to supplement the baby's diet with formula, the bottle should be given *after* the breast feeding.

DIET

While nursing, a woman's need for total calories and for calcium is greater even than in pregnancy. A nursing mother should increase her consumption of each of the four food groups, with special emphasis on meats, fruits, vegetables, and milk. Three pints of milk a day are needed to meet her nutritional needs and to compensate for the loss of fluid in the breast milk.

Some foods (garlic, onions, legumes, and cabbage, for example) seem to cause colic in babies and are best avoided. Almost all drugs pass to some extent into the breast milk; some may cause adverse reactions in infants. No medications, either prescription or over-the-counter, should be taken while nursing without a doctor's approval.

The best guide to diet while nursing is weight adjustment. Within a month of delivery, a woman should be at, or only slightly above, her prepregnancy weight. She should not gain further while nursing, nor should she lose weight.

If the mother is eating a properly balanced diet, the only supplements that may be needed for her baby are vitamin D, iron (after the first four months, if breast milk is the only food given), and fluoride. In areas where the drinking water contains less than three parts per million of fluoride, a supplement may be recommended for babies as young as two weeks.

WEANING

Although some mothers continue to nurse for up to two years, most babies show a decreased need for the breast at about six months of age and can be readily weaned to a cup. If a woman who wishes to wean her baby is producing little milk, she can simply stop all regular nursing, allowing the baby to nurse for a few seconds only if the breasts become full and uncomfortable. If she is producing a moderate amount of milk, weaning should proceed more gradually, starting with the omission of every other feeding.

If a nursing mother becomes seriously ill, or some unforeseen situation makes it necessary for her to wean the baby suddenly, several measures can make the abrupt cessation of breast feeding less painful. If it is possible to consult a doctor, he or she may prescribe hormones to suppress lactation. Otherwise, fullness and discomfort can be relieved by expressing a little milk manually or by using a breast pump. (Because the breasts are not emptied, production will gradually cease.) Reducing the fluid intake and binding the breasts firmly is a further way, but an uncomfortable one, of stopping the supply of milk.

BREAST FEEDING AND CONTRACEPTION

Ovulation and menstruation usually do not occur while a woman is nursing. However, a woman should not rely on nursing as a method of birth control. Oral contraceptives are not usually recommended for nursing mothers, as they tend to reduce the milk supply.

SUMMING UP

Human milk is the ideal food for human infants, easily digestible and highly nutritious. It has the additional benefit of providing the infant with protection from many of the bacterial and viral infections that commonly affect young babies.

Many women find breast feeding a very satisfying experience, both physically and emotionally. If, however, a woman chooses not to breast-feed, or is unable to do so, she can select from a wide variety of infant formulas and be assured that her baby will thrive.

Problems In Childhood

---

168. Feeding Your Baby

GENERAL CONSIDERATIONS

The food that infants receive during the first year of life is of great importance to their physical and emotional health. Both the amount and type of food, and the way in which it is given, are important.

Eating patterns are formed early and may persist for a lifetime. A taste for salt acquired in infancy may contribute to hypertension in middle age. Urging food on a reluctant baby, adhering rigidly to a schedule, or withholding food from a hungry infant can have long-term emotional effects. Fortunately, however, successful infant feeding is quite simple, provided that the parents are relaxed and have a basic understanding of good nutrition. With love and care, babies are well equipped to thrive.

BREAST MILK

Breast feeding is the natural way to feed an infant and is recommended to most women by their physicians. More women are breast-feeding their babies, and for longer periods, than was the case a generation ago—even though more women work outside the home than ever before. Breast milk contains an ideal mixture of the proteins, fats, sugars, vitamins, and most minerals needed by the infant for growth and development. It also contains a variety of antibodies that provide resistance to intestinal disorders and respiratory infections in the early months of life. A few days of nursing are usually needed before a regular and adequate milk supply is established, but thereafter breast feeding is simpler than bottle feeding.

During lactation, a woman needs to eat more food (approximately five hundred calories more daily), extra protein (about twenty grams more a day), and extra fluid (at least four to six glasses more a day).

469

Iron supplements for the baby are advisable by the fifth or sixth month. A nursing mother should check with her doctor as to what over-the-counter and prescription medications she can take, since many medications pass into the breast milk.

FORMULA

Not all women have the time, the inclination, or the milk to breast-feed. Bottle feeding is a very satisfactory alternative.

One advantage of bottle feeding is that the responsibility for feedings can be shared by both parents. Bottle feeding also allows parents to keep track of the exact amount of nourishment their infant is receiving, which many find reassuring. It is of the greatest importance to hold a bottle-fed baby while feeding, both to provide the infant with the needed sense of security and closeness and to avoid accidental aspiration of the formula. Infants should be allowed to regulate the volume of formula intake. Do not insist that the baby finish the bottle; infants set their own nutritional needs.

Commercial infant formulas are carefully manufactured to resemble breast milk as much as possible with respect to protein, fat, and sugar. They are available in powder, liquid concentrate, and liquid ready-to-use forms and are simple to prepare. After the age of four months, when the infant's innate reserves of iron are depleted, an iron-fortified formula should be given. Babies who are allergic to cow's milk can be fed a special formula (usually made from soy products) or goat's milk, which is highly digestible.

WATER

An infant's water requirements are relatively higher than an adult's, and care should be taken to guard against dehydration. Lukewarm boiled water should be offered to babies frequently, especially in hot weather.

VITAMIN SUPPLEMENTS

Breast-fed babies receive adequate vitamin C from their milk, but they may need vitamin A and D supplements, as well as iron supplements at five to six months of age. Bottle-fed babies should get adequate amounts of vitamins C, A, and D and iron from commercial formulas. Many pediatricians favor food sources for these vitamins, especially later in infancy. Additionally, if the local water supply is not fluoridated, infants should receive a fluoride supplement.

SOLID FOOD

From the point of view of normal growth and development, solid food is not necessary before the age of twelve months, and today is not usually introduced before six months. There is, however, no inflexible, "right" time for the introduction of solid food. It should be added to the diet when the baby is no longer satisfied with breast milk or formula alone, ideally not earlier than six months of age.

Initially, solid foods are given after the breast or bottle; later, as the baby becomes accustomed to them, they can be given in the middle or at the beginning of a feeding. New foods should be introduced one week apart in order to detect possible allergies. If a new food or texture is refused, do not force it on the baby, but try again after a few days. The first serving of any new food should be very small, perhaps half a teaspoonful; increase the quantity gradually.

Cereals are usually the first solid food to be introduced. Rice cereal seems to be especially well tolerated. Commercial baby cereals are fortified with iron. Pureed fruits are usually introduced a few weeks later, although some pediatricians advise that fruits precede cereals because babies take to them so readily. Pureed vegetables are added after two to four weeks, followed by high-protein foods such as meat,

Feeding Your Baby

Breast feeding provides an ideal balance of nutrients, plus several protective ingredients. With bottle feeding, the responsibility can be shared by both parents, and the amount taken is easily checked.

At about six months, solids are gradually introduced a little at a time. New foods should be offered at least a week apart.

By one year, the infant should be eating three meals a day and taking food from the four basic groups.

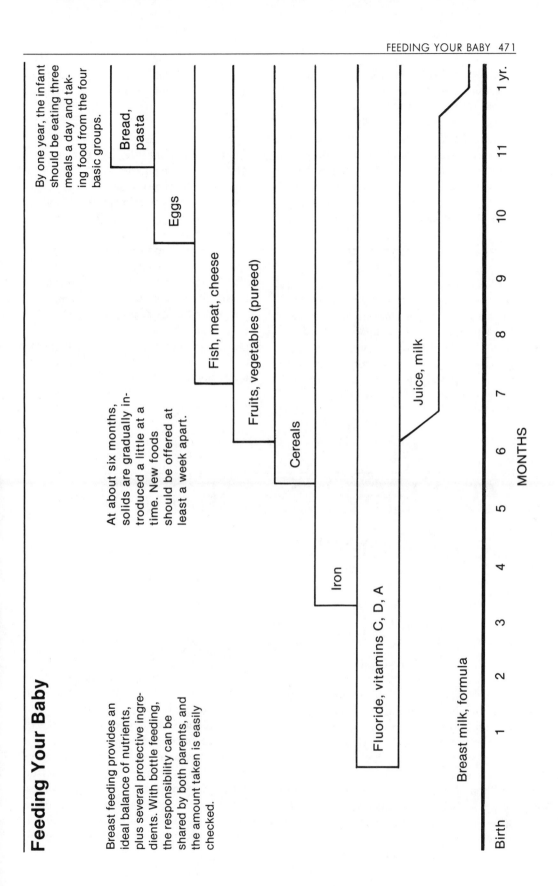

Bread, pasta

Eggs

Fish, meat, cheese

Fruits, vegetables (pureed)

Cereals

Iron

Fluoride, vitamins C, D, A

Juice, milk

Breast milk, formula

Birth 1 2 3 4 5 6 7 8 9 10 11 1 yr.

MONTHS

fish, and cottage cheese. Eggs are seldom introduced before the eighth or even the tenth month because they are more allergenic than the previously mentioned foods. Bread, pasta, and potatoes are added in the tenth and eleventh months, completing the diet. By the time the baby is a year old, he or she will be eating food from the four basic groups—and in a pattern of three meals a day.

FINGER FOODS

Slices of soft fruit, cooked carrots, biscuits, and similar foods may be offered to infants at six or seven months, so that they learn to feed themselves. When teething begins, strips of hard toast or zwieback can be given. Little will be eaten at first, but the sucking and chewing will help to develop the gums and assist in the eruption of the teeth. (Teeth should be brushed as soon as they erupt, to minimize cavities.)

SUMMING UP

A well-fed infant is happy, alert, and active, with good muscle tone and a firm layer of subcutaneous fat. A steady, age-appropriate weight gain is the best indication that he or she is receiving the proper nourishment.

Despite its importance to physical and emotional health, infant feeding is not difficult. Parents who respect their infants' signals of hunger and satisfaction, who offer their babies appropriate food in an appropriate form, and who provide a relaxed, secure atmosphere at feeding time seldom have trouble feeding their infants successfully.

169. Normal Growth and Development

GENERAL CONSIDERATIONS

Growth patterns in childhood, and the ultimate height that an individual attains, are influenced by a number of factors: heredity, the hormones and nutrients required for growth, acute and chronic health disorders, and the emotional environment of the home. In the final analysis, however, ultimate height depends on the yearly growth and the number of years during which growth occurs.

The yearly growth in height, or "height velocity," is determined by the net effects of many heriditary and environmental factors. It is not evenly spaced over the twelve months of the year, and periods of rapid growth may follow periods of slow growth, and vice versa. The duration of growth (the number of years during which growth occurs) is largely determined by the age at which a child attains puberty because the hormones which initiate the processes of puberty also terminate the processes of physical growth.

NORMAL GROWTH CURVES

Most children of the same age grow at approximately the same rate. A child who seems "too short" or "too tall" may actually have a normal growth *velocity* for his or her age. Exceptionally tall or short children, in other words, may simply represent one extreme or the other of the normal range of size. This range of normal heights in childhood has been well established and is the basis for the "growth curves" that are familiar to many parents. Doctors use these growth curves to determine whether a child has a normal growth *pattern*—a normal progression of growth over a period of time.

Only 3 percent of normal children are taller at each age than the height represented by the topmost (97 percent) line in the growth chart; 3 percent of normal children are shorter at each age than the heights represented by the bottom (3 percent) line.

The fiftieth percentile line represents the growth pattern of the "average" child: 50 percent of normal children will be taller, and 50 percent will be shorter, than children who grow at this rate. Normal growth is defined as any pattern that lies between or just outside the ninety-seventh and third percentile limits and runs parallel to the growth curves. A growth pattern which is significantly or progressively outside those limits, or crosses several percentile lines, suggests that there may be a significant growth disorder.

PUBERTY

Growth in height stops only after pubertal changes are complete. By the time of the first menstrual period (usually at the age of twelve or thirteen), the growth velocity of girls is already slowing down. Puberty starts and finishes about two years later in boys than in girls.

If puberty occurs at an unusually early age, growth will cease earlier than it does with other children the same age. Similarly, if puberty is delayed, growth will continue for a longer period of time than is the case with other youngsters the same age. The chronological age at which puberty will occur, and thus the number of years of growth potential remaining for a particular child, can be estimated by the maturity of the skeleton—the "bone age" —determined by an X-ray of the hand and wrist. Most factors that accelerate or slow growth in height have a comparable effect on the skeletal system.

FACTORS INFLUENCING GROWTH

Heredity is probably the most important single factor that determines childhood growth and adult height. A child's growth pattern is often similar to the patterns of other members of the family who are of the same sex, and he or she will usually enter into and complete puberty at about the same chronological age as other family members.

"Constitutional" factors (usually unidentifiable) result in children who are unusually tall or short during childhood and whose "bone age" is appropriate to their height. Puberty compensates to some extent for the unusual stature, terminating growth either earlier or later than would be expected for the child's chronological age. Such children often attain normal adult height. "Primordial" factors (also usually unidentifiable) result in children who are small at birth, remain short in childhood, and have "bone ages" appropriate to their chronological age. Such children enter puberty at the appropriate age and usually become small adults.

Five hormones have major influences on growth patterns: growth hormone (secreted by the pituitary gland), thyroxin (secreted by the thyroid gland), androgens (secreted by the testes and adrenal glands), estrogens (secreted by the ovaries and adrenal glands), and insulin (secreted by the pancreas). All are essential for normal growth. The androgens and estrogens result in the changes of puberty, including

Normal Growth

Boys

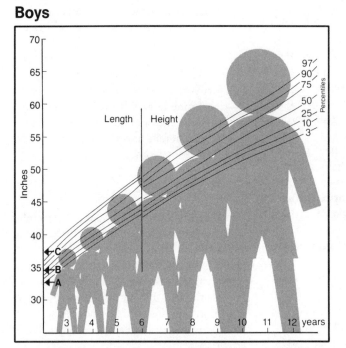

A, B, and C represent the 3rd, 50th, and 97th
percentiles in growth at a given age. Any height
between the 3rd and 97th percentile is considered normal.

Girls

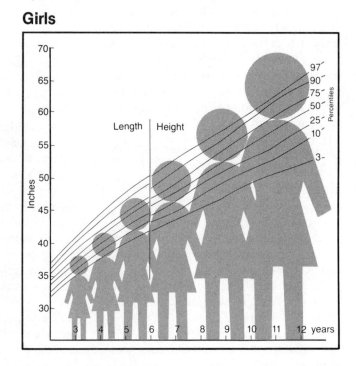

the growth spurt characteristic of early puberty. They are the agents which terminate the growth of the skeleton and, thus, end the potential for further growth in height.

Growth may be retarded by poor nutrition—and also by emotional starvation. There is evidence that both are involved in the short stature of children from families facing the many problems of unemployment, alcoholism, marital breakup, and the like. Fortunately, catch-up growth may occur if the adverse emotional environment can be corrected.

ABNORMAL GROWTH PATTERNS

Abnormally slow growth (falling progressively below the growth curve) may be caused by reduced secretion of any of the hormones required for growth. Thyroid hormone deficiency is a relatively common endocrinologic cause of significant growth failure. Fortunately, replacement of thyroid hormone is easy and inexpensive. Small supplies of human growth hormone have been available to treat growth hormone deficiency states in children during the past few years. If a deficiency of growth hormone can be proved, it may be possible for your doctor to obtain a supply for experimental purposes. There is no evidence that provision of growth hormone, thyroid hormone, or any other hormone will increase the growth rate of children who have short stature for some reason other than hormonal deficiency.

Abnormally slow growth may also be caused by either congenital or acquired disorders of the skeletal system, the liver, the kidneys, and most other organ systems. Correction of the causal disorder is usually followed by a period of increased growth velocity and some degree of "catch-up" growth. Abnormally *rapid* growth may be caused by excess amounts of the hormones required for growth or by unusually early appearance of those responsible for puberty. Disorders in the timing of puberty usually solve themselves and require no

correction. Excess hormone secretion can often be corrected; this should slow growth velocity.

Disturbances during prenatal life may result in permanent growth problems. Babies born unusually small for their gestational age (for example, a four-pound infant born at term) have limited ability to catch up. Those who are small at birth due to prematurity or multiple birth, however, often catch up to a normal size during the first year or two after birth.

Growth failure may accompany prolonged therapy with adrenal glucocorticosteroid hormones, such as cortisone. These hormones are sometimes used in treating asthma, arthritis, and other chronic disorders.

TEENAGERS—THE SHORT BOY AND THE TALL GIRL

Delayed puberty is common in boys and is usually self-correcting. If the delayed puberty is due to permanent lack of testicular function, treatment with testosterone will result in most of the normal virilizing changes of puberty. In rare cases of extreme pubertal delay, hormones similar to the testicular hormones may accelerate development and speed up skeletal maturation to the point that puberty occurs. Such treatment, however, may reduce the potential for adult height because of its effect on the skeletal system. This risk must be balanced against the psychological benefits of speeding up maturation.

In exceptional cases, excessive growth in girls may be treated by inducing an earlier puberty, thereby accelerating bone maturation and terminating growth at an earlier age than would be expected. The question of adverse reactions from the hormones used is still unanswered, and few doctors would consider such treatment unless the girl's predicted adult height was over six feet. As with treatment for delayed puberty in boys, risks must be weighed against psychological considerations.

SUMMING UP

There are many causes for unusual stature in childhood. Fortunately, the majority of them are simply variations of normal growth or in the timing of puberty, or both.

The processes of growth and development in children are well understood, and parents and children need not suffer unnecessary anxiety because of concern for present or potential growth. A review of past growth patterns, a thorough medical history, and a physical examination (supplemented where necessary by appropriate laboratory and X-ray tests) will enable a doctor to determine whether a child's current growth pattern is abnormal or simply unusual.

170. Bed-Wetting

GENERAL CONSIDERATIONS

Occasional loss of urinary control at night is normal for all children, especially if the child is sick, overly excited, or under stress. In children over the age of five or six, such accidents are likely to happen only occasionally rather than on a regular basis. However, chronic bed-wetting beyond this age, which is referred to as enuresis, is often perceived as a problem or source of embarrassment by both parent and child.

A common misconception is that bed-wetting is an intentional attention-getting device. This is not the case. It is beyond the youngster's conscious control and often leads to embarrassment and a diminished self-image. In some cases, the enuresis is caused by a specific urologic disorder and the problem will be resolved with proper diagnosis and treatment. More often, however, there are no apparent physical abnormalities, and time, patience, and understanding are the major treatments.

WHO WETS THE BED

Above all, parents should realize that enuresis is common and almost always resolves itself with time. Studies have shown that about 20 to 25 percent of all four and five year olds occasionally wet their beds. The number declines to about 10 percent by the ages of six to ten, and finally, to about 3 percent by the teen years. Therefore, it has been estimated that three to seven million schoolchildren in the United States suffer with the problem. It is important that both parents and children be aware of these numbers so that they do not feel alone. All too often, the youngster thinks he or she is the only child in the neighborhood with the problem, and this only intensifies feelings of guilt and makes the problem worse.

Enuresis has been found to disappear spontaneously in almost all children by adolescence. However, because parent and child may find waiting for such "growing out of it" difficult, a variety of treatments have been explored.

At least 80 percent of all children with enuresis are boys, and there is strong evidence of a hereditary tendency. About half of all bed-wetting youngsters have a parent or close relative who had a similar problem. Although a father may not wish to admit to his son that he suffered with enuresis as well, such an admission may help the youngster cope.

Enuresis is classified as primary in children who simply have not become dry at night by age four or five and secondary in those who have been dry for a period but revert to bed-wetting. Primary enuresis is more likely to be associated with physical causes and secondary, with psychological causes. Occasionally, both physical and psychological factors play a role.

CAUSES OF BED-WETTING

The most common cause is simply lack of bladder control. Just as some children learn to read later than others, some are late in developing the mechanisms for bladder control. The development of this neuromuscular ability cannot be accelerated by scolding and is probably hindered by scolding and its consequent anxiety.

Bladder capacity may also be a factor, and children with small bladder capacity can often be identified by their tendency to urinate frequently during the day. Bladder size will increase only with age, but the bladder is a flexible organ, and children can learn to increase their bladder capacity by holding back urination for increasing periods during the day. This increased capacity may be reflected in decreased bed-wetting at night.

Urinary tract infections may be another causative factor, especially in girls. Other organic causes include abnormalities of the genital or urinary system, spinal cord disorders, and uncontrolled diabetes.

PSYCHOLOGICAL FACTORS

Psychologists have suggested that a variety of emotional conflicts may play a role in bed-wetting. Perhaps the most common is the unconscious wish to retreat into babyhood. This is most often seen when a new baby arrives and gets a great deal of parental attention, or when the family moves to a new town and the youngster is homesick. The separation or divorce of parents also may be followed by a return to bed-wetting.

Children who suffer with enuresis are often insecure. Rather than scolding, which may only worsen the problem, parents should reassure the youngster that the problem is only temporary and express confidence in the child and maintain a general attitude of encouragement. With such thoughtful attention, professional psychological counseling is seldom necessary.

CAUSES OF BED-WETTING

PSYCHOGENIC:
- Sibling rivalry
- Family stress
- Emotional problems

ORGANIC:
- Anatomic abnormality
- Bladder or kidney infection
- Diabetes, epilepsy

FUNCTIONAL:
- Deep sleep
- Low bladder capacity

TREATMENT

Some treatment approaches have already been noted, as well as the fact that most cases of enuresis disappear with no specific treatment. If further steps are warranted, they should be discussed with the physician. For example, mechanical devices are available to wake the child at the first bit of wetting. These devices are sometimes effective in conditioning the child to wake up in response to the urge to urinate. In addition, imipramine, a drug that has been shown to prolong the dream stage of sleep and increase the tone of the sphincter muscle at the outlet of the bladder, is sometimes prescribed for older children. This medication has helped about 50 percent of those in experimental studies. However, it should not be used in children under the age of six years.

SUMMING UP

Bed-wetting is a common, if inconvenient, problem in families with young children. Family attitudes can play a significant role in the duration of the problem, and a relaxed attitude, rather than a punitive or panicky one, can make a considerable difference in a child's self-image as he or she learns to improve bladder control.

171. Diarrhea in Children

COMMON CHARACTERISTICS

Diarrhea—the abnormally frequent passage of loose, watery stools—is a symptom and not a disease in its own right. In almost all cases, it indicates the presence in the intestinal tract of an irritant that speeds up the transit time of the contents of the intestines through the bowel.

There are several different types of diarrhea. In one, illness in the gut interferes with the body's normal absorption of water. In another, there is active secretion of fluid and body chemicals. Finally, there are diarrheas in which too high a level of dissolved salts in the gastrointestinal tract causes water loss greater than water absorption, resulting in watery stools.

The chief danger of diarrhea is the excessive loss of body fluids (dehydration); therefore, the most urgent requirement is that this loss of water be brought under control. In very young patients (as in the very old), dehydration can quickly become life-threatening.

Until the beginning of the twentieth

century, diarrhea was a leading cause of infant death throughout the world. This threat has been reduced in the United States and other industrialized countries that enjoy good sanitary conditions and enlightened medical care. Elsewhere, however, diarrheal diseases still remain the leading cause of infant death.

CAUSES OF DIARRHEA

Because infants have more delicate intestines and lower immunity than older children, mild diarrhea is a common problem during babyhood. In some cases, the intestinal irritant may be an ingredient in the infant formula. In the case of breast-fed babies, the condition may result from the introduction of new foods, especially fruits and vegetables. Breast-fed babies may also respond unfavorably to an unusual food eaten by the mother.

Bacterial organisms that contaminate food and water—especially the *Salmonella* genus and the disease-causing strains of *Escherichia coli*—are often identified as the cause of diarrhea epidemics, especially in hospitals, day-care centers, and other such facilities. Most cases, however, are caused by viruses.

Other conditions responsible for childhood diarrhea are infestation with worms or other parasites, celiac disease (also called malabsorption syndrome and characterized by sensitivity to gluten, a protein found in rye and wheat flours), and food allergies. Lactose intolerance, caused by a deficiency of an enzyme essential in digesting milk, also causes diarrhea. Transient lactose intolerance frequently follows infectious diarrhea in children who usually digest milk well.

Antibiotics, which change the normal balance of different types of bacteria in the intestinal tract, often cause diarrhea. Other medications may cause irritation (castor oil is an example) or a secretory diarrhea. Diarrhea may also accompany an infectious illness not directly affecting the digestive tract, or be a response to stress.

In children approaching adolescence, ulcerative colitis is a possible cause of severe, recurrent diarrhea. This should be suspected if the stool contains blood and mucus. Regional ileitis—inflammation of portions of either the small or large intestines—may also be responsible for diarrhea in this age group.

EMERGENCY SYMPTOMS

A healthy baby may have as many as six or eight loose movements daily during the first month or so of life. However, if the number increases suddenly, if the stools are greenish, or if they contain mucus and/or blood, the doctor should be called promptly. With diarrhea of increasing severity accompanied by vomiting, the baby should be taken to the nearest hospital if the doctor cannot be reached. Since this condition can quickly lead to a critical loss of sodium, potassium, bicarbonate, and water, intravenous infusion may be essential to prevent dehydration. Signs of dehydration include dryness of lips, tongue, and mouth; decreased urine output; increasing restlessness; and as the circulation begins to collapse, cold, bluish skin.

DIARRHEA IN CHILDREN

ORAL REHYDRATION FOR INFANTS

- Stop milk and solids
- Give 5% glucose solution (add no salt) first day
- Reintroduce milk gradually over about five days
- Total daily fluid given must not exceed 40 oz. for any infant
- Feedings can be hourly or three-hourly at first, then less frequent

5% GLUCOSE SOLUTION

- Add 3 level teaspoons of glucose to 6 oz. of water

TOTAL FLUIDS PER 24 HOURS

Day	Volume of Glucose Solution (oz.)	Volume of Milk (oz.)
1	2.3 × weight (lbs.)	0.0 × weight (lbs.)
2	1.8 × weight (lbs.)	0.5 × weight (lbs.)
3	1.4 × weight (lbs.)	0.9 × weight (lbs.)
4	0.5 × weight (lbs.)	1.8 × weight (lbs.)
5	0.0 × weight (lbs.)	2.3 × weight (lbs.)

DIAGNOSIS

Mild, recurring cases of diarrhea that are linked to a certain food or foods can be prevented simply by eliminating the offending items from the diet. This may require some detective work, especially if the cause of diarrhea is an ingredient that is hidden in many foods—cornstarch, lactose, and wheat gluten are common examples. Mothers sometimes think a child has diarrhea when, in fact, the stools are normal. After weaning, toddlers sometimes have frequent bowel movements containing undigested fragments of food. If there are no other symptoms and weight gain is satisfactory, no special measures are necessary.

Correct diagnosis in other cases may depend on laboratory examination of a stool sample to determine whether the cause is a virus, parasite, or bacterial organism. Medication generally should be given only on the advice of a doctor following correct diagnosis.

TREATMENT

If mild diarrhea is present in a young child still on formula, the formula should be discontinued and your doctor consulted, particularly if the diarrhea continues or vomiting occurs.

When a stool sample of an older child contains blood or mucus, and causes such as an infectious organism, allergies, and drug reactions have been ruled out, an examination of the colon may be necessary.

SUMMING UP

Diarrhea in children is a common condition resulting from many different causes. In most cases, it is mild and self-limiting. However, when it is acute and/or chronic, the cause must be determined before proper treatment can be administered. Emergency measures are essential in cases where dehydration is imminent, especially in infants and very young children. Antidiarrheal medicines should not be administered except on the advice of a doctor.

172. Fever in Infants and Children

COMMON CHARACTERISTICS

Unlike the oral temperature of a healthy adult, which remains fairly steady at 98.6°F, the normal body temperature of infants and young children ranges anywhere from 97.1 to 100° F, depending on the time of day, the child's activity level, and the site at which the temperature is measured. As a rule of thumb, rectal temperature is 1°F higher and axillary (armpit) temperature 1°F lower than oral temperature. Any temperature over 100° or 101° indicates that the child has a fever. Most fevers in children are due to viral infections. When a child is ill, the temperature may rise to 104° or more, but the fever is usually of brief duration and, in itself, of limited medical seriousness.

When infants are sick, they may not run

high fevers. In some instances, temperature may even fall below normal. If, however, the baby looks or acts sick and the temperature is over 100°, a doctor should be consulted. Older children tend to run higher temperatures with infections; a fever over 103° orally or 104° rectally in an older baby or toddler is usually an indication to call a doctor, especially if it persists for more than a day and there are other signs and symptoms.

The degree of fever, however, does not necessarily indicate the seriousness of the illness. Some children may have a minor illness and run high temperatures, while others may be very sick and have little or no fever.

CAUSES OF FEVER

Fever itself is not a disease but, instead, is a symptom of an illness, usually an infectious one. Colds, childhood viral infections, such as chicken pox and measles, and other viral and bacterial illnesses are all common causes of fever in children. While many parents worry that a fever may cause permanent damage, this is very rare and occurs only when the high temperature is prolonged over several days or weeks and associated with a serious disease such as meningitis.

WHEN TO TREAT A FEVER

A fever is part of the body's natural defense mechanism for overcoming disease, and it usually is not necessary to try to lower it unless the temperature is over 103°, or unless the high temperature lasts longer than seventy-two hours or is accompanied by other symptoms such as nausea, vomiting or somnolence that require treatment. It is important, however, to make sure that the child consumes plenty of fluids during a fever, since dehydration is one of the problems associated with a high temperature, especially if there is also diarrhea and/or vomiting.

A doctor should be consulted—if only by phone—before giving a baby or a young child any medication to lower a fever. Aspirin or acetaminophen are the drugs recommended most often, but both should be used with caution and under a doctor's supervision. Avoid overdressing or using heavy covers and keep the room temperature comfortable but not overheated. Sponging with lukewarm water—not alcohol—will lower a temperature.

Sometimes a high fever will cause convulsions. While a fever-associated convulsion is frightening to witness, parents should remember that it is not life-threatening and is usually of short duration. In the event of a convulsion, the child should be turned on its side to prevent choking, and a doctor should be called. Some children are more prone to febrile convulsions than others; if the convulsions seem to recur whenever a child has a fever, a medication to prevent them may be prescribed.

HOW TO TAKE A TEMPERATURE

To take a temperature, a thermometer is an absolute necessity—placing your hand on a child's forehead does not provide accurate information. There are several different types of thermometers: the traditional glass mercury thermometer; digital crystal thermometers, such as those commonly used by doctors and in hospitals; and newer crystal thermometers that record temperature differences on a color register. The latter are easy to use but are not as accurate as the glass thermometers or the more expensive digital models; therefore, most doctors recommend that parents use the glass mercury thermometers. These come in two styles—one with a rounded bulb for taking rectal temperature, the other with a more elongated end for oral (under the tongue) use. Temperature should be taken rectally in a young baby, but in a toddler, the armpit (axillary) method may be used instead. This involves placing the bulb of the thermometer—ei-

HOW TO READ A THERMOMETER

When buying a thermometer, look for one with easy-to-read numbers. Most Fahrenheit thermometers have only the even numerals, with the odd numbers indicated by long bars. The shorter bars mark each fifth of a degree. In some thermometers, the mercury is red; in others it is silver. If you have difficulty reading the thermometer, try using a magnifying glass, which will make both the degree markings and mercury more visible.

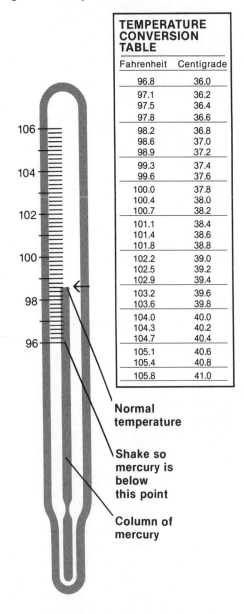

TEMPERATURE CONVERSION TABLE

Fahrenheit	Centigrade
96.8	36.0
97.1	36.2
97.5	36.4
97.8	36.6
98.2	36.8
98.6	37.0
98.9	37.2
99.3	37.4
99.6	37.6
100.0	37.8
100.4	38.0
100.7	38.2
101.1	38.4
101.4	38.6
101.8	38.8
102.2	39.0
102.5	39.2
102.9	39.4
103.2	39.6
103.6	39.8
104.0	40.0
104.3	40.2
104.7	40.4
105.1	40.6
105.4	40.8
105.8	41.0

Normal temperature

Shake so mercury is below this point

Column of mercury

ther type may be used—in the armpit and holding the arm against the chest. By the time the child is four or five years old, the thermometer may be placed under the tongue for an oral reading. Remember that there are slight differences in the temperature reading according to the method used: the rectal temperature is highest because it is taken internally, followed by oral and axillary in descending order.

Before taking a temperature, shake the thermometer so that the mercury is below the normal temperature line. When taking a rectal reading, make sure that the thermometer bulb is lubricated. The baby should be lying on his or her stomach. Gently glide the thermometer about one inch into the rectum; do not force. Hold the thermometer in place by gently pinching the "cheeks" of the baby's buttocks together with one hand. The mercury will reach its maximum level within one minute using this method.

To take an oral temperature, the bulb of the thermometer should be under the tongue and the lips closed. This method takes one and one-half to two minutes. The axillary method takes four minutes.

Many people have trouble reading a thermometer because the numbers and markings are small and sometimes the mercury is hard to see. On most Fahrenheit thermometers, only the even numbers are engraved, with the odd numbers indicated by long lines and each fifth of a degree (0.2) indicated by a shorter line. The centigrade scale may be used on some thermometers and in some hospitals. The accompanying table converts one to the other.

When a young child is sick, it is a good idea to keep a temperature log, recording it every few hours during the day. Usually the fever is lowest in the morning and rises during the day. Your doctor will want to know not only how high the fever is but also how long it has persisted and how it changes during the course of a day.

SUMMING UP

Fever—a temperature over 100° or 101° —is very common in babies and young children. It is not a disease in itself but a symptom of an illness, usually one that involves infection. Most fevers require no special treatment and will resolve themselves with treatment of the underlying disease. In some instances, steps should be taken to lower the temperature, but this should usually be done only after consulting a physician.

173. Giving Medication to Children

GENERAL CONSIDERATIONS

At one time or another, all children require some form of medication. Notwithstanding the fact that medicine has traditionally been the bane of many a child's existence, an honest, reasonable approach to giving it can prevent what should be a cooperative effort from escalating into a tug-of-war. In giving medicine to children under six, avoid excessive apologies and explanations; instead, approach the child as if his cooperation were assured.

Before starting a child of any age on a course of medication, be sure prescription instructions are clear. Ask the doctor what the drug's possible side effects are and whether it will interact adversely with certain other medications or foods. Unless the doctor advises that a medication be discontinued, give the child the entire recommended course of treatment, even if he or she appears to have recovered. And finally, throughout the course of medication, be on the lookout for overt or subtle side effects.

ADMINISTERING MEDICATION

Infants are usually given liquid medication, either by dropper or server. If the medication does not come with a calibrated liquid measure, ask the physician or pharmacist for one, and use it instead of a household teaspoon or tablespoon—these utensils are very unreliable for measuring. Don't worry if a little medicine spills or is spit up as long as the child receives most of it. Continued vomiting or discomfort after medication, however, should be promptly reported to the doctor. Also, if a dose of medication is missed, call the doctor for instructions.

The following are tips for giving different kinds of medicines:

Eyedrops
Have the child lie down, eyes closed. Put a drop in the inner corner of the eye or eyes, and, to avoid contamination, make sure the tip of the dropper doesn't touch any surface, including the eyelid. When

the child opens his or her eyes, the drops will slide into them.

Ear Drops

Lay the child down, with head slightly turned. Hold the dropper just inside the ear canal and squeeze the bulb to expel the drops. The child should lie in the same position for five to ten minutes following the administration of ear drops, so that the drops can flow down to the inner ear. A small piece of cotton may also be placed at the entrance to the ear canal to keep the drops inside.

Nose Drops

The child should tip his or her head back as far as possible. Insert the dropper into each nostril, and make sure the child's head remains tilted long enough for the drops to flow through the nasal passage. Nose drops cause a slight burning sensation in the throat; this may be uncomfortable, but it is no cause for alarm.

In giving eye, ear, and nose drops, it is best to rest the hand holding the dropper on the child's head—or, in the case of nose drops, on the chin; this way, he or she is less likely to be knocked or to have the dropper jammed into the eye or ear if he or she moves suddenly. If drops are stored in a refrigerator, you can warm them by holding them in your hand for a few minutes.

Oral Medications

Measure liquid medication carefully, using a calibrated measuring device supplied by your pharmicist or physician. Alcohol-based liquid medicines may be diluted with a small amount of water so that the taste is not overpowering. Follow other liquid medications with a piece of fruit or a drink of juice, but be sure to alternate the flavors so that the child doesn't come to associate one in particular with medicine and refuse it in the future.

If a child is unable to swallow a capsule or pill, grind it up and mix it with a very small amount of some palatable food; do not use the child's favorite foods or foods that are a usual part of his diet, however. Never, under any circumstances tell a child that pills or capsules are candy—he or she may go looking for them in your absence and help himself or herself to a handful.

THE MEDICATION ROUTINE

Try to keep the number of people giving your child medication to a minimum. Working mothers or single parents may have to rely on others to give out medication at certain times, though, so be sure the person in charge knows exactly what to do. If a child has to take medication during school hours, notify the school nurse or principal to discuss dosage, schedule, and possible side effects. Send a follow-up note as confirmation. Generally, the medicine will be kept in the nurse's office, and school personnel will take responsibility for giving it.

Children on long-term medication must develop a sense of responsibility for taking their medicine. Do not single out a child as "special" for this reason. Rather, the medication should become as much a part of a child's routine as brushing teeth. Children on long-term medication are likely to rebel at some point. Do not panic over an occasional missed dosage, but do reiterate the importance of the medication without trying to evoke guilt or fear. If the child has a consistently strong aversion to the medication, he or she may be experiencing an invisible side effect. When a child is extremely unwilling to use a medication, a talk with the physician is in order.

FURTHER PRECAUTIONS

Nonprescription drugs deserve the same care in administration as prescription drugs. They should be given only on a doctor's recommendation. Read the labels carefully, with special attention to adjustments in dosage according to the child's age and weight.

Should there be any medication left after the physician has said to discontinue it, throw it away. Never give a drug prescribed for one child to another child. Even though their symptoms appear to be similar, their illnesses and the proper course of treatment could be quite different. Once a medication course is completed, make a follow-up visit to the doctor to see if further medication is necessary.

Keep all medication well marked, retaining the pharmacist's label. Medications that must be refrigerated should be placed as far in the back of the refrigerator as possible and clearly marked *"Off Limits."* The bathroom cabinet is the worst place to store any medicines, since the hot, steamy atmosphere can lessen medicine's effectiveness. A cool, dry, dark cupboard out of children's reach is best.

The physician keeps a record of all pre- scriptions with the family medical record. It is best, however, to keep a similar personal record in the home in case of emergencies.

SUMMING UP

From time to time, almost every child will need medication of some sort. Never give an infant or very young child medicine, including aspirin and other nonprescription drugs, without first checking with your doctor. In administering a prescription drug, follow the doctor's instructions fully and do not discontinue the drug early, even if the symptoms improve. Medications should be kept out of the reach of children; if an accidental overdose should occur, call your doctor or emergency room immediately. When giving a youngster medication, be alert for any signs of possible adverse reactions and report these to your doctor.

CONVERSION CHART FOR MEDICATIONS

HOUSEHOLD MEASURE	FLUID OZ.	ML.	DRY MEASURE (G.)
Teaspoon	⅛	5.0	3.9
Tablespoon	⅜	15.0	11.7
½ cup	4	118.3	70.2
1 cup	8	236.6	140.4
1 pint	16	473.2	280.8
1 quart	32	946.4	561.6
1 gallon	128	3,785.0	2,250.0

174. Croup

Croup is the term commonly used for various forms of laryngitis (inflammation of the larynx or voice box) in young children. Spasmodic croup, the commonest type, occurs most often in children between the ages of three months and three years. Typically, the child wakens at night with a harsh "barking" cough and has difficulty catching a breath. Although frightening, spasmodic croup is not a serious problem; in most cases the attack will subside with simple measures that parents can take at home.

There are, however, other graver conditions that cause breathing difficulties in young children. Viral croup may be severe enough to require hospitalization. Another condition, epiglottitis, is life-threatening and should be considered a medical emergency. It is important that parents know when it is necessary to call a doctor about a child who is having breathing difficulties and also when and how to treat such problems at home.

SPASMODIC CROUP

During the day preceding an attack of spasmodic croup, the child may have been completely well, or may have had only a mild cold, with no cough. At night, however, the child suddenly wakes with a harsh cough, which sounds rather like a seal barking. The intake of breath is difficult and very noisy (this noisy breathing in is known as stridor). Naturally, the child becomes frightened by the lack of air, and tension contributes to the difficulty in breathing.

The cough and distressed breathing of spasmodic croup are caused by a swelling of the tissues below the larynx, partially blocking the passage of air into the lungs. Some doctors think that this swelling is the result of a mild viral infection; others feel that it is due to a type of allergic reaction.

What Parents Should Do

The best way to curtail an attack of spasmodic croup is to expose your child to steam. An effectively steamy environment can be created quickly by turning on all the hot water faucets in a closed bathroom. Alternatively, a "cold steam" vaporizer can be used. Talking soothingly to the child—while remaining calm yourself— may help to quiet him or her and halt the attack. Another way to stop a spasmodic croup attack is to take your child outside into the cool night air.

Before the child is put back in bed, the air in the room should be moisturized. Some doctors recommend that a vaporizer be used not only for the rest of the night but also for the next three or four nights, since spasmodic croup tends to recur on the first few nights after an initial attack.

If neither steam nor cool air stop the cough and distressed breathing within fifteen to twenty minutes, or if at any time there is severe difficulty in breathing, the doctor should be called immediately. If the doctor suspects that the distressed breathing is the result of a more serious condition, he or she may ask that your child be taken to a hospital emergency room at once.

VIRAL CROUP

Viral croup, more serious than spasmodic croup, is another common cause of breathing difficulty in children between the ages of three months and three to four years. It usually develops a few days after a virus infection such as influenza. Children with viral croup have the "barking" cough, stridor, and distressed breathing typical of spasmodic croup. However, they are feverish and do not improve when exposed to steam or cool air. The croup may come on gradually or suddenly at any time of the day or night. The doctor should be called.

Mild cases of viral croup can be treated at home; more severe ones usually require hospitalization. The doctor will probably recommend that your child have mist therapy to relieve the irritation in the throat. At home, this is done by placing a vaporizer in the child's room. In the hospital, your child will probably be placed in a "croup tent" for mist therapy and may also be given oxygen. Steroid drugs to reduce inflammation may be prescribed. Alternatively, the doctor may decide to treat your child with the technique known as intermittent positive-pressure breathing, in which a medication containing epinephrine is given through a face mask.

EPIGLOTTITIS

Breathing difficulties in young children may also be caused by the serious condition epiglottitis. This illness can develop at any age from infancy to adulthood, but it occurs most commonly in two to six year olds and appears to affect boys more than girls. It is more prevalent during the cooler months.

The epiglottis is a leaf-shaped flap of cartilage located at the back of the throat above the larynx. It opens to allow air to pass down the windpipe (trachea) and into the lungs; it closes like a trapdoor when swallowing to prevent food from "going down the wrong pipe." Epiglottitis (inflammation of the epiglottis) is caused by infection with the bacterium *Hemophilus influenzae.* The larynx and the tissues above it, including the epiglottis, become inflamed and swollen very quickly, often in a matter of hours. The swelling may completely block passage of air to the lungs. Thus, epiglottitis can be fatal if not treated promptly and properly.

Symptoms of Epiglottitis

The child usually first develops a fever and a sore throat. Soon after these symptoms appear, swallowing becomes difficult and painful; this often results in drooling. The child frequently sits upright or leans slightly forward with the neck extended, the mouth open, and the chin jutting out. This position opens the clogged windpipe as much as possible, making breathing easier. The child may look very sick indeed, with bluish or discolored lips or skin, especially around the fingertips, as a result of insufficient oxygen in the blood. Unlike children with spasmodic croup, those with epiglottitis seldom have a "barking" cough. Nor are the measures

TYPES OF CROUP

TYPE	SYMPTOMS	TREATMENT
Spasmodic	Harsh barking cough; difficulty breathing	Exposure to moist air (steam-filled bathroom, moisturizer, cool night air)
Viral	Barking cough following viral infection; fever; difficulty breathing	Exposure to moist air; seek emergency treatment if breathing becomes labored
Epiglottitis	Great difficulty breathing; bluish cast to lips, fingers, and toes	Seek immediate emergency treatment; breathing tube; antibiotics

effective in stopping an attack of croup of any avail.

If you suspect that your child's breathing difficulties are due to epiglottitis, it is vital to call your doctor immediately. If the doctor cannot be reached, take your child to a hospital emergency room as quickly as possible.

Treatment

The most important step in the treatment of epiglottitis is to make sure that there is a clear passageway for air to reach the lungs. In most cases, this must be accomplished either by inserting a tube through the child's nose and into the trachea (nasotracheal intubation) or by inserting a tube directly into the child's trachea through a small incision in the throat (tracheostomy). Both these procedures are usually done in a hospital's emergency room.

Once the tube is in place, your child will be carefully watched in the pediatric intensive care unit. Antibiotics will probably be given intravenously to destroy the bacteria that are causing the swelling. After two or three days, if the child has improved sufficiently, the tube will be removed from the windpipe. Once your child can keep food down, he or she will be given an oral antibiotic. It is important that this medication be taken as prescribed in order to completely eradicate the infection.

SUMMING UP

Spasmodic croup is a common, alarming, but minor condition which affects many young children. Exposure to steam or to cool air usually stops an attack of spasmodic croup quickly.

Children with viral croup have the cough and the distressed and noisy breathing characteristic of spasmodic croup but in addition are feverish. Steam and cool air are ineffective in these cases, and the doctor should be called.

If a child has a history of respiratory problems, or along with difficult breathing, a child should drool, sit with the neck and chin extended and the mouth open, and show signs of oxygen deficiency (discolored or bluish lips and skin), immediate emergency care is essential. The latter symptoms are signs of epiglottitis, a condition which can be fatal if it is not treated correctly and swiftly.

175. Diaper Rash and Other Infant Skin Problems

COMMON CHARACTERISTICS

A baby's skin is very delicate and sensitive to many types of irritation. The most common infant skin disorders are diaper rash, cradle cap, and eczema. These are mild rashes that parents can usually treat successfully at home without the aid of a physician. However, any rash that is more extensive or does not respond promptly to treatment should be seen by a doctor. An atypical rash could be a symptom of some other type of a disorder that warrants medical treatment, such as a bacterial or fungal infection, or a childhood infectious disease, such as measles or chicken pox.

DIAPER RASH

Virtually every baby suffers occasionally from some degree of diaper rash, which doctors refer to as a type of "contact dermatitis." Quite simply, it is an inflammation of the baby's skin in the diaper area due to exposure to irritating agents in the urine or bowel movements. Depending on how often diapers are changed—which may be less frequent during the night—these irritants can remain in contact with the skin for varying times. The result usually is a reddish rash, sometimes producing swollen patches, in the area around the genitals and the skin folds of the thighs. This does not necessarily mean that the infant is not being changed often enough. Some babies simply have more sensitive skin. An additional contributing factor is the use of plastic diaper covers or disposable diapers, which may seal moisture in the groin area. Finally, stool bacteria can exacerbate diaper rash by releasing ammonia from urinary urea.

Some babies may develop a rash from the soap or detergent used to wash cloth diapers; others may be sensitive to the plastic covering or other substances in disposable diapers. The first step in preventing diaper rash is pinpointing its cause, especially if it is related to the type of diaper being used.

Frequent diaper changes will usually help minimize the problem. If the baby's skin is very sensitive, avoid the use of plastic or rubber pants that can help trap moisture next to the skin. Cleanse the diaper area with a gentle soap and warm water after each diaper change. Make sure all soap is removed because it, too, can aggravate diaper rash. Baby powder helps dry the skin, and a heavy skin cream promotes healing by protecting the rash area from further contact with urine and feces. Whenever possible, let the baby go without diapers to expose the skin to the healing effects of fresh air and, if available, sunlight.

Should the rash become raw or infected, or if the infant appears very uncomfortable, check with a physician. The rash may be complicated by a yeast or fungal infection for which special medication is necessary. If cloth diapers are used, make sure they are washed in hot water and thoroughly rinsed.

CRADLE CAP

Cradle cap is a very common, mild skin disorder seen in early infancy. It is sometimes called seborrheic dermatitis, because it is related to seborrhea, a disease of the oil-producing glands of the skin that causes dandruff in adults. It produces flaky, crusty, gray- or orange-colored patches on the scalp and, sometimes, around the eyebrows. Parents should not be alarmed by this skin condition; it usually disappears spontaneously within a few months.

Washing the scalp daily with mild soap and water usually keeps flakes to a minimum. Regular, but gentle, brushing of the overlying hair also helps remove flakes. Many babies appear to enjoy this gentle, massaging stimulation. Parents need not worry about brushing the soft spot, or fontanel, on top of the infant's head. If the condition persists or becomes rather unsightly, consult a physician about a special shampoo.

ECZEMA

Eczema, an inflammation of the skin, is also called atopic dermatitis. The rash it causes is red and rough, and may become crusted. In contrast to the other rashes discussed here, eczema usually is very itchy, but scratching makes it worse.

Physicians still do not know what causes eczema. It has long been thought to be related to allergies, because many of the youngsters who are afflicted also have hay fever or asthma, or come from families with a history of allergy. However, a variety of factors unrelated to allergies have been shown to make eczema better or worse, such as sweating, skin temperature, weather, emotional stress, colds, and infections. The only clear conclusion is that children who have eczema have highly sensitive skin.

The rash usually develops at about three months of age and may last for a few months to many years. It may involve small patches or large areas of the body. In some youngsters, it recurs in adolescence and, in a few, even in adulthood. In the absence of natural remission, there is no total cure for eczema, although a number of treatments may be helpful.

The objective of treatment is to moisturize the skin and protect it from further irritation. Extended bathing is unwise because it promotes drying. Gentle lubricating lotions or ointments are recommended, as well as the use of soft clothing. Avoid wool and other irritating fabrics. The physician may also recommend removing potentially irritating substances from the home environment, such as feathers and animal hair, and elimination diets may be tried to screen for food allergies. The most common offenders are cow's milk, wheat, and eggs.

SUMMING UP

Skin rashes in infants may be troubling to both the baby and parents, but most are self-limited. The delicate skin of babies is particularly sensitive. Persistent rashes should be seen by a physician to rule out more serious conditions.

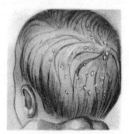

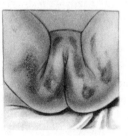

Cradle cap　　　　**Prickly heat**　　　　**Diaper rash**

176. Reye's Syndrome

COMMON CHARACTERISTICS

Reye's syndrome (pronounced *Rise*) is a disease that affects the brain, central nervous system, and liver. It occurs almost exclusively in persons under the age of eighteen and is most common in young children. Its course is always swift, of short duration, and often fatal. First recognized in 1963, much has become known since that time about the diagnosis and management of the disease, although both its cause and processes remain partially a mystery. Fortunately, Reye's syndrome is a relatively rare disease, far more often a source of fear than a present danger.

SYMPTOMS

Typically, a child will be recovering from a viral infection, usually chicken pox or the flu, when the symptoms of Reye's syndrome begin. Following a symptom-free period, ranging from several hours to a few days at the end of the viral infection, the first symptom of Reye's appears. This is usually a persistent vomiting, and usually unlike the vomiting of other childhood illnesses. At the same time, the child may feel lethargic and disoriented. Convulsion and irregular deep breathing are also common.

As the disease progresses, the youngster may become intensely agitated and delirious. Finally, the patient may lapse into a coma.

The entire course of the disease, from the onset of the viral infection to final recovery or death, takes approximately seven to ten days, and from the onset of the vomiting, only two to three days. In younger children, the disease may progress more rapidly from the early to the final stages, while in older children and teenagers, the disease will usually advance more slowly and there is a greater likelihood that it will not progress beyond the initial stages. Approximately 60 percent to 80 percent of those youngsters who become comatose will die from the swelling of the brain caused by Reye's, while nearly all patients in whom the disease does not go beyond the initial stages will eventually recover.

CAUSES OF REYE'S SYNDROME

No single, specific cause of Reye's syndrome has been identified, and it is generally thought that a combination of factors may be responsible. It seems likely that one of these factors is the viral illness which usually precedes an episode of Reye's. Environmental factors have been implicated, particularly with regard to pesticides and other environmental toxins that have a damaging effect on the liver. Recently, much attention has been given to

TYPICAL COURSE OF REYE'S SYNDROME

FIRST STAGE
*Apparent recovery from viral illness (usually chicken pox or flu)
*Onset of persistent vomiting

SECOND STAGE
*Lethargy
*Behavior change
*Disorientation, convulsions, irregular deep breathing

THIRD STAGE
*Intense agitation, delirium
*Coma

the possibility that aspirin may be a factor; however, the studies that suggested children may have been made more vulnerable by aspirin remain inconclusive. Finally, many researchers feel that a genetic predisposition is also a contributing factor.

A number of seasonal and geographic patterns have been associated with outbreaks of Reye's. Most cases occur during the fall, winter, and early spring months. The majority of cases in the United States are in the Midwest, and more often in rural than urban areas.

DIAGNOSIS

Diagnosis of Reye's syndrome is usually based on a review of the symptoms and history of illness and a number of blood tests. Typically, there are increased levels of ammonia and lactic acid in the blood. The liver may be swollen, and a liver biopsy usually shows fatty streaks in this organ.

TREATMENT

The mortality from Reye's syndrome has declined markedly in recent years, going from 40 percent in 1974 to 20 percent in 1980. This decline is attributed, in part, to a greater awareness of the disease, meaning that parents seek medical help earlier. Improved diagnostic methods and treatment also have helped lower the mortality.

The greatest danger in Reye's is increased pressure on the brain caused by swelling. Relieving this pressure is of top priority. Both drugs and physical manipulation of the skull may be used.

Drugs and infusions of glucose, as well as serum transfusions, may be needed to compensate for the liver abnormality. If Reye's syndrome is suspected, a child should be taken to the nearest hospital that has an emergency pediatric unit and a staff that is likely to be experienced in treating the disease. For example, a teaching hospital or university medical center is more likely to have the facilities and staff than a small community hospital.

SUMMING UP

Reye's syndrome is a relatively rare disease that is most often seen in young children. Any episode of persistent vomiting and other symptoms that follow apparent recovering from a minor viral illness should receive immediate medical attention. Many cases are mild and resolve themselves. Others, however, may quickly advance to a life-threatening stage. In any event, careful monitoring in a hospital is advised for all Reye's patients.

177. Eye Problems in Children

COMMON CHARACTERISTICS

While many eye problems of children may result from illness or injury, two of the more common defects are congenital and seem to run in families. The two defects are crossed eyes or walleye (technically, *strabismus*) and "lazy eye" *(amblyopia)*. While the two conditions may exist independently of each other, crossed eyes, if not corrected early enough, can lead to "lazy eye." And if "lazy eye" is neglected beyond a certain age, it can become an irreversible lifelong visual disability.

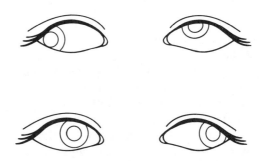

Eye position typical of crossed eyes, or strabismus. Correction involves surgical repositioning of the eye muscles.

CROSSED EYES

Crossed eyes, also called squint, is the condition in which the eyes fail to be directed simultaneously toward the object of regard. This fault in proper convergence occurs when some of the six muscles controlling eye movement fail to work together as they should.

During the first three to six months, an infant's eyes have a tendency to waver from time to time, turning inward or outward. After six months, this instability usually corrects itself. However, in some cases, the drifting continues. Depending on which muscles are involved, the deviation may be outward, inward, upward, or downward. Thus walleye is the result of the same disability as crossed eyes, and both conditions cause the brain to receive blurred or double images.

When the stimulus to maintain binocular single vision is so powerful that it overrides the faulty muscular performance interfering with the achievement of normal sight, the strabismus is said to be latent. This constant (and largely un-conscious) effort gives rise to eyestrain.

An older child whose head is habitually tilted when reading or who is constantly rubbing his or her eyes for no apparent reason, may be suffering from latent strabismus. Any such suspicion should be brought to the attention of an ophthalmologist, especially since the cause of strain may be neurological rather than merely muscular.

SURGICAL TREATMENT

Where the condition of crossed eyes is unambiguous at a very early age, surgical correction is usually recommended before the child is two years old. Early correction is considered advisable in order to prevent the complication of "lazy eye" discussed below. The operation is a relatively simple one that does not involve the eyeball. The muscles that require shortening or repositioning for the achievement of stereoscopic vision are adjusted so that the eyes become properly aligned. Hospital stay rarely extends beyond three days. Continued supervision over an extended period is always advised because in some few cases the problem may recur. The likelihood of recurrence is reduced if the child follows a routine of eye exercises designed to strengthen the weak muscles.

"LAZY EYE" OR AMBLYOPIA

"Lazy eye" is a condition in which there is a distinct difference in the visual acuity of the two eyes, with the result that the brain learns to reject the fuzzy or distorted image produced by the "poor" eye. As the rejection continues, and with increasing dependence on the "good" eye only, the child fails to develop the binocular vision essential for evaluating distance and depth, for catching a ball, and for dealing safely and competently with many other aspects of daily experience.

If this abnormality is neglected much beyond the age of six, the faulty eye deteriorates to the point where it may become impossible to rehabilitate it.

Causes

It is estimated that "lazy eye" is a problem affecting one in twenty-five children under the age of five. Uncorrected strabismus (crossed eyes or walleye) is one of the chief causes. Another cause is a marked difference in the visual acuity of the two eyes. When this is the case, the brain blocks out the "information" provided by the farsighted or astigmatic eye and depends increasingly on the accurate image presented by the normal eye.

Early Indications

Crossed eyes or walleye are easily apparent to the beholder, but in many cases, warning indications about "lazy eye" are not so obvious. An eye checkup should be scheduled promptly for a child who appears clumsy in athletics and has a tendency to trip often, or who rubs his or her eyes a lot, or whose head is held at an unlikely angle.

Treatment

Many cases of "lazy eye" are corrected by placing a patch over the "good" eye, forcing the child to use the weak one and thereby strengthening it. When a corrective lens is needed for the farsighted or astigmatic eye, the patch is attached to the eyeglass in front of the good eye. Some doctors recommend the daily use of eyedrops in combination with the patch. Whatever its original cause, "lazy eye" should not be expected to improve only through exercise without covering the "good" eye.

Surgery

When surgery is deemed essential, it should be scheduled early. Postponed beyond the age of seven, its results are less successful. An ophthalmologist who specializes in such operations should give parents detailed instructions in how best to prepare the child for the hospital experience. Parents who have doubts about the advisability of surgery should seek a second opinion, but since time is of the essence if serious deterioration is to be avoided, the decision should not be unnecessarily postponed.

STIES

A sty is an inflammation of the eyelid caused by infection or by the blocking of one of the oil (sebaceous) glands at the base of an eyelash. Sties are among the most common complaints of childhood. They are highly contagious when caused by germs, and they may originate because eyestrain leads to rubbing the eyes, often with grimy fingers. It is not unusual for children to get one sty after another if their resistance to infection has been lowered by illness.

Treatment

Compresses of lukewarm water should be applied for five minutes at a time every two hours. An eye cup should not be used since it may lead to reinfection, nor should the sty be squeezed or the eye rubbed. *No medicated ointment or drops should be used unless prescribed by a doctor.* While the sty is present, the child should not share a washcloth or towel with anyone else in the family. If home remedies are unsuccessful, the doctor should be consulted.

EYESTRAIN

Where eyestrain leading to fatigue and headaches exists without any underlying defect in vision, it may be attributable to poor lighting or to poorly focused television images. Family rules about watching television should include instructions about keeping the room semilighted and having the screen perpendicular (not angled) and at eye level. A distance of eight to ten feet is desirable but difficult to maintain since children usually want to get as close to the action as possible. Whatever the problems associated with television exposure, parents should keep in mind that, in and of itself, constant viewing under suitable arrangements causes eye fatigue only in children who need glasses.

While "too much" reading doesn't damage the eyes, it may cause eyestrain if the lighting is poor. A good reading light produces no glare and should come over the right shoulder if the book is held in the right hand, and over the left if the reader is left-handed.

EYE SAFETY

Fortunately for apprehensive parents, youngsters like to wear the wraparound eye protectors featured in sporting equipment stores. They should be encouraged to do so when bicycle riding, playing baseball or racquet games, or clipping hedges and mowing the lawn. Watertight goggles provide good protection against irritation from heavily chlorinated pools and against conjunctivitis from swimming in infected waters.

SUMMING UP

Most eye problems of children can be corrected if they are properly treated. Since early detection of a disability is critical in some cases, an eye checkup is advisable for the preschool child, especially where there is even the slightest sign of visual difficulty. No child should have to suffer from the functional handicaps—not to mention the distressing appearance—resulting from the neglect of crossed eyes or walleye. Surgery for this condition is safe and can be accomplished before complications occur. Regular eye checkups should be scheduled for school-age children to rule out the possibility that astigmatism or nearsightedness may be interfering with their academic and social progress.

178. Lead Poisoning in Children

COMMON CHARACTERISTICS

Lead poisoning in children is a serious national health problem. It affects mainly—but by no means only—young children living in poorly maintained older buildings in the inner cities.

Lead is absorbed slowly; symptoms of poisoning occur only after there has been prolonged exposure to the substance and it has accumulated in the body. In mild cases, the symptoms resemble those of flu and other viral diseases, and the problem, unfortunately, may not be recognized for what it is. If undetected and untreated, lead poisoning can have severe consequences, including permanent brain damage and even death.

Parents who are aware of the hazardous sources of lead in the home and in the neighborhood can take important preventive steps that will minimize the risk of lead poisoning in their small children.

ENVIRONMENTAL SOURCES OF LEAD

The major source of lead in the environment is house paint. Prior to World War II, paint contained as much as 40 percent lead (by dry weight). Later, a growing awareness of the health hazards of lead exposure resulted in a gradual reduction of the lead content of paints. Finally, in the 1970s, federal regulations were issued requiring that paints contain no more than 0.5 percent of lead (by dry weight). Although this measure has effectively eliminated the danger of lead poisoning from new paint, people living in older houses continue to be exposed to lead in paint that was manufactured before the regulations went into effect. The hazard is greatest in buildings that are in poor condition, where old paint cracks and peels from walls, woodwork, and other surfaces. Young children, especially those two to three and a half years old, may develop lead poisoning by putting chips of such paint in their mouths and chewing on them or swallowing them. Lead-contaminated dust may be inhaled during restoration when the old paint is being removed.

Lead-based paint is not the only environmental source of this metal. Automobile exhaust and industries that use lead as part of their manufacturing process pollute the air with lead particles, and these in turn add to the lead levels in dust and dirt. Lead is also present in substantial quantities in tap water, in processed foods (particularly canned foods that have been left open for periods of time), and in acidic foods and beverages such as vegetable juices, fruits, and cola drinks that have been stored in noncommercially glazed pottery. Yet other sources of lead are the fumes of leaded gasoline and those of car battery casings.

ACCUMULATED LEAD

The amount of lead in the diet—or in the air, for that matter—is unlikely to cause lead poisoning by itself. However, lead accumulates in the body over time. Small amounts of lead taken in from different sources can build to dangerous levels, producing a number of toxic effects. The most important of these is a blocking of the production of hemoglobin, a substance in the blood that is essential for the transport of oxygen to the cells of the body. In addition, although the body can rid itself of small amounts of lead, it cannot dispose of larger quantities of the substance. Large amounts of lead accumulating in the body tissues—particularly the bone marrow, kidneys, and brain—can cause great damage by interfering with the proper functioning of these tissues.

THE SUSCEPTIBILITY OF CHILDREN

Young children are more susceptible to lead poisoning than older children or adults for several reasons. First, they take in more of the lead that is present in the environment. Because toddlers explore the world around them by putting things in their mouths, they ingest more lead-containing dirt and dust. Also, some young children have a desire to eat nonfood substances, which may include lead paint chips and other objects coated with lead dust. Furthermore, children not only take in more lead but also retain more of what is consumed. Lastly, since lead levels are higher in the air closer to the ground, small children breathe more heavily polluted air.

SYMPTOMS OF LEAD POISONING

The earlier lead poisoning is diagnosed and treatment is begun, the greater the chances for successful therapy and complete recovery. Thus, it is very important for parents to be aware of the signs of this condition.

SIGNS OF LEAD POISONING

MILD ACCUMULATION IN BODY
*Irritability
*Inability to concentrate
*Lethargy
*Stomach cramps
*Constipation
*Occasional vomiting

SEVERE ACCUMULATION
*More pronounced lethargy
*Extreme irritability
*Frequent vomiting
*Impaired coordination
*Seizures
*Black line along gums
*Mental impairment

The signs of mild lead poisoning include crankiness, sluggishness, decreased attention span, loss of appetite, stomach pains, constipation, and occasional vomiting. Many viral infections have similar symptoms, of course, but if your child develops any of these problems—and particularly if you suspect exposure to lead paint—it is wise to seek medical advice.

Children with more severe cases of lead poisoning may become very lethargic or irritable, may vomit a great deal, may have trouble walking or seem uncoordinated, and may even have seizures. A child with any of these symptoms is in great danger of developing serious complications and should be taken to a hospital or clinic immediately.

TREATMENT

Treatment is aimed at ridding the body of excess lead. This is done primarily by means of drugs known as chelating agents, which draw the lead out of the body tissues, enabling it to be excreted in the urine. The child usually must be watched very closely for the first week after these drugs are given to make sure that there is no relapse. Additional treatments may be necessary to get rid of most of the remaining lead in the body.

PREVENTION

In most, but not all, cases of lead poisoning in children, old, peeling paint is found to be the major culprit. Therefore, as an important preventive measure (or, if poisoning has already occurred, as a vital step in treatment) this source of lead exposure should be eliminated.

Paint with a high lead level must either be completely removed or be covered with hardboard, plywood paneling, or some other fire-resistant, durable material. Applying new paint over an old surface is pointless, since the child will still be exposed to lead if the new paint chips or cracks. In some areas, landlords are required by law to remove old paint and apply new; in others, the health department or housing authority must go to court to force such renovation.

As a temporary measure, until old paint can be permanently removed or covered, all chips should be scraped off walls and other surfaces and disposed of. (Alternatively, painted areas within the child's reach can be covered with boards, adhesive-backed paper, or masking tape.) The house should be thoroughly swept and the floors cleaned with a wet mop once a week.

SCREENING

Authorities generally agree that children between the ages of one and five years who live in high-risk areas should be screened periodically for lead poisoning. Many communities provide free blood tests for lead poisoning for all young children. Your doctor or local health authority can advise you on the need for tests for your child and on how frequently they should be performed.

SUMMING UP

Young children are particularly susceptible to the toxic effects of lead in the environment. They may take in high levels of lead—frequently from paint chips, but also from diet and the air—without appearing sick. Screening tests are valuable in detecting poisoning at this early, asymptomatic stage. Symptoms of poisoning, when they appear, are easily mistaken for those of common viral illnesses. However, lead poisoning can progress rapidly to become life-threatening.

Lead poisoning can be effectively treated and its serious consequences prevented if the problem is caught early. However, measures aimed at identifying and eliminating sources of lead exposure provide the best long-term answer to this national health problem.

179. Learning Problems

GENERAL CONSIDERATIONS

Children who have difficulty in school because of an apparent inability to listen, speak, read, write, think, or do numerical calculations are likely to have learning disabilities. Fortunately, today's school systems are generally well equipped to identify and help learning disabled children. In fact, federal and state laws require that every school system employ learning disabilities teachers to offer special instruction for learning disabled youngsters. Additionally, scientists and educators have developed effective ways to identify and treat learning disabilities.

IDENTIFYING LEARNING DISABILITIES

Problems rooted in physical handicaps, mental retardation, emotional disturbance, or cultural and economic deprivation are not classed as learning disabilities. Learning problems that are unrelated to these factors are classified in four categories corresponding to the four basic steps in the learning process: input, integration, memory, and output.

Input

This is the process of perceiving and recording information in the brain. Simply put, children with perception problems have trouble seeing and hearing accurately. Those with visual perception disabilities may confuse or reverse letters, using "3" for "E" or "b" for "d." Auditory perception disabilities may cause children to misunderstand words and respond to questions inappropriately. In a normal auditory environment, with several sounds going on simultaneously, these children may have trouble focusing on any one sound.

Integration

Typical problems in this area involve sequencing—the ability to place things in their proper order—and understanding. Sequencing problems often affect spelling and reading comprehension. Children with understanding disabilities grasp only the literal meanings of words and gestures. For example, the term "horsing around" makes no sense to a child who conceives of a horse only as a large animal.

Memory

This is the storage and retrieval of visual and auditory information. A child with short-term memory problems may forget verbal instructions before he or she has a chance to carry them out. Children with long-term memory disabilities, on the other hand, forget information that should be stored permanently, such as their home address.

Output

Both language and motor communication may be affected in output disabilities. Children with language disabilities often grope for words or use the wrong word. Motor output disabilities can hamper coordination of large groups of muscles, causing problems with such activities as bicycle riding. Many children also have a problem with fine motor coordination—precise coordination for small movements—which often appears as poor, laborious handwriting.

CAUSES

Much more is known about how learning disabilities affect children than about what causes them. For some children, the cause is simply a maturational lag; they have not reached the stage in development required to succeed with a certain level of school work. These children may need extra help for only a few years, until they catch up with their classmates.

Sometimes, an as yet to be explained nervous system malfunction causes children with normal vision and hearing to misinterpret everyday sights and sounds, resulting in the input disabilities discussed earlier. Learning disabilities specialists have found ways for these children to develop strengths that can compensate for weaknesses in perception. For instance, a child whose difficulty with visualizing words prevents him from writing may get his thoughts on paper by using a tape recorder, then transcribing.

Injuries incurred before birth or early in infancy account for some later learning disabilities. Children who were born prematurely, or who experienced medical problems soon after birth, frequently need special help in school. Learning disabilities also tend to run in families. Parents often recall having reading or coordination problems similar to their children's. Additionally, learning disabilities are about five times more likely to occur in boys than in girls.

LEARNING PROBLEMS

TYPE OF DISABILITY	AREAS AFFECTED	SIGNS AND SYMPTOMS
Input	Visual perception	Writing letters and figures backwards; confusing similar words and letters; spelling words backwards
	Auditory perception	Imprecise hearing; slow or inappropriate verbal response; difficulty focusing on one sound when several sounds are going on
Integration	Sequencing	Spelling errors in which the correct letters appear in the wrong order; difficulty remembering the sequence of events in a story; problems with counting and alphabetizing
	Abstraction	Difficulty understanding double meanings and figures of speech
Memory	Short-term memory	Difficulty memorizing and remembering instructions
	Long-term memory	Difficulty remembering personal information such as address, phone number, parents' names
Output	Language	Responding to questions with slow, halting speech
	Motor	Clumsiness—trouble with walking, running, athletic activities; poor handwriting

DIAGNOSIS

School special education teams use a variety of standardized tests, including intelligence, achievement, and development tests, to evaluate children who appear to be learning disabled. A visit to the family physician or pediatrician is also advisable in conjunction with the school evaluation; the doctor should make a complete physical examination to rule out any correctable problem—such as hearing loss or poor vision—that may cause difficulty in school. Other specialists, including neurologists, mental health professionals, and ophthalmologists or optometrists, may also be consulted. All the professionals involved both in and outside school should eventually pool their findings and collaborate on developing a suitable treatment program.

TREATMENT OPTIONS

The central treatment for learning disabilities generally takes place in the school and involves the child's spending all or part of the day in a special learning disabilities class—sometimes called a resource room. There are independent learning disabilities specialists or educational therapists in most communities as well; their services may be used for children who need more help than the school can provide.

Whatever the setting for treatment, the emphasis is always on developing strengths to overcome weaknesses. Some of the strategies used include:

1. Using recorded materials as a supplement to printed materials for children with reading problems.

2. Allowing children with fine motor coordination problems to use a typewriter or tape recorder for writing.

3. Providing chapter outlines and giving tests immediately after drills for children with memory disabilities.

4. Supplying written outlines of class presentations for children with auditory perception difficulties.

5. For children with visual perception and sequencing disabilities, providing worksheets instead of requiring assignments to be copied from books or from the blackboard.

Behavior modification is often part of a learning disabilities program. Teachers give tangible rewards and privileges for good performance and behavior. When students behave or perform poorly, these rewards are withheld.

Additionally, doctors sometimes prescribe medication for children with hyperkinesis, a neurological disorder characterized by constant movement and a short attention span and often accompanied by learning disabilities (see Chapter 180, "Childhood Hyperactivity"). For reasons that are not yet understood, nervous system stimulants exert a calming effect on hyperactive children, allowing them to concentrate on school work for longer periods of time.

SUMMING UP

Although there are still many unanswered questions about learning disabilities, more and more learning disabled children are being identified and helped at an early age. With proper therapy, chances are that the learning disabled child will be able to succeed in school and beyond.

180. Childhood Hyperactivity

COMMON CHARACTERISTICS

Childhood hyperactivity—or hyperkinesis—is a rather common disorder affecting 1 to 5 percent of all American children. Hyperactivity is characterized by a constant state of physical and emotional agitation. These children usually exhibit unusual impulsiveness, incessant talking, loudness, crying spells, a need to touch everything in sight, excitability, an inability to sit still, a short attention span, and other similar behavior problems. The syndrome may arise from a variety of causes, such as an emotional disorder, genetic predisposition, a minor brain dysfunction, unrecognized learning disorders, or a physical handicap, such as a hearing loss. Many physicians believe that the central cause of true hyperactivity is an organic disorder of the central nervous system.

The disease often develops in infancy, with parents reporting an unusual level of activity. In many cases, however, the symptoms often do not become apparent until the early school years.

DIAGNOSIS

Hyperactivity is more common in boys than girls, and most children seem to outgrow the problem by the time they reach adolescence; some evidence, however, indicates that the cognitive disorders associated with hyperactivity persist into adulthood. In diagnosing hyperactivity, it must be differentiated from other childhood and behavioral problems, such as brain disorders, childhood depression, dyslexia and other learning disabilities, and hearing deficits. Therefore, before a diagnosis of hyperactivity can be reached, these other conditions should be ruled out by careful physical and neurological examination and appropriate tests.

TREATMENT

Early recognition of hyperactivity and appropriate therapy usually can keep a child functioning well enough to prevent the development of low self-esteem and frustration. In general, scolding or other forms of punishment do little good; indeed, they often make the problem worse. Trying to make the hyperactive child sit still for more than a few minutes is also futile. Behavior modification, which involves rewarding good behavior and punishing inappropriate behavior, has proven successful in some cases.

Hyperactive children may be helped by an understanding teacher skilled at coping with the problem. It is important to maintain the child at a scholastic level corresponding to his or her age and abilities. If necessary, this can be accomplished by special tutoring, either at school, privately, or by members of the family.

Drugs administered for hyperactivity consist of central nervous system stimulants such as the amphetamines. It is not understood why these drugs have a calming effect, when characteristically one would expect the opposite. Still, when certain stimulants are given to a hyperactive

SYMPTOMS OF HYPERKINESIS

INATTENTION
- Failure to complete any task
- Easy distractability
- Poor listening
- Poor concentration
- Rapid movement from one form of play to another

IMPULSIVENESS
- Acting before thinking
- Speaking out of turn in class
- Frequent shifting from one activity to another
- Not waiting turn in group games and activities
- Low tolerance for frustration
- Quick mood shifts

HYPERACTIVITY
- Running about constantly
- Climbing excessively
- Fidgeting
- Inability to stay seated
- Excessive movement during sleep
- Clumsiness

child, the calming effect is often dramatic.

The dosage of the drug must be carefully established by the physician. Intermittent therapy, with drug-free periods, is now favored over long-term continuous drug administration to avoid side effects, possible problems with growth and development, and increased tolerance to the beneficial effects of the drug.

NUTRITIONAL INTERVENTION

Whether or not nutrition is related to hyperactivity has been debated for years. At this point, the answer is still unclear, although evidence suggests that diet is not a factor in the vast majority of cases. There are, nevertheless, a number of anecdotal accounts from patients attributing marked improvement to special diets. Some doctors theorize that there may be other explanations for the improvement, such as that the child outgrew the hyperactivity or that the extra parental attention involved in preparing the special diet was beneficial. Others feel that in some patients, the problem may involve food allergies, in which a restricted diet could conceivably be helpful.

Working together to try to solve the problem often produces positive psychological benefits. There also are self-help groups for parents of hyperactive children, taking advantage of the bond uniting those who suffer from a common problem.

SUMMING UP

Childhood hyperactivity is a very trying and frustrating disorder for everyone involved. Most children outgrow many aspects of the problem by the time they are teenagers. Understanding and time spent away from a demanding hyperactive child may help preserve peace in the household. School difficulties are common because of the disruptive behavior and neurologic problems such as dyslexia that are characteristic of hyperactive children. Drugs that have a calming effect may be prescribed, especially for school-age children. Self-help and parent support groups are sources of information and resources, and such groups can be found in most parts of the country. Further information may be obtained from The New York Institute for Child Development, 215 Lexington Avenue, New York, NY 10016 (212) 686-3630, or The Association of Children with Learning Disabilities, 4165 Library Road, Pittsburgh, PA 15234.

181. Immunization for Children

GENERAL CONSIDERATIONS

Most of the childhood diseases feared by earlier generations have now been widely controlled through vaccinations. Diseases such as mumps, measles, and rubella that all children experienced as few as twenty years ago can now be prevented with vaccinations, while long-available vaccines continue to control killing and crippling diseases such as polio, diphtheria, and whooping cough.

THE FUNCTION OF VACCINES

Vaccination works on a very simple principle: A killed or weakened version of a disease-causing agent is introduced into a person's system, and, in response, the person develops antibodies to protect against the disease. Most vaccines are administered by intramuscular injection; the major exception is the polio vaccine, which is usually given orally.

The agents that immunize against diphtheria, tetanus, and whooping cough (pertussis) are given in a combined single injection. Diphtheria and tetanus vaccine contains toxiod, an inactivated form of the bacterial toxins that cause the diseases. The whooping cough vaccine consists of killed bacteria, and the polio vaccine is a live but weakened (attenuated) version of the three types of the virus that cause polio. Similarly, the measles, mumps, and rubella vaccines are made from live, attenuated virus.

Children should be routinely immunized against diphtheria, tetanus, whooping cough, polio, measles, rubella, and mumps. Immunization should begin at the age of two to three months, when an infant's immune system has developed sufficiently to respond to vaccination. (Prior to that age, antibodies passed to the fetus through the placenta may interfere with immune response.)

ADMINISTRATION OF VACCINATIONS

Conferring immunity through vaccination frequently requires more than a single dose of the killed or attenuated disease agent. Booster immunization is also needed to update earlier vaccines. The recommended schedule of immunizations for infants and young children appears in the accompanying table. In addition to the required immunizations listed, children should have a tetanus booster any time

they are at risk of contracting tetanus—for instance, after sustaining a cut from an unclean object. Rarely, a child may be exposed to diphtheria or whooping cough; however, if exposure occurs, existing immunity should be strengthened with a booster.

REACTIONS TO IMMUNIZATION

Some children feel out of sorts and unwell after a vaccination, but generally these reactions are quite mild. Restlessness and loss of appetite are the most common problems, usually lasting only a couple of days. Refusal of food for longer than two days should be investigated by a physician.

Sometimes, a lump develops at the site of the injection. This, too, should pass within a few days. Fever is a common reaction to the DTP vaccination. If a child develops a slight fever after being vaccinated, the doctor should be contacted to recommend a remedy to lower the fever.

IMMUNIZATION FOR ADOLESCENTS

All teenagers should receive a diphtheria-tetanus booster. Additionally, any teenager who has neither been infected

SCHEDULE OF REQUIRED VACCINES FOR INFANTS AND CHILDREN

AGE	TYPE OF VACCINATION
2 months	Diphtheria-tetanus-pertussis (DTP) vaccine; trivalent oral poliovirus vaccine (TOPV)
4 months	DTP; TOPV
6 months	DTP; TOPV (The third DTP vaccination is mandatory; the third TOPV optional, unless polio is endemic.)
15 months	Measles, mumps, rubella vaccines, either separately or combined in one injection
15–18 months	DTP; TOPV
4–5 years	DTP booster
5–6 years	TOPV booster
12 years	Adult-type tetanus or tetanus-diphtheria booster

with nor received vaccinations for mumps, measles, or rubella should be immunized. Mumps may be serious in persons who have reached sexual maturity, causing inflammation of the testes in 20 percent of infected men and inflammation of the ovaries and fallopian tubes in a smaller percentage of women. Also, young women who are given the rubella vaccine should not become pregnant for at least two months because of the risk of transmitting the virus to the fetus.

SUMMING UP

Immunization has greatly reduced children's chances of contracting many serious diseases, and vaccines for the remaining childhood diseases, such as chicken pox, are now being developed. It is the parents' responsibility to keep their child's immunizations up to date and obtain appropriate boosters at regular intervals.

Common Medical Emergencies

182. Cardiopulmonary Resuscitation (CPR)

GENERAL CONSIDERATIONS

Patients in many emergency situations require cardiopulmonary resuscitation (CPR) to reestablish halted breathing and circulation. CPR combines artificial respiration and external cardiac compression to keep an adequate supply of oxygenated blood pumping through the patient's system until a fully equipped emergency team takes over with definitive medical treatment. CPR alone can sustain life for an indefinite period of time, but it must be done properly and, above all, begun promptly. Permanent brain damage can occur after as few as four or five minutes without oxygen, and six or seven minutes without oxygen will cause death.

STARTING CPR

If a patient is not breathing, his circulatory system will inevitably shut down within a few minutes; similarly, a patient in cardiac arrest will rapidly lose respiratory function. Signs of cardiac/respiratory failure include a deathlike appearance, a bluish tinge to the skin, widely dilated pupils, and absence of pulses and breathing. If these signs are present, CPR should begin immediately.

CPR consists of four basic steps, known as the ABCD, that must be performed in order with no delay between steps: *a*irway opening, *b*reathing, *c*irculation, and *d*efinitive medical care.

Airway Opening

First, an unconscious patient's jaw is relaxed, and his tongue drops backward to obstruct the throat. To clear the blocked airway, turn the patient onto his back and, placing one hand beneath the neck and the other on the forehead, tilt the head and lift the neck so that the throat is extended and the chin is pointing upward. Next, remove all foreign obstructions from the mouth and throat, including dentures and stomach contents. (Vomiting may occur in an unconscious patient, and it is likely to occur during CPR.) Sometimes, breathing resumes as soon as the airway is cleared. If this happens, precautions should be taken to ward off shock, and emergency care should still be obtained. Breathing may cease again, so the rescuer should remain prepared to begin CPR.

Breathing Restored

Second, if breathing does not resume, begin mouth-to-mouth resuscitation immediately after clearing the airway. Keep the head tilted back with the hand supporting the neck, but rotate the upper hand to grasp the patient's nose, sealing it off. The nose should be sealed so that air blown into the lungs does not escape. Next, take a deep breath and place your mouth, opened wide, over the patient's. Exhale forcibly, until the patient's chest rises and the resistance of the expanded lung is noticeable. Then allow the patient to exhale passively, noting whether the chest falls. The first four breaths should be given in rapid succession without waiting for the patient's lungs to deflate completely between breaths. If the patient is receiving adequate ventilation, his chest should rise and fall with each breath, his lungs should become resistant as they fill, and his exhalation should be audible and strong enough to feel with a hand next to the mouth and nose. In the absence of these signs, check the airway for additional obstruction and make sure the head is tilted sufficiently.

Circulation Restored

Third, as soon as mouth-to-mouth respiration is instituted, external cardiac compression should begin. Ideally, the two processes should be carried out simultaneously by two different rescuers, one inflating the lungs while the other compresses the heart. If only one rescuer

The A·B·C of CPR

Airway opening **Breathing** **Circulation**

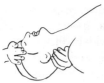

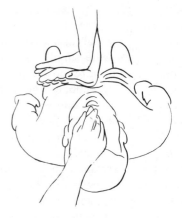

is present, however, external cardiac compression and mouth-to-mouth respiration must be alternated in a specific, rhythmic pattern.

The heart is located slightly to the left of the middle of the chest, between the sternum, or breastbone, and the spine. Pressure to the lower portion of the breastbone compresses the heart's chambers between the breastbone and the spine, producing sufficient output to keep blood circulating to the body's vital tissues. The patient should be lying on a firm surface, such as a floor or a board, for external cardiac compression to succeed.

Maintaining the correct position of the hands is essential in external cardiac compression. Kneeling at the side of the patient, the rescuer should place the heel of one hand over the lower half of the breastbone—*not* the lower tip of the breastbone. (Pressure on this point, known as the xiphoid process, may cause damage to the liver.) Place the other hand on top of the first hand, and, keeping the arms stiff, rock forward to exert eighty to one hundred pounds of pressure on the chest. Then relax. The pressure–relaxation motion should be repeated every second, with pressure lasting one-half second and relaxation one-half second. This rhythm can be maintained by counting "one-and-two-and-three-and-four-and-five-and," exerting pressure on the count and relaxing on the "and."

For every five heart compressions, the patient's lungs should be inflated once. If two rescuers are working together, one can perform the compression, counting audibly, while the other ventilates the lungs at five-second intervals. If only one rescuer is present, he may attempt to maintain a five-to-one ratio of compressions to breaths, using the "rule of five": Start by giving five strong breaths by mouth-to-mouth resuscitation, at the rate of one breath every five seconds. Then start external cardiac compression at the required rate, pausing only long enough to give the victim one breath after every five heart compressions. Try not to interrupt the

compression procedure for more than five seconds at any time.

Another option for the single rescuer is to alternate fifteen compressions at a slightly faster rate with two breaths. The faster rate is necessary to compensate for the pauses for ventilation.

For small children, cardiac compression requires only the heel of one hand and a much lighter pressure on the breastbone: For infants, it should be depressed only one-half to three-fourths of an inch, and for young children, three-fourths to one and one-half inches. The rate of compression should also be faster, up to eighty to one hundred compressions per minute.

Definitive Medical Care

Finally, trained emergency technicians should be summoned at the first sign of cardiac or respiratory distress. Basic CPR should continue, however, while emergency personnel intubate, draw blood, and administer drugs to the patient.

COMMON PROBLEMS AND MISTAKES

At the least, the common mistakes made in administering CPR render it ineffective. At the worst, they further endanger the patient. In giving mouth-to-mouth respiration, remember these four points:

1. Be aware that the patient may vomit. If vomiting occurs, turn the patient on his side with his cheek resting on the ground. Clear all stomach contents from the mouth, and continue mouth-to-mouth.
2. Tilt infants' and children's heads back gently; an exaggerated tilt could rupture a cervical vertebra.
3. Open the mouth widely, and seal it tightly over the victim's mouth.
4. Seal the victim's nose tightly.

In cardiac compression, remember:

1. Keep only the heel of one hand on the breastbone.

2. Press only the lower half of the breast-bone.

3. Press vertically, so that pressure is not exerted on the rib cage.

4. Use a smooth rhythm of compressions and relaxations.

SUMMING UP

If a patient appears to be in cardiac or respiratory arrest, follow the ABCD of cardiopulmonary resuscitation. First, provide a clear airway; second, establish artificial breathing; third, begin cardiac compres-sion; and fourth, continue until definitive medical treatment is available.

Training in CPR is available to the public from the Red Cross, the YMCA and YWCA, and similar organizations. Students work on lifelike mannequins that provide electronic feedback indicating whether procedures are successful, and experienced instructors demonstrate effective techniques. The training is usually offered at no or very low cost; more importantly, few people can effectively administer CPR without the hands-on experience provided by such training.

183. Choking Emergencies

COMMON CHARACTERISTICS

A choking emergency occurs when breathing is obstructed by an object that has "gone down the wrong way" and entered the windpipe. A choking emergency may also occur when breathing is threatened by blockage of the windpipe during an acute bronchial asthma attack. Choking is one of the leading causes of accidental death in the United States, and for children of pre-school age, it is the leading cause of accidental death in the home. Since death from asphyxiation can occur within four minutes, choking obviously is an emergency that requires on-the-spot rescue.

HOW CHOKING OCCURS

Behind the tongue in the upper part of the throat, there are two passages: the gullet, or esophagus, into which food is swallowed for transport into the stomach; and the windpipe, or trachea, through which air is transported into the lungs.

When food and drink are swallowed, a reflex action occurs that shuts off the windpipe. However, this mechanism may fail because of a confusion of signals, for example, when an individual takes a breath while talking or laughing or gasping with surprise at the same time that food is being swallowed, and the windpipe does *not* shut off. The food—or whatever else was in the mouth—may then enter the windpipe, obstructing the air passageway.

SYMPTOMS OF CHOKING EMERGENCY

The symptoms of a choking emergency can easily be mistaken for a heart attack, and because such episodes frequently occur in restaurants, the phenomenon is sometimes referred to as a "cafe coronary." In typical cases, victims become pale as they struggle for air, then they turn blue from lack of oxygen. If not treated on the spot, the victim dies in a matter of minutes.

The sign that the victim is choking rather than having a heart attack is that even though still conscious, he or she will be incapable of speaking because a chunk of food large enough to obstruct the top of the windpipe will also close off the larynx or voice box.

It has been suggested that excessive drinking can play a role in these emergencies, not only because of impaired judgment but also because alcohol dulls the gag

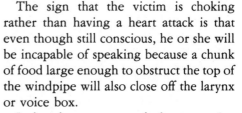

How to Perform the Heimlich Maneuver

With the victim standing or sitting:
1. Stand behind and wrap arms around victim's waist.
2. Place thumb side of your fist against victim's abdomen, slightly above the navel and below the rib cage.
3. Grasp your fist with other hand and press fist into the victim's abdomen with a quick upward thurst. Repeat as often as needed.
4. For seated victim, stand behind chair and perform maneuver as described above.
5. After food is dislodged, victim should see a doctor.

When the victim is lying down:
1. Lay victim on his back.
2. Kneel astride his hips.
3. With one hand on top of the other, place the heel of your bottom hand on the abdomen, slightly above the navel and below the rib cage.
4. Press into the abdomen with a quick upward thrust. Repeat as often as necessary.
5. Should the victim vomit, quickly place him on his side and wipe out mouth to prevent vomitus from entering lungs.
6. After the food is dislodged, the victim should see a doctor.

reflex, which normally might cause the piece of food to be expelled before it can be "inhaled."

THE HEIMLICH MANEUVER

In 1974, a simple and effective lifesaving procedure for choking victims was introduced by Dr. Harry J. Heimlich, a Cincinnati surgeon. Now known widely as the Heimlich maneuver, it can be accomplished even by a child and is something everyone over the age of ten or eleven years should know how to do.

The technique works because the accident occurs only during inhalation. Therefore, a certain amount of air has been taken into the victim's lungs at the same time that the obstructive material has been "inhaled" instead of swallowed. By using the piston principle, the volume of air is compressed sufficiently to propel the obstruction upward and out of the mouth.

Step by step, the Heimlich maneuver involves:

1. If the victim is capable of standing, the rescuer stands behind and positions his or her own fist so that the thumb is against the victim's abdomen under the rib cage and slightly above the navel.
2. Grasping the fist with the other hand, the rescuer performs a quick upward thrust into the abdomen. This pistonlike motion pushes the diaphragm upward, compressing the air in the lungs so that it is pushed upward, thereby providing the force that expels the obstruction.
3. If the first attempt is unsuccessful, the maneuver should be repeated.
4. For a seated victim near collapse, the rescuer performs the maneuver while kneeling or squatting.
5. If the victim is lying down, he or she should be turned face upward. The rescuer kneels and straddles the victim's thighs. Hands are placed one over the other so that the heel of the bottom hand is positioned between the rib cage and the navel.

A quick thrust inward and upward forces the air from the lungs.

SPECIAL CIRCUMSTANCES

Older children and baby-sitters caring for infants and toddlers should be taught to use this variation of the Heimlich maneuver in an emergency: Instead of using the fist, the thrust at the abdomen is accomplished by quickly pressing inward and upward with the index and middle fingers.

In the absence of a rescuer, a choking victim can accomplish the maneuver by putting the fist in the right place, grasping it with the other hand, and thrusting inward and upward.

SPECIAL PRECAUTIONS

Forcefully squeezing or hugging the victim can cause internal injuries and break ribs. The obstruction is not propelled outward by the manual compression of the chest but by the upward thrust of the diaphragm. Whacking the victim on the back should not be used as a substitute for the Heimlich maneuver.

PREVENTION OF CHOKING EMERGENCIES

Children

• Small objects such as buttons and earrings should not be left within reach of a baby or toddler.
• Young children should not be given peanuts, hard candies, or similar "treats," especially when they are playing or moving around.
• Children under the age of three should not be given any toys with small removable parts.
• Horseplay and hilarity during meals should be discouraged.

Adults

- Candy or chewing gum should be disposed of before engaging in tennis, running, or other active pursuits.
- Medicines in pill or capsule form should never be taken when lying down.
- Dentures should be checked regularly for necessary repairs and refitting.
- Food should be cut into small pieces and chewed thoroughly. Watch out for large pieces of rare meat!
- Avoid talking with a full mouth.

SUMMING UP

Choking emergencies can usually be prevented by using good sense and good table manners and by taking precautionary measures around young children. However, everyone in a household should learn the Heimlich maneuver and practice it so that it can be applied as a lifesaving measure if necessary.

184. Drowning and Water Safety

GENERAL CONSIDERATIONS

Some seven thousand Americans drown every year, and over a million are near victims or suffer traumatic injuries related to participation in water sports. The great majority of these accidents occur in shallow water, or within fifty feet of the shore or a swimming float.

Exercising common sense when in, near, or on the water can prevent many accidents. Being aware of the basics of water safety and emergency procedures can make the difference between life and death in the event of a serious injury or accident.

DROWNING

Drowning is specifically defined as suffocation when in or under the water. Most water accident victims die of hypoxia (lack of oxygen) or of a heart attack brought on by panic and exertion. There is seldom much water in the lungs.

Little water reaches the lungs because of the sensitivity of the larynx to foreign material entering it. When water enters the nose and mouth, a person's instinctive reaction is to cough and swallow, while at the same time taking a deep breath. If the head is submerged, large amounts of water will be swallowed and a little may be inhaled. However, as the inhaled water passes down the trachea (windpipe), an irritative response occurs in the larynx, resulting in a spasm that seals off the airway. Only about a teaspoon of water will have entered the lungs. In many cases, the drowning person remains in laryngeal spasm until he or she has stopped trying to breathe. Unconsciousness then brings a relaxation of the spasm. If this occurs while the person is still submerged, water will enter the lungs but not in large amounts, since the victim is no longer inhaling and swallowing.

The water that does enter the lungs can cause delayed problems in those who survive a threatened drowning. Fresh water is absorbed from the lungs into the bloodstream and drastically dilutes normal body salts. As a result, red blood cells may be damaged and the cells of the pulmonary membranes may rupture. Seawater, on the other hand, which has a considerably greater concentration of salt than the body fluids, tends to pull water out of the body tissues and into the lungs, causing pulmonary edema. People who have been rescued from near drowning should therefore be observed closely in a hospital for at least twenty-four hours.

RESCUE AND RESUSCITATION

The fate of someone threatened with drowning is determined largely by the speed of the rescue and the speed with which the airway is cleared and resuscitation begun. Getting air into the lungs without delay is vital.

Someone in trouble in the water may be conscious and struggling or may be unconscious, floating face downward on the surface or submerged below the surface. A drowning person who is conscious is often in a state of panic and will grab wildly at a would-be rescuer. Many double drownings have occurred when people who were not qualified to do so attempted a swimming rescue. Therefore, whenever possible, rescue should be left to those who have been trained in lifesaving techniques. If, however, such help is not available, the rule, "Throw, tow, row, and only then go," should be followed when attempting rescue of a conscious swimmer.

• Standing in shallow water, or on a sturdy dock or float, throw a rope attached to a buoyant object (a life preserver or plastic

Drownproofing

This technique preserves strength and can enable a person to survive for a long period in water. Start by taking a deep breath and holding it with face in the water and arms and legs dangling. When ready to breathe, raise the arms and spread legs. Then lower arms, bring legs together and exhale. Raise the head just enough to clear the surface and inhale. Repeat until rested enough to swim on or until help arrives.

bottle, for example) to the swimmer. When he grasps it, tow him in.

• If this fails, and a rowboat is available, row out to the victim, approaching him stern first (the stern of a boat is more stable than the bow), allowing him to climb aboard or hang on to the rail. Alternatively, hold out a pole or a spare oar to the victim and tow him ashore.

• Only if these courses fail, and only if the rescuer is capable of performing the rescue in safety to himself, should a swimming rescue be attempted.

If the victim is not breathing, mouth-to-mouth or mouth-to-nose resuscitation should be started at once, with no attempt being made to clear the lungs of any water that may be present. If the rescuer can stand, or can hold onto a float or similar object while supporting the victim, resuscitation should begin while the victim is still in the water. It should continue without interruption until the victim is breathing spontaneously. Cardiopulmonary resuscitation, if necessary, should begin as soon as the victim can be placed on a firm surface.

Once the victim is breathing spontaneously, he or she should be placed in the "recovery position" (lying prone, the arms extended at shoulder level and bent so that the hands rest beside the head, the head turned to one side, and the leg on the same side drawn up at a right angle to the torso), and kept warm. A rescuer should be alert to the probability that the victim, having swallowed a great deal of water, will vomit.

SPECIFIC PROBLEMS

Cramps

Cramps in the feet and legs and, less commonly, the stomach may occur when swimming for long periods or in cold water. Usually they are caused by a fatigued muscle that goes into spasm because of oxygen deprivation. A cramped leg or foot muscle should be stretched and mas-

saged. A cramp in the abdomen is best treated by floating until it relaxes.

Hypothermia

A drop in core body temperature, which may occur in a person submerged in cold water for a prolonged period of time, leads to a progressive decline in both mental and physical functioning, making it progressively more difficult for a swimmer to take action to save himself. On the other hand, hypothermia may contribute to survival: it slows metabolism and minimizes the effects of hypoxia. Some victims can be resuscitated with no permanent damage.

Breath-holding Blackout

In order to improve their breath-holding ability, some swimmers hyperventilate (take several deep breaths in quick succession) before entering the water. This produces a significant decrease in the level of carbon dioxide in the blood, making it possible to remain under water much longer. However, since the presence of carbon dioxide in the blood normally provides the stimulus for taking a breath, the swimmer becomes vulnerable to diminished levels of oxygen and subsequent unconsciousness.

Spinal Cord Injuries

Serious spinal cord injuries, concussions, and death can result from sliding head first into shallow water, or from accidents while diving. Water should always be tested for depth and the presence of rocks and other hidden objects before diving. A victim of a spinal cord injury, if conscious, will have paralysis or weakness or tingling sensations in the extremities. If a spinal cord injury is suspected (cuts or abrasions on the head may provide a clue), a swimmer should be removed from the water on a board and should be kept as still as possible.

BASIC WATER-SURVIVAL TACTIC

Survival floating (the "dead man's float") can be done for hours without tiring. It is a basic safety measure and should be understood and practiced by swimmers and nonswimmers alike.

PRECAUTIONS

• A careful watch should be kept on all infants and children playing near and in water.

• When boating, all nonproficient swimmers should wear Coast Guard–approved personal flotation devices (PFDs) at all times. (In accordance with Coast Guard regulations, there must be one approved PFD per person on board.)

• All water-skiers should wear PFDs or a specially designed life belt.

• Alcoholic beverages should be avoided when engaging in water activities. Alcohol impairs judgment. It also dilates the blood vessels, forcing the heart to work harder than usual.

• Swimming alone, or during a thunderstorm, or when a storm threatens, should be avoided.

• Home pool owners should install a fence around the pool area; the gate should be self-locking. (In some areas, these precautions against small children wandering alone beside a pool are required by law.) A life preserver or crook and a first-aid kit should be kept near the pool at all times.

SUMMING UP

Most drownings and near drownings can be prevented by practicing common sense and taking safety precautions in and near the water. Special care should be taken in attempting to rescue a drowning victim. All too often people who cannot swim or cannot effectively rescue the drowning person will plunge in, resulting in a double tragedy.

185. Burns

COMMON CHARACTERISTICS

There are over 2 million burn injuries annually in the United States. Of these, 75,000 are serious enough to require hospitalization, and 8,000 are fatal. The more extensive a burn, the more dangerous it is. A burn that affects more than 20 percent of the body surface endangers life. However, with modern treatments (fluid replacement, artificial skin, microsurgery, plastic surgery, and antibiotics), many of those victims whose burns would previously

have been fatal make a good recovery.

Burns are usually classified according to the degree of tissue damage. In a first-degree burn, damage is limited to the outer layer of the skin (epidermis); there is redness, tenderness, and usually some swelling. First-degree burns, although painful, usually are not serious unless large areas of the body are involved. In second-degree burns, the damage extends through the epidermis into the dermis, and blisters form. Third-degree (full-thickness) burns involve complete destruction of the skin and may extend into the underlying tissues. Many second-degree and all third-degree burns require hospitalization. The severity of a burn can easily be underestimated. Unless the burn is obviously a minor one, medical help should be sought.

The great majority of burns are thermal burns, resulting from fire, scalding liquids, steam, or excessive exposure to the sun. Chemical burns from drain cleaners, bleaches, and so on are also common. Electrical burns may be caused by touching the working parts of a home appliance with wet hands or by contact with a metal object inserted into a service outlet, fallen electric wires, or lightning.

MINOR BURNS

Minor burns occur very frequently and usually require no medical attention. Ice or cold-water compresses should be applied to the burned area for about half an hour to relieve pain. Petroleum jelly may be applied if there are no blisters, and the area may be covered with a gauze dressing for a few days.

Most sunburns are first-degree burns, but they can be very painful. The victim can be bathed in cold water to relieve the pain. He or she should be kept warm and given plenty of fluids. An extensive second-degree sunburn is a major burn and should be treated as such.

A second-degree burn that does not involve a large area should be gently cleaned with soap and water and rinsed with a salty (saline) solution. All dirt, grease, and broken skin should be removed. Burned skin that has not been broken should be left in place, since healing will take place underneath it. Blisters should be carefully opened and the skin allowed to cover the wound. More extensive second-degree burns should be treated by a doctor. The doctor may decide to leave the burn uncovered and allow the wound to dry, particularly if the hands are involved, since open treatment of this kind allows the

joints to move and helps prevent stiffness and contractures. In closed treatment, a dressing of absorbent gauze is covered by a bulky pressure dressing and held firmly in place with a bandage. If there is no infection, the dressing will be left in place until the wound has healed—usually within two weeks.

FIRST-AID MEASURES FOR MAJOR BURNS

Since most major burn victims should be moved as quickly as possible to a hospital or burn center, an ambulance should be called immediately. While waiting for help to arrive, some first-aid measures can be taken. However, it is important to stress that, when a burn is serious, it is better to risk doing too little than too much.

First-aid measures depend to some extent on the cause of the burn, but the most

Rules of Nines

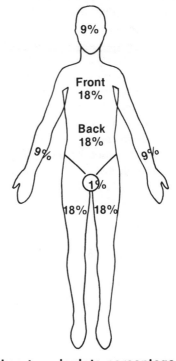

How to calculate percentage of body that has been burned

important first step—in almost every case —is to immerse the burned area in ice water or the coldest water available until the burn and the surrounding clothing are thoroughly soaked. Clean blankets or sheets can then be wrapped loosely to keep the victim warm and to prevent the burned area from being contaminated. No attempt should be made to remove clothing that adheres to the burn, and no ointment should be applied.

In serious burns, as in other major medical emergencies, the possibility of shock should always be anticipated. (Shock, in fact, is responsible for more fatalities in burn cases than is the actual damage to the tissues.) The early signs of shock include a weak, rapid pulse, clammy skin, and rapid, shallow breathing. Later, the pupils become dilated and the patient grows increasingly unresponsive. If untreated, unconsciousness and possibly death will result.

To ward off shock, the victim should be kept warm but not hot, should lie down with the feet higher than the head, and should be kept still. Every attempt should be made to reassure and calm the patient. If help does not arrive within an hour, and if the victim is conscious and not vomiting, lukewarm water or salt solution (one teaspoon of salt and a half-teaspoon of baking soda to a quart of water) should be given by mouth to maintain the fluid balance, which may be upset because of plasma leakage through the burned areas. About four ounces should be offered every fifteen minutes to an adult; half that amount to a child.

ADDITIONAL MEASURES

In chemical burns, whether of the skin or of the eye, it is important to flood the area with large amounts of cold, running water, being careful not to wash the chemical onto other parts of the body. First-aid instructions for neutralizing the chemical —if these are given on the container— should then be followed and the burn covered with a cold, wet, sterile dressing.

As long as the victim of an electrical burn is in contact with an electric current, he should not be touched. If possible, the current should be shut off immediately. Alternatively, a dry stick or a dry rope may be used to remove the wire from the victim or the victim from the wire. If this fails, a rescuer wearing rubber boots and gloves, and roped around the waist so that he can be pulled back if need be, may be able to remove the victim. As soon as the victim has been separated from the electric current, breathing should be checked, and, if necessary, cardiopulmonary resuscitation should be started (see Chapter 182, "CPR"). First-aid treatment of the burn should be delayed until the victim is breathing.

SUMMING UP

Most burns are caused by carelessness. The most frequent causes of accidental burns are smoking in bed, using flammable materials, servicing furnaces irregularly, keeping matches within the reach of children, failing to provide smoke detectors and readily available fire extinguishers, unsafe storage of chemicals, and carelessness when handling electrical appliances. Medicine has made great advances in the treatment of burns, and many lives are now saved that previously would have been lost.

186. Bleeding Emergencies

Minor external bleeding is seldom serious. The damaged blood vessel contracts, slowing the flow of blood, and a clot forms to plug the wound so that the injured vessel can heal. But in a severe wound—as when an artery is severed or torn—blood may flow so rapidly that clots cannot form. Severe and rapid blood loss (about one and a half pints in an adult, half a pint in a child) can lead to shock and, if not stopped, can be fatal in a short period of time. Therefore, the goal of emergency treatment of external bleeding is to stop the flow of blood as quickly as possible. Controlling blood loss takes precedence over most other emergency procedures.

TREATMENT OF SEVERE BLEEDING

Usually, the most effective way to stop bleeding is to apply direct pressure to the wound.

• Have the victim lie down and, if feasible, elevate the injured part. This will tend to reduce the flow of blood from the wound and forestall shock.
• If there is visible and easily removable debris in the wound, pick it out. Do not try to remove anything deeply embedded.
• Using a clean pad, a firmly rolled handkerchief, or even the fingers (the priority is to stop the bleeding; preventing infection takes second place), press hard on the wound. If the edges of the wound are gaping, hold them together at the same time as you press down. If there is anything embedded in the wound, direct the pressure around the object rather than over it.
• When bleeding stops, take a clean pad or handkerchief and tie it firmly over the wound, so as to maintain pressure. If blood oozes through this pad, do not remove it, but put more padding on top and bandage it firmly enough to stop the bleeding.
• Do not remove the dressing—that should be done by a doctor.

If direct pressure on the wound fails to stop the bleeding, or if the wound is too extensive for direct pressure to be used, it may be possible to control bleeding by applying pressure to a major artery, at a point between the wound and the heart. Such pressure points, where the arteries lie close to the surface, include the center of the groin (for leg wounds), the underside of the wrists (for hand wounds), the inside of the upper arm between the armpit and the elbow (for arm wounds), and the area directly in front of the ears (for scalp wounds). The artery should be firmly compressed against the underlying bone. Bleeding will probably not stop completely, but it will be significantly slowed, making local pressure more effective. The pressure-point technique should not be used any longer than is necessary.

A tourniquet should be applied only in extreme circumstances, as for example, when a limb is badly crushed or severed, or when bleeding cannot be controlled in any other way. In such cases, a tourniquet may be lifesaving, but in general, use of a tourniquet tends to do more damage to the wounded extremity than did the original injury. Moreover, if left in place too long, a tourniquet may result in the loss of the extremity.

A tourniquet should be positioned just above the wound and should not touch its edge. If the wound is in the area of a joint,

Applying a Tourniquet

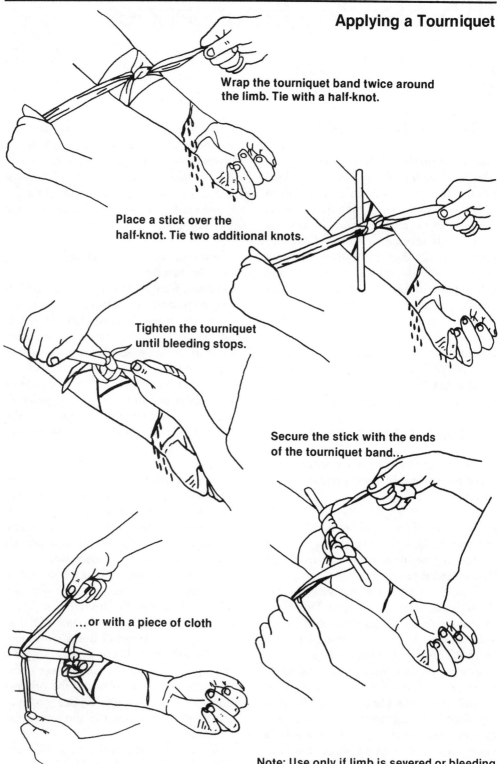

Wrap the tourniquet band twice around the limb. Tie with a half-knot.

Place a stick over the half-knot. Tie two additional knots.

Tighten the tourniquet until bleeding stops.

Secure the stick with the ends of the tourniquet band...

...or with a piece of cloth

Note: Use only if limb is severed or bleeding cannot be controlled by applying pressure.

or just below it, the tourniquet should be placed immediately above the joint.

• Fold a triangular bandage, long handkerchief, or piece of cloth until it is three or four inches thick and six to eight layers thick.
• Elevate the bleeding extremity and wrap the tourniquet band twice around it. Tie the band with a half-knot.
• Place a short stick that will not break, or a similar object, on the half-knot. Tie two additional overhand knots on top of the stick.
• Tighten the tourniquet by twisting the stick to the point that the bleeding stops.
• Secure the stick with the ends of the tourniquet band or a spare piece of cloth. It is very important that the tourniquet not be loosened after it has been applied, and that it be removed only by a doctor.

NOSEBLEEDS

A nosebleed is a common bleeding occurrence and usually a minor one, although occasionally the amount of blood lost is sufficient to cause shock. Most nosebleeds are the result of facial injuries, nose infections, or high blood pressure. These can be treated in the following way:

• Have the patient sit up so that blood trickling down the throat is not taken into the lungs.
• Apply pressure by pinching the nostrils or placing a bandage between the underside of the patient's upper lip and the gum and pressing it with the fingers.
• Keep the patient quiet. Anxiety can heighten blood pressure and increase bleeding.
• Apply an icepack over the nose.

A few nosebleeds cannot be stopped by this treatment and require a visit to the hospital for application of a special nasopharyngeal pack.

If a person is bleeding from the nose or ears following a head injury, no attempt should be made to treat the nosebleed. Instead, it should be assumed that the skull has been fractured, and medical help should be summoned at once.

INTERNAL BLEEDING

Bleeding, however slight, from any body orifice (the mouth or rectum, for example) may point to internal hemorrhage, perhaps from an ulcer, a closed fracture, or a lacerated internal organ. Signs suggesting internal bleeding are those of incipient shock: a weak or rapid pulse, cold and clammy skin, dilated pupils that respond slowly to light, thirst, anxiety, nausea, and vomiting.

Nothing can be done on the spot to control internal bleeding: medical care is needed, as soon as possible. In the meantime, it is important to keep the patient warm and still, to loosen binding clothing, to give no food or fluids, and to act in a reassuring manner.

SUMMING UP

Severe bleeding always calls for quick action to prevent extensive blood loss, shock, and eventual death. Most external bleeding can be controlled by applying pressure directly to the wound, or at a pressure point between the wound and the heart. A tourniquet should be applied only in extreme cases, such as a badly injured limb or bleeding that cannot be controlled in any other way. Internal bleeding requires medical care as soon as possible.

187. Shock

COMMON CHARACTERISTICS

Shock is a condition in which the blood pressure suddenly drops and the vital organs of the body, deprived of adequate oxygen, cease functioning—at least momentarily. Shock may be slight and transitory, as in a fainting spell. It may also be serious and prolonged, as when a person suffers an extensive third-degree burn. If severe and untreated, shock leads to death.

CAUSES OF SHOCK

Shock usually arises from one of three general causes. First, blood or other body fluids may be lost to the point that the blood pressure cannot be maintained. (This is known as hypovolemic shock.) Severe internal or external bleeding, an extensive burn, or prolonged diarrhea may all result in hypovolemic shock.

Shock may also result from disruption or disturbance of the heart's rate or rhythm, with a consequent reduced output of blood from the heart (cardiogenic shock).

A third possible cause is a sudden enlargement or dilation of the blood vessels so that, although the volume of circulating blood is not diminished, there is a relative shortage of blood. Vasodilation may occur as the result of a severe head injury, a bacterial infection, or an acute allergic reaction, among other conditions.

When shock develops, a dangerous spiral is set in motion. Poor blood supply to the brain results in dilation of the blood vessels and a further drop in blood pressure. The heart begins to fail and the brain cells, receiving progressively less oxygen, begin to die. The brain can function for only a few minutes without oxygen; thus, prolonged shock may result in permanent brain damage, even if recovery is otherwise satisfactory.

SYMPTOMS

The symptoms of shock include sweating, nausea, faintness, a rapid pulse, quick and shallow breathing, and a cold, pale, clammy skin. As the blood supply to the brain drops, the individual becomes confused and drowsy and may lose consciousness.

It is important to remember that a person in shock is not capable of doing anything to help himself. Intervention is essential, and the victim should be taken to a hospital as soon as possible. In the meantime, first-aid measures may help prevent shock from becoming more profound. The same first-aid measures, taken promptly after an accident—especially one in which there is blood loss or burn damage to the skin—may help prevent shock or at least minimize its severity.

SIGNS OF SHOCK

RESPIRATORY
*Increased rate of breathing; may be shallow or deep and irregular

CARDIOVASCULAR
*Rapid pulse (over 100 beats per minute)
*May be too faint to feel in wrist, but detectable in neck (carotid artery) or groin (femoral artery)

VISUAL APPEARANCE
*Skin pale or bluish, cold to touch
*Victim becomes apathetic and unresponsive
*Eyes become sunken, expression vacant, pupils dilated

FIRST-AID TREATMENT FOR SHOCK

• If possible, control the injury or cause of shock (for example, take steps to stop external bleeding).

• If the victim is conscious, place him on his back, face upward and with the legs raised about one foot above the hips. This will encourage blood flow to the upper body.

• If the victim is unconscious, place him in the recovery position (lying prone, the arms extended at shoulder level and bent so that the hands lie near the face, the head turned to one side, and the leg at that side drawn up so that it is at a right angle to the torso).

• Loosen tight clothing at the neck, chest, and waist.

• Wrap the victim in a blanket or coat to prevent heat loss. Do not overheat the victim or use an electric blanket, heating pad, or hot water bottle.

• Give nothing by mouth unless it will be several hours before medical help arrives. In that case, and if the person is conscious, give water or a weak solution of salt or baking powder and water.

• Reassure the victim, keep him comfortable, and do not leave him unattended.

• If necessary, give mouth-to-mouth resuscitation.

SUMMING UP

Shock is a depressed state of many vital functions. If prolonged, it is a life-threatening medical emergency that may cause death in conditions that otherwise are not grave. Shock may be caused by accidents as well as specific circumstances, such as an electrical shock or drug overdose.

188. Sports Injuries

GENERAL CONSIDERATIONS

The increased general participation in exercise and sports activities has been paralleled by an increase in sports injuries. Some are inevitable; others may be avoided through proper preparation. Even when you have an accident, it is not always necessary to see a physician. Knowing how to prevent and assess injuries, and treat minor ones, can enhance your sports participation and enjoyment.

ASSESSING INJURIES

The most common questions relate to the severity of an injury. Is it a strain or sprain? Or is it a broken bone demanding medical attention? Injuries often affect the ligaments, a site where serious damage can occur. If swelling is rapid and severe, the injury requires a physician's attention. First of all, look at the affected part. Is there obvious deformity? How does it feel? Is the pain minor or severe? Touch it. Does it move normally? Here are the most common symptoms of a fracture:

• The limb may be bent or deformed or seriously swollen.

• It may be impossible to walk on the leg or use the arm.

• The joint, such as elbow or knee, may wobble. (Torn ligaments, as well as fractures, have this effect.)

• The skin is discolored and turns red or blue.

• In rib fractures, breathing causes pain.

Sometimes, it is difficult to distinguish a fracture from a sprain. But severe pain is a good diagnostic tool for the lay person. If you believe an injury is a fracture, get medical attention right away. Do not move the affected part; use a broomstick, a board, or even a pillow, and tie it firmly to the limb to serve as a splint. Once the splint is in place, do not shift its position; also, do not attempt to straighten the injured area.

Some accidents clearly call for immediate medical attention. If a person is unconscious or has a severe cut that is gushing blood, professional attention should be sought at once. Do not try to move an unconscious person. First determine if the patient is breathing and, if not, begin basic life support. Ask if anyone knows CPR (cardiopulmonary resuscitation). Attempt to retard bleeding by applying direct pressure to the wound. Only if this method is unsuccessful, place a tour-

How to Wrap an Elastic Bandage

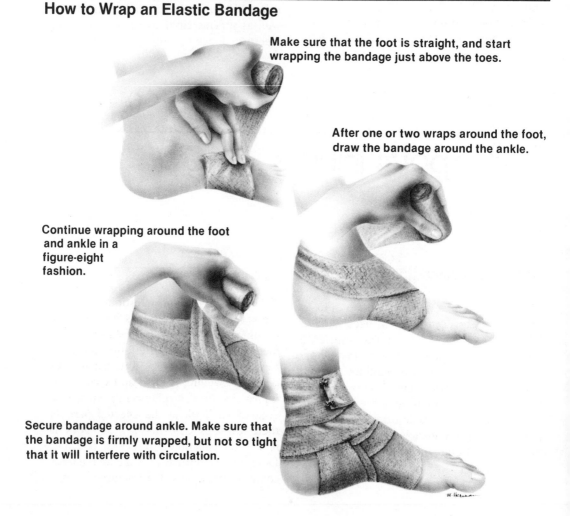

Make sure that the foot is straight, and start wrapping the bandage just above the toes.

After one or two wraps around the foot, draw the bandage around the ankle.

Continue wrapping around the foot and ankle in a figure-eight fashion.

Secure bandage around ankle. Make sure that the bandage is firmly wrapped, but not so tight that it will interfere with circulation.

niquet between the injury and the heart.

Remember, also, that neck injuries are potentially very serious and a fracture is never obvious. If there is any neck pain, numbness in the extremities, or paralysis of a limb, *do not* move the patient until the head and neck are firmly fixed with adequately placed sand bags.

SELF-CARE

The best remedy for most sprains and strains is an ice pack. When applied for fifteen minutes, several times a day, for the first day or two after the injury, ice packs help reduce swelling and ease pain. Elevating the injured limb also helps, and taking aspirin may further reduce the pain and inflammation that contribute to swelling. Do not use a heating pad or hot compresses if there is any evidence of swelling.

After the swelling subsides, apply a heating pad set on "low" to help relax muscles in the area and assist in regaining mobility. Liniment and/or hot baths may serve the same purpose and are helpful in treating muscle spasms as well. An elastic bandage may be applied after initial swelling begins to subside.

Any severe pain or persistent swelling should be reported to a physican.

PREVENTION

Many sports injuries are avoidable. The first step in prevention is to get proper training in the activity of your choice and to use the appropriate equipment. When starting a new exercise program, be sure to begin gradually. If you lead a sedentary life style, do not rush into a race or a ball game with people who exercise regularly. Thus, the second step in beginning a new sport should be to learn slowly but surely, and stay in your own league.

Before any exercise session, be sure to warm up. Ten minutes of stretching exercises can be your best sports medicine for preventing strains and improving muscle tone and flexibility. Then, follow the rules. At the first sign of fatigue or injury, stop. At the conclusion of the exercise session, don't quit abruptly. End your program with cool-down exercises to stabilize respiration and to diminish the likelihood of muscle aches or a charley horse. And keep a sweatsuit handy to slip into during rest periods between strenuous exertions or when the workout is completed. On days that you don't exercise, it is a good idea to do some stretching to reduce muscle tightening.

SUMMING UP

While sports injuries have become more common, many can be prevented or treated at home. Use common sense and caution while participating, and do not take lightly the warning signs of pain and fatigue. When a fracture or other serious injury is suspected, call an ambulance or get prompt medical attention.

189. Fractures, Dislocations, and Sprains

COMMON CHARACTERISTICS

A fracture is any break in a bone. In some fractures the bone may be cracked; in others, the pieces may be separated or bent in on one another.

A dislocation is a displacement of the bone ends that form a joint in such a way that they are no longer in proper contact.

A sprain is a partial tearing or stretching of the ligaments around a joint. (Ligaments are the tough, fibrous tissues that connect one bone with another.)

Fractures and dislocations are more serious than sprains, though they are not always more painful. Fractures and dislocations are generally caused by a severe blow, either directly (as when the kneecap is broken against the dashboard in an auto accident) or indirectly (as when the wrist is broken as the result of falling on an outstretched hand, or the hip is dislocated as the result of the knee striking the dashboard). Sprains are usually caused by twisting or stretching, though a severe twisting will sometimes result in a dislocation or even a fracture.

FRACTURES

There are two main classes of fractures: closed (simple) fractures and open (compound) fractures. In closed fractures the broken bone does not penetrate the skin; in open fractures it does. The wound in an open fracture may be only a small opening over the fracture or may be large enough for one or both ends of the broken bone to protrude. Open fractures are more serious than closed fractures because of greater blood loss and the possibility of infection.

Fractures are also classified according to the appearance of the break. *Greenstick fractures,* which occur only in children, are incomplete, passing only part way through the bone. In *transverse fractures* the fracture line is straight across the bone; in *oblique fractures* it crosses at an angle; and in *spiral fractures* it twists around and through. When the bone is broken in more than two pieces, the fracture is *comminuted;* when the broken ends of bone have been driven into each other, it is *impacted.*

A fracture can be recognized easily if the bone penetrates the skin, or if fragments of bone can be seen in the wound. Other signs and symptoms are:

- Deformity. An arm or leg may lie in an unnatural position or be bent where there is no joint.
- Pain and tenderness.
- Swelling and discoloration. Some swelling is almost always present with fractures. It may be the result of bleeding, both from inside the bone and from surrounding damaged tissues, or of increased fluid in the tissues.
- Inability to use a limb. The injured person will usually guard the injured limb and not attempt—or be unable—to use it. There are exceptions, however. Occasionally in a greenstick or impacted fracture, the injured extremity will be used almost as if it were normal.

Some fractures, such as those of the pelvis, may have no visible signs. However,

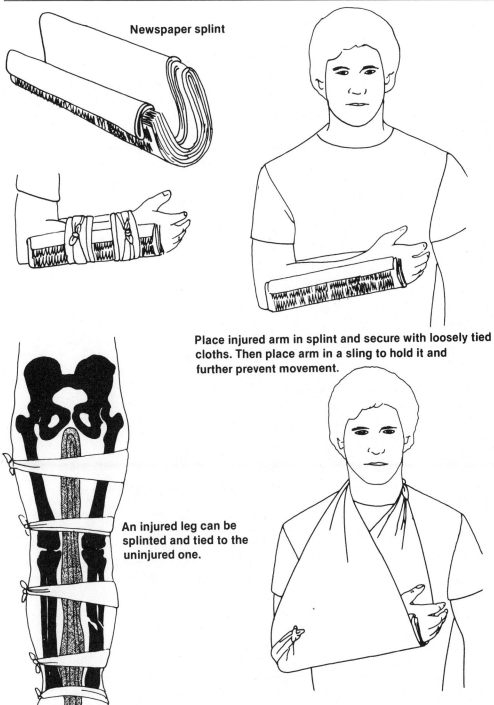

Newspaper splint

Place injured arm in splint and secure with loosely tied cloths. Then place arm in a sling to hold it and further prevent movement.

An injured leg can be splinted and tied to the uninjured one.

Splinting helps prevent fractured bones from moving and also lessens the pain and potential of injury to adjacent joints. Rolled-up newspapers with a towel for added padding make an excellent emergency splint. Newspapers or a rolled-up blanket can be used to splint a leg.

the injured person may have pain and may even go into shock from heavy internal bleeding.

DISLOCATIONS

A joint consists of the ends of two bones held in position by a joint capsule, ligaments, and tendons. In a dislocated joint, the capsule and ligaments are usually torn, and one of the bone ends is dislodged from its normal position. Some of the signs and symptoms of a dislocated joint are marked deformity, pain or swelling, pain on any attempted movement, and complete or nearly complete loss of movement.

The joints that are most frequently dislocated are the shoulder, elbow, fingers, hip, and ankle. Less often, the wrist and knee are affected.

SPRAINS

A sprain is also a joint injury. It is usually the result of twisting or stretching a joint beyond its normal range of movement, with consequent stress on the ligaments or, in serious sprains, injury to all the tissues surrounding the joint. The ankle and the knee are the two most common locations of sprains.

EMERGENCY TREATMENT OF FRACTURES AND DISLOCATIONS

If there is any doubt as to the nature of the injury, assume that it is a fracture or dislocation, since harm may result from treating either as a sprain.

• If there is severe bleeding, treat this first, by applying pressure at the appropriate pressure point (see Chapter 186, "Bleeding Emergencies").
• Do not attempt to realign a fracture or a dislocation. Instead, immobilize the injured part, either by securing it with bandages (or improvised bandages) to a sound

part of the body or, if necessary, by splinting it.
• Splints should be rigid, well padded, and preferably long enough to immobilize the joints both above and below a dislocation or fracture. A piece of wood, some folded cardboard, or a broom handle can be used as a makeshift splint. Wrap the bandage around limb and splint firmly enough to prevent movement but not so tightly as to obstruct the blood circulation.
• Do not give the injured person any food or liquids since general anesthesia may be used when the broken bone is set. Keep the person warm and still and watch for signs of shock (see Chapter 187, "Shock").
• Unless life is immediately endangered or the victim is choking on vomit, *do not* move someone who has signs of spinal injury: severe pain in the neck or spine; tingling, loss of sensation or loss of control in the limbs; or loss of bladder or bowel control.
• If the exposed bone in a compound fracture slips back on its own, inform the doctor of this, since it may have become infected during exposure.

TREATMENT OF SPRAINS

If the injury has been safely identified as a minor sprain, apply an ice pack to constrict local blood vessels. Four to six hours later, apply heat to open the blood vessels. The injured limb should be kept elevated to prevent swelling.

SUMMING UP

Fractures, dislocations, and sprains are among the most common injuries. Knowing basic first aid, including recognizing those cases in which the patient should not be moved, is important in minimizing the injury and preventing irreversible damage.

190. Poisoning Emergencies

GENERAL CONSIDERATIONS

A poison is any substance—solid, liquid, or gas—that, when taken into the body in sufficient amounts, can be fatal or can produce serious bodily harm. Even a substance that is normally beneficial can be poisonous if excessive amounts are taken.

It has been estimated that every year thousands of adults and about one million children are the victims of accidental poisoning. To these figures can be added the numbers of people who poison themselves intentionally.

Poison control centers located throughout the United States are prepared to provide emergency poison treatment information twenty-four hours a day. The phone number of the nearest center should be readily available in case of sudden need (see Directory of Poison Control Centers at the end of this chapter). In addition, every adult should know the basic guidelines about dealing with poisoning emergencies. Although there are no specific antidotes (substances that neutralize a particular poison's effect) for most poisons, there are definite procedures which may be lifesaving.

SIGNS AND SYMPTOMS OF POISONING

Some of the common signs and symptoms of poisoning are abdominal pain, nausea and vomiting, odor on the breath, excessive salivation or sweating, pupillary dilation or constriction, convulsions, dizziness, unconsciousness, shallow or difficult breathing, cyanosis (bluish skin and lips), and burns around the mouth and hands. A quick search of the area where the victim was found may reveal the remains of some food or beverage, a poisonous fungus or berry, or an empty container that will suggest what substance has been ingested. Gases may be detected by their smell, but it should be remembered many are odorless.

GUIDELINES

The first step, when poisoning is suspected, is to call the poison control center, or a doctor. (Many accidental poisonings can be treated at home, but it is better to get medical advice before instituting first-aid measures for *any* ingested poison). When telephoning, describe the substance that has been taken, if this is known, as precisely as possible, or give information from the suspect container. In addition, give the victim's size, age, and symptoms.

If advised by the poison control center, call an ambulance or drive to a hospital. Take the container and any vomited material with you.

If the victim is not breathing, give mouth-to-mouth resuscitation. If there is no response and the heart has stopped beating, begin cardiopulmonary resuscitation in addition to artificial respiration (see Chapter 182, "CPR").

If the victim is unconscious, or about to vomit, place him on his side, bend the uppermost leg and arm to prevent rolling forward, and place the other arm behind so that he cannot roll backward. Turn his head toward the ground so that he will not choke on the vomit.

HOME TREATMENT

It is sometimes possible to treat poisoning at home, following medical advice.

When the victim is conscious and has no serious circulatory or nervous system symptoms, the following steps are usually recommended:

If the poison is noncaustic (nonburning), as, for example, aspirin, barbiturates, and poisonous plants and berries, the substance should first be diluted and then vomited up. The victim should be given one or two glasses of water to dilute the poison in the stomach. Then vomiting should be induced by administering one tablespoon of syrup of ipecac (something every household should have), followed by a glass of water. The ipecac usually induces vomiting within fifteen to twenty minutes. If it doesn't, the dosage may be repeated once. If syrup of ipecac is not available, the victim can be made to gag by placing a finger or spoon handle or similar object at the back of the tongue. Be alert to the danger of the person choking on or breathing in vomitus.

If the ingested substance is caustic or acid, for example, a strong alkali such as toilet bowl cleansers, ammonia, bleach, lye, automatic dishwashing compounds, or oily, for example, kerosene, gasoline, and turpentine, *do not induce vomiting.* Corrosive material can do further damage as it is regurgitated. Instead, unless given different instructions by a doctor or poison control center, try to dilute the poison in the victim's stomach. You may also be advised to administer a so-called all-purpose antidote, which is available in drugstores. The main ingredient in this preparation is activated charcoal, a substance that has the ability to absorb many chemicals. This kind of antidote also has a buffering alkali to help neutralize acids and a buffering acid to help neutralize any alkali in the substance that may be present. It is wise to keep a can of this antidote on hand. Soothing agents such as milk, milk of magnesia, and aluminum hydroxide gel can help to decrease gastric irritation.

If the poison has been inhaled, move the victim into fresh air immediately.

HOW TO PREVENT ACCIDENTAL POISONING OF CHILDREN

Most poisonings of children are caused by the ingestion of familiar household products. Aspirin is a prime offender, as are tincture of iodine, petroleum products, ammonia and other strong cleaning compounds, bathroom antiseptics, and various automatic dishwashing compounds. Keep all such containers clearly labeled and well out of reach of children. In addition:

• Use bottles with safety caps that are difficult to open.
• When possible, buy pills or capsules that have been strip-packaged, that is, sealed in a plastic strip which must be pulled out of its box one pill at a time.
• Put a childproof safety lock on the door of every cupboard that houses a potentially lethal substance.
• Check the contents of sheds, garages, and basements.
• Never transfer a hazardous substance out of its original container. Equally, never store hazardous substances in a container that originally held food, drink, or medicine.
• Be especially alert at the peak poisoning time, which is 4 to 6 P.M.—when children are hungry and parents are usually busy.

SUMMING UP

There is no easy rule of thumb to follow when poisoning occurs. What first aid is desirable will depend on the poison, the dose, and the victim's age and size. No first-aid measures should be undertaken without first calling a doctor, except in the most extreme of circumstances.

DIRECTORY OF POISON CONTROL CENTERS

The following directory of poison control centers was compiled from information furnished by the National Clearinghouse for Poison Control Centers, U.S. Department of Health and Human Services. Facilities designated by the American Association of Poison Control Centers as regional centers are indicated by an asterisk (*).

Alabama

Northeast Alabama Regional Medical Center, 400 East 10th Street, Anniston, AL 36201 Tel: 205/236-2210

The Children's Hospital, 1601 Sixth Avenue South, Birmingham, AL 35233 Tel: 205/933-4050, 800/292-6678

Southeast Alabama Medical Center, PO Drawer 6987, Highway 84 East, Dothan, AL 36301 Tel: 205/793-8111

University of South Alabama Medical Center, 2451 Fillingim Street, Mobile, AL 33617 Tel: 205/471-7100

East Alabama Medical Center, 2000 Pepperell Parkway, Opelika, AL 36802 Tel: 205/749-3411 ext 258

John A. Andrews Hospital Emergency Room, Tuskegee Institute, Tuskegee, AL 36088 Tel: 205/727-8488

Alaska

Anchorage Poison Center, Providence Hospital, 3200 Providence Drive, Anchorage, AK 99504 Tel: 907/274-6535

Arizona

Central Arizona Regional Poison Management Center, St. Luke's Hospital, 525 North 18th Street, Phoenix, AZ 85006 Tel: 602/253-3334 (24 hours)

Arizona Regional Poison Center,* Arizona Health Sciences Center, University of Arizona College of Pharmacy, Tucson, AZ 85724 Tel: 602/626-6016, 800/362-0101 (in Arizona)

Yuma Regional Medical Center, Avenue A & 24th Street, Yuma, AZ 85364 Tel: 602/344-2000

Arkansas

Warner Brown Hospital Emergency Department, 460 West Oak Street, El Dorado, AR 71730 Tel: 501/863-2266, 501/863-2000

St. Edward's Mercy Medical Center, 7301 Rogers Avenue, Fort Smith, AR 72903 Tel: 501/452-5100 ext 2401

Sparks Regional Medical Center, 1311 South Eye Street, Fort Smith, AR 72901 Tel: 501/441-5011

Boone County Hospital Emergency Room, 620 North Willow Street, Harrison, AR 72601 Tel: 501/741-6141 ext 275 or 276

Helena Hospital, Newman Drive, Helena, AR 72342 Tel: 501/338-6411 ext 340

University of Arkansas for Medical Sciences College of Pharmacy, Slot 522, 4301 West Markham Street, Little Rock, AR 72205 Tel: 501/661-5544, 800/482-8948

Osceola Memorial Hospital, 611 Lee Avenue West, Osceola, AR 72370 Tel: 501/563-7180

Jefferson Hospital, 1515 West 42nd Avenue, Pine Bluff, AR 71601 Tel: 501/535-6800 ext 4706

California

Central Valley Regional Poison Control Center, Fresno Community Hospital and Medical Center, PO Box 1232, Fresno & R Streets, Fresno, CA 93715 Tel: 209/445-1222

Los Angeles County Medical Association, Poison Information Center, 1925 Wilshire Boulevard, Los Angeles, CA 90057 Tel: 213/664-2121 (professional), 213/484-5151 (public)

Children's Hospital Medical Center of Northern California, 51st & Grove Streets, Oakland, CA 94609 Tel: 415/428-3000

University of California, Irvine Regional Poison Medical Center, Route 32, 101 City Drive, Orange, CA 92688 Tel: 714/634-5988

Sacramento Medical Center,* 2315 Stockton Boulevard, Sacramento, CA 95817 Tel: 916/453-3692, 800/852-7221

San Diego Regional Poison Center,* University Hospital, 225 Dickinson Street, San Diego, CA 92103 Tel: 714/294-6000 (24 hours)

San Francisco Bay Area Regional Poison Control Center,* 1001 Potrero Avenue, San Francisco, CA 94110 Tel: 415/666-2845

Santa Clara Valley Medical Center, 751 South Bascom Avenue, San Jose, CA 95128 Tel: 408/279-5112

Colorado

Rocky Mountain Poison Center,* Denver General Hospital, West Eighth Avenue & Cherokee Street, Denver, CO 80204 Tel: 303/629-1123, 800/332-3073

Connecticut

Bridgeport Hospital, 267 Grant Street, Bridgeport, CT 06602 Tel: 203/384-3566

St. Vincent's Hospital, 2820 Main Street, Bridgeport, CT 06602 Tel: 203/576-5178

Danbury Hospital, 95 Locust Avenue, Danbury, CT 06810 Tel: 203/797-7300

Connecticut Poison Control Center, University of Connecticut Health Center, Farmington, CT 06032 Tel: 203/674-3456

Middlesex Memorial Hospital, 28 Crescent Street, Middletown, CT 06457 Tel: 203/347-9471

The Hospital of St. Raphael, 1450 Chapel Street, New Haven, CT 06511 Tel: 203/789-3464

Department of Pediatrics, Yale–New Haven Hospital, 789 Howard Avenue, New Haven, CT 06504 Tel: 203/785-2222

Norwalk Hospital, 24 Stevens Street, Norwalk, CT 06852 Tel: 203/852-2160

St. Mary's Hospital, 56 Franklin Street, Waterbury, CT 06702 Tel: 203/574-6011

Delaware

Wilmington Medical Center, Delaware Division, 501 West 14th Street, Wilmington, DE 19899 Tel: 302/655-3389

District of Columbia

National Capital Poison Center,* Georgetown University Hospital, 3800 Reservoir Road, Washington, DC 20007 Tel: 202/625-3333

Florida

George E. Weems Memorial Hospital, PO Box 610, Franklin Square, Apalachicola, FL 32320 Tel: 904/653-8853

Manatee Memorial Hospital, 206 Second Street East, Bradenton, FL 33505 Tel: 813/746-5111 ext 466

Halifax Hospital Emergency Department, PO Box 1990, Daytona Beach, FL 32014 Tel: 904/258-2002

Broward General Medical Center Emergency Department, 1600 South Andrews Avenue, Fort Lauderdale, FL 33316 Tel: 305/463-3131 ext 1511

Lee Memorial Hospital, PO Drawer 2218, 2776 Cleveland Avenue, Fort Myers, FL 33902 Tel: 813/332-1111 ext 5285

Pharmacy Department, General Hospital of Fort Walton Beach, 1000 Mar-Walt Drive, Fort Walton Beach, FL 32548 Tel: 904/862-1111 ext 572

Shands Teaching Hospital and Clinics, University of Florida, Gainesville, FL 32610 Tel: 904/392-3389

Citrus Memorial Hospital, 502 Highland Boulevard, Inverness, FL 32650 Tel: 904/726-2800

Department of Pharmacy Services, St. Vincent's Medical Center, PO Box 2982, Jacksonville, FL 32203 Tel: 904/387-7500, 904/387-7499

Lakeland General Hospital, Lakeland Hills Boulevard, PO Box 480, Lakeland, FL 33802 Tel: 813/686-4913

Leesburg Regional Medical Center, 600 East Dixie Avenue, Leesburg, FL 32748 Tel: 904/787-7222 ext 381

James E. Holmes Regional Medical Center, 1350 South Hickory Street, Melbourne, FL 32901 Tel: 305/727-7000 ext 675

Naples Community Hospital, 350 Seventh Street North, Naples, FL 33940 Tel: 813/262-3131 ext 2222

Parkway General Hospital, Inc., 160 NW 170th Street, North Miami Beach, FL 33169 Tel: 305/653-3333

Munroe Regional Medical Center, PO Box 6000, Ocala, FL 32678 Tel: 904/351-7607

Orlando Regional Medical Center, Orange Memorial Division, 1415 South Kuhl Avenue, Orlando, FL 32806 Tel: 305/841-5222

Bay Memorial Medical Center, 600 North MacArthur Avenue, Panama City, FL 32401 Tel: 904/769-1511 ext 415, 416

Gulf Region Poison Center, Baptist Hospital, 1000 West Moreno Street, Pensacola, FL 32501 Tel: 904/434-4611, 800/874-1555, 800/342-3222

Medical Center Hospital, 809 East Marion Avenue, Punta Gorda, FL 33950 Tel: 813/637-2529

Wuesthoff Memorial Hospital, 110 Longwood Avenue, Rockledge, FL 32955 Tel: 305/636-2211 ext 107

Memorial Hospital, 1901 Arlington Street, Sarasota, FL 33579 Tel: 813/953-1332

Tallahassee Regional Medical Center, 1300 Miccosukee Road, Tallahassee, FL 32301-8257 Tel: 904/681-1111

Tampa General Hospital, Davis Island, Tampa, FL 33606 Tel: 1-800/282-3171

Jess Parrish Memorial Hospital, PO Drawer W, 941 North Washington Avenue, Titusville, FL 32780 Tel: 305/268-6260

Good Samaritan Hospital, Palm Beach Lakes Boulevard, West Palm Beach, FL 33402 Tel: 305/655-5511 ext 4250

Winter Haven Hospital, Inc., 200 Avenue P NE, Winter Haven, FL 33880 Tel: 813/299-9701

Georgia

Phoebe Putney Memorial Hospital, 417 Third Avenue, Albany, GA 31702 Tel: 912/883-1800 ext 4159 or 4160

Athens General Hospital, 1199 Prince Avenue, Athens, GA 30613 Tel: 404/543-5215

Georgia Poison Control Center,* Grady Memorial Hospital, 80 Butler Street SE, Atlanta, GA 30335 Tel: 404/588-4400, 404/525-3323 (deaf only), 1-800/282-5846 (Georgia only)

University Hospital, 1350 Walton Way, Augusta, GA 30902 Tel: 404/722-9011 ext 2440

The Medical Center, 710 Center Street, Columbus, GA 31994 Tel: 404/571-1080

Medical Center of Central Georgia, 777 Hemlock Street, Macon, GA 31201 Tel: 912/742-1122 ext 1146

Floyd Medical Center, Turner McCall Boulevard, PO Box 233, Rome, GA 31061 Tel: 404/295-5500

Savannah Regional Poison Center, Department of Emergency Medicine, Memorial Medical Center, PO Box 23089, Savannah, GA 31403 Tel: 912/355-5228

John D. Archbold Memorial Hospital, 900 Gordon Avenue, Thomasville, GA 31792 Tel: 912/226-4121 ext 169

South Georgia Medical Center, PO Box 1727, Pendleton Park, Valdosta, GA 31601 Tel: 912/333-1110

Memorial Hospital, 410 Darling Avenue, Waycross, GA 31501 Tel: 912/283-3030

Hawaii

Kapiolani-Children's Medical Center, 1319 Punahou Street, Honolulu, HI 96826 Tel: 800/941-4411, 1-800/362-3585

Idaho

Idaho Poison Center, St. Alphonsus Hospital, 1055 North Curtis Road, Boise, ID 83704 Tel: 208/334-2241 (out of state), 800/632-9490 (Idaho only)

Consolidated Hospitals Emergency Department, 900 Memorial Drive, Idaho Falls, ID 83401 Tel: 208/522-3600

Idaho Drug Information and Poison Control Center, 777 Hospital Way, Pocatello, ID 83201 Tel: 208/234-0777 ext 2019 or 2029, 1-800/632-9490

Illinois

Rush-Presbyterian-St. Luke's Medical Center, 1753 West Congress Parkway, Chicago, IL 60612 Tel: 312/942-5969, 800/942-5969

St. Francis Hospital and Medical Center, 530 Northeast Glen Oak Avenue, Peoria, IL 61637 Tel: 309/672-2334, 800/322-5330

St. John's Hospital Regional Poison Resource Center,* 800 East Carpenter Street, Springfield, IL 62702 Tel: 217/753-3330, 800/252-2022

Indiana

Community Hospital, 1515 North Madison Avenue, Anderson, IN 46012 Tel: 317/646-5143

St. John's Medical Center, 2015 Jackson Street, Anderson, IN 46014 Tel: 317/646-8220

Cameron Memorial Hospital, Inc., 416 East Maumee Street, Angola, IN 46703 Tel: 219/665-2141 ext 146

Bartholomew County Hospital, 2400 East 17th Street, Columbus, IN 47201 Tel: 812/376-5277

St. Anthony Medical Center, Main Street & Franciscan Road, Crown Point, In 46307 Tel: 219/738-2100

St. Catherine's Hospital, 4321 Fir Street, East Chicago, IN 46312 Tel: 219/392-1700, 219/392-7203

Elkhart General Hospital, 600 East Boulevard, Elkhart, IN 46514 Tel: 219/294-2621, 1-800/382-9097 (Indiana only), 1-800/442-4571 (Michigan only)

Deaconess Hospital, 600 Mary Street, Evansville, IN 47747 Tel: 812/426-3333

Lutheran Hospital, 3024 Fairfield Avenue, Fort Wayne, IN 46807 Tel: 219/458-2211

Parkview Memorial Hospital, 220 Randalia Drive, Fort Wayne, IN 46805 Tel: 219/484-6636 ext 6000

St. Joseph's Hospital, 700 Broadway, Fort Wayne, IN 46802 Tel: 219/425-3765

Clinton County Hospital, 1300 South Jackson Street, Frankfort, IN 46041 Tel: 317/659-4731

Methodist Hospital of Gary, Inc., 600 Grant Street, Gary, IN 46402 Tel: 219/886-4710

Goshen General Hospital, 200 High Park Avenue, Goshen, IN 46526 Tel: 219/533-2141

St. Margaret's Hospital, 25 Douglas Street, Hammond, IN 46320 Tel: 219/932-2300, 219/931-4477

Indiana Poison Center, 1001 West 10th Street, Indianapolis, IN 46202 Tel: 317/630-7351 (24 hours), 800/382-9097 (Indiana only) (24 hours)

Methodist Hospital of Indiana, Inc., 1605 North Capitol Avenue,

Indianapolis, IN 46202 Tel: 317/924-3521

McCray Memorial Hospital, Hospital Drive, Kendallville, IN 46755 Tel: 219/347-1100

Howard Community Hospital, 3500 South LaFountain Street, Kokomo, IN 46901 Tel: 317/453-8444

Lafayette Home Hospital, 2400 South Street, Lafayette, IN 47902 Tel: 317/447-6811

St. Elizabeth's Hospital, 1501 Hartford Street, Lafayette, IN 47904 Tel: 317/423-6271

LaGrange Hospital, Route Five, Box 79, LaGrange, IN 46761 Tel: 219/463-2143

LaPorte Hospital, Inc., Box 250, State & Madison Streets, LaPorte, IN 46350 Tel: 219/326-1234

Witham Memorial Hospital, 1124 North Lebanon Street, Lebanon, IN 46052 Tel: 317/482-2700 ext 241

King's Daughter's Hospital, 1212 Presbyterian Avenue, PO Box 447, Madison, IN 47250 Tel: 812/265-5211 ext 131

Marion General Hospital, Wabash & Euclid Avenues, Marion, IN 46952 Tel: 317/662-4693

Ball Memorial Hospital, 2401 University Avenue, Muncie, IN 47303 Tel: 317/747-3241

Jay County Hospital, 505 West Arch Street, Portland, IN 47371 Tel: 219/726-7131

Pharmacy Department, Reid Memorial Hospital, 1401 Chester Boulevard, Richmond, IN 47374 Tel: 317/983-3014

William S. Major Hospital, 150 West Washington Street, Shelbyville, IN 46176 Tel: 317/392-3211 ext 52

St. Joseph's Medical Center, 811 East Madison Street, South Bend, IN 46622 Tel: 219/237-7264

Union Hospital, Inc., 1606 North Seventh Street, Terre Haute, IN 47804 Tel: 812/238-7000 ext 7523

Porter Memorial Hospital, 814 LaPorte Avenue, Valparaiso, IN 46383 Tel: 219/464-8611 ext 232, 312, 334

The Good Samaritan Hospital, 520 South Seventh Street, Vincennes, IN 47591 Tel: 812/885-3348

Iowa

Blank Children's Hospital, 1200 Pleasant Street, Des Moines, IA 50308 Tel: 515/283-6254, 1-800/362-2327

Mercy Medical Center, Mercy Drive, Dubuque, IA 52001 Tel: 319/589-9099

Trinity Regional Hospital, Kenyon Road, Fort Dodge, IA 50501 Tel: 515/573-7211, 515/573-3101

University of Iowa Hospital Poison Information Center,* Iowa City, IA 52242 Tel: 319/356-2922, 800/272-6477

Allen Memorial Hospital Emergency Room, 1825 Logan Avenue, Waterloo, IA 50703 Tel: 319/235-3893

Kansas

Atchison Hospital, 1301 North Second Street, Atchison, KS 66002 Tel: 913/367-2131

Dodge City Regional Hospital, Ross & Avenue A, PO Box 1478, Dodge City, KS 67801 Tel: 316/225-9050 ext 381

Newman Memorial Hospital, 12th & Chestnut Streets, Emporia, KS 66801 Tel: 316/343-6800 ext 545

Irwin Army Hospital Emergency Room, Fort Riley, KS 66442 Tel: 913/239-7777, 913/239-7778

Mercy Hospital, 821 Burke Street, Fort Scott, KS 66701 Tel: 316/223-2200

Central Kansas Medical Center, 3515 Broadway, Great Bend, KS 67530 Tel: 316/792-2511 ext 115

Hadley Regional Medical Center, 201 East Seventh Street, Hays, KS 67601 Tel: 913/628-8251

Mid-America Poison Center, University of Kansas Medical Center, 39th Street

& Rainbow Boulevard, Kansas City, KS 66103 Tel: 913/588-6633

Lawrence Memorial Hospital, 325 Maine Street, Lawrence, KS 66044 Tel: 913/843-3680 ext 162, 163

St. John's Hospital, 139 North Penn Street, Salina, KS 67401 Tel: 913/827-5591 ext 112

Stormont-Vail Regional Medical Center, 10th & Washburn Streets, Topeka, KS 66606 Tel: 913/354-6100

Wesley Medical Center, 550 North Hillside Avenue, Wichita, KS 67214 Tel: 316/688-2277

Kentucky

King's Daughter's Hospital, 2201 Lexington Avenue, Ashland, KY 41101 Tel: 606/324-2222

St. Lukes Hospital, 85 North Grand Avenue, Fort Thomas, KY 41075 Tel: 606/572-3215, 1-800/352-9900

Central Baptist Hospital, 1740 South Limestone Street, Lexington, KY 40503 Tel: 606/278-3411 ext 363

Drug Information Center, University of Kentucky Medical Center, Lexington, KY 40536 Tel: 606/233-5320

Kentucky Poison Control Center NKC, Inc., PO Box 35070, 200 East Chestnut, Louisville, KY 40232 Tel: 502/589-8222, 1-800/722-5725

Murray-Calloway County Hospital, 803 Poplar Street, Murray, KY 42071 Tel: 502/753-7588

Owensboro-Daviess County Hospital, 811 Hospital Court, Owensboro, KY 42301 Tel: 502/926-3030 ext 180, 186

Western Baptist Hospital, 2501 Kentucky Avenue, Paducah, KY 42001 Tel: 502/444-5100 ext 105, 180

Poison Control Center, Highlands Regional Medical Center, Prestonburg, KY 41653 Tel: 606/886-8511 ext 132, 160

Appalachian Regional Hospitals, Central Pharmaceutical Service, 2000

Central Avenue, South Williamson, KY 25661 Tel: 606/237-1010

Louisiana

Rapides General Hospital, Box 30101, 301 Fourth Street, Alexandria, LA 71301-7887 Tel: 318/487-8111

Doctors Memorial Hospital, 2414 Bunker Hill Drive, Baton Rouge, LA 70808 Tel: 504/928-6558

Our Lady of Lourdes Hospital, PO Box 3827, 611 St. Landry Street, Lafayette, LA 70501 Tel: 318/234-7381

Lake Charles Memorial Hospital, PO Drawer M, 1701 Oak Park Boulevard, Lake Charles, LA 70601 Tel: 318/478-6800

St. Francis Hospital, PO Box 1901, 309 Jackson Street, Monroe, LA 71301 Tel: 318/325-6454

School of Pharmacy, Northeast Louisiana University, 700 University Avenue, Monroe, LA 71209 Tel: 318/342-3008

Charity Hospital, 1532 Tulane Avenue, New Orleans, LA 70140 Tel: 504/568-5222

LSU Medical Center, PO Box 33932, 1541 Kings Highway, Shreveport, LA 71130 Tel: 318/425-1524

Maine

Maine Medical Center Emergency Division, 22 Bramhall Street, Portland, ME 04102 Tel: 207/871-2950, 800/442-6305

Maryland

Maryland Poison Center,* University of Maryland School of Pharmacy, 20 North Pine Street, Baltimore, MD 21201 Tel: 301/528-7701, 1-800/492-2414

Tri-State Poison Center, Sacred Heart Hospital, 900 Seton Drive, Cumberland, MD 21502 Tel: 301/722-6677

Massachusetts

Massachusetts Poison Control System, 300 Longwood Avenue, Boston, MA 02115 Tel: 617/232-2120 or 1-800/682-9211 (24 hours)

Michigan

Emma L. Bixby Hospital, 818 Riverside Avenue, Adrian, MI 49221 Tel: 517/263-2412

University Hospital, 1405 East Ann Street, Ann Arbor, MI 48104 Tel: 313/764-5102

Community Hospital Pharmacy Department, 193 West Street, Battle Creek, MI 49016 Tel: 616/963-5521

Bay Medical Center, 1900 Columbus Avenue, Bay City, MI 48706 Tel: 517/894-3131

Berrien General Hospital, Dean's Hill Road, Berrien Center, MI 49102 Tel: 616/471-7761

Community Health Center of Branch County, 274 East Chicago Street, Coldwater, MI 49036 Tel: 517/279-7935

Poison Control Center, Children's Hospital of Michigan, 3901 Beaubien Boulevard, Detroit, MI 48201 Tel: 313/494-5711, 800/572-1655, 800/462-6642

Mount Carmel Mercy Hospital Pharmacy Department, 6071 West Outer Drive, Detroit, MI 48235 Tel: 313/927-7000

Wayne County General Hospital, 2345 Merriman, Westland, MI 48185 Tel: 313/722-3748, 313/724-3000

Department of Pharmacy, Hurley Medical Center, One Hurley Plaza, Flint, MI 48502 Tel: 313/766-0111, 800/572-6396

St. Mary's Hospital, 201 Lafayette SE, Grand Rapids, MI 49503 Tel: 616/774-6794

Western Michigan Regional Poison Center,* 1840 Wealthy SE, Grand Rapids, MI 49506 Tel: 800/442-4571, 800/632-2727

W.A. Foote Memorial Hospital, 205 North East Street, Jackson, MI 49201 Tel: 517/788-4816

Midwest Poison Center, Borgess Medical Center, 1521 Gull Road, Kalamazoo, MI 49001 Tel: 616/383-7070, 1-800/632-4177

Bronson Methodist Hospital, 252 East Lovell Street, Kalamazoo, MI 49007 Tel: 616/383-6409, 1-800/442-4112

St. Lawrence Hospital, 1210 West Saginaw Street, Lansing, MI 48915 Tel: 517/372-5112 or 517/372-5113 (24 hours)

Marquette General Hospital, 420 West Magnetic Drive, Marquette, MI 49855 Tel: 906/228-9440, 1-800/562-9781

Midland Hospital, 4005 Orchard Drive, Midland, MI 48640 Tel: 517/631-8100

Poison Information Center, St. Joseph Mercy Hospital, 900 South Woodward Avenue, Pontiac, MI 48053 Tel: 313/858-7373, 313/858-7374

Port Huron Hospital, 1001 Kearney Street, Port Huron, MI 48060 Tel: 313/987-5555, 313/987-5000

Saginaw Regional Poison Center, Saginaw General Hospital, 1447 North Harrison Avenue, Saginaw, MI 48602 Tel: 517/755-1111

Poison Information Center, Munson Medical Center, Sixth Street, Traverse City, MI 49684 Tel: 616/941-1131, 616/947-6140

Minnesota

St. Luke's Hospital Emergency Department, 915 East First Street, Duluth, MN 55805 Tel: 218/727-6636

St. Mary's Hospital, Poison Information and Treatment Center, 407 East Third Street, Duluth, MN 55805 Tel: 218/726-4500

Fairview-Southdale Hospital, 6401 France Avenue South, Edina, MN 55435 Tel: 612/924-5000

Lake Region Hospital, 712 South Cascade Street, Fergus Falls, MN 56537 Tel: 218/736-5475

Unity Hospital, 550 Osborne Road, Fridley, MN 55432 Tel: 612/786-2200

Immanuel-St. Joseph's Hospital, 325 Garden Boulevard, Mankato, MN 56001 Tel: 507/625-4031

Fairview Hospital, Outpatient Department, 2312 South Sixth Street, Minneapolis, MN 55406 Tel: 612/371-6402

Hennepin Poison Center,* Hennepin County Medical Center, 701 Park Avenue, Minneapolis, MN 55415 Tel: 612/347-3141

Southeastern Minnesota Poison Control Center, St. Mary's Hospital, 1216 Second Street SW, Rochester, MN 55901 Tel: 507/285-5123 ext 517

St. Cloud Hospital, 1406 Sixth Avenue North, St. Cloud, MN 56301 Tel: 612/255-5617

Bethesda Lutheran Hospital, 559 Capitol Boulevard, St. Paul, MN 55103 Tel: 612/221-2301

St. John's Hospital, 403 Maria Avenue, St. Paul, MN 55106 Tel: 612/228-3132

St. Paul-Ramsey Hospital, 640 Jackson Street, St. Paul, MN 55101 Tel: 612/221-2113, 800-222-1222

United Hospitals, Inc., 300 Pleasant Avenue, St. Paul, MN 55102 Tel: 612/298-8402

Rice Memorial Hospital, 301 Becker Avenue SW, Willmar, MN 56201 Tel: 612/235-4543

Worthington Regional Hospital, 1018 Sixth Avenue, Worthington, MN 56187 Tel: 507/372-2941

Mississippi

Gulf Coast Community Hospital, 4642 West Beach Boulevard, Biloxi, MS 39631 Tel: 601/388-1919

USAF Hospital Keesler, Keesler Air Force Base, Biloxi, MS 39534 Tel: 601/377-6555, 601/377-6556

Rankin General Hospital Emergency Room, 350 Crossgates Boulevard, Brandon, MS 39042 Tel: 601/825-2811 ext 405 or 406

Marion County General Hospital, Sumrall Road, Columbia, MS 39429 Tel: 601/736-6303 ext 217

Greenwood-Leflore Hospital, River Road, Greenwood, MS 38930 Tel: 601/459-2633

Forrest County General Hospital, 400 South 28th Avenue, Hattiesburg, MS 39401 Tel: 601/264-4235

St. Dominic-Jackson Memorial Hospital, 969 Lakeland Drive, Jackson, MS 39216 Tel: 601/982-0121 ext 2345

University Medical Center, 2500 North State Street, Jackson, MS 39216 Tel: 601/354-7660

Jones County Community Hospital, Jefferson Street & 13th Avenue, Laurel, MS 39440 Tel: 601/649-4000 ext 630, 631, or 632

Meridian Regional Hospital, Highway 39 North, Meridian, MS 39301 Tel: 601/433-6211

Singing River Hospital, Emergency Room, 2609 Denny Avenue, Pascagoula, MS 39567 Tel: 601/938-5162

University of Mississippi, School of Pharmacy, University, MS 38677 Tel: 601/234-1522

Missouri

St. Francis Medical Center, St. Francis Drive, Cape Girardeau, MO 63701 Tel: 314/651-6235

University of Missouri Medical Center, 807 Stadium Road, Columbia, MO 65201 Tel: 314/882-8091

St. Elizabeth's Hospital Pharmacy Department, 109 Virginia Street, Hannibal, MO 63401 Tel: 314/221-0414 ext 101

Charles E. Still Osteopathic Hospital, 1125 Madison Street, Jefferson City, MO 65101 Tel: 314/635-7141 ext 215

St. John's Regional Medical Center, 2727 McClelland Boulevard, Joplin,

MO 64801 Tel: 417/781-2727 ext 2305

Children's Mercy Hospital,* 24th & Gillham Road, Kansas City, MO 64108 Tel: 816/234-3000

Kirksville Osteopathic Health Center, Box 949, One Osteopathy Avenue, Kirksville, MO 63501 Tel: 816/626-2266

Lucy Lee Hospital, 2620 North Westwood Boulevard, Poplar Bluff, MO 63901 Tel: 314/785-7721

Phelps County Memorial Hospital, 1000 West Tenth Street, Rolla, MO 65401 Tel: 314/364-1322

Methodist Medical Center, Seventh to Ninth on Faraon Street, St. Joseph, MO 64501 Tel: 816/271-7580, 816/232-8481

Cardinal Glennon Memorial Hospital for Children,* 1465 South Grand Avenue, St. Louis, MO 63104 Tel: 314/772-5200, 1-800/392-9111

St. Louis Children's Hospital, 400 South Kingshighway, St. Louis, MO 63110 Tel: 314/454-6099

Ozark Poison Center, Lester E. Cox Medical Center, 1423 North Jefferson Street, Springfield, MO 65802 Tel: 417/831-9746 (call collect)

St. John's Regional Health Center, 1235 East Cherokee Street, Springfield, MO 65802 Tel: 417/885-2115

West Plains Memorial Hospital, 1103 Alaska Avenue, West Plains, MO 65775 Tel: 417/256-9111 ext 258 or 259

Montana

Montana Poison Control System, Cogswell Building, Helena, MT 59620 Tel: 1-800/525-5042

Nebraska

Mid-Plains Regional Poison Center, Children's Memorial Hospital, 8301 Dodge Street, Omaha, NE 68114 Tel: 402/390-5400, 800/642-9999

(Nebraska only), 800/228-9515 (surrounding states)

Nevada

Southern Nevada Memorial Hospital, 1800 West Charleston Boulevard, Las Vegas, NV 89102 Tel: 702/383-2000 ext 221

Sunrise Hospital Medical Center, 3186 South Maryland Parkway, Las Vegas, NV 89109 Tel: 702/732-4989

St. Mary's Hospital, 235 West Sixth Street, Reno, NV 89503 Tel: 702/789-3013

Washoe Medical Center, 77 Pringle Way, Reno, NV 89502 Tel: 702/785-4129

New Hampshire

New Hampshire Poison Center, Mary Hitchcock Hospital, 2 Maynard Street, Hanover, NH 03756 Tel: 603/646-5000, 1-800/562-8236

New Jersey

Atlantic City Medical Center, 1925 Pacific Avenue, Atlantic City, NJ 08401 Tel: 609/344-4081 ext 2359

Clara Maass Medical Center, 1A Franklin Avenue, Belleville, NJ 07109 Tel: 201/450-2100

Riverside Hospital, Powerville Road, Boonton, NJ 07055 Tel: 201/334-5000 ext 186 or 187

Bridgeton Hospital, Irving Avenue, Bridgeton, NJ 08302 Tel: 609/451-6600

Camden County Poison Control Center, West Jersey Health System, Southern Division, White Horse Pike & Townsend Avenue, Berlin, NJ 08009 Tel: 609/768-6666

St. Clare's Hospital, Pocono Road, Denville, NJ 07834 Tel: 201/627-3000 ext 6063

East Orange General Hospital, 300 Central Avenue, East Orange, NJ 07019 Tel: 201/672-8400 ext 223

St. Elizabeth's Hospital, 225 Williamson Street, Elizabeth, NJ 07207 Tel: 201/527-5059

Englewood Hospital, 350 Engle Street, Englewood, NJ 07631 Tel: 201/894-3440

Hunterdon Medical Center, Route 31, Flemington, NJ 08822 Tel: 201/782-2121 ext 369

St. Barnabas Medical Center, Old Short Hills Road, Livingston, NJ 07039 Tel: 201/533-5161

Monmouth Medical Center Emergency Department, Dunbar & Second Avenue, Long Branch, NJ 07740 Tel: 201/222-2210

Mountainside Hospital, Bay & Highland Avenues, Montclair, NJ 07042 Tel: 201/746-6000 ext 234

Burlington County Memorial Hospital, 175 Madison Avenue, Mount Holly, NJ 08060 Tel: 609/267-7877

Jersey Shore Medical Center, Fitkin Hospital, 1945 Corlies Avenue, Neptune, NJ 07753 Tel: 201/775-5500, 800/822-9761

Newark Beth Israel Medical Center, 201 Lyons Avenue, Newark, NJ 07112 Tel: 201/926-7240, 201/926-7241, 201/926-7242, 201/926-7243

Middlesex General Hospital, 180 Somerset Street, New Brunswick, NJ 08903 Tel: 201/828-3000 ext 425, 308

St. Peter's Medical Center, 245 Easton Avenue, New Brunswick, NJ 08903 Tel: 201/745-8527

Newton Memorial Hospital, Emergency Room, 175 High Street, Newton, NJ 07860 Tel: 201/383-2121 ext 270, 271, or 273

Hospital Center at Orange Emergency Department, 188 South Essex Avenue, Orange, NJ 07051 Tel: 201/266-2120

St. Mary's Hospital, 211 Pennington Avenue, Passaic, NJ 07055 Tel: 201/473-1000 ext 441

Perth Amboy General Hospital, 530 New Brunswick Avenue, Perth Amboy, NJ 08861 Tel: 201/442-3700 ext 2501

Warren Hospital, 185 Rosenberry Street, Phillipsburg, NJ 08865 Tel: 201/859-1500 ext 280

Point Pleasant Hospital, Osborn Avenue & River Front, Point Pleasant, NJ 08742 Tel: 201/892-1100 ext 385

The Medical Center at Princeton, 253 Witherspoon Street, Princeton, NJ 08540 Tel: 609/734-4554

Saddle Brook General Hospital, 300 Market Street, Saddle Brook, NJ 07662 Tel: 201/368-6025

Shore Memorial Hospital, Brighton & Sunny Avenues, Somers Point, NJ 08244 Tel: 609/653-3515

Somerset Medical Center, Rehill Avenue, Somerville, NJ 08876 Tel: 201/725-4000 ext 431, 432, 433

Overlook Hospital, 193 Morris Avenue, Summit, NJ 07901 Tel: 201/522-2232

Holy Name Hospital, 718 Teaneck Road, Teaneck, NJ 07666 Tel: 201/833-3000

Helene Fuld Medical Center, 750 Brunswick Avenue, Trenton, NJ 08638 Tel: 609/396-1077

Memorial General Hospital, 1000 Galloping Hill Road, Union, NJ 07083 Tel: 201/687-1900 ext 3700

Greater Paterson General Hospital, 224 Hamburg Turnpike, Wayne, NJ 07470 Tel: 201/942-6900 ext 224, 225, or 226

New Mexico

New Mexico Poison, Drug Information, and Medical Crisis Center,* University of New Mexico, Albuquerque, NM 87131 Tel: 505/843-2551, 1-800/432-6866 (New Mexico only)

New York

Southern Tier Poison Center, United Health Services, Mitchell Avenue, Binghamton, NY 13903 Tel: 607/723-8929

Our Lady of Lourdes Memorial Hospital, 169 Riverside Drive, Binghamton, NY 13905 Tel: 607/798-5231

Western New York Poison Control Center, Children's Hospital of Buffalo, 219 Bryant Street, Buffalo, NY 14222 Tel: 716/878-7654, 716/878-7655

Brooks Memorial Hospital, 10 West Sixth Street, Dunkirk, NY 14048 Tel: 716/366-1111 ext 414 or 415

Long Island Poison Center,* Nassau County Medical Center, 2201 Hempstead Turnpike, East Meadow, NY 11554 Tel: 516/542-2323, 516/542-2324, 516/542-2325

Arnot Ogden Memorial Hospital, Roe Avenue & Grove Street, Elmira, NY 14901 Tel: 607/737-4100

St. Joseph's Hospital Health Center, 555 East Market Street, Elmira, NY 14901 Tel: 607/734-2662

Glens Falls Hospital, 100 Park Street, Glens Falls, NY 12801 Tel: 518/792-3151 ext 456

W.C.A. Hospital, 207 Foote Avenue, Jamestown, NY 14701 Tel: 716/487-0141, 716/484-8648

Wilson Memorial Hospital, 33–57 Harrison Street, Johnson City, NY 13790 Tel: 607/773-6611

Kingston Hospital, 396 Broadway, Kingston, NY 12401 Tel: 914/331-3313

New York City Poison Center,* Department of Health, Bureau of Laboratories, 455 First Avenue, New York, NY 10016 Tel: 212/340-4494, 212/764-7667

Hudson Valley Poison Center, Nyack Hospital, North Midland Avenue, Nyack, NY 10960 Tel: 914/353-1000

Finger Lakes Poison Center LIFE LINE,* University of Rochester Medical Center, Rochester, NY 14642 Tel: 716/275-5151

Ellis Hospital, 1101 Nott Street, Schenectady, NY 12308 Tel: 518/382-4039, 518/382-4309

Syracuse Poison Information Center, 750 East Adams Street, Syracuse, NY 13210 Tel: 315/476-7529

St. Mary's Hospital, 1300 Massachusetts Avenue, Troy, NY 12180 Tel: 518/272-5792

St. Luke's Hospital Center, PO Box 479, Utica, NY 13502 Tel: 315/798-6200, 315/798-6223

House of the Good Samaritan Hospital, Washington & Pratt Streets, Watertown, NY 13602 Tel: 315/788-8700

North Carolina

Western North Carolina Poison Control Center, 509 Biltmore Avenue, Asheville, NC 28801 Tel: 704/255-4490

Mercy Hospital, 2001 Vail Avenue, Charlotte, NC 28207 Tel: 704/379-5827

Moses Cone Hospital, 1200 North Elm Street, Greensboro, NC 27420 Tel: 919/379-4105

Margaret R. Pardee Memorial Hospital, Fleming Street, Hendersonville, NC 28739 Tel: 704/693-6522 ext 555 or 556

Catawba Memorial Hospital, Fairgrove-Church Road, Hickory, NC 28601 Tel: 704/322-6649

Onslow Memorial Hospital, Western Boulevard, Jacksonville, NC 28540 Tel: 919/353-7610

New Hanover Memorial Hospital, 2131 South 17th Street, Wilmington, NC 28402 Tel: 919/343-7046

North Dakota

Bismarck Hospital Emergency Department, 300 North Seventh Street, Bismarck, ND 58501 Tel: 701/223-4357

St. Luke's Hospital, Fifth Street & Mills Avenue, Fargo, ND 58122 Tel: 701/280-5575

United Hospital, 1200 South Columbia Road, Grand Forks, ND 58201 Tel: 701/780-5000

St. Joseph's Hospital, Third Street & Fourth Avenue SE, Minot, ND 58701 Tel: 701/857-2553

Mercy Hospital, 1301 15th Avenue West, Williston, ND 58801 Tel: 701/572-7661

Ohio

Children's Hospital, Medical Center of Akron, 281 Locust Street, Akron, OH 44308 Tel: 216/379-8562, 1-800/362-9922

Aultman Hospital Emergency Room, 2600 Sixth Street SW, Canton, OH 44710 Tel: 216/452-9911 ext 6203

Drug and Poison Information Center, University of Cincinnati Medical Center, Room 7701, 231 Bethesda Avenue, ML #144, Cincinnati, OH 45267 Tel: 513/872-5111 (24 hours)

Greater Cleveland Poison Control Center, 2119 Abington Road, Cleveland, OH 44106 Tel: 216/231-4455

Central Ohio Poison Center, Children's Hospital, 700 Children's Drive, Columbus, OH 43205 Tel: 614/228-1323

Western Ohio Regional Poison and Drug Information, Children's Medical Center, One Children's Plaza, Dayton, OH 45404 Tel: 513/222-2227, 1-800/762-0727 (Ohio only)

Lorain Community Hospital, 3700 Kolbe Road, Lorain, OH 44053 Tel: 216/282-2220

Mansfield General Hospital, 335 Glessner Avenue, Mansfield, OH 44903 Tel: 419/522-3411 ext 545

Community Hospital, 2615 East High Street, Springfield, OH 44501 Tel: 513/325-1255

Poison Information Center, Medical College Hospital, PO Box 6190,

3001 Arlington Avenue, Toledo, OH 43679 Tel: 419/381-3897

Mahoning Valley Poison Center, St. Elizabeth Hospital Medical Center, 1044 Belmont Avenue, Youngstown, OH 44501 Tel: 216/746-2222, 216/746-5510

Poison Control Center, Bethesda Hospital, 2951 Maple Avenue, Zanesville, OH 43701 Tel: 614/454-4221

Oklahoma

Valley View Hospital, 1300 East Sixth Street, Ada, OK 74820 Tel: 405/322-2323 ext 200

Memorial Hospital of Southern Oklahoma, 1011 14th Avenue, Ardmore, OK 73401 Tel: 405/223-5400

Comanche County Memorial Hospital, 3401 Gore Boulevard, Lawton, OK 73501 Tel: 405/355-8620

McAlester General Hospital, Inc. West, PO Box 669, One Clark Bass Boulevard, McAlester, OK 74501 Tel: 918/426-1800 ext 240

Oklahoma Poison Control Center, Oklahoma Children's Memorial Hospital, PO Box 26307, 940 NE 13th Street, Oklahoma City, OK 73126 Tel: 405/271-5454, 800/522-4611

St. Joseph Medical Center, 14th Street & Hartford Avenue, Ponca City, OK 74601 Tel: 405/765-3321

Hillcrest Medical Center, 1120 South Utica Avenue, Tulsa, OK 74104 Tel: 918/584-1351 ext 6165

Oregon

Oregon Poison Control and Drug Information Center, Oregon Health Sciences University, 3181 SW Sam Jackson Park Road, Portland, OR 97201 Tel: 503/225-8958, 1-800/452-7165

Pennsylvania

Lehigh Valley Poison Center, 17th & Chew Streets, Allentown, PA 18102 Tel: 215/433-2311

Keystone Region Poison Center, 2500 Seventh Avenue, Altoona, PA 16603 Tel: 814/946-3711

The Bloomsburg Hospital, 549 East Fair Street, Bloomsburg, PA 17815 Tel: 717/784-7121

Bradford Hospital, Interstate Parkway, Bradford, PA 16701 Tel: 814/368-4143

The Bryn Mawr Hospital, Bryn Mawr Avenue, Bryn Mawr, PA 19010 Tel: 215/896-3577

Sacred Heart General Hospital, Ninth & Wilson Streets, Chester, PA 19013 Tel: 215/494-4400

Clearfield Hospital, 809 Turnpike Avenue, Clearfield, PA 16830 Tel: 814/765-5341

Coaldale State General Hospital, Seventh Street, Coaldale, PA 18218 Tel: 717/645-2131

Charles Cole Memorial Hospital, RD Three, US Route Six, Coudersport, PA 16915 Tel: 814/274-9300

Susquehanna Poison Center, Geisinger Medical Center, North Academy Avenue, Danville, PA 17821 Tel: 717/275-6116 or 717/271-6116 (24 hours)

Doylestown Hospital, 595 West State Street, Doylestown, PA 18901 Tel: 215/345-2283

Pocono Hospital, 206 East Brown Street, East Stroudsburg, PA 18301 Tel: 717/421-4000

Easton Hospital, 21st & Lehigh Streets, Easton, PA 18042 Tel: 215/250-4000

Doctors Osteopathic Hospital, 252 West 11th Street, Erie, PA 16501 Tel: 814/454-2120

Millcreek Community Hospital, 5515 Peach Street, Erie, PA 16509 Tel: 814/864-4031

Drug and Poison Information Center, Hamot Medical Center, 201 State Street, Erie, PA 16550 Tel: 814/452-4242

Northwest Poison Center, St. Vincent's Health Center, 232 West 25th Street, Erie, PA 16544 Tel: 814/452-3232

Annie M. Warner Hospital, South Washington Street, Gettysburg, PA 17325 Tel: 717/334-2121

Westmoreland Hospital Association, 532 West Pittsburgh Street, Greensburg, PA 15601 Tel: 412/832-4000

Hanover General Hospital, 300 Highland Avenue, Hanover, PA 17331 Tel: 717/637-3711

Harrisburg Hospital, South Front & Mulberry Streets, Harrisburg, PA 17101 Tel: 717/782-3639

Polyclinic Hospital, Third & Polyclinic Avenues, Harrisburg, PA 17105 Tel: 717/782-4141 ext 4132

Capital Area Poison Center, The Milton S. Hershey Medical Center, University Drive, Hershey, PA 17033 Tel: 717/634-6111, 717/534-8955

Jeannette District Memorial Hospital, 600 Jefferson Avenue, Jeannette, PA 15644 Tel: 412/527-9300

Jersey Shore Hospital, Thompson Street, Jersey Shore, PA 17740 Tel: 717/398-0100

Conemaugh Valley Memorial Hospital, 1086 Franklin Street, Johnstown, PA 15905 Tel: 814/535-5351

Laurel Highlands Poison Center, Lee Hospital, 320 Main Street, Johnstown, PA 15901 Tel: 814/535-8255

Mercy Hospital, 1020 Franklin Street, Johnstown, PA 15905 Tel: 814/535-5353

Lancaster General Hospital, PO Box 3555, 555 North Duke Street, Lancaster, PA 17603 Tel: 717/299-5511 or 717/295-8322 (24 hours)

St. Joseph's Hospital, 250 College Avenue, Lancaster, PA 17604 Tel: 717/299-4546

North Penn Hospital, 100 Medical Campus Drive, Lansdale, PA 19446 Tel: 215/368-2100

Gnaden-Huetten Memorial Hospital, 11th & Hamilton Streets, Lehighton, PA 18235 Tel: 215/377-1300

Lewistown Hospital, Highland Ave, Lewistown, PA 17044 Tel: 717/248-5411

Nanticoke State General Hospital, North Washington Street, Nanticoke, PA 18643 Tel: 717/735-5000

Paoli Memorial Hospital, Lancaster Pike, Paoli, PA 19301 Tel: 215/648-1043

Philadelphia Poison Information, 321 University Avenue, Philadelphia, PA 19104 Tel: 215/922-5523, 215/922-5524

Philipsburg State General Hospital, Philipsburg, PA 16866 Tel: 814/342-3320

Children's Hospital, 125 Desoto Street, Pittsburgh, PA 15213 Tel: 412/681-6669

Pittston Hospital, Oregon Heights, Pittston, PA 18640 Tel: 717/654-3341

Pottstown Memorial Medical Center, 1600 East High Street, Pottstown, PA 19464 Tel: 215/327-7100

Good Samaritan Hospital, East Norwegian & Tremont Streets, Pottsville, PA 17901 Tel: 717/622-3400 ext 270

Community General Hospital, 145 North Sixth Street, Reading, PA 19601 Tel: 215/375-9115 (24 hours)

The Robert Packer Hospital, Guthrie Square, Sayre, PA 18840 Tel: 717/888-6666

Grand View Hospital, Lawn Avenue, Sellersville, PA 18960 Tel: 215/257-3611

Somerset Community Hospital, 225 South Center Avenue, Somerset, PA 15501 Tel: 814/443-2626

Centre Community Hospital, Orchard Street, State College, PA 16801 Tel: 814/238-4351

Titusville Hospital, 406 West Oak Street, Titusville, PA 16354 Tel: 814/827-1851

Tyler Memorial Hospital, RD 1, Tunkhannock, PA 18657 Tel: 717/836-2161

Memorial Osteopathic Hospital, 325 South Belmont Street, York, PA 17403 Tel: 717/843-8623

Rhode Island

Rhode Island Poison Center, Rhode Island Hospital, 593 Eddy Street, Providence, RI 02902 Tel: 401/277-5727

South Carolina

National Pesticide Telecommunications Network, Medical University of South Carolina, 171 Ashley Avenue, Charleston, SC 29403 Tel: 803/792-4201, 800/845-7633, 800/792-4201 (call collect in South Carolina, Hawaii, and Alaska)

Palmetto Poison Center, University of South Carolina College of Pharmacy, Columbia, SC 29208 Tel: 803/765-7359, 1-800/922-1117

South Dakota

Rapid City Regional Hospital-Main, 353 Fairmont Boulevard, Rapid City, SD 57701 Tel: 605/341-3333, 1-800/742-8925

McKennan Poison Center, 800 East 21st Street, Sioux Falls, SD 57101 Tel: 605/336-3894, 1-800/952-0123 (South Dakota only), 1-800/843-0505 (Iowa, Nebraska, and Minnesota)

Tennessee

T.C. Thompson Children's Hospital, 910 Blackford Street, Chattanooga, TN 37403 Tel: 615/381-4500

Maury County Hospital, 1224 Trotwood Avenue, Columbia, TN 38401 Tel: 615/381-4500

Cookeville General Hospital, 142 West Fifth Street, Cookeville, TN 38501 Tel: 615/526-4818

Jackson-Madison County General Hospital, 708 West Forest Avenue,

Jackson, TN 38301 Tel: 901/424-0424

Johnson City Medical Center Hospital, 400 State of Franklin Road, Johnson City, TN 37601 Tel: 615/461-6111

Memorial Research Center and Hospital, 1924 Alcoa Highway, Knoxville, TN 37920 Tel: 615/971-3261

Southern Poison Center, University of Tennessee College of Pharmacy, 26 Dunlap Street, Memphis, TN 38163 Tel: 901/528-6048

Vanderbilt University Medical Center, 1161 21st Avenue South, Nashville, TN 37232 Tel: 615/322-6435 (adults), 615/322-2244 (pediatric), 615/322-6455 (night line, adult or pediatric)

Texas

Hendrick Medical Center, 19th & Hickory Streets, Abilene, TX 79601 Tel: 915/677-3551

Amarillo Emergency Receiving Center, Amarillo Hospital District, PO Box 1110, 2103 West Sixth Street, Amarillo, TX 79106 Tel: 806/376-4292

Brackenridge Hospital, One Hospital Drive, Austin, TX 78701 Tel: 512/478-4490, 512/476-6461

Baptist Hospital of Southeast Texas, PO Box 1591, College & 11th Streets, Beaumont, TX 77701 Tel: 713/833-7409

Memorial Medical Center, PO Box 5280, 2606 Hospital Boulevard, Corpus Christi, TX 78405 Tel: 512/881-4559

R.E. Thomason General Hospital, PO Box 20009, 4185 Alameda Avenue, El Paso, TX 79905 Tel: 915/533-1244

Cook Children's Hospital, 1212 West Lancaster Street, Fort Worth, TX 76102 Tel: 817/336-6611

Southeast Texas Poison Center,* Eighth & Mechanic Streets,

Galveston, TX 77550 Tel: 713/765-1420 (Galveston only), 713/654-1701 (Houston only)

Valley Baptist Hospital, PO Box 2588, 2101 South Commerce Street, Harlingen, TX 78550 Tel: 512/421-1860, 512/421-1859

Mercy Hospital, 1515 Logan Street, Laredo, TX 78040 Tel: 512/724-6247

Methodist Hospital Poison Control Center, 3615 19th Street, Lubbock, TX 79410 Tel: 806/793-4366

Midland Memorial Hospital, 2200 West Illinois Avenue, Midland, TX 79701 Tel: 915/685-1111

Medical Center Hospital, PO Box 7239, Odessa, TX 79760 Tel: 915/333-1231

Central Plains Regional Hospital,* 2601 Dimmitt Road, Plainview, TX 79072 Tel: 806/296-9601

Shannon West Texas Memorial Hospital, PO Box 1879, 9 South Magdalen Street, San Angelo, TX 76901 Tel: 915/653-6741 ext 210

Department of Pediatrics, University of Texas Health Science Center at San Antonio, 7703 Floyd Curl Drive, San Antonio, TX 78284 Tel: 512/223-6361 ext 295

Medical Center Hospital, 1000 South Beckham Street, Tyler, TX 75701 Tel: 214/597-0351

Hillcrest Baptist Hospital, 3000 Herring Avenue, Waco, TX 76708 Tel: 817/756-8611

Wichita General Hospital, 1600 Eighth Street, Wichita Falls, TX 76301 Tel: 817/322-6771

Utah

Intermountain Regional Poison Control Center,* 50 North Medical Drive, Salt Lake City, UT 84132 Tel: 801/581-2151

Vermont

Vermont Poison Center, Medical Center Hospital, Colchester Avenue, Burlington, VT 06401 Tel: 802/658-3456

Virginia

Alexandria Hospital, 4320 Seminary Road, Alexandria, VA 22314 Tel: 703/379-3070

Arlington Hospital, 1701 North George Mason Drive, Arlington, VA 22205 Tel: 703/558-5000

Montgomery County Community Hospital, Route 460 South, Blacksburg, VA 24060 Tel: 703/951-1111

Blue Ridge Poison Center, Box 484, University of Virginia Medical Center, Charlottesville, VA 22908 Tel: 804/924-5543 (collect calls accepted) (24 hours)

Danville Memorial Hospital, 142 South Main Street, Danville, VA 22201 Tel: 804/799-2100 ext 3869

Fairfax Hospital, 3300 Gallows Road, Falls Church, VA 22046 Tel: 703/698-3600, 703/698-3111

Hampton General Hospital, 3120 Victoria Boulevard, Hampton, VA 23661 Tel: 804/722-1131

Rockingham Memorial Hospital, 738 South Mason Street, Harrisonburg, VA 22801 Tel: 703/433-9706

Stonewall Jackson Hospital, Spotswood Drive, Lexington, VA 24450 Tel: 703/463-9141

Lynchburg General Marshall Lodge Hospital, Inc., Tate Springs Road, Lynchburg, VA 24504 Tel: 804/528-2066

Northampton-Accomack Memorial Hospital, Nassawadox, VA 23413 Tel: 804/442-8700

Riverside Hospital, 500 J. Clyde Morris Boulevard, Newport News, VA 23601 Tel: 804/599-2050

DePaul Hospital, Granby Street & Kingsley Lane, Norfolk, VA 23505 Tel: 804/489-5288

Petersburg General Hospital, Mount Erin & Adams Streets, Petersburg, VA 23803 Tel: 804/862-5000

U.S. Naval Hospital, Portsmouth, VA 23708 Tel: 804/398-5898

Central Virginia Poison Center, Medical College of Virginia, PO Box 763 MCV Station, Richmond, VA 23298 Tel: 804/786-9123

Roanoke Memorial Hospital, PO Box 13367, Belleview & Jefferson Street, Roanoke, VA 24033 Tel: 703/981-7336

King's Daughter's Hospital, PO Box 3000, 1410 North Augusta Street, Staunton, VA 24401 Tel: 703/885-6848

Waynesboro Community Hospital, 501 Oak Avenue, Waynesboro, VA 22908 Tel: 703/942-4096

Williamsburg Community Hospital, Drawer H, 1238 Mount Vernon Avenue, Williamsburg, VA 23185 Tel: 804/253-6005

Washington

Children's Orthopedic Hospital and Medical Center,* 4800 Sandpoint Way NE, Seattle, WA 98105 Tel: 206/634-5252

Deaconess Hospital, West 800 Fifth Avenue, Spokane, WA 99210 Tel: 509/747-1077, 1-800/572-5842

Mary Bridge Children's Hospital, South L Street, Tacoma, WA 98405 Tel: 206/272-1281 ext 259

Central Washington Poison Center, Yakima Valley Memorial Hospital, 2811 Tieton Drive, Yakima, WA 98902 Tel: 509/248-4400, 1-800/572-9176

West Virginia

West Virginia Poison System, 3110 MacCorkie Avenue SE, Charleston, WV 25304 Tel: 1-800/642-3625, 304/348-4211

Wisconsin

Luther Hospital, 310 Chestnut Street, Eau Claire, WI 54701 Tel: 715/835-1515

Green Bay Poison Control Center, St. Vincent's Hospital, 835 South Van Buren Street, Green Bay, WI 54305 Tel: 414/433-8100

St. Francis Medical Center, 700 West Avenue South, LaCrosse, WI 54601 Tel: 608/784-3971

Madison Area Poison Center, University Hospital and Clinic, 600 Highland Avenue, Madison, WI 53792 Tel: 608/262-3702

Milwaukee Children's Hospital, 1700 West Wisconsin Avenue, Milwaukee, WI 53233 Tel: 414/931-4114

Wyoming

Wyoming Poison Center, DePaul Hospital, 2600 East 18th Street, Cheyenne, WY 82001 Tel: 307/635-9256

Common Medical Tests

---

191. The Exercise Tolerance Test

WHY AND HOW THE TEST IS USED

The exercise tolerance or stress test is a means of indirectly measuring the heart's work capacity. Specifically, it is a means of gauging the heart's ability to deliver oxygen-rich blood to the muscles as they work progressively harder. It is also a way to estimate the ability of the blood vessels surrounding the heart (coronary arteries) to supply blood to the working heart muscle.

The stress test consists of monitoring the heart's rhythm, pulse rate, and blood pressure while an individual goes through a series of increasingly demanding physical exercises, which usually involve walking on a treadmill or pedaling a stationary bicycle. In addition to measuring cardiovascular fitness, the test also helps diagnose possible cardiac abnormalities that are not present while at rest or during normal activities.

An exercise test is generally administered as part of a diagnostic work-up for suspected heart disease, or following recovery from a heart attack or heart surgery. It also may be recommended for people who are about to embark upon a vigorous program of exercise or in preparation for designing a cardiovascular conditioning program. This may be particularly advisable for people who have been relatively sedentary, are over the age of thirty-five or forty, and have one or more risk factors predisposing them to heart disease. These include cigarette smoking, diabetes, a family history of heart attacks or strokes, high blood pressure, and elevated levels of blood cholesterol and other blood fats.

TEST PROCEDURE

The test subject should wear comfortable, nonconstricting sports clothes and flat heels (preferably sneakers or running shoes). Most patients will be instructed not

549

to eat for at least two hours before the test. Check with your doctor about taking medications before the test time, since these may affect the outcome of your ability to exercise. There is no anticipated discomfort involved, so you should relax and approach the test much the way you might any physical activity. The test usually takes between thirty and sixty minutes, depending upon the exact procedure used by the doctor or testing facility.

The test should be performed in a doctor's office, hospital, clinic, or other medically approved setting. Exercise tests are sometimes administered at exercise clubs, YMCAs or other such facilities; if this is the case, you should make sure that a doctor or approved health care professional trained in administering exercise stress tests supervises the procedure. For most people, an exercise test does not involve

An exercise stress or tolerance test measures the heart's performance while exercising at increasing levels of exertion. Before the test, electrodes leading to an electrocardiogram (ECG) monitor will be attached to the chest. The test itself may be performed on a treadmill, as illustrated here, or on an exercise bicycle. In either instance, the patient will be asked to exercise at increasing intensity until a target heart rate is reached or until the patient becomes tired. Changes on the ECG also may lead to discontinuing the test.

any risk if it is properly administered and the patient is carefully monitored.

At the beginning of the test, the doctor or center staff member takes an electrocardiogram (ECG) while you are in a resting position. Then the electrodes for a continuous or computerized ECG will be attached at various points of the chest with tape. Depending upon the circumstances, other monitors or devices may be attached to measure other functions such as respiration, blood pressure, and lung capacity. After the various measuring devices are attached, the treadmill or bicycle is started at a slow speed. Every few minutes, at regular intervals, the speed and/or inclination is increased until the subject's heart rate reaches a predetermined rate. If the subject shows extreme fatigue, cardiac disturbances, or other symptoms before reaching that level, the test will be stopped.

NORMAL AND ABNORMAL RESPONSES

The normal range of responses to this kind of test are generally as follows:

1. Systolic blood pressure (the peak pressure during the heart's pumping cycle) may rise to as high as 190 to 220 mm. Hg.
2. Heart rate will range from 180 to 200 beats per minute in a young adult down to 160 in a person over sixty years old.
3. Symptoms experienced at peak effort might include fatigue or nausea but not chest pain or other signs of coronary distress.

Some abnormal responses might include:

1. A drop in systolic blood pressure, which suggests inadequate pumping by the heart.
2. An increase of the heart rate at a lower than normal "work" level.
3. Changes in the ECG that indicate a possible cardiac abnormality.
4. Chest pain, disturbances in the heart

rhythm, or other possible symptoms of heart disorders.

It is important to remember that all of these figures, both positive and negative, fall within a range. There are no absolute correct numbers that fit everyone. In addition, it is possible to have a response that indicates an abnormality yet have a perfectly normal heart, an occurrence referred to as a false-negative result. The opposite—a false-positive result—also may occur. Your doctor will know whether or not you have a healthy level of cardiovascular fitness by interpreting the figures within the overall context of your full physical examination and medical history.

RESULTS AND FOLLOWUP OF TESTING

The results of an exercise tolerance stress test can help a doctor to diagnose heart disease and determine the safe limits of physical exercise. Setting such parameters is especially important for someone who has had a heart attack, suffers from angina, or has undergone heart surgery.

Such tests can also help evaluate cardiac fitness and can be used in developing an exercise prescription or conditioning program. Depending upon the outcome of the test, a person may be advised to step up or decrease a particular activity or perhaps to try another, more appropriate form of ex-

ercise. The test may also be useful for evaluating an individual's response to medication.

Often, the results can prompt someone to change a life style that does not promote cardiac health. Smoking, consuming a high-fat, high-calorie diet, and leading a generally sedentary existence may all contribute to poor cardiovascular health. An unfavorable test is a tangible way of illustrating how diet and social patterns can definitely lead to serious health problems.

SUMMING UP

An exercise tolerance stress test is best given by a doctor who is familiar with the procedure. If you choose to take such a test at a nonmedical facility, it is important first to check out its credentials and standing with the medical community. An improperly administered test is of little use to you or your physician. Although there is no such thing as an infallible way of measuring cardiovascular efficiency, the exercise tolerance test is considered to be one of the simplest methods of judging the heart at work. If a heart's activity is strong and constant under conditions of hard exercise, then it is reasonably safe to assume that it can function well under day-to-day conditions.

192. Cardiac Catheterization and Angiography

COMMON CHARACTERISTICS

Cardiac catheterization is one of the most informative tests used in evaluating the heart. It generally follows numerous other tests, such as routine chest X-rays, electrocardiograms, an exercise stress test, blood tests, and evaluations of thyroid and lung function. If the results of these tests indicate the possibility of heart disease, then cardiac catheterization may be recommended to provide your doctor with more precise information about both the severity and the exact location of any defect or abnormality in or around your heart—information that cannot be obtained by any other noninvasive method at the present time. It is almost always done before open heart surgery, particularly coronary bypass operations and heart valve replacements. Cardiac catheterization also may be performed as a followup after heart surgery or treatment of a heart attack.

WHAT IS LEARNED?

Cardiac catheterization enables the doctor to measure the blood pressure and oxygen content of each of the four chambers of the heart. It is also used to take blood samples from each part of the heart. It can identify the exact location of any abnormal openings in the heart walls. It can also measure the heart's ability to contract and give information about the performance of the heart muscles in pumping the blood.

Cardiac catheterization may be combined with angiography, in which a dye opaque to X-ray is introduced through the catheter and its progress through the heart is monitored and filmed. With the aid of the dye, certain abnormalities that would not otherwise be recognizable may be seen and analyzed. Congenital malformations, blood clots inside the heart, and blocked or partially blocked arteries all can be detected by angiography. The combined tests provide detailed information about the anatomy of the blood vessels which serve the heart muscles (the coronary arteries).

WHAT IS INVOLVED?

In cardiac catheterization, a thin, flexible tube called a catheter is introduced into the bloodstream through a small incision made in the patient's arm or upper leg, or both places. The catheter is threaded through blood vessels until it reaches the coronary arteries, or until it reaches the chambers of the heart.

Prior to cardiac catheterization, the doctor who is to perform the test examines the patient. At this time, the patient should tell the doctor, if he has not already done so, about any allergies, medications, or any abnormal tendency to bleed. The patient also may be asked to sign a paper consenting to the test. If the catheter is to be introduced through the upper leg, that area will be shaved. Immediately preceding the test, the patient may be given a mild sedative.

The actual procedure will usually take from one and a half to two hours. It is performed in a hospital, in a room known as the catheterization laboratory, or cath lab. The patient is awake and fully conscious at all times. An electrocardiograph machine will monitor the patient's heartbeat continuously. Other information will be recorded by various highly sensitive instruments, including an X-ray television monitor.

During cardiac catheterization the patient should feel no significant pain. Sometimes he will feel his heart skip a beat as the

Special cameras are used to view the arteries and heart structures during catheterization. To make X-ray films of the coronary arteries (angiograms), radiopaque material is introduced through the catheter and then photographed in a rapid series of shots to provide a permanent record.

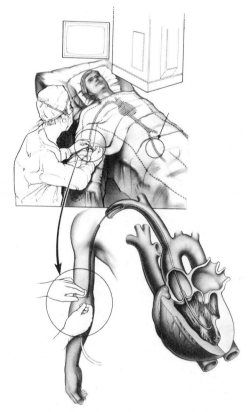

In cardiac catheterization, a thin, flexible tube (catheter) is introduced into a vein in the arm or an artery in the leg (or both) and threaded through the blood vessels until it reaches the coronary arteries or the chambers of the heart.

catheter is passed through it. If the test is combined with angiography, a slight discomfort may also be felt by the patient, along with a sensation of warmth and an acrid taste in the mouth when the dye is inserted into the bloodstream. But these symptoms will last only a few moments. The patient may not even know when the catheter is introduced, as the area of entry will be under a local anesthetic.

As the catheter progresses through the bloodstream, the patient may watch its advance as it is monitored on a television screen. At certain stages of the procedure the patient may be asked to take a deep breath, or to cough. This is to increase the performance level of the heart mildly for analysis purposes.

At the close of the procedure the catheter is withdrawn by the same route through which it entered. The points of incision in the leg or arm are sealed with stitches, which are removed after five or six days. The patient remains in the hospital overnight for observation. During this period feelings of weakness or nausea may occur, possibly accompanied by a fever. These symptoms will subside after a few hours.

POTENTIAL RISKS

Cardiac catheterization and angiography are not surgical procedures and have a relatively small risk factor. Occasionally, there may be some slight bleeding at the site of catheter entry. Rarely, the procedure may cause disturbances of the heartbeat, or the patient may react adversely to the injected dye. However, the medical staff involved in the procedure will be closely monitoring the patient and are normally able to deal with any problem immediately and effectively.

SUMMING UP

Cardiac catheterization is a relatively common test used to study the internal structures of the heart and coronary arteries as well as to assess certain aspects of heart function. It is generally a safe procedure if performed in the proper setting by a physician experienced in its administration. The patient experiences little if any discomfort but can expect to be hospitalized overnight for observation.

193. Tests of the Upper Gastrointestinal Tract

GENERAL CONSIDERATIONS

There are numerous tests for diagnosing problems of the upper gastrointestinal tract. One or more of these tests may be recommended for such signs and symptoms as difficulty in swallowing, unexplained vomiting, frequent heartburn or gnawing pain, unexplained weight loss, or internal bleeding. These tests can detect the presence of abnormalities such as hiatus hernia, polyps, ulcers, tumors, or strictures, as well as some disorders in the functioning of the digestive tract. As a rule none of these tests is painful, though they do cause discomfort. Most can be done either in a doctor's office or on an outpatient basis.

UPPER GASTROINTESTINAL (GI) SERIES

This a series of tests for which the patient drinks a barium "milkshake," a compound that resists X-rays and therefore shows up in marked contrast on X-ray film. As the mixture progresses through the digestive tract, contours and abnormalities can be observed in X-ray. The test is usually done in a radiologist's office and lasts from thirty minutes to about six hours. The patient is placed on an X-ray table and asked to take a swallow of the barium sulfate mixture, which has a somewhat unpleasant chalky taste.

The first part of the series is examination of the esophagus. This test is known as a barium swallow, or esophagography, and takes about thirty minutes. The doctor watches on the fluoroscope for an X-ray view of what happens as the barium moves down the esophagus. He or she may take both spot films and movies from different angles.

The series continues as more barium is swallowed to fill the stomach. Since air must be swallowed during this part of the test, the patient may be given a perforated straw so that air will enter the stomach as the barium is sipped. The doctor will probably tilt the table, palpate the stomach, and apply abdominal pressure, either by hand or by a flat device attached to the X-ray unit, in order to spread the abdomen for better X-ray positioning. This part of the GI series also takes about thirty minutes.

The small bowel examination is usually given in conjunction with the upper GI series because the barium must pass through the upper tract to reach the small intestine. This examination lasts from two to six hours, depending on how long it takes the barium to pass through the small intestine. X-ray pictures are taken at intervals of about thirty or sixty minutes. It would be wise to bring reading matter, knitting, or something else that can be done while waiting.

The upper GI series is considered to involve little or no risk. The only aftereffect is that stools may be white for two or three days.

Another radiographic barium test, hypotonic duodenography, is usually administered to patients with persistent upper abdominal pain. During this procedure, barium is instilled by a catheter passed through the nose into the duodenum.

ENDOSCOPY OR GASTROSCOPY

A flexible, fiberoptic tube is passed through the throat into the upper gastrointestinal tract to permit closer observation. The tube transmits light to the area being viewed and conveys the image to the viewer. It has attachments that allow the doctor to take biopsy specimens, apply suction, remove foreign objects, inject air, take pictures or movies, and even clean the lens. The procedure may be done in the hospital, on an outpatient basis, and lasts from fifteen minutes to an hour. A local anesthesia will either be sprayed into the throat or gargled. A relaxant drug may also be given. Once the patient swallows the tube into the esophagus, observations can be made. The tube is then moved further, into the stomach and the duodenum.

Since there is a slight risk of perforating some part of the digestive tract during this procedure, any sharp pain should be reported.

As a precaution, the patient may be kept in the hospital for several hours after the test for observation. Eating will not be permitted for about four hours, when the gag reflex returns. Since the sedation makes driving dangerous, transportation home should be prearranged.

GASTRIC SECRETION STUDIES

Tests of the gastric juices are generally used to gain information about the possible presence of ulcers. These tests require insertion into a nostril of a nasogastric tube, through which gastric juices can be extracted. Once the tube is in place a number of tests may be carried out. The commonly done twelve-hour night secretion test must be administered in the hospital. Shorter tests can be given on an outpatient basis. Once the nasogastric tube is in place, there may be discomfort but should not be any pain. After the tube is withdrawn, the nostril may feel sore and the patient may

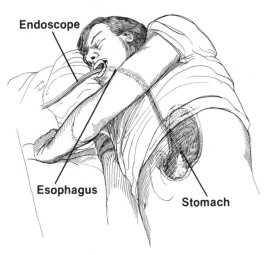

Endoscope

Esophagus

Stomach

In endoscopy, a test usually done in the hospital on an outpatient basis, a flexible, fiberoptic tube is passed through the esophagus and into the upper gastrointestinal tract. The tube transmits light to one area of the tract and conveys an image of that area to the viewer.

suffer from a minor sore throat. Complications, though unusual, have been known to occur. They are most often related to irritation caused by the tube.

Two other tests of gastric juices are the acid perfusion test (also called the Bernstein test), whose purpose is to distinguish chest pains caused by digestive tract problems from those caused by cardiac disorders, and the esophageal acidity test, which evaluates the operation of the sphincter between the esophagus and the stomach. Both tests involve the insertion of cath-

eters into the esophagus, in the acid perfusion test, through the nose, and in the esophageal acidity test, through the mouth. Each test takes forty-five minutes to an hour.

SUMMING UP

A number of tests are now available to diagnose accurately disorders of the esophagus and stomach. Most can be done in a doctor's office and involve little or no risk, although some may be uncomfortable.

194. Tests of the Lower Gastrointestinal Tract

GENERAL CONSIDERATIONS

Problems of the lower gastrointestinal tract are signaled by such signs and symptoms as lower abdominal pain, altered bowel habits, a history of constipation or diarrhea, rectal bleeding, and blood, pus, or mucus in the stool. Tests of the lower gastrointestinal tract can detect such abnormalities as colorectal cancer, ulcerative colitis, and polyps. These tests cause varying degrees of discomfort and fatigue and, in some cases, mild to severe cramps.

BARIUM ENEMA

Barium is a compound that is resistant to X-rays and therefore shows up in marked contrast on X-ray film. A barium enema allows a doctor to visualize the

large intestine (colon), and can aid in the diagnosis of colorectal cancer, inflammatory bowel disease, polyps, diverticulitis, ulcerative and granulamatous colitis, and structural changes in the large intestine. If a barium enema is given along with an upper gastrointestinal series (including a barium swallow), the enema should be administered first because the barium mixture may take days to pass through the body and can interfere with other X-ray studies.

Barium enemas can be given either in a hospital, or in a doctor's office. The procedure usually takes from thirty minutes to one hour. The doctor will give prior instructions for cleaning out the bowel.

A tube is inserted through the anus and into the rectum. Then, the doctor will watch through a fluoroscope for a view of what happens as a mixture of a compound of barium is run into the large intestine. The patient will be turned in different directions to allow gravitational flow of the liquid everywhere. Filling defects (places where the normal outline of barium should be seen but isn't) will suggest the presence of growths and other abnormalities. As the bowel fills, the doctor may apply abdominal pressure to separate overlapping loops of intestine so that any lesions may be seen.

After the doctor has finished X-raying, the patient will be helped to the bathroom to evacuate. The thin barium film that will remain on the wall of the intestine will be needed when more X-rays are taken to detect the presence of problems in the mucous membrane lining of the large intestine.

Finally, if the doctor suspects the presence of polyps on the intestinal wall, he or she may distend the colon with air so that air-contrast pictures can be taken.

A barium enema is an uncomfortable and tiring procedure. As the barium runs in, the patient will experience a sensation of fullness, may suffer from cramps, and will have a great urge to defecate. Breathing slowly and deeply should reduce the discomfort. If the patient cannot control the urge to defecate, it should be realized that the doctor will take this in stride.

After the enema, stools may be white for two or three days. If they become impacted, enemas and laxatives will help. Only very rarely do more serious complications occur.

PROCTOSIGMOIDOSCOPY

The purpose of this three-part procedure is to see directly into the lower part of the large intestine. Doctors recommend this procedure to persons forty years of age and over as a matter of course, since it is a highly effective method for detecting colorectal cancer. Proctosigmoidoscopies can also help to detect inflammations, in-

fections, ulcerative bowel disease, hemorrhoids, polyps, and abscesses.

Proctosigmoidoscopy is easily performed in the doctor's office and takes from ten minutes to a half-hour. If a biopsy is taken or a polyp is removed, the procedure will take somewhat longer. Prior instructions will be given about controlling food intake and cleaning out the bowel.

After having the patient assume either a knee-chest or a left-side position, the doctor will perform a digital examination to see if the anal sphincters are dilated. Then he or she will gently insert a ten- to twelve-inch sigmoidoscope into the anus so that the distal sigmoid colon and rectum can be seen. After that, a two and three-quarters-inch proctoscope will be inserted into the anus so that the doctor can examine the lower rectum and anal canal.

This procedure is moderately uncomfortable: the instruments may feel cool; the patient may have muscle spasms of the intestinal wall and lower abdominal pain, as well as an urge to defecate. Again, correct breathing should help ease the discomfort.

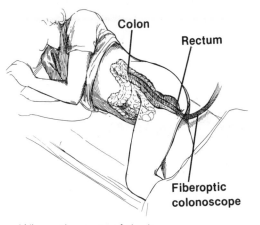

Colon

Rectum

Fiberoptic colonoscope

When other tests of the lower gastrointestinal tract are inconclusive, colonoscopy is indicated. A flexible endoscope is inserted into the rectum and up through the colon. Besides allowing the doctor to view the entire large intestine, the endoscope can also collect specimens of tissue for laboratory examination.

COLONOSCOPY

A colonoscope is a long, thin, flexible endoscope that allows the doctor to get a direct view of the entire large intestine and to obtain biopsy specimens. It is useful in detecting inflammatory or ulcerative bowel disease and lesions and for locating lower gastrointestinal bleeding. This procedure is indicated when the results of the barium enema and the proctosigmoidoscopy are inconclusive.

This procedure is usually performed in the hospital but can be done on an outpatient basis. The doctor will give preliminary instructions similar to those given before the proctosigmoidoscopy. About two hours before the colonoscopy, which may take from a half-hour to two hours, either a tranquilizer or a sedative may be given to help the patient relax.

There may be a strong urge to defecate as the cool colonoscope is first inserted and advanced. Again, this urge can be relieved if the patient breathes deeply and slowly through the mouth. A small amount of air may be introduced to distend the wall and provide a better view; no effort should be made to control escaping air.

As the colonoscopy progresses, the doctor may use suction to remove blood or secretions and use a forceps or brush to obtain specimens. When the colonoscopy is over, as a matter of course, the patient will be observed for the rare signs which might point to bowel perforation. If a polyp has been removed, it will be normal for a small amount of blood to appear in the stool.

SUMMING UP

Modern fiberoptic instruments, which include the long, flexible tubes fitted with lights and magnifying devices, have greatly changed the diagnosis of various bowel disorders. Examinations using these instruments include proctosigmoidoscopy and colonoscopy—tests that enable a doctor to look into the entire length of the colon. Although the examinations are uncomfortable, they are capable of detecting tumors and other problems in their earliest, most treatable stages.

195. Mammography

COMMON CHARACTERISTICS

Mammography is an X-ray visualization of the breasts. The technique is used to detect cysts and tumors, some of which may be too small to be felt in a physical examination, and to determine whether these growths are benign or malignant. Mammography is very accurate—only a very small percentage of malignancies is missed. It does, however, have a high rate of false-positive results, and any suspicious findings on a mammogram should be confirmed by a biopsy.

RISKS AND BENEFITS

When mammography first came into general use, the radiation dosage was quite a high one, and there was much disagreement among doctors as to whether the benefits of the technique justified its risks. The dose now used is very low (0.1 to 0.3 rads), and it now seems clear that the benefits to be derived from mammography outweigh any risks involved in the radiation exposure. The American Cancer Society and National Cancer Institute recently revised their recommendations for mammography and now suggest that women have it on a yearly basis after the age of forty or forty-five.

A few years ago, there was a good deal of controversy over whether the radiation in mammography posed a risk of causing the very cancer the test is intended to detect. Since then, numerous studies have been done to see whether women who have undergone mammography have a higher incidence of breast cancer. To date, no such increase has been found. Also, the amount of radiation administered has been decreased and is now less than that involved in an ordinary chest X-ray.

Since younger women have denser breast tissue than that seen in older women, mammography is not as useful before the age of thirty-five. It is generally recommended that a woman have a baseline mammogram between the age of thirty-five and forty, which can be used in later years to note any changes. Women at high risk for breast cancer—those with cystic breast disease or a family history of breast malignancies, for example—should be screened at an earlier age and more frequently than others.

THE PROCEDURE

Mammography is generally done in the radiology laboratory of a hospital or clinic, on an outpatient basis. The test itself takes about half an hour.

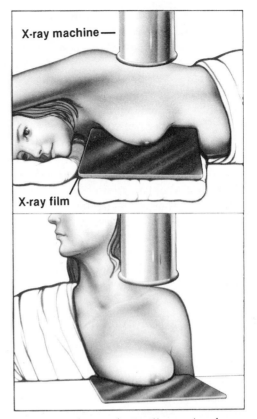

X-ray machine —

X-ray film

Mammography is a breast X-ray taken from several angles.

You will be asked to remove all jewelry and clothing above the waist and will be provided with a gown that opens in front. If you have used talcum powder, creams or body cosmetics on your breasts, you may be asked to wash, as these substances are likely to cause false-positive results.

Sitting on a chair in the X-ray laboratory, or standing, you will be asked to rest one breast on a plate above an X-ray cassette. The laboratory technician will probably spend some time positioning the breast so that folds and wrinkles are minimized. A compression device, usually a smooth plastic shield, will be placed over the breast and a little pressure applied. You will be asked to hold your breath while a radiograph is taken, giving an up-and-down view of the breast tissue. The machine will then be rotated, the breast compressed again, and another photograph taken from the side. The whole procedure will be repeated for the second breast.

The films will be developed immediately and checked for readability. You will probably be asked to wait while this is done, in case a particular view of the breast has to be repeated.

Benign cysts show up on a mammogram as well-outlined, regular, clear spots, often in groups and usually in both breasts. Malignant tumors appear as irregular, opaque areas with ill-defined edges, generally solitary and in one breast only. If such a suspicious area is seen, a biopsy will be necessary to confirm or rule out the presence of cancer.

OTHER TESTS FOR DETECTING BREAST CANCER

Two techniques, one using light, the other using sound, are being developed to detect breast cancer and other breast diseases. Both are accurate and can be repeated as often as needed and without risk.

Transillumination of the breast (also called diaphanography) uses infrared light, directed through the breast and photographed on infrared film, to examine the tissues. The denser the tissue, the darker its color on the film. Malignant tissues appear brown or black, benign tumors red, and fluid-filled cysts as bright spots. Diaphanography is somewhat less reliable than mammography. Although the detection rate is high, this technique cannot distinguish cancer from the lumps of benign mastitis (inflammation of the breast) or from a hemorrhage in the tissues. It is currently being used by a few specialists only.

In ultrasonography, a transducer focuses a beam of high-frequency sound into the breast. The sound wave returns as an echo that varies in intensity with the density of the underlying tissues and is translated into visual form by a computer. Ultrasound is especially valuable for diagnosing very small tumors, for distinguishing cysts from tumors in dense breast tissue, and for examining the area close to the ribs, which is difficult to study with radiography. The technique, still largely experimental, promises to be even more accurate than mammography.

196. The Pelvic Examination

COMMON CHARACTERISTICS

An internal pelvic examination is a routine part of the annual gynecological checkup for women of childbearing age and of the regular (usually biannual) checkup for older women. The primary purpose of the examination is to detect any tumors (benign or malignant) of the cervix, uterus, or ovaries. It is also done to confirm pregnancy and to aid in the diagnosis of numerous gynecological problems.

The examination also involves collecting samples of cells shed from the surface of the cervix and vagina—a Pap smear—for later laboratory analysis for any abnormalities. This has become an important screening tool for cervical cancers.

BEFORE THE EXAMINATION

If the pelvic examination is to include a Pap test, you will be asked not to douche or use any vaginal medication for twenty-four hours prior to the examination.

In the doctor's office or clinic, you will be asked to empty your bladder (the urine specimen will usually be examined in the laboratory for the presence of albumen [protein], sugar, and bacteria). Having taken off all your clothes, including your bra and panties, you will be given a hospital-type gown or a sheet to wear and asked to lie on the examination table in the lithotomy position—that is, with your buttocks at the edge of the table, your knees bent, and your legs supported by knee or heel stirrups.

The examination has several distinct parts. The first is an inspection of the external genitals, the vulva. The doctor (or nurse practitioner) will check the vulva for irritations, lumps and swellings, pubic lice, discoloration, and any abnormal discharge. The labia will be separated, and the doctor will examine the vaginal and urinary openings. If you have had a child, you may be asked to "bear down," or "strain as if you were trying to move your bowels"; this effort demonstrates the strength, or weakness, of the muscles of the pelvic floor. Usually, before beginning the external examination, the doctor will gently touch the inside of the upper thigh, so that you will not startle.

SPECULUM EXAMINATION

The doctor will then insert a warmed speculum into the vagina at a forty-five-degree angle, rotate it, and open it. (It will be lubricated with water rather than jelly, since the latter may interfere with the Pap test.) The speculum, a metal instrument that looks like a pair of shoehorns hinged together, is used to hold the walls of the vagina apart. Through it, the doctor can see the vagina and cervix and make a visual check for inflammation, discoloration of the mucous membrane, abnormal bleeding, signs of infection, and any growths or lesions.

If a Pap test is being done, the visible part of the cervix will be gently scraped with a spatula to obtain tissue to be sent to the laboratory. (Pressure on the cervix may cause a little, brief discomfort.) A smear of discharge for laboratory culture and to test for gonorrhea will be taken, and the speculum will be withdrawn.

BIMANUAL PALPATION OF THE UTERUS

By placing the index finger of one hand in the vagina and the fingers of the other on the abdomen, the doctor can palpate (examine by touch) the internal organs. He or she will gently and continuously shift the position of the fingers in order to determine the size, shape, and consistency

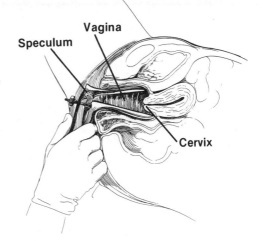

During a pelvic examination, the doctor or nurse practitioner inserts a speculum into the vagina to separate the vaginal walls, permitting a visual inspection of the cervix and vagina.

of the uterus, ovaries, and fallopian tubes and to locate any growths, irregularities, evidence of inflammation, or other abnormalities.

Palpation of the uterus is not usually uncomfortable, but there may be some slight pain when pressure is placed on the ovaries. It is helpful to the doctor—and much more comfortable for you—if you relax as completely as possible during the bimanual examination.

RECTOVAGINAL EXAMINATION

This is the final part of the examination and, for many women, the most unpleasant. The doctor places his or her index finger in the vagina and the middle finger in the rectum, palpating the back of the uterus and cervix for lumps and tender or hard places. The finger in the rectum will also be feeling for rectal lesions and noting the tone of the rectal sphincter muscle. As the doctor withdraws the finger from the rectum, you may feel that you are going to have a bowel movement, but this will not occur.

AFTER THE EXAMINATION

The results of the Pap test will usually be known within three days. These results are generally grouped into four categories: class 1—no abnormal cells; class 2—some abnormal cells, usually caused by inflammation; class 3—suspicious cells; classes 4 and 5—cancer cells. It is important to remember that both doctors and laboratories vary in the way they describe these classifications, that the distinction between different types of cells is often unclear, and that a "positive" Pap test does not necessarily mean a malignancy. For all class 3, 4, and 5 results, however, a repeat Pap test will be made, and if the abnormality persists, a biopsy and further tests to rule out cancer will be needed.

SUMMING UP

Although somewhat unpleasant, a regular pelvic examination is an important part of a woman's health maintenance program. It is the best means of detecting cervical cancer in its early, most treatable stages. It also is important in detecting infection and abnormalities of the ovaries, uterus, and other pelvic organs.

197. Computerized Tomography

COMMON CHARACTERISTICS

Computerized tomography, commonly referred to as CT or CAT scan, is a relatively new and highly sophisticated diagnostic technique that, while it uses X-rays, differs in many important ways from a conventional X-ray examination. First introduced for evaluating the brain, CT scanning is now being used to examine all parts of the body.

The technique produces a series of

cross-sectional images (the word *tomography* is derived from the Greek *tome,* a cutting or slice), making it possible to see tumors, abscesses, ulcers, cysts, and many other conditions deep within such internal organs as the pancreas and liver. Because of its unique sensitivity to variations in tissue density, CT scanning is able to distinguish benign from malignant tumors and gray from white brain tissue. Within the brain, CT can also see areas of inflammation, atrophy, and infarction (dead tissue resulting from complete blockage of the blood supply).

In addition to detecting conditions and structures that cannot be seen on conventional X-ray, CT scanning reduces the need for several dangerous invasive diagnostic procedures that were previously necessary to detect brain abnormalities. Moreover, radiation exposure is minimal.

Unlike conventional radiography, CT scanning does not use film. Instead, a scanner and a detector rotate around the patient, with the scanner sending a series of focused X-rays through a thin cross section

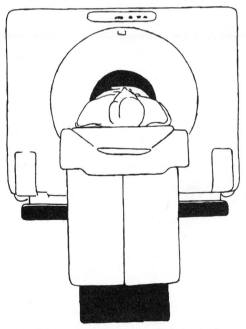

Patient in position for scan of abdominal area.

of the body with each rotation. The detector, which is mounted directly opposite the scanner, picks up the X-rays and measures the amount of radiation that has been absorbed by the intervening tissues. These measurements, hundreds of which can be made in a very short period of time, are then analyzed by a computer. Based on the amount of radiation that has been absorbed, the computer calculates the density of the tissues, expressing different densities in terms of different colors (or different shades of gray). Displayed on a viewing screen, the computer printout provides highly detailed and often striking three-dimensional images of internal body structures.

CT scanning of the body may be done with or without the use of a radio-iodine contrast medium, whose function is primarily to highlight blood vessels and allow for greater visual discrimination. Contrast, however, is usually required for CT scans of the head.

THE PROCEDURE

CT scanning is done in a hospital or radiology clinic usually on an outpatient basis. The time required for the test varies with the part of the body being examined; it seldom takes more than an hour.

If a contrast medium is to be used, or if the radiologist wants to leave open the possibility of using it, the patient will be asked to fast for four hours prior to the test. Otherwise, no preparation is necessary other than the signing of a consent form.

For the examination, the patient may be asked to remove some or all clothing and put on a hospital gown and to take off jewelry and eyeglasses. The patient will lie down on a radiographic table and will be secured with some kind of restraining device; if the head is to be scanned, it will be placed in a cradle and secured with a strap. The patient is placed in the center of the large circular apparatus that houses the scanner. During the test, one should relax and keep as still as possible. After each scan, the table will move automatically, so that the patient is in the correct position for the next one.

A contrast medium, if used, may be given either orally or by injection, depending on which part of the body is to be examined. In a brain scan, the contrast medium will be injected into a vein in the arm. (A known hypersensitivity to iodine or to shellfish is a contraindication to the use of a contrast medium.) Occasionally there are side effects to the contrast medium. These, which generally occur within five to ten minutes, include nausea, dizziness, a flushed sensation, and a salty or metallic taste in the mouth. If such reactions occur, you should report them to the radiologist immediately.

The equipment used in a CT scan is formidable and frequently noisy. The procedure, however, is completely painless. The patient will be alone for the test, with the radiologist and the CT technician monitoring the examination from an adjacent room.

After the examination, the scans will be checked by the radiologist to make certain that they are complete and contain the information requested by the doctor. Occasionally, a scan may have to be repeated or an additional one made.

ADVANTAGES OF THE CT SCAN

The introduction of computerized tomography has, quite literally, revolutionized diagnostic medicine. It is now possible to detect painlessly and accurately a wide variety of tumors or cysts involving a number of internal organs, most notably the pancreas, liver, colon, and kidney. Brain examinations, once inaccurate and highly uncomfortable, can now be done with greater accuracy and no discomfort using a CT scan. In addition to abnormal growths, the scan can detect such things as inflammation, ruptured blood vessels, and changes characteristic of senility.

SUMMING UP

Computerized tomography has emerged as a major diagnostic tool in the last decade and is now available in most parts of the country. Increasingly sophisticated machines have made it possible to expand the use of CT scanning to include the entire body, with the exception of the heart and other organs that are in constant motion.

198. Lung Function Tests

COMMON CHARACTERISTICS

Use of the stethoscope tells the doctor whether the patient's breathing sounds normal. A series of chest X-rays tells the doctor what the lungs look like. Lung (or pulmonary) function tests provide objective evidence of how efficiently the respiratory system is working. As they become increasingly sophisticated, these tests become more and more valuable as disease detectors, capable of locating the beginnings of tissue damage many years before the patient has any symptoms of a lung disorder.

As a totality, pulmonary function tests provide information about how the different cardiopulmonary diseases affect the interrelated and individual processes involved in breathing. Where disease is discovered, testing at regular intervals shows the rate at which the disease is progressing and provides the doctor and patient with evidence of the effectiveness of treatment over a long period.

Particularly in regard to the two most common obstructive airway diseases, chronic bronchitis and emphysema, for which early treatment is critical, the U.S. Surgeon General's second Report on Smoking and Health, issued in 1979, stressed the new developments that facilitate prompt diagnosis. It was pointed out that lung function testing is now so refined that the first signs of tissue impairment can be "detected in the tiniest branches of the tracheobronchial tree in air channels with diameters of two millimeters or less."

HOW THE LUNGS FUNCTION

To understand the various lung function tests and their clinical significance, it is helpful to have a picture of what happens during the process of normal breathing.

Air passes through the nose or mouth and enters the lungs by way of the trachea (windpipe). The trachea divides into the left and right bronchial tubes (the bronchi) from which the air passages (bronchioles) branch, becoming smaller and smaller. The terminal bronchioles lead into the respiratory bronchioles, from whose walls the alveolar ducts branch to permit air to enter the alveolar sacs. The walls of the alveoli are only one cell thick, and it is through these walls that gases are exchanged between the air in the alveoli and the blood in the pulmonary capillaries.

The air capacity of the lungs depends on the health of these minuscule air sacs and the efficiency with which they function. In obstructive lung diseases, these airways are impaired.

Breathing is controlled automatically, but when the doctor says, "Take a deep breath and hold it," the act is volitional. However, as the concentration of carbon dioxide in the blood rises, the respiratory center of the brain demands the expulsion of the breath so that an intake of fresh air can immediately follow.

CATEGORIES OF TESTS

Since no single lung function test can assess all aspects of pulmonary function, a battery of tests is essential if every step of the respiratory process is under investigation. However, the device known as a spirometer measures a number of lung functions with sufficient accuracy to provide the doctor with a basis for diagnosing and differentiating some of the more common

Patient undergoing an examination with a spirometer. The graph printout gives measurements such as the lungs' total air capacity and ventilation.

lung diseases, especially when combined with X-ray evidence.

WHAT THE TESTS MEASURE

Four different aspects of *volume* are measured by a spirometer: tidal volume (the amount of air breathed in and out during a single normal respiration); inspiratory reserve volume (the amount of additional air that can be breathed in following a normal intake of breath); expiratory reserve volume (the amount of air that can be expelled from the lungs immediately following a normal expiration of breath); and residual volume (the amount of gas left in the lungs after a maximum effort to expel the breath).

Another significant measurement is *total air capacity*, the total amount of air in the lungs at the time immediately following the maximum intake. This amount also includes the maximum amount of air that can be expelled *after* maximum intake and the amount of gas remaining in the lungs following such an effort (residual volume).

In diseases which cause lung tissue to become scarred, the air spaces will have decreased, resulting in a decrease in lung capacity. On the other hand, where partial airway obstruction (characteristic of asthma and emphysema) results in the trapping of air in the lungs, there is likely to be an increase in the residual volume, that is, in the amount of gas remaining in the lung following a maximum effort to expel the lung content.

Another lung function test evaluates *ventilation*. This is the process of exchange of oxygen and carbon dioxide as respiratory action moves air into and out of the alveoli. The person who ventilates normally maintains an adequate exchange of the two gases. However, when an individual hypoventilates (as in chronic obstructive emphysema, for example), the volume of air circulating in and out of the lungs decreases; inadequate exchange in the alveoli

results in a raised carbon dioxide level and a lowered oxygen level.

COMPUTERIZED SPIROMETRY

In recent years, measurements of the lung functions described above have been refined by the use of computerized spirometry. These sophisticated instruments can be programed so that they not only provide diagnostic information but also analyze its meaning in terms of abnormalities of function. Many hospitals, including small ones, and many private doctors now offer this type of pulmonary screening, either as part of a routine checkup or, when hospitals are involved, as part of community health programs.

AIR DISTRIBUTION TEST

This test is usually done in a hospital or special laboratory since it involves complicated monitoring equipment. The purpose of the test is to evaluate the pattern of air distribution in the lungs. Once air has been inhaled, the distribution to the millions of alveoli should be uniform if a normal balance is to be maintained in the exchange of gases at the capillary level. While uneven distribution may be heard through a stethoscope, a more refined estimate is usually based on the use of a radioactive gas (xenon) that shows up clearly in a lung scan. The test scan reveals the imbalance between ventilation and blood flow that leads to respiratory insufficiency.

DIFFUSION TEST

Diffusion tests measure the passage of gas across the alveolocapillary membrane. They are especially useful in distinguishing patients with asthma and chronic bronchitis from those with emphysema. In the two former diseases, diffusion capacity is likely to be nearly normal, but emphysema results in impaired diffusion because of the destruction of alveolar surfaces. In measuring diffusion capacity, carbon monoxide is used (in harmless amounts) because of its high affinity for hemoglobin, thereby enabling the tester to evaluate the rate of oxygen exchange in the blood.

SUMMING UP

Most serious lung diseases follow an insidious course over a very long period before they produce symptoms, and by the time they do, tissue damage may be irreversible. So that asymptomatic damage can be detected early and monitored for developments, lung function tests should be part of all regular health checkups. In addition, symptoms such as a nagging cough, chest pain, shortness of breath, or any other manifestation of lung trouble should be promptly evaluated by a doctor whose office is equipped for lung function testing. Young people who smoke should be screened on a regular basis.

199. Biopsy

COMMON CHARACTERISTICS

A biopsy is the removal of a specimen of living tissue, from any part of the body, so that it may be examined in detail under a microscope. The purpose of a biopsy is to help in establishing a diagnosis, as, for example, when there are symptoms that suggest cancer. Sometimes a biopsy will indicate that surgery is necessary and will suggest the type and extent of surgery that should be performed. Often, however, a biopsy makes it possible to avoid surgery by showing that a suspected malignancy is in fact benign, or that a condition exists that can be treated medically rather than surgically.

Biopsies are of two basic types, incisional (a cutting *in*) and excisional (a cutting *out*).

INCISIONAL BIOPSY

In an incisional biopsy, a sample of tissue is removed from a lesion, or from one of several lesions, or from a hidden lesion. (When tissue is sampled from a hidden lesion, the procedure is called a closed or blind biopsy.) An incisional biopsy may be done, under local anesthetic, in a doctor's office, in an outpatient surgical clinic, or at the bedside of a hospitalized patient. Depending on the technique used and the part of the body from which the tissue is being taken, the procedure may take from five minutes to a little more than half an hour.

After the tissue specimen is removed, it is immediately placed in a fixing solution to preserve it. It is then sent to a laboratory, where it is sliced to extreme thinness, stained, and examined under a microscope by a pathologist. Your doctor receives the pathologist's report one to several days later.

EXCISIONAL BIOPSY

In an excisional biopsy, abnormal tissue is cut away completely, rather than simply sampled. An excisional biopsy may be done under local anesthetic and in the same settings as an incisional biopsy. It may also be done under general anesthesia in an operating room. An open biopsy under general anesthesia is generally done when the results of a closed biopsy or some other diagnostic test (a CT scan, for example) suggest that a tissue mass should be completely removed.

During an open biopsy under general anesthesia, the tissue specimen is examined very rapidly. A specimen is sent directly from the operating room to the pathologist, who examines and sections it, then selects a section for quick freezing. That frozen section is cut into microsections, rapidly stained, and examined for malignancy. The pathologist reports the results to the surgeon within minutes. If malignant cells are found, the surgeon may decide to operate immediately in order to remove all the abnormal tissue.

COMMONLY USED BIOPSY TECHNIQUES

Excision

The biopsy, done with a scalpel, removes the whole lesion and thus combines diagnosis with treatment. Among the tissues commonly biopsied by excision are the skin, the mouth, and the lymph nodes.

Needle

Numerous tissues may be biopsied with a cutting needle, among them the bone and bone marrow, the breast, the lymph nodes, lungs, liver, kidney, and thyroid. In a percutaneous (through the skin) liver biopsy, for example, a cutting needle is inserted between the ribs; then, as the patient holds an exhaled breath, it is quickly introduced into the liver and quickly withdrawn, carrying with it a core of tissue.

Aspiration

The bone marrow and breast may also be biopsied by aspiration. A flexible hollow needle and a special syringe are used to withdraw specimens.

Punch Incision

A punch or forceps is used to remove a core from the center of a lesion. In a punch biopsy of the skin, for example, the surrounding area is pulled taut and the punch is pressed into the lesion and rotated. Another common target for punch biopsy is the cervix.

Endoscopic

Fiberoptic instruments designed for the examination of the interior of such hollow organs as the rectum, colon, larynx, and lung are frequently used to take tissue samples (by means of special auxiliary attachments) for microscopic analysis. For example, in what is called a transbronchial biopsy, multiple specimens of lung tissue can be taken through a fiberoptic bronchoscope.

DISCOMFORT AND RISKS

Biopsies, which of necessity involve cutting, puncturing, or punching, bring some degree of anxiety, discomfort, and risk. Tranquilizers, sedatives, and anesthetics are very helpful in reducing anxiety and the discomfort of the procedure. Any postbiopsy soreness or pain can be minimized with the aid of analgesic medication.

The risks involved in biopsy depend on the specific procedure. They may be simply annoying, such as urination difficulties after prostate biopsy, or sutures following a biopsy of the skin. On the other hand, they are occasionally more serious—for example, bleeding, infection, organ puncture, or pneumothorax (air in the pleura, the membranes that envelop the lungs and line the walls of the chest cavity). If your biopsy carries a risk of such problems, you

BIOPSY

TYPE OF BIOPSY	EQUIPMENT	TISSUES INVOLVED	ADVANTAGES	RISKS
Excision (superficial) (entire lesion removed surgically)	Scalpel	Easily accessible tissues (e.g., skin), using local anesthesia	Combines diagnosis with treatment	Pain, infection, bleeding
Excision (deep) (entire lesion removed surgically)	Scalpel	Many deeper tissues, using general anesthesia	Combines diagnosis with treatment	Debilitation post-anesthesia; pain, infection, bleeding
Needle (core of tissue removed)	Cutting needle	Bone, bone marrow, breast, kidney, liver, lymph node, lung, pleura, prostate, synovial membrane, thyroid	Avoids need for exploratory surgery; usually provides a representative specimen	Pneumothorax, bile peritonitis, bone fracture, organ puncture, trauma to nearby tissues, pain, infection
Aspiration (tissue sample aspirated)	Aspiration needle, needle guide, syringe	Bone marrow, breast	Avoids need for surgery; in breast cysts, combines diagnosis with treatment	Bleeding, infection, pain; in area of sternum, puncture of major blood vessels
Punch incision (specimen from core of lesion removed)	Punch or forceps	Skin, cervix	Avoids need for surgery; provides representative sample	Pain; "seeding" of malignant cells; vaginal discharge
Endoscopic (tissue sample removed)	One of a variety of scopes (e.g., sigmoidoscope, bronchoscope)	Any accessible hollow part of the body (e.g., colon, lung)	Avoids surgery; provides representative sample	Discomfort, bleeding, infection

will be watched closely until the danger period has passed.

SUMMING UP

A biopsy is done to help establish a diagnosis, usually when symptoms suggest a malignant condition. New techniques make it possible for biopsies to be performed on even the deepest internal organs without open surgery. Biopsy is not risk-free, but serious complications are rare.

200. Tests for Allergic Reactions

GENERAL CONSIDERATIONS

One out of every ten people suffers from allergies. Many of these are relatively minor and can be lived with. Others, however, may be disabling or even life-threatening, as in the case of severe allergic asthma or hypersensitivity to bee stings.

Allergic responses can be triggered by almost any substance one comes in contact with. Pollen, animal dander, certain foods, and exposure to sun are common examples. People who suffer from allergies usually know what triggers a response and learn to avoid the offending substance. But there are some people who are allergic to many different substances, some of which may not be readily apparent. In these cases, tests to detect the allergen(s) may be advised.

IS IT AN ALLERGY?

Before undergoing any tests to identify specific allergens, one must first determine whether the complaint is, indeed, due to an allergy. Many conditions mimic allergies. An itching skin rash on the feet, for example, is usually assumed to be from athlete's foot. But if treatment for a fungal infection fails to clear up the problem, the possibility of an allergic response to something in the shoes or stockings (contact dermatitis) should be investigated (see Chapter 99, "Allergic Skin Rashes").

Food allergies are another area of common misdiagnosis. Most allergic reactions to foods take the form of hives or other skin responses or hay fever-like symptoms. Sometimes, however, the allergy will involve the digestive tract, producing symptoms such as nausea, vomiting, or indigestion. Persistent symptoms involving the digestive tract should be investigated by a doctor. If food allergies are suspected, eliminating the offending items from the diet will solve the problem (see Chapter 98, "Food Allergies").

In any event, whenever allergies are suspected, a physician should be consulted. Although some children seem to outgrow their allergies, the opposite is more often the case; the allergies worsen with time. Also, special precautions should be taken by people with allergies, especially when taking drugs. Doctors always should be told of any allergies before prescribing a drug. Having used a drug without problems is no guarantee that an allergic response will not be triggered by future administration. Many times, a drug such as aspirin or an antibiotic will have been used for years and then suddenly will trigger a serious allergic reaction. *People who suffer from allergies should remember that they may potentially become allergic to almost any substance.* This does not mean they should go through life afraid to try new things or live in constant fear of an allergic attack, but it

In skin tests for allergic response, a number of different allergens are usually tested at the same time. The allergens may be applied directly to the skin and then covered with a patch, or applied just under the skin in a tiny scratch. In either case, a positive response is noted by formation of a welt or wheal.

does mean that common-sense precautions should be taken.

TESTING FOR ALLERGIES

All allergy testing involves exposing the body to the suspected allergen and then noting the response. The testing may involve using skin patches, tiny skin scratches, or a blood test called RAST, or radioallergosorbent test.

Skin Patch Test

In this test, the skin is exposed to extracts of the suspected allergen. The testing may be done on the arm or back, and several different substances may be tested at the same time. The allergen is applied directly to the skin and held in place with a patch of either cellophane for liquid allergens or linen or blotting paper for solid substances. This is covered with an adhesive patch and left in place for a specified period of time. If the allergen produces a welt or itching rash, a positive reaction to the allergen is assumed. No response means the individual probably is not allergic to the substance.

Skin Scratch Test

This is similar to the patch test except the allergen is applied to a small scratch. A tiny scratch about one-eighth of an inch is made in the skin (again, usually the arm or back), and the allergen is applied. It may be in a paste form or powdered. If the individual is allergic to the substance, a response in the form of a welt or red wheal will appear within ten to thirty minutes.

Caution should be used in scratch tests to ensure against a severe allergic response triggered by the test itself. This is particularly true in testing for hypersensitivity to drugs and insects. The tests always should be performed in a medical setting where a severe response can be quickly treated.

RAST

The radioallergosorbent test is relatively new and has several advantages over the older skin tests: it is considered more objective and accurate and is less painful. It also does not involve the danger of provoking a severe allergic response.

A RAST involves taking a sample of the patient's blood serum and exposing it to a number of different cellulose disks containing various allergens. If the patient is allergic to a particular substance, the IgE (gamma-E globulin) in the serum will bind to the particles of allergen. To determine whether this has happened, a radioactive anti-IgE antibody is added to the disk and then subjected to further testing to measure the amount of radioactivity in the substance. The higher the level of radioactivity, the greater the allergic response.

SUMMING UP

Many people mistakenly assume that allergies are a trivial problem. Although most people can adjust to their allergies by avoiding the offending substances, care must be taken to avoid severe reactions. In some cases, desensitization may be recommended (see Chapter 97, "Hay Fever," and Chapter 100, "Insect Stings"). In any instance, testing to identify the allergens may be required as a positive step in helping the patient live with the problem.

Appendix A
Understanding Medical Terms

Practically all medical and surgical terms of international usage derive from Greek, although a few come from Latin. Most have two or three parts—prefixes, roots, and suffixes. A knowledge of these components makes it easier to understand the terms used by doctors. Some of the more common are given here.

PREFIXES

PREFIX	MEANING	EXAMPLE
a-, an-	without	asymptomatic—without symptoms
ad-	near, toward	adhesion—toward each other
anti-	against	anticoagulant—acts against clotting
bi-	two	bifocal—two lenses
chlor-; chloro-	chlorine; green	chlorinated—treated with chlorine; chlorophyll—green coloring
co-, con-	with, together	coitus; conjugate—coupled or acting together
contra-	against	contraindicated—not indicated
cyan-, cyano-	blue	cyanotic—bluish skin
di-, dia-	through	diarrhea
dys-	bad, difficult	dysarthria—difficulty in speaking
ect-, ecto-	outer, outside	ectopic—in an abnormal position
end-, endo-	inner, containing	endocranium—lining of the skull
ep-, epi-	upon, in relation to	epicolic—over the colon
erythr-, erythro-	red	erythrocytes—red blood cells
eu-	good	euphoriant—inducing good feeling
ex-	out, away from	excretion
extra-	outside of	extraocular—outside the eyeball
hol-, holo-	whole, complete	hologram—a three-dimensional image
hom-, homo-	same	homogeneous—having the same qualities

(Continued)

PREFIX	MEANING	EXAMPLE
hyper-	excessive	hyperthyroidism—excessive production of the thyroid hormone
hyp-, hypo-	under, deficiency of	hypoglycemia—low blood sugar
leuk-, leuko-	white	leukemia—proliferation of white blood cells
melan-, melano-	black, dark	melanoma—a malignant tumor of dark pigment
met-, meta-	after, next, between, among	metatarsus—the foot bones between the ankles and the toes
met-, meta-	change, evolution	metastasis—transfer of disease from one organ to another
ne-, neo-	new	neonatal—pertaining to newborn infant
orth-, ortho-	straight, correct	orthodontics—corrective dental work
peri-	around	pericardium—membranes surrounding the heart
pre-	before	prenatal—before birth
pro-	before, forward	prolapse—falling or sinking down of an organ
post-	after	postpartum—after childbirth
re-, retro-	again, back	regurgitate—bring up again; retroflexed—bent backward
sub-	under, below	subnormal
super-	excessive, above	supersaturated
sym-, syn-	together	symbiotic—living together; syndrome
trans-	across	transmission

ROOTS RELATING TO ANATOMY AND MEDICINE

ROOT	MEANING	EXAMPLE
acr-, acro-	extremity, peak	acrophobia—fear of heights
aden-, adeno-	gland	adenoma—glandular tumor
andr-, andro-	man	androgen—male hormone
arthr-, arthro-	joint	arthritis—joint inflammation
bronch-, broncho-	windpipe	bronchoscope—an instrument used to view the windpipe
cardi-, cardio-	heart	cardiac—pertaining to the heart

(Continued)

ROOT	MEANING	EXAMPLE
cerebr-, cerebri-, cerebro-	brain	cerebral—pertaining to the brain
chol-, chole-, cholo	bile, gall	cholecystitis—inflamed gallbladder
col-, coli-, colo-	colon	colonitis—inflammation in the colon
cyst-, cysto-	bag, bladder	cystitis—urinary bladder inflammation
cyt-, cyto-	cell	erythrocyte—red blood cell
derm-, derma-, dermo-	skin	dermatitis—skin inflammation
encephal-, encephalo-	brain	encephalitis—inflammation of the brain
enter-, entero-	intestines	enteritis—intestinal inflammation; dysentery
gastr-, gastro-	stomach	gastrectomy—removal of the stomach
gyn-, gyno-	woman	gynecology—study of women
hem-, hema-, hemo-	blood	hemophilia—an inherited bleeding disorder
hepat-, hepato-	liver	hepatotoxic—destructive to the liver
metr-, metro-	uterus	endometrium—inside the uterus
my-, myo-	muscle	myopathy—muscle disease
narco-	numbness, stupor	narcosis—drug-induced stupor
nephr-, nephro-	kidney	nephritis—kidney inflammation
neur-, neuro-	nerve	neuritis—inflammatory nerve disorder
ophthalm-, ophthalmo-	eye	ophthalmoscope—instrument used to examine the eyes
oste-, osteo-	bone	osteoporosis—thinning of bone tissue
ot-, oto-	ear	otomycosis—ear infection
path-, patho-	disease	retinopathy—disease of the retina
phleb-, phlebo-	vein	phlebitis—vein inflammation
phobia	fear	agoraphobia—fear of open spaces
pneum-, pneumo-	lungs	pneumothorax—gas in the membrane around the lungs
proct-, procto-	anus, rectum	proctotomy—rectal incision
psych-, psycho-	mind	psychotherapy—treatment of mental illness
rhin-, rhino-	nose	rhinitis—inflammation of the nasal mucous membrane
sarc-, sarco-	flesh	sarcosis—fleshy tumors
scler-, sclero-	hard	scleroderma—hardening of the skin
somat-, somato-	body	somatomotor—pertaining to bodily movements

stern-, sterno-	breast	sternotomy—cutting through the breastbone
traumat-, traumato-	wound	traumatic epilepsy—seizures caused by brain injury
ur-, uro-	urine	uremia—retention of urine

WORD ENDINGS RELATING TO HEALTH AND DISEASE

SUFFIX	MEANING	EXAMPLE
-algia	pain	neuralgia—pain along a nerve
-cide	kill	fungicide—agent to kill fungi
-ectomy	cutting out, surgical removal	tonsillectomy—removal of tonsils
-genic	producing	allergenic—causes allergic response
-gram	drawing, recording	electrocardiogram—record of electrical heart waves
-iasis	diseased condition	psoriasis—recurring skin disease
-itis	inflammation	colitis—inflammation of the colon
-logy	science or study of	endocrinology—study of the glands
-lysis	loosening, breaking down	hemolysis—destruction of blood cells
-oma	tumor	melanoma—tumor of pigment cells
-osis	disease condition	arteriosclerosis—hardening of the arteries
-ostomy	creating an opening	colostomy—an opening created to empty the colon
-otomy	incision	hysterotomy—incision in the uterus
-plasia	formation	dysplasia—abnormal tissue formation
-rrhea	flow	leukorrhea—white discharge
-rrhagia	excessive discharge	menorrhagia—excessive menstruation
-scope	instrument for viewing	laryngoscope—instrument for viewing the larynx

Appendix B
Voluntary Health Organizations

The following organizations and agencies provide educational materials to both the lay public and health-care professionals, conduct seminars and workshops, and support education and research in their field of interest. Many also provide patient counseling and support groups and offer a variety of rehabilitation services.

Aging

The Gerontological Society of America, 1835 K Street NW, Washington, DC 20006 Tel: 202/466-6750

National Clearinghouse on Aging, 330 Independence Avenue SW, Washington, DC 20201 Tel: 202/245-2158

National Council of Senior Citizens, Inc., 925 15th Street NW, Washington, DC 20005 Tel: 202/347-8800

National Council on the Aging, Suite 504, 1828 L Street NW, Washington, DC 20036 Tel: 202/223-6250

Alcoholism

Al-Anon Family Group Headquarters, PO Box 182, Madison Square Station, New York, NY 10159 Tel: 212/481-6565

Alcoholics Anonymous, Inc., Room 219, 175 Fifth Avenue, New York, NY 10010 Tel: 212/473-6200

National Clearinghouse for Alcoholism Information, PO Box 2345, Rockville, MD 20852 Tel: 301/468-2600

National Council on Alcoholism, Inc., 733 Third Avenue, New York, NY 10017 Tel: 212/986-4433

Anorexia Nervosa

National Association of Anorexia Nervosa and Associated Disorders, Box 271, Highland Park, IL 60035 Tel: 312/831-3438

Arthritis

The Arthritis Foundation, 3400 Peachtree Road NE, Atlanta, GA 30326 Tel: 404/266-0795

Asthma and Allergy

American Lung Association, 1740 Broadway, New York, NY 10019 Tel: 212/889-3370

Asthma and Allergy Foundation of America, 1707 North Street NW, Washington, DC 20036 Tel: 202/293-1260

Blood Diseases

Leukemia Society of America, Inc., 800 Second Avenue, New York, NY 10017 Tel: 212/573-8484

National Hemophilia Foundation, 19 West 34th Street, New York, NY 10001 Tel: 212/563-0211

National Sickle Cell Disease Program, Division of Blood Diseases and Resources, National Heart, Lung, and Blood Institute, National Institutes of Health, Room 504, Federal Building, 7550 Wisconsin Avenue, Bethesda, MD 20205 Tel: 301/496-6931

Cancer

American Cancer Society, Inc., National Headquarters, 777 Third Avenue, New York, NY 10017 Tel: 212/371-2900, 212/595-4490 (night line)

Cancer Counseling and Research Center, Suite 140, 6060 North Central Expressway, Dallas, TX 75206 Tel: 214/692-6311

Damon Runyon-Walter Winchell Cancer Fund, 33 West 56th Street, New York, NY 10019 Tel: 212/582-5400

Living With Cancer, Inc., PO Box 3060, Long Island City, NY 11101 Tel: 212/241-4100

National Cancer Institute, Cancer Information Clearinghouse, Office of Cancer Communications, Building 31, Room 10A18, 9000 Rockville Pike, Bethesda, MD 20205 Tel: 301/496-4070

Child Abuse and Neglect

American Humane Association, 9725 East Hampden, Denver, CO 80231 Tel: 303/695-0811

CALM, Child Abuse Listening Mediation, Inc., PO Box 718, Santa Barbara, CA 93102 Tel: 805/682-1366, 805/963-1115 (hot line)

Clearinghouse on Child Abuse and Neglect Information, PO Box 1182, Washington, DC 20013 Tel: 202/245-2856

Childbirth/Maternity Care

International Childbirth Education Association, Inc., PO Box 20048, Minneapolis, MN 55420 Tel: 612/854-8660

Maternity Center Association, 48 East 92nd Street, New York, NY 10028 Tel: 212/369-7300

Childhood Life-Threatening Illnesses

The Candlelighters Foundation, 2025 Eye Street NW, Washington, DC 20006 Tel: 202/659-5136

The Compassionate Friends, Inc., National Headquarters, PO Box 1347, Oak Brook, IL 60521 Tel: 312/323-5010

National Sudden Infant Death Syndrome Foundation, 310 South Michigan Avenue, Chicago, IL 60604 Tel: 312/663-0650

New York City Program for Sudden Infant Death, 520 First Avenue, New York, NY 10016 Tel: 212/686-8854

Sudden Infant Death Syndrome (SIDS) Clearing House, Suite 600, 1555 Wilson Boulevard, Rosslyn, VA 22209 Tel: 703/522-0870

Cystic Fibrosis

Cystic Fibrosis Foundation, Suite 558, 3384 Peachtree Road NE, Atlanta, GA 30326 Tel: 404/233-2195

Diabetes

American Diabetes Association, Inc., Two Park Avenue, New York, NY 10016 Tel: 212/683-7444

Joslin Diabetes Center, One Joslin Place, Boston, MA 02215 Tel: 617/732-2400

The Juvenile Diabetes Foundation, 23 East 26th Street, New York, NY 10010 Tel: 212/889-7575

National Diabetes Information Clearinghouse, Box NDIC, Bethesda, MD 20205 Tel: 202/842-7630

Digestive Diseases

American Digestive Disease Society, Suite 217, 7720 Wisconsin Avenue, Bethesda, MD 20014 Tel: 301/652-5524

National Digestive Diseases Education and Information Clearinghouse, Suite 600, 1555 Wilson Boulevard, Rosslyn, VA 22209 Tel: 703/522-0870

National Foundation for Ileitis and Colitis, Inc., 295 Madison Avenue, New York, NY 10017 Tel: 212/685-3440

Drug Abuse and Narcotic Addiction

Do It Now Foundation, PO Box 5115, Phoenix, AZ 85010-5115 Tel: 602/257-0797

Drug Abuse Clearinghouse, Room 10A53, 5600 Fisher's Lane, Rockville, MD 20857 Tel: 301/443-6500

Narcotics Education, Inc., 6830 Laurel Street NW, Washington, DC 20012 Tel: 202/722-6740

Epilepsy

Epilepsy Foundation of America, Suite 406, 4351 Garden City Drive, Landover, MD 20785 Tel: 301/459-3700

Epilepsy Institute, Suite 308, 225 Park Avenue South, New York, NY 10003 Tel: 212/677-8550

Family Planning/Sex Information

The Alan Guttmacher Institute, 360 Park Avenue South, New York, NY 10010 Tel: 212/685-5858

Association for Voluntary Sterilization, Suite 2300, 703 Third Avenue, New York, NY 10017 Tel: 212/986-3880

Emory University-Grady Memorial Hospital, Family Planning Program, 80 Butler Street SE, Atlanta, GA 90303 Tel: 404/588-3680

Human Life and Natural Family Planning Foundation, 1151 K Street NW, Washington, DC 20005 Tel: 202/393-1380

National Clearinghouse for Family Planning Information, PO Box 2225, Rockville, MD 20852 Tel: 301/881-9400

Planned Parenthood Federation of America, Inc., 810 Seventh Avenue, New York, NY 10017 Tel: 212/541-7800

Population Council, Inc., One Dag Hammarskjold Plaza, New York, NY 10017 Tel: 212/644-1300

Sex Information and Education Council of the United States, Suite 801, 80 Fifth Avenue, New York, NY 10011 Tel: 212/929-2300

Fertility

American Fertility Society, Suite 101, 1608 13th Avenue South, Birmingham, AL 35256 Tel: 205/933-7222

Resolve, Inc., PO Box 474, Belmont, MA 02178 Tel: 617/484-2424

Genetic Diseases

March of Dimes Birth Defects Foundation, 1275 Mamaroneck Avenue, White Plains, NY 10605 Tel: 914/428-7100

National Clearinghouse for Human Genetic Diseases, Suite 500, 805 15th Street, Washington, DC 20005 Tel: 202/842-7617

National Genetics Foundation, 555 West 57th Street, New York, NY 10019 Tel: 212/586-5800

National Tay-Sachs and Allied Diseases Association, Inc., 122 East 42nd Street, New York, NY 10168 Tel: 212/661-2780

Growth Disorders

Human Growth Foundation, 4930 West 77th Street, Minneapolis, MN 55435 Tel: 612/831-2780

Handicapped/Rehabilitation

American Coalition of Citizens with Disabilities, Inc., Suite 201, 1200 15th Street NW, Washington, DC 20005 Tel: 202/785-4265

American Physical Therapy Association, 200 South Service Road, Roslyn Heights, NY 11577 Tel: 516/484-0095

Closer Look, PO Box 1492, Washington, DC 20013 Tel: 202/833-4160

Federation of the Handicapped, 211 West 14th Street, New York, NY 10011 Tel: 212/242-9050

Goodwill Industries of America, Inc., 9200 Wisconsin Avenue NW, Washington, DC 20014 Tel: 301/530-6500

March of Dimes Birth Defects Foundation, 1275 Mamaroneck Avenue, White Plains, NY 10605 Tel: 914/428-7100

The National Easter Seal Society, 2023 West Ogden Avenue, Chicago, IL 60612 Tel: 312/243-8400

National Paraplegia Foundation, 333 North Michigan Avenue, Chicago, IL 60601 Tel: 312/436-4776, 312/321-1629 (night line)

National Rehabilitation Information Center, Catholic University of America, 4407 8th Street NE, Washington, DC 20017 Tel: 202/635-5822

National Spinal Cord Injury Association, 369 Elliot Street, Newton Upper Falls, MA 02164 Tel: 617/964-0521

People-to-People Committee for the Handicapped, Vanguard Building, 6th Floor, 1111 20th Street NW, Washington, DC 20210 Tel: 202/653-5024

Rehabilitation International, U.S.A., 20 West 40th Street, New York, NY 10018 Tel: 212/869-9907

Spina Bifida Association of America, 343 South Dearborn Street, Chicago, IL 60604 Tel: 312/663-1562

United Cerebral Palsy Association, 66 East 34th Street, New York, NY 10016 Tel: 212/481-6347

Health Information

National Health Information Clearinghouse (NHIC), PO Box 1133, Washington, DC 20013 Tel: 800/336-4797, 703/522-2590 (collect in Virginia)

Hearing and Speech Disorders

Alexander Graham Bell Association for the Deaf, 3417 Volta NW, Washington, DC 20007 Tel: 202/337-5220

American Speech-Language-Hearing Association, 10801 Rockville Pike, Rockville, MD 20852 Tel: 301/897-5700

Deafness Research Foundation, 55 East 34th Street, New York, NY 10016 Tel: 212/684-6556

National Association of the Deaf, 814 Thayer Avenue, Silver Spring, MD 20910 Tel: 301/587-1788

National Association for Hearing and Speech Action, Suite 1000, 6110 Executive Boulevard, Rockville, MD 20852 Tel: 301/897-8682

Heart Disease

American Heart Association, 7320 Greenville Avenue, Dallas, TX 75231 Tel: 214/750-5300

Kidney Disease

National Association of Patients on Hemodialysis & Transplantation, Inc., 156 William Street, New York, NY 10038 Tel: 212/619-2727

National Kidney Foundation, Inc., Two Park Avenue, New York, NY 10016 Tel: 212/889-2210

Learning Disabilities

American Association on Mental Deficiency, 5101 Wisconsin Avenue NW, Washington, DC 20016 Tel: 202/686-5400

Association for Children with Learning Disabilities, 4156 Library Road, Pittsburgh, PA 15234 Tel: 412/341-1515

Federation for Children with Special Needs, Suite 338, 120 Boylston Street, Boston, MA 02116 Tel: 617/482-2915

Medical Alert

Medic Alert Foundation International, PO Box 1009, Turlock, CA 95380 Tel: 209/668-3333

Mental Health/Retardation

American Mental Health Foundation, Two East 86th Street, New York, NY 10028 Tel: 212/737-9027

Association for Retarded Citizens National Headquarters, 2501 Avenue J, Arlington, TX 76011 Tel: 817/640-0204

Kennedy Child Study Center, 151 East 67th Street, New York, NY 10021 Tel: 212/988-9500

National Association for Mental Health, 1800 North Kent Street, Arlington, VA 20006 Tel: 703/528-6408

National Clearinghouse for Mental Health Information, Public Inquiries Section, Room 11A-21, 5600 Fishers Lane, Rockville, MD 20857 Tel: 301/443-4513

Neurotics Anonymous International Liaison, Inc., PO Box 4866, Cleveland Park Station, Washington, DC 20008 Tel: 202/628-4379

Nerve and Muscle Disorders

Muscular Dystrophy Association, 810 Seventh Avenue, New York, NY 10019 Tel: 212/586-0808

Myasthenia Gravis Foundation, Inc., Two East 103rd Street, New York, NY 10028 Tel: 212/889-8157

National Multiple Sclerosis Society, 205 East 42nd Street, New York, NY 10017 Tel: 212/986-3240

Parkinson's Disease Foundation, New York Neurological Institute, 650 West 168th Street, New York, NY 10032 Tel: 212/923-4700

Psoriasis

The National Psoriasis Foundation, Suite 200, 6415 SW Canyon Court, Portland, OR 97221 Tel: 503/297-1545

Respiratory Diseases

American Lung Association, 1740 Broadway, New York, NY 10019 Tel: 212/889-3370

Vision Disorders/Blindness

American Association of Workers for the Blind, Inc., 1511 K Street NW, Washington, DC 20013 Tel: 202/347-1559

American Foundation for the Blind, Inc., 15 West 16th Street, New York, NY 10011 Tel: 212/620-2000

Associated Blind, Inc., 135 West 23rd Street, New York, NY 10011 Tel: 212/255-1122

Better Vision Institute, Inc., 230 Park Avenue, New York, NY 10017 Tel: 212/687-1731

Appendix C
Comprehensive Cancer Centers

The following institutions have been designated Comprehensive Cancer Centers by the National Cancer Institute. To earn this designation, the institution must meet certain criteria, including support of a strong research program in the prevention, diagnosis, and treatment of cancer; an ability to participate in integrated, nationwide clinical trials; and the capacity to perform advanced diagnostic techniques and treatment modalities.

Alabama
Comprehensive Cancer Center, University of Alabama in Birmingham, University Station, Birmingham, AL 35294 Tel: 205/934-6612

California
UCLA Jonsson Comprehensive Cancer Center, UCLA Center for Health Sciences, 10833 Leconte Avenue, Los Angeles, CA 90024 Tel: 213/825-5412 (professional), 213/824-6017 (public)

University of Southern California, Comprehensive Cancer Center, 2025 Zonal Avenue, Los Angeles, CA 90033 Tel: 213/224-7626

Connecticut
Yale University Comprehensive Cancer Center, 333 Cedar Street, New Haven, CT 06510 Tel: 203/436-3779

District of Columbia
Cancer Research Center, Howard University Hospital, 2400 Sixth Street NW, Washington, DC 20059 Tel: 202/636-5700

Vincent T. Lombardi Cancer Research Center, Georgetown University Medical Center, 3800 Reservoir Road NW, Washington, DC 20007 Tel: 202/625-7066

Florida
Comprehensive Cancer Center for the State of Florida, University of Miami School of Medicine, Jackson Memorial Medical Center, 1475 NW 12th Avenue, Miami, FL 33136 Tel: 305/547-7707 ext 203

Illinois
Cancer Center, Health Sciences Building, 303 East Chicago Avenue, Chicago, IL 60611 Tel: 312/266-5250

Illinois Cancer Council, 36 South Wabash Avenue, Suite 700, Chicago, IL 60603 Tel: 312/CANCER-1 (Illinois only), 312/346-9813 (out-of-state)

Rush-Presbyterian-St. Luke's Medical Center, 1753 West Congress Parkway, Chicago, IL 60612 Tel: 312/942-6642

Cancer Research Center, University of Chicago, 905 East 59th Street, Chicago, IL 60637 Tel: 312/947-6386

University of Illinois, PO Box 6998, Chicago, IL 60608 Tel: 312/996-8843, 312/996-6666

Maryland
The Johns Hopkins Oncology Center, 600 North Wolfe Street, Baltimore, MD 21205 Tel: 301/955-3636

Massachusetts

Sidney Farber Cancer Institute, 44 Binney Street, Boston, MA 02115 Tel: 617/732-3150, 617/732-3000

Michigan

Comprehensive Cancer Center of Metropolitan Detroit, 110 East Warren Avenue, Detroit, MI 48201 Tel: 313/833-0710 ext 378

Minnesota

Mayo Comprehensive Cancer Center, 200 First Street SW, Rochester, MN 55901 Tel: 507/284-8285

New York

Roswell Park Memorial Institute, 666 Elm Street, Buffalo, NY 14263 Tel: 716/845-4400

Columbia University Cancer Research Center, College of Physicians & Surgeons, 701 West 168th Street, New York, NY 10032 Tel: 212/694-6900

Memorial Sloan-Kettering Cancer Center, 1275 York Avenue, New York, NY 10021 Tel: 212/794-7984

North Carolina

Comprehensive Cancer Center, Duke University Medical Center, Durham, NC 27710 Tel: 919/684-2282

Ohio

The Ohio State University Comprehensive Cancer Center, Suite 302, 410 West 12th Avenue, Columbus, OH 43210 Tel: 614/422-5022

Pennsylvania

Fox Chase/University of Pennsylvania, Comprehensive Cancer Center, 7701 Burholme Avenue, Philadelphia, PA 19111 Tel: 215/728-2717

Texas

The University of Texas Health System Cancer Center, M.D. Anderson Hospital and Tumor Institute, 6723 Bertner Avenue, Houston, TX 77030 Tel: 713/792-3030

Washington

Fred Hutchinson Cancer Research Center, 1124 Columbia Street, Seattle, WA 98104 Tel: 206/292-6301

Wisconsin

The University of Wisconsin Clinical Cancer Center, 600 Highland Avenue, Madison, WI 53706 Tel: 608/263-8600

Appendix D
Comprehensive Pain Clinics

The following list of pain centers and clinics, compiled by the Committee on Pain Therapy of the American Society of Anesthesiologists, offers a broad range of diagnostic and therapeutic modalities.

Alabama

Brookwood Medical Center Pain Management Center, 2022 Brookwood Medical Center Drive, Birmingham, AL 35209 Tel: 205/877-1569

Pain Center, University of Alabama in Birmingham, Kracke Building, 1920 Seventh Avenue South, Birmingham, AL 35233 Tel: 205/934-6174

Arizona

St. Joseph's Hospital Pain Center, 350 West Thomas Road, Phoenix, AZ 85013 Tel: 602/241-3474

Pain Clinic, University of Arizona Hospital, University of Arizona Health Sciences Center, 1501 North Campbell Avenue, Tucson, AZ 85724 Tel: 602/626-6239

California

New Hope Pain Center, 100 South Raymond Avenue, Alhambra, CA 91801 Tel: 213/570-1607

Pain Treatment Center, Scripps Clinic Medical Institutions, 10666 North Torrey Pines Road, La Jolla, CA 92037 Tel: 714/455-8898

Pain Control and Health Support Services, Loma Linda Anesthesiology Medical Group, Inc., PO Box 962, Loma Linda, CA 92350 Tel: 714/796-0231

Pain Therapy and Evaluation Unit, Jerry I. Pettis Memorial Veterans Hospital, 11201 Benton Street, Loma Linda, CA 92357 Tel: 714/825-7084 ext 2273

Pain Management Program, VA Medical Center, 5901 East Seventh Street, Long Beach, CA 90822 Tel: 213/498-6233

Pain Diagnostics and Rehabilitation Institute, 2210 West Third Street, Los Angeles, CA 90057 Tel: 213/383-8485

Pain Management Center, BH-111 Center for Health Sciences, UCLA School of Medicine, Los Angeles, CA 90024 Tel: 213/825-4291

Lawrence Pain Control Group, 7535 Laurel Canyon Boulevard, North Hollywood, CA 91605 Tel: 213/983-0697

Los Medanos Community Hospital, 2311 Loveridge Road, Pittsburg, CA 94565 Tel: 415/432-2200

University of California, Davis, School of Medicine, Professional Building, Room 253, 4301 X Street, Sacramento, CA 95817 Tel: 916/453-2424

Pain Management Center, San Bernardino Community Hospital, 1500 West 17th Street, San Bernardino, CA 92411 Tel: 714/887-6333

Pain Unit, San Diego VA Medical Center, 3350 La Jolla Drive, San Diego, CA 92161 Tel: 714/453-7500

Saint Francis Memorial Hospital, 900 Hyde Street, San Francisco, CA 94109 Tel: 415/775-4321

St. Mary's Hospital, 450 Stanyan Street, San Francisco, CA 94117 Tel: 415/668-1000

Orthopaedic Pain Center of San Jose, Cambrian Park Plaza, 14438 Union Avenue, San Jose, CA 95124 Tel: 408/371-2137

Walnut Creek Hospital, 175 La Casa Vista, Walnut Creek, CA 94598 Tel: 415/933-7990

Colorado

Boulder Memorial Hospital Pain Control Center, 311 Mapleton Avenue, Boulder, CO 80302 Tel: 303/441-0507

Pain Clinic, University of Colorado Medical Center, 4200 East Ninth Avenue, Box B113, Denver, CO 80262 Tel: 303/394-7078

Connecticut

Arthur Taub, MD, PhD, 60 Temple Street, New Haven, CT 06510 Tel: 203/789-2151

Delaware

Delaware Pain Center, 249 East Main Street, Newark, DE 19711 Tel: 302/738-0262

District of Columbia

Georgetown University Medical Center, 3800 Reservoir Road, Washington, DC 20007 Tel: 202/625-0100

Florida

Pain Treatment Center, Baptist Hospital of Miami, 8900 North Kendall Drive, Miami, FL 33176 Tel: 305/596-6552

University of Miami School of Medicine, Department of Neurological Surgery,
PO Box 016960, Miami, FL 33101 Tel: 305/547-6946

The Pain Center, Mount Sinai Medical Center, 4300 Alton Road, Miami Beach, FL 33140 Tel: 305/674-2070

Rehabilitation Institute, 1164 Normandy Drive, Miami Beach, FL 33141 Tel: 305/866-4424

Georgia

Atlanta Pain Control and Rehabilitation Center, Inc., 315 Boulevard NE, Suite 100, Atlanta, GA 30312 Tel: 404/653-4632

Emory University Pain Control Center, Center for Rehabilitation Medicine, 1441 Clifton Road NE, Atlanta, GA 30322 Tel: 404/329-5492

The Pain Rehabilitation and Biofeedback Center of West Georgia, Inc., 8954 Hospital Drive, Suite 100-C, Douglasville, GA 30134 Tel: 404/949-1222

Savannah Pain Control and Rehabilitation Center, 5354 Reynolds Street, Suite 518, Savanna, GA 31405 Tel: 912/355-4568

Illinois

The Center for Pain Studies, Rehabilitation Institute of Chicago, 345 East Superior Street, Chicago, IL 60611 Tel: 312/649-6011

Illinois Masonic Medical Center, 836 West Wellington Street, Chicago, IL 60657 Tel: 312/975-1600 (neurosurgery), 312/975-1600 (anesthesiology)

Rush Pain Center, 1725 West Harrison Street, Chicago, IL 60612 Tel: 312/942-6631

The Pain Treatment Center, Lake Forest Hospital, 660 North Westmoreland, Lake Forest, IL 60045 Tel: 312/234-5600 ext 5561

Pain Management Clinic, Methodist Medical Center, 221 NE Glen Oak, Peoria, IL 61636 Tel: 309/672-5950

Pain Center, Marianjoy Rehabilitation Hospital, 26 West 171 Roosevelt Road, Wheaton, IL 60187 Tel: 312/653-7600 ext 284 or 267

Indiana
Center for Pain, Community Hospital Rehabilitation, 1500 North Ritter Avenue, Indianapolis, IN 46219 Tel: 317/353-5987

Pain Rehabilitation Center, St. Joseph's Medical Center, PO Box 1935, 811 East Madison, South Bend, IN 46634 Tel: 219/237-7360

Kentucky
Louisville Pain Clinic, 326 Medical Towers South, Louisville, KY 40202 Tel: 502/587-6523

Louisiana
Hotel Dieu Pain Rehabilitation Unit, 2021 Perdido Street, New Orleans, LA 70112 Tel: 504/588-3477

Shreveport Pain and Rehabilitation Center, 1128 Louisiana Avenue, Shreveport, LA 71101 Tel: 318/227-2780

Massachusetts
Boston Pain Center, Massachusetts Rehabilitation Hospital, 125 Nashua Street, Boston, MA 02114 Tel: 617/523-1818 ext 110

New England Rehabilitation Hospital, Two Rehabilitation Way, Woburn, MA 01801 Tel: 617/935-5050

University of Massachusetts Medical Center, 55 Lake Avenue, Worcester, MA 01605 Tel: 617/856-0011

Maryland
Pain Treatment Center, The Johns Hopkins Hospital, 601 North Broadway, Baltimore, MD 21205 Tel: 301/955-6405

Sinai Hospital of Baltimore, Belvedere and Greenspring Avenues, Baltimore, MD 21215 Tel: 301/367-7800

Neurobiology and Anesthesiology, Branch NIDR/NIH, National Institute of Dental Research, Building 30, Room B18, National Institutes of Health, Bethesda, MD 20205 Tel: 301/496-6804

Associated Pain Consultants, 8808 Cameron Street, Silver Spring, MD 20910 Tel: 301/565-2633

Michigan
Ingham Medical Center Back and Pain Clinic, 401 West Greenlawn Street, Lansing, MI 48910 Tel: 517/374-2360

Minnesota
Golden Valley Health Center, 4101 Golden Valley Road, Golden Valley, MN 55422 Tel: 612/588-2771

Minneapolis Pain Clinic, Pain Rehabilitation Program, 4225 Golden Valley Road, Minneapolis, MN 55422 Tel: 612/588-0661, 612/347-4548

Parkview Treatment Center, 3705 Park Center Boulevard, Minneapolis, MN 55416 Tel: 612/929-5531

University of Minnesota Hospitals, Neurosurgery Department, 420 Delaware Street SE, Minneapolis, MN 55455 Tel: 612/373-8785

Mayo Pain Clinic, 200 Second Street SW, Rochester, MN 55901 Tel: 507/284-8311

Pain Management Center, St. Mary's Hospital, Rochester, MN 55901 Tel: 507/285-5921

Mississippi
The UMC Multidisciplinary Pain Clinic, University of Mississippi Medical Center, 2500 North State Street, Jackson, MS 39216 Tel: 601/987-6560

Nebraska
Nebraska Pain Management Center, University of Nebraska Hospital, 42nd and Dewey Avenue, Omaha, NE 68105 Tel: 402/559-4354

New Jersey

C.N.S. and Pain Management Institute, PA, 405 Northfield Avenue, West Orange, NJ 07052 Tel: 201/736-3434

New York

Lourdes Hospital, 169 Riverside Drive, Binghamton, NY 13905 Tel: 607/798-5111

Pain Treatment Center, Montefiore Hospital and Medical Center, 111 East 210th Street, Bronx, NY 10467 Tel: 212/920-4440

Kingsbrook Jewish Medical Center, 86 East 49th Street, Brooklyn, NY 11203 Tel: 212/756-9700 ext 2907

Pain Therapy Center, Maimonides Medical Center, 931 48th Street, Brooklyn, NY 11219 Tel: 212/270-7182

Anesthesiology Pain Treatment Service, Department of Anesthesiology, Columbia-Presbyterian Medical Center, 622 West 168th Street, New York, NY 10032 Tel: 212/694-7114

Hospital for Joint Diseases, 1919 Madison Avenue, New York, NY 10035 Tel: 212/650-4570

Upstate Medical Center, State University Hospital, 750 East Adams Street, Syracuse, NY 13210 Tel: 315/473-4720

North Carolina

Pain Center, NCMH Box 106, University of North Carolina, North Carolina Memorial Hospital, Chapel Hill, NC 27514 Tel: 919/966-4716

Duke Pain Clinic, Box 3094, Duke University Medical Center, Durham, NC 27710 Tel: 919/684-6542

North Dakota

T.N.I. Pain Clinic, 700 First Avenue South, Fargo, ND 58103 Tel: 701/235-5354 ext 65

Ohio

Pain Control Clinic, University of Cincinnati Medical Center, B4 Pavilion, 234 Goodman Street, Cincinnati, OH 45267 Tel: 513/872-5664

The Ohio Pain and Stress Treatment Center, 1460 West Lane Avenue, Columbia, OH 43221 Tel: 614/488-5971

Medical College of Ohio Hospital, Toledo, OH 43699 Tel: 419/381-3815

Youngstown Osteopathic Hospital, 1319 Florencedale Street, Youngstown, OH 44505 Tel: 419/744-9200

Oregon

Sacred Heart General Hospital, 1200 Alder Street, Eugene, OR 97401 Tel: 503/686-6854

Northwest Pain Center Program, Northwest Pain Center, Suite 170, 10615 SE Cherry Blossom Drive, Portland, OR 97216 Tel: 503/256-1930

Pain Clinic of Good Samaritan Hospital, Suite 171, 2222 NW Lovejoy Street, Portland, OR 97210 Tel: 503/229-7461

Pennsylvania

Pain Control Clinic, Charles Cole Memorial Hospital, Coudersport, PA 16915 Tel: 814/274-9527

Pain Control Center of Temple University, Temple University Hospital, 3401 North Broad Street, Philadelphia, PA 19140 Tel: 215/221-2100

Pain Control Clinic, Room 9408, Presbyterian University Hospital, Desoto at O'Hara Streets, Pittsburgh, PA 15213 Tel: 412/647-3680

VA Medical Center, University Drive "C," Pittsburgh, PA 15240 Tel: 412/683-3000

South Carolina
VA Medical Center, Garner's Ferry Road, Columbia, SC 29291 Tel: 803/776-4000

Tennessee
Pain Clinic, Faculty Medical Practice Corp., 66 North Pauline, Memphis, TN 38105 Tel: 901/528-6638

Texas
University of Texas Medical Branch, 301 University Drive, Galveston, TX 77550 Tel: 713/765-1227
Chronic Pain Treatment Program of B.C.M. at the Methodist Hospital, 6516 Bertner Boulevard, Houston, TX 77030 Tel: 713/468-8967
Pain Clinic, Medical Center Del Oro Hospital, 8081 Greenbriar Street, Houston, TX 77054 Tel: 713/790-8100
Pain Control and Biofeedback Clinic, Department of Anesthesiology, Baylor College of Medicine, Texas Medical Center, Houston, TX 77030 Tel: 713/790-5796
Anesthesia Pain Clinic, The University of Texas Medical School, 6431 Fannin Street, Houston, TX 77030 Tel: 713/792-5577
The University of Texas Medical School, Division of Neurosurgery, 6431 Fannin Street, Houston, TX 77030 Tel: 713/792-5760
Wilford Hall USAF Medical Center, Lackland AFB, TX 78236 Tel: 512/670-7100
Texas Tech University School of Medicine, Health Sciences Center Hospital, 3601 Fourth Street, Lubbock, TX 79430 Tel: 806/743-3111
Anesthesia Pain Clinic, Suite 306, 4499 Medical Drive, San Antonio, TX 78229 Tel: 512/692-0101
Anesthesia Pain Clinic, The University of Texas Health Science Center, 7703 Floyd Curl Drive, San Antonio, TX 78284 Tel: 512/691-6664
Scott and White Clinic, Scott and White Hospital, 2401 South 31st Street, Temple, TX 76501 Tel: 817/774-2111
Hohf Clinic and Hospital, 1404 East Hiller Street, Victoria, TX 77901 Tel: 512/573-7468

Utah
Stewart Rehabilitation Center, McKay-Dee Hospital, 3939 Harrison Boulevard, Ogden, UT 84409 Tel: 801/627-2800

Virginia
University of Virginia Pain Center, Box 293, University of Virginia Medical Center, Charlottesville, VA 22908 Tel: 804/924-5581
Medical College of Virginia, Virginia Commonwealth University, 1200 East Broad Street, Richmond, VA 23298 Tel: 804/786-9000

Washington
The Pain Center, Swedish Hospital Medical Center, 747 Summit Avenue, Seattle, WA 98104 Tel: 206/292-2013
Pain Clinic, RC-76, University of Washington, 1959 NE Pacific Street, Seattle, WA 98195 Tel: 206/543-3236

West Virginia
West Virginia University Pain Clinic, West Virginia University Medical Center, Morgantown, WV 26506 Tel: 304/293-5411

Wisconsin
Pain and Health Rehabilitation Center, Route 2, Welsh Coulee, La Crosse, WI 54601 Tel: 608/786-0611, 608/784-3420
Pain Clinic, University of Wisconsin Clinical Science Center, 600 Highland Avenue, Madison, WI 53792 Tel: 608/263-8094

Chronic Pain Management Program, Mt. Sinai Medical Center, 950 North 12th Street, Milwaukee, WI 53233 Tel: 414/289-8653

Curative Rehabilitation Center, 9001 West Watertown Plank Road, Milwaukee, WI 53226 Tel: 414/259-1414

Appendix E
Sleep Disorders Centers

The following centers and clinics specialize in the management of sleep disorders and will answer questions related to particular therapeutic problems.

California
Sleep Disorders Center, Holy Cross Hospital, 15031 Rinaldi Street, Mission Hills, CA 91345 Tel: 213/365-8051 ext 1497

Sleep Disorders Center, University of California, Irvine Medical Center, 101 City Drive South, Orange, CA 92688 Tel: 714/634-5776

Sleep Disorders Program, Stanford University Medical Center, Stanford, CA 94305 Tel: 415/497-7458

Florida
Sleep Disorders Center, Mt. Sinai Medical Center, 4300 Alton Road, Miami Beach, FL 33140 Tel: 305/674-2613

Illinois
Sleep Clinic, Northwestern Memorial Hospital, 250 East Superior Street, Chicago, IL 60611 Tel: 312/649-2458, 312/649-2650

Sleep Disorders Center, Rush-Presbyterian-St. Luke's Medical Center, 1753 Congress Parkway, Chicago, IL 60612 Tel: 312/942-5440

Louisiana
Sleep Disorders Center, Psychiatry and Neurology, Tulane Medical School, New Orleans, LA 70112 Tel: 504/588-5231

Maryland
Sleep Disorders Center, Baltimore City Hospital, Baltimore, MD 21224 Tel: 301/396-8603

Massachusetts
Sleep Disorders Center, Department of Neurology, University of Massachusetts Medical Center, Worcester, MA 01605 Tel: 617/856-3968

Michigan

Sleep Disorders Center, Henry Ford Hospital, 2799 West Grand Boulevard, Detroit, MI 48202 Tel: 313/678-2233

Minnesota

Sleep Disorders Center, Hennepin County Medical Center, 701 Park Avenue South, Minneapolis, MN 55415 Tel: 612/347-6289

New Hampshire

Sleep Disorders Center, Box 7770, Dartmouth Medical School, Hanover, NH 03755 Tel: 603/646-2213

New York

Sleep-Wake Disorders Center, Montefiore Hospital, 111 East 210th Street, Bronx, NY 10467 Tel: 212/920-4841

Sleep Disorders Center, Department of Psychiatry, SUNY at Stony Brook, Stony Brook, NY 11794 Tel: 516/246-2561

Ohio

Sleep Disorders Center, Cincinnati General Hospital, Cincinnati, OH 45267 Tel: 513/572-5087

Sleep Disorder Center, Mt. Sinai Medical Center, University Circle, Cleveland, OH 44106 Tel: 216/421-3678

Sleep Disorders Center, Department of Psychiatry, Ohio State University, Columbus, OH 43210 Tel: 614/421-8260

Oklahoma

Sleep Disorders Center, Presbyterian Hospital, NE 13th at Lincoln Boulevard, Oklahoma City, OK 73104 Tel: 405/271-6312

Pennsylvania

Sleep Disorders Center, Western Psychiatric Institute and Clinic, 3811 O'Hara Street, Pittsburgh, PA 15261 Tel: 412/624-2246, 412/624-2040 (night line)

Sleep Disorders Center, Department of Neurology, Crozer-Chester Medical Center, Upland-Chester, PA 19013 Tel: 215/447-2689

Tennessee

BMH Sleep Disorders Center, Baptist Memorial Hospital, Memphis, TN 38146 Tel: 901/522-5651

Texas

Sleep Disorder and Research Center, Baylor College of Medicine, Houston, TX 77030 Tel: 713/790-4886

Sleep Disorders Center, Metropolitan Medical Center, 1303 McCullough Street, San Antonio, TX 78212 Tel: 512/223-4057

Appendix F
Eating Disorders Self-Help Groups

California
Anorexia Nervosa and Related Disorders (ANRED), Box 1012, Grove City, CA 93433, Gene Ann Rubel, President, Tel: 805/773-4303 (24-hour hotline)

Anorexic/Bulimic Support, UCLA Neuropsychiatric Institute, 760 Westwood Plaza, Los Angeles, CA 90024, Karen Lee-Benner, RN, MSN, Tel: 213/825-0173

Anorexia Self-Help Group, Las Encinas Hospital, Pasadena, CA 94307, Paul E. Laemmle, Psychologist, Tel: 213/795-9901

Colorado
Ft. Collins–Anorexic/Bulimic Support, 424 Spinnaker Lane, Ft. Collins, CO 80525, Marsha Kaplan, Tel: 303/223-3914

Florida
Anorexic/Bulimic/Family Support, Mental Health Association of Dade County, Inc., 800 Brickell Plaza, Miami, FL 33131, Susan Marks, Tel: 305/379-2673

Georgia
American Anorexia Nervosa Assn. of Atlanta, 3533 Kingsboro Road, NE, Atlanta, GA 30319, Ann Bradshaw, President, Tel: 404/233-7058

Hawaii
Honolulu-Anorexic/Bulimic Support Hope, Chapter of ANAD, University of Hawaii at Honolulu, Anada Mangialetti, Tel: 808/947-3384, Kevin Lawson, Tel: 808/261-6689

Indiana
South Bend–Anorexic/Bulimic Support, University of Notre Dame, Health Services, South Bend, IN 46556, Dan Rybicki, Ph.D., Susan Stibe, Ph.D., Tel: 219/239-7497

Illinois
Anorexia Nervosa and Associated Disorders (ANAD), Suite 2020, 550 Frontage Road, Highland Park, IL 60093, Vivian Meehan, President, Tel: 312/831-3438

Kentucky
Louisville-Family/Anorexic/Bulimic Support, Association for Anorexia Nervosa and Bulimia, 1017 King Arthur Lane, Louisville, KY 40222, Jane Pfeifer, Tel: 502/425-1494

Maryland
Baltimore-Anorexic/Bulimic Support, Maryland Association for Anorexia Nervosa and Bulimia, 222 Gateswood Road, Lutherville, MD 21093, Ann Boyer, Tel: 301/252-7407

Bethesda-Parents Group, Cedar Lane Unitarian Church, 9601 Cedar Lane, Bethesda, MD 20814, Becky Edmonson, Tel: 301/493-8301

Massachusetts

Lincoln Center–Anorexic/Bulimic Support, The Anorexia Nervosa Aid Society of Massachusetts, PO Box 213, Lincoln Center, MA 01773, Patrica Warner, President, Tel: 617/259-9767

Michigan

Detroit-Anorexic/Bulimic/Family Support, Orchard Hills Psychiatric Center 23800 Orchard Lake Road, Farmington Hills, MI 48024 Peggy Debelak, Tel: 313/474-1144

Mississippi

Treatment Information Referrals, 315 Venetian Way, Hattiesburg, MS 39401, Mrs. Barbara Fisher, Tel: 601/583-6201

Missouri

Bulimia, Anorexia, Self-Help (BASH), Suite 206, 522 New Ballas Road, St. Louis, MO 63141 Tel: 314/567-4080

Nebraska

Omaha-Parent Support, Children's Rehabilitation Institute, Family Rehabilitation Department, 444 So. 44th St., Omaha, NE 68131, Daniel Baker, Ph.D., Tel: 402/559-7490

New Jersey

American Anorexia Nervosa Association, 133 Cedar Lane, Teaneck, NJ 07666, John A. Atchley, MD, President, Estelle B. Miller, MSW, Vice-President, Tel: 201/836-1800

New York

Albany-Troy Self-Help, 21 Paul Holly Drive, Loudonville, NY 12211, Anne C. Wang, President, Tel: 518/462-4583

Center for Study of Anorexia Nervosa, One West 91st St., New York, NY 10024, William Davis, MD, Tel: 212/846-6810

Ohio

Columbus-Anorexic/Bulimic/Family Support, The Bridge Counseling Center, 4897 Karl Road, Columbus, OH 43229, Belinda Berkowitz or Paula Butterfield, Tel: 614/846-6810

National Anorexic Aid Society (NAAS), Box 29461, Columbus, OH 43229, Patrica Howe, President, Tel: 614/895-2009

Oklahoma

Norman-Anorexic/Bulimic/Family Support, 511 Manor Dr., Norman, OK 73069, Marta Burr or Mary Jo Burr, Tel: 405/329-0136 (evenings), Levita Pierce, Tel: 405/321-4048 (days)

Pennsylvania

Abington-Hope (Helping Ourselves with Preoccupied Eating), Chapter of ANAD, Anorexic/Bulimic Support, 1174 Highland Ave., Abington, PA 19001, Nina Perlingiero Randall, MD, Tel: 215/887-7426, Mary Beahan, Tel: 215/659-4669

American Anorexia Nervosa Assoc. of Phil., Philadelphia Child Guidance Clinic, 34th and Civic Center Boulevard, Philadelphia, PA 19104 Tel: 215/387-1919

Tennessee

Knoxville-Family Support, 8612 Springfield Drive, Knoxville, TN 37919, Mrs. H. L. Minnich, Tel: 615/693-4923

Virginia

Riverside Hospital Clinic CMHC, 420 J. Clyde Morris Boulevard, Newport News, VA 23601, Mary Ann Sipe, Coordinator, Tel: 804/599-2582

Washington

Everett-Anorexic/Family Support, Anorexia Foundation Association, 3211 Nassau #3, Everett, WA 98201, Agnes L. Cavelero, Tel: 206/259-3386

INDEX